Travels and Researches in Native North America, 1882–1883

Herman F. C. ten Kate, Jr.,
The Hague, ca. 1881–1882
(Hovens collection)

Travels and Researches in Native North America, 1882–1883

Herman ten Kate

Translated and edited by Pieter Hovens, William J. Orr, and Louis A. Hieb

Published in cooperation with the
University of Arizona Southwest Center

UNIVERSITY OF NEW MEXICO PRESS ◆ ALBUQUERQUE

A University of Arizona Southwest Center Book
Joseph C. Wilder, Series Editor

◆◆◆◆◆

11   10   09   08   07   06   05   04   1   2   3   4   5   6   7

LIBRARY OF CONGRESS CATALOGING-IN-PUBLICATION DATA

Kate, Herman F. C. ten (Herman Frederik Carel), 1858–1931.
    [Reizen en onderzoekingen in Noord-Amerika. English]
    Travels and researches in native North America, 1882–1883 / Herman ten Kate ;
translated and edited by Pieter Hovens, William J. Orr, and Louis A. Hieb.— 1st ed.
        p. cm.
    "Published in cooperation with the University of Arizona Southwest Center."
    "A University of Arizona Southwest Center book."
    Includes index.
    ISBN 0-8263-3281-1 (cloth : alk. paper)
  1. Southwest, New—Description and travel. 2. Mexico—Description and travel.
3. Baja California (Mexico)—Description and travel. 4. Indians of North America—
Southwest, New—Social life and customs. I. Hovens, Pieter. II. Orr, William J.
III. Hieb, Louis A. IV. University of Arizona. Southwest Center. V. Title.
    F786.K21K38 2004
    917.904'2—DC22

                                    2003027913

◆◆◆◆◆

*Publication of this book was aided by a
subvention from the National Museum
of Ethnology, Leiden, the Netherlands.*

Lithographs are by Pieter Haaxman (1854–1937).

Book design and type composition by Kathleen Sparkes
The body type in this book is Sabon 10/15
The display type is Adobe Arcana Manuscript

••••••••••

Dedicated to

WILLIAM J. ORR,
1944–2002

•••••••

Contents

Preface

BETWEEN NOVEMBER 1882 AND DECEMBER 1883 THE DUTCH ANTHROPOLOGIST Herman Frederik Carel ten Kate (pronounced *ten Kah-tuh*) traveled across North America to study traditional Indian tribes and their fate in the aftermath of the settling of the frontier. This journey took him to the Iroquois of upstate New York; the Yaquis of Sonora; most southwestern tribes of Arizona and New Mexico; the Chemehuevis, Southern Paiutes, and Southern Utes of the Great Basin; several Southern Plains native peoples, and some of the Five Civilized Tribes in Indian Territory, Oklahoma. Ten Kate undertook small-scale archaeological excavations and carried out somatological, ethnographic, and linguistic fieldwork among these tribes, most of whom were recently forced to settle on reservations in the American West. In 1885 the academic publishing house of E. J. Brill in Leiden printed Ten Kate's travel narrative *Reizen en Onderzoekingen in Noord Amerika* (Travels and Researches in North America). The author intended to publish an English translation at a later date, but research and work across the globe prevented him from getting around to it.

Ten Kate's extensive narrative of travel, adventure, and research in the American West is a bountiful historical source of scientific data on the natural environment, archaeological remains, physical characteristics, traditional material culture and customs, language, and tribal history of Indians. In addition, his account vividly portrays the development of the frontier West, and the author frequently describes and comments on the role of explorers, the army, colonists, miners, railroads, and, finally, tourists in this historical process. Central to this story are Indian-white relations, from the "Indian wars" to the civilization policies of the American government, reform organizations, and missionary societies. Unfortunately, Ten Kate's narrative received little attention in its time because it was published in Dutch.

For about a century Ten Kate's book gathered dust on library shelves in the United States and in Europe, where North American Indian studies traditionally had received scant attention in academia. When in the 1980s interest in the history of anthropology blossomed, three separate initiatives on both sides of the Atlantic Ocean began to produce an English translation of Ten Kate's work. When Lou Hieb, Bill Orr, and I learned about one another's efforts, we decided to join forces. The length of time that has passed since then can only be explained by the commitments stemming from our regular jobs and private lives. Although he saw the almost finished manuscript, Lou and I greatly regretted that Bill Orr did not see the book in print, as he lost his fight against cancer in 2002. We had come to appreciate him as a fine colleague, a thorough historian, and an amazing linguist, able to translate the seemingly endless sentences Ten Kate wrought in nineteenth-century academic and literary language.

Bill Orr translated the primary Dutch text of Ten Kate's book. I provided my own translations of several parts to Orr, notably the Iroquois account, which was published in two separate articles in Dutch and French scientific journals. Bill's translation was reviewed for accuracy and nuance. All three editors shared the annotation. To introduce Ten Kate and his work and to position him and his studies within the history of anthropology, Lou Hieb and I wrote an introductory essay, most of which is based on my 1989 Ph.D. thesis on Ten Kate and his North American Indian studies. A bibliography with the most relevant and important of Ten Kate's writings is added as an appendix to the essay. An itinerary of his 1882–1883 journey of fieldwork through the American West concludes the introductory section of this book.

In the translation of Ten Kate's book we interfered little with the original text. Sometimes we combined short paragraphs into one, broke extremely long paragraphs into smaller parts, or divided very long sentences for easier reading. Ten Kate's phonetic transcriptions of Indian words were adapted from Dutch to English.

All the original endnotes of the 1885 edition are included in the English translation, indicated as HtK 1885. Corrections and additions that Ten Kate published four years later in an article were also added to the notes and are separately identified as HtK 1889. We have retained these notes mostly in their original form. In addition, the original text has been annotated extensively by the editors. We indicated additions to Ten Kate's notes with "Eds." Our colleagues might find the book slightly overannotated, but we hope the book will also appeal to a wider, nonprofessional audience with a specific interest in the American West and its native peoples.

My research for the biography of Herman ten Kate was partially funded by the Netherlands Research Council (NWO). I received financial backing for subsequent research from the National Museum of Ethnology (Leiden), the Leiden Ethnological Fund, the Foundation of Art and Science (The Hague), the American Embassy (The Hague), and United Airlines (Amsterdam). Their support is hereby gratefully acknowledged. The Laboratory of Anthropology/Museum of Indian Arts and Culture and the School of American Research in Santa Fe and the Harold S. Colton Research Center/Museum of Northern Arizona in Flagstaff provided highly appreciated research opportunities by offering research associateships in environments conducive for anthropological research.

I thank the following people for their generous practical support and professional advice during various stages of the research: Duane Anderson, Rogier Bedaux, Bruce Bernstein, Ilse Boon, Jean Collins, Richard Conn, Mary Davis, Paul van Dongen, Steven Engelsman, Christian Feest, Alan Ferg,

Willem Fermont, Ben Grishaver (photography), Anneke Groeneveld, Tilly de Groot, Willem van Gulik, Menno Hekker, Lou Hieb, Kit Hinsley, Nel van Hove, André Köbben, Lammert Leertouwer, Meg MacDonald, Elliott McIntire, Sid and Rose Margolis, Gertti Nooter, Arthur Olivas, Jarich Oosten, Marian Rodee, Steve Rogers, Wim Rosema, Richard Rudisill, Karl Schwerin, David Stuart-Fox, Bill Sturtevant, Karen Taschek, Raymond Thompson, Leo Triebels, Albert Trouwborst, and David Wilcox.

The research on Ten Kate's life and work would not have been possible without the support of these individuals and institutions. I have been continually pleasantly surprised by the readiness and generosity of American colleagues and institutions to assist in a variety of ways with this and subsequent research. Last but not least, the research also would not have been possible without the continued support of my wife, Jeanne, over many years.

—*Pieter Hovens*
Leiden, 2003

PART ONE

Editors' Introduction

1. Herman F. C. ten Kate, Jr., The Hague, ca. 1881–1882 *(Hovens collection)*

2. Ely S. Parker (ca. 1880), Seneca sachem and Commissioner of Indian Affairs during the administration of President Ulysses S. Grant *(National Museum of Ethnology, Leiden)*

3. Yaqui Indian man, Guaymas, Sonora, March 1883; picture taken to illustrate physical type *(photograph by Alfredo Laurent; National Museum of Ethnology, Leiden)*

4. Pascual, Yuma chief, ca. 1880–1882 *(photograph by E. A. Bonine; courtesy of World Museum, Rotterdam)*

5. Frank H. Cushing, U.S. government anthropologist and Zuni Priest of the Bow
*(photograph by James Wallace Black, Boston, 1882; courtesy of Fray Angélico
Chavéz History Library, Museum of New Mexico, Santa Fe)*

6. Zuni woman carrying an olla with a "rain bird" design *(photograph by William Henry Brown, ca. 1880; National Museum of Ethnology, Leiden)*

7. Herman ten Kate in Apache camp, Arizona, summer 1883 *(photograph by Constant Duhem; National Museum of Ethnology, Leiden)*

8. White Mountain Apache playing a violin, San Carlos, summer 1883
(photograph by Constant Duhem; National Museum of Ethnology, Leiden)

9. Navajo Indians (seated) and Jemez Indian, one holding a "rain god" *(photograph by William Henry Brown, ca. 1880; courtesy of World Museum, Rotterdam)*

10. Ute chief Ouray and his wife Chipita, 1880 *(photograph by Mathew Brady, Washington, D.C.; National Museum of Ethnology, Leiden)*

11. Dr. Thomas A. Bland (seated, left) of the National Indian Defense Association with delegation in the capital, including Sioux chief Red Cloud (seated, right) *(photograph by Johnson Brothers, Washington, D.C.; National Museum of Ethnology, Leiden)*

12. The Rijksmuseum voor Volkenkunde [National Museum of Ethnology] in Leiden, the Netherlands, where Herman ten Kate's ethnographic collections are curated *(Hovens collection)*

The Science of the Indians

Herman ten Kate, Anthropology, and Native American Studies

PIETER HOVENS AND LOUIS A. HIEB

Introduction

ON NOVEMBER 5, 1882, THE YOUNG DUTCH ANTHROPOLOGIST HERMAN TEN KATE disembarked in New York Harbor, intent on beginning a research journey among Native American tribes of the Southwest and the Southern Plains that would last about a year. In his applications for grants for this endeavor from the government of the Netherlands and several scientific societies in Holland and France, he had stressed the urgent need for an investigation into what remained of the traditional native cultures because the traditional ways of life of many aboriginal societies in North America were on the brink of disappearing. This salvage approach characterized not only Ten Kate's but also much of late-nineteenth-century anthropological research as the effects of Euro-American colonial expansion, commercial exploitation, and cultural suppression were increasingly felt all across the globe, particularly in the United States and Canada. While this process was taking place, the new academic discipline of anthropology was emerging in Western Europe and North America.

However, Ten Kate's research agenda extended far beyond ethnographic salvage. To determine the physical characteristics of the American Indians, he measured pigmentation, stature, and head form and attempted to identify the most prevalent physical types. When the opportunity arose, he collected skeletal material, which he sent to the Musée du Trocadéro in Paris. Ten Kate was an accomplished linguist and recorded tribal vocabularies and data on ethnic synonymy. He also described and collected material expressions of native life and sent about 400 ethnographic specimens to the Rijks

Ethnographisch Museum (National Museum of Ethnology) in Leiden (Hovens et al., in preparation). With his data on physical types, languages, and customs, he hoped to contribute to the discussion on the origin of the American Indians and the relationships between tribes. Another major interest of Ten Kate's was the impact of western civilization on tribal societies, and he frequently inquired about government policies and their effects on those societies. Combining his insights into native cultures and western impacts on them, he tried to establish the characteristics of Indian personality structure and the American "type," or national character. Such a broad research program was rather exceptional but stemmed from the intellectual background of Ten Kate's family, his multidisciplinary academic training at European universities, and his wide-ranging interests, culminating in an inclusive, nondelimiting science of the Indians (Hovens 1989:45–51).

Biography: Childhood and Student Years, 1858–1882

Herman Frederik Carel ten Kate, Jr., was born in Amsterdam on February 7, 1858. His father was a popular painter who received royal patronage from King William III. The Ten Kate family was blessed by the Muses, counting many painters and literary men among its members. Ten Kate grew up in The Hague and in 1875 registered at the Art Academy, following in his father's footsteps. He was interested in anatomy and during his first year received a prize for an anatomical drawing. The winter of 1876–1877 was spent in the Mediterranean on the island of Corsica in the company of Charles William Meredith van de Velde, a friend of his father. Erudite Van de Velde, a man who had seen the world and a physician, painter, cartographer, and humanitarian, impressed his young companion with stories of foreign lands and peoples. He touched on Ten Kate's interest in the native peoples of the Americas, sparked by the juvenile literature of his day. Ten Kate was an avid reader of the novels of James Fenimore Cooper, Mayne Reid, and Gustave Aimard. On his return to the Netherlands, he informed his surprised but supportive father that he had decided on a scientific career, which would enable him to travel and carry out scientific research among peoples and in cultures outside Europe (Heyink and Hodge 1931:415; Hovens 1989:15–18, 192–96).

Ten Kate registered at the University of Leiden in 1877, where he studied Indonesian ethnology, non-western languages, medicine, geography, geology, and paleontology. At the university he came under the scientific and humanitarian influence of the first professor of ethnology in the Netherlands, Pieter Johannes Veth (1814–1895). At Leiden museums Ten Kate studied cranial collections of Malay peoples. He also embarked on the study of North American Indians by reading the few scientific publications that were available and examining some ethnographic specimens at the National Museum of Ethnology. Ten Kate compensated for his scant study materials by reading American newspapers reporting on recent developments in Indian-white relations. The campaign of the American army against Chief Joseph and his Nez Percés encouraged Ten Kate to write a critical article about federal Indian policy, his first publication on Native North Americans (Ten Kate 1878; Hovens 1989:18–29, 1991a).

Following the advice of his tutors, in 1879 Ten Kate continued his medical and physical anthropological studies at the renowned École d'Anthropologie in Paris, where he attended courses taught by Paul Broca, Paul Topinard, and Ernest-Théodore Hamy. He also carried out somatological research on several osteological collections and for a time undertook research in criminal anthropology. At the Musée d'Histoire Naturelle de l'Homme he heard the lectures of Armand Quatrefages and continued his linguistic studies at the École des Langues Orientales Vivantes. The 1879 World Exposition in the French capital afforded him the opportunity to see the exhibits of foreign lands and peoples. He was given access to the ethnographic collections at the Musée d'Ethnographie du Trocadéro by his teacher and Hamy, the founder of the institution. The number of North American artifacts at the museum was limited at the time but increasing at a steady rate, such as through the acquisition in 1881 of the specimens collected by Alphonse Pinart. Paris had become a center of Americanist studies as a result of the work of Alexander von Humboldt in the capital city (1804–1827). Specialized interest in American studies was institutionalized in 1857 by the founding of the Société Américaine and the creation in 1863 of the American Archeological Committee within the Société d'Ethnographie. Ten Kate became a lifelong member of the biennial Congrès International des Américanistes, which had been established by the Société Américaine in 1875 (Williams 1985; Hovens 1989:29–35; Dias 1991).

During 1880–1881, the first semester, Ten Kate studied at the University of Berlin. In the German capital he attended Adolf Bastian's lectures in ethnology but also took classes in zoology, paleontology, and historical geography. Bastian was able to show Ten Kate only a little of the North American ethnographic collections; most were in storage because of the construction of a new museum, planned to be completed in 1886. Alexander and Wilhelm von Humboldt had been instrumental in fostering Americanist interests in Germany. Most of their natural history collections were deposited at scientific institutions in the capital. Wilhelm von Humboldt and his pupil Johann C. E. Buschmann specialized in Amerindian linguistics. Bastian introduced Ten Kate to Rudolf Virchow, who put the research facilities of the Berliner Gesellschaft für Anthropologie, Ethnologie, und Urgeschichte at his disposal. There the young student also examined skulls of Mongolian peoples, as he did at the Anatomical Museum (Kutscher 1966; Hovens 1989:35–38; Zimmerman 2001:4–6, 172–200).

Ten Kate continued his studies at the University of Göttingen in the spring of 1881, where he took classes in medicine, zoology, and geography and examined skulls of Mongolian peoples. Ernst Ehlers, Ten Kate's anatomy and zoology professor, acted as curator of the university's ethnographic collections and showed the aspiring Americanist James Cook's 1778 Northwest Coast collection, which had so impressed Goethe in 1801, and part of the 1832–1834 Northern Plains assemblage donated by Prinz Maximilian von Wied. Finally, Ten Kate spent the academic year 1881–1882 at the University of Heidelberg, where he read anatomy, zoology, and paleontology and probably also botany. After defending his comparative craniological study of Mongolian peoples, he received a Ph.D. in zoology on April 28, 1882 (Ten Kate 1882; Hovens 1989:38–41).

Ten Kate had long been planning an exploratory fieldwork journey to the United States and northern Mexico and sought and received scientific guidance and practical advice from his tutors in Leiden (Veth, Kan), Paris (Hamy), and Berlin (Bastian). Limited material support came from the Netherlands Geographical Society and the Société de Géographie in Paris. The Holland Association of Sciences (Haarlem) and the Department of the Interior (The Hague) provided him with funds to purchase Indian artifacts for the Leiden museum. However, most of the cost of his first fieldwork was borne by his generous and always supportive father.

Southwest Research

After visiting several Iroquois reservations in upstate New York (Ten Kate 1883a, 1883b; Hovens 1984), Ten Kate went to the Bureau of American Ethnology at the Smithsonian Institution in the capital. There he made the acquaintance of director John Wesley Powell. The creation of the bureau in 1879 crowned the efforts of the Smithsonian's first director, Joseph Henry, to develop an institution devoted to the study of Indian cultures before they completely vanished under the onslaught of western civilization. However, the bureau emphasized long-term qualitative research on language, prehistory, and ethnology, sending out its personnel for prolonged periods of fieldwork among different tribes, including the American Southwest (Hinsley 1981; Hovens 1989:53–54, 95, 101, 202–3).

From Washington, D.C., Ten Kate set out for the Southwest, traveling by train. In St. Louis he visited Monk's Mound, the most visible vestige of what remained of the prehistoric Mississippian city of Cahokia. By way of Little Rock and Dallas, he arrived in El Paso, Texas, on Christmas Day, 1882, and began preparations for his research among the native peoples of the Southwest. His book about his yearlong investigations into the physiques, languages, lifeways, and current conditions of the Indian tribes he visited, published in Dutch in the Netherlands in 1885, stands out as one of the major early scientific descriptions of Indians of the Southwest (Ten Kate 1885a). The region had already been subject to several decades of scientific surveys, but these explorations had been largely concerned with the environment rather than the peoples and cultures of the area. It was not until 1870 that scientific anthropology began, of which Ten Kate became a representative.

In 1873 John Wesley Powell visited the Moqui (Hopi) villages and published an account titled *The Ancient Provinces of Tusayan* (1875). Shortly after Powell's visit, General George Crook also visited the Hopis. His aide, Captain John Gregory Bourke, wrote *The Moquis of Arizona: A Brief Description of Their Towns, Their Manners, and Customs* (1874). Archaeological surveys by W. H. Holmes and William H. Jackson, participants in the Geological and Geographical Survey of the Territories instituted by Dr. Ferdinand V. Hayden, documented the extensive ruins in the Four Corners area between 1874 and 1877 and increased public and governmental interest in the region. Swiss-born Albert Samuel Gatschet analyzed the data on southwestern Indian languages collected by the survey of Captain George M. Wheeler (1872–1879) and in 1877 joined Powell's Rocky Mountain Survey (Fowler 2000:38–92). Ten Kate repeatedly draws on the works of these early investigators and adds his own observations and findings.

The Bureau of American Ethnology had come into being on March 3, 1879, when Congress combined four independent surveys to create the United States Geological Survey and, at the same time, transferred to the Smithsonian Institution the results of various anthropological fieldwork previously pursued by those surveys under instructions from the Department of the Interior. Smithsonian secretary Spencer F. Baird appointed Powell, who had contributed the most to the field researches, to be director, and thus began a more systematic effort to study the somatology, philology, mythology, sociology, habits and customs, technology, archaeology, and history of the American Indians. In 1882 Powell enlisted Ten Kate's assistance in obtaining ethnolinguistic data for the *Handbook of North American Indians* the bureau was preparing.

On August 1, 1879, the Smithsonian sent a collecting expedition to the Hopi and Zuni villages. The party was led by Colonel James Stevenson and included his wife, Matilda, photographer John K. Hillers, and Frank Hamilton Cushing, the young curator of the Department of Ethnology at the National Museum. Cushing, a talented naturalist but completely without training in ethnology, stayed with the Zunis for four and a half years, learned their language, and was adopted into the tribe. In this way he was able to understand the organization and ideology of a Native American society as no other non-Indian before him. Although Alexander Middleton Stephen was to spend nearly fifteen years (1879–1894) at Keam's Canyon observing the Navajos and, later, the Hopis and Dr. Jeremiah Sullivan was even more a participant in Hopi social and ceremonial life, it was Cushing who initiated ethnology in the Southwest and became the example par excellence of the anthropologist as participant observer. Ten Kate's visit to Zuni, "one of the shining points of my voyage," proved to be the beginning of a friendship with Cushing that was to last until Cushing's death in 1900 (Hinsley 1981:81–231; Hovens 1988; 1989:119–25; 1995).

For a number of years following the initial 1879 venture, Colonel Stevenson led collecting expeditions to the Southwest to gather pottery, textiles, and other examples of material culture from the Pueblos, prehistoric and present. Beginning in 1879 Matilda Coxe Stevenson spent some time each year at Zuni in a study of women's roles, domestic life, and children and from this research published *The Religious Life of the Zuni Child* (1887). Ten Kate met the Stevensons at Fort Defiance, Arizona, in August 1883 as Colonel Stevenson was preparing for an archaeological survey in Canyon de Chelly.

Alexander M. Stephen's name appeared in the 1880 census as an "explorer" and "prospector" living with trader Thomas V. Keam. Stephen was prospecting at the time of Ten Kate's visit, but the Dutch anthropologist examined a large collection of pottery assembled by Keam that Stephen was analyzing for a catalog titled *The Pottery of Tusayan*. After Jeremiah Sullivan left in 1888, Stephen became the local authority on the Hopis. In 1891 he was employed by Jesse Walter Fewkes, director of the Hemenway Southwestern Archaeological Expedition, to record information on the Hopis (Stephen 1929, 1936; Graves 1998:152–60; Hieb and Diggle 2002).

In 1880 Dr. Washington Matthews, an assistant surgeon in the United States Army, was assigned to Fort Wingate on a four-year tour of duty. With support from the Bureau of American Ethnology he began his study of Navajo language, religion, and material culture. Matthews was gathering materials for his paper "Navajo Names for Plants" (1886) at the time of Ten Kate's visits to Fort Wingate, and the two men made a field trip together. Although Stephen published several articles on the Navajos and assisted Matthews in his study of the Navajo language, Matthews's accounts of several Navajo chantways provided the foundation for twentieth-century studies of Navajo ritual (Faris 1990; Halpern and McGreevy 1997).

Brothers Cosmos and Victor Mindeleff produced a number of the most important archaeological and ethnological studies to appear in the early Annual Reports of the Bureau of American Ethnology. Victor Mindeleff surveyed the architecture of Zuni in the 1881–1882 field season and the Hopi villages between August 1882 and February 1883. Both brothers were in the East preparing exhibits when Ten Kate reached northern Arizona during the summer of 1883. The Dutch anthropologist was also interested in aboriginal architecture, prehistoric and historic, and recorded his observations on both, commenting on the earlier publications of the Mindeleffs.

Adolph Bandelier arrived in Santa Fe in 1882 and was to spend more than a decade working in New Mexico and Arizona. Ten Kate and Bandelier traveled only days apart during part of 1883, the latter on a survey of prehistoric sites for the Archaeological Institute of America. However, they were to meet later, both working on the staff of the Hemenway Expedition. Ten Kate regarded Bandelier's *The Delight Makers* (1890), along with Cushing's writings, to be among the few valid descriptions of American Indian life produced in the nineteenth century, combining realism with empathy.

Captain John Gregory Bourke returned to the Hopi villages in 1881 and with assistance from Sullivan produced his well-known book *The Snake-Dance of the Moquis of Arizona* in 1884. Although Ten Kate knew of Bourke's account when he published his own account of the Walpi dance, he let his stand unaltered as an independent observation. Bourke, Stephen, and the Mindeleffs were the only fieldworkers Ten Kate did not meet (McIntire and Gordon 1968; Hovens 1989:116–18; Porter 1986:95–111; Fowler 2000:117–33).

Ten Kate traveled through the Southwest in 1882–1883 to carry out his researches at a crucial time for the history of American anthropology and the frontier. He was able to draw on these fieldworkers for information, and he managed to be at the right place, at the right time: in La Paz, Guaymas, and Hermosillo for the Yaqui Pascola, at the Hopi villages to witness the Snake Dance twice, in Tucson when General Crook returned from his successful campaign against the Chiricahua Apaches in northern Mexico, in Santa Fe at the time of the Tertio-Millennial celebration, and in Tahlequah, Indian Territory (Oklahoma), when the Cherokee National Council had just convened. Ten Kate had a few days, at most a few weeks, to spend with any tribal group. However, with both an artist's and an anthropologist's appreciation of the rich sensate differences in the physiology, language, and culture of the peoples he met, he was well equipped to develop a systematic and remarkably detailed account. His 1885 book is the first general introduction to the native peoples of the Southwest. That the book is relatively unknown is attributable to the language in which it was written, Dutch, and its rarity. Fewer than ten copies are known to exist in North American libraries.

Ten Kate also met and provided descriptions of a number of other interesting scholars, professional men, and travelers in the Southwest, including Reverend C. H. Cook, a longtime missionary among the Pimas; Lyman Belding, an ornithologist and naturalist engaged in research in Baja California; Reverend John Menaul, a Presbyterian missionary who established a press at Laguna Pueblo in 1877; Professor A. H. Thompson, who had accompanied Powell on the second Colorado River expedition; Captain Richard Henry Pratt, recruiting Indian students in Oklahoma for his Carlisle Indian Boarding School in Pennsylvania; and Indian agents and commanders of military forts. Of all those he encountered, two men in particular were to fascinate Ten Kate: Te-na-tsa-li, or Medicine Flower—Frank Hamilton Cushing, and Oyiwisha, or He Who Plants Maize—Dr. Jeremiah Sullivan.

The fact and fiction of Frank Hamilton Cushing's stay at Zuni have been the subject of numerous studies. Twenty-two when he arrived at Zuni, one year older than Ten Kate, Cushing's initial stay was for two and a half years, interrupted only by trips to Fort Wingate, the Hopi and Havasupai Indians, and nearby archaeological sites. In 1882–1883 he published *My Adventures in Zuni*, which, as Joan Mark has emphasized, was more than it appeared to be at first: "On the surface a simple account of his adventures, it was actually a careful description of the cycles of Zuni life interwoven with the story of his own slow penetration into it. He took the reader through the seasons of the year in Zuni and through the cycle of human life, from his 'birth' into Zuni society to, at the end, the death and burial of an aged Zuni who had been his friend" (Mark 1980:101–2; Hovens 1989:119–27).

In October 1881 Cushing was initiated into the sacred order of the Priesthood of the Bow and later became Head War Chief. As such he became involved in a number of political controversies on behalf of the tribe. In 1882 Cushing took a group of Zunis to the East and, while there, married Emily Tennison Magill. By October he had returned to Zuni with his wife, her sister, and a cook and resumed his work, in spite of frequent illness, until 1884. Ten Kate's portrait of Cushing and his residence adds a significant account of the circumstances of his fieldwork. The two anthropologists befriended each other, and in 1887–1888 Ten Kate served on the Hemenway Southwestern Archaeological Expedition, led by Cushing, carrying out excavations in southern Arizona and on the Zuni reservation. Their letters provide an insight into their personal and professional friendship as well as into Cushing's handling of professional relationships with his major employer and sponsor (Hovens 1988; 1989:119–27, 138–50; 1995).

Jeremiah Sullivan, M.D., was relegated to footnotes during the period—apparently for political reasons—yet he provided valuable ethnographic material to a number of ethnologists who visited the Hopi between 1881 and 1888. Jeremiah Sullivan was the son of Hopi agent John H. Sullivan, who served from October 1880 to February 1882. The younger Sullivan joined his father on Christmas Day 1880. He sought at once to provide medical assistance to the Hopi and in early 1881 moved onto First Mesa, where he lived until 1888. Efforts by the next Hopi agent to evict the young doctor led to the establishment of the Moqui (Hopi) reservation in December 1882. By then the Hopi agency was abandoned and Jeremiah Sullivan was free to participate in Hopi life undisturbed.

Ten Kate visited the Hopi villages for only five days but provides a rich account of Hopi language and culture, thanks to Dr. Sullivan, who had compiled a Hopi vocabulary for the Bureau of Ethnology and recorded Hopi narratives and songs. After leaving the Hopi villages, Sullivan completed his medical training at the University of Louisville in 1894 and then served as a physician in southern Idaho (Hieb and Diggle 2002).

The early history of American anthropology is firmly rooted in the Southwest, where Ten Kate spent most of his time doing fieldwork. His studies from this period and region offer a rare and personal view of Native Americans, frontier life, and anthropology as a newly emerging science of man. Comparatively little anthropological research was being undertaken at that time on the Southern Plains, or Indian Territory, where the Dutchman conducted investigations among the Cheyennes, Arapahos, and Comanches at the end of his journey. This was also true of the southern Great Basin, where Ten Kate visited the Chemehuevis, Las Vegas Paiutes, and Southern Utes. In these regions he pioneered the anthropological research of the first generation of professional fieldworkers with relevant scientific training and institutional affiliations (DeMallie and Ewers 2001; Hovens and Herlaar, in press).

Ten Kate's Anthropology

Ten Kate's academic training and most of his scientific research took place in the last quarter of the nineteenth and the first two decades of the twentieth century. At this time the relatively new science of anthropology received academic recognition, emerging from a variety of specializations within already established disciplines, notably anatomy, linguistics, philosophy, archaeology, and history. The emergence of a new academic discipline from a nondelimiting field is not only characterized by an emerging consensus in the scientific community about a novel subject and field worthy of scientific inquiry but also by divergent theories and research methods existing at the same time and competing with one another in the absence of a generally accepted theory or evidence. Ten Kate's anthropology is characteristic of this paradigmatic struggle within the newly emerging academic discipline at the turn of the century (Harris 1968:19–24; Stocking 1987, ch. 7; 2001:303–14).

Ten Kate's academic training in the Netherlands, France, and Germany, especially in the fields of medicine and zoology, was in the positivist tradition. He learned a mainly nonevolutionary comparative anatomy with a strong quantitative taxonomic orientation, using newly developed measuring instruments for anthropometric research. His tutors warned students against unwarranted theorizing when solid empirical data were lacking. Human physical evolution was regarded by many academics as metaphysics because sufficient empirical data to prove such an interpretation of human physical development were not available. At the École d'Anthropologie in Paris only a nonqualitative polygenist development of the races of man was accepted, counteracting a quantitative biological determinism or reductionism. In Germany, Ten Kate was trained in Kantian empiricism, and Bastian lectured against the concept of biological evolution, stressing instead the existence of a common biological and spiritual humanity, as demonstrated by empirical studies. Ten Kate's positivist attitude toward the study of man was thus firmly consolidated, as exemplified by his physical anthropological studies, in which he rejected racial inequality and biological interpretations of criminal behavior. As such, Ten Kate became a characteristic representative of the polygenetic or physical anthropological paradigmatic tradition, due to both his humanistic family background and his academic training (Hovens 1989:215–20; Stocking 1992:249; 2001:207–17; Zimmerman 2001:68, 116–17, 122).

Early academic anthropology was interdisciplinary by reason of its historical roots. The new discipline emerged in the last quarter of the nineteenth century, and its early practitioners came from many scientific fields, all drawing from their own specialized knowledge. However, most of these nonspecialized anthropologists were prepared to cross disciplinary boundaries in the search for new solutions to questions regarding the development of man and culture. This approach was exemplified by Ten Kate's studies of non-western languages, geography, and ethnology, as well as his later active involvement in archaeological excavations in Arizona, New Mexico, and Argentina and his studies of historical sources. As such, Ten Kate's anthropology oscillated between the hominid anthropology of his medical teachers in Leiden, Paris, Göttingen, and Heidelberg and the humanid anthropology of Veth in Leiden and Bastian in Berlin, which developed into four-field anthropology as recognized academic disciplines in Europe and North America around the turn of the twentieth century. Ten Kate's emphasis on the importance of developing an applied anthropology also contributed significantly to an interdisciplinary approach (Hovens 1989:18–41, 198–200, 210–25; Darnell 2001:9–10).

Despite his lifelong reservations about the theory of hominid evolution, Ten Kate at times seemed to subscribe to social Darwinist views of the evolution of culture during his early career. This is exemplified in some qualitative judgments of tribal cultures as primitive, backward, and inferior and western civilization as advanced, progressive, and superior. However, he explicitly regarded these differences not as insurmountable but only as difference of degree, stressing the fundamental psychic unity of mankind as propagated by Bastian. The tension between Social Darwinism and the psychic unity of mankind is evident in much of Ten Kate's scientific work, and this tension is maintained by the "different but equal" polygenist tradition in which Ten Kate was immersed in Paris.

Ten Kate's idealism was reflected in his insistence on the inclusion of psychology in the cross-cultural study of man. It was his impression that personality was only partially hereditary and that environment, socialization, and experience were major factors in shaping people not only as individuals but especially as representatives of cultural groups, foreshadowing the culture-and-personality tradition of the 1930s. He criticized Lucien Lévy-Bruhl's theory of "prelogical" thinking among native peoples and stressed that the tribes among whom he carried out fieldwork were equipped with essentially the same intellectual faculties as the working classes in Europe.

Although the theory of evolution provided a framework for a diachronic theory of culture, a synchronic theory of culture was still in the making during Ten Kate's years of training and his early research career. Edward B. Tylor's comprehensive definition of culture dated only from 1871.

In the Netherlands culture theory was slow to develop due to the complexity of the native societies in colonial Indonesia. This resulted in specialized studies in linguistics, common law, and religion, thus slowing the emergence of cross-cultural theory (Held 1953:867–68; Ellen 1976:312–13; Josselin de Jong 1980:243–45). Not until the final decades of the century did a comparative theory of culture develop and gain acceptance, with ethnology becoming firmly established as a new academic discipline.

The lack of a unified theory of culture was an important factor in the fragmented nature of much of nineteenth-century ethnography, including Ten Kate's, but other factors also contributed to this situation. The realization that native cultures were rapidly disintegrating and disappearing as a result of western colonial and commercial expansion became firmly ingrained in the scientific consciousness of many European academics in the late nineteenth century. Bastian once remarked that it was an irony that ethnology emerged as a science precisely at a time when its subject matter, nonwestern cultures, was on the verge of disappearing. Fieldwork resulting from this awareness usually consisted of short visits to peoples to acquire their remaining traditional artifacts for museums and to obtain as much data on traditional customs as feasible, thereby documenting only the most visible traits of culture. Such hit-and-run ethnography usually resulted in unsystematic studies of limited importance (Hinsley 1981:34–42; Koepping 1983:107; Hovens 1989:45–47, 170).

Lack of funding for long-term fieldwork was another contributing factor to the paucity of systematic ethnographic research in the late nineteenth century. Ten Kate was well aware of the scientific limitations of his own salvage ethnography and that of others, and he advocated long-term association with peoples and participation in their daily lives as a fundamental requirement for scientific cultural analysis. At the same time he recognized the importance of the work of armchair anthropologists, culling data from a variety of descriptive works to try to develop a comparative theory of culture. True to his personal inclination, he aptly stated that ethnology needed to become a "science of experience," as demonstrated by the work of Frank H. Cushing, Washington Matthews, Franz Boas, and James Mooney. His own North American fieldwork early in his career was the rite of passage that initiated him into the emerging anthropological communities in the Netherlands, France, and the United States and confirmed his status as an anthropologist. Later in his career Ten Kate developed relationships with Robert H. Lowie and Alfred L. Kroeber, whose ethnographic studies and cultural analyses he came to appreciate (Ten Kate 1885a:197, 280–82, 456; 1900:769; 1927a; Stagl 1985:289–91; Hovens 1989:125–27, 210–15).

Nineteenth-century travelers, fieldworkers, and even armchair anthropologists were continually confronted with the vagaries of civilization, wreaking worldwide havoc among tribal cultures. With Social Darwinism the worldview of the day, they accepted the irrevocable course of colonial expansion of European nations across the globe, encapsulating nonwestern societies economically and, wherever possible, politically, eventually assimilating them culturally. However, public and scientific opinion split over policies regarding native peoples. The disinterest of the general public had its academic counterpart in value-free science, avoiding or rejecting moral stands. Those advocating the establishment of western civilization supported governmental aboriginal policies aimed at cultural assimilation and the missionary programs of the churches aimed at Christianizing the heathen peoples. Others pointed out the negative impact of western civilization on native peoples and called for an enlightened policy to prevent it. A few rejected assimilation and Christianization and demanded that native peoples be protected from the inroads of western culture and left alone to develop on their own terms.

His training at academic centers of major European colonial powers and his interest in North American Indian studies motivated Ten Kate to monitor and study not only U.S. Indian policy but also the development of the policies of the major western colonial powers aimed at native peoples. At the University of Leiden, Professor Veth instilled the value of the practicality of science in colonial government but also advocated an ethically justified policy toward native peoples, based on general standards of human rights. During his many journeys across the globe, Ten Kate was also able to witness firsthand the impact of Dutch, French, and British colonial regimes on native peoples. While living and working in Japan, Ten Kate was confronted with Japanese colonialism on mainland Asia. He wrote about his experiences and expressed his critical views on colonial policy in a series of publications (e.g., Ten Kate 1878, 1889a, 1901, 1911a, 1915, 1916a).

Ten Kate condemned imperialism as based on the uncivilized principle of the survival of the fittest. Europe, the United States, and Japan had disproved their moral superiority by the atrocities committed against tribal and nonwestern peoples and by drawing the world into the Great War. As a social Darwinist he recognized that peoples of intellectual superiority would dominate peoples lagging behind. This was a "biological necessity," but he also regarded this an "anthroposociological problem" since it meant genocide, slavery, and destitution. Ten Kate resolved this dilemma by stressing the moral imperative that the intellectual superiority of civilized nations implied a moral responsibility vis-à-vis tribal peoples to treat them justly, protect them from harm, and introduce only developments that were beneficial to them. Ten Kate's social Darwinism was clearly mitigated by his emphasis on ethical standards, especially humanistic principles. In his view the scientists carried explicit responsibility in pointing out the moral obligations of civilization (Ten Kate 1889a; 1916a:11, 16; Hovens 1989:156–64, 210).

The only domain of western civilization in which Ten Kate did not lose faith completely was that of science. He emphasized the need to develop an effective applied anthropology, thereby echoing stances taken by contemporaries such as Bastian and Thurnwald in Germany and Steinmetz, Kohlbrugge, and Van Eerde in the Netherlands. He was convinced that a scientific anthropology would make possible native policies that both preserved cultural diversity and improved the living conditions of tribal peoples. However, a scientific approach provided only sound analyses but did not suffice to bring about effective policies. The latter required humanistic moral standards and emotional involvement with the tribal peoples. He rejected ethnocentric philanthropy and sentimental romanticism, pointing out that emotional involvement should be based on the native people's own vision of their societal development; hence he approached a principle of "action anthropology." In displaying a paternalistic humanism and relativistic rationalism, Ten Kate proves to be an exponent of a small but prominent group of contemporary anthropologists with progressive ideas who were receptive to native values and visions as a foundation for colonial policies and development (Ten Kate 1916a:79–84; Van Capelle 1928; Hovens 1989:220–25).

Because science is an integral part of western culture, Ten Kate recognized that science, too, was no stranger to ethnocentric pretensions and served to legitimize and facilitate exploitation of nonwestern peoples. He advocated not only an applied anthropology but explicitly demanded a partisan anthropology aimed at the improvement of the fate of colonized peoples. He was well aware that this demanded the moral courage to speak out against government policies and the missionary creeds of the churches, a courage he found sadly missing among many of his colleagues, especially in the United States. As a widely traveled man, he had clear ideas what a partisan and applied anthropology might realize in colonial situations: the maintenance of traditional economies, the improvement of material conditions, the provision of health care, the education of native peoples in their own language, the recognition of existing social structures, the training of native peoples so they could adequately face the new challenges of the colonial situation, and protection against efforts at Christianization, a thoroughly modern stance (Ten Kate 1915; 1916a; Hovens 1989:169–80, 221–26).

For Ten Kate anthropology was not only the science of nonwestern man but also a vehicle for critical self-reflection on western culture. In the confrontation between western civilization and nonwestern native peoples he became aware of the tragic dimension of his own culture and society. Contemporaries regarded views such as Ten Kate's as unscientific and even dangerous. However, his scientific training and positivist empiricism enabled him to keep the intellectual distance required of serious scholarship, a stance largely uncompromised by empathy and emotional involvement with native peoples and their fate and consideration of their own aims regarding societal development. In this regard Ten Kate's anthropology is embryonically modern and exemplifies his scientific and human stature.

Ten Kate embarked on his academic career at a time when the new academic discipline of anthropology was struggling to define its identity. From the clutches of the various brands of anatomy and philosophy, new sciences of man struggled forth, notably a hominid and a humanid anthropology. Ten Kate was educated in both, straddling traditions and competing paradigms as expressed in the four-field anthropology so characteristic of his work and rare among European practitioners. As such, and also because he was an Americanist, he fit more into the American anthropological tradition.

Despite thorough training in a positivist approach to the science of man, Ten Kate never fell victim to the illusion of a pure, value-free science generally or biological reductionism specifically. His liberal and humanistic social background and broad academic education shielded him from materialist views and made him realize the moral dimensions of science. He combined his positivist science and multidisciplinary approach with an explicit idealism shared by few of his contemporaries. This was especially expressed in his continual propagation of not only an applied but a partisan anthropology on behalf of native peoples. His social Darwinism, so prevalent in his time, was qualified with an idealism that would eventually lead to a tragic fate later in life.

Ten Kate's Native American Studies

Ten Kate's studies of Native Americans encompassed all four fields of anthropology. During his physical anthropological fieldwork, Ten Kate conducted observations on physical types; the color of skin, hair, and eyes; hair types; artificial deformation of the head; and so on. He took anthropometric measurements from many Indians, often only after overcoming initial opposition. To ensure the representativeness of his samples, he traveled to remote areas of reservations. He also took photographs and collected pictures to illustrate physical types. For his measurements he made use of anthropometric instruments developed at the École d'Anthropologie in Paris. His final somatic typology included five types or varieties: a Pueblo type (Pueblo, Hopi, Zuni), a Red Indian type (Arapaho, Cheyenne, Comanche), an unnamed third type (Ute, Kiowa), a Baha type (with Melanesian characteristics), and a Mongolian type, found especially among Indian women, whose somatological homogeneity he emphasized. Ten Kate was always careful to base his conclusions about intertribal relationships on as broad a database as possible, using the results of physical anthropological, archaeological, ethnolinguistic, ethnographic, and ethnohistoric research. He collected a few Indian skulls and received several craniums from colleagues and friends; he donated these to the museum in Paris (Ten Kate 1884a, 1884b, 1884c; 1885a; 1892a; 1917a, 1917b; 1931; Hovens 1989:75–94).

During his research in the Southwest in 1882–1883, Ten Kate did little archaeological work. He recorded prehistoric ruins he encountered in the field, noted their meaning to contemporary Indians, and tried to interpret them on the basis of scientific research carried out by others, Indian oral traditions, and the insights he gained on intertribal relationships. Only in Baja California did he excavate in caves and middens, assisted by ornithologist Lyman Belding (Belding 1885; Van der Pas 1977; Hovens 1989:131–37; 1991b).

In 1887–1888, as a member of the interdisciplinary Hemenway Southwestern Archaeological Expedition, Ten Kate took part in excavations at Los Muertos and other Hohokam sites in south-central Arizona and at Hawikuh, a prehistoric Zuni town. A small collection of Hemenway artifacts was donated to the National Museum of Ethnology in Leiden. Ten Kate acted as chief physical anthropologist and was assisted by Jacob Wortman of the Army Medical Museum, with whom he undertook a study of the hyoid bone. He continued his earlier anthropometric research among several southwestern tribes (Pimas, Maricopas, Zunis), further increasing the size of his tribal samples. His visit to the Pimas was recorded on a tribal calendar stick kept at Gila Crossing and collected by Frank Russell. This is probably a unique example of native recording of anthropological fieldwork. The 1887–1888 period includes a carving of a crooked bone on the mnemonic device, which Russell's informant said referred to a stranger "who counted the bones of the people." Ten Kate's findings seem to support Emil W. Haury's theory of a Saladoan immigration into Hohokam territory. However, Ten Kate also pointed to Piman oral traditions suggesting a Hohokam-Piman cultural continuity. Unaware of the fact that changes in burial practices, from cremation to interment, could explain these opposing interpretations, Ten Kate adhered to the empirical evidence and emphasized the necessity for further interdisciplinary research to answer this question. It was Ten Kate's lifelong frustration that his Hemenway work went largely unrecognized (Ten Kate 1888a, 1889b, 1889c; 1890a; 1892a; Russell 1907:60; Hrdlicka 1919:117–19; Hovens 1989:131–54; 1995; Hinsley and Wilcox 1995; 1996; 2002).

Ten Kate's ethnolinguistic studies were rather modest in scale and depth. However, he regarded comparative studies of Indian languages as an essential instrument in unveiling relationships between tribes and possibly contributing to resolving the origin of the aboriginal population of the Americas. On his visit to the Bureau of American Ethnology in 1882, it was probably Powell who requested Ten Kate to compile vocabularies among the tribes he was going to visit. For transcription of tribal languages he used the standard word lists of the bureau, elaborated the phonetic alphabet developed by Powell with symbols from the alphabet of Karl Lepsius, and covered a number of sounds with six symbols of his own design. He studied the vocabularies and the grammar of Indian languages comparatively and in a number of cases came to the same conclusions as earlier researchers about the relationships between tribes. In other instances he indicated linguistic relationships that were confirmed in later studies (Ten Kate 1884d:355; Hovens 1989:95–104).

Of lasting importance are Ten Kate's studies of ethnic synonymy, following the example set by Albert S. Gatschet (1877) with his studies of the Yuman-speaking tribes and the work of Otis T. Mason and James Mooney at the Bureau of American Ethnology. A prime motive for this research was to eliminate the terminological confusion in much of the historical and anthropological literature. That his work was valued by contemporaries as well as in more recent times is shown by Frederick Webb Hodge's use of Ten Kate's findings for the first *Handbook of American Indians North of Mexico* (1907–1910) and in the Smithsonian Institution's new twenty-volume *Handbook of North American Indians,* in which the subject of ethnic synonymy is treated under a separate heading in the chapter on each tribe (Ten Kate 1884d, 1885a; Sturtevant 1978–present; Hinsley 1981:155–58; Hovens 1989:100–102).

Ten Kate's first year of fieldwork in the United States (1882–1883) was in reality a journey of recognizance during which he tried to get a general and representative idea about Indian peoples, their physical characteristics and cultural backgrounds, and their condition under white domination. Combined with a salvage orientation, his enterprise resulted in a hit-and-run ethnography and subsequently a severely fragmented description of tribal cultures. However, some of these fragments proved to be of lasting value, especially when he was able to observe certain traditions firsthand, encountered an informant willing to elaborate on certain customs, or devoted extra time to a subject that captured his special interest (Hovens 1989:105–30).

Indian games and sports were a phenomenon that received more than average attention from the young anthropologist, perhaps because the games and sports were easily observable and were performed intensely by Indians whose subsistence at that time was largely government rations. Ten Kate also made a point of collecting objects used in hoop-and-pole games, gambling, and ball games. He provided Cushing with the data on games and sports when his friend was preparing an exhibit for the International and Cotton States Exposition in Atlanta (1895). Ultimately he delivered his materials to Stewart Culin to be used for his colleague's monumental monograph on North American Indian games (Ten Kate 1885a; Culin 1907; Hovens 1989:110–14).

Ten Kate also focused on social organization, although his fieldwork went little beyond listings of clans, moieties, and marriage rules. The only exception was the organization of the Southern Cheyennes, which he could study in more detail because he was able to enlist the services of good interpreters and informants. These data provide interesting material for a comparative study, using similar data obtained during fieldwork by James Owen Dorsey and E. Adamson Hoebel (Ten Kate 1885a:359–62; Dorsey 1905; Hoebel 1960; Hovens 1989:110–13).

A recurrent theme in Ten Kate's work is the criticism of travelers and scientists who expressed negative views about Native American societies generally and the position of women and treatment of children particularly. He repeatedly stressed the caring and affectionate upbringing of children he witnessed and also pointed out that women's roles were not only defined by the internal division of labor but also by clan membership, often providing protection against mistreatment after marriage. In addition, in certain tribes women played a prominent political role, signifying a more prominent position (Ten Kate 1885a:115, 364–65, 459; Hovens 1989:113–14).

Ten Kate also reprimanded writers who declared that tribal peoples had no religion and lived only by superstition and without morality. He pointed out that all tribal peoples had fundamental religious concepts that guided and ordered their daily lives and recurring rituals. In addition, he stressed that a certain degree of religious pluralism prevailed in tribal societies since he had encountered and heard about religious skeptics. This he regarded as another expression of the fundamental psychic unity of mankind (Ten Kate 1885a).

Ethnographic research in the field of religion was a difficult affair because Indians generally shielded this sphere of life from outsiders. Ten Kate tried to elicit myths from his informants. In this he was successful several times, but most of his notes are lost. Only the Cherokee and Zuni oral traditions he published survive (Ten Kate 1885a:426–28; 1889d; 1917c). Rituals provided another opportunity to study Indian religious concepts, but opportunities to witness ceremonies were not always available. However, Ten Kate was able to be present at two important events in 1883: the Snake Dance at Walpi, which he witnessed in the company of Jeremiah Sullivan (Oyiwisha) and Thomas V. Keam, and the Kakokshi Dance at Zuni. He managed to describe both rituals in some detail, thus contributing valuable data for a comparative study using other early descriptions (McIntire and Gordon 1968; Hovens 1989:114–19, 140).

In 1888, when employed by the Hemenway Expedition, Ten Kate, who had recently completed his medical studies, researched medicinal practices at Zuni. Unfortunately, only a few fragments of his notes survive. He stressed the empirical knowledge of medicine men, especially in the case of mechanical afflictions such as wounds and broken bones. Knowledge of internal afflictions was limited, and treatment was sought in the realm of the supernatural, notably a variety of curing ceremonies focused on identifying and neutralizing witchcraft. Ten Kate noted that both western physicians and native shamans were able to contribute to the healing process by the effect on patients of their powers of suggestion. In addition, medicine men possessed pharmacological knowledge, using potent medicinal herbs in treatment. Finally, Ten Kate observed the clairvoyance of several Indians. He proved to be an accomplished physician and scientist when he concluded that ignoring the phenomenon was as unscientific as believing in it (Hovens 1989, 124).

Ten Kate considered his stay at Zuni the high point of his journey. He regarded this oasis in the desert as a microcosm of aboriginal life, the people at the individual and collective level at one with each other, the natural environment, and the cosmos, socially, physically, and spiritually. Indelibly etched in his mind were the scenes of the women carrying painted ollas on their heads, descending to the river to draw water; the exotic calendric ceremonials with masked and colorfully attired dancers; the women and men working, manually adept and mentally inspired, on their delicate pottery and fine jewelry; the old storytellers sharing the ancient tribal legends around an evening fire; the reverent rituals of the societies of the priests. Nowhere did Ten Kate come closer to an understanding of Indians as fellow men than in Zuni, where he observed and analyzed the interaction between the individual and tribal society in a uniquely sensitive manner. As such, Zuni became instrumental in making sense of larger things for him, as it has done for many other anthropologists and other intellectuals since (Ten Kate 1885a:273–306; Hovens 1989:119–25, 209; McFeely 2001:167–68).

During his travels and researches Ten Kate purchased ethnographic artifacts with the funds provided for this purpose by the government of the Netherlands and the Holland Association of Sciences. He reported on the conditions for collectors in the field, the resistance to be overcome in obtaining certain objects, and the rapid replacement of traditional artifacts by western goods. His collections were deposited with the National Museum of Ethnology in Leiden. In addition he bought specimens with private funds but in the course of his life donated or sold these to the Leiden museum. A catalog of the Ten Kate collection, totaling approximately 400 artifacts from upper New York State, the Southwest, and the Southern Plains, is in preparation. To document Indian culture and history, the Dutch anthropologist also took and collected photographs, which were deposited at the anthropology museums in Leiden and Rotterdam (Kaemlein 1967:132–44; Hovens 1989:106–10, 164–66; Hovens and Groeneveld 1992; Hovens et al. in preparation).

While studying in France, Ten Kate learned about Count de Gobineau's views on qualitative mental differences between peoples and cultures. However, the Dutch student agreed with the criticism of white and western supremacist thought expressed by his Parisian tutors. In Berlin his ideas about culture and personality were greatly influenced by Bastian's concept of the psychic unity of mankind. In his studies of Native American tribes, Ten Kate presented evidence for this principle by showing that Indian lives were not only regulated by formal rules but also by etiquette, that humor was frequently used as a mechanism for social control, and that Indians were sensitive to fashion. He explicitly addressed the question of Indian personality, since popular imagery often denied Native Americans the most common human characteristics. Such imagery carried over into science, and the Dutch anthropologist criticized contemporaries such as Lucien Levy-Brühl in France and J. C. Van Eerde in the Netherlands, who argued that tribal people's thought was "prelogical" because they were unable to recognize causal relationships. He stressed that the intellect of the lower classes in Europe was quite similar to that of tribal peoples, that only gradual differences existed between peoples and groups, and that feelings of white superiority should be checked by critical self-analysis (Ten Kate 1885a; 1916a:5–10).

Ten Kate also noted intertribal differences in personality, referring to the uncomplicated, carefree, and optimistic character of the Yumans of the Colorado River Valley, the persistent reserve of the Utes, and the seriousness of the Zunis. Ten Kate stressed that personalities across cultures differed because they were shaped by living conditions, socialization, and experience, thus rejecting a simplistic biological determinism. He regarded the difference between the personalities of tribal peoples and white westerners not as fundamental but as gradual. His ethnopsychological typology of tribes is an early expression of the culture-and-personality tradition that gained wider acceptance since in the 1930s (Hovens 1989:127–28; Spindler 1978).

In his North American research, Ten Kate was much concerned with establishing relationships between tribes on solid empirical grounds and even hoped to contribute to the solution of the question regarding the origin of the Indians. He took an interdisciplinary approach and used physical anthropological, linguistic, and ethnographic data. Always cautious not to speculate without sufficient hard data, he never ventured far beyond arguing for intertribal relationships on linguistic grounds and Asian-American relationships on the basis of physical type. Boas encouraged Ten Kate to publish a criticism of Brinton's controversial views on the indigenous American origin of the Indians in *Science* but shied away from publishing Ten Kate's reaction to Brinton's rebuttal due to the Philadelphian's stature in the scientific community (Ten Kate 1888b, 1892b; Brinton 1888, 1890, 1894; Darnell 1988:110–14; Hovens 1989:151–52; Baker 2000).

Ten Kate was one of the first anthropologists to study Indian imagery in western art and literature, much earlier than David H. Bushnell of the Bureau of American Ethnology, often credited as the founder of this special field (Ewers 1967). Ten Kate analyzed the work of some early but mostly contemporary writers and artists. Those who took liberties with the portrayal of the natural environment, physical type, material culture, and customs of the Indian peoples could count on his firm criticism and sometimes even condemnation of their work. However, with his background in the arts and the humanities, Ten Kate recognized artistic achievement. In his opinion only a few people were able to combine realism with artistic ability, and their work he considered of immense and enduring value to science and society. To this category belonged artists George Catlin, Karl Bodmer, Paul Kane, Rudolf Friedrich Kurz, Henry F. Farny, and Frederic Remington and writers Washington Irving, Helen Hunt Jackson, and Marah Ellis Ryan. Ten Kate felt his colleague Adolph Bandelier had also succeeded in this field with the fictional *The Delight Makers* (1890). Some of the early Taos painters, such as Eanger Irving Couse and Joseph Henry Sharp, received at least honorable mention from Ten Kate. Apart from pioneering in this field, the lasting value of Ten Kate's work may be deduced from the fact that one of his main publications on this topic was reprinted repeatedly until quite recently. Throughout his life and work the imagery of native peoples in art and literature remained a recurring topic (Ten Kate 1910, 1911b, 1912a, 1913, 1919, 1920a, 1922a, 1970, 1973; Hovens 1989:185–96, in preparation).

Ten Kate's efforts to find academic employment in the United States met with no success, a source of extreme disappointment for him. The professionalization of anthropology was only embryonic in his time, resulting in few positions at universities, museums, and research institutions. Ten Kate attributed his lack of success in this field to the fact that he was a European, an impression strengthened by private comments of Belgian-born Charles Rau at the Smithsonian Institution. John Wesley Powell's aversion to physical anthropology and a formal division of labor between the Smithsonian and the Army Medical Museum were other factors, the latter the result of Joseph Henry's determination to keep his institution free from politically damaging scientific discussions about monogenism versus polygenism. However, Ten Kate's critical views on Indian policy, repeatedly stated in private and in public, could also have been decisive barriers to employment. He always advocated a strongly partisan anthropology on behalf of native peoples vis-à-vis colonial and national governments (Hovens 1989:200–207).

In the American West, Ten Kate witnessed the disastrous effects of colonialism on native tribes: exploitation and poverty, powerlessness and apathy. Government and churches allied to carry out a relentless policy of destruction of Indian cultures, using unjust laws and policies, an exploitative and repressive system of administration, and repressive mission schools to banish all traces of traditional beliefs and practices and turn Indians into mainstream Americans at any cost. Ten Kate was realistic in recognizing that the wheels of history could not be turned back, but he expected and in his writings demanded a just and equal treatment of native peoples by the federal government and the various religious denominations. He called for respect for native cultures and a humane and just policy based on the interests of the Indian tribes (Ten Kate 1878, 1885a, 1889a, 1901, 1911a, 1916a). Thus Ten Kate proved to be an early advocate of self-determination, a stance situating him outside the public, political, and scientific mainstream of his day. He joined the National Indian Defense Association (NIDA), which advocated similar policies. Ten Kate's article in its periodical *The Council Fire* (1889) caused an outcry among reform organizations that condemned foreign comments on domestic policy. However, Ten Kate continued to express his views in Dutch and German periodicals, recruited supporters in Europe for the NIDA, and promoted publications and views of other Indian advocates such as Helen Hunt Jackson, Frank H. Cushing, and James Mooney (Ten Kate 1889a, 1889e, 1889f; Dozy 1889; Schmeltz 1889; Priest 1975:169; Prucha 1976:89–90; Hovens 1989:177–80, 195–96, 224). In 1910 Ten Kate was among a small group of anthropologists vocally speaking out against the deportation and enslavement of the Yaquis in Mexico. He wrote President Theodore Roosevelt to request his intervention but was dismayed about the noncommittal answer he received from the White House (Ten Kate 1911a; Spicer 1980:158–61; Hovens 1989:177).

Ten Kate strongly rejected the plea for a value-free anthropology as advocated by Pliny Earl Goddard and criticized the passive attitude of the majority of his American colleagues about Indian policy. He regarded John Wesley Powell as the pallbearer of the interests of the federal government. Although his Bureau of American Ethnology had done valuable ethnological research, it had shied away from practicing an applied anthropology, although its charter included such a mandate. Only Frank H. Cushing and James Mooney had showed moral courage by expressing controversial views based on the priority of Indian rights and the value of cultural pluriformity, a stance that had effectively ended Cushing's fieldwork among the Zunis (Ten Kate 1889a; 1916a; Hinsley 1981:148–49; Hovens 1989:177–80, 220–25; 1995:642).

During his fieldwork Ten Kate faced the question of the future of the Indians, as did his American contemporaries involved in scientific studies, government policy, charitable work, and missionary endeavors (Dippie 1982; Scheckel 1998). On the basis of his observations he concluded that the process of miscegenation and acculturation was progressing among all tribes as such and that the high fertility of these unions speeded it up. However, he also pointed out that temporal and cultural factors within Indian communities and between Indian and white society determined its course, the Iroquois and Pueblo peoples being cases in point. But although the degree of miscegenation could vary between tribes, the direction of the process was obvious among all: a gradual dilution of Indian physical types and the corresponding dilution of Indian lifestyles with western elements. He regarded this process as continuous and irreversible and concluded that the Indians would not die out as a race but would gradually be incorporated into the American population without visible physical and cultural trace. This view was shared by prominent contemporary Indians and scientists, and John Wesley Powell aptly formulated it thus: "Civilization overwhelms Savagery, not so much by spilling blood as by mixing blood" (Powell 1885:436).

The question remaining and foremost in the minds of many of Ten Kate's contemporaries in politics and science was the capacity for civilization of the Indians. After considering all the arguments in the debate and analyzing his own observations, Ten Kate concluded that the Indians were intellectually and socially capable of mastering the difficult transformation from savagery to civilization. He rejected the necessity of physical miscegenation as he had witnessed full-bloods who had adopted western culture and were comfortable with their new lifestyle. In taking this view he opposed many contemporaries, including those in his scientific community, who regarded the Indians as an inferior race. Ten Kate admitted the superiority of the white race but restricted it to demography, sheer numbers, and modern technology (Ten Kate 1885a:402–30, 462–63; 1927a:107–8; Hovens 1989:180–82).

A Life in Anthropology

After his first great American research journey, Ten Kate pursued his career and carried out fieldwork in Scandinavia, Surinam, the Caribbean, Algeria, Mexico, Sri Lanka, Indonesia, Australia, the Tonga and Society Islands, Hawaii, China, Argentina, and Paraguay, publishing the results of his researches in European and American scientific serials and in two travel and research itineraries (1894a; 1925). With Lindor Serrurier, the director of the National Museum of Ethnology in Leiden, he founded the physical anthropological journal *Notices Anthropologiques*. His fieldwork was financially supported by his wealthy friend Prince Roland Bonaparte, several scientific societies in Holland, the governments of the Netherlands and the Dutch East Indies, employment for several years by the Museo de La Plata in Argentina as curator of physical anthropology (1893–1894, 1895–1897), and his own increasingly modest means. To his great regret, a number of efforts to find employment with the Bureau of American Ethnology or other American scientific institutions in the 1880s and 1890s failed, despite recommendations by Frank Cushing and Washington Matthews. Ten Kate's fieldwork across the globe and the study of relevant scientific and historical sources were facilitated by his command of many European as well as several major non-European languages, including Arabic, Malay, and Japanese. The Dutch anthropologist was truly a citizen of the world, and in Paris he was known as "l'homme qui n'est jamais là, où est sa dernière adresse?" His ethnological, archaeological, zoological, and botanical collections from the Americas and around the world helped to enrich museums in Leiden, Rotterdam, Utrecht, Paris, and Berlin (Hovens 1989:200–207; 2001; Hovens et al. in preparation).

Ten Kate's romantic inclination, exemplified by his artistic and scientific work, hardly qualified him for a bourgeois existence. He never felt at ease in the salons of The Hague, Leiden, and Paris, and only academia provided a niche for self-realization for such estranged as him. However, fieldwork was the prime opportunity for Ten Kate to realize his romantic yearning for faraway exotic places and peoples. Whatever the hardships in deserts and mountains, in the sweltering tropics or the chill of the Andes, in his diaries he extolled the grandeur of nature, feeling at home alone in the field, one with his untamed environment. He equally felt at ease with the peoples he visited. His captivating personality and intelligence were quickly realized and usually resulted in a generous welcome, which he accepted without reservations. He showed respect for his hosts by trying to learn their ethos, anxieties, and aspirations. Fieldwork enabled Ten Kate to break through the constraints of pretentious bourgeois Victorian society in a romantic search for a pristine environment, untouched by western civilization, awakening the soul of the primeval man of nature that lives in every man (Hovens 1989:207–10, 271–79).

Between 1898 and 1919 Ten Kate practiced medicine in Japan, principally serving the European enclaves of Nagasaki and Yokohama, meanwhile studying Japanese culture and pursuing his North American Indian studies from his armchair. He married Kimii Fuji in 1906, and during their four-year (1909–1913) European interlude, Ten Kate concentrated on his anthropological writings. With Franz Boas he debated the stability of physical types both privately and publicly. In 1911 he declined the offer of the University of Utrecht to become professor of Indonesian ethnology, as his wife had trouble adjusting to the European way of life and his own health deteriorated because of the cold and wet climate. In 1913 the couple returned to Japan and Ten Kate set up medical practice in

Ashiya, near Kobe, now mainly serving Japanese patients. During those first decades of the twentieth century, Ten Kate grew increasingly dissatisfied with global developments that he witnessed on his many travels, most importantly the degradation of native peoples under western and Japanese colonialism and the rapidly increasing mechanization of life. He had little patience with "progress" and clung to his older memories, his "mundo de saudade," which he cherished dearly (Boas 1912; Ten Kate 1912b, 1912c; Hovens 1989:90–91, 225–27).

The major part of his physical anthropological work during that period and the final part of his working life was concerned with physical types and skin color. He had become an authority on pigment spots, a subject about which he published a number of articles. With Daniel G. Brinton he debated the origin of the American Indians, rejecting his American colleague's theory of European origins. With Franz Boas he exchanged views on the stability of physical types, stressing general stability versus immutability. He befriended Ales Hrdlicka, creating a bond that remained strong for a long time. The American anthropologist appreciated the efforts of his Dutch colleague to get access to the remains of *"Pithecantropus erectus,"* which Eugene Dubois eventually effectively blocked. Later Ten Kate was a frequent contributor to the National Museum of Ethnology's periodical *Internationales Archiv für Ethnographie,* and as a prominent member of the Royal Netherlands Geographical Society he published numerous short articles, research notes, and book reviews in that society's journal, often on Americanist subjects (see Hovens 1989:271–79 and Ten Kate bibliography following this essay).

The Great War deeply shocked Ten Kate emotionally and morally, as did the sudden death of his Japanese wife in the influenza epidemic of 1919. From then on he suffered from recurring depressions caused by his disillusion with civilization, an increasing sense of professional failure, and growing existential insecurity, the latter the result of progressively exhausting private financial means. He became intellectually homeless, an aimless wanderer living a "vie errante," traveling around the world to visit friends and familiar places in search of a Paradise Lost, his "mundo do saudade," enclaves of which he had known during his earlier journeys across the globe but that were now irrevocably lost as a victim of the onslaught of western civilization. From that time on he was hardly able to do productive scientific work and only able to finish a few studies on which he had been working for many years. Returning to Europe in 1919 by way of the United States, he wandered restlessly across the continent, trying unsuccessfully to concentrate on his writing. He lived alternately in the Netherlands, Switzerland, France, and Italy and in 1925 published a popular book with his travel narratives, which gave him some satisfaction. He spent the last years of his life in Tunisia in deteriorating health because of a lifelong cardiovascular affliction and impoverished, barely surviving off his own slender means and on funds raised by friends and colleagues in the Netherlands. Death came as salvation at the Villa Tanit in Carthago on February 5, 1931 (Hovens 1989:15–41, 197–215, 225–31, 282).

Ten Kate, the man and the scientist, was honored in a plethora of obituaries by friends and colleagues from both sides of the Atlantic, who stressed his many qualities, notably his erudition and moral courage (e.g., Snelleman 1930; Van Capelle 1931; Friederici 1931; Heyink and Hodge 1931; Kohlbrugge 1931; Rivet 1931; Steinmetz 1931; Mendes Corrêa 1932). Because of his extensive firsthand experience with fieldwork in North America and wide-ranging studies in different scientific fields of a nondelimiting anthropology, Ten Kate was recognized as one of the leading European experts in the field of North American Indian studies in the decades around the turn of the twentieth century.

Epilogue

Herman Ten Kate was a unique representative of the pioneer period of academic anthropology. He was among the first professionally trained anthropologists and straddled all four fields that would later come to characterize American anthropology and the new interdisciplinary study of man. His work exemplifies the competing paradigms that characterize a nascent academic discipline as well as revolution in scientific thought. Ten Kate became an early and strong advocate of participant observation as the ideal strategy for anthropological research. The Dutchman was an anthropological entrepreneur in that he crossed borders and frontiers worldwide and carried out fieldwork on different commissions and his own initiative in all continents, a truly remarkable feat. His ethnographic collection from North America is one of the earliest in Europe assembled in the context of professional anthropological fieldwork. Ten Kate also pioneered the study of what was then called the exotic genre in art and literature, a precursor to modern anthropological studies of imagery.

Ten Kate's liberal family background and predominantly empiricist academic training resulted in an idealistic stance that informed his applied and partisan anthropology. With only a few others he stands out from the ranks of contemporary colleagues in his vocal criticism of colonialism, strong emphasis on the necessity of an applied anthropology, and public advocacy of the human rights of native peoples around the world, a truly modern stance for an anthropologist in the 1880–1920 period.

Ten Kate's published itineraries reveal much of the man behind the scientist. They are written in an attractive literary style and still make for captive reading for present-day scientists and laymen. The irony and sarcasm so frequent in his early works turn into cynicism in his publications after the Great War, the human cataclysm that broke his spirit. However, as a student of man and a man of science, he was a unique representative of the pioneer era of academic anthropology.

◆◆◆◆◆

References

Baker, Lee D. 2000. "Daniel G. Brinton's success on the road to obscurity." *Cultural Anthropology* 15 (3):394–423.

Bandelier, Adolph F. 1890. *The delight makers*. New York: Dodd, Mead and Company.

Belding, Lyman. 1885. "The Pericué Indians." *West-American Scientist* 1 (4):21–22.

Boas, Franz. 1912. "Changes in the bodily form of descendants of immigrants." *American Anthropologist* 14:530–62.

Bourke, John Gregory. 1884. *The Snake-Dance of the Moquis of Arizona*. New York: Scribners.

Brinton, Daniel G. 1888. "On the alleged Mongolian affinities of the American race." *Science* (September 14):325.

———. 1890. *Essays of an Americanist*. Philadelphia: Porter & Coates.

———. 1894. "On various supposed relations between the American and Asian races." In *Memoirs of the International Congress of Anthropology*, ed. C. S. Wake, 145–51. Chicago: Schulte.

Culin, Stewart. 1907. *Games of the North American Indians*. Washington, D.C.: *Annual Report of the Bureau of American Ethnology 24*.

Darnell, Regna 1988. *Daniel Garrison Brinton: The fearless critic of Philadelphia*. Philadelphia: University of Pennsylvania Publications in Anthropology 3.

———. 2000. *Invisible Genealogies: A History of Americanist Anthropology*. Lincoln: University of Nebraska Press.

DeMallie, R. J., and John C. Ewers. 2001. "History of ethnological and ethnohistorical research." In *Handbook of North American Indians: Plains*, ed. R. J. DeMallie, 13(1):23–43. Washington, D.C.: Smithsonian Institution.

Dias, Nélia. 1991. *Le Musée d'Ethnographie du Trocadéro, 1878–1908: Anthropologie et Muséologie en France*. Paris: Editions du CNRS.

Dippie, Brian W. 1982. *The vanishing American: White attitudes and U.S. Indian policy*. Middletown, Conn.: Wesleyan University Press.

Dorsey, James Owen. 1905. *The Cheyenne*. Chicago: Field Columbian Museum Anthropological Series 9.

Dozy, G. J. 1889. "Voor Recht en Menschelijkheid: The National Indian Defense Association." *De Tijdsspieghel* 3 (10):141–50.

Ellen, Roy F. 1976. "The development of anthropology and colonial policy in the Netherlands, 1800–1960." *Journal of the History of the Behavioral Sciences* 12:303–24.

Ewers, John C. 1967. "Fact and fiction in the documentary art of the American West." In *The frontier re-examined,* ed. J. F. McDermott, 79–95. Urbana: University of Illinois Press.

Faris, James C. 1988. *The Nightway: A history and a history of documentation of a Navajo ceremonial*. Albuquerque: University of New Mexico Press.

Fowler, Don D. 2000. *A laboratory of anthropology: Science and romanticism in the American Southwest, 1846–1930*. Albuquerque: University of New Mexico Press.

Friederici, Georg. 1931. "Herman F. C. ten Kate." *Ethnologischer Anzeiger* 2 (7):294–95.

Gatschet, Albert Samuel. 1876. *Zwölf Sprachen aus dem Südwesten Nordamerikas*. Weimar: Böhlau.

Graves, Laura. 1998. *Thomas Varker Keam: Indian trader*. Norman: University of Oklahoma Press.

Halpern, Katherine Spencer, and Susan Brown McGreevy, eds. 1997. *Washington Matthews: Studies of Navajo culture, 1880–1894*. Albuquerque: University of New Mexico Press.

Harris, Marvin. 1968. *The rise of anthropological theory: A history of theories of culture*. London: Routledge and Kegan Paul.

Held, G. Jan. 1953. "Applied anthropology in the Netherlands." In *Anthropology today,* ed. A. L. Kroeber, 866–79. Chicago: University of Chicago Press.

Heyink, J., and F. W. Hodge. 1931. "Herman Frederik Carel ten Kate." In *American Anthropologist* 33:415–18.

Hieb, Louis A., and Susan E. Diggle. Forthcoming. "A question of authorship: A. M. Stephen's catalogue of the Keam Expedition [1884]." *Kiva*.

Hinsley, Curtis M. 1981. *Savages and scientists: The Smithsonian Institution and the development of American anthropology, 1846–1910*. Washington, D.C.: Smithsonian Institution Press.

Hinsley, Curtis M., and David R. Wilcox, eds. 1995. "A Hemenway portfolio." In *Journal of the Southwest,* special issue, 37 (4).

———. 1996. *The Southwest in the American imagination: The writings of Sylvester Baxter, 1881–1889*. Tucson: University of Arizona Press.

———. 2002. *The lost itinerary of Frank Hamilton Cushing*. Tucson: University of Arizona Press.

Hodge, Frederick Webb. 1907–10. *Handbook of American Indians north of Mexico*. Bulletin of the Bureau of American Ethnology 30. Washington, D.C.: U.S. Government Printing Office (2 vols.).

Hoebel, E. Adamson. 1960. *The Cheyennes: Indians of the Great Plains*. New York: Holt, Rinehart and Winston.

Hovens, Pieter. 1984. "Between survival and assimilation: The visit of the Dutch anthropologist Herman ten Kate to the Iroquois in 1882." In *North American Indian studies 2: European contributions to science, society and art*, ed. P. Hovens, 36–42. Aachen-Göttingen: Alano Verlag—Edition Herodot.

———. 1988. "The anthropologist as enigma: Frank Hamilton Cushing." *European Review of Native American Studies* 2 (1):1–5.

———. 1989. *Herman F. C. ten Kate (1858–1931) en de antropologie der Noord Amerikaanse Indianen* (Herman F. C. ten Kate and the anthropology of the North American Indians). Ph.D. diss., University of Nijmegen. Krips: Meppel.

———. 1991a. "Veth, Pieter Johannes (1814–1895)." In *International dictionary of anthropologists*, ed. C. Winters, 727–28. New York: Garland.

———. 1991b. "The origins of anthropology in Baja California: The fieldwork and excavations of Herman F. C. ten Kate in 1883." *Pacific Coast Archaeological Society Quarterly* 27 (4):15–22.

———. 1995. "Ten Kate's Hemenway Expedition diary, 1887–1888." In *A Hemenway Portfolio* (special issue), eds. C. M. Hinsley and D. R. Wilcox. *Journal of the Southwest* 37 (4):635–700.

———. Forthcoming. *A portrait of Native America: Henry C. Balink and the art of Taos and Santa Fe*.

Hovens, Pieter, et al. Forthcoming. *North American Indian art and material culture: The Ten Kate collection*. Catalog.

Hovens, Pieter, and Anneke Groeneveld. 1992. *Odagot: Photographs of American Indians, 1860–1920*. Amsterdam: Fragment Uitgeverij.

Hovens, Pieter, and Jiska Herlaar. In press. "Early anthropology in the Great Basin: The 1883 fieldwork of Herman ten Kate." *Journal of the Southwest*.

Hrdlicka, Ales. 1919. *Physical anthropology: Its scope and aims; its history and present status in America*. Philadelphia: The Wistar Institute.

Josselin de Jong, P. E. 1980. "The Netherlands: Structuralism before Lévi-Strauss." In *Anthropology: Ancestors and Heirs*, ed. Stanley Diamond, 243–58. The Hague: Mouton.

Kaemlein, Wilma. 1967. *An inventory of Southwestern American Indian specimens in European museums*. Tucson: Arizona State Museum.

Koepping, K. P. 1983. *Adolf Bastian and the psychic unity of mankind*. St. Lucia: University of Queensland Press.

Kohlbrugge, J. H. F. 1931. "Een merkwaardig zwerversleven: Dr. H. F. C. ten Kate." *Tijdschrift voor het Onderwijs in de Aardrijkskunde* 9:59–63.

Kutscher, Gerdt. 1966. "Berlin als Zentrum der Alt-Amerika Forschung." *Jahrbuch der Stiftung Preussicher Kulturbesitz* 4:88–122.

Mark, Joan. 1980. *Four anthropologists: An American science in its early years.* New York: Science History Publications.

Matthews, Washington. 1886. "Navajo names for plants." *American Naturalist* 20:767–77.

McFeely, Eliza. 2001. *Zuni and the American imagination.* New York: Hill and Wang.

McIntire, E. G., and S. R. Gordon. 1968. "Ten Kate's account of the Walpi Snake Dance." *Plateau* 41:27–33.

Mendes Corrêa, A. A. 1932. *Herman ten Kate: um Amigo de Wenceslau de Moraïs.* Pôrto: Instituto de Antropologia, Universidade do Pôrto.

Porter, Joseph C. 1986. *Paper medicine man: John Gregory Bourke and his American West.* Norman: University of Oklahoma Press.

Powell, John Wesley. 1885. "From savagery to barbarism." In *Transactions of the Anthropological Society of Washington* 3:173–96.

Priest, Loring B. 1975. *Uncle Sam's stepchildren: The reformation of United States Indian Policy, 1865–1887.* Lincoln: University of Nebraska Press.

Prucha, Francis Paul. 1975. *American Indian policy in crisis: Christian reformers and the Indians, 1865–1900.* Norman: University of Oklahoma Press.

Rivet, Paul. 1931. "Herman F. C. ten Kate." In *Journal de la Société des Américanistes* 23:236–42.

Russell, Frank. 1907. *The Pima Indians.* Washington, D.C.: Annual Report of the Bureau of American Ethnology 26.

Scheckel, Susan. 1998. *The insistence of the Indian: Race and nationalism in nineteenth century American culture.* Princeton, N.J.: Princeton University Press.

Schmeltz, J. D. E. 1889. "The National Indian Defense Association and The Council Fire." In *Internationales Archiv für Ethnographie* 2:109.

Snelleman, Johan F. 1930. "Ten Kate is in Carthago gestorven." In *West-Indische Gids* 12:501–2.

Spicer, Edward H. 1980. *The Yaquis: A cultural history.* Tucson: University of Arizona Press.

Spindler, George, ed. 1978. *The making of psychological anthropology.* Berkeley: University of California Press.

Stagl, Justin. 1985. "Feldforschung und Ideologie." In *Feldforschungen,* ed. H. Fischer, 289–310. Berlin: Dietrich Reimer Verlag.

Steinmetz, S. R. 1931. "Ter nagedachtenis aan Dr. H. F. C. ten Kate." In *Tijdschrift van het Koninklijk Nederlands Aardrijkskundig Genootschap* 48:487–91.

Stephen, Alexander M. 1929. "Hopi tales," ed. Elsie Clews Parsons. In *Journal of American Folklore* 42:2–72.

———. 1936. *Hopi journal of Alexander M. Stephen,* ed. Elsie Clews Parsons. New York: Columbia University Contributions to Anthropology 23.

Stevenson, Mathilda Coxe. 1887. "The religious life of the Zuni child." In *Fifth Annual Report of the Bureau of Ethnology,* 533–55. Washington, D.C.: U.S. Government Printing Office.

Stocking, George W. 1987. *Victorian anthropology.* New York: Free Press.

———. 1992. *The ethnographer's magic and other essays in the history of anthropology.* Madison: University of Wisconsin Press.

———. 2001. *Delimiting anthropology.* Madison: University of Wisconsin Press.

Sturtevant, William C., ed. 1978–present. *Handbook of North American Indians.* Washington, D.C.: Smithsonian Institution (20 vols.).

ten Kate, Herman (see Ten Kate bibliography in appendix).

Van Capelle, H. 1928. "Dr. Herman F. C. Ten Kate." *Nienne Rotterdamsche Courant,* June 20.

———. 1931. "Dr. Herman F. C. ten Kate, 1858–1931." *De Wandelaar* 3:110–14.

Van der Pas, Peter. 1977. "In search of the original Californian: Herman ten Kate's expedition to Baja California." *Journal of San Diego History* 23 (3):41–51, 81–92.

Williams, Elisabeth A. 1985. "Anthropological institutions in nineteenth century France." *Isis* 76:331–48.

Zimmerman, Andrew. 2001. *Anthropology and antihumanism in imperial Germany.* Chicago: University of Chicago Press.

·····

Ten Kate Bibliography

This partial bibliography lists Ten Kate's publications on North American Indians, including his publications referred to in the introduction. A full bibliography is listed in Hovens 1989, 269–79. Translations of major Dutch titles are bracketed.

ABBREVIATIONS

AA *American Anthropologist*
BSA *Bulletins de la Société d'Anthropologie de Paris*
IAE Internationales Archiv für Ethnographie (Leiden)
JSA *Journal de la Société des Américanistes* (Paris)
TAG *Tijdschrift van het Koninklijk Nederlandsch Aardrijkskundig Genootschap*
        [*Journal of the Royal Netherlands Geographical Society*]

1878
Amerikaansche toestanden [American affairs]. *Omnibus* 10:366–69.

1882
Zur Craniologie der Mongoloïden: Beobachtungen und Messungen. Berlin: L. Schumacher.

1883
a. Een bezoek bij de Irokeezen [A visit to the Iroquois]. *TAG* 7:202–6.
b. Quelques observations sur les Indiens Iroquois. *Revue d'Anthropologie* 6:279–83.
c. Een Nederlandsch reiziger in de Vereenigde-Staten van Noord Amerika. *TAG* 7:19–20
        (letter, December 17, 1882, from St. Louis, Missouri).
d. Visite chez les Papagos. *Revue d'Ethnographie* 2:89–90 (letter, January 7, 1883,
        from Tucson, Arizona).

e. Mesures d'Indiens Papagos. *Revue d'Ethnographie* 2:90–91.

f. Brief van den reiziger Ten Kate. *TAG* 7:57 (letter, January 21, 1883, from La Paz, Sonora).

g. Quelques observations ethnographiques recueillis dans la presqu'île californienne et en Sonora. *Revue d'Ethnographie* 2:321–26.

h. Reis door Noord Amerika van den heer H. ten Kate Jr. *TAG* 7:79 (letter, March 19, 1883, from La Paz, Sonora).

i. Les Indiens de la presqu'île de la Californie et de l'Arizona. *BSA* 6:374–76 (letter, March 21, 1883, from La Paz, Sonora).

j. Brief. *TAG* 7:121–23 (letter, June 12, 1883, from Tucson, Arizona).

k. Indiens de la Sonora et de l'Arizona. *BSA* 6:634–37 (letter, June 19, 1883, from Tucson, Arizona).

l. Observations sur les Indiens du Nouveau Mexique et du Colorado. *BSA* 6:801–7 (letter, October 4, 1883, from Trinidad, Colorado).

m. Indiens des Etats-Unis du sud-ouest. *BSA* 6:898–900 (letter, December 5, 1883, from Washington, D.C.).

1884

a. Sur quelques crânes de l'Arizona et du Nouveau-Mexique. *Revue d'Anthropologie* 7:486–92.

b. Matériaux pour servir à l'anthropologie de la presqu'île californienne. *BSA* 7:551–69.

c. Materiales para servir a la antropologia de Baja California. *Annales del Museo Nacional de Mexico* 1 (4):5–16 (translation of 1884b).

d. Sur la synonymie ethnique et la toponymie chez les Indiens de l'Amérique du Nord. *Verslagen en Mededeelingen der Koninklijke Akademie van Wetenschappen, afdeeling Letterkunde* 1:353–63.

e. Notes sur l'ethnographie des Zunis. *Revue d'Ethnographie* 3:161–63.

f. Reis van Dr. Ten Kate Jr. (letters, September 10, 1883, from Santa Fe; October 3, 1883, Cheyenne-Arapaho Agency, Indian Territory; November 28, 1883, St. Louis). *TAG* 1:161–65.

1885

a. *Reizen en onderzoekingen in Noord Amerika* [*Travels and researches in North America*]. Leiden: E. J. Brill (see also 1889g).

b. Notes sur l'ethnographie des Comanches. *Revue d'Ethnographie* 4:120–36.

1886

Description d'un crâne d'Indien Moqui. *Archives Néerlandaises des Sciences Exactes et Naturelles* 20:14–19.

1887

Sur quelques objets trouvés près de Guaymas, Mexique. *Revue d'Ethnographie* 6:234–38.

1888

a. Eenige mededeelingen omtrent de Hemenway Expeditie [Some communications
 on the Hemenway Expedition]. *TAG* 6:216–24.

b. On the alleged Mongolian affinities of the American race: A reply to Daniel G. Brinton.
 Science 12:227–28.

c. Schrijven van Dr. H. F. C. ten Kate aan de redactie (letters, February 26, 1888, from
 Camp Baxter, Arizona, and May 9, 1888, from Camp Hemenway, Arizona).
 TAG 5:316–18.

d. Schrijven van Dr. H. F. C. ten Kate aan de redactie (letter, August 21, 1888, from
 Camp Cibola, New Mexico). *TAG* 5:536–37.

e. Schrijven van Dr. H. F. C. Ten Kate aan de redactie (letter, December 12, 1888, from
 The Hague). *TAG* 6:105–6.

1889

a. A Foreigner's view of the Indian question. *The Council Fire* 12, n.p.

b. The Hemenway Southwestern Archaeological Expedition. *IAE* 2:48–49.

c. Fouilles archéologiques aux Etats-Unis et au Mexique (letter, December 23, 1888, from
 The Hague, Netherlands). *Comptes-rendues de la Société de Géographie de Paris,
 séance du Janvier 18, 1889,* 51–54.

d. Legends of the Cherokees. *Journal of American Folklore* 2:53–55.

e. Ansichten eines Ausländers über die Indianerfrage. *Das Ausland* 23:441–44 (translation
 of 1889a).

f. Iets over het Indiaansch vraagstuk in de Vereenigde Staten [Notes on the Indian question
 in the United States]. *TAG* 6:582–88 (translation and expansion of 1889a).

g. Verbeteringen en aanvullingen van *Reizen en onderzoekingen in Noord Amerika* [Corrections
 and supplements to *Travels and researches in North America*].
 TAG 6:232–43.

h. (book review) James Owen Dorsey—*Osage traditions. IAE* 2:239.

i. (book review) Otis T. Mason—*The Ray collection from the Hupa reservation. IAE* 2:239.

j. (book review) Washington Matthews—*The Mountain Chant. IAE* 2:175.

k. Ethnographische and Anthropologische Mittheilungen aus dem Amerikanischen
 Südwesten und aus Mexiko. *Zeitschrift für Ethnologie* 21:664–68.

1890

a. (with Jacob L. Wortman) On an anatomical characteristic of the hyoid bone of the
   Precolumbian Pueblo Indians of Arizona. In *Comte-rendu du Quatrième Congrès
   International des Américanistes, Berlin 1888*, 263–70. Berlin: W. H. Kühl.

b. Zuni fetiches. *IAE* 3:118–19.

1892

a. Somatological observations on Indians of the Southwest. *Journal of American Ethnology
   and Archaeology* 3:119–44.

b. Sur la question de la pluralité et de la parenté des races en Amérique. In *Comte-rendu
   du Huitième Congrès International des Américanistes, Paris 1890*, 288–94. Paris:
   Ernest Leroux.

1894

a. *Verslag eener Reis in de Timorgroep en Polynesië* [*Report of a journey to the Timor
   Archipelago and Polynesia*]. Leiden: E. J. Brill.

b. Parallels between the Shiwian or Zunian culture and that of the Calchaquis. *IAE* 7:142–43.

1900

(obituary) Frank Hamilton Cushing. *AA* 2:768–71.

1901

(book review) Georg Friederici—*Indianer und Anglo-Amerikaner*. *TAG* 18:89–90.

1907

a. On pigment spots in newborn children. *AA* 9:433–36.

b. (book review) Georg Friederici—*Skalpieren und ähnliche Kriegsbräuche in Amerika*.
   TAG 24:474–78.

1908

a. (book review) Georg Friederici—*Der Tränengruss der Indianer*. *TAG* 4:2–4.

b. The house of Tcuhu. *AA* 10:174–75.

1910

Sur quelques peintres ethnographiques dans l'Amérique du Sud. *Sumarios de las Conferencias y
   Memorias presentadas al XVII Congreso des Americanistes a Buenos Aires*.

1911

a. Slavernij in een republiek [Slavery in a republic]. *Vragen des Tijds* 37 (1):397–408.

b. On paintings of North American Indians and their ethnographical value. *Anthropos* 6:521–45.

c. (book review) Observations au sujet des *Recherches anthropologiques de la Basse Californie* par le Dr. P. Rivet. *L'Anthropologie* 22:37–40.

d. Encore l'anthropologie de la Basse Californie. *L'Anthropologie* 22:374–75.

1912

a. Schilder-teekenaars in Nederlandsch Oost- en West-Indië en hun beteekenis voor de land- en volkenkunde [Artists in Dutch East and West India and their relevance for anthropology]. *Bijdragen tot de Taal-, Land- en Volkenkunde van Nederlandsch-Indië* 67:441–515.

b. Nachtrag zu *Schädelform und Umwelteinflüsse* von Moritz Alsberg. *Archiv für Rassen- und Gesellschaftsbiologie* 9:357–59.

c. Antwort Dr. H. ten Kate's. *Archiv für Rassen- und Gesellschaftsbiologie* 9:630.

1913

Exotisme in de kunst [Exoticism in art]. *Elsevier's Geïllustreerd Maandschrift* 46:179–94, 256–69, 346–63.

1915

Een paar woorden over het beschavingswerk onder primitieven [A few words on civilization work among primitive peoples]. *TAG* 32:350–55.

1916

a. *Psychologie en ethnologie in de koloniale politiek* [*Psychology and ethnology in colonial policy*]. Amsterdam: J. H. de Bussy.

b. Dynamometric observations among various peoples. *AA* 18:10–18.

1917

a. Mélanges anthropologiques: Indiens de l'Amérique du Nord. *L'Anthropologie* 28:129–55.

b. Mélanges anthropologiques: Indiens de l'Amérique du Nord. *L'Anthropologie* 28:369–401.

c. A Zuni folktale. *Journal of American Folklore* 30:496–99.

1918

Notes on the hands and feet of American natives. *AA* 20:187–202.

1919

De Indiaan in de letterkunde [The Indian in literature]. *De Gids* 83 (3):63–128.

1920

a. (editor and translator) Indiaansche minnebrieven [Indian love letters] door Marah Ellis Ryan. *De Indische Gids* 42:696–717.

b. De Noord Amerikaansche Indiaans als bondgenoot in de oorlogen der blanken [The North American Indian as an ally in the wars of the whites]. *TAG* 37:681–87.

1922

a. (book review) W. H. Holmes—*Handbook of aboriginal American antiquities. De West-Indische Gids* 3:58–61.

b. (obituary) James Mooney. *JSA* 14:216–17.

c. The Indian in literature. *Annual Report of the Smithsonian Institution for 1921,* 507–28. Washington, D.C. (abridged translation of Ten Kate 1919).

d. (obituary) James Mooney. *TAG* 39:522–23.

1923

(book reviews) Het Museum of the American Indian en zijn publicaties (F. H. Cushing—*Zuni breadstuff*; M. Harrington—*Cuba before Columbus*; M. Harrington—*Religion and ceremonies of the Lenape*). *TAG* 40:500–505.

1924

a. (book reviews) Het Museum of the American Indian en zijn publicaties (M. Harrington—*Cherokee remains on the Upper Tennessee River*; A. Skinner—*Notes on Iroquois archaeology*; R. P. Bolton—*Indian paths in the Great Metropolis*; F. G. Speck—*Beothuk and Micmac*; M. H. Saville—*Turquois mosaic art in ancient Mexico*). *TAG* 41:87–92.

b. (book reviews) De Hendricks-Hodge expeditie (F. W. Hodge—*Turquois work of Hawikuh*; F. W. Hodge—*Circular kivas near Hawikuh*). *TAG* 41:260–64.

1925

Over land en zee: schetsen en stemmingen van een wereldreiziger [*Across land and sea: sketches and moods of a world traveler*]. Zutphen: W. J. Thieme & Cie.

1927

a. (book review) Kroeber's ethnologische onderzoekingen in Californië [A. L. Kroeber—*Handbook of the Indians of California*]. *TAG* 44:95–108.

b. (book review) Bruno Oetteking—*Skeletal remains from Santa Barbara. Mensch en Maatschappij* 3:132.

c. (book review) Edward W. Gifford—*California anthropometry. Mensch en Maatschappij* 3:324–27.

1931

(book review) Florence Hawley—*Prehistoric pottery and culture relations in the Middle Gila. AA* 33:268–70.

POSTHUMOUS REPRINTS

1970

The Indian in literature. *Indian Historian* 3:28–32 (partial reprint of Ten Kate 1922c).

1973

The Indian in literature. In *The American Indian reader: literature,* ed. Jeannette Henry, 111–21. San Francisco: Indian Historian Press (partial reprint of Ten Kate 1922c).

1977

a. My journey to the peninsula of Baja California. *Journal of San Diego History* 23 (3):53–81 (translation of 1885a, 43–95).

b. Somatological observations on Indians of the Southwest. *Journal of American Ethnology and Archaeology* 3:117–44; New York: AMS Press (reprint of 1892a).

1979

Materiales para servir a la antropologia de Baja California. *Calafia—Revista de la Universidad Autonoma de Baja California* 4 (1):7–20 (translation of 1883g).

Itinerary of Herman ten Kate, 1882–1883

1882 ◆◆◆

OCTOBER

21 Departure from the Netherlands

NOVEMBER

5 Arrival in New York City
Meeting with Ely S. Parker
Washington, D.C.: meetings with Major John Wesley Powell, James Mooney,
and Charles Rau at the Bureau of American Ethnology; visits to Department
of the Interior and the War Department; meetings with George M. Wheeler
of the U.S. Geological Survey;
Stay with Emil Bessels at Yale University

DECEMBER

Fieldwork on Tuscarora Indian Reservation, Lewistown, New York State; guest
of Caroline Parker/Mrs. Mount Pleasant; receives name of Odagot (Clear Light)
in adoption ceremony; fieldwork on Cattaraugus (Seneca) Indian Reservation,
Erie County; visit to Thomas Orphan Asylum

19 Departure from New York City

21 Visit to Monk's Mound (Cahokia), near St. Louis

22 Departure from Little Rock, Arkansas; farewell to father

25 Arrival in El Paso; visit to Fort Bliss

27–29 Fieldwork among Tiguas at Ysleta del Sur

31 Departure from El Paso; New Year's Eve in Deming

1883 ◆◆◆

JANUARY

  1 Arrival in Tucson

  2 Visit to camp Lowell

 3–7 Fieldwork among Papagos at San Xavier del Bac

  9 Departure from Tucson; to Mexico via Nogales

10–11 Stay in Hermosillo

  11 Arrival in Guaymas; visit to Yaqui *ranchería*

  16 Across the Gulf of California to La Paz on Baja California

17–March 18

  Archaeological explorations of caves, graves, and rock art sites
on Baja California and islands in the Gulf of California, partly with ornithologist
Lyman Belding

MARCH

20–22 Fieldwork at Yaqui village near La Paz and observation of Easter festivities, including the
pascola dance

  23 Return to Guaymas

  24 Observation of Yaqui Easter festivities at El Rancho near Guaymas; collaboration with
photographer Alfredo Laurent

APRIL

  3 Return to Hermosillo; trip to Ures

 9–11 To United States by way of Calabasas; first encounter with Apaches

12–15 Travel preparations in Tucson

  17 Arrival in Yuma

17–20 Fieldwork on Fort Yuma Indian Reservation

  22 Encounter with Apache-Yumas

29–May 13

  Fieldwork among Mohaves and Chemehuevis on the Colorado River Indian Reservation
and Fort Mohave Indian Reservation

MAY

14–18 Visit to Southern Paiutes in El Dorado Canyon and on Cottonwood Island

20–21 Visit to Walapai camps in Kingman area

21–26 To Phoenix by way of Ash Fork and Prescott

  27 Archaeological survey east of Phoenix

JUNE

1–7   Fieldwork among Pimas on Gila River Indian Reservation

8   Visit to Casa Grande ruins

10–13   Fieldwork among Papagos at San Xavier del Bac

14–24   Travel preparations; meeting with General Crook; hires photographer Constant Duhem for research among Apaches

26   Visit to Fort Thomas

27–July 12   Fieldwork on San Carlos Apache Indian Reservation

JULY

14–17   Fieldwork on White Mountain Apache Indian Reservation

21   Arrival in Albuquerque: acquaintance with Frank H. Cushing; visit to Indian School

22–25   Santa Fe; Tertio-Millennial Celebration; visits to Pueblo camps around town; attendance of *matachina* and other dances of Indians from Jemez and San Juan

26   Visit to Tesuque Pueblo

28–31   Visit to Las Vegas–Hot Springs

AUGUST

1   Acquaintance with Professor A. H. Thompson in Santa Fe

5   Visit to Laguna Pueblo

6–10   Fieldwork on Navajo Indian Reservation; visits to Fort Wingate and Fort Defiance; acquaintance with Washington Matthews

12   Keam's Canyon Trading Post; acquaintance with Thomas Varker Keam

13–16   Fieldwork on Hopi Indian Reservation; acquaintance with Jeremiah Sullivan; observance of Snake Dance at Walpi and Mishongnovi

17   Study of Alexander M. Stephen's collection of Anasazi and Hopi pottery at Keam's Canyon Trading Post

19–25   Fieldwork among Navajos in the Fort Defiance area; acquaintance with Colonel James Stephenson and Matilda Coxe Stevenson

27   Visit to Fort Wingate; joins Washington Matthews on ethnobotanical collecting trip

28–September 6   Fieldwork in Zuni Pueblo; stay with Frank H. Cushing

SEPTEMBER

8–16   Santa Fe

18–30   Fieldwork on Southern Ute Indian Reservation

OCTOBER

9–17   Fieldwork on Cheyenne-Arapaho (Darlington) Indian Reservation; meets Captain
       Richard Henry Pratt

18–26 Anadarko Indian Agency and Fort Sill: fieldwork among Comanches, Kiowas,
       Wichitas, Caddos, and Apaches

31–November 9
       Stay in Dallas

NOVEMBER

  9   Journey from Dallas to Caddo, Indian Territory

9–13   Fieldwork among Choctaws, Caddo region

14–16 Fieldwork among Creeks in Eufala region

16–22 Fieldwork among Cherokees in Vinita and Tahlequah; attends meetings of
       Cherokee National Council; visit to Cherokee Male Seminary

DECEMBER

 16   Back in the Netherlands

PART TWO

HERMAN TEN KATE

Travels and Researches in Native North America, 1882–1883

TRANSLATED BY WILLIAM J. ORR,
WITH
CONTRIBUTIONS BY PIETER HOVENS

Introduction

IF WE CONSIDER THE VARIETIES OF PEOPLES IN VARIOUS REGIONS of the earth who still live wholly or partially in a state of nature and ponder: which of these races is destined to vanish first within a relatively short time span, our attention then promptly turns to those peoples whose territories, due to their natural condition, attract a steady influx of civilization. Primarily on that section of the western hemisphere extending northward from the Tropic of Cancer to form an immense continent do we encounter those peoples whose demise is imminent. Perhaps nowhere is scientific investigation more urgent than among the aboriginal inhabitants of North America.

Long so persuaded, I spent some time mulling over plans for a journey of ethnological exploration to these regions. Only during the winter of 1881–82, however, when I was living in Berlin and Paris, did this idea take on more definite contours, particularly after discussions with Professor Bastian[1] and Doctor Hamy.[2] The following spring I informed Professor Kan, secretary of the Netherlands Geographical Society,[3] of my decision to go to North America on my own that very same year. As a result, some time later, in September—after I had presented to the aforementioned society an itinerary, which gained the board's approval—I was named a delegate of the society and at the same time granted a stipend of 500 guilders.

Together with the director of the Rijks Ethnographisch Museum in Leiden, Mr. L. Serrurier,[4] the board was also able to obtain material support from the government by providing me 1,000 guilders. It also succeeded in arousing interest in the itinerary from the Dutch Academy of Sciences in Haarlem, which awarded me 500 guilders for the purchase of ethnographic specimens. In October 1882, shortly before my departure, I was at the same time named *"délegué temporaire"* of the Société d'Anthropologie in Paris, on the motion of Professor Topinard.[5]

The primary goal of my journey was an anthropological-ethnographic investigation of various Indian tribes, which are scattered across the southwestern United States and the adjoining sections of Mexico. It was a question, first of all, of gaining information about their physical traits, morphological as well as physiological, through precise, methodical investigation, and, if possible, thereby bring the issue of their origin and relationship a step closer to resolution.[6] This investigation necessarily included observations of a general ethnological character, concerning not just morals and customs, but also regarding the capacity for civilization and the growth of the Indian population. Finally, it entailed the creation of an anthropological-ethnographic collection.

Although I have attempted to relate the most significant results of my investigations in free-form sketches of land and people in the pages that follow, these largely consist of the unadorned narrative of various journeys, based on notes in my diary.[7]

Although the literature about the United States and Mexico is already quite extensive, one would have to agree that in our homeland the knowledge of these lands—of the more uncivilized areas, at least—is still limited to just a small circle. This fact and awareness that, to the best of my knowledge, there is no original travel narrative of any scope in our language about the "Great Southwest" and northern Mexico prompted me to compose the narrative of my "Kreuzfahrten zum Sammelbehuf auf transatlantischen Feldern der Ethnologie" [Cruises for the Purpose of Collecting on Transatlantic Fields of Ethnology].

Given the nature of the subject, Indians, primarily, will be discussed in these travel sketches. But those who think they will be reading adventures on the order of Cooper or Aimard[8] will be disappointed. Though chances for perilous encounters on the "frontier" are not infrequent, I could carry out my ramblings without difficulty.

In the following pages I have, as a rule, cited various sources relating to the subjects discussed only when other authors' points of view and my own differed. Thus one will find citations for only a small portion of the pertinent literature. Just as one should not expect a study here of sources, neither should one expect a comprehensive description of land and people because I have generally limited myself to describing only what I experienced based on my own observation, unless the information was provided me by reliable persons who, through a long residence in the regions, were fully familiar with the prevailing conditions.

Above all, my sketches will be incomplete as regards the religion and traditions, the language and spiritual life of the Indian. To collect reliable data from that realm, much more time is necessary than what I had at my disposal. My own experience has taught me the accuracy of what the well-traveled Pechuel-Loesche has recently recounted in this respect.[9]

But, generally speaking, my work might have increased in comprehensiveness and value if I had not continually stood entirely on my own and did not have to defray the costs of the journey largely from my own resources. Let no one conclude that I am appealing for the reader's support for my work, as writers customarily do. Recalling a certain mot of Locke,[10] I regard that as without purpose. What I have reported regarding the plan and content of this book was meant as an aid to comprehension for the reader.

The actual results of the journey have already appeared in part[11] and should continue to be published in French. All ethnographic objects I collected are located in the National Ethnographic

Museum in Leiden.[12] The small collection of zoological specimens was given to the National Museum of Natural History in the same city. As a delegate of the Société d'Anthropologie in Paris, I was obliged to deliver all that I collected in the field of physical anthropology to the Musée Broca.[13]

I do not want to conclude this introduction without a word of sincere gratitude to all, organizations and individuals, who supported me by advice and deed in my endeavors. Not just in my homeland, but in France and America, too, many provided offered their services to me. Though I must attest my recognition of more people without providing their names, here I do want to call attention to the special kindness and consideration of the American officers at the military posts in the Far West; thanks especially to then commander in chief of the army, W. T. Sherman, who provided a general letter of recommendation.[14]

I am particularly indebted to Capt. George M. Wheeler in Washington, to whom I was recommended by the Geographic Society, for the best maps of and information about the regions I traveled through, and to Captain Emmet Crawford, of the Third Cavalry Regiment, for the energetic assistance provided me during my visit to the Apache Indians in Arizona.[15]

Finally, let me express my warmest acknowledgment to Messrs. Gaston J. Vives and H. von Borstel in La Paz, Jules Simoneau at San José del Cabo, Prof. A. H. Thompson in Washington, J. Sullivan at Hualpé, Frank H. Cushing in Zuni, William Eubanks at Tahlequah, William P. Ross in Vinita, and last but not least, to my spry traveling companion on the California peninsula, Mr. Lyman Belding.

The plates appurtenant to this work were lithographed by Mr. P. Haaxman, artist in the Hague,[16] based on photographs and sketches.

·····

NOTES

1. Adolf Bastian (1826–1905), Ten Kate's teacher and one of the leading German anthropologists of the day, was a professor at the University of Berlin and a founder of the Berlin Museum für Völkerkunde. *Neue Deutsche Biographie* (Berlin: Duncker und Humblot, 1953–2001, 20 vols.), 1:626–27; K. P. Koepping, *Adolf Bastian and the Psychic Unity of Mankind* (St. Lucia: University of Queensland Press, 1983). Cf. Pieter Hovens, *Herman ten Kate en de antropologie der Noord Amerikaanse Indianen* (Meppel, Krips, 1989), 35–36, 45–46, 212–13.

2. Ernest Théodore Jules Hamy (1842–1908) was since 1880 a curator of the Ethnographic Museum of the Trocadéro in Paris. Hovens, *Herman ten Kate,* 32; Elisabeth A. Williams, "Art and Artifact at the Trocadéro: Ars Americana and the Primitivist Revolution," in *Objects and Others: Essays on Museums and Material Culture,* ed. C. W. Stocking (Madison: University of Wisconsin Press, 1985), 146–66.

3. Cornelius Marius Kan (1837–1919), one of Ten Kate's teachers, was a professor of geography at the University of Amsterdam and one of the founders of the Netherlands Geographical Society. Hovens, *Herman ten Kate,* 21, 50.

4. Lindor Serrurier (1846–1901) was a curator and later director of the Netherlands Ethnographical Museum in Leiden. He was later married to Ten Kate's older sister, Madelon. Hovens, *Herman ten Kate,* 25, and Hovens, "Lindor Serrurier," in *International Dictionary of Anthropologists,* ed. C. Winters (New York: Garland Press, 1991), 632–33.

5. Paul Topinard (1830–1911), who had spent several years in the United States, was a leading exponent of the French physical school of physical anthropology. Ten Kate had studied craniology with Topinard in 1879. Hovens, *Herman ten Kate,* 30, 31; see also E. A. Williams, "Anthropological Institutions in 19th Century France," *Isis* 76 (1985):331–48.

6. Herman ten Kate (HtK), 1885: Generally, I have recently laid out the goal and requirements of such an investigation in the Tijdschrift van het Aardrijkskundig Genootschap, VI. 254 et seq.; 1882. Eds.: For an extensive methodological analysis of Ten Kate's North American fieldwork, see Hovens, *Herman ten Kate,* 45–73.

7. HtK 1885: Some preliminary reports regarding my journey and the results obtained, directed to the Geographical Society from America, were included in vol. VII of the Tijdschrift. Also the Bulletins of the Société d'Anthropologie, 1883, published some of my letters directed to the aforementioned institute.

8. Gustave Aimard (1818–1883), a French writer, participated in Raousset-Boulbon's expedition in Sonora. His adventures were the basis for a score of adventure novels, many with American themes.

9. HtK 1885: "Ethnologische Forschung," in *Verhandlungen des vierten Deutschen Geographentages in München.* Eds.: German anthropologist and geographer Eduard Pechuel-Loesche (1840–1913) was the author of works on the ethnography of West, Central, and South Africa, partially based on his own expeditions. As a university professor he taught ethnology at Jena and geography in Erlangen. *Deutsche Biographische Enzyklopädie,* eds. W. Killy and R. Vierhaus (München: K. G. Saur, 1995–2000, 12 vols.) (1998), 7:586–87.

10. Presumably John Locke (1632–1704), the English philosopher. Ten Kate's reference is obscure.

11. HtK 1885: In chronological order:

    "Quelques observations ethnographiques recueillis dans la presqu'île californienne et en Sonora." *Revue d'Ethnographie,* vol. II, 1883, 321 ff.

    "Notes sur l'ethnographie des Zuñis," ibid., vol. III, 1884, 161 ff.

    "Matériaux pour servir à l'anthropologie de la presqu'île californienne." *Bulletins de la Société d'Anthropologie de Paris,* 1884, 551 ff.

    "Sur quelques crânes de l'Arizona et du Nouveau Mexique." *Revue d'Anthropologie,* 1884, 486 ff.

    "Sur la synonymie ethnique et la toponymie chez les Indiens de l'Amérique du Nord." *Verslagen en Mededeelingen der Koninklijke Akademie van Wetenschappen, afd. Letterkunde,* 3rd series, 1884, vol. 1, 353 ff.

12. HtK 1885: A list of what was collected is contained in the *Nederlandsche Staats-Courant,* March 25, 1884, no. 72, and May 10, no. 111. Eds.: This list does not include the artifacts Ten Kate purchased with his own means and later donated or sold to the museum in Leiden. A catalog of all of Ten Kate's North American collections is currently in progress.

13. HtK 1885: An account provided in the *Bulletins de la Société d'Anthropologie,* 1883, pp. 599, 687, and 1884, p. 571.

14. General William Tecumseh Sherman (1820–1891) gained recognition for his exploits in Georgia during the Civil War. Subsequently he became commander of the Division of the Missouri and advocated and carried out campaigns against the Plains Indians. From 1869–1884 he was commander in chief of the U.S. army. Robert G. Athearn, *William Tecumseh Sherman and the Settlement of the West* (Norman: University of Oklahoma Press, 1956).

15. During the 1870s Lt. George Montague Wheeler (1842–1905) led several expeditions in the Southwest and California that surveyed over a third of the territory west of the 100th meridian, produced numerous maps, and uncovered archaeological and scientific information. William H. Goetzmann, *Exploration and Empire* (repr. New York: Norton, 1978), 467–88.

    After a long career as an Indian fighter, Emmet Crawford (1844–1886) was appointed commander of the San Carlos Apache reservation in 1882 and played a key role in training Apache scouts. Bernard C. Nalty and Truman R. Strobridge, "Captain Emmet Crawford: Commander of Apache Scouts, 1882–1886," *Arizona and the West* 6 (1964):30–40.

16. Pieter Haaxman (1854–1937) had studied art with Herman ten Kate, Sr., the anthropologist's father. He was known primarily as a painter of still lifes and miniature portraits. Hans Vollmer, ed., *Allgemeines Lexikon der bildenden Künstler des XX Jahrhunderts*, 6 vols. (Leipzig: VEB E. A. Seeman, 1953–62), 6:3.

CHAPTER ONE

From New York to Guaymas

A ROUGH, STORMY FIFTEEN-DAY VOYAGE ACROSS THE OCEAN ended with my landing at New York on November 5, 1882, affording a brief, final glance at the splendid "Indian summer" with its colorful woods and clear skies. I hurriedly visited the most important cities of the eastern states and then admired the magnificent Niagara waterfall in its winter garb.[1]

In December 1882 I had the opportunity to pay my respects to Cooper's heroes, the Iroquois, when I visited two of their reservations in western New York State.[2] A reservation is an area specifically set aside for Indians by the United States government. I obtained necessary information on the Iroquois Indians from Mr. Ely S. Parker, a completely civilized *sachem* (chief) of the Senecas, one of the six nations constituting the Iroquois. Recommended to him by respected authorities, I found him to be a man of high education and breeding. These qualities gained Parker the rank of general in the American army, and during the Civil War he was on General Grant's staff. He is married to a white woman and lives in New York, where he occupies a government position.[3]

General Parker was the first Iroquois I saw. He was tall and of athletic build and about sixty to sixty-five years of age. He had a pronounced Mongolian physiognomy, and the first impression he left was that of a Chinese. Most notable were the extremely small brown eyes. His nose was large, wide, and crooked; the forehead high, vaulted, but somewhat receding. His mouth and chin were covered by a thin graying beard, and he had thick raven black hair, also graying. His skin color approximated numbers 26 and 33 of Broca's chromatic scale, but also had a peculiar reddish tinge.[4] His hands were much darker. Mr. Parker's grandfather was a white man, but his physical type, and that of his sister and brother, whom I met later, had the most pronounced Indian features when compared to the type of other Iroquois.

Mr. Parker was an expert on the history and customs of his people and had assisted the well-known ethnologist L. Morgan with his book *The League of the Iroquois*.[5] He advised me to visit three of the eight Iroquois reservations of New York State, those of the Tuscaroras, the Senecas and others on the Cattaraugus River, and the Onondagas near Syracuse. Weather conditions, especially the abundant snowfall, allowed me to visit only the first two. In these parts the Iroquois are least intermixed and have retained some of their old customs. Before I try to recount my visit, it is appropriate to provide some general information about the Iroquois.

The Iroquois of the Confederacy of Five Nations (later Six Nations) call themselves among other names *"Onkwé Honwé,"* meaning "true people, real people."[6] In pre-Columbian times they lived in the extensive region of mountains, woods, rivers, and lakes that now constitutes the states of New York and Pennsylvania, from the Hudson River to the Great Lakes. They were feared by all neighboring tribes because of their ferocious warfare. They annihilated several tribes and also engaged the whites in desperate battles before they witnessed the gradual conquest of their ancestral lands. With the Hurons or Wyandots in Canada, the Nottoways in Carolina, and several smaller tribes they constituted a distinct linguistic group. Some people think they have found linguistic similarities in the language of the Cherokees, originally from the Carolinas, Georgia, and Tennessee.[7] The continually increasing power of the whites eroded the might of the Iroquois, and two-and-a-half centuries of contact with white civilization have resulted in the state in which they now find themselves: that of a peaceful, civilized, largely agricultural people, which has lost much of its original character because of intermixture with the blood of the conqueror.

There has been much debate about whether the Indians are decreasing or increasing in number. It is generally claimed that the Iroquois are now more numerous than ever before. Their number, excluding certain groups of mixed bloods who live among the whites, could be 13,600—6,900 of whom live in Canada. Based on what I have seen and what I know from other sources, it seems to me that the Indians are increasing in number only because of miscegenation. The race that is multiplying is not really Indian anymore; they are mixed bloods in varying degrees. The Indian is not dying out in the actual sense of the word but is slowly but surely being absorbed by the white population. After a certain amount of time he will cease to exist as a separate race. This reminds me of the story of a traveler who visited the Huron Indian village of Jeune Lorette near Quebec and did not see a single Indian there. Researches, by Professor Wilson of Toronto, if memory serves me rightly, have disclosed that there is only one full-blooded Huron among the 200 or 300 inhabitants.[8] It was different with the Indians I had seen so far. Many of them, especially the older ones, seemed to be pure-blooded.

Let me now try to inform the reader about my visit and give a firsthand description of the Iroquois. The purpose of my visit to these Indians was to familiarize myself with their physical type before traveling to the Indians of the American West and to establish the extent to which they had retained their old customs, religion, and language. After the publications of Colden[9] and Morgan, it is not possible to tell something completely new about the Iroquois. The ethnographic information I weave through my account has no pretense of originality but was given to me by several people, Indians and whites.

I first traveled to the Tuscaroras, the sixth nation of the Iroquois, who live in a small area seven to eight miles northeast of the Niagara Falls. Their number is over 400; about fifty Onondagas also live among them. The road runs through the town of Suspension Bridge; Lewiston is on the left, and the view to the west is of steep, silent, and pine-clad banks of the Niagara River, which rushes on to Lake Ontario. Forests and undergrowth, mostly oak, here and there closed off by rough wooden fences, and fields, intermittent solitary farmhouses, mostly constructed from wooden planks, painted white, are the images one sees from the sleigh that hurries across snow and ice, swept along by the ice-cold northwesterly wind.

After more than a one-and-a-half-hour journey, a few minutes after crossing the reservation boundary, we arrived at the house of Chief John Mount Pleasant. It was also built of wooden planks, painted white, and consisted of several small rooms; all were on the ground floor. Stories were lacking. The old sachem, a mixed blood of English-Iroquois descent, was married to General Parker's sister.[10] With Parker's recommendation, my traveling companions, members of my family, and I were kindly welcomed in the living room and introduced by Mrs. Mount Pleasant to the chief and some Senecas who were present.[11] When I told her about the purpose of my visit, she gave me all the information I asked for, expressing herself in flawless English.

She was an attractive stout woman of over fifty, and her face betrayed more white blood than that of her two brothers. Her grandfather was a white man. Coming from an old Seneca family, of which the famous chiefs Red Jacket and Cornplanter were members, she bears the title of Ge-Keats-sau-sa, or Queen, and, like her brother Ely, is an expert on the history, traditions, and customs of her people. In her bookcase I noticed *Types of Mankind,* by Nott and Gliddon, Lyell's *Elementary Geology,* and Morgan's ethnological works. Thanks to her, I was able to visit Indian homes and witness family life during three trips across the reservation. Through her I also gained access to the council, the church, and the school.[12]

Miss Lay, or, to call her by her Seneca name, Gar-hor-noh (the Half-Opened Door), was a slim young girl. She and her father sang several religious hymns for us in the Seneca language, accompanied by a Seraphine organ. Speaking about old customs on another occasion, I was adopted into the Seneca tribe. When I was speaking about old customs, I asked one of the Senecas from the Cattaraugus reservation, whom I knew to be a pagan, to perform a traditional dance or song. After some hesitation and an exchange of words in their language, he left the room but returned before long dressed in Indian attire, which was fragmentary in places. The upper part of the body was clad in a shirt that reached down to the middle of his thighs. Attractively decorated leggings and moccasins covered his calves and feet. He wore a feather headdress and had painted his face black. Mrs. Mount Pleasant informed me that I would be adopted into the foremost clan of the Senecas, that of the Wolf, to which she herself also belonged and as the result of which I would become her brother. We sat down in a circle. Odâgot (Bright Light), the Indian whose name I would receive, began with an ode to the Senecas, stating among other things that they were fierce warriors and that they could even walk away with an enemy tomahawk lodged in their body. Subsequently he took us whites by the hand and made us stand up while he mumbled some unintelligible words and pointed upward. Now Bright Light gave me the peace pipe and seated me next to him. He took my right hand and slowly we moved up and down several times while he sang a hushed monotonous song and shook his rattle of turtle shells. The old Tuscarora sachem and Mr. Lay, the chairman of the Senecas at Cattaraugus, joined in Odâgot's song in dull, short tones. Finally I was led back to my place and received a small necklace of wampum from Mrs. Mount Pleasant as a token of my adoption.

Many Indian tribes have a practice of distinguishing different clans, or *gentes,* among themselves, just like the Scots once did. Among the Iroquois especially this practice has remained alive. Every tribe of the Confederacy (Mohawks, Senecas, Oneidas, Onondagas, Cayugas, and Tuscaroras) has eight different clans, each of which is named after an animal. Among the first five, that of the Wolf is the most prominent, among the Tuscaroras that of the Bear. People belonging to the same clan cannot marry each other. Much of the traditional tribal government is still intact. There is no chief over the entire confederacy, but every tribe has a chief sachem. The Indians at Cattaraugus are an exception: they have a council that is presided over by a chairman who is elected annually. About half of the Indians at Cattaraugus are non-Christians and most live in a place called Newtown. On specific dates there are feasts such as the White Dog Sacrifice and the Corn Festival.[13]

Unfortunately the weather was very bad and prevented me from staying at Cattaraugus longer or visiting the Onondagas. One should realize that there are no real villages or hamlets on these reservations; at best only two or three houses are situated next to each other, and most are spread out over the whole reservation area, making a trip by sleigh impossible. All I could do was visit one of the sachems, Nicholson Parker, and the Thomas Orphan Asylum.

The Cattaraugus reservation, situated in Erie County, extends westward from the picturesquely situated little town of Gowanda to Lake Erie. Its southern border is the Cattaraugus River. The route from Gowanda to the asylum is lovely. On the right are low hills covered with clusters of dark conifers, on the left bottomlands and the winding Cattaraugus. Several times the almost completely straight road climbs and falls across a mostly level plateau, which is covered by low bushes among which one can see many charred tree stumps. Occasionally an isolated Indian farm, built from roughly hewn planks or logs, breaks the monotony of the surroundings. Now and then a horse-drawn sleigh with a bronzed rider passes on the other side of the road. It takes an hour's ride from Gowanda to get to the asylum.

The institution for poor Indian children and orphans was founded by Mr. Philip Thomas and the Reverend Asher Wright. Founded in 1855, it came under state control in 1875. Children of both sexes from all Iroquois tribes are cared for and educated here until they are sixteen years old. At the time of our visit, there were about a hundred of them. The director, a Mr. Van Valkenburgh, who despite his Dutch name does not speak one word of Dutch, and his wife showed us around. I only want to point out that the children are very bright, quickly forget their native language, and show an inclination for mechanical work, such as fine writing, drawing, and needle-work. Many of the girls also have musical ability. Many of the children show clear signs of white parentage, particularly their lighter hair and lighter-colored eyes. From Mrs. Wright, the widow of the missionary who spent almost half a century among the Senecas, I received a Seneca grammar and vocabulary compiled by her late husband. It is a rather rare book, and the Reverend Wright was the first to write in this language.[14]

Sachem Nicholson Parker informed me that the name "Cattaraugus" was derived from a word to describe the peculiar smell produced by the mud and stones in the river. The 150 Cayugas and the few Onondagas and Tuscaroras who live among the Senecas on the Cattaraugus reservation all speak Seneca with each other. They have intermarried with the Senecas and are losing their nationality, as is the case everywhere else where one tribe is the most numerous and absorbs the remainder. Marriages across tribal lines are very common among the Iroquois. Exogamy is prevalent among many tribes and explains the presence of different physical types within a tribe. Relations between different Iroquois tribes in New York and Canada, even with Oneidas in Wisconsin and a few Senecas in the Far West, are maintained. Frequent visits take place, also in the interest of the Confederacy.

Nowadays the Iroquois wear white men's clothing, without exception. Traditional items of material culture are very hard to find. With difficulty I was able to acquire a traditional wooden cradle among the Tuscaroras. However, they do make boxes and beaded baskets, which they sell to the stores in Niagara Falls and other places, but the European influence on these objects is evident. The moccasins of soft leather, the original Indian footwear, are the most characteristic traditional item remaining.

The diffusion of the language is gradually decreasing. Many young people, though they can understand their language, are unable to speak it. English, learned in school, is gaining ground. I had a good opportunity to hear Tuscarora when I visited a Mennonite church where a young Indian minister delivered a sermon in that language. It sounded strange and harsh with deep guttural sounds and numerous consonants, among which the sound *k* was prevalent. Often it sounded as though a word was suddenly broken off and swallowed. No one has ever been able to write Tuscarora, and the other Iroquois who speak dialects of the same language do not understand it. Some American ethnologists doubt whether the Tuscaroras are Iroquois, because of their language especially. The only thing certain is that they were adopted into the Confederacy about 1713 and that they came from North Carolina. Some have argued that their language is similar to Welsh, and Bancroft, among others, cites a strange case. I could learn nothing from the Indians about such a relationship. However, it can be argued on good grounds that the ancient inhabitants of Wales knew America long before Columbus.[15]

Even if one finds the Iroquois only in a few places in the territory where he was once uncontested master, but where according to an eloquent chief "the bones of my people lie banished in their own land," numerous places have derived their names from the Indians, especially the Senecas. Mr. Orsamus Marshall, who maintained relations with the Indians of New York State for many years and whom I had the privilege of meeting in Buffalo, provided an overview of mostly very fitting Indian place names in his study *The Niagara Frontier.*[16] I want to point out a few. The Senecas call the Niagara Falls *Detgahskohses,* meaning "place of the high fall." They never called them *Niagara,* which according to Schoolcraft means "thundering waters." This word seems to be of Mohawk derivation and should be pronounced as "Nyahgarah." It is supposed to mean "neck," referring to the connection between the two walls. The origin of the term *Seneca* lies shrouded in obscurity. They call themselves *Nandowahgaah,* or "the people from the big hill." Nevertheless, one has tried to deduce the name *Seneca* from this, with intermediate terms *Sonnondowaga* and *Sonnontooan,* names used by the Jesuits. *Onondawaah* is "big hill," and the *s* or *ts* as prefix connotes a possession. The suffix *gaah* means "people."

On the basis of my observations on both reservations, I will try to offer my conclusions about the Iroquois type, limiting myself to what in modern anthropology are called the physical "descriptive" characteristics. I did not establish anthropometric characteristics, because to a great extent we know these. Gould[17] conducted measurements on 508 Iroquois and found that their stature averaged 1.73 meters, which places them among the "races of high stature" category. Another anthropometric characteristic noted by Gould is the proportionally longer upper extremities in comparison to Europeans or even mulattos. In this respect the Iroquois occupy a position between the latter and the Negroes. Their cephalic index is known. On the average they are dolichocephalic, and I was able to verify this on the basis of a number of old skulls in the museum in Philadelphia.

When I began to distinguish different types, I based my determinations on those individuals whose genealogy I knew, for instance Mrs. Mount Pleasant and both of her brothers. Among the other Iroquois, I searched for individuals who looked like them, and while searching and analyzing I found other types and many varieties that would be difficult to describe. Excepting the numerous mixed bloods of different grades, it seems to me that there are two or three main types. One is of more than average stature and of athletic build, with very small eyes, a reddish yellow complexion, and on average a Mongolian facial form. The other is smaller, less robust, with larger eyes, lighter skin color, and finer facial features. A third type is intermediate and probably the result of intermixture. Among this group were individuals looking like Chinese, but they were neither tall nor had the reddish complexion of the first type. Some types made me think of Liplaps as they showed a certain degree of prognathism of the upper jaw.[18] One woman reminded me of a Batak woman I knew in The Hague.

The skin color, that is, of the face (as I did not see the upper body or extremities), varied among the Iroquois between the numbers 23, 25/26, and 32/33 from Broca's chromatic scale. That of the eyes was between 1 and 3, although the peculiar warm tinge of the Indian eye is beyond reproduction. The sclerotica was yellowish. The characteristic fold of the Mongoloid races in the inner eye, which completely or partially covers the caruncle *(l'oeil bridé),* I saw on several adults and several children. Often the average-sized teeth showed decay and discoloration. About half the people I saw had a rudimentary earlobe, but their ears were of average size.

It goes without saying that the Iroquois had black hair; some had very thick hair that nearly stood on end. Only mixed bloods with a high degree of white blood wore mustaches; others had sparse mustaches. Among the mestizos, especially among the women and girls, types with fine facial features and attractive build were observed. The Iroquois, and Indians in general, have few children. As for diseases they suffer from, primarily scrofula is endemic among children.

The Iroquois' tone of voice was peculiar: deep, guttural, and nasal at the same time, although they barely raise their voices while talking. The young girls and children whom I heard singing several times had rather heavy and deep voices. I think I also noted that the American white woman has a deeper voice than her European sister.

Not for long would I have to endure the horrors of a North American winter because already on December 19 I left "the East" with its snow and ice behind and on the wings of steam sped off to Little Rock, the capital of the state of Arkansas. By morning we have departed bustling, smoky St. Louis in its winter finery. Following the right bank of the Mississippi River toward the south for a while, the train before long heads in a more westerly direction among the nearly unbroken forests of oak and pine trees, which still blanket a sizable part of this region so rich in minerals. Before reaching Little Rock after midnight, we pass through nothing but small cities and hamlets lost in the endless forests. By now the outward appearance of the inhabitants shows that we are getting closer and closer to the West. The farther south we go the warmer it gets, with light rainfall, and when we wake up the next morning, a bright sun caresses the pleasant streets of Little Rock with its rays.

Little Rock is charmingly situated on the high right bank of the Arkansas River. Its appearance resembles that of most small American cities, with its low houses mostly furnished with flat roofs, with elevated and roofed wooden sidewalks running alongside the entire length of the street. Due, however, to its fine location in a rolling, heavily wooded landscape it has attractive features, to which the bustle in the unpaved, sandy streets of the motley population, comprising roughly 16,000 people, contributes. Along with merchants from the eastern states, one encounters frontier dwellers from the West and, along with Negroes and mulattos, the sons of the Celestial Empire [the Chinese].

On December 22 I bid farewell to my blood relatives returning to the homeland,[19] and I set out alone on the journey to the Far West. That day I reach Texarkana on the Texas border, after having traveled continuously through a landscape that in its main features fully resembles the one between St. Louis and Little Rock. During the evening and the next morning, numerous emigrants from all parts of the world, most of them looking extremely shabby and decrepit, throng into the station. To this is connected an inferior hotel, where I spend the night. Afterward it's "Westward ho!" again through oak forests and plains across Texas in a long train ride lasting two days and two nights to the Mexican border.

Toward evening, at Elmo, the eye beholds for the first time open plains after the route has been going all day long through dense oak and pine forests, during which we have already passed

Jefferson and Marshall, the most important towns along the line. While it is dark we move beyond Dallas and Fort Worth, the most prosperous cities in this part of Texas, and I spend the night in the comfortable sleeping car until the next morning, when the sun in all its splendor rises above the silent plain and illuminates the distant limestone mesas[20] with splendid purple tints. In the cool morning hours we stop at Abilene, a small town consisting of wooden dwellings, and have an awful breakfast. Then the train rushes onward again across the vast plains, which are blanketed with short, parched grass and leafless mesquite bushes *(Acacia)*. Now and then steep, bare table-shaped mountains of limestone rise. Upon them there are ever more prickly cactuses the farther west we go, making us realize that we are in another climatic zone. Herds of horned cattle have now replaced the bison, which once traversed these barren stretches by the thousands, but you can still see the small herds of dainty antelope. Not far from the Colorado station I behold a herd of at least sixty head among the mesquites. The Comanche, once lord and master of these plains, has vanished forever and been forced to seek a new homeland farther north, between the Red and Canadian rivers.[21]

After Colorado numerous colonies of prairie dogs *(Cynomys ludovicianus)* appear, and the nopal *(Opuntia)* becomes larger and more frequent.[22] Shortly after we put Big Spring behind us, the landscape takes on a different character, more like desert. Amidst the drifting sand, which recalls our dunes, the yucca,[23] too, which has already earlier emerged, begins to acquire larger dimensions and is especially plentiful in the area around the Pecos River, which we cross late in the afternoon. At Toyah (i.e., mountain), whose name is evocative of the Comanches, we have supper, and we see the sun's final rays illuminating the rugged silhouette of the Guadalupe Mountains. By the light of the moon, looming marvelously radiant in the Texas sky, the train wends its way through the remote, endless plains to eventually halt early in the morning of December 25 in El Paso, my journey's destination.

El Paso makes a startling overall impression on the visitor. The low houses with flat roofs and adobe walls,[24] which are frequently whitewashed, reveal its Mexican origin, while the nearly uninterrupted roofed sidewalks at the edge of the street running along the facades recall the American influence. The Central Hotel, where I stay, is an old Mexican building with a *zaguán*[25] and a patio[26] furnished with galleries along which the rooms are situated.

Since the Southern Pacific Railway reached the Rio Grande,[27] the population of El Paso has grown considerably because it is a natural commercial entrepôt for Mexico, given its location. Even in earlier years some commerce had already been taking place, and the name [*El Paso* means "the pass"] thus refers to the old ferry, situated at the shallows of the sandy river. The recently opened railway to Chihuahua, to be extended from there to the Mexican capital, will surely contribute to elevating El Paso to a thriving commercial city within a few years. In many places tall redbrick buildings for warehouses are already rising up above the low adobe dwellings of the Mexicans, and a horse-drawn railway has recently linked the American with the Mexican bank.

Old El Paso is situated on the Mexican side and is by preference called "Paso del Norte," but El Paso itself, formerly called "Franklin" by the Americans, has a predominantly Mexican population too.[28] Among the many who came here to seek their fortune are a number of Chinese and a few Negroes as well. El Paso was, and still is, though to a lesser extent, what people in the West call a "hard place," that is, a place teeming with drinking and gambling dens where a large part of the drifting population of adventurers spends its time. Fights, frequently ending in manslaughter and murder, are the order of the day.

El Paso is situated at an altitude of approximately 3,500 feet[29] along the sandy banks of the Rio Grande, whose bed is constantly changing because of the wind blowing across the sand. Here the river is merely narrow and full of sandbanks, between which the muddy water flowing southward slowly makes its way. The banks are overgrown primarily with *álamos (Populus monilifera)* and mesquite bushes, and higher up in the valley of the Rio Grande, which is very wide here, on the mesas and the rugged mountain slopes one primarily encounters greasewood *(Obione canescens),* whose odor to some extent recalls the cistus plant [rock rose].[30]

Because of the Christmas festivities on the day of my arrival, there was a huge noisy commotion in Paso del Norte since a bullfight was to take place that afternoon. Numerous Mexicans with broad-brimmed sombreros (hats of fine straw or of gray felt) and draped in serapes (multicolored shawls) thronged around the tables where monte (a certain card game) was being played or listened, while sitting or strolling, to the strumming of a guitar. Numerous small shops with fruits—bananas, watermelons, and sugarcane—or *dulces* (sweets) were set up on a sandy square and drew numerous visitors. The bullfight, which took place in an arena made of rough unpainted boards, differed only slightly from other performances of the same kind so often described. But certainly it is not often the case that a camel takes part in a bullfight, and indeed so effectively that with vigorous kicking and tremendous leaps, it not only holds many bulls at bay but, in doing so, at the same time throws its rider, to the tremendous delight of the jubilant spectators.

The next day I went to Fort Bliss, a military post situated about three miles[31] to the northwest of El Paso along the Rio Grande.[32] Usually the military posts of the United States in the West do not deserve the name of fort because they are not fortified, and it would be impossible to defend them effectively. They are nothing but military posts of rather varying defensible properties, mostly constructed according to a fixed plan. In the middle there is an open square with a flagpole, which is bounded by a rectangle formed by the barracks and stables, the commandant's quarters, the officers' quarters, and the hospital, along with some warehouses and sheds. Only the building material varies, depending on the area where the post is situated. Fort Bliss, too, resembled all the other posts I later had the opportunity to see. Because of often recurrent malaria, it has the reputation of being insalubrious.

Upon request, I received from the commanding officer the directions needed to visit the Indians in Isleta, and the next day I arranged to have a wagon bring me to the aforementioned place.[33] Isleta is situated about eight miles southeast of El Paso. Here the broad valley floor is completely transformed into a plain, if one leaves the foothills[34] of the sierra[35] out of consideration. The sandy road winds its way through the chaparral (brush) of mesquites and álamos, and while riding one enjoys a splendid view of the distant mountains of Chihuahua, which, with their pointed crests, stand out sharply against the fixed blue of the cloudless sky. After roughly two hours of riding, we are in Isleta del Paso, where I register at a humble inn of adobe and am assigned a soiled bed for the night in a tiny room next to various other people.

Except for a very few houses, Isleta consists of adobe dwellings, scattered and widely separated from each other. This is one of the oldest places in North America and, just like Paso del Norte, has a very old church that, viewed from a distance, recalls a fortress because of its massive slanting walls. On the inside this church has a peculiarly hewn ceiling with crude pictures, consisting of plain, artless decorations in red paint, from which the Indians' taste is readily evident.

The population is predominantly Mexican and Indian. Except for the large sombrero of yellow straw and gray felt, mostly with a peaked crown, and the multicolored serape, there is nothing distinctive anymore about the residents' everyday attire. The short jackets, the wide trousers split at the outside hem to allow the riding boots to be seen—all that has vanished for good to make way for tasteless modern European dress. This is not just true for El Paso and Isleta, but for all the places where I encountered Mexicans later in my journey.

The Indians of Isleta del Paso are the southernmost of all Pueblo Indians in the United States. They are about forty families strong, some of whom live in Mexico. These Indians speak the same language as their northern brethren in Isleta and Sandia in New Mexico. For no adequate reason, Oscar Loew reckons them among the Tanos tribe.[36] I discovered, however, that they call themselves Tiwa, and later investigations by Bandelier establish that not far from Paso del Norte live Indians who speak a Tehua language and, linguistically, are unquestionably related to the Tiwas of Isleta.[37] *Tehua, Tewa,* and *Tiwa* are definitely local expressions for the same word that is supposed to mean "house."[38] The Tiwas of Isleta no longer live in an original pueblo (city, village) of houses, consisting of two or three stories and furnished with terraces, but in small adobe dwellings just like the Mexicans. Nominally, at least, they are all Roman Catholic, but among the elderly people there are still many who quietly abide by their old religious concepts.

A German merchant, who was pointed out to me by an officer from Fort Bliss and was personally acquainted with many Indians thanks to his lengthy residence in Isleta, informed me that the Indians were now engaged in bringing the final days of the year to a festive end. They were dancing every day from midday to late at night, in the process clearly mingling in an odd way their ancient pagan customs with the religion they later adopted. Around 5 P.M. the racket began. From ten to fifteen men and boys, holding rattles made from gourds, hopped up and down alternately behind or next to each other in a tightly closed row, without, however, leaving their place and practically without lifting their feet. Now and then, in time to the rhythm from the monotonous chanting, the dancers bent their upper body strongly to the side and stretched the right arm with the rattle out to the ground. All this is accompanied by monotonous droning from a leather drum. The Indian beating the drum and a couple of the most prominent people from the tribe stood behind the row of dancers and did not budge. They were all bare-headed, and many had smeared part of their faces with red paint. They did not wear special attire, however. In various places in the village the same dance is repeatedly performed, always starting in front of the entryway to the church. During the three days of my stay in Isleta, I could observe these dances. Otherwise I spent my time taking walks through the village and paying visits on various Indians. At the same time, though, I had the unpleasant experience of making the acquaintance of the numerous enraged dogs, a bastard version of all sizes and varieties, that can be found in every Indian village.

What especially catches one's attention are the artificial irrigation canals (acequias), by means of which the inhabitants—not just Indians, but other people as well—irrigate their fields. The water coming from the Rio Grande is channeled between the cultivated fields through ditches one or more meters wide, with high banks. If one wants to irrigate the land, the bank is temporarily breached and the water gushes over the ground. Near many dwellings one finds storage places for grain and corn, consisting of a scaffolding of dead tree trunks with heavy branches laid crosswise over them. Sometimes the provisions are stored between the broad branches of an álamo [cottonwood].

Whenever I visited the Indians' dwellings, the people were polite and friendly, which was certainly due in good part to the fact that I knew the merchant L., already mentioned above, and could converse with them in Spanish. Beginning with the *gobernador* (governor) José Maria Durán, I made the acquaintance of all the most prominent Indians.

The governor was a marvelous old Indian, tall in stature with long raven black hair. It was in his home that I photographed him and his wife, along with some of his friends. It occurs to me that of the Tiwa Indians whom I was able to observe at Isleta, approximately half are of pure Indian blood, notable among the more elderly. To all appearances, they are genuine brachycephalic types, as a rule, with the back of the head quite flat and with raised parietal bones. Based on stature and facial shape, we may distinguish at least two main types among these Indians, leaving the intermediate forms out of consideration. The first type is tall and slender in build and has sharp features and a bent nose. The old governor is a good representative of this type. The second type is small and more heavyset in build, less handsome, and has a short, straight, sometimes slightly turned-up nose, with the root very deep set. Prognathism of the lower jaw is a not infrequent occurrence in this type. Both types have small eyes, brown in color, in various shades. I noticed a skin fold in the inside corner of the eye, partially covering the caruncle, in the case of a few children. The facial color comes closest to the numbers 30, 44, and 45 on Broca's table of colors. The darkest among these Indians fall between the numbers 37 and 43. The same is true for their hands and feet.

Once and for all, I must here point out the incorrectness of the term "redskins," a term that is not only very popular but even has found its way into the scholarly literature. The Indians do not have red skin, any more than Hindus, Javanese, Malayans, or Polynesians, and I believe that it can be safely assumed that the North American Indians have all the skin tints of the aforementioned races and are frequently even lighter in color. Among the Moqui [Hopi] and Zuni Indians, I have seen women who had a lighter complexion than many of their sisters in southern Europe. However, among a great many Indian tribes a custom exists of smearing part of their faces with a red pigment, making the inaccurate name "redskins" common currency.

It took some effort to find ethnographic items, but finally one evening I turned up a few with a very old Indian called Bernardo who, after protracted negotiations, sold me his war bonnet *(emóh)* decorated with feathers and round leather shield *(gweeyèr),* along with a big drum *(póhojèt)* coated with red paint and a [drum] stick *(làh).* The next day he expressed remorse over the sale of his bonnet, associated with the recollection of so many campaigns against the Apaches, but with effort I hung on to what I had acquired and, in addition, was still able to obtain one of his graying locks of hair. I also took a photograph of him, as well as of his wife and two daughters. He had been able to impart a warlike appearance to himself for the occasion by smearing his face with red and yellow paint and putting on an American officer's coat, which he received as a gift from the commandant of Fort Davis.[39]

As I mentioned above, the Indians of Isleta have almost completely abandoned their original attire. Only the old men wear their hair rolled together in back in a short, stiff tail, which is wrapped with some material or other. Moccasins[40] (Indian footwear) of brown leather, with thin soles and without any ornamentation, are still widely worn.

Although it was again rather warm during the day, there was still a freeze during the night, just like what had already occurred in El Paso.

As for the vertebrate animals, the fauna in the Isleta area, except for the fishes, consists of the same animals one encounters in nearly all the desert regions of the southwestern United States and northern Mexico.[41] Hares *(Lepus callotis)* and rabbits, so-called cottontails *(Lepus sylvaticus),*[42] appear rather frequently in the sandy foothills of the sierra, but at the same time the hunter must be careful not to disturb the rattlesnake, which, like the horned lizard *(Phrynosoma),* can be found in large numbers. Quails *(Ortyginae)* can be found all over the chaparral. Now and then the chaparral cock *(Geococcyx),* a ground cuckoo, dashes across the field when he is startled by your appearance.[43]

On the evening of December 29, I returned to El Paso, where, early on the morning of the 31st, I left with the immigrant train to Deming in southern New Mexico, from there to head toward Tucson in Arizona. There are practically no passengers on the train. I try to start a conversation with a Chinese, who says he has to go to "Kamelee," meaning the station Cambray.[44] Our conversation dragged because of our mutually inadequate knowledge of the language and thus came to an end with me offering the worthy Mongol a draught of whisky from my canteen, an offer he requited by presenting me a sweet-and-sour jam. Strauss, the name of a small stopping place in the dreary, remote desert that surrounds us here, seems a parody of the celebrated waltz king.[45] We follow our way across the plateau of the Sierra Madre, which consists of arid plains with short grass and greasewood. As we pass freakish formations of reddish sandstone, our eyes behold far to the northeast the splendid shapes of the Organ Mountains. The plain is everywhere covered with small isolated mountain ranges or mountains standing by themselves, which often have the shape of a blunt cone, and the farther we go the more frequent the yucca becomes. After we have lunch at Cambray and my Chinese traveling companion stays behind, we arrive in Deming two hours later.

Deming owes its emergence just a couple of years ago to being the junction point of the Southern Pacific Railway and the Atchison, Topeka & Santa Fe line coming from the north. Minerals can be found in the area besides. But Deming consists of only about fifty wooden houses without upper floors and some linen tents, a large part of which are saloons and "hotels." In the "streets" of Deming you encounter practically nothing but men, as, indeed, in all the "cities" of the West, where women are definitely a rare commodity. From the outward appearance of the bearded, rough fellows in broad-brimmed hats, almost without exception with revolvers on their hips, you can see that one is in the West, in the land where the right of the strong is practically the sole right. Judging from their appearance, there are many men of whom one could then say: "Light and free was his touch upon the trigger; heavy indeed the mortality incident to that lightness and freedom."

Because the express train heading west leaves only the next morning, I spend a lonely New Year's Eve in Deming. On New Year's Day 1883 the splendid, ever cheerful New Mexico sun shines on the rugged landscape between Deming and Stein's Pass, not far from the Arizona border, which has mostly the same character as between the first-named place and El Paso.[46] Once through Stein's Pass, one's gaze is fixed on the dreary San Simon Plains to the north and on the 7,000-foot-high Chiracahua Mountains to the south, which in some places are blanketed with snow. Just a few years ago these mountains were the last refuge of Cochise, the dreaded chief of the Apaches. Heading out from here, his handful of warriors divided up, spreading death and terror among the settlers of southern Arizona, until Cochise eventually had to bend before superior power in 1872 and surrender to government troops with the greater part of his followers.[47] Although Cochise has since died and a number of his old warriors have gone to the "happy hunting ground," the Chiricahuas, reinforced by Apaches of various bands, have almost continually harassed the government, and the 1883 campaign, to which I will return in a subsequent chapter [chapter 5], was carried out in large part by Chiricahuas.

In Bowie, Arizona, we have lunch and after a continued train ride across high plateaus and hilly country with saguaros *(Cereus giganteus)*[48] and yuccas, we arrive that evening, New Year's Day, in Tucson, where I check into the Palace Hotel, which leaves much to be desired in every respect, despite its grandiose name and notwithstanding the fact that its owner is a "colonel."

Tucson is situated on a high sandy plateau (2,500 feet) at the foot of the Santa Catalina Mountains. It is an ugly adobe city of Mexican appearance. It has nothing to attract the foreign visitor. It is dreadfully hot most of the time. The streets are sandy, dusty, and without shade. The water is bad—to say nothing of other inconveniences. Tucson has approximately 7,000 residents, mostly Mexicans. Part of the American population resides there just temporarily and consists primarily of gamblers and adventurers, whom one can find every afternoon and evening in the smoky saloons and gambling houses. Among the loyal frequenters of such halls are also various Chinese, some of whom run laundries in the city or are cooks. Often one encounters Papago Indians in the streets, who have come to sell firewood and pottery.[49] Although they can scarcely be distinguished from the lower classes of Mexicans because of their attire and often their external appearance, one can immediately recognize them from their manner of walking behind each other instead of next to each other.

1. Saguaro cacti
near Tucson.

The name *Tucson* is derived from the Pima language: *Stjukson* = black spring[50] and is pronounced "Tuksón" by the Mexicans and "Tussón" by the Americans. Tucson's origins are somewhat murky. It seems that around 1694 the Spaniards established a military post on the place where the city is now to protect the mission of San Xavier to the south. Others assume that the valley of Santa Cruz was colonized around 1560 and that Tucson owes its origin to this. In that case, after Santa Fe, which was founded in 1550, Tucson would be the oldest city in the United States.[51] A few miles to the north of Tucson lie the ruins of what appears to have once been a city.[52] Whether one must look for old Tucson there or whether present-day Tucson is identical with it, I cannot judge. In earlier times the Apaches tried repeatedly, though in vain, to capture Tucson, which certainly did not help draw colonists to these parts. Only in recent years, after the opening of the railway line linking Tucson with Texas and California,[53] has it been revived from its languishing existence as a military post, and the population, which numbered a mere four hundred shortly after the Mexican evacuation in 1856, gradually climbed to its present number. Seven miles to the northeast lies Camp Lowell,[54] a military post directly at the foot of the majestic Santa Catalina Mountains, which consist of granite and gneiss. There I call on the commanding officer, General C.,[55] who gives me the instructions needed to visit the Papago Indian reservation and at the same time have the opportunity to see a dress parade (inspection) of the garrison.

On January 3, I hire a buggy (a light wagon for two with very narrow wheels) so that, equipped with my anthropometric instruments and hunting rifle, I can proceed to the Papagos of San Xavier. The route first leads across the sandy greasewood plains, then through dense woods of massive mesquite trees until the brush comes to an end a short distance from the old mission. The terrain rises, and one notices before long the ancient church lying at the foot of a hill, while on the right the Indians' huts are spread out far and wide like a gigantic prairie dog village. Before long I receive a hospitable welcome in the rancho[56] of Mr. Berger, the sole white man, who lives on the reservation and is married to a Mexican woman.[57] His rancho, which is surrounded by some farmland, is a short distance from the church and provides a good vantage point for gaining an idea of the surrounding landscape.

San Xavier is situated on a sandy plateau, which forms the entry to the valley of the Rio Santa Cruz and is broken up in countless places by isolated hills of volcanic origin. To the north the horizon is bounded by the steep slopes of the Santa Catalina Mountains, which are bathed in a purple glow every evening at sunset.[58] To the east and south the delicate lines of the Santa Ritas stand out against the fixed sky, and the dense mesquite forests extend from San Xavier to their base. To the west is the rolling plain blanketed with prickly chaparral flora, merging into the arid deserts of Papaguería. The old church, which lies half in ruins, and the huts of the Papagos, which are mostly laid out without order or regularity southwest of the church, provide the landscape's sole decor.

The mission of San Xavier del Bac[59] was founded by the Jesuits at the end of the seventeenth century, probably shortly after the foundation of Guevavi by Juan Maria Salvatierra and Father Kino.[60] Guevavi, now completely abandoned, was the first mission that arose in present-day Arizona. During an Indian uprising that began in 1751 and ended in 1754, in which the Pimas took part,

San Xavier was abandoned. A few years later, after the Jesuits were expelled by the Spanish government in 1767, the mission came into the hands of Franciscan priests, who in 1783 were the founders of the present church, the construction of which was completed only fourteen years later.[61]

The church, whose style mostly corresponds to that which was referred to as the "baroque" around 1700, is built entirely of red brick and its entire surface was once obviously plastered over. The ground plan has the shape of a Latin cross and the inside measurements are 105 x 27 feet. The beautifully ornamented facade points toward the south but has fallen into an advanced state of decay. Not much more can be recognized of the Franciscans' coat of arms, nor of the statue of St. Francis of Assisi, nor of the other decorations covering two pairs of triangular half columns on both sides of the portico. Above the front nave rise two towers, of which only the western one is finished. The cornice continues all along the flat roof, partly by a balustrade, party by an open ornamental border. A ball-shaped dome arises above the back nave. There is something very picturesque about the ensemble, an impression reinforced when one enters the church and the eye views a wealth of shadings and a lovely play of colors, which yields nothing to Saint Mark's in Venice. The main altar, in luxuriant baroque style, is beneath the dome. One can still see traces of old frescos on the lateral walls of the main structure. Although everything has deteriorated and is partially decayed, since 1859 French priests have assumed the pastoral leadership of the old mission, and every two weeks there is a religious service held in Spanish, which is attended by a large number of Papagos.[62]

As might be expected, the Indians of San Xavier have abandoned most of their ancestral customs. In attire they can hardly be distinguished from the Mexican rural population, and perhaps the sole difference consists in the way the Papago women wear the head cloth fastened to their heads in ancient Egyptian fashion. All the men have cut their hair short, and they all wear hats. When not going barefoot, both sexes wear leather sandals. The Papagos who live near San Xavier contrast favorably with their other fellow tribesmen who live in the arid and still imperfectly known Papaguería and are still semisavage in some ways.[63] The few individuals from these western settlements—such as Piragua, Santa Rosa, and Tecolote—I was able to see in San Xavier had faces painted red and longer hair and struck me as more timid and suspicious than the other Indians.

The Papagos and the Pimas are basically the same tribe. Not only are they greatly similar in appearance, manners, and customs, but they speak the same language belonging to the Pima-Opata family, with slight dialectical variations. The Papagos call themselves *Tóno-Oohtam*, that is, desert people. I do not know the derivation of the name *Papago*. In some works it is said that it signifies "cut hair" because the Indians converted to Christianity set themselves apart from the others in this manner. People who are thoroughly familiar with the Pima language assured me, though, that this etymology is absolutely incorrect.[64] The Pimas call themselves *A'kémorl-Oohtam*, "river people," because they live along the Gila River. For this reason they were formerly called *gileños* as well.[65] The name *Pima* or *Pimo* is possibly derived from the language of the Yaqui Indians.[66] The old bond of friendship is still maintained by both tribes and considerably strengthened by intermarriage.

On the reservation there are usually no more than 250 to 300 Papagos present. According to government reports, the remaining 5,700 in their ranks are spread west and southward across Papaguería, but it is very difficult to determine which Indians belong to the United States and which to Mexico because in the Papago-Pima settlements of Arizona and Sonora people are constantly wandering back and forth, something that is impossible to keep under close control. As far as official reports about Indian population statistics are concerned, one must proceed with caution. In the course of this account, I hope to return to this issue.[67] The number of Pimas and Papagos in Sonora is estimated at approximately 20,000.

The American government shows little interest in the Papagos. They receive no rations or yearly donations but provide their own sustenance, mainly from agriculture. They grow wheat, barley, oats, and corn, along with watermelons. What they do not require from the harvest for their own use, they sell to whites, just as they do firewood from their reservation and even baskets and pottery they manufacture.

The Papago village near San Xavier consists of approximately ninety dwellings, nearly forty of which are in the old style with the shape of a blunt beehive. The remainder are square huts of adobe or bundles of branches and belong to the more enterprising segment of the population. The huts of the old stamp have an almost purely circular floor plan and consist of a solid wood frame, over which branches and twigs are attached along the sides and on top, with sand heaped up on the sides. The only opening is a small bow-shaped entrance about 1 meter high and thus so low that one cannot enter and exit the dwelling except by crouching very low. A screen woven from

2. Papago hut at San Xavier, near Tucson.

branches, without handles, serves as a kind of door. One of these huts I measured was 2.30 meters high, 4.70 wide, and 4.80 deep. Most Papago huts have roughly the same dimensions.

The household utensils in the dwellings are a curious hodgepodge. Baskets and clay pots of their own making are found in every hut, along with grinding stones, metates, and *manitas*[68] for corn and grain, but along with these you will find wooden trunks and boxes, linen articles, empty vegetable cans, and broken bottles. Ascencio, the most important chief, himself has a table in his house, but he does not yet own a bed. He finds a mat and a couple of goat skins adequate.

The Papagos' basketry is primarily of two kinds: the first kind is prettier than the other and is very tightly woven together from willow sprigs and ornamented with tasteful dark meandering lines. The shape is best compared to a very deep, round dish without pedestal. The measurements greatly vary, just like those of the second variety, which is less ingenious and consists of square little baskets of rectangular or square shape, which are with or without lid, depending on their function. Baskets play a major role in the domestic life of the Papagos because they hold all kinds of items for household use, in addition to provisions and sometimes even water.

The pottery consists of plump pots, somewhat oval in shape and generally of a light reddish brown color. In nearly every house or each hut of southern Arizona and northwest Sonora one finds a number of ollas or pots of Papago make, serving especially as water containers.

One of the most characteristic items still generally found among the Papagos is the carrying basket, or *quijo* (Papago, *kjéoh*), which one repeatedly encounters with the women. The quijo is a trap-shaped net prepared from plant fibers, which is spread out between four long sticks that are bound at the bottom end and extend outward toward the top. Although the quijo, upon which sometimes heavy burdens such as firewood are borne, is balanced on one's back, the hauling strap rests against the forehead. Support while walking is provided by a fork-shaped stick *(sahrkuh),* which is used at the same time to prop up the basket when it is loaded or the carrier puts down her load for a moment. The younger and more coquettish the woman or girl is, the lovelier the red-dyed sahrkuh is ornamented with leather fringe or colorful pieces of cloth.

Mothers carry small children not on their backs nor in their arms but on their side, with the child resting on its mother's hipbone and tightening its legs around her waist while it is propped up by its mother's hand.

Although the Papagos are archenemies of the Apaches, whom they call *Ohp,* they have not been inimical to the whites during the last hundred years any more than the Pimas have, and both tribes have provided Americans and Mexicans effective assistance in many a pursuit of the Apaches, their common foe. Barely twelve years ago San Xavier was made unsafe by the raids of the Apaches, who held out in the Santa Rita Mountains, and the fortified hills one finds in the vicinity of the Papagos' village demonstrate how these Indians were always ready for an attack by the Apaches.[69] An ancient custom still in vogue among them and the Pimas at the present time can serve as an example of the deep contempt the Papagos have for their enemies. Every warrior from the Papago tribe who has killed an Apache must undergo a kind of purification procedure,

3. Papago women with
   burden baskets
   (after a photograph
   by Henry Buehman
   and Company, Tucson,
   ca. 1880).

consisting of him keeping apart for forty days[70] on an isolated spot outside the village where food is brought to him by friends.

In the rancho of my host, the Swiss whom the Papagos call Don Juan[71] and who is on a very friendly footing with them, I began my anthropological investigations the day after my arrival. "La Luz," a very elderly but still vigorous Papago woman, came to the rancho every morning to fill the ollas with fresh water, afterward receiving some tortillas[72] with coffee as recompense. Don Juan's wife knew a little Papago and after a long chat was able to persuade old Luz to allow me to make an outline of her hand and foot. She showed some anxiety about the shiny instrument with which I wanted to measure her head, and she could not be persuaded to remove her head cloth. That same noon, at mealtime, I could expand my knowledge in that, after considerable effort, I measured the heads of two shy young girls and could make some additional observations. However, they would not allow this until I had first carried out the same manipulations with Don Juan's wife. When I was ready, they peered at me with a kind of shy wonder and eventually burst out in nervous laughter.

During my walks through the village, I had no less difficulty and, even with Don Juan's assistance, could induce only six men to let themselves be measured. We began our attempts with the chief, Ascencio, who, though he did not agree to be measured himself, joined us when we continued our walk and persuaded some other young men to let me examine them. While I was busy, a throng of young and old gathered around us, and I was stared at with undisguised amazement. Now and then they broke out in raucous laughter, and their pleasure knew no bounds when I took a multi-colored piece of cloth out of my sack and asked them for the names of the different colors, then repeating the words to make sure I got the pronunciation right. To my regret, I did not have the opportunity to measure their limbs because none of the Indians present would agree, for money or a small gift, to disrobe, even partially. All that I could obtain were cranial measurements, observations regarding the color of skin and eyes, outlines of hands and feet, as well as a couple of hair samples.

The eight Papagos I measured had an average cranial index of 81.26 and were thus sub-brachycephalic.[73] But the Papagos have different skull shapes, as was later evident to me from the examination of some Papago skulls and from observations during a second visit. As a rule, the Papago nose is well formed, gently curved, and not strongly protruding. Now and then a short, straight nose appears. The cheekbones are somewhat prominent, especially in the case of the women, but by no means to the extent they are among the Apaches. Moderate prognathism of the upper jaw, and of the teeth as well, occurs now and then. The dark eyes are small and the caruncle at one moment is in both, then in just one of the inside corners of the eye, partially covered with a fold of skin. The Papagos' skin color is brown with a warm tint, roughly matching the numbers 29, 30, and 37 of Broca's chromatic scale for the face—mostly somewhat darker for the hands and arms.

The Papagos' physiognomy mirrors their principal character traits: amiability and idle insouciance. Even the unusually drawn-out, somewhat lisping manner with which the Papago speaks his melodious language seems to be an expression of his natural disposition. If there is no particular motive to rouse him from his apathetic state, the Papago spends his time *dolce far niente* [Italian: sweetly doing nothing]. These Indians do little hunting, and one of the few physical exercises they have is a kind of ball game with a ball of hard rubber being continuously kicked about by two men trotting across a large stretch of land. A crowd of spectators on horseback and on foot follows the two players at the same pace. That was the first thing about the Papagos I got to see upon my arrival at San Xavier, and still vivid in my memory is the shouting band of bronzed chaps running across the sun-drenched plain.[74]

Just like Indians everywhere, the Papagos are avid smokers, of cigarettes especially. Drunkenness is not uncommon. The Papagos one sees carrying on business in Tucson not infrequently succeed in obtaining strong drink, and sometimes their drinking bouts end in a tussle among themselves or fights with their Mexican half brothers. Although in United States territory there is a high penalty on the books for selling strong drink to Indians, the law is frequently a dead letter.

Facing the slope of a small hill, no more than a pistol shot's distance south of the Papago village, lie a number of old Indian graves where those among them who were not baptized are laid to rest. The Catholic Papagos are buried on the other side of the village. These old graves consist of huge chunks of lava in piles. The body, which is placed in a sitting or crouching position with all the owners' paraphernalia, is first surrounded by a stone wall. When the wall is somewhat higher than the body's head, thick branches are laid across, and then a number of bundles of sticks cross-wise over them, while these in turn are covered with heavy stones so that the whole thing looks like a huge stone heap 1 to 1½ meters high. Stones marked with incised figures, including many shaped like spirals, lie on top of some graves. Now and then one notices an olla intentionally broken lying next to the graves or one finds among the stones a necklace of colored beads as offerings for the dead. When I had visited these graves, I could not withstand the temptation of daring to try to get hold of a skull. But I had to be careful, for who knows what these otherwise so peaceful Indians might do if they noticed that someone had desecrated their fathers' graves!

I soon informed Don Juan of my plan, and, as a result, one fine morning, shortly before day-break, we headed to the graves in a roundabout way, armed with a long hook, a bag, a candle, and with our guns too—so we would be ready for anything that might occur. No other sound than the dying howl of the coyotes (*Canis latrans*) troubled the stillness of the cool night as we carefully proceeded to break apart stone by stone a grave we had already selected by day for our depredation because of its favorable location. Eventually when he had made an opening large enough to stick one's head through, we lit the candle and looked inside. There sat the skull of a valiant warrior star-ing grimly at us, but before long the hook sat on his jawbone and I yanked the head from the trunk. I had to abandon my attempt to get hold of other parts of the skeleton because in the east day was already dawning, and we had to carefully seal the grave, which was also speedily accomplished thanks to help from the powerful Don Juan. Before the sun rose above the horizon, I had safely brought my treasure to the rancho.[75]

It is obvious that, apart from baskets and ollas, very few ethnographic items can be found among the Papagos. After long searching I found a wooden club and a bow with arrows, the points of which consisted of cut glass. Fortunately, during a later visit to the Pimas, I could get a better idea of the Papagos' former state.

The chapparal in the neighborhood of San Xavier harbors an abundance of small game. It is also a genuine pleasure to roam about through field and brush in the cool morning hours or toward nightfall with your hunting rifle and try your luck on hares and cottontails or on lovely blue-gray doves, which you can shoot by the dozen, and *godornizes* [i.e., *codornizes,* or partridges] (Ortyginae), who break the silence with their calls. There are just a few small flocks of wild ducks in the creek,[76] which now wends its way among the dense mesquite bush, then through the grassy plain. Hardly have you fired a shot than you can see one or more *auras (Cathartes),*[77] more rarely a *quelele (Polyborus cheriway)*, flying above your head in a wide orbit.[78] Don Juan is a passionate hunter, and the time I do not spend in the Papago village we are together in the field. I would have gladly tarried longer at this pleasant spot, but I still had a long journey ahead of me. So on January 7 I returned to Tucson, to depart two days later, because on the 16th I had to board at Guaymas for La Paz, in Lower California, where I would meet my next traveling companion, Mr. Belding. I retrace my steps to Benson, a new town along the railway, and there, after a brief delay, take a freight train to Nogales on the Mexican border. Every freight train in America has a car at the rear end (caboose) set aside for passengers, who are not permitted to bring along anything other than hand baggage, however.

Slowly and steadily climbing, the train heads in a southwesterly direction through the magnificent high country that spreads out between the mineral-rich Santa Rita Mountains in the west and the Whetstone and Huachuca Range in the east, which bound the horizon on both sides with their jagged peaks. In the middle of the day, at a small station whose name eludes me, practically all my fellow travelers leave the caboose to take a seat on a couple of mail coaches standing in readiness, which will take them to Tombstone, forty miles to the east. Tombstone is a flourishing mining town of still recent date, situated in an area that certainly is among the richest in Arizona.

The route leads through high grassy meadows, and gradually dark stone oaks appear, which, illuminated by the midday sun, imbue the rolling landscape with considerable enchantment. Although this region was seized from the wild Apaches some years ago, settlements are still sparse. Now and then we can see a lone rancho along a mirror-smooth puddle or a babbling brook, next to which the colorful horned cattle are feasting on the tender grama grass (Chlorideae). Off in the distance, from amidst the dark foliage, a vertical smoke column at one time rises high into the transparent air. Possibly it indicates the spot where a hunters' camp has been set up because above it a couple of bald auras soar in wide circles, coveting their share of the booty.

Evening falls, and the cool mountain air rushes through the windows, in front of which I sit staring dreamily outside. It seems like the train's pace is slackening, and we stop suddenly. The conductor and brakeman[79] look up astonished and jump out of the caboose. Following their example, I can see that our car is standing alone on the track; of the locomotive and the rest of the train nothing can be seen. Presently, it appears that the iron hook linking us to the other cars is broken, and the train has gone on unaware of this. The officials head up the track with their lanterns and break the deathly silence with loud shouting, but without luck because the train has vanished behind the bends in the line, which here runs along rocky walls. Eventually, after a half hour, while we are thinking about what needs to be done, the locomotive comes slowly steaming back and, after the damage is repaired to the extent possible, we soon continue our journey and at 9 P.M. reach Nogales.

Following the shimmering from illuminated tents that I see a short distance from the depot, I head "cityward" and before long I sit down for a frugal meal that is placed in front of me by a greasy fellow with dangling, disheveled hair. I then look the place over more closely and see that Nogales consists of nothing more than a number of canvas tents and huts of sticks and branches, half of which are bars and "restaurants," except for a couple of saloons that are built of planks. I enter one of these tents to take a closer look. About twenty bronzed men with savage features, mostly Mexicans, with the broad-brimmed sombreros on their heads, draped in their colorful serapes, are standing or sitting around the monte tables, a game in which some dark-eyed señoritas of questionable reputation are also involved. Others sit on benches or empty barrels smoking their cigarettes, while some others, drinking their mescal[80] or whiskey at the counter, stand listening to the sometimes dreamy, sometimes passionate strains of a guitar. Everything is illuminated by the ruddy glow of a pair of smoking torches, which are fastened to the tent poles, forming a tableau worthy of the brush of a Salvator Rosa.[81]

I continue my evening stroll and find Mexicans sitting silently around the flickering fires burning in front of their houses, but the foul-tempered dogs, who get plenty of beatings and little to eat, make things so difficult for me that I give up further strolling about Nogales and sit down on the ground in front of the small wooden station, where neither chair nor bench can be found. Absorbed in thought, I observe the course of the stars along the dark silhouettes of the nearby mountains until it is time to board the train that will take me to Hermosillo. Unfortunately there is only one train that takes this route during the night, but I had to choose between this and the long dusty ride with the mail coach, through a country that is not among the safest. Mexican customs makes things very difficult for me by making me open and empty out all my luggage, but, to their annoyance, without result. I quickly fall asleep on one of the matted benches of the nearly empty car while the train speeds southward.

Awakening at daybreak, I see that we are darting through a sandy plain, which is bounded on the right and left by low, nearly bare mountains and is covered with a chaparral of *pitahuayas (Cactus pitahuaya)*,[82] paloverdes, and mesquites. Before long the white "Bell Mountain" rises up in the distance. Cultivated fields and orchards line the route, and a few moments later I am in Hermosillo. After having worked my way with difficulty through a throng of shouting and quarreling coachmen and porters and having brought my baggage to safety, I step into an old covered wagon and flit along lanes and streets—where the fragrance of orange trees, borne through the fresh cool morning air, wafts toward me—until we stop at the Hotel Francés, where a number of Americans have taken up residence.

After breakfast, which is partially representative of Mexican cuisine and partially of French, my first labor is to ascend the "Bell Mountain," from which one has a broad view of the city and the surrounding area. This mountain—or rather hill, because it is only a few hundred feet high—is situated on the southwest side of the city and is partly enclosed by it. The rock is a kind of white marble. When one strikes with a loose stone on one of the huge blocks covering the downward slope, the largest of which have rolled to the bottom, there is a sound like a bell. This is the derivation of the name "Bell Mountain" or "Cerro de la Campana." The slopes are covered with the brush usual to these regions, while now and then one encounters the white shells of *Bulimus* and *Cylindrella* varieties between the rocks.

Hermosillo is situated in a vast elevated valley on the left bank of the Rio Sonora, which is practically without a drop of water during the dry season. The area around the city has a parched and arid appearance, but where they have been able to irrigate the land artificially, the vegetation appears as fresh and luxuriant as one could expect only in a warm climate. Now and then the crowns of magnificent palms jut up high from the green *huertas* (gardens), where the dark foliage of the orange trees mingles with the vivid green of the broad-branched *huamóches*. Gigantic nopals *(Opuntia)*, which often reach a height of five to six meters, enclose practically all the huertas like a double wall.

Hermosillo owes its existence to the mission of Pitic, founded in the previous century, and kept this name until 1830, when it was elevated from a "presidio" to a city and received the name "Villa de Hermosillo."[83] The city does not look unattractive and consists in large part of adobe dwellings without floors and with flat roofs. Instead of glass windows, the houses have iron bars *(rejas)* spaced widely apart, which like the windows themselves mostly reach straight down to the ground. The city's layout is quite spacious and regular, but many houses lie in ruins—in the poor neighborhoods especially. The main street exiting onto the Alameda (public promenade) has young orange trees along its whole length, which are laden with ripe fruits. The Alameda, which is surrounded by walls, is no longer used as a promenade but seems to have been transformed into a kitchen garden for the city. Just like all cities of Spanish origin, Hermosillo, too, has its plaza, with benches and a fountain in the middle, where in the evening, after the scorching daytime heat, the populace comes to seek relief. Between 12 and 5 P.M. one therefore sees very few people in the streets, except for Indian *peones* (workers and servants), who primarily belong to the Yaqui and Mayo tribes.[84] These peones and the lean, furious dogs, which swarm in the back streets especially, are the sole creatures who defy the sun's searing rays. In the case of these dogs, hot weather by itself seems to encourage contentiousness because they have vowed never-ending pursuit of the numerous black and mottled pigs, which you can encounter again and again in the streets and doors of the dwellings.

Facing Hermosillo, along the other edge of the dry riverbed—because here one can hardly speak of a bank—lies Pueblo de Seri, where a mission of Seri or Ceri Indians was once established.[85] My hope of seeing individuals from this tribe in Hermosillo was not fulfilled. Now and then some of them come to the city from the coast to sell pelican skins, which they know how to prepare in a lovely way. Usually they then use the proceeds to get good and drunk. Many a Seri loses his life in Hermosillo because they are intensely hated by the Mexicans and other Indians for their treacherous ways. The Seris are probably the oldest inhabitants of the state of Sonora but by constant warfare with other tribes have seen both their territory and their number gradually reduced. Most of them—just a few hundred—have finally occupied the island of Tiburon, which they certainly will not be allowed to hold much longer.[86]

An event that still lives on in the memory of many a Hermosilleño is the seizure of the city by a handful of French filibusters under Count de Raousset-Boulbon. Here, perhaps, it is appropriate to say a word about an undertaking that was often discussed in France as well as Mexico thirty years ago. In 1850 a number of twists of fate had cast the young Raousset-Boulbon on the shores of

California just recently opened. But fortune, which so many had vainly sought there, did not smile on the energetic nobleman either. His plan of founding a French colony in Sonora and there exploiting the rich but abandoned mines, in particular, came to fruition in 1852. Supported by the Compañia Restauradora, which had been formed in agreement with the government, Raousset landed in Guaymas with 270 followers organized on a military footing. From the beginning, intrigues of the Mexican authorities and the complications growing out of these made the enterprise go awry with mishaps. After a number of vicissitudes in the interior of Sonora and, driven to extremes by the actions of the Mexican government, they eventually resorted to hostilities, which began with the storming of Hermosillo by the French on October 14, 1852. From then on one can say that the colonizing venture degenerated into a filibustering excursion, which, after repeated suspension and negotiations with the Mexican government, ended two years later with the defeat and capture of Raousset-Boulbon's entire corps. Charged with conspiracy and insurrection, he himself was shot on August 12, 1854.[87]

Because the seat of the governor of Sonora, formerly established in Ures, was transferred to Hermosillo, and the city, besides that, has been situated since 1881 along the railway line linking Guaymas and the United States, Hermosillo has developed very rapidly—to the fullest extent possible in a country such as Mexico. Many Americans have flocked to the numerous mines of Sonora to seek their fortune; a number of French and Germans have established themselves in Hermosillo as well. The city numbers between 8,000 and 9,000 inhabitants.

On the morning of January 11, I bade farewell to Hermosillo and took a seat on the train to Guaymas, which is just four hours away by rail. The route displayed the same character as above Hermosillo: lonely monotony as far as the eye could see. One could see some cultivated land and cattle only in the vicinity of isolated small stations, which usually consist of just a few pathetic branch huts or adobe sheds. Only toward the end, as you near the seacoast, does the route become more interesting. The mountains move closer together, and over long rocky railway dikes you pass the many bends and inlets forming the bay of Guaymas. The city has an enchanting location at the foot of steep, reddish brown porphyry cliffs and on the north and west side is almost completely surrounded by them. There is something Austrian about the locale and appearance of Guaymas, and people who know Aden find much similarity between the two places.[88] From Guaymas you do not have a view out to the open sea because the bay, where just a few ships lie at anchor, is completely enclosed by the steep, bare cliffs and precipices of Cape Haro. Present-day Guaymas is little older than fifty years and perhaps owes its origin to the old San José mission, where El Ranviejo is now.[89]

The city derives its name from the tribe of the now extinct Guaymas Indians, whose language, according to Alphonse Pinart, belonged to the Pima-Opata family.[90] Guaymas is a small, neglected city, which lies partly in ruins. The *muelle*, or quay, the wide plaza planted with oleander, and a couple of long, wide streets running parallel are thus the most important sections. The houses resemble those of Hermosillo and are covered with white and yellow plaster. On the northwest side of the bay is the Yaqui Indians' ranchería,[91] which for the most part consists of squalid huts of straw and branches. The part of the city bordering the ranchería exemplifies the worst kind of filth. With each footstep you encounter piles of garbage, which largely consist of innumerable empty oyster shells and fish bones, between which starving, mangy dogs and emaciated pigs run around rummaging about, often disputing their loathsome meal with the bald-headed auras. Given such conditions, it is hardly surprising that Guaymas now and then is ravaged by *tonto,* a form of yellow fever, and frightful depredations the yellow fever wrought in the summer of 1883 are additional evidence of the deleterious effect of this filth.

The actual working class of Guaymas consists primarily of Yaqui Indians, whose number in Sonora is estimated at 12,000. They hire themselves out as carriers, servants, and laborers and are quite a sight on the wharves and streets in their loose, white clothing and with their large straw hats. Their actual homeland is on the Rio Yaqui, but one encounters these Indians ranging from San José on the California peninsula to the Gila River in Arizona. But it is difficult for a foreigner to visit their settlements around and near Belem, where their chief lives. Cajèm or Cahèm, as he is called, is, in fact, extremely suspicious and, as much as possible, closes off the region he rules over from Mexicans and foreigners.[92] Many a person, so I was told, who had wanted to take a look among the Yaquis has never returned from their country. Later, recounting my stay in La Paz and my second visit in Guaymas, I will have the opportunity to refer to these Indians in more detail.

The "Hôtel" Cosmopolita, where I was accommodated, is maintained by a Frenchman from Pau. The person who runs the hotel bar is a French nobleman, an ex-officer from the African army. The "Cosmopolita" is situated on the spot where Raousset was shot and is residence for a number of short-time guests only, the majority of whom are Americans who develop the mines of Sonora.

South of the city, between the foot of the bare porphyry cliffs and the seashore, the old cemetery is situated in the middle of groves of thorny mesquites in a state of total neglect. No tombstone has not been violated, no sepulchral column does not lie in ruins. Raousset-Boulbon, too, lies on the field of the dead. Just like the other graves, no flower adorns the exile's resting place, but the withered branches of a thornbush, the emblem of his life, are spread across the grave.

If you climb the 1,400-foot-high hill that rises behind the city, you will be amply rewarded for your effort by the magnificent view observed from the summit. In front of you lies the sleeping city with its *azoteas* [tile roofs] and patios, sweltering under the hot sun; behind them the blue bay, with rocking boats and rocky capes that separate it from the sea. If you look northward, then your eye discerns the pale environs of San Pedro Island and the California coast off in the mist. Behind you lies the rugged, lonely sierra with its numerous crevices and caves, where the melodious call of the canyon wrens (*Cathertes* [sic]) is the only sound breaking the somber silence.[93] In the numerous inlets and coves the bay of Guaymas harbors a large number of seabirds, and I cannot withstand the temptation to cross the bay now and then in a small sailboat and with help from my hunting rifle subject their plumed inhabitants to closer scrutiny.[94]

Before I left Guaymas, the Mexicans apparently intended to provide me an example of their national vice by stealing two of my bags, which, in addition to my field pharmacy, included some maps, books, and instruments, which it is impossible for me to replace in Guaymas. All efforts to

4. Yaqui Indian day laborer, Guaymas, Sonora (after a photograph by Alfredo Laurent, 1883).

retrieve what was stolen were futile and ended with the judge threatening to throw me in jail if I continued to insist I had been robbed.

On the morning of January 15, at daybreak, a cannon shot thundered, announcing the arrival of the long-awaited steamboat *Mexico*. But there was no thought of departure this day because there was so much to unload and reload that the Yaquis were busy all day long and part of the next morning. On the morning of the 16th I was rowed out to board at 11 o'clock, and a few hours later the *Mexico* was under steam. The bay is very shallow because soundings during the departure revealed a depth of 3 to 4 fathoms. Soon afterward we had reached the open sea but for some time kept the mountainous coast of Sonora in view. Although the Gulf of California in olden times was called the Vermillion Sea (Mar Bermejo), from this height I could not perceive the slightest hint of a red color. Numerous dolphins accompanied the ship, just like they did on the Atlantic Ocean, now diving and rising up again from the foam of the graceful waves. On the morning of the 17th we traveled between the bare, abandoned coast of Lower California and the volcanic islands San José, San Francisco, and Espiritu Santo, anchoring in the bay of La Paz after a calm journey of nearly twenty hours.

NOTES

1. During this part of his journey, Ten Kate visited scientific and governmental institutions in the Northeast to consult with colleagues and government officials about travel and fieldwork in the American West. In Washington he made the acquaintance of Major John Wesley Powell, Charles Rau, and James Mooney at the Bureau of American Ethnology. He was requested to gather linguistic material for the bureau and received several letters of recommendation. At the Interior and War departments he received letters of recommendation from Indian Commissioner Hiram Price and General William T. Sherman for Indian agents and fort commanders, ordering their employees to assist the foreign scientist with travel arrangements, accommodation, and interpreters. Emil Bessels was his host at Yale University. Ten Kate also visited Philadelphia. See Ten Kate's letter of December 17, 1882, in *Tijdschrift van het Aardrijkskundig Genootschap* 7 (1883–84):19–20, and P. Hovens, *Herman ten Kate en de Antropologie der Noord Amerikaanse Indianen* (Meppel: Krips, 1989), 51–54.

2. The following section recounting Ten Kate's visit to the Iroquois reservation was not part of his book *Reizen en Onderzoekingen in Noord Amerika* (Leiden: E. J. Brill), 1885. Rather the editors have inserted primarily a translation of his article "Een bezoek bij de Irokeezen," *Tijdschrift van het Aardrijkskundig Genootschap* 7 (1883):202–6, with some reliance on a shorter French-language article on the same subject: "Quelques observations sur les Indiens Iroquois," *Revue d'Anthropologie* 6 (1883):279–83. For a discussion of Ten Kate's research in upper New York State, see Pieter Hovens, "Between Survival and Assimilation: The Visit of the Dutch Anthropologist Herman Ten Kate (1858–1931) to the Iroquois," *North American Indian Studies 2: European Contributions to Science, Society, and Art*, ed. P. Hovens (Aachen and Göttingen: Edition Herodot, 1984), 36–42.

3. Ely S. Parker (1828–1895) was named Hasaneanda at birth. He studied civil engineering and worked for Henry Rowe Schoolcraft and Lewis Henry Morgan as interpreter and informant during their ethnographic research. In 1851 Parker became chief sachem of the Senecas. During part of President Grant's administration (1869–1871) he was the first Commissioner of Indian Affairs of Indian descent. William H. Armstrong, *Warrior in Two Camps: Ely S. Parker, Union General and Seneca Chief* (Syracuse: Syracuse University Press, 1978).

4. HtK 1885: Paul Broca, *Instructions anthropologiques*. Paris, 1875. Eds.: Paul Broca (1824–1880), one of Ten Kate's teachers, was one of the leading theorists of the French school of anthropology, focusing on the study and interpretation of physical differences among the races of humanity and stressing the need for precise measurement. Francis Schiller, *Paul Broca: Founder of French Anthropology, Explorer of the Brain* (Berkeley: University of California Press, 1979). The chromatic scale Ten Kate refers to appears as an endpaper in Paul Broca, *Instructions générales pour les recherches anthropologiques* (Paris: V. Masson et fils, 1865); Hovens, *Herman ten Kate*, 30–31, 77, 217.

5. Lewis Henry Morgan (1818–1881) was a successful corporate lawyer in Rochester, New York. His scholarly interests focused on the Iroquois, and his acquaintance with Ely S. Parker enabled him to learn about the culture of the Five Nations. The results of his research were published as *League of the Ho-de-no-sau-nee or Iroquois* in 1851 (Rochester and New York: Sage and M. H. Newman). Morgan gave up his legal career and embarked on studies of the evolution of culture, thereby laying the theoretical basis for evolutionary anthropology in North America. Carl Resek, *Lewis Henry Morgan: American Scholar* (Chicago: University of Chicago Press, 1960).

6. The Iroquois Confederacy was founded before 1630 to end intertribal warfare. It originally consisted of five nations: Senecas, Cayugas, Onondagas, Oneidas, and Mohawks. The Tuscaroras, who had moved north from North Carolina, joined the league as the sixth nation in 1722.

7. Ten Kate is referring to the Iroquoian language family.

8. Sir Daniel Wilson (1816–1892), a Scottish-born archeologist, historian, and educational reformer, became a professor at Toronto University in 1853 and eventually president in 1881. *Dictionary of National Biography* (Oxford: Oxford University Press), 21:560–61. The story about the visit to the Huron village comes from Wilson's *Prehistoric Man: Researches into the Origin of Civilization in the Old and New World*, 2 vols. (London: Macmillan, 1876), 2:281–82.

9. Cadwallader Colden (1668–1776) was an Irishman who became governor of New York. In that capacity he was responsible for Indian affairs. His scholarly inclinations resulted in a two-volume study of the Iroquois Confederacy: *The History of the Five Indian Nations, Depending upon the Province of New York in America*, 2 vols. (London: T. Osborne, 1747). *Dictionary of American Biography* (New York: Scribner, 1943–73), 4(1):256–57.

10. John Mount Pleasant (more frequently Mountpleasant) was the leading chief of the Tuscarora Indians and the owner of a large and prosperous farm on the Tuscarora reservation. He was a widower when he married Gen. Parker's sister Caroline. Armstrong, *Parker*, 105.

11. It could not be determined who all of Ten Kate's traveling companions were. However, it is certain that he was accompanied by his father, H. F. C. ten Kate, Sr. (1822–1891), a well-known and popular artist. Inspired by literary works and his experience among the Iroquois, Ten Kate, Sr., painted a multipaneled picture with scenes from Indian life. He accompanied his son on his journey west until Little Rock, where he stayed behind to visit acquaintances before returning to Europe. Hovens, *Herman ten Kate*, 15–16, 236–37.

12. Caroline G. Parker (ca. 1830–1892) was the sister of Ely S. Parker, later Mrs. John Mountpleasant. Named Ga-hah-no at birth, she studied at Brockport and Cayuga academies in New York and later at Albany State Normal School. She contributed to Lewis Henry Morgan's ethnographic research and is pictured in Morgan's *League of the Ho-de-no-sau-nee, or Iroquois*, wearing articles of clothing he collected for the state of New York. Elisabeth Tooker, *Lewis Henry Morgan on Iroquois Material Culture* (Tucson: University of Arizona Press, 1994), 60–84; also Pieter Hovens and Anneke Groeneveld, *Odagot: Photographs of American Indians, 1860–1920* (Amsterdam: Fragment Uitgeverij, 1992), 42, 107.

13. The White Dog Sacrifice was part of the midwinter ceremonials during which two dogs were ritually strangled and then burned. Their spirits carried the Iroquois' prayers to the gods. The Green Corn Ceremony took place when the first corn ripened and was in essence a thanksgiving ritual and feast. Lewis Henry Morgan, *League of the Iroquois* (repr., New York: Corinth Books, 1962), 198–205, 215–17.

14. The Thomas Orphan Asylum was founded in 1855, a joint venture of the Society of Friends, the American Board of Foreign Missions, and the Seneca tribal council. Missionary Asher Wright and his wife, Laura, took the initiative, and funds were provided by Baltimore philanthropist Philip Thomas. Wright began missionary work among the Senecas in 1831. He studied their language, devised a phonetic system for its transcription, and translated the four gospels into Seneca. He established a press for religious and social publications. Wright died in 1875, and the asylum came under federal control. Pieter Hovens, "Between Survival and Assimilation," 40–41.

15. Ten Kate probably refers to the story of the Welsh prince Madoc who, according to oral tradition, fled the civil wars of Wales ca. 1170 by sailing west and settling in America with a small group of followers. G. A. Williams, *Madoc: The Making of a Myth* (London: Eyre Methuen, 1979).

16. Orsamus Holmes Marshall (1814–1884) was a historian of the aboriginal inhabitants of western New York. He was personally acquainted with Red Jacket and other chiefs and from them got much of the data for his works. *Appleton's Cyclopedia of American Biography,* 7 vols. (New York: Appleton, 1888–1901), 4:221. Ten Kate is referring to Holmes's *The Niagara Frontier* (Buffalo: Historical Society, 1881).

17. Benjamin Apthorp Gould (1824–1896), a distinguished American astronomer, was noted especially for his charting of the southern skies and the application of photography to astronomy. The anthropological work Ten Kate refers to was a sidelight to his career, the outgrowth of his work for the U.S. Sanitary Commission during the Civil War. Gould published anthropometric data of military recruits, including Indians, in his *Investigations in the Military and Anthropological Statistics of American Soldiers* (New York: U.S. Sanitary Commission, 1869). *Dictionary of Scientific Biography,* 16 vols. (New York: Scribner, 1970–80), 5:479–80.

18. Derisory term from the days of Dutch domination in Java referring to mixed-blood descendants of early Portuguese and, later on, other European settlers.

19. See note 11.

20. HtK 1885: Table-shaped elevations of land, resulting from the effect of water.

21. By the Treaty of Medicine Lodge (1867) the Comanches, Kiowas, and Kiowa Apaches were assigned a reservation in the territory adjacent to Fort Sill in what is now Oklahoma. In 1874 many Comanches revolted against the arrangement but were defeated and forced into final submission. T. R. Fehrenbach, *Comanches: The Destruction of a People* (New York: Knopf, 1974), 463 ff. See also chapter 9 of Ten Kate's travel narrative for a fuller discussion of these events.

22. *Cynomys ludovicianus,* blacktail prairie dog; nopal is prickly pear cactus.

23. HtK 1885: The part of the stem of the various yucca species (including *Y. baccata,* Spanish bayonet or dagger) that is underground, along with the roots, and contains a sticky sap that has purgative properties to a high degree. According to Oscar Loew [see note 36], it contains saponine, just like most agave species. Pieces from the roots of these plants are often used in the Southwest as soap and are known under the names of amole and soapweed.

24. HtK 1885: Clay dried in the sun.

25. HtK 1885: Great entry gateway; kind of vestibule.

26. HtK 1885: Open space between the walls; Fr. *cour.*

27. In the spring of 1880. Ira G. Clark, *Then Came the Railroads* (Norman: University of Oklahoma Press, 1958), 195.

28. El Paso del Norte on the Mexican side is present-day Ciudad Juárez.

29. HtK 1885: 1 English foot = 0.30479 meter.

30. *Populus monilifera* is *Populus deltoides,* or marsh cottonwood. *Obione canescens* is *Atriplex canescens,* or four-wing saltbush, and chamisa is *Ericameria nauseosa.*

31. HtK 1885: 1 English mile = 1,609 meters. Let it be noted once and for all that in the Southwest, just like the areas I traveled through in Mexico, most distances provided are based on a very superficial estimate from the residents. Opinions regarding distances often greatly vary. The estimate, of course, heavily depends on the means of travel and the circumstances under which the distance is traveled. It goes without saying that the properly measured distances by rail constitute an exception.

32. Initially established in 1849, this post received its name in 1854 from Captain William Wallace Smith Bliss, an adjutant and later son-in-law of General Zachary Taylor. The fort has occupied five different sites but at the time of Ten Kate's visit was situated at Hart's Mill. Robert W. Frazer, *Forts of the West* (Norman: University of Oklahoma Press, 1965), 143–44.

33. Isleta Pueblo near El Paso was one of several settlements of transplanted Indians along the Rio Grande that came into being after the great Pueblo Revolt of 1680 in New Mexico forced pueblos loyal to the Spanish to flee south. The Tiwa-speaking Indians of Isleta del Sur were taken mainly from Isleta Pueblo, south of Albuquerque, with some Piro admixture. Their mission Corpus Christi de los Tihuas de Ysleta was established in 1682. These Indians long succeeded in resisting absorption into the Mexican population and in preserving customs closely resembling those of their original pueblo in New Mexico. Nicholas P. Houser, "Tigua Pueblo," in *Handbook of North American Indians: Southwest*, ed. A. Ortiz (Washington, D.C.: Smithsonian Institution, 1983), 9:336–42.

34. HtK 1885: Hills at the foot of the mountain, mostly of sedimentary origin.

35. HtK 1885: Mountains.

36. HtK 1885: *Petermann's Geographische Mittheilungen* 1876, p. 213. Eds.: Oscar Loew (1844–1941), a German chemist, emigrated to the United States in 1867 and during the 1870s participated in three surveying expeditions led by Lieutenant George M. Wheeler through the Southwest. He published English-language works on the geology and mineralogy of the Southwest, and in German geographical journals he serialized reports of the expeditions in which he took part. (Ten Kate here is referring to Loew's article "Lieutenant G. M. Wheeler's Zweite Expedition nach Neu-Mexiko und Colorado, 1874," *Petermann's Geographische Mittheilungen* 22, 1876.) Loew later returned to Germany, where he achieved distinction as an organic chemist and plant physiologist. M. Klinkowski, "Oscar Loew (1844–1941)," *Berichte der Deutschen Chemischen Gesellschaft* 74, Abteilung A (1941):115–36; *Neue Deutsche Biographie,* 20 vols. (Berlin: Duncker & Humblot, 1953–2001), 15:72–74.

37. Swiss-born Adolph Francis Bandelier (1840–1914) was the first American scholar to undertake serious archaeological and historical investigations into Pueblo civilization and Spanish colonization of the Southwest during the period 1880–1892. Although both were traveling and working in the Southwest in 1883 and their paths nearly crossed, Ten Kate and Bandelier only met later as scholarly collaborators during the Hemenway Expedition, after which they corresponded. On Bandelier's life see Charles H. Lange and Carroll L. Riley, *The Life and Adventures of Adolph F. Bandelier* (Salt Lake City: University of Utah Press, 1996).

38. Ten Kate is mistaken. There are four linguistic families or languages represented among the Puebloan peoples: Uto-Aztecan, Zuni, Keresan, and Kiowa-Tanoan. The Tanoan languages include Tewa, Tiwa, and Towa. *Tehwa* is one of several Spanish forms of *Tewa*. The name *téwa* has no meaning in Tewa except as a linguistic or ethnic label. However, it is sometimes used, by extension, to refer to a village, as in "Tigua Pueblo" (Ysleta del Sur Pueblo) or "Tewa" (Hano, on the Hopi First Mesa). Fred Eggan, "Pueblos: Introduction," in *Handbook: Southwest*, 9:235.

39. This post, just north of present-day Fort Davis, Texas, was founded in 1854 and named in honor of Jefferson Davis, then secretary of war. Its purpose was to protect the El Paso–San Antonio route and deter Comanche and Apache raiding. The fort was abandoned in 1891. Frazer, *Forts,* 148. For Ten Kate's collection of Tigua artifacts, cf. Bill Wright, *The Tiguas: Pueblo Indians of Texas* (El Paso: Texas Western Press, 1993), 16–18.

40. HtK 1885: Names like these, to which one can also add *wigwam* = hut, *squaw* = woman, *papoose* = child, *powwow* = council, are derived from the Indians of the N.E. states (Algonquins) but have by now gained currency over the entire West thanks to American immigrants. Many Indians there use these expressions themselves in their conversations with whites. Eds.: The term "squaw" is now considered as pejorative by Indians and scientists alike but still retains some popularity among the general public.

41. HtK 1885: According to Loew, one can distinguish three kinds of deserts west of the Mississippi. (1) Treeless plains covered with grass, the actual prairie; (2) semideserts, treeless with little or no grass but with low shrubs (*Atriplex*, saltbush, *Artemisia*, sagebrush, *Aplopappus* [= *Haplopappus*]); (3) genuine deserts with extremely sparse or partially without vegetation. The greatest part of the region traveled by me belongs to the genuine or semidesert, as will be more apparent from the account. Eds.: Oscar Loew, "Lieutenant Wheeler's Expedition durch das südliche Californien im Jahre 1875," *Petermann's Geographische Mittheilungen* 22 (1876):335.

42. *Lepus callotis*, white-sided jackrabbit; *Lepus sylvaticus* is an obsolete name for *Sylvilagus* gray, the genus name for cottontails and close relations.

43. That is, the roadrunner.

44. Cambray, New Mexico, was a small railway village between Las Cruces and Deming in present-day Luna County. It survived until the creation of Interstate 10, which bypassed it. Robert Julyan, *The Place Names of New Mexico* (Albuquerque: University of New Mexico Press, 1996), 23.

45. Strauss, in Doña County, New Mexico, was sixteen miles northwest of El Paso. Julyan, *Place Names of New Mexico*, 343.

46. In the late nineteenth century, travelers to California taking the southern route through New Mexico passed through a canyon in the northern Peloncillo Mountains that came to be called Stein's Pass after Major Enoch Stein, U.S. Dragoons, who camped there in 1856. The Southern Pacific Railroad chose another route through the Peloncillo Mountains nine miles south and the settlement there was also called Stein's Pass until 1905, when the name was shorted to Steins. Julyan, *Place Names of New Mexico*, 341–42.

47. In 1861, after his band was falsely accused of taking Americans hostage, Cochise (ca. 1805–1874) became involved in a decade-long conflict, a struggle involving both depredations by the Apaches and a series of bloody clashes with the U.S. Army. In 1872 Cochise agreed to a truce—though hardly a surrender, as Ten Kate suggests—and settlement on a reservation in southeastern Arizona. Edwin R. Seward, *Cochise* (Norman: University of Oklahoma Press, 1991).

48. *Cereus giganteus* = *Carnegieia gigantea*, saguaro.

49. The Papago (or Tohono O'odham) Indians belong to the Uto-Aztecan linguistic group. Concentrated in southern Arizona and adjoining areas in northern Mexico, they preserved friendly relations with whites and served the Americans as scouts and allies in the struggle with their traditional enemy, the Apaches. In 1874 they were granted a small reservation centered around the San Xavier del Bac mission, but they mostly lived outside of its confines. Winston P. Erickson, *Sharing the Desert: The Tohono O'odham in History* (Tucson: University of Arizona, 1994), 74 ff.

50. Later, during his participation in the Hemenway expedition, Ten Kate learned from his Pima interpreter Hótontóahim that the name *Tucson* actually means "black foot" (HtK 1889, 233).

51. Santa Fe was founded in 1609, but St. Augustine, Florida, founded in 1565, is actually the oldest continuously settled city in the United States. Tucson's origins reach back to the end of the seventeenth century, when Father Eusebio Kino (see note 60) named the site San Cosme de Tucson, but the city's formal foundation dates only from August 20, 1775, when Don Hugo O'Connor established the Spanish presidio San Agustín del Tucson on the east bank of the Santa Cruz River. C. L. Sonnichsen, *Tucson: The Life and Times of an American City* (Norman: University of Oklahoma Press, 1982), 7–9.

52. This is probably San Agustín de Oiaur, which was a thriving Pima village when Father Eusebio Kino visited it in 1698. Kino noted that the village consisted of 177 houses and had fields rich in corn, beans, watermelons, and squash. Fay Jackson Smith, John Kessell, and Francis Fox, *Father Kino in Arizona* (Phoenix: Arizona Historical Foundation, 1966), 14, 44.

53. Tucson was linked to the Southern Pacific Railroad on March 20, 1880. Marshall Trimble, *Arizona: A Panoramic History of a Frontier State* (Garden City, New York: Doubleday, 1977), 132.

54. Originally established in the city of Tucson and called the post of Tucson, this base was renamed Camp Lowell in 1866 and was moved to a site south of Rillito Creek in 1873. It was elevated to fort status in 1879 but abandoned in 1891. Frazer, *Forts,* 10–11.

55. "General C" is Eugene Asa Carr (1830–1910), a decorated veteran and breveted brigadier general in the Civil War, who later took part in campaigns against the Apaches, Sioux, and Cheyenne. Carr was commandant of Camp Lowell between September 1882 and March 1883. James T. King, *War Eagle: A Life of General Eugene A. Carr* (Lincoln: University of Nebraska Press, 1963).

56. HtK 1885: Rural dwelling, farmstead, hut.

57. A small hill opposite the San Xavier mission belonged to the Martinez family, Mexicans who managed to retain possession even though other families were required to move when the San Xavier Indian reservation was established. The owner's daughter, Maria, married the jeweler John Berger, noted here, who later became an Indian agent on the reservation. Will C. Barnes, *Arizona Place Names* (Tucson: University of Arizona Press, 1960), 272; Erickson, *Sharing the Desert,* 88.

58. The author later noted that the Pima name for the Santa Catalina Mountains is "Pápat" (HtK 1889, 233).

59. HtK 1885: *Bac* does not mean "a place where there's water nearby," as I find cited by a writer, but can be derived from *wagh (bac), wáhki,* "ruin." Also *bac* denotes a certain type of grass. Eds.: *Bac* in Pima and Papago means "house" or "ruins." Barnes, *Arizona Place Names,* 326.

60. Juan Maria de Salvatierra (1648–1717), born in Italy, emigrated to Mexico. After teaching in Puebla, he dedicated himself to Jesuit missionary work in what is now Arizona and Baja California. His writings about Baja California have been translated: Juan Maria de Salvatierra, *Selected Letters about Lower California,* trans. and ed. Ernest J. Burrus (Los Angeles: Dawson's Book Shop, 1971), and Miguel Venegas, *Juan Maria de Salvatierra of the Company of Jesus* (Cleveland: Arthur H. Clarke Company, 1929). Eusebio Kino (1645–1711), who was born in Tyrol, entered the Society of Jesus in 1665 and was sent to Mexico as a missionary in 1681. After unsuccessful endeavors in Baja California, Kino first visited the territory that is now Arizona in 1691 and made forty subsequent expeditions, exploring the region as far north as the Casa Grande ruins and as far west as Yuma. He carried out extensive missionary activity among the Pimas, converting some 4,000 and teaching them agriculture. Herbert Eugene Bolton, *Rim of Christendom: A Biography of Eusebio Francisco Kino* (New York: Macmillan, 1936).

61. The site of San Xavier de Bac was first visited by Father Kino in 1692. Kino also began construction of a church in 1700, which was never completed. A mission was finally built in 1732, but a quarter century later it was replaced by an adobe structure, which remained until the present church was finished in 1797. Howard R. Lamar, *The Reader's Encyclopedia of the American West* (New York: Thomas Y. Crowell, 1977), 1086.

62. At this time, San Xavier belonged to the diocese of Santa Fe, whose archbishop, Jean Baptiste Lamy, faced with the dismal standards of the local clergy, brought many French and other European priests to the Southwest in an effort to revitalize the church. Paul Horgan, *Lamy of Santa Fe* (New York: Farrar, Straus & Giroux, 1975).

63. HtK 1889: A visit to the region in April 1888 showed me that the aridity of Papaguería is only relative. Water is indeed scarce, but one nevertheless finds extensive grassy plains and in the high mountains, which consist of igneous rock, many trees—such as oaks, ash, and various varieties of conifers.

    Also, whites who are engaged in mining live in a few places, e.g., in Quijotóa, so, at the very least, the incomplete knowledge I referred to is only relative. What is certain is that for no single part of Papaguería has any kind of reliable map been published, as I have experienced to my chagrin. Southwestern Arizona has not yet been visited by the U.S. Geological Survey.

    The Papago Indians I encountered besides in the smaller villages, in Quijotóa, Cabábi, and Fresnal, were not "half savage" but, as far as I could determine, stood at the same level of development as the Papagos of San Xavier. But even though the Papagos are more "civilized" than the Pimas, I found them very suspicious, reserved, and intractable (HtK 1889, 233).

    Eds.: Ten Kate, like most of his contemporaries, was an evolutionist, as is clear from his use of categories such as "savage" and "civilized." For a modern perspective on the different ecological adaptations of historic Pima and Papago peoples, see Bernard L. Fontana, "Pima and Papago: Introduction," *Handbook: Southwest*, 10:134.

64. HtK 1889, 233: According to Adolph Bandelier (*Verhandlungen der Gesellschaft für Erdkunde zu Berlin,* 1885, nos. 5 and 6) the name *Papago* is derived from "Pápap-votam." Bandelier assumes that the Pima-Opata family, or at least the actual Pima, must be included in the Shoshone (Nahuatl) group.

65. HtK 1885. A subdivision of the Apaches likewise carried the name of *Gileños.*

66. The name *Pima* was apparently given to the *Akimel Oodham* (river people) by the Spanish, who derived the word from the Pima word for "nothing," *pimahaitu.* Bernard L. Fontana, "Pima and Papago: Introduction," *Handbook: Southwest*, 10:134.

67. HtK 1889, 233: In large part the Papago village in San Xavier actually has a population in constant flux because the agricultural land—the only land at the reservation—which belongs to many, is in the immediate vicinity and because those who come to Tucson to trade mostly stay in San Xavier. The part of the Papago reservation that is near San Xavier—which is not large—is the only habitable part. The remaining or greater part of the reservation is uninhabitable because of the lack of water—again an example of the way the American government proceeds in allotting land to the Indians.

68. The stone quern is known as a metate, the roller as a mano—or here manita.

69. HtK 1889, 234: The fortified hills one finds in the "vicinity of the Papagos' village" are most likely not from the Papagos, and, at the very least, certainly not from the historic Papagos. Keeping in mind similar fortifications in the Sacaton Mountains and the petrographs that are found there as well as near San Xavier, after my second visit in 1888, I regard them instead as the work of the prehistoric race, which for the time being I will call the "Shiwian" (cf. *Tijdschrift van het Aardrijkskundig Genootschap,* 6).

The petrographs reported on in chapter 5, for example, in the canyon near Fort Apache, are probably also of prehistoric origin.

Eds.: Various hypotheses have been put forward regarding these "fortified hills," or *trincheras,* with "defensive refuge" as the most plausible explanation. David R. Wilcox and Jonathan Haas, "The Scream of the Butterfly: Competition and Conflict in the Prehistoric Southwest," in *Themes in Southwest History,* ed. George J. Gumerman (Santa Fe: School of American Research Press, 1994), 221.

70. Later corrected to four days (HtK 1889, 234).

71. I.e., John Berger.

72. HtK 1885: Cakes of cornmeal resembling thin pancakes that take the place of bread among the Mexicans. They are nutritious and tasty.

73. HtK 1885: Compare *Revue d'Ethnographie* of Dr. Hamy; vol. 2, p. 89.

74. HtK 1885: Later I saw the same game played by Mexicans, not far from San José del Cabo on the California peninsula. Whether we were dealing here with an ethnographic *survival,* dating from the time of the Pericués, or whether this game was introduced to the peninsula I could not determine.

75. HtK 1885: This skull is described in *Revue d'Anthropologie* of Topinard, p. 486. Eds.: Many nineteenth-century anthropologists collected skeletal materials for research purposes. However, some scientists collected such materials because museums paid for the acquisition and thus reduced the costs of fieldwork by the financial compensation offered. Cf. Robert Bieder, *Science Encounters the Indian: The Early Years of American Anthropology, 1820–1880* (Norman: University of Oklahoma Press, 1986), 64–67; Hovens, *Herman ten Kate,* 80–82.

76. The "creek" is the Santa Cruz River shortly before the initiation (1887) of a series of irrigation projects, which, when combined with woodcutting, overgrazing, and other activities, "led to the rapid degradation of the Santa Cruz floodplain and the ultimate destruction of the river itself." Thomas E. Sheridan, *Los Tucsonenses: The Mexican Community in Tucson 1854–1941* (Tucson: University of Arizona Press, 1986), 67–68.

77. *Cathartes aura* (Linnaeus), turkey vulture.

78. *Polyborus cheriway = Caracara cheriway* (Jacquin), caracara.

79. HtK 1885: Railway official charged with oversight of the brake equipment.

80. HtK 1885: A drink distilled from various types of agave that is colorless and in taste somewhat resembles gin.

81. Salvator Rosa (1615–1673), an Italian painter and engraver, was noted for painting in yellow brownish tones and for work evoking a certain eerie atmosphere. Ulrich Thieme and Felix Becker, *Allgemeines Lexikon der bildenden Künstler,* 37 vols. (Leipzig: A. Seeman), 29:1–3.

82. There are two types of pitahaya—the sour (*Lemaireocereus gummosus* [Engelm.] Britt. and Rose, dagger cactus) and the sweet (*Lemaireocereus thurberi* [Engelm.] Britt. and Rose, organ pipe cactus). Peter W. Van der Pas, "In Search of the Original Californian: Herman ten Kate's Expedition to Baja California," *Journal of San Diego History* 23 (1977):41–92, 85, n. 41.

83. A Seri mission, La Santisima Trinidad del Pitic was founded ca. 1700 across the Rio Sonora from the site of modern Hermosillo but abandoned sometime after 1704. Later, as Spanish settlements pushed down the Rio Sonora, a royal fort (presidio) was established in the water gap at Pitic in 1742 and shortly thereafter the mission of San Pedro de la Conquista or "Pueblo de San Pedro de la Conquista de Seris" (later abbreviated to "Pueblo Seri"). Both fort and mission were designed primarily for protection of the settlements against the Seri. The town's name was changed in 1828 in honor of a

general from the state of Jalisco, José María Gonzalez de Hermosillo. *Diccionario Porrúa de Historia, Biografía y Geografía de Mexico*, 2 vols. (Mexico: Porrúa), 1:976; W. J. McGee, "The Seri Indians," *Annual Report of the Bureau of American Ethnology* (Washington, D.C.: U.S. Government Printing Office, 1897), vol. 17, pt. 1, 72–73, 93; Paul M. Roca, *Paths of the Padres Through Sonora* (Tucson: Arizona Pioneers' Historical Society, 1976), 172–73.

84. The Yaqui and Mayo speak mutually intelligible dialects of Cahita and occupy a region of coastal Mexico, now part of southern Sonora and the state of Sinaloa: the Yaqui living north of Arroyo de Cocoraqui, principally along the Yaqui River, and the Mayo south of the Arroyo de Cocoraqui, along the El Fuerte and Mayo rivers. Perhaps 30,000 in the early 1600s, the Yaqui population, thanks to recurrent epidemics, had dropped to about 14,000 by the time of Ten Kate's visit. In 1887 the Mexican military occupied the region and dispersed the population throughout Mexico and the southwestern United States. The Mayos long tolerated incursions by the Spanish and later Mexican mestizos, but in 1880s they revolted and were promptly pacified and, like the Yaquis, dispersed. Though their population numbered around 25,000 in the 1600s, the Mayos were decimated by smallpox and other diseases, so that their population had dropped by the middle of the eighteenth century to 6,500 and only recovered its former numbers in the twentieth century. Edward H. Spicer, "Yaqui," *Perspectives in American Indian Culture Change* (Chicago: University of Chicago Press, 1961), 1–93; "Yaqui," N. Ross Crumbrine, "Mayo," *Handbook: Southwest,* 10:250–75.

85. See note 83.

86. In the nineteenth century the Seri Indians occupied the area between the Rio Magdalena and Rio Matope and Tiburon Island. Beginning in the 1750s the Seris started a series of wars against the Spaniards and later Mexicans, which led to a drastic loss of their population and reduction of territory to Tiburon Island and the closely adjoining coast. Thomas Bowen, "Seri," *Handbook: Southwest,* 10:230–49.

87. HtK 1885: For more details I can refer to the captivating biography by Henry de la Madelène, *Le Comte Gaston de Raousset-Boulbon, sa vie et ses aventures d'après ses papiers et sa correspondance,* rev. ed. (Paris, 1876). Eds.: Gaston de Raousset-Boulbon (1817–1854) was born in Avignon. He lived for a while in Algeria but returned to France after the revolution of 1848 and the creation of the Second Republic, edited a newspaper, and engaged in politics. In 1850 he emigrated to California. His adventures in Sonora were in essence as Ten Kate describes them. After the French invasion of Mexico in the 1860s, his remains were exhumed and returned to his homeland. See Rufus Kay Wyllys, *The French in Sonora (1850–1854): The Story of French Adventurers from California into Mexico* (Berkeley: University of California Press, 1932).

88. HtK 1885: The illustration that Felix Oswald, *Streifzüge in den Urwäldern von Mexico,* etc., p. 5, provides of Guaymas is completely inaccurate. Eds.: The author is citing from a German translation of *Summerland Sketches, or Rambles in the Backwoods of Mexico and Central America* (Philadelphia: J. B. Lippincott, 1880), by Felix Leopold Oswald (1845–1906), an American author.

89. The mission San José de Guaymas was founded in April 1701 by Father Salvatierra but soon after abandoned. It was reestablished in 1751 but burned a few years later by Apaches and then abandoned. Roca, *Paths of the Padres,* 309–12; see also *Diccionario Porrúa,* 1:936.

90. During the 1870s Alphonse Pinart (1852–1911), a French explorer and ethnographer, visited Alaska, the Pacific Northwest, California, Arizona, and Mexico. Here Ten Kate is citing Pinart's article "Voyage en Sonora," *Bulletin de la Société de Géographie* 20 (1880):197.

91. HtK 1885: Collection of huts, a hamlet.

92. José Maria Leyva (1839–1887), known as Cajeme, had been embroiled with the State of Sonora after he established an independent tax collection system. The refusal of Mexican authorities in 1882 to surrender perpetrators of an assassination attempt against him resulted in open rebellion, which led to his eventual capture and execution. Ramón Corral, "Biografía de José Maria Leyva Cajeme," *Obras Historicas* (Hermosillo, 1959), 147–92.

93. I.e., *Catherpes mexicanus,* canyon wren.

94. HtK 1885: Other than gulls of various genera, including *L. heermanni* [*Larus heermanni* Cassin, Heermann's gull], one finds cormorants (*Phalacrocorax* [Brisson]), grebes *(Podiceps),* and especially many pelicans (*Pelecanus fuscus* [*P. occidentalis* Linnaeus, brown pelican] and *erythrorhyncus* [*P. erythrorhyncus* Gmelin, white pelican]). I found that in the gullet of the latter lives a bird lice from the genus *Menopon,* which, upon closer examination by Dr. Piaget, appears to be a new species. (Notes from the Leiden Museum, vol. VI, p. 111.) In the flat coastal stretch that bounds Cape Haro on the landward side and that is blanketed with dense brush and saguaros, you can encounter multitudes of the half-white *Lepus callotis.* Of songbirds you can find the most important, numerous specimens of *Harporhynchus* [*Toxostoma,* thrasher] *(Methriopterus),* and *Campylorhynchus* [cactus wren] varieties here.

   Between the countless loose boulders covering the beach you find, primarily at ebb tide, a number of sea animals. Most numerous are snails of the genera *Fusus* [*Fusinus* Rafinesque], with *F. ambustus* Gould [*Fusinus ambustus* Gould, 1853]; *Nassa* [*Nassarius* Duméril] with *N. luteostoma* Kien [*Nassarius (Arcularia) luteostoma*] [Broderip & Sowerby, 1829]; *Conus; Ceritheum* [i.e., *Cerithium* Bruguière] with *C. varicosum* Sow. [*Cerithidea valida*] (C. B. Adams, 1852); *Turritella,* including *T. goniostoma* Valenc. [i.e., *Turritella gonostoma* Valenciennes, 1832]; *Nerita; Trochus* with *T. rugosus* [*Tegula (Chlorostoma) rugosa* (A. Adams, 1853)]; next are shell animals, represented by *Porcellana, Sesarma, Alpheus,* and others. The coast teems especially with a large, very mobile type of isopod.

CHAPTER TWO

On the California Peninsula

THE PENINSULA EMERGING FROM THE BLUE WAVES of the Pacific Ocean along the west coast of Mexico, reaching a length of 160 geographical miles,[1] is one of the most forgotten corners of the earth. Discovered in 1533 by a certain Fortun Ximenez, at the site of present-day La Paz, it was until 1602 visited intermittently by Cortés, Ulloa, Alarcón, Cabrillo, and Vizcaino as well.[2] Their voyages, however, were little more than coastal reconnaissance. They did not provide much more fresh knowledge about the land itself than the undertakings that followed since their primary purpose was hunting for pearls in the "Vermilion Sea." More exact knowledge of the country's interior and its inhabitants dates only from 1683, the moment when priests set foot on the peninsula. The works of Miguel Venegas, Jacob Baegert, and Francisco Saverio Clavijero are in many respects still the best sources on Lower California.[3] After the Jesuits had to leave the Spanish possessions following a decree by Charles III in 1767, the peninsula again plunged into oblivion.

Following a visit to the southern part of the country in 1826, Duhaut-Cilly was the first to again provide some information about the nature and products of the land, while a few seafarers, including Belcher and Du Petit Thouars (1839), Duflot de Mofras (1843), and Kellett (1846, 1849–1850), later carried out coastal reconnaissance.[4] The English conchologist, Hugh Cuming, who visited the peninsula around 1830, was probably the first to do so with natural history in mind.[5] Reigen and Rich came after him with the same intention and eventually in 1858 the Hungarian von Csiktapolcza Xántus, who in April and May that year undertook a journey across the peninsula from San Bartolomé on the west coast to La Paz. Later, between 1859 and 1862, he stayed on at Cape San Lucas in the service of the United States Coast Survey for the purpose of making tidal observations. In addition, during this period he was busy in the realm of natural history and assembled an abundant collection.[6] E. Guillemin-Tarayre, a member of the French scientific commission for the exploration of Mexico, visited La Paz, Triunfo, and vicinity in 1865, primarily with an eye to the products of the land and mining.[7]

J. Ross Browne, Dr. William M. Gabb, and Dr. F. von Loehr in 1867 traveled through Lower California on a mission of the Lower California Company, which in 1866 had purchased the peninsula between 24°20' and 31°. This is the only great journey of exploration that was ever undertaken in Lower California and extended across the entire length of the peninsula.[8] Dr. Gabb is the first since Clavijero who provides us with definite, though also sparse reports about the former inhabitants, that is, the Cochimí Indians in the center of the peninsula.[9]

Six years later, in 1873–1874, the first complete and accurate coastal survey of Lower California was undertaken by the American warship *Narragansett* under Captain G. Dewey.[10] Dr. Th. H. Streets, who took part in this expedition, carried out observations in the areas of natural history and geology at that same time.[11]

Then another interval of nearly seven years follows, and the American Lyman Belding continues the investigations of Xántus, Streets, and their predecessors. The first time Mr. Belding visited the California peninsula was in the spring of 1881, when he carried out a zoological survey, primarily in ornithology, along the west coast, including the island Cerros or Cedros to the north of Cape San Eugenio. The most important result of this journey was determining that the ornithological fauna to the north of latitude 28° is wholly identical with that of Upper California in the area around San Diego. From December 1881 to May 1882 Belding returned to the peninsula and, in fact, to that part situated south of La Paz. His investigations were crowned with success because not only did he more carefully elucidate Xánthus's observations, but he increased our knowledge of Lower California fauna and flora at the same time by discovering various new species.[12] The following pages will provide a more detailed account concerning Mr. Belding's third journey, when I was his traveling companion for much of the time.[13]

From the foregoing overview it appears that, despite the journey of Ross Browne and his traveling companions, our geographical knowledge of the interior is still not as precise as one might wish. A detailed map of the interior based on astronomical observation is most desirable. Precise observations in the general physical-geographical realm, except for the geognostic ones under the mandate of the Lower California Company, have never been carried out. With the exception of the peninsula south of latitude 24°40', our information about natural history, both zoology as well as botany, is still incomplete. This is true not just for the interior but for the coast as well because the tract of land between Santa Rosalia Bay and the Tropic of Cancer, for instance, has never been investigated from a zoological vantage. No more than for the east coast do we know where the boundary between the San Diego avifauna and that of the peninsula itself begins.

In particular, the eastern half of the region, which extends to the north of latitude 30°, is a terra incognita in every respect. Where the Calamahué with its white peak rises to an altitude of 3,000 meters and the savage mountain Cocopas dwell in undisturbed freedom, a scientist-traveler has never penetrated, and over these deserts extends a mysterious veil.[14] The same is true for the region between 113 and 114° longitude west (from Greenwich) and latitudes 27 and 28°.

Anthropological and ethnographic investigation of Lower California north of 24°40' is still desirable, too. If I have succeeded in clearing up the horizon for the part south, what remains is still shrouded in total obscurity. The numerous pictographs that, according to Clavijero, may be found in the mountains between latitudes 27 and 28° have never found anyone to describe them, and neither on the peninsula nor on the islands has anyone tracked down what remains of the original inhabitants. There can be no doubt that a rich find will reward the future visitor in this realm. What I observed in this regard in the south of the country and on the island Espiritu Santo justifies this assumption. Now let us return to our actual narrative.

Viewed from the sea, La Paz offers an attractive view. The white houses, nestled among the verdant palms, álamos, and huamóches;[15] the numerous watermills; the sandy, sloping beach; the mass of boats bobbing on the blue waves; and the colorful bustle of the crowd on the pier leave a very favorable first impression. No sooner had I landed than one of the first people I met was Mr. Belding, who was about to sail on the *Mexico* to San José del Cabo. He had finished his business in La Paz and, aware that I, too, would later be coming to San José, had decided to await my arrival there so we could continue the journey together.[16] We then parted in the hope of soon seeing each other again, and before long I was accommodated in the same room that had been Mr. Belding's taxidermy laboratory the month before. Señor Don Gaston J. Vives, a young Mexican of French extraction, with whom I was staying, immediately offered me his services, which I eagerly accepted. No one, however, knew the area better than he, and I still recall with satisfaction the pleasant hours spent in his company.

La Paz owes its origin to a mission among the Pericué Indians, established in 1720 by the fathers Ugarte and Bravo.[17] Because of the warlike character of the Indians, the mission had to be abolished after just a few years, and only about a century later did present-day La Paz arise on the ruins of the old mission.

The city is situated on the sandy plateau that bridges the beach and the sierra. The houses, which Xánthus called tastefully built(!), look just like those of Guaymas but do not leave the impression of neglect and decay. On the contrary, there is something cheerful and tidy about the main streets of La Paz, which are planted with shady álamos. There is no pavement. A wooden sidewalk runs along both sides near the houses of the main street, but between them one finds just loose sand. The most important buildings are the city hall, the barracks, and the main church, which all face the plaza. Except on the days that the steamboats between Guaymas, Mazatlán, and San Francisco put in at port—and that happens only twice a month—a deathly stillness pervades La Paz, and the shores and streets are deserted. The outskirts of the city, which stretch upward all along the bay, consist of wretched straw huts, occupied by Yaqui and Mayo Indians, who have migrated from the mainland. The entire population of the municipality La Paz, of which the city has the largest part by far, amounts to nearly 4,000 inhabitants.[18] On the north side the bay of La Paz merges into the Gulf of California. On the east side it is bounded by the mountainous peninsula that extends from the San Lorenzo strait to near La Paz. On the south and west side it is enclosed by a sandy beach, which divides directly opposite La Paz, forming a peninsula called Mogóte or Mojóte in the shape of a gigantic, somewhat bent T. A large part of this sandy

coast is blanketed with compact forests of mangroves *(Rhizophoracae)* and is the abode of numerous ocean fowl.

At the same time Raousset-Boulbon was in Sonora with his freebooters, a similar expedition
took place under the American adventurer "General" William Walker in Lower California. On
November 3, 1853, landing with the bark *Caroline* at La Paz, he and a handful of freebooters took
the city, jailed the authorities, lowered the Mexican flag, and declared Lower California a separate
republic with him as president. But in January 1854 everything changed when Lower California
and Sonora constituted themselves as a united republic. In March and April of the same year, Walker
made another attempt from the north, in league with a hundred filibusters under Watkins.[19] But,
assailed by Mexican troops while returning via San Tomás, Walker crossed the frontier, where on
May 6, 1854, he surrendered to the American authorities. Although Walker was brought to trial,
nothing came of this. A couple of years later he set out again on a freebooter expedition to
Nicaragua.[20] Like so many places in Mexico, La Paz, too, was repeatedly the scene of minor revolutions, ending just as quickly as they erupted.

I spent the ten days that elapsed before a favorable opportunity to head for the uninhabited island Espíritu Santo presented itself with various jaunts on land and sea, accompanied mostly
by Señor Gaston Vives. The first priority was to turn up Indian relics, the second to collect zoological specimens. It was on the beach south of La Paz, at ebb tide especially, that I found a number
of spear points and arrowheads of various shapes and sizes. Most were damaged, particularly due
to the kind of stone of which they were made—porphyry, as a rule. Where the beach rose up to
form a sandy embankment and brush began growing, there were numerous scattered piles of empty
shells, primarily oyster shells, the contents of which had once certainly provided the Indians with
food. Despite my investigations, I could not find any tools in these rubbish heaps, but I still believe
that a prolonged search of a large number of these places would turn up some items. Clearly the
former Pericúes once had settlements along this beach.[21] Also, somewhat farther inland at Las
Garzas, the huerta where Vives had his fields of sugarcane, I came into possession of a couple of
spear points. Las Garzas is also a good place to make natural history collections and give vent to
your desire for hunting.[22]

Along the sandy ground, with which they share compatible coloration, the horned frog
(Phrynosoma sp.) scampers about, and the rattlesnake[23] slithers between the chaparral of *pitahuayas*
[*pitahaya*] and *cardones (Cereus giganteus* [thistle])—the latter plant riddled with numerous holes from
the Gila woodpecker *(Centurus uropygialis).*[24] *Huitachoches* and *huitacochones (Campylorhynchus*
and *Methriopterus)* chime in with their melodious call, while with nearly every footstep one drives off
a dove or two (including *Chamaepelia passerina)* with warbling and flapping wings. As the shots fall,
the *quelele (Polyborus cheriway)* rejoices at the prospect of spoils, while its relation, the slender and
much less common *Aesalon columbarius,* is the terror of smaller birds (including *Pipilo* [towhee],
Tyrannus [kingbird], and *Porzanna* species).[25] Hares *(Lepus callotis)* are not uncommon. Vives and I
tried in vain to spot the very rare bird *Rallus beldingi,*[26] discovered by Belding,[27] and though we sat

deathly still for some hours near a pool in a mangrove forest, we never had the satisfaction of getting the timid bird within range.

I was more fortunate during our jaunts in the bay in a small sailboat. In particular, various species of gulls (including *Larus occidentalis, L. delawarensis, L. heermanni,* and *L. philadelphiae)* are numerous all along the coast.[28] Cormorants *(Phalacrocorax)* are not as common as the pelicans, who are often perched in dense rows along the beach or soaring up in the air, suddenly darting directly downward when their acute eye perceives in the clear sea a fish that catches their fancy. High up in the air and seldom within range the frigate bird *(Tachypetes minor)* hovers in stately movement during flight; it is called *tijereta* by the Mexicans because of the shape of its tail.[29] Only by reaching the edge of the mangrove forest above wind and without making any noise can one get in range of it because it sometimes alights on the branches. Once I shot a specimen of *Sula cyanops* between La Paz and Pichilingue, which was probably an *"Irrgast"* [errant guest] because none of the Mexicans to whom I showed the bird had ever seen it. Nor had Belding ever encountered it in this area. Sometime later I saw a second specimen of this *Sula,* but I could not get hold of it.[30]

Among the plenitude of fish abounding in the Gulf of La Paz, I will name just *Conger niger, Aphorista atricauda, Tetrodon geometricus, Diodon hystrix,* etc.[31] The Mexicans often catch fish with harpoons.[32] Sharks are not uncommon and make swimming very dangerous—as do the *manta raya,* a gigantic ray, and the *tintorera,* a giant cephalopod.[33] Between La Paz and Pichilingue lies a reef of fragile coral *(Fungia* and *Poecilopora),* where at ebb tide one can observe numerous starfish, sea urchins *(Encope,* sp.), and holothurians. At ebb tide the shores of the gulf, especially the Mojote peninsula, provide the collector an abundant catch in shells.[34]

On January 25 the north wind, which had been blowing for several days now, eventually completely subsided, and the sky, which during this period was mostly overcast, this morning formed a brighter and lovelier dome than ever above the tranquil bay. We took advantage of the favorable opportunity to have everything in readiness for the long-planned expedition to Espiritu Santo. Already by noon the *Soledad* or *Petit Coco,* a sailboat belonging to Vives that he used for pearl fishing, had our provisions and extra equipment on board. We were just waiting for a favorable south wind, which began picking up in the evening, and at 9 o'clock we started our expedition under darkness. Apart from Vives, our traveling company consisted of Señor Sepúlvida, our captain; Señor Uzárraga, a judge in La Paz; and two Mexican sailors. Also Duc, Vives's trusty dog, joined the entourage.

The *coromuel,* or south wind, was not filling our sails, despite the captain's prompting by whistling, so we had to ply the oars if we hoped to land in Espiritu Santo the next morning.[35] Fortunately, a more powerful wind arose, and when we awoke on the 26th we lay in the *ensenada* (cove) of La Gallina along the west coast of the island. There were just a few fishermen at work near us, and I had the chance to see how the divers, attired in diving suits, retrieved oysters from the bottom. Just a few years ago this occupation was carried out exclusively by naked divers, but now the diving suit has found its way to this remote corner of the earth too. While examining some oysters, I found a couple of decapods from the genera *Remipes* and *Pontonia* inside their shells. Probably they have strayed among the pearl oysters because these crustaceans are not known to be parasites.[36]

After we had breakfast we rowed farther on to a point called Las Cuevitas, where we made our first landing. The landing occurred in a very small canoe, which consisted of a hollowed-out tree trunk, and in the beginning I had difficulty keeping my balance and avoiding tumbling into the water, gun and all. I explored two caves I saw in the slope overhead in hopes of finding Indian graves, but without success. An exhausting excursion that I made with Gaston at noon under scorching heat across rocks and through ravines turned up nothing as well. For the first time, however, I could observe the black hare *(Lepus californicus richardsoni, bennetti),* which here appears in the wild.[37] Toward evening we headed southward for a while and anchored in the Ensenada de la Candelera, probably so named because of the vague resemblance of the rock columns along the coast, evidently of porphyry, to a candlestick.

The next morning I went ashore and photographed a couple of scenes not far from our landing place. Candelera is one of the few places on Espiritu Santo where fresh water can be found, justifying the assumption that Indians once lived here. Nor had we been clambering over the rocks and exploring some caves for very long when to my great satisfaction I found a skull along with some long bones. The skull lay half buried in the sand, covering the floor of the cave, and unfortunately, while it was being dug out, part of the rather severely weathered skull bones separated. The bones bore clear signs of having once been covered with red pigment. The skull shape was markedly dolichocephalic, and everything pointed to a race of limited development. Relying on old writers, we can indicate from which of the now vanished Indian tribes these bones came. The Pericués or Péricu Indians were the same tribe as the Edués or Edu from the south and, in addition to Espiritu Santo, inhabited the surroundings islands and coast.[38] The Coras were a subdivision of the Pericués. There is nothing in Venegas or Clavijero, however, regarding the mode of interment among these Indians.[39]

It was an auspicious day because at noon, when I resumed my searching with Sepúlvida and one of the sailors, we found in three different caves in a ravine emptying into the small bay of Cardoncito a rather large quantity of human bones—again including a dolichocephalic skull, probably from a woman. Practically all these bones, to the extent they were not too severely weathered, displayed the same red color as the previous ones, though much more intense. There could no longer be any doubt that these bones were deliberately colored this way, and the possible influence of the soil was ruled out. Upon closer examination, the red pigment appeared to be iron ochre. All these bones lay scattered about in helter-skelter fashion, exposed on the floor of the caves. Manufactured items were not to be found. I found only some half-decayed plant fibers, probably from the mescal.[40]

This midday excursion was one of the most onerous ones of my entire journey. For many hours we had to clamber over jagged lava blocks—now climbing, now descending—under the sun's fierce heat. My hands were lacerated from contact with the thorny chollas *(Opuntia)* and cardones. My feet felt like they were on fire, and I reached the seashore at sunset dead tired.

Because of the proximity of the tropics, twilight in these parts is very brief, lasting just a few minutes longer during the summer, and by 6:30 it is already dark. For a long time we sit in the dark, staring outside, while our little hulk bobs up and down and the stars follow their eternal course along the pinnacle. The seabirds squabble over a resting place for the night and make the secluded rocks echo with their shrieking calls. But before long their cries die down, and the lapping waves, which slosh the bow, lull us to sleep.

Es murmeln die Wogen ihr ew'ges Gemurmel.[41]

The following morning we set our course for Ensenada de la Ballena and carry out our investigations. A long valley opens out into this bay, and on the floor one finds the dried-out bed of a mountain stream. Here a wilderness of giant cactuses, pitahuayas, chollas, and dense brush spreads out, and it is the refuge of choice for a large number of black hares, wild doves, and woodpeckers *(Centurus uropygialis)*. In the southern valley wall I explored a number of caves, but without success. Sepúlvida, who had headed out in a different direction, was luckier and at noon brought me to a cave where he had made an excellent find. There the bones of at least four fully grown persons and a child lay together in a disorderly heap, and here, too, most of them again displayed the same red color as the ones that preceded them. Some of the bones were so moldy that they fell apart when touched.

At the beach of Whale Bay there are a number of stone dams, which are certainly for catching fish. At flood tide they are underwater. By ebb tide part of the receding water still remains inside the stone enclosure, and later, after it slowly slips between the piled-up stones, the remaining fish and crustaceans become easy prey for the Yaqui Indians, who have built these dikes. Now and then one finds shells of huge turtles lying along the beach, and many times we can see these animals in the sea along the coast. They are difficult to get within range, however, because they immediately dive below the water to surface farther on.

In the summer the Yaquis often visit this island when they are fishing for pearls, and we repeatedly find traces of their stay. Later, in the afternoon, we set our course for the wide bay of San Gabriel and cast anchor there shortly before sundown. At this elevation a broad sandy plain cuts across Espiritu Santo. Because of the dense brush, one cannot see the eastern shore, however. And here I again encountered many stone piles and dried branches, which indicated the spot where the Yaqui fishermen spent the night to protect themselves against mosquitoes during the unbearably hot summer.

Along the beach of San Gabriel one can collect numerous and often lovely shells just as one can along the aforementioned coves. Of gastropods the genera *Strombus, Fusus, Oliva, Nassa, Natica, Vermetus,* and *Bulla* are particularly well represented. A small, white *Oliva* species, which is very numerous in some places, is called *arroz de mar* (sea rice) because of its shape and size. On land one often runs across *Bulimus.* The genera *Lucina* and *Cytherea* represent, in addition to *Ostrea,* the lamellibranchs. As for cephalopods I found only a shell of *Argonauta.* The spots between the mangroves teem with white *garzas* [herons] *(Garzetta candidissima),*[42] and at the same time a few pelicans appear. In the plain there were black hares again, which here appeared in profusion and of which we laid up a goodly supply with our weapons one very turbulent morning.

The exploration of the caves in the nearby mountains unfortunately turned up nothing. So I had to be content with photographing a couple of scenes along the coast, and the next morning we sailed to Dispensa Bay, the one farthest south, one along the west coast of Espiritu Santo. Had the Mexicans' claims proved true, I should have found gigantic human bones here but, as was to be expected, I found nothing. Possibly the numerous shark vertebrae, which I encountered on the beach, gave rise to this claim.[43] The points we visited during our last landing on the island also included a regular volcanic cone, reddish in color, which here had penetrated the layers of Tertiary sandstone forming the primary mass of the island and had already caught my attention while we were steaming past on the *Mexico*.[44] From the south coast we had marvelous views of the majestic mountains along the strait of San Lorenzo and Cerralbo Island.

Because the east coast of Espiritu Santo is steep and there is no place where one can find fresh water, we saw no point in a visit there and on the 30th, around 2:30 P.M., turned back. Because of a strong contrary wind (coromuel), we went no farther that day than the bay of Pichilingué. The next morning we visited the small island, which is opposite the bay, to take a look at the salt pans *(salinas)*. In several places along the gulf coast, on Carmen Island especially, considerable salt is extracted. On the sandy ground, near the saline, I found over a surface of several meters a number of large stones, which were laid according to the pattern of a maze. Our captain told me that this was part of a Yaqui game and they called it *"la casa de Montezuma"* [Montezuma's house].[45]

Before long a favorable breeze arose, and that afternoon at 2 o'clock we returned safe and sound to La Paz. After I had developed my negatives and had organized the items collected, I began making preparations for my expedition to San José. Vives had been able to find me a guide in the person of Don Juan de Dios Angúlo, someone who knew the country like the back of his hand and who had a fine reputation on the peninsula because of the effective part he played in the American war of 1847–1848 and in the defense of Lower California against Walker. Don Juan was a vigorous old man of sixty-seven years, tall in stature, with a thick, long beard and a bald head. There was something dignified in his bearing and demeanor, and his appearance inevitably brought an Arab to mind.

Before long we settled on remuneration, and on February 6, well before sunup, we were mounted up and on the way to the rancho Las Playitas. A mule, which carried my baggage and photographic equipment, was guided by a Mexican boy of twelve or fourteen years, named Valentín, who was riding a small, emaciated horse. The horses on the peninsula are mostly small and unimpressive and can make no claim to being handsome. On the other hand, all of them have the good qualities of horses who have been tempered by rough experience. Inured against all fatigue, they can comfortably go half a day without water and fodder and require no care because covering up an overheated horse, rubbing, and currying are not done in Lower California.

As the morning began to dawn, I saw that we were on a wide, sandy road, which was lined on both sides by tall cardones and pitahuayas[46] and a dense chapparal. At 10 A.M. we reached Las Playitas, Don Juan's rancho, romantically situated in a sunny valley of light gray granite mountains. After a hearty meal of chili con carne (a roasted hash [hachis] of beef or venison with Spanish pepper), *frijoles* (brown beans), tortillas, and cheese, I took a closer look at the region. The nearly desiccated arroyo (creek, stream, mountain stream), the bed of which consists of grit from heavily weathered granite, winds its way behind the rancho along the foot of the mountains through the dense brush, above which the slender crowns of some palms are swaying off and on. Marjoram, damiana *(Bigelovia),*[47] and salvia fill the air with their fragrant aromas. The babbling of the brook and the buzzing from the fluttering wings of the hummingbird *(Calypte costae)* are the only sounds ruffling the calm.[48] With unprecedented delight one revels in this profusion of shapes and colors of a semitropical nature, and while one wanders through the meadows daydreaming, the hours pass by with unprecedented swiftness.

Around 4 P.M. we continued our journey to Triunfo, while Valentín had gone ahead with the pack mule. The road is now worse, filled with rough spots, climbing and descending and leading now and then through a dry arroyo. At one point along the route the majestic shapes of the heavily wooded Sierra Laguna rise up along the azure horizon, then vanish again in the shade of sturdy huamóche trees and fragrant *binoramas* (a mimosacea). Calabásas and San Blas are the only rancherías we pass through. In the latter town the residents were noisily celebrating a fiesta, which nearly cost me my baggage, as I later found out. Valentín, however, who had come through San Blas with the pack mule late that evening, a few hours after us, had eluded the disorderly conduct of some drunken fellows only with difficulty. They were already cutting through the *lariates,*[49] which attached the baggage to the mule, when Don Juan's return soon gave them pause for thought. After he had accompanied me to Triunfo, he had immediately retraced his steps, concerned about Valentín's long absence, and then had luckily rescued the muchacho (boy).

Lower California is one of the safest areas of Mexico. Highway robbery is not a widespread occurrence, as it is in other states. A contributing factor for this is certainly that there is actually no regular traffic of travelers and goods in the interior.

This day I had been in the saddle nearly ten hours, and in my very exhausted state I lay down to rest almost immediately after arrival at a simple hostel. I had barely gotten up the next morning when I was summoned to a sick child. Although Triunfo has a couple thousand inhabitants, there is still no doctor nor apothecary, and it is natural that they should seek advice from every stranger whom they think can provide medical assistance. As a matter of fact, I was able to provide the help requested, and willy-nilly I thus began my practice.

Triunfo, which owes its existence to the discovery of silver mines about twenty years ago, has an enchanting location amid granite mountains partially overgrown with vegetation. It looks like a typical Mexican town and is built in quite regular fashion. The mines, one of which I visited that afternoon, are exploited by an English company, headed by Mr. H., and for the moment are the only ones in the peninsula earning a profit.[50] The mine workers include a number of Yaqui Indians as well.

At 8 A.M. we said goodbye to Triunfo, reaching San Antonio with its white houses after roughly an hour of riding. It is marvelously situated between the mountains among the verdure of huamóches and orange trees. After leaving San Antonio the route again rises, and once one has reached the saddle between the mountain, one can look back on the peaceful little town with its white houses, radiant in the morning sun. The wide valley of Aguas Calientes lies before you, spreading out toward the east to the sea, where one can see the rugged mountainous mass of Cerralbo Island laid out in full view. Off in the west high mountains tower up, blanketed to the very top with vegetation. Having reached the bottom, we halt for a moment near the Aguas Calientes rancho, near which, as the name indicates, there is a warm spring, which, to judge from its taste, includes traces of hydrogen sulfide. Under the canopy of palm leaves in front of the rancho, various deer hides are hung out to dry, and, according to the *ranchero*'s testimony, there are certainly numerous deer in the vicinity.

We continue our ride part of the way past the rancho La Venta mostly through and along an arroyo wending its way through the dense thicket, halting under the foliage of an oak to take our midday meal. Around 4 P.M. we reach San Bartólo, which is nestled romantically against a steep mountainside. Semitropical nature seems to have lavished its entire bounty on this spot, titillating the traveler's eye with indescribable enchantment. Sugarcane fields join banana trees, and the dark foliage of the orange blossoms, which are laden with glowing fruit, vies with the stately crown of the palms and wild fig trees to create a view one will never forget.

We water our horses at the clear stream flowing through San Bartólo and continue the journey through a long valley of gray granite rocks to the rancho de la Ensenada [ranch of the cove], which is not far from the level seashore. Our supper is frugal and consists only of a couple of tortillas with cheese because the poor inhabitants themselves do not have much. But this is not a problem because the fatigue of the journey causes me promptly to doze off under the veranda of palm leaves, to the murmuring refrain of the waves along the secluded shore. Early in the morning we head out again and follow the coast to Tecolote, a small rancho, where we have breakfast, and at the same time I have the opportunity to add some shells to my collection.

The route now leads across sandy ground, which in large part is covered with Brazil wood, and well before midday we have reached Los Martyres. It consists of nothing more than isolated ranchos, lost in the vast fields of sugarcane blanketing the plain. We dismount by one of these ranchos. Before long the horses are unsaddled, and I am on the way with a Mexican boy to the sandstone hills, full of caves and crevices, rising up not far from the seashore, to look for other *"indicios de la gentilidad,"*[51] as Don Juan referred to them. It cost me many a bead of sweat before I had found the magnificent male skull, with jaws to match, and some long bones, which clearly were an *"indicio"* that in former times Indians had lived here. Los Martyres owes its name to the fact that once a couple of missionaries were burned alive here by Indians.[52] A noteworthy characteristic of this skull was again the pronounced dolichocephalic and Melanesian features, setting it apart. In contrast to the skulls found in Espiritu Santo, this one was not colored red.

Later that afternoon I went to the seashore, where a number of large granite blocks lie spread across the sand, and augmented my shell collection with a number of fine specimens of *Dolium*, inside which a small hermit crab often lives; *Cypraea;* etc. I made the return trip to the rancho through the dense thicket blanketing the hills along the coast, and the abundant doves provided food needed for our supper. Here, too, the white garza *(Garzetta candidissima),* the red cardinal *(Cardinalis virginianus igneus),* and the mockingbird or *zenzóntle (Mimus polyglottus)* frequently appeared.[53]

It was cool that evening, and after the meal we gathered around a crackling wood fire that was burning under a shed by the corral.[54] One of those who came looking for shelter in front of the fire before nightfall was a strange personage thirty to thirty-five years old. His outward appearance was totally wild. Long blond hair hung over his shoulders in a disheveled mass, while his timid face was covered by a rough, bushy beard. He was wrapped in rags and had sandals on his feet. When I asked for information about him, I was told that he was an American of German ancestry who for some years now had been wandering on foot as a vagabond through the peninsula. He lived entirely from the hospitality of the country folk, who regarded him as a kind of harmless lunatic. No one knows anything about his antecedents and how he got here. He sat staring pensively into the fire and gave only disjointed answers to our questions. As we smoked our cigarettes and related hunting adventures, of which our host was an inexhaustible source, the hours slipped by.

After we had spent the night by the fire wrapped in our serapes, I left the next morning on horseback for the mountain range, accompanied by one of the peones from the rancho. Our host had told me that there were painted rocks along the eastern slope of the sierra, and my steps were now directed that way.

In the interim Don Juan and Valentín left with the baggage for Las Cuevas, a rancho on the way to Santiago, where I would later find them. After a ride of a few hours in the hot sun, the guide led me into the dense brush to the left of the narrow footpath along the mountainside we had followed thus far, and before long I stood facing a huge granite block standing off by itself. Above an area more than $2^{1}/_{2}$ meters wide and $1^{1}/_{2}$ meters high, this block was covered with a large number of red vertical stripes placed next to each other, which were mostly effaced, however. In addition, there was an olla, so it would seem, faintly discernable, as well as a couple of other figures of indeterminate form. The front of these paintings faced east.

When I had taken a photograph, which was not easy because of the character of the terrain, the peon then led me to a second rock, situated higher up the mountainside in the midst of the bushes, on the premises of the rancho El Sauce. This granite rock was painted with approximately twenty red fish and other animal shapes, which were difficult to discern. All told, they occupied an area 2 meters wide and 1 meter long. The front part, too, again faced east. The broad trunk of a wild fig tree *(zalate)* had grown up right in front of the rock since the time when the Indian artist had last been working there and kept some of the figures from view. Because it was impossible to set up the photographic apparatus on the steep slope, overgrown with dense brush, I made only a sketch of the figures.[55] Around 3 P.M., famished, I reached Las Cuevas, where I met Don Juan, and after halting a couple of hours we continued our journey. The route now led through a wide *cañada* [ravine] of yellowish sandstone, with us repeatedly passing through arroyos. Once the cañada is behind us, we reach a sandy plateau and on our right the majestic Sierra Victorio rises before our eyes. An hour and a half later, at dusk, we have reached the little town of Santiago. We seek accommodation with a subprefect, who also runs a grocery store, where the counter provides a bed for the night. Santiago—in full Santiago de las Coras—owes its origin to a mission founded in 1723.[56] The warlike character of the natives put the mission's existence in jeopardy many times and was vented especially in a violent 1734 uprising in which two priests were killed. With its abolition in 1795, the converted Indians from the Cora tribe were transferred to Caduaño and San José. Here in Santiago there is nothing left to recall this era; even the old church has vanished. It has 2,000 inhabitants and is one of the most important towns in this part of Lower California.

Before we continued the journey on the morning of the 11th, I visited a nearby lagoon, where, besides wild ducks and a stilt walker *(Himantopus mexicanus)*,[57] we encountered turtles *(Pseudemys)*.[58] Our first stop is at the fine rancho Agua Caliente, situated at a splendid spot beneath the shade of sturdy oaks. Evidently there was once an Indian settlement here because, when I went digging along the sandy bank of a creek, some old cylindrical stones (manitas and metates) used for preparing corn turned up.[59] I also came into possession of a fine flint arrowhead and had the opportunity to shoot a gray fox with my revolver. After a hearty meal at the hospitable table of the old *señoritas-rancheras,* we continued our ride to La Palma across sandy plateaus and cañadas. Caduaño is the first inhabited place we pass.[60] It has a very enchanting location against the green slope of the mesa among slender palms and heavily laden orange trees. We pass Miraflores with its white houses and its sole sandy street, and shortly after the bloodred sun has set behind the rim of the mountains, we reach the rancho La Palma, which is situated along the edge of a sandstone mesa. At a short distance from there another plateau rises up again until Santa Anita. It is called the Yéneca, which—again according to Don Juan— is an old Indian word signifying "green plain."

The next morning we continue our journey across Santa Anita and Santa Catarina to San José. On the right the jagged peak of San Lázaro rises up, and out in front of us, off in the distance, we sight the ocean. In the middle of the day we stop for a couple of hours at Santa Catarina. No sooner is it known that a foreign *naturalista* has dismounted than I am summoned to the most prominent resident, who is lying in his sickbed, but help I cannot provide, for his days are numbered. Toward 5 P.M. we have reached San José, where Mr. Belding was impatiently awaiting my arrival. I have promptly rented a room in an unoccupied, dilapidated house, which is filled with bales of dry damiana, making the atmosphere unbearable.[61] But there are no other dwellings to choose from, and there is no inn.

San José del Cabo is in a rolling, fertile valley a short distance from the sea. At this altitude the valley, which is watered by a clear stream, almost looks like a plain. Toward the east and west a low row of hills arises, and northward there is lowland broken up by numerous arroyos and cañadas, which we passed through from Los Martyres on. San José is a moribund and dreary dump with dilapidated houses and wretched huts. The site where the mission of this name, established in 1730, once stood is situated a few miles northwest and is known as San José Viejo.[62] In San José one encounters a very motley population to which nearly every corner of the globe has provided its contingent. Besides Mexicans, who make up the bulk of the population, there are mulattos and zambos,[63] inhabitants of the Philippines and Chinese, Americans and Chileans, French and Germans. Many are sailors who deserted from whaling ships. Others are castaways on the ocean of life who have sought refuge in this remote corner of the earth.

We spent most of the three days that passed before undertaking the journey to the Sierra Victorio in minor hunting trips in the area around San José. One moment the ducks from the San José creek, the next moment partridges and doves drop from the murderous lead of our guns. Here the Mexicans call partridges *chicuacuas* because of the sound they make.[64] The ground cuckoo *(Geococcyx californianus),* here called *churéa,* appears in the plain now and then.[65] This bird has an astonishingly rapid gait and only rarely uses its short wings to momentarily lift itself slightly above the ground. According to popular belief, the churéa fights snakes and is immune to their venom as well, which perhaps can be explained by the exceptionally thick layer of fat covering the chest and abdomen of these birds.

On the flat, sandy seashore, where there is a constant heavy surf, a number of pelicans *(P. fuscus)* appear. Often one sees them perched among the mangroves huddled pathetically together. The animal seems to be pining away, and the countless dead pelicans one encounters by the pools leads one to suspect that another reason apart from hunters' lead enters the picture. In fact, on closer investigation we found a large number of worms *(Ascaris spiculigera* Rud.) in these birds' stomachs. Another bird from these regions, which one often sees only around evening, is the *tapacamina,* a small variety of nightjar *(Chordeiles acutipennis texensis).*[66]

Among the distinctive plants in the area around San José, I will mention just *Selaginela lepidophylla,* which sometimes blankets entire hillsides in the arroyos.[67] This plant has hygroscopic qualities to the highest degree, which has gained it the name *siempre viva* [always alive] among the Mexicans. Dried specimens, placed in water years later, start growing again and take on their dark green color.

The San José is the largest river of this area and in its clear waters harbor some species of fish, such as *Mugil albula, M. brasiliensis,* and *Agonostoma nasutum,* called *trucha* [trout] by the Mexicans; in addition, *Gobius banana* and *G. sagittata, Philypnus lateralis, Dormitator somnolentus,* and *Centrophanes robalito,* the *liza* of the Mexicans, which sometimes glides above the water.[68] Two or three kinds of small snakes can apparently be found in the San José, but *Tropidonotus validus tephropleura* was the only one Belding collected.[69] In addition, there is a small turtle *(Pseudemys ornata)* and, among crustaceans, numerous tiny shrimp *(Palaemon).*[70]

For Belding the expedition to the central mountain range, which we undertook on February 15, had ornithological investigations as its primary goal. For my part, I wanted to investigate whether the now vanished Indians in the sparsely visited sierra might have left a few traces behind. At 1 P.M., with warm, splendid weather, we left, guided by Don Juan and with Valentín and the pack mule in the rear. Following our route via Santa Catarina, where I once visited my patient, we reached the rancho El Desecho after a long ride in the moonlight. Here we spent the night. The next morning a heavy north wind was blowing, which lasted all day and cooled the atmosphere considerably. Along the already familiar La Palma, we headed to Rancho Viejo, not far from Miraflores, whose owner was a demented old man of almost ninety years. We sent Valentín to Miraflores to summon our mountain guide, and an hour later Francisco, "El Tintero," appeared on his fiery, half-tamed bay. Belding had already traveled previously with this man in the sierra and knew him to be an experienced *montañero* [mountain man]. The nickname "El Tintero," the inkwell, he owed to his dark complexion. We then agreed to head for Agua Caliente on that same day and travel to the sierra the next morning, while Don Juan and Valentín would head to La Palma to await our return.

In gathering information about the "heathen period," in which I was constantly engaged among the Mexicans, I often heard about the ruins of a "painted house," the "Casa Pintada," which was somewhere high up in the mountains. The stories greatly varied, however, and no one had ever seen the "Casa Pintada" until I eventually found out that the owner of the rancho El Carrizal would provide explanations. So our steps were first directed toward El Carrizal. The road there was steep and arduous and led continuously along the mountain slope, so that, after about four hours of riding, we reached the humble rancho, which is situated in the mountains like an eagle's aerie. Here the slope was partially overgrown with vines, and the white wine the ranchero let us sample had a marvelous flavor. Viniculture has begun in various regions of the peninsula and with optimal results, because the wine one has obtained up to now in Los Dolores as well does not suffer in comparison to that of Upper California.

El Carrizal had obviously once been the abode of Indians because the ranchero pointed out to us on the rocky ground a number of large, bowl-shaped cavities that served as a mortar for mashing corn. It seemed that the ranchero really knew something about the "Casa Pintada," but he told us beforehand that nothing remained of a building. Before long we were on horseback again, and, with him as our guide, we headed there. The terrain was extremely difficult for a rider, and the narrow, rugged mountain path was often so steep that we could not stay in the saddle. At first the vegetation consisted primarily of *Cereus* species, which at higher altitude completely ceased, making way for a marvelous parklike forest of oak trees, whose crowns jostled back and forth vigorously in the heavy north wind. At the spot where a creek trickles down from rock to rock, clusters of *taco* palms rose above the fresh grassy carpet blanketing the ground. Ascending, we had splendid vistas of the mountains, plains, and cañadas—like a gigantic relief map bounded by the sea. Now and then we encountered herds of wild pigs, which here feast on the marvelous sweet acorns blanketing the ground in spots. Eventually we pass through a section of the sierra where the nearly white granite rocks are blanketed in the most colorful fashion with a kind of reddish brown lichen,[71] and shortly afterward we halt at a spot that is called the "Casa Pintada," according to our guide."[72] Despite my searching I find nothing resembling ruins. Only a half-decayed wooden fence marks the spot where there once appeared to have been cultivated land, and loose rocks covered with red moss were strewn all over the ground.

No solid information can be gleaned from the disjointed responses the guide provides to my questions. His story that the Jesuits had formerly exploited mines somewhere in the mountains and refined the metals here strikes me as unlikely. Instead, I assume that an ordinary rancho once stood here, which was called "Casa Pintada" because of the rocks from the surrounding area covered with red moss, which, at a distance, leave somewhat the impression of painted objects. From this pointless excursion I am once more confirmed in my judgment about how little reliance can be placed in the Mexicans' tales. Before we began the descent, we shot as many doves as we needed for our supper, and flushed and exhausted we reached El Carrizal at dark.

We spent the night under the palm leaf shed, shivering from the cold because most of the guests are directed to sleeping quarters outside the house since the rancho itself is frequently too small to accommodate, in addition to the usually numerous family, even one more guest as well. The next morning we returned to Agua Caliente to retrieve the pack mule with provisions, and that afternoon we turned again toward the mountains. We steadily climbed through the dense brush until the narrow, barely negotiable mountain pass exits into a narrow valley, which is enclosed by steep rocky walls. Somber oaks hem the deserted banks of the clear mountain stream, and when evening approaches we begin setting up camp. Numerous swallows *(Tachycineta)* hover above the water in graceful circles,[73] and when night has spread its veil, the tree frogs and crickets raise their voices to a uniform chant, which only comes to an end when dawn tints the rocky walls and, shivering, we once more poke the wood fire to prepare our frugal breakfast.

Then we head onward along a nearly untrodden steep path, which later vanishes, and clamber along a mountain ridge, the slopes of which are covered with short grass and oaks. It is an utter wilderness where the eye discerns nothing but mountain and forest. A couple of deer cross our path. At that very moment a shot detonates from Belding's never erring rifle, and one of them drops, badly hit. We immediately climb down to pursue the second deer. We soon find it in a shallow ravine, and a second later it lies rattling on the ground, felled by a shot from my hand. With astonishing proficiency, Francisco in short order has gutted both deer, and our trusty mule toils under the double burden of our baggage and the quivering flesh from the spoils of the hunt. Clearly the burden is heavy for him. Somewhat farther on, at a steep point, he loses his footing and tumbles down a ravine. The rocks roll down, the branches crack, Francisco utters a thousand curses, and long ears snorts fretfully. Before long he is lying against a tree trunk, unhurt but with half his load gone. Part of the base of my photographic apparatus is smashed, and we recover only half of the precious venison.

A half hour later we are on the move again. Toward the middle of the day we camp on a green mountain plain that is completely surrounded by oaks and palms. We "hobble"[74] the horses and after the meal we head off in different directions into the wilderness. The season is not far enough along yet to allow us to see the animal kingdom in all its plenitude. Insects, especially, are scarce and represented almost exclusively by numerous tiny red ant species and a louse fly *(Lipoptena)*, which I find on the hide of the deer we killed.[75] Along with a couple of spiders and some brachiopods, these insects are the only arthropods we had a chance to see. Nor do we find fish at this altitude, except for the trucha *(Agonostoma nasutum)*. On the other hand, a small water snake *(Tropidonotus)* appears in the calm shaded creeks, and of lizards we find just a few specimens of *Gerrhonotus multicarinatus*.[76] Here we again encounter the tree frog *(Hyla regilla),* which we have already noted.[77] Some of the birds inhabiting these forests belong to those that are unique exclusively to the peninsula south of La Paz. I will note, first of all, the "cape robin" *(Merula confinis),* primarily inhabiting the pine tree zone, which we were not able to see this time.[78] Since 1860, when Xánthus was reported to have shot this bird in Todos Santos, no one has seen a specimen of *Merula.* Some weeks before our journey, however, Belding succeeded in shooting two specimens of this rare bird in the northern part of these mountains (Laguna) and thus establishing beyond doubt that this *Merula* species definitely does not warrant the name of "cape thrush." The source of this error is probably that Xánthus was stationed at Cape San Lucas and sent everything he collected there to museums.[79]

The largest mammal in these mountains is the deer *(Cariacus macrotus),*[80] which roams in small herds and is seldom disturbed by hunters because only on rare occasions do the Mexicans enter the rugged, uninhabited sierra. Maybe in days past the mountain sheep *(Ovis montana)* occurred as well because hunters told us that they had found horns here, which, judging from the description, could hardly have belonged to anything but this animal.[81] The American lion *(Felis concolor),*[82] here called *onza* and not to be confused with *F. onza,* the American tiger,[83] occurs only rarely—to judge from what Francisco says. On the other hand, the lynx *(Felis rufa)* and fox *(Urocyon cinereo-argentatus)* are far more common.[84] During the night, by the campfire, we can hear the call of an owl (Mex. *lachusa* [i.e., *lechuza*]) and though we try to get within range in the moonlight, it does not show itself.

At 9:30 the next morning we break camp to head higher up into the sierra. At times we are forced to dismount because the slope is too steep or the brush too thick, and even then we cannot move ahead except with difficulty. The same sunny weather and the same lofty blue sky vaults above the green oak bushes and lush mountain meadows, through which we slowly move ahead in single file. After an exhausting hike of four hours, we make a halt at the edge of an oak forest where there is a little meadow hemmed in between heavily overgrown mountain slopes, at an altitude of approximately 3,910 feet. For four days we camp here and make excursions into the nearby area, hunting for deer and fowl from early in the morning until nightfall.[85] The flora never varies, but now and then *madroño (Arbutus menziesi)* appears.[86] Now and then a yucca shows itself. There are numerous forms of mimosa, but we see few blossoms. Only a small red species of lupine peers between the long grass in spots, while the *Geranium* appearing here is not yet in bloom. Various species of ferns adorn the moist banks of the streams, which are seldom illumined by a ray of sunlight because the branches of the mighty oaks intertwine, forming a dense arch of live vegetation, where there is shade and quiet and you gladly lie down to escape the scorching midday heat.[87] In many places near our camp the granite rocks are covered with the same lovely lichens as was the case near the "Casa Pintada."

The loathsome auras constantly hover around our camp to feed on the venison, sliced by Francisco into long, thick strands and suspended on a *lazo* [a rope] to dry in the sun. Along with

Mexican cheese and crackers, a kind of biscuit, venison roasted on a long stick is also the unvarying fare during our stay in the sierra. At night there are lynxes and foxes, which make shrieking meows and howl, but the flickering of the wood fire and the sound of our voices overawe them.

At nightfall I climb one of the hills blanketed with vegetation, overlooking our campsite, and sit down, gazing at the silent mountains and valleys illuminated by the moon's soft silver light. The evening wind caresses the crowns of the palms and the grass at your feet. There is rustling in the oak leaves while the profound silence of the wilderness, with its thousands of nameless voices and sounds, puts the stamp of the most grandiose solitude on everything. Then images of times past loom up before your spirit. You think of your homeland, of those dear to you who are far away, and of the life full of privation and struggle that lies ahead. Although a feeling of melancholy and doubt in your own power overwhelms you as well, 'tis only for a moment. . . .

> *Ein süsser Zauber war auf mich gekommen,*
> *Ich wusste nicht, wie meiner Brust geschehen,*
> *Was ich geheim im Mondenlicht vernommen,*
> *Das wird mir ewig durch die Seele gehen.*[88]

So you sit for hours in reflection until the cool evening air from the mountains reminds you to seek out the campfire flickering over yonder among the trees.

I discovered not the slightest indications that Indians had once lived in these mountains. Possibly this wilderness was but rarely trodden by them. Just like the present-day Apaches, they harbored a mysterious dread of heavily wooded mountains and the thunderstorms frequently hovering above them. But perhaps this is where we must seek out the mountains of Acaragui, which the mythology of the Pericués tells us about, where Quaayayp, the son of the world creator Niparaya, was born of the maiden Anayicoyondi.[89]

Photography did not work out as I might have wished. Although I tried to repair the broken pedestal, the camera still lacked the stability needed when focusing, and all the negatives I prepared on this excursion were apparently ruined.

On the morning of February 23 we started back, which involved even more difficulties than getting there, and after an arduous daylong march we reached Agua Caliente around evening, to depart again the next morning and head for Miraflores. Starting out from there, I visited two painted rocks in the Boca San Pedro, while Belding put the finishing touches on the preparation and organization of his ornithological catch. The pictographs in question are two *leguas*[90] from Miraflores along the rugged mountainous path leading to Todos Santos along the west coast. Roughly half the surface of both rocky colossi was covered with a large number of red figures, the majority of which had been effaced over time, however. Yet three red hands and a large number of large red stripes of various sizes were still recognizable.[91]

Having returned to Miraflores, I lend a helping hand to Belding, who is still constantly busy, and while we sit down under the roof of our humble dwelling, a throng of curious Mexicans presses toward us. But this is not the first time we are stared at like beings from another planet. While one is writing, reading, eating, smoking, or whatever, there are always a couple who stand impassively, watching one's slightest movements with the greatest attentiveness.

After we had vainly tried that evening to bring a dwarf owl *(Micrathene whitneyi)* into range under moonlight, we spend the night in the company of cockroaches and scorpions.[92] The next morning I am taken to various sick people, and shortly afterward we gallop off toward La Palma, accompanied by "El Tintero," who sees us off. We find Don Juan in La Palma, and by evening we have returned to [San] José.

A day and half later I am again with Don Juan on the path to Los Frailes along the seacoast east of San José, where I hope to find human bones in the surrounding sandstone caves. From Santa Catarina on, it is a monotonous ride across the rugged sandstone ground, which is only sparsely covered with brush and yuccas. We look around in the dark a long time before we find shelter for the night. In the morning we glimpse the same scenery from the day before. Now and then one can hear the waves breaking on the southern shore, like the rolling of thunder in the distance. When we have the abandoned rancho El Tule behind us, the route leads for a while along the beach, which is covered with dunes of low height.

Near the rancho El Salado we leave the coast and climb the foothills of the sierra, where Don Juan loses his way and we wander around in the brush a few hours until the isolated mountainous masses of Los Frailes and Cape Pulmo rise up in front of us along the coast. It is already nightfall when we reach a hut made of branches, where a group of pearl fishermen are preparing their meal. One of them leads us to a rancho lying at the foot of Los Frailes, which is abandoned by the inhabitants for fear of the storm forecast by Weggins.[93] Only a single muchacho has stayed behind, and only reluctantly does he bring us some dried meat and allow us to spend the night underneath the shed.

The next morning the sky is overcast and there is abundant rain, an unusual phenomenon at this time of year. The actual rainy season in Lower California starts only in June and ends in October. Don Juan and the muchacho look dejectedly at each other and ask me what I think of Weggins's storm forecast. I promptly reassure them, and when the rain ceases after a few hours, we mount our horses. We search through a number of caves and crevices in a narrow valley with steep sandstone walls, but there is no trace of human bones there, no more than in the rocks of Los Frailes, consisting of crumbling gray granite. This entire stretch of coast is an image of barren, dreary isolation, enhanced even more by the monotonous splashing of the waves on the sandy shore.

Disappointed, I head back after a miserable lunch. The sky is as cloudy as ever, and the atmosphere is oppressively warm. We spend the night in a small, wretched hut, whose poor inhabitants can barely provide us a tortilla. Under a steady stream of rain, we continue on our way on March 2. The horses hung their heads dejectedly and were just as hungry as we were an hour later when we reached the rancho El Chino and enjoyed a hearty breakfast, which was put in front of us by the graceful daughter of the house, a señorita of not yet eighteen summers. I am deluged by questions about Paris and the fashions, the balls, and theaters, and as I tell her about all these fine things, she heaves a sigh as her thoughts wander toward all these unattainable ideals. Stranger! Do not look too deeply into those dark moist eyes if you want to keep your peace of mind because oh, how lovely Mexican women are!

The sky has cleared up—back onto horses again, then off we go! In the course of the afternoon we wander off track because the mountains, which were our landmarks thus far, remove themselves from our view because of the heavy clouds. A steady rain falls in torrents, and in the middle of an impenetrable forest of cardones and pitahuayas darkness overtakes us. We disentangle ourselves from this labyrinth with great care and eventually come upon the dry bed of an arroyo. Don Juan explains that he no longer knows the way, and there is nothing else to do but spend the night in this spot. We unsaddle the horses and lie down along the edge of the streambed. My straw sombrero and my serape are drenched, and shivering from the cold, I try to start a fire, but the wood is too damp to burn, and so the night passes by without food or drink, without fire or light, until finally, after hours, which seem like ages, the morning dawns. Slowly the sky clears up and we jubilantly greet the sun. A couple of hours pass by before we have dried our damp clothing and have rounded up the horses that strayed. As we stand ready to ascend, a couple of Mexicans who are out deer hunting appear on horseback. They put us on the right track, and eventually we reach San José and partake of tortillas, frijoles, and coffee, which are a taste delight after a twenty-four-hour fast.

Three more days pass before we can resume our journey because heavy rains tie us down in San José. I spend this time acquiring information for the journey ahead, for which Mr. Jules Simoneau, consular agent of the United States, is of the greatest help to me. During my absence he had, at my request, collected as well a number of plants, which in these regions are used as medicines for various illnesses and which perhaps it would be useful to analyze.[94]

My medical practice is expanding as well because there is no doctor here. Many people still recall how the traveler Xánthus provided help in many cases. Because I, too, am a naturalista and thus, according to them, an *hombre quien mucho sabe* ("a man who knows a lot"), now and then I am called on for consultation, often unwillingly. Things get so out of hand that a couple of times sick horses are brought to me!

I have often been surprised how the quack remedies so widespread in Europe and the United States have found their way even to this remote corner of the world. Holloway and Brandt, Mother Seigel and Airy, and whatever other names the inventors of "infallible remedies" may have were often encountered in various homes, and many times I was asked for an opinion about them. Obviously my response was unfavorable, and, to my satisfaction, not infrequently did I watch this or that panacea being hurled to the ground with a vehement gesture.

On March 6, around 11 A.M., we bade farewell to San José and headed straight through the sierra to Todos Santos, on the west coast. Under gently falling rain we moved ahead, first through the valley, then through the mountains. Don Juan, always silent, was up in front. Then came Belding on his tall white horse, with the rifle over his shoulder and whistling a Strauss waltz. I followed on a small mustang. And finally Valentín, dirty and shabby as ever, closed the train with a pack mule.

We head through a mountain pass where Alamitos and Ascención, two small ranchos, lie hidden, and at nightfall we halt by La Parrita. Because it is raining, we are forced to spend the night in the wretched hut and share the little room with some men, women, children, and a number of emaciated dogs, the everlasting nuisance of every rancho. But these animals have their value, too, because their constant ravenous hunger drives them to consume all refuse. Moreover, they are the archenemies of the *zorrillo* (skunk, *Mephitis putorius*), which always roams around the huts at night, hoping for spoils.[95] The Mexicans harbor a great dread of the skunk because, as I have noted above,[96] it is thought their bite results in hydrophobia.

One of the Mexicans knows about a couple of painted rocks near La Parrita, but only reluctantly does he agree to take us to the spot. Just as on previous occasions, my question about *piedras pintadas* (painted rocks) is answered with *¿quien sabe?* (who knows?), and a suspicious glance is cast my way. The reason for this is obvious because in Lower California there is a rather widespread popular belief that buried treasure is hidden in some places, left behind by the Jesuits when they departed the country, and the strange red signs, encountered here and there on the rocks, are supposed to indicate where the hidden treasures can be found. Many times I also encountered numerous pits in the area around these rocks, proof that people had been looking for the treasures. I always achieved my purpose by stating that if I discovered a treasure, I would give it to whomever brought me to the place with the *pinturas*. We used the same approach this time, too, and after a difficult journey, with one of the Mexicans having to cut a path through the bushes with a machete (long knife shaped like a sword), we reached on foot a couple of huge alabaster blocks, not far apart from each other, on a mountain slope in the Rincón de San Antonio. On the smallest stone I found just a few red-colored signs, which could not be explained. On the flat wall, on a surface 3 x 7 meters, the second stone had a large number of pictographic characters, which were partially effaced, however, and whose significance was obscure.[97] For both stones the painted surface was pointed roughly toward the northwest.

In digging underneath and along the side of the large block, we found a couple of red-colored human bones, ribs, and finger phalanges. On the way back we were overtaken by a heavy downpour that thoroughly drenched us, and after [stopping for] a meal we headed on. In the evening we reach the rancho San Felipe, in a wide valley of sandstone and limestone, between which dark lime comes into view now and then, and the next day we continue our ride through a landscape of unrelenting monotony. Always the same pillar cactuses, chollas, and chapparal flora, which extend without letup across the mountainous terrain. The only landmark we can see is the white peak of lofty Calaveras Mountain.

At 4 P.M. we reach the rancho El Zorrillo, from where we can see Cape St. Lucas. Not far from the hut is the Cañada de las Calaveras or de los Defuntos [Gully of the Skulls or the Departed], at the end of which some shallow caves can be found a couple of meters above ground level in the severely weathered rocks. As the name would lead one to surmise, the following morning, while digging, we quickly turned up some loose red-colored human bones, and with further work there emerged something like a flexed skeleton of a child roughly twelve to fifteen years old. The face was turned toward the ground, and between the bark and the fibers of the king's palm covering the bones were laid a pair of fashioned oyster shells. These bones were not colored. In the immediate vicinity Mr. Belding found an incomplete male skeleton including a skull,[98] which again displayed the same Melanesian character as the ones I earlier uncovered and once again was colored red.[99] It was a robust skull with an index of 61.45 and a distinct *torus occipitalis*. Our Mexicans, including the ranchero of Zorrillo, had observed our actions not without some aversion, primarily because, according to them, it was possible that these bones had belonged to *"cristianos."* But when they did not see the cross on the skulls that, according to popular belief, is found on the forehead of every Christian, they were reassured and convinced that here we were handling the *"calaveras de gentiles"* (heathen skulls).

Satisfied with this find, we continued our journey to Candelario. After the long ride through the endless cardones and pitahuayas, Candelario with its slender royal pines, willows, and sugarcane fields rises up before one's eye like an oasis. Various ranchos are situated here in the valley, where the inhabitants are engaged primarily in the preparation of *panoche.*[100] We spend part of the next day to track down a cave high in the sierra, where, amidst a rats' nest, we nevertheless found a number of elongated bones, shoulder blades, and a sacrum of Indians. In the course of the afternoon, we continued along our route, which now led across steep, rugged mountainous paths and again through arroyos and cañadas. Once in a while we startled a deer from its afternoon nap, and chicuacuas crossed our path. For a long time we had in view the Pacific Ocean, whose blue mirrorlike surface merged with the misty horizon far in the west. Toward evening we passed the Arroyo del Medio, where we watered our horses, and set up our night camp somewhat farther afield. Nothing disturbed our sleep except for the distinctive howling of the coyotes at the break of day.

Except for *pinole*[101] we have no provisions with us; so we take our guns to shoot a couple of partridges, and an hour later we have a hearty breakfast. By the middle of the day we reach the rancho San Jacinto, situated in a wide fertile valley. A swiftly flowing bubbly mountain stream, surrounded by willows and palms, wends its way across the rocky bed. To the east rises the mighty crest of the Sierra Victorio, whose highest peaks are covered with a cloudy veil. Everything is resplendent in the tropical sunshine. Nature exudes peace and tranquility.

After Agua Caliente, San Jacinto is the largest rancho I visited on the peninsula. It is a large building erected from whitewashed stones with a high veranda, which is supported by stone columns. In front of the building the huerta with flowers and plants reaches to the creek, while on the east side are some outbuildings, dwellings for the peones and the corrals.

My visit to San Jacinto had a specific goal. The proprietress of San Jacinto, who spends her days here with two grown children, was also one of the very few people in this part of the country who were regarded to be pure-blooded Indians. She was large and robust in appearance and, in spite of her age, showed traces of gracefulness. The profile was finely etched. The fine nose was gently curved, the lips thin. Her forehead receded somewhat. The eyes were small. The cheekbones protruded; the ears were large. Her skin color was dark yellow. In no way do her two children from a union with a Spanish father look different from other Mexicans. I had to content myself with this superficial observation and dared not investigate the tribe of which she was one of the last descendants because it certainly would have given offense had I called her an Indian.[102]

Every Mexican, no matter how hybrid, regards himself as being of pure Spanish descent and, even if he knows the opposite to be the case, feels insulted if one states that he is an Indian or a mestizo. Apart from a few exceptions, only the Yaquis and Mayos in the south of the peninsula are still regarded as Indians. Based on what I have seen of the rural population, though, I am persuaded that except for the aforementioned tribes for whom this is not their home, a number of Indians and half-blood Indians, who are descendants of the old Pericués, still appear here in the southern part of Lower California. But all these Indians have forgotten the language, religion, traditions, and customs of their people and are partially or fully Hispanicized. There are Indians and mestizos who are not aware, and sometimes do not want to know, that they are Indians and mestizos. The Pericué *people* have ceased to exist, but the *blood* of the Pericués still flows through the veins of the present-day inhabitants.

But it would be impossible to pursue the genealogies of all the people and to indicate even to a partial extent the presumptive type of the original inhabitants because a large part of the California population comes from the most diverse areas of Mexico and even from South America. In addition, there are a number of Malay descendants from the Philippines distributed throughout the population and totally merged with it, something contributing to no small extent toward making the issue of the original California type even more complicated. Thus the only definite anthropological data for this part of the peninsula are the cave bones that one encounters here in the mountains.

Restraining our thirst for knowledge about the genealogy of San Jacinto's owners was perhaps the reason for the superbly hospitable reception we enjoyed, and after a hearty farewell we continued our journey to Todos Santos on March 12. The landscape we pass through in an alternately westerly and northwesterly direction has a somewhat different character now. The area is flatter, more open, and the brush is more low lying, while a species of yucca appears in profusion. On the right we have an uninterrupted view of the central mountain range—which in its various sections bears the name of Sierra Laguna, Victorio, San Francisco, and San Rafael—and on the left of the Pacific Ocean. Palmar, a rancho, and Pescadero, a small hamlet not far from the sea, are the only places we pass before reaching San Pedro on the coast. We meet a young Mexican, for whose father in Todos Santos I have a letter of recommendation, and we finish the final leguas of our journey together. On many bushes here we encounter the greenish gray *orchilla*, a lichen from which a lovely red dye is prepared. The export of this plant to the United States is a primary source of livelihood for those living along the coast.

At nightfall we reach Todos Santos and are promptly and hospitably received into the dwelling of one of the most prominent residents. An evening of music is instituted in our honor, with the lovely daughter of the house offering the finest example of her virtuosity at piano playing. Belding plays Strauss waltzes on the violin to the immense delight of those present, while Don Juan, roused by Belding's example, entertains us with his vigorous baritone in a romance that he accompanies on the guitar.

The next morning we get a close look at Todos Santos. It is an enchanting spectacle because it is in a wide valley that heads out toward the sea. The houses resemble those of San José, and the church of the ancient mission still lies largely in ruins. This mission, identical with that of Santa Rosa, was founded among the Guaycuru Indians in 1733 by Father Tamaral.[103] All products of the subtropical zone appear abundantly in this part of the country. Sugarcane and bananas, pomegranates and tamarinds, orange trees and palms cover much of the valley.

The coast near Todos Santos is sandy and to the north, as far as the eye can see, the flat seacoast stretches outward bounded by a low-lying row of dunes. The awesome mass of water from the Great Ocean breaks on these beaches with tremendous force, and from afar one can already hear the surf, like the rumbling of thunder. The rolling waves pummel the rocks of mica schist, which slice the silent beach to the south and impotently surge back again, foaming and splashing, to resume at once their ceaseless struggle.

Here and there small lagoons with brackish water, ringed by mangroves and *yerba de flecha,* extend along the coast. The *palo* or yerba de la flecha (arrow weed) has poisonous properties, which the Californians exploit for catching fish. The twigs are split open and tossed into the water, and promptly thereafter the fish appear in a stunned condition on the surface of the water, where they are easily collected.[104] Clavijero has already reported about this plant but says that though the California Indians were aware of its poisonous properties, they did not use it on their arrows. On the other hand, according to him, the Indians of Sonora made use of the yerba de flecha to poison their arrows.[105]

With all due haste we head back to the aforementioned rancho San Pedro belonging to our host at Todos Santos to track down remains of the original inhabitants in the area nearby. Accompanied by young Díaz, I quickly found some caves again high in the rocky walls, which contain a number of red-colored human bones. Among other things, I again came into possession of two nearly intact skulls, which had the same features as the ones discovered earlier. Under the heap of loose bones strewn in disorderly fashion on the floor of the caves, I found fibers here and there from palm leaves and some pieces of palm bark, which clearly had served as covering for the bones.[106]

A short distance from the rancho is a spot that is also associated with the now vanished Indians. It is a gigantic rocky block of mica schist standing alone, the surface of which is covered with a countless number of loose stones. This rock is known to the present-day residents by the name of Piedra de los Viejos (Old People's Rock) and is thus the subject of a tradition. When the Indians went fishing, one by one they tossed a stone on this rock. If the stone stayed in place, that was regarded as an auspicious sign for fishing. If the stone rolled back from the slanting surface of the rock, then that was regarded as a sign that whoever had thrown the stone would meet with misfortune on the catch and would do better not to take part.

Having returned to Todos Santos, we set up our main headquarters in the lowly schoolhouse, which was closed because of vacation. We rented a couple of cots to serve as beds, brought our horses back into the corral, and set up our laboratory between the benches. It was at Todos Santos that I got a chance to see the second specimen of a genuine Indian from the peninsula. He was usually known by the name of "Concha" (Shell), although his baptismal name was Juan Villanueva and he passed for a full-blooded Guaycuru. Despite all my efforts to gain some definite information about his descent, all my attempts foundered on Concha's reluctance. He maintained that he did not know what tribe he came from and stubbornly refused to let himself be measured. Only with the greatest effort, and particularly with the help of our guide Don Juan, did I succeed in photographing him and obtaining a small lock of his hair for a peso (approx. 2.50 guilders). Concha was small and somewhat misshapen in stature. He was very broad-chested, while his extremities were slender but muscular. He had, in addition, crooked legs. His forehead was receding with pronounced eyebrow ridges, and he seemed to be dolichocephalic. Tangled, curly locks hung down on both sides of his face, which was dark in color and surly in expression. His nose was large and bent but handsomely shaped. His large mouth was framed by a thin gray mustache and goatee. Finally, his ears were large with very elongated lobes.

On March 15 we said farewell to Todos Santos and headed back to La Paz. A short distance from Todos Santos we passed the ruins of an old church (Templo de San Juan), which consists of nothing more than a couple of thick stone walls.[107] Until we reach the rancho Juan Marqués in the evening, the route leads through a nearly flat sandy region, which is blanketed with the usual monotonous flora. *Spiacevole ed orrido* (unpleasant and horrible), as Clavijero rightly labels the peninsula's general appearance, and it is the same now. But the mesquite trees appear more abundantly in this area than elsewhere, and today their fine foliage provides fodder for our animals because there is no grass, any more than there is water. Before we make a halt at Juan Marqués, we move through a forest of extremely high cardones, such as we have not yet encountered anywhere. The ranchero with whom we spent the night complained about the ever increasing aridity of the country, and before long he may be forced to leave the area. On earlier occasions I had repeatedly heard observations about the continuing scarcity of rain and the drying up of streams and ponds. Where just ten years ago cattle were grazing in lush meadows, one now encounters a parched, dry region. So it seems that Lower California is undergoing the same slow process of desiccation that Loew noted with regard to Arizona, New Mexico, and the bordering region.[108] If this situation does not change, it is clear that one day the California peninsula will become uninhabitable.

Early the next morning Belding departs alone, heading straight for La Paz, because I have plans of viewing some pictographs near Agua Tapada, and for him the area is devoid of further interest. With Don Juan and Valentín, I follow the route through a landscape having the same character as the day before and around midday reach Carrizal, a collection of ranchos and insipid, whitewashed houses in the middle of a completely flat, dry area.

Before continuing the thread of my narrative I cannot refrain from making a few observations regarding reports about the area between Todos Santos and La Paz by Xánthus, the traveler already mentioned several times previously.[109]

To begin with, Xánthus says that Todos Santos and La Paz are "only a few miles" apart. The shortest-possible distance is at least forty miles, and the wretched, bad route, which Xánthus regards as "well built," nowhere has "solid bridges," spanning "ditches and streams." "Carefully tended gardens and parks" extend "far and wide" neither to "the right" nor "the left," and of the "tasteful villas," along with the "plain huts" that one encounters along the way, neither Belding nor I have observed a single one. What one sees "far and wide" is the everlasting monotony of pillar cactuses, interrupted in places by nothing more than a miserable rancho.

Xánthus speaks of a place, called Marqués, that consists of "houses of two and three stories" and that must be roughly a day's journey north of La Paz. Between these two places he found, as he put it, "many ruins," and "in many places there were, in addition to countless potsherds, clearly recognizable signs of canals with which this now infertile land was once irrigated." Before leaving La Paz, I had tried to obtain all available information regarding this Marqués and the nearby ruins, but people who had detailed knowledge of the country—including Messrs. Viosca, the American consul, and Von Borstel—had never heard of any such thing. The only Marqués known to them was Juan Marqués between Carrizal and Todos Santos. It is certain that not the slightest trace of ruins, irrigation canals, or potsherds can be found there.

Furthermore, the Hungarian traveler reports on "Timpa," which is supposed to be on the northwestern rim of the valley of Todos Santos and consists of a "two story-high building" and purportedly serves as "protection for the plantation against the Indians." But these Indians from the "Piñolero tribe" supposedly do not mind the "fortress," and "descend from the mountains" driving "herds of cattle" before them "under the very mouth of Timpa's cannons." Where this Timpa is supposed to be is a mystery to me, and where the Piñolero Indians dwell I have been unable to determine in spite of all investigations in situ and into the literature on hand. So much for Xánthus regarding an area that I visited with a traveling companion. Neither Mr. Belding nor Don Juan, whom I had informed about Xánthus's travel account, has found anything to corroborate his assertions.

I will conclude my observations regarding Xánthus's reports with what he says about the Gulf of California's coastal dwellers. According to him, from La Paz to latitude 28°N one encounters "the descendants of the former tribe of the Marihopo Indians." Neither from Venegas, Baegert, nor Clavijero have I been able to find this tribal name among the California Indians. Moreover, people who have been navigating the Gulf coast for years fishing for pearls could tell me nothing about the "Marihopos." That here it might be a question of the Cocópa Indians, who live along the lower course of the Colorado River, or of the Maricopas along the Gila River is beyond doubt. Moreover, much of Xánthus's information regarding the area of Lower California between San Bartolomé along the west coast and La Paz strikes me as unlikely when compared with other writers',[110] but because I was not familiar with these areas from my own observation, I want to withhold a definite judgment.

After we have stopped for refreshment at Carrizal during the hottest afternoon hours, we resume our ride and around 4:30 reach the rancho Agua Tapada, situated along the western rim of the low granite range separating it from Las Playitas. The ranchero has just felled a lynx with his machete, and Don Juan, who wants to give me a token of his regard at the conclusion of the journey, buys the hide and gives it to me as a present.

The next morning I get a look at "Los Monos" (the Figures, the Portraits). On a lone block of white granite lying alongside the dry bed of an arroyo, like countless others, I find some animal forms depicted in red, including a deer and a couple of rabbits, and after I have taken a sketch of these pictographs[111] we continue our journey to Las Playitas. We pass in succession the ranchos Santa Rita, Las Tijeras, and Novillo, Don Juan's paternal home, where we make a short stop, and I have the opportunity to admire the guitar playing of one of the *señoras*. One of the residents of Novillo is suffering from rheumatism, and a hairless dog, resting against his feet, serves as a remedy. In this country these so-called Chinese dogs are reputed to cure various painful ailments by simply lying next to the afflicted body part.[112] On most ranchos in the neighborhood of Triunfo and La Paz there are a number of male and female Yaqui and Mayo Indian servants, and at the aforementioned places I have the opportunity to expand my anthropological observations. Palmar, with its swaying palms and fields of waving corn, is the last place we visit before we return to Las Playitas around 4 P.M.

From Don Juan's son I notice that spiritualism numbers its adherents even in Lower California. During my previous visit I had provided him medical assistance, but because the remedy did not work rapidly enough in his opinion, he had sought assistance from the spirit of a holy man, who had provided him an infallible remedy. To counter my skepticism, the next morning at my departure he gives me an old, battered book on poltergeists, expressing the wish that this may be of use to me when I am among the *"bárbaros."*

On March 18 I have returned to La Paz. Because Belding is thinking of heading across the sea to Mulegé along the west coast of the gulf, to spend a short time there and then return to San Francisco, I decide to depart the peninsula on the next ship. In view of the difficulty of continuing my investigations north of La Paz under present conditions, I will resume my journey in the United States. Several days must pass, however, before the steamship *Sonora* is expected to arrive, and we pass this time packing the collection and undertaking short sailing and rowing excursions in the bay.

In addition, I visit the Yaqui quarter to supplement my observations among these Indians. Easter festivities are drawing near, and the Yaquis are having a merry time of it. Song and dance are the order of the day, with the *pascóla* particularly popular. The pascóla is danced by a single man to the music of a violin and a flute. The dancer is unclad, apart from the hips, which are covered by a cloth. His face is covered with a wooden mask, which is colored black and is decorated with white figures, including a cross. In his right hand the dancer holds a *sonagay,* a kind of oblong tambourine, which he strikes on the palm of his left hand now and then. The *taynuhboi* is wrapped around his ankles, making a gentle rattling-rustling sound as he moves his feet—not unlike the sound of a rattlesnake. The taynuhboi consists of a string of tightly interwoven, silky, silver-white chrysalises of a *Saturnia*, into which some small stones have been placed. The dancer hardly budges from his spot though he moves the extremities of the body vigorously, and the steps he carries out automatically bring the American minstrels to mind. The melody as well is probably largely of Spanish origin, as is already evident from the violin.[113] The Yaqui Indians' stay on the California peninsula goes way back because Clavijero already mentions that the Yaquis' women were very much sought after among the Pericúes—all the more so because the number of men among the latter tribe by far outnumbered that of women.[114]

Among the Yaquis one encounters two main physical types, one of which with its sharp features, prominent nose, and generally tall stature recalls the type frequently encountered among the Plains Indians. As a rule, the second type is smaller and more heavyset in stature, has broader, coarser features, and often has a straight, somewhat blunt nose. The nine Indians whom I was able to measure in La Paz had a cranial index varying between 75 and 91, from which the existence of two main elements was equally well apparent. Their complexion was brown, in shades coming closest to the numbers 29, 30, 37, and 44 on the chromatic table. Among the Mayos, a tribe very closely related to the Yaquis but with only a few representatives in California, there appear many individuals with lighter skin color and, as I learned from a reliable source, with blue eyes now and then.

From a linguistic standpoint the Yaquis and Mayos belong to the Cahita-Tepehuana family, which is related to that of the Pima-Opata.[115] The language is very melodious because of the many vowels. All Yaquis speak Spanish. Indeed, these Indians have been under the influence of Spanish priests for so long that all of them are now Catholic. Although they have Christian baptismal names, they often have surnames from animals or plants. The Yaquis call themselves *Giaki* (*g* hard), frequently written *Hiaqui* by the Spaniards, according to the practice of pronouncing the *h* as *g*. The Yaquis and Mayos, who number approximately 600 in La Paz, form an entity to themselves and have no relation with their brethren on the mainland. They seem to have completely abandoned their tribal alliance and to recognize no chief either. Their ranchería closely resembles the one in Guaymas but is tidier.

On the evening of March 22 the *Sonora* dropped anchor in La Paz, and the following afternoon we said farewell to our friends. For a long time I continued gazing upon the mountainous coast, which was enveloped in dark blue tints at evening and eventually receded from my view because of the nocturnal veil. The days of weal and woe, full of carefree pleasure but also filled with deprivation—they seemed to me by now like a long, unforgettable dream, and when I finally cast to the distant shore one last farewell greeting while leaving the deck, I could not repress the silent wish to "meet again." Thirty hours after leaving La Paz, we had returned to Guaymas.

Notes

This chapter was originally translated and ably annotated by Peter W. van der Pas, "In Search of the Original Californian: Herman ten Kate's Expedition to Baja California," *Journal of San Diego History* 23 (1977):41–92. The editors gratefully acknowledge their use of some of the annotations from this work; the translation, however, is entirely our own.

1. In English miles, the peninsula is approximately 775 miles long.

2. After the conquest of Mexico, Hernán Cortés actively organized expeditions to Baja California. Ortun Jiménez, a pilot of Cortés, sailed into the Bay of La Paz in 1533 and is thus credited as the discoverer of Baja California. Cortés later sent Francisco de Ulloa to explore the area. In 1539 he sailed around the peninsula. Hernando de Alarcón, a Spanish sea captain, set out from Acapulco in May 1540 as the ocean-borne component of Coronado's expedition. Alarcón lost contact with Coronado but in the course of his travels explored the coasts of Baja California and eventually navigated the Colorado River as far north as present-day Yuma. Juan Rodriguez Cabrillo was captain and Bartolomé Ferrero pilot of a 1542–1543 expedition that explored the Pacific Coast of North America as far north as Oregon's Rogue River. Sebastiano Vizcaino explored the coast and interior of Baja California in 1596, also attempting unsuccessfully to establish a settlement in the La Paz region. In 1602 Vizcaino undertook a more well-known voyage of exploration up the California coast as far north as latitude 41 degrees. David J. Weber, *The Spanish Frontier in North America* (New Haven, Conn.: Yale University Press, 1992), 40–42; Hubert Howe Bancroft, *History of the North Mexican States and Texas*, vol. 1: *1531–1800* in *Works*, 39 vols. (San Francisco: History Company, 1875–90), 90–93; Herbert Eugene Bolton, ed., *Spanish Exploration in the Southwest 1542–1706* (New York: Scribner, 1908), 3–39, 43—134.

3. Miguel Venegas (1680—1764), a Jesuit writer and native of Puebla, was the author of *Noticias de California* (Madrid: Viuda de M. Fernández, 1757); English trans.: *A Natural and Civil History of California*, 2 vols. (London: J. Rivington & J. Fletcher, 1759). *Diccionario Porrúa de Historia, Biografía y Geografíía de Mexico*, 2 vols. (Mexico: Porrua, 1970), 2:2244. The Alsatian-born Johann Jakob Baegert (1717–1772) was a Jesuit missionary in Baja California between 1751 and 1767. After the expulsion of the Jesuits from Mexico, Baegert published *Nachrichten von der amerikanischen Halbinsel Californien* (Mannheim: Churfürstliche Hof- und Academie-Buch-Druckerei, 1772); English trans.: *Observations in Lower California*, M. M. Brandenburg and Carl L. Baumann, eds. (Berkeley: University of California Press, 1952). Francisco Xavier Clavijero (1731–1787), born in Veracruz, entered the Jesuit order and served in Valladolid (now Morelia) and Guadalajara. After the expulsion of the Jesuits, he took refuge in Italy, where he wrote *Storia antica del Messico*, 4 vols. (Cesena: G. Biasini, 1780–81), one of the most important early histories of Mexico, and *Storia della California* (Venice: M. Fenzo, 1789), the work to which Ten Kate is referring. This highly informative work—which was not, however, based on firsthand experience—has been translated as *The History of Lower California*, trans.S. E. Lake, ed. A. A. Gray (Riverside, Calif.: Manessier, 1971).

4. Auguste Bernard du Hautcilly (1790–1849) was captain of the *Héros*, a French vessel that undertook a commercial voyage around the world, including extensive visits to both Upper and Lower California. He later wrote an account of his visit: *Voyage autour du monde principalement à la Californie et aux îles Sandwich pendant les années 1826, 1827, 1828 et 1829*, 2 vols. (Paris: Arthus

Bertrand, 1834–35). Sir Edward Belcher (1799–1877), later an admiral in the British navy, was captain of the *Sulphur,* which surveyed the coasts of South and North America in 1836–1839. Belcher returned to England in 1842 after crossing the Pacific and authored an account of his voyage: *Narrative of a Voyage Round the World Performed in HMS* Sulphur *During the Years 1836–42,* 2 vols. (London: H. Colburn, 1843). *Dictionary of National Biography,* 22 vols. (London: Oxford University Press, 1885–1922), 4:142–43. Abel Aubert Du Petit-Thouars (1793–1864) was a French naval commander best known for establishing a French protectorate over Tahiti (1842). In 1837–1839, as captain of the *Créole,* he undertook a voyage of exploration to the islands of Oceania, during which he presumably cruised the coast of Baja California. *Dictionnaire de Biographie Francaise,* 18 vols. (Paris: Letouzey et Ané, 1933),12:343–44. Eugène Duflot de Mofras (1810–1884), a French diplomat and writer, was posted between 1839 and 1842 in Mexico. During this period he visited the Californias and Oregon, the basis for his *Exploration du territoire de l'Orégon, des Californies et la Mer Vermeille,* 2 vols. (Paris: Arthus Bertrand, 1844); English translation: *Duflot de Mofras' Travels on the Pacific Coast* (Santa Ana, Calif.: Fine Arts Press, 1937). *Dictionnaire de Biographie Francaise* 11:1410. Sir Henry Kellett (1806–1875), who eventually became a vice admiral in the British navy, from 1845 commanded the *Herold,* a surveying vessel that surveyed the northern coast of South America. *Dictionary of National Biography,* 10:1230.

5. Hugh Cuming (1791–1865), after moving to South America in 1819 and settling in Valparaiso, Chile, built his own yacht and cruised along the Pacific coast of the Americas in 1826. *Dictionary of National Biography,* 5: 295–96.

6. Frederick Reigen, a Belgian who resided in Mazatlán from 1848 to 1850, collected fourteen tons of shells. Thomas Ritchie, an English carpenter who had lived in Cape San Lucas since 1829, assisted later researchers in their scientific investigations. John Xántus (1825–1894), after participating in the unsuccessful Hungarian revolt against Austrian rule (1848–1849), fled to the United States in 1851. After joining the army in 1855 he became involved in natural history surveys in the West and was eventually sent to California to pursue this work. Following his discharge he was sent by the U.S. Coastal Survey to undertake tidal surveys in Baja California, where he continued his natural history collecting for the Smithsonian Institution. In 1864 Xántus returned to his homeland. Henry Miller Madden, *Xántus: Hungarian Naturalist in the Pioneer West* (Linz: Oberösterreichischer Verlag, 1949), 97–152. See also the editor's introduction to John Xántus, *Travels in Southern California,* trans. and ed. Theodore Schoenman and Ruth Benedek Schoenman. (Detroit: Wayne State University Press, 1976), 11–19.

7. Edmond Guillemin-Tarayre (1832–1920), a French geologist, wrote two works on northern Mexico: *Explorations mineralogiques des régions mexicaines* (Paris: Imprimerie Nationale, 1869) and *Description des anciennes possessions mexicaines du nord* (Paris: Imprimerie Nationale, 1871).

8. The company was organized in 1864 and received the grant to colonize the territory from the government of Benito Juárez shortly afterward. John Ross Browne (1821–1875), who headed the survey, was a traveler and writer who settled in California in the 1840s and later participated in government surveys of the region. William More Gabb (1839–1878), an American paleontologist, had carried out extensive geological surveys in California during the early 1860s. F. von Lühr was from the Freiberg (Germany) School of Mines. See Arthur Walbridge North, *The Mother of California, Being an Historical Sketch of the Little Known Land of Baja California, from the Days of Cortez to the Present, etc.* (San Francisco and New York: Paul Elder, 1908), 81–82. *Dictionary of American Biography,* 23 vols. (New York: Scribner, 1943–73), 2(1):167–68; 4(1):81–82.

9. HtK 1885: Albert S. Gatschet, "Der Yuma-Sprachstamm," in *Zeitschrift für Ethnologie*, 1877, pp. 385, 387. Eds.: All the languages spoken within the Central Desert are placed in a single subgroup of the Yuman linguistic family, which the Jesuits identified as Cochimi. Modern linguists prefer Peninsular Yuman to identify this group of closely related languages. William C. Massey, "Tribes and Languages of Baja California," *Southwestern Journal of Anthropology* 5 (1949): 272–307.

10. George Dewey (1837–1917), celebrated for his destruction during the Spanish-American War of the Spanish squadron at Manila and capture of the city, recounted his voyage to Baja California, many years earlier in his career, in his memoirs, *Autobiography of George Dewey, Admiral of the Navy* (New York: Scribner, 1916), 145–49. He also published an account of his survey: *Remarks on the Coasts of Lower California and Mexico* (Washington, D.C.: U.S. Government Printing Office, 1874).

11. Thomas Hale Streets (1847–1925) wrote *Contributions to the Natural History of the Hawaiian and Fanning Islands and Lower California* (Washington, D.C.: U.S. Government Printing Office, 1877).

12. Lyman Belding (1829–1917) was a pioneering California ornithologist and the author of *Land Birds of the Pacific District* (San Francisco: California Academy of Sciences, 1890). Several birds bear his name, most notably Belding's jay. See his obituary in *Auk* 35 (1918):106; also Van der Pas, "In Search," 48–50.

13. In a subsequent article the author called attention to accounts of Belding's third journey appearing in *Annual Report of the Smithsonian Institution* (1883):21 and the *West American Scientist*, San Diego, Calif., 1, no. 4 (1885) (HtK 1889, 234).

14. The Cocopas are speakers of a language of the Yuman family who live on the lower Colorado River and its delta in the southwestern United States and northwestern Mexico. As a result largely of recurring epidemics during the period of Jesuit missions (1697–1767), the Peninsular Yumans of the Central Desert area were extinct well before Ten Kate's journey to the southern cape region of Baja California. There is no evidence that the Cocopas ranged south into the Calamahué Mountains during historic times. Anita Alvarez de Williams, "Cocopa," in *Handbook of North American Indians: Southwest,* ed. A. Ortiz (Washington, D.C.: Smithsonian Institution, 1983), 10:99–101; William C. Massey, "The Cultural Distinction of Aboriginal Baja California," *Homenaje a Pablo Martínez del Río* (Mexico: Instituto Nacional de Antropología e Historia, 1961), 411–22.

15. That is, *huamúche* = *guamúchil* = *Pithecollobium dulce* (Roxb.) Benth., a tree that grows on both coasts of Mexico and reaches a height of twenty-five meters. It has greenish white or yellowish flowers. Its wood is used for building, its roots as a cure for dysentery, and its leaves as an abortifacient. Maximino Martínez, *Las Plantas Medicinales de México* (Mexico City: Ediciones Botas, 1939), 141–42.

16. Ten Kate had received a letter of recommendation for Belding from Director Spencer F. Baird of the Smithsonian Institution. The letter had informed Belding about Ten Kate's itinerary so that they could meet and possibly carry out fieldwork together. Pieter Hovens, *Herman ten Kate en de Antropologie der Noord Amerikaanse Indianen* (Meppel: Krips, 1989), 54.

17. Juan de Ugarte (1660–1730), born in Tegucigalpa, was a Jesuit missionary who spent the last thirty years of his life working in Baja California missions. Jaime Bravo (1683–1774), who was born in Spain, began missionary work in Baja California in 1704. The foundation of the mission at La Paz was one of his main achievements. *Diccionario Porrúa de Historia, Biografía y Geografía de México,* 2 vols. (Mexico: Porrúa, 1970), 1:289; 2:2190–91.

18. HtK 1885: The entire population of the peninsula amounts to about 23,000 inhabitants = 0.1 per square kilometer. More than half the population lives in the southern district, also the most fertile one in Lower California.

19. William P. Watkins, who had been Walker's law partner in Maryville, California, in 1851–1852.

20. The Mexican adventure of William Walker (1824–1860) was in essence as Ten Kate described. In 1855 Walker invaded Nicaragua, made himself president in 1856, and was driven out the following year. An attempt to return to power in 1860 resulted in his capture and execution. William O. Scroggs, *Filibusters and Financiers: The Story of William Walker and His Associates* (New York: Russell & Russell, 1969).

21. The Pericués existed as a tribe and as a language distinct from all others on the peninsula. They occupied the Cape region perhaps as far north as La Paz and including the Gulf islands of Cerralvo, Espiritu Santo, and San José. A revolt against missionization, followed by diseases, led to the demise of this people. Massey, "Tribes of Baja California," 279–82.

22. HtK 1885: As is known, the California peninsula, just like Sonora, is part of the central district of Wallace's nearctic region. Eds.: The English naturalist Alfred Russell Wallace (1823–1913) is best known for developing simultaneously with Darwin the theory of evolution by means of natural selection. *Dictionary of Scientific Biography*, 18 vols. (New York: Scribner, 1980–1990), 14:133–40. Ten Kate is referring to Wallace's pioneering work in zoogeography, *Geographical Distribution of Animals*, 2 vols. (New York: Harper, 1876), 2:79. Wallace defined the nearctic region as including Canada, the United States, and the central plateau of Mexico.

23. HtK 1885: *Crotalus adamanteus atrox* is the most frequently appearing variety; then *C. mitchelli* and *C. enyo*. The last two varieties, to the best of my knowledge, do not occur north of La Paz. Eds.: *Crotalus adamanteus atrox* = *C. atrox*, western diamondback rattlesnake. Contrary to Ten Kate's supposition, *Crotalus mitchelli*, the speckled rattlesnake, is also found in the American Southwest. *Crotalus enyo*, which has no common name, is widespread in Baja California, especially in the Cape area, but is found up to El Marmól. Barry L. Armstrong and James B. Murphy, *The Natural History of Mexican Rattlesnakes* (Lawrence: University of Kansas, Museum of Natural History, Special Publication no. 5, 1979), 16, 29.

24. Pitahayas, fruit-bearing cactus, *Hylocereus* sp. *Cardones:* In Baja California there are two species that go by this name: *Pachycereus pringlei* and its smaller cousin, *Pachycereus pecten-aboriginum*. Though the *cardón* resembles the American saguaro, it is not the same cactus. See Maximino Martínez, *Baja California* (Mexico: Ediciones Botas, 1947), 132–33. *Centurus uropygialis* (Baird), Gila woodpecker.

25. *Huitachoches* and *huitacochones:* The *cuicacoche* (in Mexican Spanish *huita, cuita,* etc., are interchangeable) is a songbird, somewhat smaller than a thrush, with a yellow breast and abdominal feathers and the rest gray and black. *Campylorhynchus brunneicapillum* (Lafresnaye), cactus wren. Van der Pas, "In Search," 91. Also in Mexico several species of thrushes from the genus *Toxostoma* go by names such as *cuicacoche, cuitlacoche,* and *huitlacoche.* See Lilian R. Birkenstein and Roy E. Tomlinson, *Native Names of Mexican Birds* (Washington, D.C.: U.S. Department of the Interior, 1981), 67. *Chamaepelia passerina* = *Columbigallina passerina pallescens* (Baird), ground dove; *Aesalon columbarius* = *Falco columbarius* Linnaeus, pigeon hawk; *Porzanna carolina* (Linnaeus), rail.

26. *Rallus beldingi* = *R. longirostris beldingi* Ridgway, clapper rail.

27. HtK 1885: *Proceedings of the National Museum,* vol. 5, p. 345.

28. *Larus occidentalis* Audubon, western gull; *Larus delwarensis* Ord, ring-billed gull; *Larus philadelphia* (Ord), Bonaparte gull.

29. *Tachypetes minor = Fregata minor,* minor frigate bird. The Spanish word *tijeras* means "scissors."

30. *Sula cyanops = S. dactylatra californica* Rothschild, blue-faced booby.

31. *Conger niger = Leptocephalus conger* (Linnaeus), conger eel; *Diodon hystrix* Linnaeus, porcupine fish.

32. HtK 1885: Baegert, *Nachrichten von der amerikanischen Halbinsel Californien,* Mannheim, 1773, describes this method of catching fish by the now vanished Guaycuru Indians of the peninsula.
    Eds.: See Baegert, *Observations in Lower California,* 176.

33. *Tintorera* means a shark, where Ten Kate here seems to be referring to an octopus or squid, both cephalopods.

34. HtK 1885: I found specimens of the following shells, which Dr. R. Horst, curator at the Museum of Natural History at Leiden, was kind enough to identify:
    Gasteropoda.
    Strombus, a few varieties, including *S. granulatus* Sow. [= *S. (Lentigo) granulatus* Swainson, 1820], *S. gracilor* Sow. [Erby, 1825], and *S. galateus* Wood [= *S. galateus* Swainson, 1823].
    Murex, various species, including the lovely *M. nigritus* Phil. [= *Muricantus nigritus* Philippi, 1845], *M. bicolor* Valenc. [= *Hexaplex erythrostomus* Swainson, 1831] with pinkish mouth and *M. princeps* Sow. [= *Muricanthus princeps* Broderip, 1833].
    Cancellaria and *Fusus,* with several species. *Terebra* with *T. variegata* Gray. *Nassa* with *N. luteostoma* Kien [= *Nassarius luteostoma* Broderip and Sowerby, 1829].—*Purpura.*
    Cassis, including *C. coarctatus* Wood [= *Cassis (Levenia) coarctata* Sowerby, 1825] and *C. abbreviatus* Lam [= *Cassis (Semicassis) centiquadrata* Valenciennes, 1832].
    Dolium, with *D. latilabre* Kien.—*Onisca.*
    Columbella, including *C. strombiformis* Lam. [Arck, 1922], *C. haemastoma* Sow. [Erby, 1832] and *C. meleagris* Ducl. [= *Columbella fuscata* Sowerby, 1832].
    Oliva with *O. lineolata* Gray [= *Olivella dama* Wood, 1828], the magnificent *O. porphyrea* L. [*Oliva porphyria* Linnaeus, 1758] and *O. venulata* Lam [= *Oliva (Oliva) spicata* Roding, 1798] in numerous specimens.—*Olivella.—Rapana.*
    Conus in various species, including *C. brunneus* Wood and *C. interruptus* Brod. [= *Conus (Ximeniconus) Ximenes* Gray, 1839]—*Mitra.*
    Cypraea, various species such as *C. solandri* Gray [= *Trivia (Pusula) solandri* Sowerby, 1832], *C. albuginosa* Gray [= *Cypraea (Erosaria) albuginosa* Gray, 1825], *C. pustulata* G. [= *Jenneria pustulata* Lightfoot, 1786], *C. Sowerbyi* K. [= *Cypraea (Zonaria) annettae* Dall, 1909], the latter in numerous specimens.
    Natica, including *N. quadrifuscata* Gray.
    Sigaretus.—Cerithium, with various species, including *C. maculosum* Kien. [= *Cerithium (Thericum) maculosum* Kiener, 1841] and *C. varicosum* Sow. [= *Cerithidea valida* (C. B. Adams, 1852)].
    Nerita, with some species.—*Trochus.—Crucibulum,* with *C. spinosum* [*Crucibulum (crucibulum) spinosum* Sowerby, 1824]. *Credidula.—Dentalium.—Bulla.*
    Lamellibranchiata.
    Placuna.—Pecten.—Spondylus.—Modiola.—Hemicardium.—Cardita (Lazaria).— Venus.—Cytherea, with various species.—*Tellina.—Meleagrina.—Pholas.*

35. The term *coromuel,* referring to a wind coming from the northwest, is a corruption of the name of the English pirate Cromwell, who periodically sailed down from the San Francisco area and devastated the Mexican coasts at the time these winds occurred.

36. HtK 1889, 234. That is only true for *Remipes* because it appears to be well known that *Pontonia* occurs as a parasite.

37. *Lepus californicus,* black-tailed jackrabbit. *L. californicus richardsoni* and *L. californicus bennetti* are varieties that appear in central California and San Diego respectively. On the other hand, *Lepus insularis* Bryant, black jackrabbit, inhabits only the island of Espiritu Santo, and undoubtedly this is what Ten Kate saw. See F. R. Hall and K. R. Kelson, *The Mammals of North America,* 2 vols. (New York: Ronald, 1959), 1:281, 284–85.

38. HtK 1885: Venegas, *Noticia de la California,* Eng. ed. vol. I, pp. 55, 56, and Clavijero, *Storia della California,* vol. 1, p. 109. Regarding the manners and morals of the Pericués and other tribes that once dominated the peninsula, I must refer to these two writers, as well as to Baegert, op. cit., who more specifically describes the Guayacuri Indians, however.

39. The Coras were a tribe composed of several rancherías who spoke Huchiti and occupied the coastal area along the Gulf from La Paz Bay to Las Palmas Bay and the mouth of the Arroyo de Santiago. Massey, "Tribes of Baja California," 275–76.

40. All the burials excavated by Ten Kate in southern Baja California belong to the prehistoric Las Palmas culture, probably its latest phase. Primary burials were common during the Las Palmas I phase, for which a radiocarbon date of 1120 B.C. is available. Secondary burials, accompanying staining of skeletal remains with ochre and wrapping in fronds of the Mexican fan palm *(Washingtonia robusta),* bound with agave cordage, was common in the Las Palmas II phase, which yielded a radiocarbon date of A.D. 1300. Pieter Hovens, "The Origins of Anthropology in Baja California: The Fieldwork and Excavations of Herman ten Kate in 1883," *Pacific Coast Archeological Society Quarterly* 27, no. 4 (1991):18.

41. "The waves murmur their eternal murmuring." Eds.: We have not been able to identify the author of this verse.

42. *Garzetta candidissima = Leucophoyx thula brewsteri* (Thayer and Bangs), snowy egret.

43. HtK 1885: The sharks in the Gulf of California reach an extraordinary size. According to Ross Browne, some should have the dimensions of a medium-size whale.

44. HtK 1885: Indicated as "Red Mound" on Dewey's hydrographic map.

45. Ten Kate (1908) later elaborated on the "casa de Montezuma" game and compared it to similar games among the prehistoric Hohokam Indians and historic Pima tribe of south-central Arizona. The Pima name for the labyrinth pattern is "House of Tcuhu," after a cultural hero sometimes identified with Montezuma. Herman ten Kate, "The House of Tcuhu," *American Anthropologist* 10 (1908):174–75.

46. HtK 1885: The fruits of the pitahuaya were the principal nutriment of the original inhabitants for a couple of months of the year.

47. From the characteristics Ten Kate later provided (note 61), this plant would appear to be *Turnera diffusa* Willd. See Martínez, *Las plantas medicinales,* 116–18.

48. HtK 1885: Besides this species of hummingbird, one also finds a second one in Lower California, namely *Basilinna zantusi* [= *Hylocharis xantusii* (Lawrence), Xantus's hummingbird], found exclusively on the peninsula. Along the west coast where Belding found a specimen of *Calypte annae* on Cerros Island a third type also appears. The Mexicans call the hummingbird *chuparosa,* rose sucker. Eds.: *Calypte costae* (Bourcier), Costa's hummingbird; *Calypte anna* (Lesson), Anna's hummingbird.

49. HtK 1885: Lariates are sturdy ropes of tightly interwoven strips of leather. Some are also made of *pita,* the dried fibers from agaves and yuccas. From the same material one makes rough, sturdy items used for various purposes.

50. Since 1862 the mines were run by the Triunfo Mining and Commercial Company, then the Hormiguera Mining Company, and finally the El Progreso Mining Company. Van der Pas suggests Mr. H. may have been E. F. Harris. Van der Pas "In Search," n. 63 and 64.

51. HtK 1885: Literally "signs of pagan life."

52. In October 1734 Fathers Lorenzo Carranco and Tamaral were murdered by Indian insurgents in Santiago and San José. Both their bodies were then burned after great indignities were visited upon them. H. H. Bancroft, *North Mexican States,* 458.

53. *Cardinalis virginianus igneus = Richmondena cardinalis ignea* (Baird), cardinal; *Mimos polyglottos* (Linnaeus), northern mockingbird.

54. HtK 1885: Open horse or cattle stall that consists solely of a wooden enclosure.

55. HtK 1885: See *Revue d'Ethnographie* of Hamy, vol. II, pp. 323–24.

56. Santiago de las Coras, a mission established by the Jesuit Ignacio Maria Nápoli, failed and was moved from Santa Ana and reestablished at Aiñiní in the territory of the Pericúes and Misión de Santiago became Pericú.

57. HtK 1885: Xánthus mentions this bird as appearing in the "Sierra de Santiago"; although this probably is a synonym for the Victorio Mountains, this bird does not appear in the mountains in Belding's opinion. Eds.: *Himantopus mexicanus* (Müller), black-necked stilt.

58. A genus of basking turtles.

59. Manitas and metates were in widespread use in Mexico, not just among Indians. The manita is the roller, the metate the stone quern.

60. HtK 1885: According to Don Juan, *Caduaño* or *Cadoaño* is an Indian word, signifying "green chasm."

61. HtK 1885: The already often mentioned damiana (*Bigelovia* sp.) is an aphrodisiac. In addition, this plant is exported to the United States, where a liqueur is distilled from it. HtK 1889, 234: Besides the *Bigelovia* species in the American Southwest, there are other plants, too, which are stamped with the general name damiana but nevertheless belong to other genera and families, e.g., the Turneraceae, with *Turnera aphrodisiaca,* well known in the American pharmacopoeia. Eds.: See note 47.

62. Misión de San José del Cabo was founded in 1730 by Padre Nicolás Tamaral but was moved because of poor soils downstream to a place the Pericú called Añuití.

63. Offspring of blacks and Indians.

64. I.e., *chacuacua.* This is probably *Lophortyx californicus* (Shaw), California quail, which inhabits the region and makes a loud "chi-ca-go"-like sound. See Van der Pas, "In Search," 89, n. 91; National Geographic Society, *Field Guide to the Birds of North America,* 2nd ed. (Washington, D.C.: National Geographic Society, 1987), 218.

65. *Geococcyx californianus* (Lesson), roadrunner.

66. *Chordeiles acutipennis texensis* (Lawrence), lesser nighthawk.

67. *S. lepidophylla* (Hook & Grev.) spring, resurrection plant.

68. *Mugil albula* = *M. cephalus*, Linnaeus, common mullet; *Mugil brasiliensis*, Agassiz, liza; *Agonostoma nasutum* = *Agonostomus nasutus*, Günther, trucha; *Gobius banana* = *Awaous taiasica* (Lichtenstein); *Gobius sagittata* = *G. sagittula* (Günther); *Philypnus lateralis* Gill, aroma del mar. *Dormitator somnolentus* is perhaps *D. maculatus* (Block), (Guavina Mapo), *Centrophanes robalito* is probably *Centropomus robalito* (Jordan & Gilbert), Constantino.

69. *Tropidonotus validus tephropleura* = *Natrix valida celaeno* (Cope), Cape water snake. Roger Conant, *A Review of the Water Snakes of the Genus* Natrix *in Mexico* (New York: American Museum of Natural History Bulletin vol. 142, article 1, 1969), 111–24.

70. *Pseudemys ornata* = *Chrysemys ornata*, ornate slider.

71. HtK 1885: According to Dr. J. G. Boerlage, who was kind enough to identify these lichens for me, it is *Amphiloma murorum* Hoffmannii, and indeed a minor variant of this related to *A. pusillum* Mass.

72. HtK 1885: According to barometric observation about 3,350 English feet above sea level.

73. *Tachycineta thalassina* (Swainson), violet-green swallow.

74. HtK 1885: Hobbles are fetters of leather or other material with which the forelegs of beasts of burden in the field are bound during a halt to prevent them from running away. In addition side hobbles are sometimes applied between the fore- and rear legs for animals who are more inclined than others to wander too far away.

75. Louse flies live off the blood of warm-blooded animals. *Lipoptena cervi*, however, is a European species only later introduced into the New World.

76. *Gerrhonotus multicarinatus*, southern alligator lizard.

77. *Hyla regilla*, Pacific tree frog.

78. *Merula confinis* = *Turdus confinis* (Baird), San Lucas robin.

79. HtK 1885: *M. confinis* is probably a nonmigratory bird in the mountains of Laguna. This is also true, but with absolute certainty, for a couple of titmouse species (*Lophophanes inornatus cineraceus* [= *Parus inornatus cineraceus* (Ridgway)], plain titmouse and *Psaltriparus grindae* [= *P. minimus grindae* (Ridgway), common bushtit]), discovered by Belding. My traveling companion had not yet established the identity of a *Sitta* species, probably *S. carolinensis aculeata* [*Sitta carolinensis* (Latham), white-breasted nuthatch].

    Another constant resident of these forests is the lovely snowbird (*Junco bairdi* [= *J. Bairdi* (Ridgway), Baird's junco]), first observed by Belding. The *pito real* of the Mexicans (*Melanerpes formicivorus angustifrons* [= *Melanerpes formicivorus angustifrons* (Baird), acorn woodpecker]), a woodpecker frequently occurring here, surpasses its relation the *carpintero* [woodpecker] in magnificence of color with shiny black, yellow, and red and in addition is the only woodpecker of Lower California that lives on oak trees. Doves, including *Columba fasciata* [= *C. fasciata* (Say), band-tailed pigeon], frequently appear.

    The description of the species discovered by Belding can be found in *Proceedings of the U.S. National Museum*, March 1883, pp. 154 ff. As already noted, these birds, along with the aforementioned *Sitta* and *Melanerpes* and seven others, including *Geothlypis beldingi* [= *G. beldingi* (Ridgway), Belding's yellowthroat] (Ibid., vol. 5, p. 344), make up that part of the avifauna of Lower California that is exclusively characteristic for the southern part of the peninsula.

    On Belding's authority, I avail myself of this opportunity to point out an absurdity perpetrated by Xánthus, who in 1858 alleged (*Petermanns Geographische Mittheilungen*, 1861, p. 140) that on the California peninsula approximately 300 species of birds were counted, while now, twenty-five years later, barely 200 species are known, approximately 100 of which are residents. Most of these species are numerous.

80. HtK 1885: Mule deer or black-tailed deer of the Americans. The Mexicans presuppose two or three species of deer, but according to Belding this distinction rests exclusively on the animal's age, which can be determined from the antlers, and there is only one species of deer, at least in the south of the peninsula. Eds.: *Cariacus macrotus* = *Dama hemionus,* black-tailed deer or mule deer.

81. *Ovis montana* = *O. canadensis,* bighorn sheep.

82. *Felis concolor,* mountain lion.

83. I.e., the jaguar, often called *tigre* in Spanish-speaking countries.

84. *Felis rufa* = *Lynx rufus,* bobcat; *Urocyon cinereo argentatus,* gray fox.

85. HtK 1885: The highest point we reached in these mountains was approximately 4,500 feet. The highest peak of this mountain range is 6,200 feet (Dewey).

86. *Arbutus menziesii* Pursh, coast madrono.

87. HtK 1885: Regarding the floral-geographical character, I derived the following from Belding's notes, kept during his first visit to the sierra (Laguna) as well during our journey together.

    Rubus [bramble] (*rivularis?*) not below 4,500 English feet altitude.

    Heteromeles arbutifolia [toyon, Christmas berry] not below 4,500 English feet altitude.

    Ribes sanguineum not below 4,500 English feet altitude.

    Arbutus menziesi not below 4,000 English feet altitude.

    Mimulus luteus from 3,000 English feet and above.

    Castilleia sp. from 2,500 English feet and above.

    Populus sp. from 2,000 English feet and above.

    Quercus [oak] sp. from 3,000 English feet and above.

    Quercus sp. (*palo encino* of the Mexicans).

    Quercus grisea [*Q. grisea* (Liebmann), gray oak] (*roble* of the Mexicans).

    Pinus sp. not below 3,500 English feet altitude.

    Nolina sp. not below 3,000 English feet altitude.

    In addition, the following ferns:

    Polypodium vulgare.

    Nothochlaena ferruginea.

    Pellaea ternifolia.

    Pellaea angustifolia.

    Adiantum capillus veneris.

    Asplenium trichomanes [maidenhair spleenwort].

    Asplenium aurantium.

    Nephrodium patens.

    Nephrodium mexicanum.

    Nephrodium karwinskianum.

88. A sweet magic came upon me / I knew not what passed in my breast / what I secretly espied in the moonlight / that will pass forever through my soul.

89. HtK 1885: Venegas, op. cit., vol. II, p. 89. English ed.

90. HtK 1885: 1 legua or Spanish mile = 6,349 meters.

91. HtK 1885: See the illustration in *Revue d'Ethnographie of Hamy,* vol. II, pp. 323–24. Eds.: See note 55.

92. *Micrathene whitneyi* (Cooper), elf owl.

93. HtK 1889, 234. E. Stone Wiggins (not Weggins) is a well-known, or rather notorious, weather forecaster in Ottawa, Canada, whose forte is making the most alarming weather forecasts in the newspapers, which usually do not come to pass, either in part or at all.

94. HtK 1885: For two of these plants Prof. E. A. van der Burg, director of the Pharmaceutical Laboratory at Leiden, was kind enough to make a couple of extracts. One plant, the *golondrina* of the Mexicans, a species of *Euphorbia* (probably *E. prostrata*), is used against snakebite. One drinks a liquid extract from it and places the leaves and fine twigs containing a white milky sap on the wound.

   According to Prof. v. d. B., the liquid extract primarily contains tannic acid, vegetable acid, gum, and sugar. The alcoholic extract appeared to consist primarily of resins, chlorophyll, and tannic acid but does not contain alkaloids, just like the former.

   The other plant, the *confituría* of the Mexicans, which could not be identified with certainty because of the incomplete condition in which the specimens brought to me existed, is applied in the same way but as medicine against the bite of the *zorrillo (Mephitis putorius),* of which madness (*rabies mephitica* Hovey) can be the result, according to them.

   The liquid extract of this plant principally comprises a bitter material, sugar, vegetable acid, and some tannic acid; the alcoholic extract consisted primarily of bitter material and chlorophyll in addition to a small quantity of resin and tannic acid, but just like the liquid extract, it does not contain alkaloids. Although the modus operandi of the golondrina on the body is unknown, we can assume, based on the investigations of Dr. B. J. D. Irwin, that this plant really possesses medicinal properties, which Mexicans as well as Indians ascribe to it. See *American Journal of Medical Sciences,* January 1861.

   HtK 1889, 234. Dr. H. C. Yarrow took a single sample with the alcoholic tincture of a golondrina species *(Euphorbia maculata)* to investigate whether the plant is really an antidote for snakebite, and with a negative result, in fact. Nevertheless, Yarrow rightly notes that the experiment "can hardly be considered a fair test." See *Forest and Stream, A Weekly Journal of the Rod and Gun.* New York 1888, vol. XXX, no. 19, p. 370.

   Eds.: The name *golondrina* is used for both *Euphorbia prostrata* and *E. maculata.* Confituría is one of many names for *Lantana camara* Linnaeus, which grows throughout Mexico and which in some regions such as Sinaloa is regarded as an antidote for snakebite. Martínez, *Las plantas medicinales,* 306–8, 366.

95. *Mephitis putorius = Spilogale putorius,* eastern spotted skunk.

96. See note 94.

97. HtK 1885: See illus. *Revue d'Ethnographie,* loc. cit.

98. HtK 1885: Now in the Smithsonian Institution in Washington (no. 61398). Eds.: Ten Kate later referred the reader to *Annual Report of the Smithsonian Institution,* 1883, 204 (HtK 1889, 234).

99. Back in Paris at the Ecole d'Anthropologie, Ten Kate studied the Baja California skulls, assisted by Léonce Manouvrier, and found them in some aspects resembling Melanesian craniums, suggesting the possibility of prehistoric Melanesian contacts. Paul Rivet especially was a staunch defender of such interethnic connection. Hovens, "Origins of Anthropology," 17; Herman ten Kate, "Observations au sujet des 'Recherches sur la Basse Californie' par Dr. P. Rivet," *L'Anthropologie* 22 (1911):37–40.

100. HtK 1885: Raw sugar.

101. HtK 1885: Roasted corn, finely ground and mixed with sugar. A small quantity, mixed with water, provides a tasty nutritious dish. Pinole is the foodstuff par excellence of traveling Mexicans.

102. Belding provided an interesting, complementary account of this incident:

> *It was a prime object with my companion Dr. H. Ten Kate, of the society of anthropology of Paris, and myself as well, to find a living representative of the original Lower Californian, which we probably found on the Rancho San Jacinto, owned by the Vallerino family. But we could get no positive or definite information concerning this Indian woman, who must have been about seventy-five years old, although from La Paz to Cape San Lucas she was universally reputed to be a pure blooded Indian. She differed widely from the Yaquis and other Indians from the east s ide of the Gulf, being of good stature, robust form and dark complexion, with a cranium which resembled those found in the caves.*

> Dr. H. Ten Kate offered to photograph the hacienda and its occupants, hoping by this means to get her photograph, but his diplomacy failed, although backed by our distinguished guide, Don Juan Dio Angoula, who had long been a friend of the family.

> We saw three of her children who were good examples of the better class of Mexicans, their father having been a Mexican or Spaniard. This woman is probably the only living pure blooded native south of 24 degrees 30 minutes. (Lyman Belding, "The Pericue Indians," *The West-American Scientist* 1 [1885]:21–22

103. HtK 1885: According to Clavijero, the Guaycuru formed an autonomous tribe of which the Coras formed a subdivision. But it appears that "Guaycuru" at the same time was the nickname of the Pericués. See my "Matériaux," etc., p. 554. Eds.: There were three languages in the area visited by Ten Kate: Guaicura, Huchiti, and Pericú. Most of the Sierra Giganta and the Plains of Magdalena were the territory of Guaicurus; the country surrounding La Paz and the mountainous regions of the Cape district were held by the Huchiti-speaking peoples (Pericúes, Coras, Aripes, and Huchitis); the Cape itself and the big islands east of La Paz were held by the Pericúes. As Ten Kate notes, Clavijero included the Huchitis as a member of the Guaycura language. Massey, "Tribes of Baja California," 272–307. Nicolás Tamaral (1687–1734) was born in Seville and came to Mexico in 1712. He began missionary work in Lower California in 1717. He founded San José del Cabo in 1730, and here he was later martyred (see note 52). Bancroft, *North Mexican States*, 437–38.

104. HtK 1885: Ratzel, *Aus Mexico*, p. 185, reports poisonous liana tendrils that are used by the Indians of Tehuantepec for the same purpose. Eds.: Friedrich Ratzel (1844–1904) was a German geographer and anthropologist.

105. Clavijero, *History of Lower California*, 55.

106. HtK 1885: In "Matériaux, etc.," I provided a detailed description with illustrations of these and other cave bones I discovered.

107. Todos Santos was the site of two successive missions: Santa Rosa de las Palmas (founded in 1733) and Nuestra Señora del Pilar de la Paz (founded in 1749 by Padre Sigismundo Taraval). The latter gradually came to be called Todos Santos.

108. See Lieutenant G. M. Wheeler's "Zweite Expedition nach Neu-Mexiko und Colorado, 1874," *Petermann's Geographische Mittheilungen* 21 (1875):447; 22 (1876):212.

109. HtK 1885: *Petermann's Geographische Mittheilungen*, 1861, 136–41.

110. HtK 1885: One finds even greater nonsense in Bates-Hellwald, "Central America," etc. (*Stanford's Compendium of Geography and Travel*), London 1878, p. 42, where it is claimed that, before the arrival on the peninsula of the Spaniards, the Maricopas in the north and the Chichimecas farther south lived from Mulegé to Cape San Lucas but later took over the district near the highlands of Sonora and Chihuahua!

111. HtK 1885. Depicted in *Revue d'Ethnographie,* vol 2., p. 325.
112. HtK 1889, 234. Actually it is better to call these animals Mexican dogs because there is at least one race of hairless dog native to Mexico.
113. The Yaqui pascola performances are in essence secular dancing and clowning at ceremonies such as children's funerals, saint's days festivities, weddings, and—as in this case—Holy Week ceremonies. For a historical account of the Yaqui-Christian ritual organizations and calendrical ceremonies, see Edward H. Spicer, "Yaqui," in *American Indian Culture Change* (Chicago: University of Chicago Press, 1961), 49–67.
114. Clavijero, *History of Lower California,* 350–51.
115. The most recent classifications of Uto-Aztecan languages identify the Piman languages as members of the Tepiman branch and Opatan and Cahita (which includes Mayo and Yaqui) as members of the Taracahitan branch. Wick R. Miller, "Uto-Aztecan Languages," in *Handbook,* vol. 10, ed. A. Ortiz, 113–24.

CHAPTER THREE

Through Sonora to Yuma

Along the Colorado River

THE TEMPERATURE AT GUAYMAS HAD RISEN SINCE MY ABSENCE and was noticeably higher than that of La Paz. Because the city is surrounded on all sides by mountains, which a hundred times over reflect from their bare walls the solar warmth received, the heat there during the midday hours is often unbearable, especially during the summer, and the thermometer not infrequently climbs to 104 degrees in the shade.

On the first day of Easter there was a bullfight in El Rancho, a settlement some distance from Guaymas, and a colorful, turbulent throng was crowding between the stalls and stores with sweets and the tents, where games of chance were in full swing. The Yaquis, many of whom were in an uproarious mood because of the excessive consumption of mescal, danced the pascóla, as though possessed, to the sound of screeching violins and rattling *sonáges*. A select public was in attendance in the wooden arena. Everything that the *beau monde* [beautiful people] of Guaymas had to offer in the form of black-haired señoritas and caballeros had flocked in to attend the *corsos de toros*, and among the officers could also be found the governor of Mexico's west coast, the very much dreaded General Carbó.[1] May the reader spare me a description of this bullfight, which came to an end with one of the toreadors being tossed into the air by a bull, and from which he escaped with a broken nose.

Belding was waiting for an opportunity to sail across the gulf again and continue his investigations in Mulegé, while for my part I tried to broaden my knowledge among the Yaquis. Mr. Laurent, a photographer, was very helpful to me [in this], and we succeeded in taking photographs of a number of these Indians.[2] But they were not willing subjects. "One dies soon," the Yaquis insisted when I asked them why they did not want to be depicted. For many the desire for monetary reward was more powerful than superstition, and hesitantly they placed themselves in front of the apparatus. It was amusing to note their amazement when we showed them the negatives a moment later and they recognized their likeness feature by feature. Once one of them agreed to pose, it was not difficult to take measurements and make additional anthropological observations.

It was in Guaymas that I abandoned further photography of my own. A number of my negatives were in such condition that making good positive prints was out of the question. According to Laurent, my plates were not adapted for a journey in this region. Many were damaged by transport by mule over the rugged paths and full of tiny pits from the fine dust getting into everything. In others the gelatin coat came loose during the developing, probably the result of the intense heat. In many places the water was brackish and alkaline and unsuitable for making chemical solutions, and because I would be encountering the same water in Arizona and New Mexico almost continually, I foresaw nothing but wasted effort. Another difficulty was that the dark slide did not close well and during use snapped open continually—as a result, hazing up the plates. In addition there was the difficulty of working without an assistant and the enormous expense of transporting heavy chests with glass plates, chemicals, etc.[3]

Among the people I got to know in Guaymas was Mr. Emeric, a railway official, who made an important discovery when the railway was being extended along the seacoast. It was an animal figure—apparently an Indian fetish cut from greenish white stone, probably representing a turtle. Some other objects found at the same site, which I later saw in the Smithsonian Institution in Washington, matched the stone animal fetishes we are familiar with from the Santa Barbara islands.[4] The other objects were several fragments of polished green stone, apparently knives, but the use of which is not entirely clear. An investigation that I undertook at the discovery site led to no result.

Several days passed by while I gathered information regarding further expeditions, and the outcome was that I had to abandon my plan of visiting the Seri Indians on Tiburón Island. Mr. A., a distinguished resident of Guaymas, who had just returned from exploration of the island with a view to exploiting it, assured me that at present because of the Seris' hostility and temerity there was nothing he could accomplish among them. Intimidated by his military escort, the Indians scattered and sought refuge in the mountains, but certainly the life of a solitary traveler venturing on their shores would be in jeopardy. As is evident from the ethnographic objects Mr. A. found in their hastily abandoned settlements, the Seris have certainly changed least among the Indians of Sonora. Their most important weapons are long, poisoned arrows with points of iron, which they steal from the ranchos between Hermosillo and the seacoast. They fashion crude pottery and make use of very distinctive canoes, consisting of bundles of reeds bound together.[5]

I then resolved to visit some settlements of the Opata Indians outside of Ures,[6] though the unsettling news about the Apache war made the undertaking of this journey, too, unlikely. The Apaches, however, had left their hideouts in the Sierra Madre and, divided into small bands, passed through the countryside killing and plundering.[7] They had even ventured onto the railway near Querobabi and made the whole area between Ures and the Gila River unsafe.

On April 2 I bade farewell to Belding and returned to Hermosillo, which I left again the following night with the mail coach heading for Ures. As the sun appeared above the horizon, we trotted merrily along through a blossoming stretch of countryside with vast fields of waving grain and luxuriant poplars. Here we are in the most flourishing districts of Sonora, and the hamlets and haciendas, of which I will mention just El Molino and San Luis, have a population that is more prosperous than other Sonorans. Repeatedly we cross the sandy bed of the Sonora River, and the more the heat intensifies, the denser become the gray dust clouds along the route. All my fellow travelers are armed with Winchester carbines and revolvers of every caliber so as to give the Apaches a warm welcome, should that prove necessary.

We have left behind us Gavilán, inhabited mostly by half-breed Opatas, as the hills covered with saguaros loom closer and we must pass through a sunken road. The wagon driver enjoins us to hold our guns in readiness and plies the whip to the mules, and at a frantic pace we rush through the narrow passage. The hail of arrows and bullets we had somewhat anticipated did not transpire and, covered with froth and dust, he halted our mules a little while later at Guadalupe. We refresh our thirsty throats, and around 2:30 P.M. we are in Ures, where I get off at the modest *fonda* [hotel] of Señor Bouvion. The hotel keeper is a French sailor who deserted and former traveling companion of Raousset-Boulbon. The guests are mainly American prospectors[8] and miners. Just previously, one of them fought with Apaches. He has killed two of them and shows us a war trophy, the bloody scalp of one of his assailants.

Since the seat of government has been transferred to Hermosillo, Ures's prosperity has declined considerably, and the city has been partially depopulated. It is the image of dismal abandonment, and with each footstep one takes in the silent, sandy streets, one encounters an adobe dwelling crumbling in ruins. Ures, too, owes its existence to a mission, San Miguel. According to Alphonse Pinart, the name is supposed to mean "red mesa" in Pima because of the reddish color of the soil.[9] The wide valley, in which Ures is situated, is bounded by bare mountains, and, just like the foothills of the sierra, is blanketed mostly with mesquite bushes.

A good part of the day I roam around the area with my Winchester to test the effect of pointed bullets on the long-eared, half-white specimens of *Lepus callotis* and at the same time to provide the *"table d'hôte"* with game—certainly no idle luxury since there was "d—d poor grub," as one of the prospectors rightly remarked. As evening approaches, the "boys" organize a ball. Until well into the night, the feet of the blond-haired *americanos* and the black-haired señoritas stomp and shuffle on the clay floor of the dance hall, to the strumming of the *guitarras* and the stroking of the violins.

The Apaches are the daily topic of conversation. The Cajón, a long, narrow chasm a few leguas north of Ures on the road to Arispe, is permanently occupied by a strong military detachment in order to put an end to the Indians' treacherous attacks on travelers. But elsewhere the lords of the mountains go their way unimpeded. There a band of soldiers, themselves half Indian, walking about in sandals, move silently out of the city because the news has just arrived that the Apaches have plundered a rancho four leguas from the city and massacred the inhabitants. But don't worry.

The Apaches are as swift as the wind of their sierra, and when the troops reach the site of calamity, the robbers are dividing up their booty, safe and far away at some secluded spot.

Based on all I heard, it would have been foolhardy to head north or eastward from Ures, and to avoid losing any more time, I return to Hermosillo after a stay of two and a half days. In Hermosillo, too, it has become considerably hotter since January, and the vegetation of the plaza, profuse in flowers, is resplendent in its full leafy raiment. In the calm evening hour, by the twinkling starlight and murmuring fountains, Hermosillo's beau monde gathers to seek respite in the pleasant cool air, caused by the ocean wind, which wafts over western Sonora during the evening, supplanting the scorching daytime heat. This is the only time when Mexican women and girls from the better classes appear on the streets, at the end of a day spent in dreamy repose.

On April 9 I leave Hermosillo by train and the next morning, twelve hours later, get off at the American border station Calabasas.[10] Here, too, fear has gripped the hearts of the inhabitants because shortly before, the Apaches have appeared in the vicinity. Military force has been summoned in all due haste, and the cavalry encampment lends Calabasas an unusual flurry of activity.

Besides the hotel and the railway station, Calabasas, once a Pima mission, consists of a dozen wooden houses and linen tents. It is situated at the confluence of the Santa Cruz River and Sonoita Creek on a grassy high plateau, surrounded on all sides by mesas, which are completely covered with loose igneous rock and farther on are transformed into majestic mountains, on whose pale brown slopes the eye discerns not a trace of vegetation. In the area surrounding the creek and pools, the abode of wild ducks, stand cottonwoods with wide branches, whose verdure, along with that from the reeds of the puddles, is practically all there is in the entire area. The mesas are blanketed with an uninterrupted grassy carpet. But it is arid, and the mesquite brush, clusters of which now and then break up the wavy lines of slopes, is not yet resplendent in its summer attire. But farther on, inside and close by the canyons, one encounters the juniper tree and a couple of cactus species, *bisnagas* and nopals *(Echinocactus*[11] and *Opuntia)*.

The temperature of Calabasas differs noticeably from that of Hermosillo, and the morning of my arrival I am shivering from the chill in my light clothing. Various mines already known from olden days, including that of Planchas de Plata, are near Calabasas. Only in recent years, though, has it been possible to exploit them without repeated interruptions stemming from Apache enmity.

The troops on hand, arrivals from Fort Thomas,[12] include some Apache scouts in the service of the United States who support the troops in the pursuit of their more independent tribal compatriots. These are the first Apaches I see, but two of them, as it later turned out, were so-called Apache-Yumas, who in appearance and language are quite distinct from the actual Apaches.[13] Early in the morning they have returned from a "scouting party" and are now sauntering about through the only "street" of Calabasas. I buy a reed flute from one of them, but he cannot be persuaded to play it for me. The actual Apache is by far the most interesting figure of the three. He is of medium height, but slender and lithe as a panther. Except for a white cotton jacket and a loincloth, he wears nothing else. His bare, somewhat crooked, muscular legs are enveloped in high animal-skin top boots of domestic make. A red headband holds his raven black locks in place. He has regular features, and his nose, though somewhat flat, is slightly bent, but the breadth of the jawbones and the tininess of his dark eyes are striking. What thoughts passed through my mind on seeing the first Apache, a specimen of the tribe I had read about so often as a boy and had heard so much about the last few weeks!

I stayed in Calabasas no longer than necessary to await the mail coach leaving for Tucson, and the next day I began the fifty-nine-mile-long journey. I cannot deny that the Santa Cruz Valley did not live up to my expectations after the glowing description Froebel provided.[14] The valley is very wide and surrounded by nearly bare mountains. The floor of the valley, which is intersected by the Santa Cruz across its entire length, is covered with expansive meadows of grama and other grasses, and luxuriant álamos and prickly mesquites alternately adorn the sandy edges of the little stream. Now and then an adobe rancho looms up along the sandy and dusty route, and when we are about four miles out of Calabasas the old church of the abandoned mission of Tumacácori appears on the left at the foot of the mountains among the trees.[15]

Ten more miles and we reach Tubác, a miserable hole of adobe dwellings, part of which is situated on a minor elevation. The unattractive church lies nearly in ruins. On the whole, Tubác's appearance bespeaks decline and decay. But Tubác, which owes its origin to a Jesuit mission, was once a rather lively and flourishing place, the center of a wealthy mining district. However, this came to an end with the outbreak of the Civil War in 1861, and Tubác, already repeatedly ravaged by the Apaches, now stood completely exposed to plundering.[16]

We have changed the mail horses, and we continue through Canóa, where we have lunch, then through Sauríta[17] and along San Xavier, known to me from old, which we pass several miles on our left, however. Now greasewood in large part replaces mesquites, and before long the white steeples and houses of Tucson, radiant in the midday sunlight, emerge from the clouds of dust. It is the same uncomfortable Tucson of three months ago, but the heat there has intensified considerably, and the sparse trees are resplendent in their leafy attire. One of the first people I encounter on the street is my old acquaintance Ascencio, the chief of the Papagos. We heartily shake each other's hand, and shortly afterward I also encounter Don Juan Berger, my fellow grave robber, again.

Suddenly we hear rumbling, like from a drum, and shouting. A crowd gathers, and before long we can see a band of Papagos, in red paint, who have improvised a scalp dance. One of them holds a scalp on a long stick, and in the middle some Indians sit hunkered down while they pound on baskets turned upside down and with monotonous hand clapping make the dancers rotate in the circle. Word has it that shortly before a Papago had killed an Apache and that they were celebrating this feat of arms this way. But I got the impression that this was nothing more than speculating on the anti-Apache sentiments of the Tucsonians, and in fact they received many a "bit"[18] and quarter from the numerous spectators. I could not help but view the jesters with aversion. All this was so little in keeping with the image I had formed—from books!—about the Indian character.

I had many letters to read and many to answer, and so nearly four days passed with this as well as preparations for my upcoming journey, so that on the evening of April 16 I took my seat on the train to Yuma, 247 miles to the west, and the next day, shortly after sunup, greeted the Colorado, the colossal stream of the remote Southwest.

Yuma is a city of contrasts. Next to an American hotel by the railway station, where one can encounter ladies and gentlemen dressed in the latest fashions of San Francisco and New Orleans, rises the shabby complex of straw and adobe houses of the Mexicans. A few steps from the railway bridge, on the other side, are the clay and branch huts of the Yuma Indians, whom one can encounter on the platform unclad and in body paint. To the east and west one can depart Yuma twice a day in a luxurious and comfortable railway car. To the north and south, on the other hand, one cannot leave without exposing oneself to the perils of a desert journey, and then only when a freight wagon leaves to bring provisions to the isolated settlements along the banks of the river.

Yuma has declined since the completion of the Southern Pacific Railroad.[19] Now it is just a place where travelers briefly stop to eat a hurried meal at the station. Once it was one of the largest towns on the overland mail, where travelers, after months of exposure to the privations and perils of the desert journey, stayed awhile to recoup their energy before the second stage of their journey.

Yuma, which is 126 feet above sea level, consists primarily of a single straight, very wide street full of loose sand and with unattractive squat adobe houses with flat roofs. The surrounding area is bare and dismal and consists of low-lying hills of conglomerate and gray sand without tree or shrub. The wooden territorial prison is situated on the hill at the mouth of the Gila, emerging from the east and here uniting with the Colorado. Fort Yuma with its white and light green houses is situated on a barren hill on the opposite side, along the California bank of the Colorado. With the carefully tended cottonwoods in places, they offer a not unattractive view.[20] Looking in both directions along the river, you can see the abundantly irrigated bottomland of the winding stream, moving with moderate swiftness, dispatching its muddy, brownish gray mass of water to the Gulf of California. Except toward the east, where the arid Gila Desert vanishes off in the dusk-shrouded distance, a row of freakishly shaped mountain peaks enveloped in purple tints, resembling so many fortifications, arises all around along the horizon. Yuma is undeniably one of the hottest places in North America, a condition to which its location amid two genuine deserts at the same latitude as the Sahara contributes to no small extent. Although the climate can generally be characterized as very dry, summer, particularly July and August, is nevertheless the wet season. Scorching sandstorms blowing out of the desert are a common phenomenon in Yuma. They frequently last three days, though they abate around nightfall, and, according to Loew, usually register a temperature of 40°C.[21]

Soon after my arrival I went to the fort's commanding officer to facilitate my investigations with the Indians, and shortly afterward, accompanied by him, I made my first tour through their settlements.

Hernando de Alarcón (already mentioned in the previous chapter), who discovered the Colorado River in 1540, must have been the first white man to come into contact with the Yumas. In 1700 Father Kino visited the Yumas, whom he calls "Cutganes," and founded a mission among them, which was destroyed shortly afterward, however. Next came Father Gonzaga in 1746 and

Father Garces in 1771, and it appears that only in 1780 were a couple of missions again founded among the Yumas, one of which must have been established at the site of the present-day Fort Yuma.[22] That same year, however, the Indians put an end to the missions for good, and except for Don José Cortés, who in 1799 traveled along the Colorado River and estimated the number of Yumas at 3,000,[23] it appears that these Indians were visited by no known traveler before Bartlett and Whipple traveled through these areas in 1849—and from that point on dates the beginning of linguistic and ethnological investigations among this tribe.[24] In 1850 a military post was established among the Yumas to protect the emigrants traveling to California from their attacks. In the years that followed there had been a series of hostilities between the Indians and the white colonists, until the latter in 1853 became so securely established that, under the protection of the fort Colorado City arose, which was later renamed Arizona City—and eventually Yuma.

Since the beginning of the historical epoch the confluence of the Gila River with the Colorado was the center of the Yuma settlements, and these Indians could boast of dwelling on the very same soil as when Alarcón traveled up the Colorado nearly three and half centuries ago. But time has not been without its effects, and the last thirty years especially—the period the Yumas have been in continual contact with "civilization"—have determined their fate. In 1855 Whipple estimates them at 5,000, while the government reports from more recent years list their number as over 900.[25] The Yumas and their brethren the Mohaves, whom I have also been able to get to know from my own observation, have preserved the ways of their fathers almost unchanged.

I had a surprising first impression of the Yumas.[26] A band of half-nude, painted young men were engrossed in the *ohtoorbook* game. On the sunny bank of the river the merry group of bronzed figures with their fluttering hair and colorful G-strings[27] formed a tableau like the ones Catlin painted so faithfully.[28] The game consisted of two men trotting next to each other, each armed with a very long wooden stick that they held in front of themselves, running some distance after a rapidly rolling wooden ring *(kahptzorr)*, tossed by one of them, and then suddenly hurling the sticks ahead simultaneously so that the ring was stopped in its course. Without letup they began the course as before, and the players always made the same movements. It was not entirely clear to me, however, whether the sticks had to go through the ring or whether they must remain lying next to it.[29] Möllhausen, a member of the Whipple Expedition who witnessed this game among the Mohaves in 1854, relates that they threatened to bash in his skull if he did not leave the playing field.[30] Fortunately, the Yumas were of more mild disposition, and I could move about unmolested in their midst.

The Indians' huts are all on the western bank of the river, among the green bushes of the mesquite, whose fruits provide part of their diet. The huts consist of tree trunks and bundles of branches covered with a layer of earth. They are very low, and the floor is often somewhat lower than ground level. One does not encounter a consistent shape among these huts: there are round ones, oblong ones, and rectangular ones, high and low ones, but all of them have more or less flat roofs and are made of the same building materials. As has been noted already, the Yumas live primarily from the fruit of mesquites, of which there are two varieties: the *Prosopis juliflora* DC, or *algarroba* of the Mexicans with long pod fruits, and the *P. pubescens* Benth., called screw bean by the Americans because of the fruit's shape.[31] The fruits of both varieties have a large amount of glucose. They are first roasted, finely ground with the metate, and then kneaded and baked into cakes. Grass seeds, too, are prepared in the same way.[32] In addition, the Yumas grow corn, wheat, and watermelons, while their animal nutriment consists primarily of rabbits, rats *(Neotoma floridana),*[33] partridges, and fish.

Generally the Yumas' physique can be characterized as handsome. Both sexes have a sturdy build, and the men are mostly tall in stature.[34] They have regular facial features and a pleasant expression. There is something joyous and good-hearted in the gaze of their bright dark eyes, and the hearty laughter, which so often displays their strong handsome teeth, inspires confidence.

It goes without saying that one encounters various cranial types among the Yumas as well, but if here I attempt to provide an idea of their outward appearance, I have the most commonly occurring type in mind. They have receding foreheads, and the men have pronounced eyebrow arches. The shape of the back of their heads recalls that of the Pueblo Indians because of the pronounced flattening and the prominence of their side bones. Just like them, the Yumas are brachycephalic, obvious even on sight.[35] Their noses are straight, moderately long, and somewhat flattened. The mouths are rather large but without prominent lips. Their chins are flat and broad.

The Yumas' skin color can be called light and generally matches number 30 on the chromatic table. The men wear their luxuriant black hair in a large number of long braids hanging down their backs and wrapped at the tips with tiny red ribbons. The women's hair hangs down in disheveled fashion, and they do not wear it as long as the men; at the same time it is snipped off flat along the forehead above the eyebrows. Old men and women cut their hair short and do not paint their bodies at all. Many men, especially when they are young, paint all or part of their faces with blue, red, or yellow colors and have the entire length of their bare legs smeared with these colors as well. The women do not paint themselves but tattoo their chins with two to four vertical blue stripes, likewise with six or eight, sometimes less, blue dots in single or double rows in between. The children, even babies, are often painted in the most colorful fashion and festooned with beads or shells just like their mothers. Blue seems to be the Yumas' favorite color because every variety of the beaded necklaces and bracelets both sexes wear is blue and has a number of white beads, often arranged into tasteful designs. Of the cotton materials the Indians buy in Yuma, the blue ones are very much in demand.

As a rule, the men go around unclad except for a G-string dangling like a long tail. The women's upper body is nude and, besides a short skirt of blue, red, or multicolored cotton they usually wear an apron of black and red wool, *altahwahdeek,* reaching down to their knees, which hangs down in long twisted fringes while the somewhat longer apron *(njahwehgai),* covering the body from behind, is prepared from willow bark. Both sexes go around barefoot, but in the summer, when the sun makes the sand unbearably hot, they wear leather sandals.

From morning until evening I was with the Yumas and thus had the opportunity to observe them in their comings and goings at all hours of the day. My faithful *cicerone* [guide] was a beautiful Indian who spoke excellent Spanish and called himself Miguel. I was unable to learn his Indian name.[36] With him I went around to nearly every hut of the village and astonished the Indians with my questions. They were delighted when I tried out their dishes and professed to find them very tasty. Their amusement was displayed in roars of laughter when I read aloud the Yuma vocabulary collected at the time by Whipple and then asked them the names of the colors.

The Yumas call themselves *Kutchán* or *Kutzán*. Their language is very melodious because, as a rule, a consonant is followed by a vowel, but the Yuma language does have some pronounced guttural sounds, which occur so often in the American [i.e., Indian] languages. *A, i,* and *u* occur most frequently, and diphthongs are rare. Frequently, vowels from the same word will be pronounced differently, something I later noticed among many other tribes. Thus not infrequently *o* was exchanged for *u, e* with *a* and *i, d* with *t,* and *b* with *p.* The accent falls primarily on the last syllable.[37]

Everyone very quickly realized that I wanted to see all possible objects of Indian fabrication, and various people now came by with different items for sale. Things are different now, though, than in the days of Columbus, when one could barter an old knife and a couple of beads for the finest things the Indians had. The Yumas wanted cash—and no bits or quarters but whole dollars, and not just a few of them. If I pointed out to Miguel that the prices were much too high, then he would ask: *"No le gustan los Yumas?"* (You don't like the Yumas?)

For all that, however, I did obtain a small collection of the most important items of Yuma industry, such as pottery painted with black-and-reddish-brown ornamentation, beadwork, and items of clothing, as well as a board for carrying children *(gomáhradeewah),* conforming to the model one encounters among most Indian tribes, though with minor

5. Yuma woman with basket, ca. 1880 (after a contemporary photograph).

modifications. In many huts I encountered basketry that closely resembled that of the Papagos and, as I could later see, that of the Chemehueves as well. Because I received contradictory responses to my query whether the Yumas made these baskets themselves, I assume that they get them by barter with the aforementioned tribes.

The Kutcháns' weapons consist of handsomely painted bows and arrows with long iron points and short wooden clubs *(keeleeahgwai).* They have just a few firearms and do not know how to handle them either, in this regard presenting a stark contrast to other Indians such as the Apaches. This was most evident to me when Miguel and I went rabbit hunting and I handed him my repeating rifle (Winchester 45). At first he wanted me to fire a couple of shots, then took it but handed it back, saying: *"Tengo miedo"* (I'm afraid). He was not afraid of my double-barreled hunting rifle, however. To avoid spending a lot of time tracking game, Miguel set fire to the brush over a certain expanse, and all kinds of rabbits, partridges, or doves sitting concealed quickly came into view and many easily fell into our hands. This custom of hunting is in vogue among many Indians, including the Diggers in California and the Chemehueves.

The most important person among the Yumas is the chief Pascual, a lean graying old man of gigantic stature, already mentioned in 1849 by Whipple.[38] In his hut I met a young Indian painted from head to toe, who had already impressed me earlier with his excellent English accent. When I asked where he had learned this, he told me that he had roamed throughout the world as a circus clown and later had been a hotel attendant in an American city and thus had learned not just English, but French and a little Italian too; he spoke Spanish in addition. For his part, he posed me questions about my visit among the Yumas. When I related that my people wanted to know how the Yumas lived and what they made and that all I related regarding the Yumas would still be known long after the Yumas would have become civilized— that met with approval, and all of this was translated for old Pascual in my presence.

The office of chief among the Yumas does not appear to be hereditary. The most intelligent Indian and the one most suited to the office, in the people's opinion, is elected. Thus Miguel, for

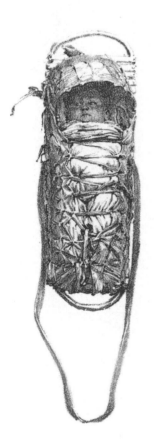

6. Yuma baby on cradle board, ca. 1880.

instance, was selected to succeed old Pascual one day, and he was already occupying the position of subchief.[39] When I asked where the Yumas came from, they replied that their fathers had always dwelled along the "river" *(gahweel)*,[40] just like their neighbors the Cocopas and Mohaves. However, the Maricopas who lived near the Yumas sixty years ago had to leave the Colorado because of discord and conflict with the latter and had sought refuge farther east among the Pimas.[41] Although the old feud now seems forgotten, the Maricopas have permanently established themselves in their new homeland but still maintain bonds of friendship with the Yumas through reciprocal visits and through marriage too. The few Maricopas and Cocopas I was able to see completely matched the Yumas in outward features.

The Yumas cremate their corpses and, with them, everything that has belonged to the deceased. I will provide more details about this custom when I get to my visit to the Mohaves. To judge from their appearance, the Yumas are a basically healthy race, but many of them suffer from syphilis, which assumes a mild form, however. The herbaceous diet and the strong skin secretion in this exceptionally dry area probably contribute to this. In some children traces of syphilis and scrofula were clearly discernable from their eyes and teeth.

Song and dance play an important role in the life of these Indians. Because I had a better opportunity to observe both of these among the Mohaves, for now I do not want to expand on this point. The musical instruments I saw consisted of gourd rattles *(gnahl)* and reed flutes *(alooweel)* with painted carvings. A dice game, evidently played only by women and called *otóchuh-ee*, consists of four little bits of wood approximately twenty centimeters long painted with black figures.[42]

In contrast to the Papago women, the squaws of the Yumas carry their children on their backs, but down low so that the little one rests on the mother's usually strongly developed posterior and puts its little legs around her hips while she supports her delicate burden with her arms crossed in back. If the child is too small to be borne in this manner, then the carrying board upon which it is tightly bound is laid flat on the mother's head. These models prove that the pronouncement of Ploss,[43] according to whom all North American Indian women carry their children *dos-à-dos* [back to back], thus setting themselves apart from nearly all other peoples, is far too general. I saw women carrying burdens, e.g., bundles of sticks, on their backs by means of a hauling strap fastened to the middle of their heads.

Women's lot among the Yumas is quite tolerable and in no way corresponds to the dreary picture painted by many writers regarding the Indians generally. Certainly the Yumas are polygamous and their morals before marriage quite loose,[44] but from this it does not necessarily follow that the lot of women is wretched. Their activities are limited primarily to the preparation of food, caring for children, and making pottery. For the rest they are free. They take part in many of the men's pastimes, in song and dance. The women's outward appearance, too, does not indicate poor treatment or oppression. Everywhere I encountered gaiety and banter.

On the second day of my stay in Yuma, a heavy wind arose from the west at 2 o'clock and filled the atmosphere with a drab haze from the myriad grains of sand swept up from the Mohave

Desert. At the same time the atmosphere was oppressive, and the thermometer registered 90°F in the shade. Toward evening the wind abated, but the following morning it started up again with redoubled fury to rage all day long and to subside again at nightfall. In view of this phenomenon, all Indian huts have their front facing east.

Because I wanted to head for the Mohaves' reservation upstream and there was no regular traffic with Yuma, I eagerly took advantage of a sudden opportunity to leave. An Italian store-keeper,[45] who was sending a freight wagon to a rancho near Ehrenberg, was quite willing to provide me a free ride there, and on April 21 I bade farewell to my Indian friends and to Miguel, who had kept me company to the very end. We had a ride of 130 miles ahead of us to Ehrenberg. About 3 1/2 miles from Yuma we crossed the Gila River. Because the water had risen considerably and the wagon was heavily laden, it got stuck deep in the sand in the middle of the river, and the water came close to flowing over horses and wagon. With great effort our six horses eventually hauled the wagon to the bank, and we extricated ourselves with a wetting, but part of the load, including my baggage, was damaged.

All day we trudged step by step under a scorching sun through an arid, sandy region covered with arrow weed and mesquites. Before nightfall we camped at an abandoned rancho, not far from the Colorado, upon which the moon casts its silver sheen at night. At 6:30 A.M. we headed out again and this day traveled through a landscape that was at least as arid as some areas in Lower California. The first place we reached is Castle Dome Landing, situated along the river and consisting of a couple of huts and a store, where I replenished my provisions with a can of tomatoes and some onions.[46]

There are a couple of so-called Apache-Yumas here, representatives of the tribe whom one could best call Mountain Kutchán and who are now settled on the San Carlos reservation. In appearance they match the River Kutchán to some degree but were smaller in stature.[47]

We pass the bare Chocolate Mountains, consisting of reddish stone, and halt for a while by a miners' camp in the so-called Silver District. We started our campfire this evening at Morton's Landing, a small settlement of recent date.[48] The next morning one of my traveling companions stays behind here, and the two of us continue our journey. The river now stays constantly in view and affords a lovely panorama with the fierce play of sunlight on its multicolored rocky banks. Partridges are abundant in the mesquite bushes; these shrubs mostly appear where the rocky ground changes over to dirty yellowish sand. Rabbits are scarce.

The driver had formerly been with the well-known archaeologist Stephens in Central and South America,[49] before that time had scoured the seas on a whaling ship, then had been a soldier, except that with twelve other occupations he had had thirteen misfortunes—and to pass the time he tells me many an episode from his active life. Off in the distance, where a whirling dust cloud rises like a gigantic column above the scorched ground,[50] he shows me the spot where he once nearly perished of thirst and was rescued from certain death by some prospectors. Thus a half day in these parts without drinking is also a veritable torment because, due to the exceptionally strong perspiration, the feeling of thirst is almost continually sustained, and I drank repeatedly from the brown, muddy river water, which under normal circumstances would have aroused my aversion.

Late in the afternoon the western horizon again darkens because of the desert dust being lifted up, and shortly afterward the hot wind covers us with a layer of fine sand. The wind persists for a long time after we have pitched camp and at the same time scatters the light branches with which we sustain the campfire. Our supper, too, does not turn out any better because the sides of bacon that I sit down to fry are blown out of the pan, and the coffee, already less than perfect, is made even muddier by the sandy torrent. Fortunately, the wind slackens appreciably later on, and nothing disturbs our sleep other than the barking of a couple of big dogs who come visiting us from a nearby rancho.

The next morning before 6 o'clock we break camp. After a couple of hours of riding in the cool morning air, we halt for a moment by a lagoon of brackish water, where some wild ducks and grebes flee upon our approach. We water the horses because we will find no more water before evening. The area we are now traveling through is an arid desert of unbroken sandy mesas, which are covered far and wide with loose chunks of lava. The unsightly paloverdes with their smooth, sea green bark and miniature leaves and the lank ocotillos *(Fouquieria splendens),* which besides numerous thorns bear red bells, are, along with individual pillar cactuses, the most typical plants of the area. The only living thing we see is a coyote, which promptly breaks off his flight to gaze at us with curiosity. The wind torments us without letup all day long and again abates in the evening when we reach Ehrenberg, our journey's destination. The little town is almost completely abandoned and because there is no hotel, we start up a fire along the "main embankment" in the center of the "city" and pass the night "on the street." Shivering from the cold, I boil my coffee the next morning and then take a closer look at the place.

Ehrenberg dates from 1863 and was once a busy place because it was one of the main points along the stage line between Arizona and California and had connecting lines to Wickenburg and Prescott. But in large part the railway has robbed Ehrenberg, too, of a source of livelihood, as did the exhaustion of the placers (metal quarries, mines) nearby, with the result being that the other mail line was eliminated. Of the 500 residents it once numbered, barely fifty remain. The others have sought their refuge in other towns and have left nothing but a dilapidated heap of wretched adobe houses, some of which are temporarily occupied by some loafing Mohaves of both sexes.[51]

My traveling companion crosses the river at noon with the wooden ferry to reach Blythe's Ranch, his destination. I accompany him there. Because of the large-scale construction of irrigation canals, this settlement, situated 7 1/2 miles west of Ehrenberg along the edge of the Mohave Desert, has cost thousands of dollars, perhaps a waste of money because the water does not get here and thus the soil remains infertile. Having returned from this little *"Abstecher"* [side trip] on California territory, and being alone, I have no choice but to be patient and wait at Ehrenberg until I find the opportunity to continue the journey to the reservation. I seek accommodation with "French Frank," a Breton who has been buried alive in this dismal place for many years and gains his livelihood tending a small garden. "French Frank," too, has been a sailor and has a turbulent life behind him. Three whole days I share his sober meals with *soupe maigre* [watery soup] and weak tea—three days abundant in tedium and privation.

I spend my time tracking quails, doves, and cottontails, primarily on the California bank, which is overgrown with cottonwoods and willows and with arrow weed and mesquites farther inland. In addition, hummingbirds, attractively colored lizards, and ants are all I observe of animal life in this area—except for nightjars *(Antrostomus),* here called *poorwill*. I also get to know the few Mohaves who have set up their huts in the vegetation opposite Ehrenberg.

On April 28 I can finally leave, thanks to the arrival of a driver from Yuma, with whom I begin the ride at 1 o'clock in a buckboard (light wagon, where, in addition to front seats for two persons, there is room for goods) hitched to two mules. The landscape has the same arid features as it did south of Ehrenberg. Where Olive City once stood, you now find just a couple of adobe walls, and some miles farther on one travels through the now deserted streets of La Paz, which was depopulated because the placers were no longer productive and the landing place silted up.[52] In the evening we make "dry camp," that is, camp without water, among the mesquite bushes, and at daybreak continue on our way. By 9 A.M. we have reached the agency.[53] Although I look like a tramp[54] because I have not changed clothes for a week, I am received with the greatest courtesy by the agent, thanks to the letter of recommendation from the Commissioner of Indian Affairs,[55] and for nine days I have my headquarters here.

The Mohave and Chemehueve Agency, or Parker (to call it by its post office name), is situated in the heart of the reservation, like an abandoned outpost of civilization in an endless desert. It consists of a squat adobe building with a flat roof and verandas. On the one side it is bounded by a compound with stables and sheds for provisions, on the other side by school buildings and some small outbuildings. The whole complex is surrounded by tall cottonwoods. The sandy plain, covered primarily with mesquites, spreads out in all directions. A few miles away, toward the east, it is bounded by mesas overgrown with greasewood, while to the west, a quarter mile from the agency, the Colorado flows past. The horizon is bounded by bare mountaintops tinged reddish, yellow, and gray, freakishly shaped and evidently consisting of porphyry. Elsewhere, along the entire course of the Colorado, there is likewise nothing but bottomland, which owes its fertility to the periodic inundation of the river—the result of strong atmospheric precipitation—and is habitable. Consequently, all Indian settlements are near the water.

Rabbits, kangaroo mice, doves, partridges, and black birds *(Quiscalinae)* appear frequently around the agency, as does the very dangerous side viper [i.e., sidewinder], a small rattlesnake *(Crotalus cerastes* Halowell),[56] which made me stay on my guard many times while hunting.

According to the government report of 1882, there are 1,026 Indians present on the reservation, 811 Mohaves and 215 Chemehueves, the latter being established in the northwestern corner of the reservation along the California bank.[57] A few years ago the United States government had also brought the largest part of the Hualapai Indians onto this reservation and compelled them to stay by force of arms. But the troops, who in time were recalled, had hardly turned their backs when the Hualapaís to a man left their place of exile and returned to their beloved mountains.[58]

One of the first excursions I made from the agency was to a village of the Chemehueve Indians, about twelve miles from there. Although in historic times these Indians have inhabited the same areas as the Mohaves, they are in appearance, character, and language totally different from them and in reality nothing but the southernmost tribe of the very widespread family of the Pah-Utes, as their name of *Tontewaits* = "southern," "the southerners" indicates.[59] They are not as large and robust and have flatter faces than the Mohaves. The backs of their heads jut out prominently, and some have high skulls bordering on acrocephaly. The fourteen men whom I persuaded to be measured, under the pretext that the government would be giving them hats, had an average cranial index of 87.30 and were thus strongly brachycephalic. Those with the shortest skulls still registered 83. Many of them have thin mustaches, which are sometimes clipped above the lip so only the tips of the mustache remain at the corners of their mouths. At the present time most Chemehueves cut their hair short and wear hats, just as they have for the rest preserved practically nothing else of their traditional attire; so, after long searching I could acquire nothing more than a pair of leather boots *(pagáp)* of Indian make for my collection.

The lovely, often waterproof basketry the Tontewaits weave closely resembles that of the Papagos, but in place of the kjéoh they use a densely woven basket shaped like a funnel. Their pottery resembles that of the Yumas and Mohaves, as do their huts. When I visited the chief, known to the Americans by the name of Thomas, he was sitting in a "sweat hut" with his face painted red but wearing a black hat, in the company of a number of other Indians playing cards. One of the first things the Indian, a passionate dice player by nature, adopts from the "white man's ways" is card playing.

Most Chemehueves understand and speak some Spanish and English. Their own language sounds much harsher than the very melodious Mohave and is difficult to transcribe. In their dealings with the Mohaves, most Chemehueves use the former's language; only rarely does a Mohave speak Chemehueve.

The Mohaves' villages and settlements are distributed along the riverbank at various distances from the agency and completely resemble the Yumas' settlements described above. Here, too, one finds near the huts some large round baskets of willow twigs that rest on poles a few feet above-ground. The provisions of mesquite beans are kept in these baskets. In addition, the Mohaves keep hidden storage areas for corn and wheat to guard against starvation in the event of a poor harvest. For this purpose they have a designated "seed man," who collects a certain portion of the harvest from each Indian, bringing it to a safe place.

The chief of the Mohaves living on the reservation is Hookerau (Fast Boat), a magnificent specimen of an Indian, 1.86 meters tall and weighing 220 pounds, with whom I am on the best of terms. He is the first person who allows himself to be measured, and after word has gotten out that the chief has done this, it is not difficult to get a number of young bucks[60] to follow his example. But I have little success with the Mohave ladies, and only with great difficulty do I persuade a couple of former beauties to submit to my manipulations. As a rule, Mohave girls and young women can be characterized as pretty. With their black locks and brown tint, their dark gleaming eyes filled with mischief and love of life, their red lips on which a childlike laughter so often plays, and the delicately curved lines of their slender bodies, they provide in their natural simplicity a fitting image of the "peerless dark-eyed Indian girl" so eloquently intoned by Joaquin Miller.[61]

The Mohaves, too, are polygamous, and before marriage the young girls enjoy complete freedom. Syphilis is very widespread and occurs more commonly among the younger Indians than the older ones, which would lead one to assume that the whites (primarily soldiers) helped spread this disease. Just like the Chemehueves, the Mohaves often have bad teeth, dirty white in color with lots of irregularities.

Half-blood Indians are encountered no more among the Mohaves than among the Yumas because children born from a union of whites and Mohave squaws are, as a ruled, killed. Among the Chemehueves, on the other hand, mestizos are often encountered, and the unions of whites with women from this tribe are quite common. More than one Chemehueve has left her tribe to follow her white spouse to a mining camp or small frontier town.

The Mohaves' children are nurtured for an exceptionally long time by their own mothers, and very often I saw children who, though they had been walking for some time now, had not yet been weaned. It is likely that the nursing of the children is prolonged for this length of time to prevent the return of the menses, which for this naturally fertile race is promptly followed by a new pregnancy.

Although infirm and deformed persons are very seldom found among the Mohaves, they do appear now and then. Thus—to digress from my account for a moment—I saw an Indian hunchback at Fort Mohave.

The Mohaves, particularly the women, love animals. Several times I saw women petting and pampering dogs and chickens. Here they provided a favorable contrast to the Mexicans, who practically let their dogs starve to death and mistreat them besides. The Mohaves' dogs, generally a small type from all different breeds, looked mostly well fed and sometimes even wear ornaments from their masters. I recall having seen a large dog who wore a lovely collar with long leather fringes.

The attire of the Mohaves from both sexes closely resembles that of the Yumas, and it is primarily the young bucks who paint themselves. The women especially, both among the Mohaves as well as the Chemehueves, paint around their eyelids with blue dye. They say they do this to protect against the sunlight and thus to be able to see farther. The Mohaves and Yumas both have the custom of cleansing their hair with mud from the river. The hair is loosened, covered completely with a gray, wet mass of mud, and then bound up as high as possible. This coating stays a couple of days until everything dries out. Then the hair is undone, carefully brushed, freed from unwelcome guests, and worn again in the usual way—glistening, blacker than ever. Seen from a distance it is as though this head, coated with light gray mud, is powdered.

One sees the young bucks nearly always with a long pole *(ookahnuh)* resembling a large so-called sixpence and serving to bat in front of them a leather ball *(milekjái)* the size of a medium-sized potato. This game is called *ookáhnuh* or *ookáhnk.* Another game *(toowuhdooljk),* which I saw being played almost every evening by a number of boys who sat crouching around a fire, to some extent recalls our *"slofje onder."*[62] But here a couple of pieces of wood tied together were hidden and then passed behind the players' backs, and someone from the row seated facing then had to guess who had the sticks. That was joined with vigorous movements of the upper body, with the arms remaining crossed, while a monotonous chant was heard from the players. There was also another game called *chejayresoowárwk,* which is played during the evening by boys and girls. A row of boys and girls standing opposite each other, but only one or two paces from each other, walked slowly up and down in time to a chant so that now one and then the other row walked on. While the walking was going on, the players in one of the rows had assumed a crouching position, from which they lifted themselves up suddenly at a given moment with a loud shout and then stopped chanting.

Two years ago an Indian school was opened at the agency. Though the Indians at first seemed unwilling to send their children there, most later changed their minds. Now a rather large number of boys and girls from both tribes are being instructed by two women teachers. According to them, the Chemehueve children are more intelligent than those of the Mohaves, and the boys from both tribes are noticeably smarter than the girls. Moreover, the character of each tribe is revealed through the schoolchildren. Thus the Chemehueves are very headstrong, do not easily forget a punishment, and nourish resentment a long time. The Mohaves, on the other hand, though quite impressionable and short-tempered by nature, quickly forget an episode, and before long their natural humor reasserts itself. Some children show a bent for music. There is a Chemehueve girl called Topáhlja who unquestionably has a bent for plastic arts. Without ever having benefited from instruction, she models small busts and animal shapes from clay, with no other assistance than from her slender fingers. Her pencil drawings, too, reveal a fine eye and a sure hand.

The children are faithful visitors to my room. At every hour of the day a little group is standing around me. The shyer ones, mostly girls, peer through the opened window or around the corner of the door. Little Hooktahreemay (Fox Paw) especially, with his roguish dark peepers and pleasant jests, is less inhibited than the others, and when I go rabbit hunting at dusk often accompanies me with his bow and arrows. With the interpreter Joolevéekah (Two Ropes), a young Mohave with handsome features, I visit all the villages in the area, where I have abundant opportunity to see the Indians at home.

Their limited household implements include the grinding stones *(ahgpáy* and *hamoostséé)* with which they finely grind corn or wheat; the *achmó,* a wooden mortar to mash mesquite beans; some painted earthen pots and earthen scoops *(kahmootah)*; and a couple of baskets, probably originating from their neighbors, the Chemehueves. Besides the aforementioned foodstuffs, the Mohaves boil a sweet beverage from the leaves of the willow tree (probably *Salix longifolia*).[63] They also eat fish,[64] and besides rabbits they hunt rats *(Neotoma)*[65] and kangaroo mice *(Jaculus* [= *Zapus*]) as well and most likely eat them too. They are very fond of mule meat, which they rarely obtain, however. I will not easily forget with what relish and eagerness a band of Mohaves got hold of a mule that lay down to die, how they disemboweled it in short order, and how it disappeared inside their stomachs.

The Mohaves are not really a hunting race because the Colorado Valley, poor in game, provides little that would allow them to live off the bounty of hunting. Big game, such as antelope and mountain sheep, are absent because the grass they need is lacking. That is also why the Mohaves' livestock is extremely scanty and consists of just a hundred horses and some cows. In addition, they keep chickens.

The Mohaves own a few crude wooden flat-bottom vehicles, which they have probably imitated from the Americans, but at the same time they own a few canoes made from hollowed-out tree trunks.[66]

The American government organized a weekly distribution of flour, salt, and beef during the fall, winter, and spring. Although, according to the government reports, the Yumas and Cocopas belong to the same reservation as the Mohaves, they receive no rations because only rarely do they come to the agency.

Just like the Yumas, the Mohaves cremate their corpses.[67] On the same day I left the reservation a cremation took place. The agency physician, Dr. C. C. Webb, who attended this ceremony, was later kind enough to provide the following information by letter:

> The first thing that caught my attention, when I arrived at the spot, was the lamentation of a group of Indians, which could be heard nearly a mile away. My arrival had caused some commotion among the Mohaves, and before long a circle formed around me until one of the chiefs spoke. When the interpreter I had with me translated his speech, I realized that they regarded me as an intruder and wanted me to leave. But when I promised them that I would not tell "Washington"[68] anything I saw, they hesitantly agreed, after considerable discussion among themselves, that I could stay. The body lay in the sand in front of a hut and was completely enveloped in a blanket so that nothing of its face or limbs was visible. It was surrounded by approximately three hundred Indians of both sexes and every age, roughly a third of whom served as mourners. Some of these mourners lay flat on the ground. Others were kneeling and jerking their bodies back and forth. Still others stood with their arms stretched above their heads, producing a monotonous hand clapping which could be heard without interruption. There was one man there who delivered a loud, long address with wild gesticulations.
>
> The section of the Indians present not taking part in the lamentations stood grouped in two rows between the spot where the body lay and the funeral pyre, so that there was space left between them. Roughly an hour passed, when six Mohaves, three on each side, lifted up the body and slowly carried it to the funeral pyre, followed by a throng of mourners who, with violent gestures and wringing of hands, filled the air with their sad cries.
>
> After the bearers had reached the funeral pyre, they lifted the body up three times and then laid it flat on its back on a hollow area of the funeral pyre formed by the bundles. The hollow was then filled with wood so that the body was completely and fully covered. The mourners and both ranks, which the retinue had passed between, now formed a double circle around the

funeral pyre and walked around it three times. Then the fire was lit; and when the pyre was fully ablaze, the dead man's belongings—articles of clothing, blankets, jewelry, baskets, etc.—were tossed into the flames. Then the horse of the deceased was brought forward and three times was led as closely as possible around the fire, to then have its neck arteries slit open not far away. After the horse had bled to death, it too was laid on a woodpile and cremated. All during this time the heart-rending lamentation of the spectators continued, and at the same time they bent their upper bodies now backward, now forward.

The Needles, a well-known mountain group on the left bank of the Colorado, are regarded as the abode of the spirits by the Mohaves. They believe that there they will enjoy eternal youth and there will be an abundance of juicy watermelons. I cannot say with certainty whether the Mohaves bring the ashes of their bodies to these sacred mountains, but it has been ascertained that they sometimes go there to lay down watermelons as an offering to the dead. All my efforts to learn more about their religion foundered on the Indians' unwillingness to provide me further information. So with reservations I accept that the Mohave name for the Needles is *Hohkeeampáypáy,* as one of them assured me.[69] The name *Mohave* in its full form, *Hahmookháhváy,* means "three mountains."[70] Whether the name is related to the Needles and their mountain paradise I cannot determine.

Just like the Yumas, the Mohaves—and the Chemehueves, too—believe in the power of the "evil eye." Many innocent people, and not infrequently women and children, are put to death because they had cast a spell on a sick person or because a fatal prophecy had brought on displeasure and fear from other Indians.

As is the case for many Indian tribes, the Mohaves' medicine consists primarily of "sweating out" and "squeezing away" the illness. The former takes place in the "sweat lodge"—among the Mohaves a large, half-subterranean chamber of sticks, branches, and sand—in which piles of large stones are heated to incandescence and water is then poured over them, resulting in hot steam filling the closed room, making the patient break out in a sweat before long.[71] At the same time, the sweat lodge is not uncommonly the tribe's council chamber. The "squeezing away" is a genuine massage, whereby the patient lies flat on the ground while another person kneels and carries out the artificial operation.

On May 7 the quiet, monotonous life at the agency was momentarily interrupted by the arrival of the steamboat, which once a month navigates the Colorado from Yuma to Fort Mohave, and I had to choose between an immediate departure or waiting a month. I chose the former, and before long I was on board the gigantic, strange steam colossus with its flat keel and its double deck that looks as though it were resting on scaffolds. At 1 P.M., with a temperature of more than a hundred degrees, the awesomely huge rear wheel (stern wheel), which is nearly as wide as the boat itself, sets itself in motion; heaving, creaking, trembling, and groaning the *Mohave* proceeds on its way north.[72] The passengers consist of a military pharmacist with his family. The crew is made up of fifteen Mohaves, while the cargo consists primarily of merchandise for the fort. An Indian positioned at the stern carries out constant soundings by means of a long stick and loudly calls out the number of feet or inches separating the flat keel of the boat from the sandy river bottom.

The riverbanks are monotonous in form, and all around, the eye discerns nothing but desolate mesas of conglomerate and cliffs with sheer walls. After approximately four hours of steaming, we stop for a while at Aubrey's Landing, which consists of a couple of wretched houses,[73] and then continue the journey until 7 o'clock, when it turns dark, laying at anchor by the bank to wait for morning.

The Indians go ashore and start a fire because the evening is chilly. Because of the many shallow spots, the journey on the river by dark is too perilous, and so we continue our journey only at daybreak. Again there is an alternation between sheer rock walls in all variegations and sandy banks with cottonwoods, willows, and mesquites, which appear in large number, particularly in Chemehueve Valley, where the river valley widens considerably. We stop for a moment to bring in wood, and some Chemehueves, men and women, are sitting by the landing place. This stretch, one of the most fertile along the entire Colorado, was once inhabited by the Chemehueves, but the Indian Department, altruistic as ever, thought that the arid reservation was more suitable for civilizing the Chemehueves and forced them to leave the valley *en corps* [in a body, en masse].[74] A few individuals, too attached to the land of their childhood, later returned to settle next to white settlers.

Toward 10 A.M. we pass the Mohaves' Eden, the Needles, a group of jagged reddish rocks, where the valley narrows, and we steam through a canyon. All during the day we repeatedly collide with sandbanks, and once we remain stranded on a sandbank for more than an hour. At 7 P.M. we reach the point where the railway bridge of the still incomplete Atlantic and Pacific Railway is under construction and lay at anchor. Early in the morning we steam on, and at 10 o'clock we land at Fort Mohave,[75] where I am soon thereafter accommodated in an empty officer's quarters, thanks to the commandant's solicitude.

The fort, which consists of a collection of adobe dwellings, is situated on a roughly seventy-foot-high bench of conglomerate along the eastern riverbank. There is some vegetation in the sandy bottomland, but the mountains, which appear on every corner of the horizon, are bare. To the northeast the eye discerns the tower-shaped peaks of trachyte and rhyolite at Unions Pass, which have a reddish glint in the pale sunlight.

Investigations of Oscar Loew, who visited a section of the Colorado Valley as a member of the Wheeler Expedition in 1875, have shown that Fort Mohave is one of the hottest places on earth, whose temperature is exceeded by just a few degrees in the Sahara. In Fort Mohave the average temperature during the warmest month is 34.2°C (93.6°F). A temperature of 122° was repeatedly observed, while at night the thermometer seldom registered less than 90°.[76] Because of the exceptional dryness of the air, dew is something unknown across the entire Southwest (with the exception, of course, of the high mountainous stretches), and the dryness of the atmosphere, which permits free transpiration and perspiration, is precisely why one tolerates the heat so much better than in the moist tropical regions.[77]

That group of Mohave Indians, roughly 700 in number, who preferred to perish rather than go to the reservation, has settlements in the area around the fort and stands under [the authority of] other chiefs, the most prominent of whom is Ampotumkwittelsjitsje, called Potetsjitsje in abbreviated fashion by the Americans.[78] He is the son of the great chief Iritéba and succeeded his father after his death.[79] He is much revered and loved by the Indians. Seldom if ever have I seen a nobler type than this young chief. Small and slender in figure, he has a totally different physiognomy from the other Mohaves. He has a pale complexion. His deep, reflective eyes and the finely cut face, with a profile as handsome as a Greek image, arouse sympathy and instill confidence. Below him is Mayoemehaí, a genuine beggar of sly countenance, who lacks all of Potetsjitsje's attractive features and at every turn comes begging to me for this or that item. The interpreter is Maseháyewee,[80] called "Lying Jim" by the soldiers. He is as bad as his aforementioned chief, but he is immensely useful to me.

The five days of my stay at Fort Mohave, I spent visiting some nearby Indian camps, during which the commanding officer was kind enough to loan me his own horse, the only one at the garrison. And with it I made a trip to Murray's Ranch on the Nevada bank. The two most important events during this time, however, were a powwow I had with the Mohaves and an Indian dance party I had organized through the intercession of Captain H. and Masseháyewee. The purpose of the powwow, which took place under the veranda of the house where I was lodging, was to add to my measurements and observations among the Mohaves and to propose a dance and feast to them at the same time.

With the first I did not think I would succeed because when the Indians realized that they had been called together so they could be examined and touched, many were indignant and a disapproving murmur made its way through their ranks. Mahyoomahaí took the floor to ask what impelled me to make such a strange proposal—who was I, and where did I come from? If I came to poke fun of the Mohaves' ignorance they would not speak, for he had heard that I was a medicine man and thus knew more than the Mohaves. But he added that if I paid the Mohaves well, he would once more take the matter under advisement. Captain H. saved me from my predicament by reading in a loud voice my letter of recommendation from General Sherman and adding what was necessary—all this was translated by "Lying Jim" to his tribal compatriots.

That had its effect, and when I then distributed tobacco among the crowd, I could at last proceed and measure a number of them. But with Ampotum Quitahtchitsjuh a difficulty developed in that he did not want to let himself be touched by a white man in the presence of his subjects. After chatting awhile I got him to go to my room, where he allowed himself to be measured in Captain H.'s presence.[81] The morning cost me dearly because, in addition to paying the chief and the interpreter two to three dollars, each Indian who let himself be measured received a quarter, and thus I was out twelve dollars (roughly thirty guilders). My proposal that I would treat the Mohaves to coffee with sugar and white bread if they later would agree to perform some dances was greeted with satisfaction, and when I was ready to leave, Jim told me that the Mohaves still found me "a pretty good doctor" and that I wasn't as bad as I at first seemed to be.

Two days after the powwow, during the evening, a throng of roughly 170 Indians—men, women, and children—came to the fort. I had arranged for nearly 500 small loaves to be baked and at the same time twenty-five gallons (about 113 liters) of warm coffee with sugar to be added, and this was distributed to the Indians at the door of the canteen. Then they headed to the two huge fires that the commandant at my request had ordered to start in a large space near the hospital. When they had made themselves at home and I had then passed around a quantity of tobacco, the dancing began.

One of their dances consisted of a row of men and women facing each other and positioned close together moving slowly up and down to the monotonous sound of a chant and a rattle (achnáhlya). The space where they were constantly moving backward and forward in alternation took up just a few meters. The row of women was always in a crouching position, that of the men only toward the end of the dance, when everybody stuck their heads together, uttered a kind of growling noise, and then chanting and dancing both came abruptly to an end. Another dance consisted of the rapid rotation of several chanting bucks and squaws, gathered hand in hand around Indians, also chanting, who were in the middle of the circle. The finest dance consisted of a number of men, arrayed in two rows facing each other, up and down poised sideways in rhythm with a sorrowful chant. Then they grabbed the hands of the person standing next to them and leaned against each other with the underarm, then abruptly bent over forward, and, in time to the chant, shifted the left leg in turns forward and backward while the right leg remained in place.[82]

The half-moon hovered high above the silent banks of the stream and until deep in the night the chanting of the Indians reverberated around the flickering fires.[83] If ever people have approached Rousseau's ideal state of felicity, the Mohaves must be the ones. Children of the moment, content in the present and unconcerned about the future, their life passes by like a carefree dream. Now and then sickness and sorrow make their rounds among them. Both inflict wounds, but these quickly heal, and the childlike cheerfulness promptly returns like the sun of their homeland after a sandstorm or downpour. But this dreamlike existence will not endure much longer. "Civilization," which has already taken root at several points along the silent stream, will spread. With the railway will come throngs of fortune hunters, unprincipled and avaricious, who will settle on their best lands and burrow through their mountains for gold. . . . There will be more sickness and sorrow. Death will cut a more rapid swathe than before. Discord, falsehood, greed, treachery will prevail among that people, who will scatter and in the course of time dissolve into the turbid stream of "civilization."

On the evening of May 13 the steamboat *Mohave* returned from the agency with the Indian inspector, General C. H. Howard, on board.[84] At the agency I already had the pleasure of meeting Mr. H., and because he was planning to visit the Pah-Utes, who live farther upstream, I decided to accompany him. The next morning, at the break of dawn, the boat moved off again. All day we steam along the banks, which have the same character as the ones already described above. Now and then we see a beaver, which dives off into the stream at our approach, or a lone wolf along the bank. Among the Mohaves the beaver seems to be the object of a certain reverence because supposedly they never kill one deliberately, and they try to foil the white beaver trappers in every way possible.

We pass Hardyville, which consists of a single house and where the northernmost settlements of the Mohaves can be found.[85] That afternoon we reach Bowlder [*sic*] Rapids, where the shallow riverbed is strewn with a large number of boulders. Because we could not steam past them, an anchor on a very long rope is fastened by the Indians on the bank some distance ahead of us, and before long the boat pulls through the rapids with jolts and bumps. Just before evening we reach Cottonwood Island, where no cottonwood can be seen, however, and the mesquites became scarce as well because the few Pah-Utes living on the island earn their livelihood primarily by providing firewood for the boats. On the western bank facing the island rises a high mountain, upon which, according to tradition, the Pah-Ute paradise once could be found. But they brought upon themselves the wrath of the Great Spirit by killing a good chief and, as punishment, were expelled from their magnificent, bountiful Eden into the scorching hot river valley down below.

The early morning hours of the 15th were spent loading wood, and several Pah-Utes arrived along the bank. They are more or less attired in "citizen's dress" and do not have the handsome build nor the wide-eyed look and pleasant features of the Mohaves. One of them has a fine bow, which is decorated on the inside with numerous plumed scalps from quails.

At 9 o'clock we continue our journey and about an hour later reach Painted Canyon, where steep, splendidly variegated rocky walls of reddish and grayish yellow igneous rock surround the drab stream. Six miles before we reach El Dorado Canyon, we again have to pass some rapids. The banks, now closer to the water, become steeper and higher, and now and then sheer rocks of conglomerate and sandstone tower up. At nightfall we anchor before El Dorado Canyon, where a mining camp has been set up, and Mr. Howard and I visit the mill, where silver ore is refined from a nearby mine.

The next day General Howard called together the Pah-Utes living here to learn more about their situation, but for lack of a good interpreter not much came of this powwow. Moreover, they seemed suspicious, and the brother of the momentarily absent chief proved unwilling to answer questions posed him. Clearly he dreaded that our arrival had something to do with a removal to a reservation because the few words he deigned to utter were: "I love that land (Cottonwood Island); I spent my childhood there."

The Pah-Utes, who call themselves "Nu," that is, "people," are only a hundred strong on Cottonwood Island and El Dorado.[86] To judge from the individuals I saw, they are of medium height, some even short in stature, and though lean, muscular and "tough" in outward appearance. Two types seem to occur among them, one of which has a short, blunt, slightly turned-up nose, the other a bent nose and is probably identical with the type so widespread among the Plains tribes, which has, indeed, been referred to as the "redskin type." The blunt-nosed type has a receding forehead but without pronounced eyebrows and is more or less prognathous, especially the lower jaw. Just like the Chemehueves, they allow only the tips of their thin black mustaches to grow. The women—who, in contrast to their Mohave sisters, often have slightly bent noses but are just as good-looking—have very prominent cheekbones, however. Almost all wear white man's attire; just a few remain who let their hair grow long and wear head cloth and white leather moccasins. The latter bear a very close resemblance to those of the Chemehueves. A number of Pah-Utes work for the Americans at the mill, while many squaws live with the whites and have given birth to a number of half-breed children.

When General Howard's "talk" was over, I tried to solicit information from them and collected a short vocabulary of their language at the same time.

The Nu live partly from hunting, including the mountain sheep *(Ovis montana)*. Beyond that, grass seed and mesquite beans are their chief nutriment. The root of the jimson weed *(Datura)* is chewed as a narcotic, with a state of delirium frequently ensuing. In addition, the Pah-Utes are heavily enthralled with strong drink, which, thanks to civilization, they can now buy from the Americans. Their dwellings are merely huts of tree branches, and their entire industry consists of making baskets and funnel-shaped carrying baskets of willow bark.

Just like their neighbors, the Mohaves, whom they call "Ayats," that is, "the handsome ones," the Pah-Utes cremate their corpses. In years past they took scalps and had many battles with the Mohaves. In the past ten years, though, there have been no large-scale hostilities. Many mountains along the Colorado, for example, Mount Newberry, were dreaded by them because of the evil spirits dwelling upon them.

As for their language, this bears a very close resemblance to Chemehueve and is possibly identical to it.[87] As was to be expected, I later discovered many Pah-Ute words among the Utes and Comanches. For example, *pah,* "water," *káni* or *káne,* "hut," *mamma, mamáts,* "woman," etc. Moreover, in the three languages some numbers match, for example:

	Pah-Ute	Ute	Comanche
one	sójoes	soewis	sámes
two	wai	wain	wáhat
three	pai	pain	páhaste

The word for *five* is related to the word for *hand,* as it is in so many languages. So, *five* in the three languages is respectively *máneghi, maínegen,* and *mówe; hand* is *moáve, moev, mamóo.*[88] Many sounds are extremely difficult to replicate with our letters—for example, the final consonants in *papágh,* "river," and *sagwagágh,* "blue," which correspond to some extent to the Malay-Arabic *ghain* (as *gh* or *gr*).

Some writers have maintained that the peculiar condition of the Colorado Valley explains the unique physical and psychological character of the Yumas and Mohaves. But then the question must be raised why the Chemehueves and Pah-Utes, who live in exactly the same surroundings, differ so dramatically from these two tribes in appearance, character, and lifestyle. It is indeed possible that the Yumas and Mohaves have lived considerably longer in the hot Colorado Valley and that the Pah-Ute tribes with individual character traits recalling the northern Plains Indians, who came from the north only later, have not yet experienced the far-reaching influence to which the Yuma-Mohaves have been exposed for centuries.

El Dorado Mill is situated in the state of Nevada at the mouth of a lateral canyon, which extends outward toward the western riverbank.[89] The walls of the canyon largely consist of conglomerate—just like all mesas in these parts, the remnants of old sedimentary formations—while now and then enormous blocks of igneous rocks of various structure obstruct the canyon. If one climbs the surrounding mountains, then the eye descries the bleak wilderness of an immense rocky labyrinth. As the setting sun lets its light play on the bare, multicolored mountains and calls up thousands of tints of violet and amber, red and yellow, as though by a stroke of magic, then you would fancy viewing a dream image, and, forgetting everything, one gazes ecstatically at the endless sea of mountains—an image of repose and immobility.

We are accommodated in the adobe dwelling of Mr. M., the manager of the smelting works, because the *Mohave* has once again steered to Cottonwood to fetch a second supply of wood for the smelting furnaces. On the afternoon of the 16th, it is oppressively hot, and the wind we had been hoping for, which was supposed to take us in a small sailboat to Black Canyon situated fifteen miles upstream, did not appear. The following day a strong wind blows from the south, filling the air with sand; it has been accompanied by rain showers. The temperature has dropped considerably, and all day long the sun only once illuminates the gray landscape surrounding us. We visit the silver mine, which is west of the mill at the end of the canyon in the mountains. At the rim of the canyon arise some gigantic earthen pillars of conglomerate with a rock block as a capital—mute testimony to the effect in these regions of the periodic heavy rainfall.

On the morning of May 18 we again board the *Mohave,* setting our course for Cottonwood Island, which we reach after a two-hour journey. Having arrived here we must follow our southern course in a different way because the steamer now heads northward again to the Virgin River, a right tributary of the Colorado, to fetch mountain salt. With Mr. Howard, Captain Polhemus, superintendent of the steamboat line, and an Indian, I take my place in a rowboat, and during the scorching hot afternoon we sail down the river in swift journey to Fort Mohave, which we reach $3^{1}/_{2}$ hours later (a distance of ca. fifty miles). During the journey I could not help but think admiringly of Powell and Thompson, who in 1869–1872, as the first scientific travelers, carefully investigated the entire upper course of this river with its tremendous canyons and dreadful rapids and revealed to the world of science a wonderland of geological phenomena.[90] Little did I suspect that a couple of months later I would have the privilege of being with an expedition of Mr. Thompson's for a short time.[91]

·····

Notes

1. In October 1878 José Guillermo Carbó (1841–1885) was named military chief in Sonora; shortly afterward he ousted Governor Mariscal. In 1881 Carbó was named commander of the military zone comprising Sonora, Baja California, Sinaloa, and Tepic. *Diccionario Porrúa de Historia, Biografía y Geografía de México,* 2 vols. (Mexico: Porrúa, 1970), 1:360.

2. Alfredo Laurent, a studio photographer in Guaymas, Mexico, ca. 1882–1883. During a tour of Sonora he photographed Apaches who had been captured after escaping from the San Carlos reservation in Arizona.

3. HtK 1885: See *Tijdschrift van het Aardrijkskundig Genootschap,* vol. VII, pp. 122, 123.

4. HtK 1885: See the illustrations in *Revue d'Ethnographie,* vol. I, pp. 31, 32. A close comparison of these objects with those I have in my possession has brought me back to the opinion that these are not of Guaymas Indian origin. Moreover, most of the objects reported by the Smithsonian Institution were illustrated and described by me. See *Tijdschrift van het Aardrijkskundig Genootschap,* vol. VII, p. 121. HtK 1889: The animal effigy, cut from white stone with a greenish shade, probably representing a turtle and apparently an Indian fetish, was described and illustrated by me (fig. 31/32) in the *Revue d'Ethnographie* of Hamy, vol. 6, 1887, pp. 234–38. This fetish, which really does represent a turtle (*Sphargis coriacea* [= *Dermochelys coriacea,* leatherback]), is now found in the Ethnographic Museum of the Trocadéro in Paris. See my "Sur quelques objets Indiens trouvés près de Guaymas (Mexique)," loc. cit., and *Annual Report Smithsonian Institution* 1883, pp. 21 and 24.

5. At the time of Ten Kate's travels, the Seris occupied the arid central coast of Sonora as well as the Islas Tiburón and San Esteban in the Gulf of California. Although Seri, as a language, is generally assigned to the Hokan stock, it is often classified as an isolate. Nearly half of the 500 to 600 Seris were killed during the Encinas War (ca.1855–1865) with 250 to 300 living in scattered bands in the early 1880s. Thomas Bowen, "Seri," in *Handbook of North American Indians: Southwest,* ed. A. Ortiz (Washington, D.C.: Smithsonian Institution, 1983), 10:230–49.

6. The Opatas of central and eastern Sonora spoke two languages: Teguina, or Opata proper, and Eudeve. The Opatas lived in mission towns in narrow but fertile valleys, well watered by permanent streams. Seemingly eager converts to Christianity, they allied themselves with the Spanish against the Apaches. In the early nineteenth century, however, they were involved in several revolts against Mexican authority, which led to the demise of Opata culture and the assimilation of the group. Spanish replaced Opata by the mid-nineteenth century. Thomas B. Hinton, "Southern Periphery: West," *Handbook,* 10:319–22.

7. During the 1870s the American authorities attempted to settle various Apache tribes, scattered throughout Arizona and New Mexico, primarily onto the San Carlos reservation in southeastern Arizona. Because the land was hot, malarial, infertile, and lacking in game, the Apaches hated it. During the 1870s there were repeated breakouts by disgruntled bands, which proceeded to raid, plunder, and massacre in the Southwest, then flee to Mexico. The most important escape, however, occurred in 1881, when Chiricahua Apache bands under the leadership of Juh, Nana, and Geronimo (augmented by additional breakouts in 1882) concentrated in the Sierra Madre. From here they also carried out raids in Mexico. (See chapter 5 for a fuller discussion of specific events, incidents, and leaders.)

8. HtK 1885. People who search for mineral-bearing sites—be it for precious metals, copper, or coal.

9. Pinart, "Voyage en Sonora," *Bulletin de la Société de Géographie* 20 (1880):203.

10. Formerly a Spanish ranch, Calabasas was converted in the 1850s into quarters for American troops, only to be abandoned in the 1860s. In the 1880s, when there were rumors the branch line of the American railway would pass through here, the settlement grew again. When Nogales was instead chosen, the site was abandoned. W. Barnes, *Arizona Place Names* (Tucson: University of Arizona Press, 1960), 315.

11. *Echinocactus horizonthalonius,* eagle's claw cactus.

12. This fort, named after Brigadier General Lorenzo Thomas, was established in August 1876 on the site of the present-day town Geronimo but moved in 1878 to the site of the present-day town of the same name. Robert W. Frazer, *Forts of the West* (Norman: University of Oklahoma Press, 1965), 12.

13. A group of Yumans—said to be of Yuma, Mohave, and Yavapai mixture—who occupied an area of the Colorado River south of the Yavapais before most were moved to the Rio Verde reservation (Arizona) in 1873 and then to the San Carlos reservation in 1875. According to Gatschet, they spoke a dialect of Yavapai. Albert S. Gatschet, "Tulkepaia," in *Handbook of American Indians North of Mexico,* ed. Frederick Webb Hodge, 2 vols. (Washington, D.C.: U.S. Government Printing Office, 1910–12), 2:836.

14. Julius Froebel, *Seven Years Travel in Central America* (London: R. Bentley, 1859), 493–94. Froebel (1805–1893), a German radical republican, fled to America after the failure of the 1848 revolutions in Central Europe. During the 1850s he traveled widely in North and Central America and published the account of his journeys, *Aus Amerika,* 2 vols. (Leipzig: J. J. Weber, 1857–58), translated as cited above. *Dictionary of National Biography* 22 vols. (London: Oxford University Press, 1885–1922), 5:644–46.

15. This site was first visited by Fathers Kino and Salvatierra in 1691 but only developed into an important mission at the end of the eighteenth century under Franciscan control. The church Ten Kate refers to was built between 1790 and 1822. Because of constant Apache raids, the mission was abandoned around 1840. H. R. Lamar, *New Encyclopedia of the American West* (New Haven, Conn.: Yale University Press, 1998), 1199.

16. The presidio of San Ignacio de Tubác was established in 1752 to protect missions and peaceful Indians of the area but later relocated in Tucson. A military post was reestablished there in 1862 and permanently abandoned in 1868. Frazer, *Forts,* 13.

17. Sahuarita Ranch became the center of a small settlement (school, post office, stage station) with the ranch house becoming a hotel, which served the stage line in the early 1880s. Barnes, *Arizona Place Names,* 347.

18. HtK 1885: One-eighth of a dollar; this term is in vogue only in the Southwest.

19. Yuma was linked to the Southern Pacific Railroad in 1877. Marshall Trimble, *Arizona: A Panoramic History of a Frontier State* (Garden City, N.Y.: Doubleday, 1977), 131–32.

20. Fort Yuma was established in 1850 to monitor the Yuma Indians and as a military supply center. It was abandoned in May 1883, right after Ten Kate's visit, as the railway obviated the need for a supply depot. Frazer, *Forts,* 34–35.

21. Loew, "Wheeler's Expedition durch das südliche Californien im Jahre 1875," *Petermann's Geographische Mittheilungen* (1876), 22:411.

22. Francisco Garcés (1738–1781) was sent as a missionary to the Province of Sonora in 1768. From his station at San Xavier del Bac, he made four expeditions to points along the Gila and Colorado rivers

between 1768 and 1774. By early 1781 the Mission of La Purisima Concepción (across the river from contemporary Yuma) and the town and mission of San Pedro y San Pablo de Bicuñer, five leagues upstream, were officially established. On July 17–18, 1781, the Indians rebelled, killing over 100 Spaniards, including Father Garcés, and another seventy-four were captured and later ransomed. *Dictionary of American Biography*, 23 vols. (New York: Scribner, 1943–1973), 4:132. James Officer, *Hispanic Arizona, 1536–1856* (Tucson: University of Arizona Press, 1987), 57.

23. José Maria Cortés y de Olarte, *Views from the Apache Frontier: Report on the Northern Provinces of New Spain*. trans. John Wheat, ed. Elizabeth A. H. John (Norman: University of Oklahoma, 1989), 102. Cortés (d. 1811) was a military engineer who served on the Spanish northern frontier from 1796 to1799.

24. John Russell Bartlett (1805–1886) headed the U.S.-Mexican boundary survey between 1850 and 1852 and published an account of his work: *Personal Narrative of Explorations and Incidents in Texas, New Mexico, California, Sonora, and Chihuahua Connected with the United States and Mexican Boundary Commission During the Years 1850, '51, '52, and '53*, 2 vols. (New York: D. Appleton, 1854). Amiel Weeks Whipple (1817–1863) was a surveyor in an 1849 boundary commission survey on which he made observations in the area around the junction of the Gila and Colorado rivers. He later joined the Bartlett commission. Francis R. Stoddard, "Amiel Weeks Whipple," *Chronicles of Oklahoma* 28 (1950):226–34.

25. Many of the peoples Ten Kate discusses in chapter 3 are Yuman speakers, including, south to north, the Cocopa, Quechan, Mohave, and Pai. Of these the Quechan were and are popularly known as "Yuma." Ten Kate is in error regarding population figures. Whipple's actual estimate was 3,000. A. W. Whipple, Thomas Eubank, and William W. Turner, *Report upon the Indian Tribes* (Washington, D.C., 1855), 17, 18. The Quechan ("Yuma") population is estimated to have been 4,000 at the time of Spanish contact but declined to about 3,000 due to European diseases and increased warfare. The decline continued, reaching 2,000 in 1872 and 1,100 to 1,200 in the 1880s. See Robert L. Bee, "Quechan," in *Handbook: Southwest*, 10:97.

26. The Quechan (Yumas) occupy an area near the confluence of the Gila and Colorado rivers, their aboriginal territory now divided between the states of Arizona and California. Accounts of the Quechan, 1780–1860, portray them as growers and gatherers rather than hunters who occupied a number of scattered settlements or rancherias that shifted location seasonally. Warfare against the Cocopas (south) and the Maricopas (east) appears to have been economically motivated: slaves could be traded for horses or other goods. Bee, "Quechan," in *Handbook: Southwest*, 10:86–98.

27. HtK 1885. A cloth covering the sexual organs, the perineum, and the crack in the buttocks, which is fastened in front and in back by a loincloth or belt.

28. George Catlin (1796–1876) was one of the first artists to visit the trans-Mississippi frontier and paint Indians from various tribes. He also authored *Letters and Notes on the Manners, Customs, and Conditions of the North American Indians*, 2 vols. (London, 1844; repr., New York: Dover, 1973), which presented a highly favorable and romanticized portrait of Native Americans. William H. Truettner, *The Natural Man Observed: A Study of Catlin's Indian Gallery* (Washington, D.C.: Smithsonian Institution Press, 1979). For illustrations of the kind Ten Kate is referring to see vol. 2, plate 252.

29. This is in essence a variant of the hoop and pole game played through the continent north of Mexico. Stewart Culin, *Games of the North American Indians* (New York: Dover, 1975), 420–527, 526 for the Yumas.

30. Heinrich Balduin von Möllhausen (1825–1905), a German traveler, artist, and author, made several journeys in the American West, often as a member of U.S. government expeditions. After his return to Germany, he became a celebrated author of adventure novels with the West and Indians as their central themes. Andreas Graf, *Der Tod der Wölfe: Das abenteuerliche und das bürgerliche Leben des Romanschriftstellers und Amerikareisenden Balduin Möllhausen, 1825–1905* (Berlin: Duncker und Humblot, 1991). The incident Ten Kate refers to is noted in Möllhausen's *Diary of a Journey from the Mississippi to the Coasts of the Pacific with a United States Government Expedition,* 2 vols., trans. Percy Sinnett (London: Longman, Brown, Green, Longmans & Roberts, 1858), 2:260.

31. *Prosopis juliflora* (Swartz) DeCandolle, true mesquite; *P. pubescens* (Bentham, Tornillo).

32. C. D. Forde, *Ethnography of the Yuma Indians* (Berkeley: University of California Press, 1931), 114, suggests this was *Sporobolis airoides* (Tarr), "a grass which seeds plentifully and flourishes in this region on alkaline soils."

33. *Neotoma floridana,* eastern wood rat.

34. HtK 1885: I could persuade only a single Yuma to let me measure his height. This one was 1.75 meters tall. Most of his tribal compatriots, however, were evidently taller.

35. HtK 1885: The three Indians whose heads I could measure had indices of 82, 89, and 89.

36. His Indian name was Scared Eagle. See also note 39.

37. HtK 1885: What is recounted here is generally applicable to the Yuman languages. See A. S. Gatschet, "Der Yuma Sprachstamm," *Zeitschrift für Ethnologie* (1877), 365.

38. Although he had earlier fought against the Americans, Pascual was appointed chief of the Yumas by the local military commander, Captain Samuel Heintzelman, in 1852. Celebrated as a cunning but valiant warrior, Pascual also proved to be an excellent judge and administrator. He died in 1887. For a photograph see Robert L. Bee, "Quechan," in *Handbook: Southwest,* 10:94. Eugene J. Trippel, "The Yuma Indians," *Overland Monthly* 13 (1889):567. See also Amiel W. Whipple, *The Whipple Report,* repr. ed. (Los Angeles: Westernlore Press, 1961), 58, 63.

39. Miguel actually succeeded Pascual in May 1887. Pascual's son did not want the honor of being chief, as this would have interfered with profitable commercial activities. Trippel, "Yuma Indians," 568; also cf. Pieter Hovens, "The Yuma Indians: A Comment," *Journal of California and Great Basin Anthropology* (1985), 7 (2):270–71.

40. HtK 1885: Humboldt already indicated how primitive peoples have geographic names only for things that could be confused with others. The Orinoco, Amazon, and Magdalena are simply named "the river," while the Indians use separate names for the smaller tributaries. *Ansichten der Natur,* 1849, vol. I, p. 254.

41. Prior to their confinement on reservations, the Maricopas, a Yuman-language group that numbered about 350 at the time of Ten Kate's journey, occupied the Gila River Basin in western and central Arizona. According to Maricopa traditions, they once lived along the Colorado and then migrated east. This migration, however, would have occurred well before white exploration. Henry O. Howard and Marsha C. S. Kelly, "Maricopa," *Handbook: Southwest,* 10:73, 75.

42. There is some question about the derivation of the term *otóchuh-ee,* which other investigators were not able to find among the Yumas or related tribes. Stewart Culin, *Games of North American Indians* (New York: Dover, 1975), 210.

43. HtK 1885: *Das kleine Kind vom Tragbett bis zum ersten Schritt.* Berlin, 1881, p. 53.

44. HtK 1885: *Roganti mihi quemdam Yuma-Indianum, quomodo horas vespertinas degere solerent, hic respondit: "Música y cazar mujeres"* (Hisp. = Lat. *Musica et venari mulieres*). *Apud Yuma (postea etiam apud Yabipai-) Indianos luce palam vidi juvenes puellasque alteram in alterius brachiis arctissimo amplexu jacentes, nec multum meum adventum morantes.* [When a certain Yuma Indian was asked on my behalf how they passed their evening hours, he responded: *"Musica y cazar mujeres"* (Music and chasing women). Among the Yuma Indians (later again among the Yabipai), I saw young men and women out in the open lying in the tightest embrace in each other's arms, practically oblivious to my approach.] Eds.: Ten Kate, like other nineteenth-century travelers and ethnographers, recounted indelicate matters dealing with sex, childbirth, and bodily functions in Latin, a language that women readers, then educated differently from men, did not usually understand.

45. HtK 1885: Someone who has a place of business where one can find items of every kind but primarily groceries, clothing, and tools. Almost everywhere in the West where there is a small settlement of whites, one finds a store to which a small bar is always attached.

46. This community near mining camps in the Castle Dome Mountain region was used to ship ores by steamer to Yuma. After 1883 mining diminished and the town eventually vanished. Will Barnes, *Arizona Place Names,* 320.

47. In the nineteenth century the term *Apache-Yumas* was applied to the Yavapai, a Yuman-language tribe that originally occupied parts of central and western Arizona. In 1865 the Talkapayi branch of the Yavapai settled on the Colorado River reservation, but in 1875 the bulk of the tribe was required to settle on the San Carlos reservation, created primarily for the Apaches. (See also references to "Apache-Yumas" in chapter 5). Sigrid Khera and Patricia S. Mariella, "Yavapai," in *Handbook: Southwest,* 10:38–41, 53.

48. Morton's Landing (briefly known as Pacific City), fifty-two miles north of Yuma on the Colorado River, was a landing place for freight for the Silver District and Reduction. Richard E. Lingenfelder, *Steamboats on the Colorado River, 1852–1916* (Tucson: University of Arizona Press, 1978), 80–81.

49. That is, John Lloyd Stephens (1805–1852), the American traveler whose visits to Yucatán and southern Mexico in 1839 and 1841 and whose travel accounts—*Incidents of Travel in Central America, Chiapas and Yucatán* (co-authored with Frederick Catherwood, many editions)—made the Mayan ruins well known in North America and Europe.

50. HtK 1885: These oblong, funnel-shaped clouds—really violent sandstorms—are a frequently occurring phenomenon in the arid deserts of the Southwest. Above all they arise when a stream of air forcibly descends into an immobile mass of air.

51. Ehrenberg was founded and named in memory of a German engineer, Hermann Ehrenberg (1816–1866), who came to Arizona in 1854 and surveyed the surrounding area, after his death by shooting. In 1870, before experiencing the decline noted by Ten Kate, Ehrenberg had about 230 residents. It is now a ghost town with nothing remaining but the cemetery and the barely visible foundations. Barnes, *Arizona Place Names,* 374; Dan Thrapp, ed., *Encyclopedia of Frontier Biography,* 4 vols. (Glendale: Arthur H. Clark, 1988), 1:455.

52. Olive City (also called Olivia) consisted of nothing more than a ten-by-twelve-foot house that later vanished. Barnes, *Arizona Place Names,* 382.

53. HtK 1885: "Agency" is the name for the place on an Indian reservation inhabited by some whites, where the government agent and some officials are established. Usually there is a post office, a store, and sometimes a school for Indian children.

54. HtK 1885: Vagabond, vagrant.

55. Hiram Price (1814–1901), a prominent Iowa banker and Republican politician, who had twice served in Congress, was Commissioner of Indian Affairs between 1881 and 1885. An advocate of Indian assimilation of the white man's ways, Price, during his tenure, forbade many traditional Indian customs such as plural marriage, dances, and shamanism. *Dictionary of American Biography* 8 (1):212–13; Robert M. Kvasnicka and Herman J. Viola, *The Commissioners of Indian Affairs, 1824–1977* (Lincoln: University of Nebraska Press, 1979), 173–79.

56. *Crotalus cerastes* (Hallowell), sidewinder.

57. See Jonathan Biggs, "Report of Agents: Colorado River Agency, Arizona," *Annual Report of the Commissioner of Indian Affairs* (Washington, D.C.: U.S. Government Printing Office, 1882), 1.

58. The Walapais, a Yuman-speaking group with close cultural affinities to the Havasupais and Yavapais, occupied an extensive territory in northwestern Arizona. In 1882, following a period of warfare and epidemic diseases, a U.S. army census counted 667, perhaps only a third of their number originally. Thomas R. McGuire, "Walapai," *Handbook: Southwest,* 10:25.

59. Chemehuevi and Southern Paiute are closely related Southern Numic (Uto-Aztecan) languages.

60. HtK 1885: *Buck* is what the Americans call every Indian capable of fighting. *Kid,* actually "young goat," is what they call a boy. Eds.: The term *buck* is now considered pejorative by Indians and whites alike but generally used in Ten Kate's day.

61. Cincinnatus Hiner Miller (1839–1913), who took his pen name from the famous California desperado Joaquín Murietta, was the author of several volumes of poetry, evoking romantic images of the West and celebrating its beauty and freedom—work highly regarded in his day but largely forgotten now. Lamar, *American West,* 732–33.

62. This is in essence the same as the Indian game described but using a slipper instead of pieces of wood.

63. *Salix longifolia* = *S. interior* (Rowlee), sandbar willow. This species, however, is not found farther west than Louisiana and Texas.

64. HtK 1885: I do not know the reason why Gatschet, op. cit., p. 344, says that the Mohaves eat no fish, but this assertion is utterly erroneous.

65. *Neotoma,* wood rats or pack rats.

66. HtK 1885: Milhau, in Gatschet, op. cit., p. 346, says that the Mohaves have no canoes!

67. HtK 1885: W. J. Hoffman, *Tenth Annual Report U.S. Geological and Geographical Survey,* 1876, p. 472, says—totally erroneously—that the Mohaves bury their dead.

68. HtK 1885: The Indians usually mean the American government or the president himself.

69. HtK 1885: Loew, *Petermann's Geographische Mittheilungen,* 1876, p. 421, calls the Mohave heaven *ohkeeáhmbohva.*

70. This is not so certain. A modern expert notes: "The translation of the name Mohave as 'Three Mountains' is a guess based on knowledge of the Mohave words *hamók* three and *ʔaví* mountain, but these words do not appear in *hàmakhá.v* and would in any case have to be used in the order *ʔaví.hamók* to give the meaning." Kenneth M. Stewart, "Mohave," *Handbook: Southwest,* 10:69.

71. HtK 1885: In Finland and Scandinavia, where I have since had a chance to visit such steam baths, they are a very old custom.

72. The second of three vessels with this name, the *Mohave,* launched in 1876, was the largest steamboat ever run on the Colorado and the only double-decker. In outward appearance the *Mohave* resembled the palatial riverboats of the Mississippi, but her interior furnishings were less ornate. She drew only

a foot of water, allowing her to make trips to the mouth of the Virgin River, nearly 600 miles up the Colorado. Richard E. Lingenfelder, *Steamboats on the Colorado River, 1852–1916* (Tucson: University of Arizona Press, 1978), 53, 56.

73. This landing point, founded around a mining settlement at the mouth of the Bill Williams River, was named after Francis Xavier Aubrey (1824–1854), a noted freighter. The site was largely abandoned shortly after its founding in 1864 and by the time of Ten Kate's visit consisted only of a post office, saloon, and hotel. Today no trace remains of this settlement. Barnes, *Arizona Place Names,* 202.

74. Ten Kate's account is at odds with more recent ethnohistoric reconstructions of the movements of the Chemehuevi people. The Chemehuevi originally ranged over the Mohave Desert, hunting and gathering, but earlier in the nineteenth century moved into the Colorado River at the sufferance of the Mohave. After war broke out between the two tribes in 1865, many Chemehuevi moved to the Colorado River reservation or into the Chemehuevi Valley. Kenneth M. Stewart, "A Brief History of the Chemehuevi Indians," *Kiva* 34 (1968):9.

75. Fort Mohave was established opposite present-day Needles, California, in April 1859 for protection against the Mojave and Paiute Indians. It was converted into an Indian school in 1890, which was abandoned in 1935 with all buildings later being demolished. Frazer, *Forts,* 11–12.

76. Loew, "Wheeler's Expedition durch das südliche Californien," 412.

77. HtK 1889:235. Dew cannot occur in the Southwest during the summer; in the winter, however, it is a common phenomenon, at least in s. Arizona.

78. Mohave chief Ampotumkwittelsjetsje or Potetsjitsje, son of Iriteba, was succeeded by his son Pete Lambert in 1890. Ampodqualachichi (Hide Behind the Dust) is mentioned in "Last Mohave Chief Dies," *Desert Magazine* (December 1847):31.

79. The Mohave chief Iretaba (1805–1874) was particularly friendly to whites. He had, for example, served as a guide to the Ives and Whipple expeditions in the 1850s. In 1863–1864 he traveled to Washington (via Panama) and even met President Lincoln. He continued to espouse friendly relations with the whites even in the face of serious personal provocation. Dan L. Thrapp, *Encyclopedia,* 2:704–5; Arthur Woodward, "Irataba—Chief of the Mohave," *Plateau* 25 (1955):53–68.

80. HtK 1885: I.e., *Clunis puellae* [girl's buttocks]. Among nearly all Indian tribes one finds people with names whose meaning, according to our notions, is obscene.

81. HtK 1885: From my anthropological observations I derive the following conclusions:

By far the majority of Mohaves are genuinely brachycephalic. Among the forty heads I measured, only three subdolichocephalic ones occurred. The average cephalometric index is 87.07, the maximum 98.82.

The majority of the Mohaves have the same cranial and facial shape as the one already briefly described for the Yumas. Among both tribes one finds a couple of types as well that deviate from the most commonly occurring ones—namely one with a bent nose and another with a turned-up nose. These types are frequently mingled and give rise to a number of varieties difficult to define.

Among the women there is more uniformity of type. Among them bent noses are quite rare. As a rule, their noses are straight and relatively shorter than those of the men. The nose root is frequently somewhat compressed.

The ethnic entities, Mohaves and Yumas, undoubtedly consist of the same anatomical multiplicities and can thus be regarded as physically identical. On the face of it, I would not be able to distinguish any Mohave from a Yuma, of whatever sex.

Most Mohaves are tall in stature. The average figure from thirty-eight measurements of both sexes is 1.73 m.

The complexion of these Indians varies between the numbers 22/30, 29/30, and 30 of Broca's chromatic scale; the color of the underarm between 36/37, 42/43, and 43.

Among both tribes, and later among the Maricopas as well, I saw some individuals who, though full-blooded Indians, had rather thick beards. A couple were of a type that recalled the Mongolian and that one could perhaps comprehend as a fourth type from these tribes.

Many Mohaves have very hairy legs, particularly lower legs.

82. HtK 1885: This was a part of the ceremony, somewhat vaguely described by Dr. Webb, that takes place during cremation.

83. HtK 1885: Loew, *Geographische Mittheilungen,* 1876, p. 421, reports a scalp dance of the Mohaves. Despite all my efforts I could learn nothing about it from the Indians.

84. General Charles H. Howard, of Glencoe, Illinois, was an Indian inspector in the Office of United States Indian Service, Department of the Interior, reporting to the Commissioner of Indian Affairs, 1881–1885. U.S. Department of the Interior, *Biographical and Historical Index of American Indians and Persons Involved in Indian Affairs* (Boston: G. K. Hall & Co., 1966), 4:240.

85. Situated nine miles above Fort Mohave, this miners' community was founded by Captain William H. Hardy (1823–1906). It numbered about twenty people in 1870 and still existed earlier in this century, but today few traces remain. Barnes, *Arizona Place Names,* 212; Thrapp, *Encyclopedia,* 2:615–16.

86. John Wesley Powell wrote: "This desolate land is the home of a great family of tribes speaking different dialects or languages of the same stock. They call themselves Nu-mes, Nu-intz, Nu-mas, Shi-ni-mos, Nu-nas, etc., all doubtless variations of the same word. We will call them Nu-mas." Cited in *Anthropology of the Numa: John Wesley Powell's Manuscripts on the Numic Peoples of Western North America, 1868–1880,* eds. Don D. Fowler and Catherine S. Fowler, *Smithsonian Contributions to Anthropology,* no. 14 (Washington, D.C.: Smithsonian Institution Press, 1971), 5.

87. See note 59.

88. Ute (including Southern Paiute) and Comanche are Numic (Uto-Aztecan) languages.

89. El Dorado City, Nevada, at the mouth of El Dorado Canyon, was a frequent destination of the steamboat *Mohave.* The area became the scene of the great Colorado River Rush of 1862, following the discovery of rich silver lodes in El Dorado Canyon in the spring of 1861 and of gold placers in Laguna de la Paz soon after. Lingenfelder, *Steamboats,* 31.

90. HtK 1885: *Exploration of the Colorado River of the West and Its Tributaries,* Washington, 1875. Eds.: John Wesley Powell (1834–1902), one of the most celebrated western explorers and scientists, undertook two epochal journeys down the Colorado, in 1869 and 1871. Later he was for many years head of the U.S. Geological Survey and the Bureau of Ethnology. Almon Harris Thompson (1839–1906), Powell's brother-in-law, accompanied Powell on the second expedition. Between 1871 and 1878 he mapped the Colorado River region. In 1879 he became chief geographer of the United States Geological Survey, where he continued working until his death. William H. Goetzmann, *Exploration and Empire* (New York: Knopf), 530–76. J. Cecil Alter and Herbert E. Gregory, "Diary of Almon Harris Thompson," *Utah Historical Quarterly* 7 (1939):3–140, esp. p. 5.

91. See chapters 6 and 7.

CHAPTER FOUR

From the Colorado to the Pima Indians

GENERAL HOWARD DEPARTS THE NEXT MORNING FOR LOS ANGELES in California, while I leave the fort with a military ambulance—my destination being the terminus of the still unfinished Atlantic and Pacific line. After a dusty ride of nearly five hours, we reach a camp of linen tents and wooden barracks. This place is christened with the name "the Needles" and is a station-to-be along the new rail line. At night I spread out my blanket in a little corner of the "French restaurant," otherwise linen tent, where one can obtain bad whiskey and even worse food. The next day I go a couple of miles farther with a buckboard to reach the construction train, which, after a twelve-mile ride, brings me to a point whence a passenger and freight train runs to Albuquerque in New Mexico.

The landscape surrounding us can perhaps be best described as follows:

Sandhills to right of them
Sandhills to left of them
Sandhills in front of them[1]

At 5 P.M. I reach Kingman, a small frontier town, and find accommodations with "Colonel" S., who has a store. Up to now I have forgotten to mention that the number of people in the United States bearing titles is legion. Among any hundred middle-aged men, at least twenty are "colonel," "major," "captain," or "judge": "generals" are rarer. Every citizen who had led an irregular unit during the war, even for a brief period, has officer's rank. And even though a number of years have passed since these ephemeral corps commanders shone on the battlefield—whether in reality or in their imaginations—they are quite intent on being named by their titles, whether they run a store, a bar, or a miserable rancho. One should not assume that a judge needs to be DCL [doctor of civil law] or even BCL [bachelor of civil law]. Everyone who is chosen by the vox populi and called upon to serve as judge in a court case can exercise jurisprudence. As a rule, these gentlemen educated in the law are "good judges of whiskey." Not being a man of the profession, I must withhold judgment about their other qualifications.

Kingman, an insignificant complex of white linen tents and wooden sheds—all told, certainly occupying less place than a Dutch fair—is situated in a high valley, whence far to the south and east the eye discerns for the first time again mountains covered with pine trees. Before long I am called to a poor "judge," who is bedridden from severe pneumonia in one of the tents, though I come just in time to witness the final hours of his mortal struggle.

Near Kingman is a small encampment of Hualapai Indians. They are genuine loafers, whiskey-drinking beggars whose squaws engage in prostitution. With a young Hualapai buck, the "colonel's" mule driver, and another Indian I head on foot one warm morning to another Hualapai camp in the mountains, about ten miles south of Kingman. Here one finds grass and numerous varieties of *Opuntia* in bloom, while white, yellow, red, and blue flowers scattered among the grass reinvigorate one's eye and the gentle southern breeze wafting against one is laden with fragrant odors. When one has seen nothing but arid, drab deserts for weeks on end, the view of the verdant landscape is doubly attractive.

The narrow and barely accessible Indian footpath, which leads across brown sandstone mesas and through crevices, makes for an exhausting walk in the scorching sun. All of a sudden, in the spacious grassy valley, the wretched hut of Leve-Leve, the chief of the Hualapais, stands before us.[2] Leve-Leve is hunting, but I do encounter his son-in-law, a couple of squaws, and two children. The hut is actually nothing more than a shelter of paloverde branches and twigs standing in a half circle, over which some pieces of old canvas and a couple of Navajo blankets are spread. Leve-Leve's son-in-law is an intelligent Indian with whom I can converse because he understands a little English. I pose various questions to him, and this is basically what he tells me:

There are approximately 700 Hualapai or Walapai, that is, "Forest People," and although they are supposed to have a reservation (where it actually is not even the Indian inspector himself knows!), they are scattered far and wide in northwestern Arizona.[3] Among other places, they have encampments around and near Mineral Park, Hackberry, and Peach Springs, mining camps, and frontier towns, where they are becoming more and more demoralized by civilization, otherwise known as whiskey and venereal disease. Until a few years ago they displayed an indomitable obstinacy in opposing white settlement and cost the Americans, both troops as well as settlers, many a struggle. In particular, Cerúm or Seroom, a chief still alive, was the soul of the resistance. Due to the occupation, however, of their best lands by the settlers and the growing scarcity of game, the Hualapais, hungry and discouraged, eventually had no choice but to seek government support, which they were provided with during the winter months of 1879–81.[4] The Hualapais are now poorer than ever, but they struggle as best they can to provide their own sustenance, supporting themselves through their own efforts. Their primary food is the root of mescal *(Agave)*, which they call *wee-áhl*. After that, there is the fruit of a yucca species *(maynáht)* and grass seeds *(celay-a)*.

The latter are collected by the squaws with the *áh-váhjuh*, a tool woven from young twigs, which is held in the right hand while they move along the grass stalks and toss the seed in a small basket, which they hold in their left hand. From time to time this small basket is then emptied into a larger carrying basket. The mescal I enjoyed, to the Indians' immense satisfaction, was sweetish. Their water jugs *(sowáh-ah)*, which often hold several liters, consist of tree twigs and are covered with a thick coat of red resin. They are carried with handles made of horsehair. The Hualapais prepare fine blankets or cloaks *(coohooluh)* of rat skin, which they exchange with the Mohaves and other tribes. Their footwear closely resembles that of the Pah-Utes. Most Hualapais wear the white man's attire more or less in its entirety, but they have long loosely hanging hair, sometimes held together, in the men's case, by a red or purple headband. Although these Indians recall the Mohaves in appearance, they have shorter and wider faces, and some individual physiognomies, as was later evident, recalled the Apaches. They, too, are smaller, more slender, and less handsome than the Mohaves.

Having returned to Kingman, that evening I take a seat on the train to Ash Fork and from there take the mail coach to Prescott. After being taken by rail through a secluded stretch of land where yuccas appear in profusion, the next day at sunup I find myself in Ash Fork, a frontier town like hundreds of others. Here I am in the heart of northern Arizona, an area that has only been opened to the world in the last two years by the construction of the Atlantic and Pacific Railway. Grass-covered hills extend far and wide, alternately covered with lovely juniper trees, so-called cedars. To the southwest arises an isolated mountaintop, probably Mount Floyd, whose reddish-colored slopes are covered by clusters of dark firs. I have free time that evening and, with my Winchester in hand, I roam around among plains and hills, but the antelope I hope to encounter do not appear. But here, too, I again encounter turkey buzzards *(Cathartes aura)*, the hunter's inseparable companions.

At 8:30 P.M. I take a seat in an old covered wagon and make the journey to Prescott. The route, or what goes by that name, is indescribably bad, and all night long I am jolted every which way in the most ungentle fashion. In Chino, a post station, which we reach in the chilly early morning hours,[5] there are the endless rolling plains with *Juniperus* [juniper]. Then the mail coach rolls through a grassy high plateau, bounded off in the distance on both sides by granite rocks overgrown with pine trees. When I descry the snow-covered crowns of the San Francisco Mountains along the dusky horizon far to the northeast, I am vividly reminded of the Alps. After a sleepless night and a ride of about fourteen hours, I ride into the town of Prescott. The adobe houses, so drab and misshapen, have here given way to nice wooden dwellings, surrounded by a sea of splendid pine tree forests.

Prescott, which came into existence in 1864, is about 5,300 feet above sea level. It is a quiet, pleasant, rural community with about 2,000 residents and the principal town of the territory. Nearby is Fort Whipple, the headquarters of the troops stationed throughout Arizona.[6] The temperature here is magnificent. With deep breaths I take in the fresh mountain air, doubly bracing after the searing heat I have experienced the past few months.

The day after my arrival, I climb Thumb Butte, a steep rock, which rises above the dark forests a couple of miles west of Prescott. The peak is readily visible from the city, just like Granite Peak situated more to the north. At the southern foot of the gigantic fissured rocky cone consisting of andesite, at the spot where it turns into a wide plateau, I found the remnants of crude walls in three different places; these consist of stones loosely piled on top of each other, which could not be very clearly distinguished from one another, however. I presume that these crude ruins are the remnants of an Indian defense works.

On the morning of May 25 I leave for Phoenix, situated 126 miles south of Prescott. Except for the driver, again a "colonel," I am the sole passenger on the mail coach, this time a big red Concord coach. The landscape, through which the rugged, rocky road winds its way, consists of unbroken grass-covered mountains and sprawling pastures and continually descends until reaching Phoenix. At Big Bug,[7] a rancho, we have lunch. And at Bumble Bee,[8] a collection of houses and corrals at the entrance to Black Canyon, the garrulous old "colonel" leaves me to make way for another driver. The area around Bumble Bee, which is overgrown with mesquites and chollas, abounds in hares and rabbits. Over a terribly bad route—because it cannot be called a road—we follow the eastern rim of Black Canyon, which is approximately twelve miles long. The bandits, who so often make this chasm unsafe, fortunately leave me unmolested. The farther south we go, the more numerous become the columns of *Cereus,* and near Gillett, where I partake of a frugal meal, we reach a nearly flat terrain.

On the 26th, as the radiant morning sun floods the landscape with a stream of light, we are in a sandy plain covered with greasewood, bounded by barren hills. At Desert Station, eighteen miles above Phoenix,[9] we have breakfast, and four miles before we reach the last-named place, we move through an old irrigation canal, which the people of the *casas grandes* once used to water their lands. From there a long, sandy road leads through dense and luxuriant mesquite and álamo growth to Phoenix, which I have soon reached. With its lovely lanes of poplars with wide branches, with the houses of wood and adobe spread out between them, Phoenix has a pleasant appearance. Many Mexicans live there, and now and then one sees a Pima or Maricopa in the streets, teeming with saloons. It is dreadfully hot, and because I am weary from the long ride, I spend most of the day sleeping in my "hotel."

The next day I hire a buggy to visit the Indian ruins situated between Phoenix and Tempe. The first, a distance of one and a half miles from east Phoenix, is now barely recognizable as more than a ruin and consists of some heavy adobe walls buried under a pile of sand, while in the area nearby a number of painted potsherds and manitas can be found. The second rubble heap is about five miles farther east and somewhat sprawling. The description Hodge provided in *Arizona As It Is*[10] does not hold up any longer. The walls have now fallen into ruin, and the buildings' floor plan is difficult to recognize. Far and wide extend the drab heaps of crumbling walls, with thousands of potsherds,[11] frequently handsomely painted, strewn across the ground between them. Where an impressive Indian city once appears to have stood, nature has reasserted its claims, and dense batches of gray *Artemisia* brush glitter among the ruins.[12] Not far from there arises a gigantic volcanic cone, standing isolated in the plain overgrown with saguaros and paloverdes.

From Phoenix, I cross the Rio Salado with the mail coach that afternoon and then the Gila River where a Pima village, at the foot of the Sierra d'Estrella [*sic*],[13] rises above the sunny plain like a collection of anthills. Against my will I am forced to spend the night at Maricopa Station because I have missed the train to Tucson.[14] The following day, however, I make my entrance again into the dusty hotbed where the heat has become unbearable and the thermometer at noon registers 110°F in the shade. I leave it again as quickly as possible and on the evening of May 31 find myself in Casa Grande, whence I head to the Pima reservation the following day.

Within a few hours a two-horse wagon took me through a sandy flat covered with *Artemisia, Obione,* and saguaros to the agency, a short distance west of the post station Sacaton.[15] There are just a couple of buildings: a dwelling with two stories, a school building under construction, and the adobe dwelling of Antonio, the aged chief of the Pimas. Around them [are] a number of huts in the shape of flat beehives, in the main resembling those of the Papagos. Along the northern bank of the Gila, in the immediate vicinity of the agency (which is on the southern bank, however), extend the Indians' abundant grain fields. The government agent, Dr. Jackson, whose hospitality I enjoy for a week, promptly introduces me to Rev. C. H. Cook, a missionary, and two interpreters, Luis and Antonito, or—to call the latter by his Indian name—Hotontóahim (Evening Thunder), and I take turns going around among the various Pima settlements with them.[16]

The Pimas (or *A'kemorl-oohtam*) of Arizona, who are a part of the so-called Pimeria Alta (Upper Pimeria), share a reservation with the Maricopas along both banks of the Gila and another one, not as large, along the Salt River to the east of Tempe. Their number is estimated at approximately 3,900, that of the Maricopas at about 300.[17] Ever since one can recall, these Pimas have lived at peace with the whites, and for the overland mail travelers, who in former days traveled along this route to California, their villages served many times as a refuge against the hostile Apaches. Only during the recent Civil War, in which a number of allied Indians of various tribes participated, did the Pimas, too, fight in the southern camp—so I understand.[18]

Nearly all the Pimas had moved into their summer quarters and were living under roofs made of branches in the fields where they performed their work. Their dark "beehives" were nearly all abandoned, and nowhere did I find many Pimas together because they were scattered over great distances far and wide. At first sight one would never look for the brethren of the Mexicanized Papagos among these half-naked "savages." Only a few male Pimas are attired in "citizens' dress"; most go about unclad, like the Mohaves, or wear short colorful cotton shirts. The women wear a short skirt of dyed cotton, fitting tightly around their legs, and mostly a short white jacket recalling an Indian *kabaai* but with pouf sleeves. The men usually wear their hair after the fashion of the Mohaves in long, abundant braids hanging down their backs, which the older men sometimes take up and wind together with a colored cloth, giving the whole thing the appearance of a turban. Formerly the beautifully woven, colorfully dyed *kaywoot*[19] or head cloth was used, but the Pimas now find it easier to buy red or multicolored foulards in a store than to make a *giwud* by a slow, laborious process.[20] The women wear their hair hanging down over their foreheads, cut right above the eyebrows, while otherwise it is worn hanging loosely but not longer than approximately thirty centimeters. That of the bucks is more than twice as long.[21]

They try to enhance the luster of their hair by smearing a mixture of mesquite gum[22] and black earth on it. It is not uncommon for the young bucks to smear alkaline earth, so often found on the ground, over the hair on top of their heads. Sometimes the children have cut all their hair short on their temples, the top of their heads, and the nape of their necks, except for a few solitary locks. Most people of both sexes have blue tattoos on their faces, especially around the eyes. A horizontal stripe from the outside corner of the eye going across the temples often appears. Some young bucks smear their faces with a red dye, probably iron ochre, which they find in the mountains. As is the case for most Indian tribes, the Pimas are proud of their hairdos, and they will not shear them off at any price. In their case, too, the men put more work into their "toilette" than the women.

As regards the Pima [physical] type, there are two distinct types among them, in addition to transitional forms. The first, with handsome features, usually with a slightly bent nose, and of small or medium stature is the "redskin type" in its finest form. The second is large in stature with gross features, receding forehead, and often prognathous. Straight and, not uncommonly, slightly up-turned noses are often characteristic of this type. Generally the first type most often tends to be more brachycephalic, or at least mesaticephalic, than the second one, which is dolichocephalic.[23] The stature of twenty-three male Pimas I measured varied between 1.64 m and 1.83 m. Their complexion is, as a rule, identical to no. 30. The color of their arms or thighs matches the numbers 29, 30, and 43 of the chromatic scale.

If I had to choose between the beauty of the Mohave and the Pima women, then certainly I would bestow the palm of honor on the latter. I have seen girls and young women who, attired in European fashion, could easily pass for Spanish or Italian.

The Pimas still retain the beliefs of their fathers and, notwithstanding the more than eleven-year missionary work of Rev. Cook, not a single Pima has publicly converted to the Christian faith. But the worthy missionary is honored and loved, and when he preaches Sundays in the villages, a dense throng of Pimas stands listening attentively. How much influence his words have I am not in a position to say, however. But I will mention that drunkenness and immorality among the Pimas have increased during the most recent years. The people practicing the doctrine preached to them, of whom they so often see representatives in Phoenix and Casa Grande, are hardly in a position to make them form a high estimation of Christianity.[24]

The Pimas acknowledge a Supreme Being whom they call Chehwita-mahke (Earth Prophet),[25] but they worship his son Seuh-heu (Suhu, Sugh-ha), who survived a great deluge and repopulated the earth. Seuh-heu killed the evil spirit, after which he had to fast sixteen days to cleanse himself from the impure contact. Now he is in the land of the rising sun, where all good Pimas go after death. Siwanno, the descendant of Seuh-heu, led the Pimas to power and greatness, but disunity and powerful enemies led to their downfall.[26]

The Pimas believe that they were created in the land where they now dwell and have a tradition that part of their nation traveled southeast. Individual writers, such as Spring[27] and Pinart,[28] regard the Pimas as the descendants of the people who built the casas grandes, and the latter leaves open the possibility of their kinship with the Pueblo Indians. I have found nothing to corroborate this opinion. If I rightly recall, the Pimas themselves attribute the building of the casas grandes to the Onavas, a tribe in Sonora related to them.[29] Neither in manners and morals, nor language and appearance, do the Pimas have anything in common with the Pueblo tribes. The peculiar, pronounced brachycephalic skull shape with flat rear head, which one encounters so often among the Pueblos, I have not encountered among the Pimas and Papagos. The only skull I know of from a casa grande, discovered by Pinart, is distinguished, on the other hand, by the aforementioned characteristics.[30]

The Pimas seem to possess a clan system. At least they have "coyote gentes" and "buzzard gentes," *Pahn-kech-emk* and *Neuy-kech-emk,* perhaps because the coyote and the buzzard (or the eagle) warned the Pimas' ancestors that the great flood was imminent.[31] These gentes, or whatever one chooses to call them, are distinguished by the manner in which the child addresses its father. The Pahn call "father" *apáp* or *mahm,* the Nuey, on the other hand, *vahv,* while the common word for father is *awk* or *auk.* I remember reading somewhere—the source has slipped my mind—that the Pimas have a masculine and feminine language. That is incorrect; the differences are limited to just a couple of interjections.

During my journeys, following directions from the interpreter, I came upon a cave, which was high up on a mountainside consisting of lava, approximately eight miles to the northwest of the agency. In this cave, not far from the entrance, I found an oblong basket of yellow straw, which was clearly set down there on purpose. Opening the basket, I found inside a number of feathers tied together, bracelets and necklaces of beads, short arrows, bands or rings of sinew, along with some rags, for which it was impossible to give a name. Back in the cave, which was filled with a powerful ammoniac air, stood a bundle of old arrows, most of which had lost their tips. When I asked Evening Thunder whether this was the work of the Pimas, he at first denied this, but when I wanted to take the basket with me, he resisted, repeatedly muttering, "People come to visit." I had to use all my powers of persuasion to induce him to let me take the basket, but he made me promise that if anyone later asked for it, I would surrender it to that person without delay. And that is, indeed, what happened. A couple of days later an old Pima presented himself to me and asked for the basket back. When I handed it to him, his face brightened and, removing a couple of the objects from the contents, he looked at them with eager eyes and pressed them close to his heart. He allowed me to remove an item and keep the bundle of old arrows as well. Then he looked at me with a grateful gaze, shook my hand, and cheerfully departed with the basket under his arm, taking it back to where it belonged.[32]

As I later discovered, one quite often finds caves like these in the mountains of Pimeria Alta and Baja, and usually they are closely related to Indian legends. Not infrequently rock paintings, too, are encountered nearby.[33] In the small chains of granite hills, which spread out to the southeast of the agency, I found on the loose blocks of rock that covered some mountainsides an immense number of incised signs, already partially effaced by time. They were mostly human and animal shapes, very crude and primitive in design. Those here bear a close resemblance to the ones that Bartlett[34] depicts and that this traveler discovered along the Gila between Yuma and the Maricopa villages.

The Pima reservation has a large number of ruins of casas grandes and ancient irrigation canals, which apparently indicate how dense this area's population once was. These ruins fully resemble the ones encountered near Tempe, and here, too, an innumerable quantity of potsherds are strewn across the ground. As time passes, stone axes are becoming rarer because they are collected by the Pimas and put to various uses.

Ruins often seem to be the object of a certain awe on the part of the Pimas because I several times found some small heaps of stones, obviously of later origin, piled on top of each other around the collapsed walls. Between the stones lay broken-off branches of greasewood or bead ornaments. Hotontóahim could not explain why these ruins were revered. When I asked him about the meaning, the unvarying refrain was that he knew nothing about them.

While looking through these rubble heaps, I was nearly bitten by a rattlesnake, which lay coiled among the rocks. Disturbed in its sleep, it had already raised its head and unwound to angrily strike the person disturbing its repose. It took only a moment to jump back and fire both barrels of my hunting rifle at the monster. When the smoke cleared, an unrecognizable bloody mass marked the spot where the snake had been sleeping.

"Mexican Luis," the other interpreter, a Papago Indian from Sonora, was in many ways less withdrawn than Hotontóhaim and carried his love of "king dollar" so far that he even helped me steal a Pima skull. The method of interment among the Pimas differs markedly from that of the Papagos because they dig a deep pit and lower the body in a sitting position while the space remaining is filled with branches and stones. Finally, a pile of sand and bundles of sticks is heaped on top of it. The skull I got hold of, however, was not buried in the usual manner.[35] Because the person to whom it had belonged had been killed by the Apaches, his corpse had been left lying there, and nothing but a pile of rocks was laid on top of that. In days past, when a Pima was slain in battle in the land of the Apaches, his body was cremated.

The belief in witches and bewitched persons is quite common among the Pimas, as it is among so many Indian tribes, and just before my arrival another sorcerer had been put to death. The Pimas have a superstitious dread of owls, which is probably related to the information Spring provided: that according to popular belief, an owl carries the souls of the dead to the other world.[36]

The Pimas' technology corresponds to that of the Papagos, but they have forgotten various arts too. Besides the kaywoot, the lovely head cloth, which one sees now and then, the Pimas wove fine blankets and made moccasins, where they now wear leather soles. As I already noted, their huts also matched the original Papago huts, but among the Pimas the entrance always faces east, perhaps because the land of *Say-ahluh-takkeah,*[37] the "rising sun"—their paradise—is in the east.

Since 1872, when General Howard concluded a mutual peace treaty with a number of tribes, the Pimas have halted their everlasting struggle against their archenemies the Apaches.[38] So homemade weapons, except for bows, are now very rare too. Like the Papagos, the Pimas used a club[39] made from hard mesquite wood and a round, thick leather shield *(káwats),* painted on the outside with colorful figures. After searching a long time I eventually found an old Pima who was willing to surrender his shield—for four dollars, I think—because the few elderly warriors who still had one did not want to part with the trusty companion and protector, bound up with the memory of so many campaigns.

The only Pima dance I got to see was the already described pascóla of the Yaqui Indians, which they have most likely learned from them because some of the Indians from this tribe live among the Pimas.[40] I pass over a number of minor details from the life of the Pimas and only wish to report that they are familiar with a game *(keensùh)* that greatly resembles the *otóchùh-ee* and *ootahá* of the Yumas and Mohaves. They also play a game like soccer with balls *(sónjikjo)* consisting of the gum from greasewood and sand.[41] The use of matches is not yet so widespread that it has completely displaced the fire stick *(áywaytahkoot),* which consists of the soft dry wood of the giant cactus.

As for the names of colors, I would just briefly mention that the Pimas, like many Indians, have just one and the same expression for *green* and *blue,* namely *stjötik* or *stjöthik,* but for "green" *wahsay,* "grass," is placed in front—thus "grass-blue" for "green." For "color" as an abstract concept, they have the word *óhotök.*[42]

A number of place names have been borrowed from the Pima language. Besides "Styukson" (Tucson), already mentioned, we find "Ariz(s)on-a," "little spring"; "Arivaca" from *ari,* "small," and *vac (bac),* a type of grass, the latter word being found in "S. Xavier del *Bac*" and probably in Tu-*bac.* In addition, "Arivaypa," "small fountains," from *vaypa,* plural of *bávia,* "fountain"; "Arituava," probably from *toeák,* "mountain," "hill," a word that we encounter in *tsjoemakákork* (Tumacácori) and a name that signifies "unequal" or "bent peak."[43] The Gila River is called *A'kemorl,* "stream," by the Pimas, from *morl,* "flow," "stream."[44] The Casa Grande ("de Montezuma") they call *wak, wakh,* or *wahki,* that is, "ruins."[45]

Of the tribes they are familiar with, the Pimas call the Maricopas *Oöpáp* or *Ohpáp;* the Apaches, Návajos, and Hualapais together *Ope, Ohp;* the Yumas, *Yoom;* the Mohaves, *Náksat;* the Chemehueves *Ah'alakát,* "small bows"; the Pah-Utes *Auölasús,* "mescal shoes"; the Onävas, *Tsjoefkwátam,* "hare eaters."

Of the Maricopas, I was able to see only isolated individuals and thus will refrain from describing them. These Indians must be very backward—at the same time lazier, dirtier, and just as primitive as the Pimas. Some of them live in the same huts as those of the Pimas.[46] They cremate their dead.[47] In outward appearance they closely correspond to the Yumas. I also saw some individuals who were of the very hirsute type found now and then among Yumas and Mohaves. The Maricopas call themselves *Pipátsje,* "people." They call the Pimas *Techpás* and the Pápagos *Techpamais.* The Gila River they know by the name of *C'has* or *Gas (ch* acute).[48]

On the morning of June 8, I said farewell to the agency and with a buggy headed to Walker's Ranch, about fifteen miles east on a sandy plain blanketed with mesquite, *Obione,* and *Artemisia* brush, to visit the well-known Casa Grande in the area nearby. Mr. J. D. Walker is one of the few whites who speaks the Pima language fluently, and a stay of more than twenty years in this area has gained him the unlimited confidence of the Pimas, for whom he was an excellent counselor in many difficult cases.[49] Much of the information I provided above regarding the Pimas I owe to Mr. Walker.[50]

No writer who has written about antiquities of the American Southwest has failed to mention the Casa Grande, the so-called red house *(Chichilticale)* of Montezuma.[51] In 1540 Coronado, on his memorable journey from Culiacán to the "Seven Cities of Cíbola," visited a building that he called Chichilticale and that can hardly have been anything other than the present-day "Casa Grande." Castañeda provided a fleeting description of it.[52] But Father Mange, who visited this place in 1697 with Father Kino, was the first to provide a comprehensive description of it.[53] Between the Casa Grande as Father Mange saw it and the Casa Grande of today, however, is a vast difference because during the two intervening centuries the walls have deteriorated considerably.

Approximately a mile to the south of Walker's Ranch, in the yellow, sandy plain among the mesquites, arises the abandoned ruin, which is seventeen meters wide and twelve meters deep while the current height is approximately fourteen meters. The walls are 1.10 to 1.20 meters thick and consist of a kind of fine adobe, as hard as cement. The entire surface of the walls, both on the inside and the outside, is completely smooth and has a distinctive faint reddish tinge, which was probably added after the completion of the structure.

One now finds only a hint of two stories. Of the round wooden beams from a variety of pine trees supporting the ceilings, scarcely a single one can still be found. The ground plan consists of five rooms of roughly equal size, three of which are situated in the middle of the building and one each on the north and south sides. The three middle rooms running parallel to the longitudinal axis of the building are interconnected, while the outermost two of these rooms each has an exit to the outside—just like the north and south rooms, which form a right angle to the longitudinal axis of the casa.

On the east side, a short distance from the main building, stand the remnants of a heavy adobe wall, while a little farther, on the southern perimeter, stand two similar higher walls. On the northeast side are various rubble heaps buried under the sand, indicating the place where buildings once stood. In the area one can find potsherds scattered far and wide, many of which are painted. Now and then seashells, which have been worked on, can be found in the piles of earth. Obviously we are dealing here not with the ruins of an isolated building, but with those of an entire village, of which the Casa Grande is still the sole house that has not been ruined by the ravages of time.[54]

It cannot be said with certainty from which people these ruins originated, but for various reasons we can assume that the present-day Pueblo Indians are the closest relatives of the "Casa Grande builders."[55]

That the name "House of Montezuma" is utterly incorrect is fairly obvious. The Casa Grande has nothing in common with the Aztecs or their king Montezuma—although that is a popular belief of sorts among the Americans and appears in print in trashy popular works such as those of Cozzens,

Hodge, and Hinton.[56] The name *Chichilticale,* an Aztec word meaning "red house," and that of Montezuma were given to the ruins in question by the first Spanish explorers who came from Mexico. For those familiar with only the most important Indian civilization, the Tolto-Aztecan, it was quite natural that, in encountering vestiges reminding them of what they had observed in Mexico, they would think of the Aztecs and connect Aztec names to their discoveries.[57]

I spent the night in Mr. Walker's hospitable home and the next morning, June 9, left in his company for Florence, ten to twelve miles east of the rancho.[58] The area around Florence is one of the most fertile regions of Arizona. Rolling fields of alfalfa grass, corn, and wheat—interrupted by stout, shady cottonwoods and willows—line the southern bank of the Gila River. Far to the northeast, dimly visible through the warm trembling layers of air, the Pinal Mountains, so abundant in mines, rise up along the horizon.

Florence, which has nothing in common with the capital of Tuscany other than its name, recalls Phoenix because of its sandy streets planted with cottonwoods with adobe houses as well as its scorching heat, but it is smaller and more tranquil. Mexicans comprise a considerable part of the population. With every footstep one encounters Papagos in the streets, who have a small camp south of the city not far away. In addition, one encounters a few Yaquis in Florence. The Gila flows above the city, a quarter of an hour's walk away, between low sandy banks overgrown with willows.

I stayed just a few hours in Florence and in the afternoon took the mail coach leaving for the Casa Grande station. We pass Adamsville and Sanford, small "towns" that are totally abandoned,[59] like La Paz and Olive City along the Colorado, and, after a dusty ride of four hours through the sandy torrid plains, reach Casa Grande, which I leave the following morning on the train to Tucson.

Then I spend four days with my old friend Berger and the Papagos of San Xavier, four days rich in sport. I also commit grave desecration again—and on June 16 have returned to Tucson with my stolen booty—two intact skulls.[60]

*****

Notes

1. After Alfred Lord Tennyson's "The Charge of the Light Brigade" (1854), stanza 3.

2. Leve-Leve, identified as the Walapai "peace chief," played a prominent role in Walapai–U.S. government relations beginning in 1869. Henry F. Dobyns and Robert C. Euler, *The Walapai People* (Phoenix: Indian Tribal Series, 1976), 45–47.

3. The 1882 army census lists 667 Walapai. This is one of the few instances when official bureaucratic sources and Indian sources agree on the number of tribespeople. Pieter Hovens, "De Walapai Indianen van Arizona," *De Kiva* 29 (1) (1992):1–5.

4. The Walapais first came into contact with Anglo-Americans in the 1850s. Conflicts with settlers came to a head after the discovery of gold in Prescott and the influx of prospectors. The war Ten Kate refers to lasted between 1867 and 1869. Not only Cherum but Leve-Leve, too, played leading roles. The Walapai were given their present reservation only in 1883, which perhaps explains Ten Kate's confusion about its location. Thomas R. McGuire, "Walapai," in *Handbook of North American Indians: Southwest,* ed. A. Ortiz (Washington, D.C.: Smithsonian Institution, 1983), 10:25–37; Hovens, "Walapai Indianen," 2–5.

5. Chino was four miles west of Seligman at the head of the Big Chino Valley. Barnes, *Arizona Place Names,* 92.

6. Fort Whipple was established in December 1863. Designed to protect the nearby gold-mining districts, it had various locations near Prescott. It was finally degarrisoned in 1913. Robert W. Frazer, *Forts of the West* (Norman: University of Oklahoma Press, 1965), 14–15.

7. So named because miners who first entered the area encountered walnut-size bugs by a nearby creek. Barnes, *Arizona Place Names,* 334.

8. Bumble Bee, in present-day Yavapai County, got its name from prospectors who in 1863 discovered a bumblebee nest full of honey. The settlement was a stage station in Ten Kate's day and a town of about sixty even as late as 1948, but today the site is totally abandoned. Barnes, *Arizona Place Names,* 336.

9. Ten Kate errs. This is not the Desert Station, which was established on the Butterfield Overland Stage route in late 1858 and also served as a stop on the Prescott-Ehrenberg stage line. In the area mentioned by Ten Kate was a place called Desert Well. The canal Ten Kate saw was probably in Cave Creek or possibly New River. Barnes, *Arizona Place Names,* 179; on Hohokam canals, see J. B. Rogers, "Prehistoric Cultural Variability in the Hohokam Northern Periphery," in *Hohokam Settlement and Economic Systems in the Central New River Drainage, Arizona,* eds. D. E. Doyle and M. D. Elson (Phoenix: Soil Systems Publications in Archaeology, 1985), 4:249–96.

10. Hiram C. Hodge was the author of *Arizona As It Is; Or, The Coming Country* (New York: Hurd and Houghton, 1877).

11. HtK 1885: J. R. Bartlett, *Personal Narrative of Explorations and Incidents in Texas, Etc.,* New York, 1854, vol. 2, depicts a number of old potsherds he found along the Gila, closely matching the ones mentioned above. Eds.: This site is probably La Ciudad, which was partially excavated in the 1920s by Frank Midvale. It is now under St. Luke's Hospital in Phoenix. David Wilcox, *Frank Midvale's Excavations at La Ciudad* (Tempe: Arizona State University Archaeological Field Studies 19, 1987).

12. HtK 1889: As appears from the investigations of the Hemenway Expedition, the Indian ruins between Phoenix and Tempe are entirely of the same type as those of Casagrande, near Florence, and come from the same race or people.

The "valleys"—actually nothing but shallow furrows winding their way through a sandy plain—of the Gila and Salado [Salt] rivers teem with clusters of such ruins. Especially those that are between Tempe, Mesa City, and the Maricopa Mountains are significant. Eds.: This site is now known as Pueblo Grande, the most important Hohokam site in the Salt River Valley. David Wilcox, "Pueblo Grande in the Nineteenth Century," in *Archaeology of the Pueblo Grande Platform Mound and Surrounding Features,* eds. C. E. Downum and T. W. Bostwick (Phoenix: Pueblo Grande Museum Anthropological Papers 1, 1993). On Ten Kate's fieldwork during the Hemenway Expedition, see Pieter Hovens, "Ten Kate's Hemenway Diary, 1887–1888," *Journal of the Southwest* 37 (1995):635–700.

13. The author later corrected this to Sierra de Estrella and added: "The Pima name for this mountain range is Kómert. Seen from afar, this mountain range is only bare, as was evident to to me from a visit in 1888, when I was able to observe it close up. The sparse vegetation consists primarily of saguaros *(Cereus),* cholla or choya, paloverde, and mescal, of which the last-named plant was collected here by the Apaches in former years. Grass, too, occurs because, according to the Pimas, the mountain sheep and deer can be found in this sierra. The rock that I noticed in various places was rough-grain granite" (HtK 1889, 235).

14. This was originally a junction point on the Southern Pacific Railway where passengers who wanted to travel to Phoenix or Tucson got off to transfer to stage lines. Barnes, *Arizona Place Names,* 299.

15. Now Sacate. Barnes, *Arizona Place Names,* 305.

16. Dr. A. H. Jackson served as agent to the Pimas and Maricopas, 1882–1884. *Annual Report of the Commissioner of Indian Affairs* 1883::5–7. Charles H. Cook (1838–1917), born as Karl Koch in Germany, emigrated to the United States in 1855 and after becoming a missionary moved to Arizona in 1870, where he established a mission among the Pimas. Cook lived among them for forty-one years and compiled a dictionary of their language. Minnie A. Cook, *Apostle to the Pima Indians: The Story of Charles H. Cook* (Tiburon, Calif: Omega Books, 1976).

17. HtK 1889: On the reservation along the Gila River no Maricopas have been living among the Pimas for years now. Although according to the government reports the Maricopas live together with a number of Pimas on the reservation along the Salt River, there were, at least in May 1888, no Maricopas on the reservation. Instead, their three most important villages lay outside the boundaries of the area set aside for them, two villages even several miles SW of Phoenix and thus a considerable distance from the reservation.

    The government report estimate of the number of Maricopas as being about 300 in 1882 is probably too high. During my short stay among this tribe the number, according to my estimate, amounts to about 200. Eds.: Agent Roswell G. Wheeler reported the Maricopa population in 1882 to be 331; Agent A. H. Jackson reported, "Maricopas off of reservation (actual number)" to be 574 in 1883. *Annual Report of the Commission of Indian Affairs* (1882):9; (1883):5.

18. During their brief occupation of Tucson in 1862, a Confederate detachment under Major Sherod Hunter took various supplies from the government agent at the Pima villages. Hunter's efforts to persuade the Pimas to join the southern camp were unsuccessful, however. L. Boyd Finch, *Confederate Pathway to the Pacific* (Tucson: Arizona Historical Society, 1996), 125–30.

19. Spelled *kéwoet* in the Dutch original. Dean Saxton, Lucille Saxton, and Susie Enos, eds., *Dictionary: Papago/Pima–English, O'othham–Mil-gahn; English–Papago/Pima, Mil-gahn–O'othham,* 2nd rev. & enl. ed. (Tucson: University of Arizona Press, 1983), give the spelling as *giwud.*

20. The *giwud* consisted of a double-weave headband in blue, red, yellow, and white cotton with braided fringe at the ends. It was worn over the hair, which was long and twisted into rolls. Paul H. Ezell, "History of the Pimas," *Handbook: Southwest* 10:158, fig. 10.

21. HtK 1889: The *kaywoot* is worn not only around the head but is used as a sash at the same time. Also small children are tightly fastened to the carrying board with the *kaywoot,* and in former times, when the Yumas still wore white blankets, the *giwud* served as a belt. In the Pima village Komertkewóótsje, by the Sierra de Estrella along Gila Crossing, I managed to see one of these ancient blankets. This was very coarse, woven from cotton, and white in color.

22. HtK 1885: The bark of the mesquites includes a gum, which in many respects is like the well-known gum arabic. For this reason the mesquites are also called gum trees.

23. HtK 1889: From my 1888 anthropometric observations on 279 Pimas (men, women, and children), it appears that in round numbers 42% are dolichocephalic, 21% mesatichephalic, and 35% brachy-cephalic. From my second visit to the Pimas, it also seems to me that there are more types occurring among them than those observed in 1883. Thus the Mongolian-Apache type occurs several times among them, as does the Pueblo type with compressed nose root and prognathism of the upper mandible. This last type is rare, however. Many children display Mongolian facial features. Eds.: See also Ten Kate's "Somatological Observations on Indians of the Southwest," *Journal of American Ethnology and Archeology* 3 (1892):119–44, for a detailed anthropometric study of the Pimas and the Southwestern tribes, conducted in 1887–1888 as a member of the Hemenway Southwestern Archeological Expedition, and Pieter Hovens, "Herman ten Kate's Hemenway Diary, 1887–1888," *Journal of the Southwest* 37 (4) (1995):635–700.

24. Over the long run Cook's influence does seem to have been more significant than Ten Kate suggested. "An enduring and pervasive consequence of the missionary couple's work [i.e., of Cook] was the elimination of large areas of Pima supernatural concept, and Pima religious culture took on a strong flavor of Presbyterian Christianity." Paul H. Ezell, "History of the Pima," *Handbook: Southwest,* 10:158.

25. HtK 1889: *Chehwita-mahke,* better pronounced *Tsjerwúrtemahke.*

26. For other versions of the Pima original myth, see Frank Russell, "The Pima Indians," *Annual Report of the Bureau of American Ethnology* (Washington, D.C.: U.S. Government Printing Office, 1908), 26:206–38.

27. HtK 1885: *Globus* 1877, p. 282. Eds.: The article in question is John A. Spring, "Die Pima Indianer in Arizona," *Globus* 32 (1877):281–83, 295–99. Virtually the same article was later republished in English: A. M. Gustafson, ed., *John Spring's Arizona* (Tucson: University of Arizona Press, 1966). The Swiss-born Spring (1845–1924) was a soldier and educator in frontier Arizona.

28. HtK 1885: *Bulletins de la Société de Géographie de Paris,* 1877. Eds.: This article has been translated: Alphonse Louis Pinart, *Journey to Arizona in 1876* (Los Angeles: Zamorano Club, 1962), 37.

29. The Onavas, who take their name from a village of this name, are a lowland division of the Mexican Pimas. Timothy Dunnigan, "Lower Pima," *Handbook: Southwest,* 10:217–29.

30. HtK 1885: Cf. De Quatrefages and Hamy, *Crania Ethnica,* p. 465, and *Revue d'Anthropologie,* 1884, pp. 490, 491. HtK 1889: Later investigations of A. Bandelier, Cushing, and myself have brought to light that the Pimas, at least in an ethnographic sense, appear to be more closely related to the Pueblo Indians than I first suspected. In the very ancient customs and practices of the Pimas, individual items (e.g., the use of feathered prayer sticks and sacrificial caves, agreement in symbolism) recall the Pueblos. Moreover, the Pima language apparently must be included among the Shoshone family, to which various other Pueblo tribes, in addition to the Moquis, probably still belong.

The hut construction of the Pimas most likely represents the first stage of Pueblo house construction, what Cushing has called "basket-adobe work." Thus one could properly regard the Pimas as Pueblo Indians who stagnated in their development. What has been said above regarding the Pueblo type occurring sporadically among the Pimas seems to strengthen this opinion. But the present-day, as well as the prehistoric, Pueblo Indians are significantly more brachycephalic than the Pimas. In January 1888 I dug up a skull (fragment) near the Casa Grande, which was brachycephalic, just like the one found by Pinart. Furthermore, the hundreds of skulls excavated by the Hemenway Expedition from the ruins of Los Muertos, Las Acequias, Los Guanacos, and other ruins of the Casa Grande type and at Hálonawan, near Zuni, are for the most part brachycephalic. See Eenige mededeelingen omtrent de Hemenway-expeditie, *Tijdschrift van het Aardrijkskundig Genootschap,* vol. VI, 1889.

31. HtK 1889: The coyote and buzzard gentes of the Pimas are in all probability not clans, but phratries.

32. Pima grain baskets were made of wheat straw but, more typically, were round in form. Yucca is the more frequent material used in all other Pima baskets. Russell, "Pima Indians," 131–47; Bert Robinson, *The Basket Weavers of Arizona* (Albuquerque: University of New Mexico Press, 1954), 30–31.

33. HtK 1889: The cave described here is undoubtedly an offertory cave, and my statement that in the nearby area red paintings are frequently encountered is confirmed by the fact that, according to Cushing's investigations, by far most red paintings or petroglyphs are rituals, which are related to the offerings or are of later date. The Hemenway Expedition found the ritualistic petroglyphs distributed from Central Arizona to Papagueria.

In April 1888 I found an interesting offertory cavern of the Papagos high in the Baboquivari Mountains. There, too, I found numerous arrows, but these were in a close circle, sticking vertically into the ground and thus not bound together like those in the Pima grotto. Eds.: See also Hovens, "Ten Kate's Hemenway Diary," 673–77.

34. HtK 1885: Op. cit. vol 2.

35. HtK 1885: I have described this skull in the *Revue d'Anthropologie,* 1884, pp. 486 ff.

36. John A. Spring, "Die Pima Indianer in Arizona," *Globus* 32 (1877):295.

37. HtK 1889: *Say-ahluh-takkeah;* better yet, *Siáree-táhkjo,* whereby the *r* is pronounced.

38. In 1872 General Otis Oliver Howard negotiated a peace treaty ending the decades-long war between the U.S. government and the Chiricahua Apache chief Cochise. Howard also made peace between some Apaches and their enemies, the Pimas and Papagos. See David Roberts, *Once They Moved Like the Wind: Cochise, Geronimo, and the Apache Wars* (New York: Simon & Schuster, 1994), 98–102; Dan L. Thrapp, *The Conquest of Apacheria* (Norman: University of Oklahoma Press, 1967), 111.

39. HtK 1889: The Pima name for *club* is *sónjik* or *sóntjik.*

40. HtK 1885: *Sunt e.g., plerumque feminae gentis Yaqui, quae apud Pimas munere obstetricis funguntur. Feminae parturientes cruribus passis humi sedere solent, alia ei femina abdomen premente. Partus fit in parvo tugurio, ramis hunc ad finem sedulo exstructo, segregato ab habitatione proprie dicta. Eodem modo feminae menstruantes segrari solent.* [There are, for example, several women from the Yaqui tribe who serve among the Pimas in the office of midwife. Women giving birth are accustomed to sitting with their legs stretched out on the ground, with another woman pressing their abdomen. Childbirth occurs in a small hut, expressly built for this purpose, segregated from the dwelling. In the same fashion, menstruating women are customarily segregated.]

41. For a more detailed description, see Stewart Culin, *Games of the North American Indians* (Washington, D.C.: 24th Annual Report of the Bureau of American Ethnology, 1907), 670–71. Ten Kate gave his field notes on Indian sports and games to Frank H. Cushing and Stewart Culin when they were organizing the Smithsonian Institution's contribution to the International and Cotton States Exhibition in Atlanta in 1895. Culin subsequently used Ten Kate's data for his monumental monograph. Hovens, *Herman ten Kate en de Antropologie der Noord Amerikaanse Indianen* (Meppel: Krips, 1989), 110.

42. The word for *color* in O'odham (Pagago/Pima) is given as v.t. *mahsith, mahsithchuth*; n. *mahs, mahschu, mahstag.* Saxton, Saxton, and Enos, *Dictionary: Papago/Pima–English,* 77.

43. Compare Barnes, *Arizona Place Names* (1935), 138, 457.

44. HtK 1889: *Morl.* This word is also pronounced *meurl* and *murl.*

45. HtK 1889: The Casa Grande is also called *Síwannoki* or *Síwanki,* "house of Síwanno." With *Wahki* is meant more strictly speaking the ruin of "Casablanca" on the Pima reservation, ten miles NNW from Sacaton.

46. HtK 1889: The huts of Maricopas, indeed, match those of the Pimas in the main, but the entrance is mostly square and supported as well as covered with slender beams.

47. The Maricopas are Yuman-speaking people who traditionally occupied locales along or near the Gila River and its tributaries in what is now southern Arizona. The Maricopas shared much in common with both the Quechan and the Mohave: patrilineal or bilateral descent and emphasis on personal dreams, cremation, and floodwater agriculture. The languages of the three groups are closely related. And as Ten Kate's narrative makes clear, the material culture of the Maricopas was in essence the same as that of the Quechan and the Mohaves. These similarities reflect common origins and sustained contact over a long period. Henry O. Harwell and Marsha C. S. Kelly, "Maricopa," *Handbook: Southwest,* 10:70.

48. HtK 1889: The Maricopa name for *Gila River* is also pronounced "Chasj."

49. John D. Walker (1840–1891), after his discharge from the army in 1864, moved to Tucson and became a trader to the Pimas. He developed a thorough knowledge of their language and became so immersed in their culture that he later became a Pima chief. By the time of Ten Kate's visit he had also served in public office and achieved success in mining. Dan L. Thrapp, *Encyclopedia of Frontier Biography,* 4 vols. (Glendale, Calif.: Arthur H. Clarke, 1988–1994), 3:1499.

50. HtK 1885: Among other things, Mr. Walker provided me the figures for eighty-seven length measurements of male Pimas, from which I find an average figure of 1.753 m; max. 1.854, min. 1.52.

    Practically everything Bancroft says about the Pimas in his *Native Races* is derived from information from Walker. Eds.: That is, Hubert Howe Bancroft, *The Native Races of the Pacific States of North America,* 3 vols. (New York: Appleton, 1875), 1:530–33. Bancroft (1832–1918) was a prodigious collector of manuscripts and author and editor of thirty-nine volumes of histories of western America, Mexico, and Native American cultures. Jo Tice Bloom, "Hubert Howe Bancroft," in *Historians of the American Frontier,* ed. John R. Wunder (New York: Greenwood, 1988), 56–64.

51. The ruins at Casa Grande were built sometime after 1150, at the beginning of what archaeologists term the Classic period of the Hohokam, when people left the outlying settlements and concentrated in the large riverine villages such as Casa Grande. Walled compounds enclosing houses and flat-topped structures called platform mounds also, as here, sometimes included great houses. The Great House ("casa grande") Ten Kate visited and that is called Casa Grande today was completed before 1350. It was made of caliche mud and stood four stories high. Like other great houses,

Casa Grande was situated at the end of a major canal, and the village probably had a significant role in the maintenance and use of the irrigation system. David R. Wilcox and Lynette O. Shenk, *The Architecture of Casa Grande and Its Interpretation,* Arizona State Museum Archaeological Series no. 115 (Tucson: University of Arizona, 1977).

52. Pedro Castañeda accompanied Coronado on his southwestern expedition and authored the primary account of the journey. Coronado merely mentioned but did not describe Chichilticale, where Castañeda provides a few details. George Parker Winship, ed., *The Journey of Coronado, 1540–1542* (Boulder, Colo.: Fulcrum, 1990), 143–44, 177–78.

53. Juan Mateo Mange (1670–1727?), who was born in Aragon and emigrated to Mexico in 1692, accompanied Father Kino on major journeys, many of them to what is now Arizona, between 1694 and 1701. He was the author of *Luz de tierra incognita en la America Septentrional y Diario de las Exploraciones en Sonora* (1721) (Engl. trans. *Unknown Arizona and Sonora* [Tucson, Arizona: Arizona Silhouettes, 1954]). See pp. vii–viii for biographical information and *Diccionario Porrúa de Historia, Biografía y Geografía de México,* 2 vols. (Mexico: Porrúa, 1970), 2:1246.

54. HtK 1889: Contrary to the opinion of others, including most recently Alphonse Pinart (*Bulletin de la Société de Géographie de Paris,* 1877, p. 237) and myself, Cushing's investigation in 1888 has established that the Casa Grande does not actually consist of adobe, i.e., in the usual sense of a construction material in blocks, as adobe is prepared in wooden molds. Rather the Casa Grande seems to be constructed by means of "basket adobe" work, whereby a shell of wood and basketry was filled and covered with adobe made by hand and other pottery. This "adobe," used in the building of the casa, consists of a kind of natural cement, rich in alkalis, which the ground itself provides.

The Casa Grande was in all likelihood one of those "large citadel and temple buildings in the middle of groups of dwellings inside a space enclosed by walls." And the building complex, of which the Casa Grande was the center, formed one of those numerous urban groups of six or seven, which were based on a mythological-sociological division.

The Casa Grande is the most complete remnant of the typical "temple-citadel" of the Shiwi culture within the realm of the United States and is thus rightly regarded by Cushing as typical of the adobe ruins of the Southwest.

An old irrigation canal in the vicinity of the ruins is still clearly recognizable.

The people who once built the Casa Grande belonged to the Shiwi race, whose most complete descendants are the present-day Zunis. Cf. "Eenige mededeelingen omtrent de Hemenway-expeditie," *Tijdschrift van het Aardrijkskundig Genootschap,* vol. VI.

Close, systematic excavations in the Casa Grande group of ruins should certainly provide surprising results. The Hemenway Expedition will probably bring the task to completion one day.

55. There has been considerable debate about the origins of the Hohokam as well as the "abandonment" of the Salt-Gila Basin by the end of the Classic period (ca. 1350). A "gap," a lack of cultural continuity, appears to exist between the end of the Hohokam Classic period and the peoples and cultures encountered in the area in the mid-1500s. However, the present-day Pueblo Indians appear to be physically and cultural separate from the "Casa Grande builders," the Hohokam. Linda S. Cordell, *Prehistory of the Southwest* (New York: Academic Press, 1984), 69–70; Patricia L. Crown, "The Hohokam: Current Views of Prehistory and the Regional System," in *Chaco and Hohokam: Prehistoric Regional Systems in the American Southwest,* eds. Patricia L. Crown and W. James Judge (Santa Fe, N.Mex.: School of American Research, 1991), 135–57.

56. Samuel Woodworth Cozzens (1834–1878), a Massachusetts lawyer, had served as a district judge in New Mexico from 1858 to 1860. He was the author of *The Marvelous Country; Or, Three Years in Arizona and New Mexico, the Apache's Home* (Boston: Lee and Shepard, 1873). The work in question seems to have been drawn from sources other than his own experience, has a fictionalized style of narrative, and is characterized by some inaccuracy. Thrapp, *Encyclopedia,* 1:333. Richard Josiah Hinton (1830–1901) was the author of *The Handbook to Arizona* (San Francisco: Payot, Upham, and Co., 1878). On Hodge see note 10.

57. HtK 1885: When Hodge, *Arizona as It Is,* New York, 1877, p. 180, says that the Pimas assured him that Moc-te-zu-ma built the Casa Grande, this says nothing for his reliability.

58. HtK 1889: According to later measurement with the odometer by one of the members of the Hemenway Expedition, the distance is exactly nine miles.

59. Adamsville was established by settler Charles Adams in 1866 and by 1870 had grown to 400 people. It was given the name "Sanford" by government authorities, but the local residents continued to call it by its old name—hence Ten Kate's reference to two towns. The town later declined and by now has completely ceased to exist. Barnes, *Arizona Place Names,* 289.

60. HtK 1885: These skulls, too, I described in *Revue d'Anthropologie,* loc. cit.

CHAPTER FIVE

Among the Apaches

IN TUCSON THERE WAS A MOOD OF EXCITEMENT
about the favorable outcome of General Crook's campaign against the Apaches, particularly after
the long uncertainty over the fate of his expedition. To better understand the situation, a brief ret-
rospect is in order.

In April 1883 the American authorities had made an alliance with their Mexican counter-
parts to do whatever possible to put an end, once and for all, to Apache hostilities, which had already
been going on several months. As a result, the celebrated Indian fighter General George Crook with
a column about 1,000 men strong, consisting largely of Apache allies, crossed the Mexican border,
heading from San Bernardino to the heart of the Sierra Madre.[1] This mighty range with its deep
chasms and dense forests, which arises like a natural fortress along the frontiers of Sonora and
Chihuahua, had always been the Apaches' refuge after their raids. Here in their colossal fortress,
where the white man had never set foot, they felt themselves secure. Little did they suspect that the
"gray fox" (General Crook) would head so far across the Mexican border, and they particularly
did not anticipate that one of their own, a captive warrior, would commit treason by showing him
their hiding place.[2]

After a single battle of minor significance and a march, which presented exceptional difficulties because of the condition of the terrain and its lack of trails, the Apaches' hiding place—situated
like an eagle's nest on the highest ridge of the mountain chain east of Babispe, roughly seventy miles
from the American border—was taken by surprise. Completely surprised and unnerved at the sight
of so many of their tribal compatriots in hostile confrontation, the Apaches soon gave up without a
struggle and surrendered. Although there were roughly 330 Indians in the rocky fortress, the number
of warriors amounted to barely thirty. Among them, however, were Loco, Nané [Nana], and Benito
[Bonito], chiefs whose names had filled the land with terror for so long.[3] Roughly eighty warriors
were absent. General Crook understood very well that if he wanted to be assured of a favorable

outcome, he had to have them in his hands too. So he let the Indians know that their lives would be spared if they saw to it that the still missing warriors, including the chiefs Juh and Geronimo, came and surrendered at the San Carlos reservation.[4] Nané accepted the terms, and before long the Apaches were on their way to San Carlos as prisoners, where I would be seeing them before long.[5]

Already on June 19 General Crook made his entry into Tucson and for a period of three days was regaled in a festive manner. On two different occasions I had the privilege of meeting with the general, and because my path led to San Carlos at the outset, I asked him if I could undertake more detailed observations of his war captives there. With a readiness one has come to expect in American officers, General Crook provided me with an excellent letter of recommendation to Captain Crawford, who would be arriving in San Carlos a few days later with his scouts, soldiers, and captives.[6]

To make my stay there as productive as possible, I arranged for the photographer C. Duhem, a Frenchman, to accompany me for a short time.[7] For the reasons already mentioned I had given up on photography myself. A few days passed as I arranged for packing and dispatching the collection assembled during my earlier journey and made the necessary preparations for the next one.

Finally, on June 25 we are ready, and I bid farewell to scorching hot Tucson. We follow the railway, by now familiar to me, to the Bowie station and, while riding, have the opportunity to observe a lovely mirage in the desert. Once my eye perceives the gleaming watery surface of a lake to the south. Along the misty banks, blending with the horizon and the desert sand, sway trees of various shapes and sizes. The rapid course of the train makes further observations impossible, and after a ride of nearly five hours we leave the car at twelve noon.

After much rummaging about, I hire a buckboard, which should take us to Salomonville on the Gila. A couple of hours later we are on our way under a downpour, cutting across the San Simon Plains in a northwesterly direction. The sandy plain, covered with mesquite and greasewood, is bounded on the right by the dreary, barren Peloncillo Mountains, which, according to Loew, consist primarily of basalt and rhyolite,[8] while on the left the Pinaleño chain extends outward from the railway to Graham's Peak with its densely overgrown slopes, which is already visible from a distance. The only animal we see is a coyote, which slinks around in the neighborhood of Billy's Wells, a miserable rancho, where we take our midday meal and water the horses.[9]

At midnight we continue the journey, but by our arrival at Salomonsville, which consists of just a few adobe houses, we find everything closed and not a living soul "on the street."[10] All our calling and banging on the doors and windows is to no avail, and there is nothing left for us to do but lie down on the ground in the corral, in the company of horses and sheep. The next morning Mr. Salomon, the master of Salomonsville, offers us breakfast and a vehicle to reach Fort Thomas. For six hours we trot along a dusty route, following the winding Gila, and by afternoon have reached the military post, which is just inside the boundary line of the Apache reservation, between barren mountains and mesas, in a plain overgrown with mesquite.[11]

Thomas is not a healthy place to stay. The Gila provides the only drinking water, which is brackish—likewise the source of malaria, the recurrent scourge of the garrison. From the commandant

I request and receive a military ambulance to go to San Carlos the next morning. The night is so oppressively hot that we cannot stay inside the sleeping quarters provided us and drag the cots outside. On the 27th at 6 A.M. we take our place in the ambulance hitched to four splendid mules, and again it moves ahead along the sandy, hot banks of the muddy Gila. Dense cottonwoods rise up now and then along the edge of the water, and the high pillar cactuses are the only vegetation adorning the arid slopes of the mountains, volcanic in origin. We see nary a living thing along the route before approaching the neighborhood of San Carlos, which we reach at 3 o'clock, covered with dust.

Already from afar the eye discerns the Indians' numerous branch huts and the soldier's white tents along the sprawling mesa, desiccated as an ash heap. In between and situated far apart [are] two large ugly buildings: the agency and the officers' quarters. The rigid, stern face of the government agent, "Judge" W., becomes even sterner when I hand over my letter of recommendation from the Indian Department. But however much he would have liked to, he dare not send us back: the letter is tantamount to an order. He points us to a large filthy room, where there is nothing to be seen but four white walls, wooden ceiling, and ditto floor. But that evening, when we want to find a pair of cots or something to wash up with, there is nothing. One of the employees—the carpenter, I believe—takes pity on us and brings what we request. But agent W. erred thinking he would intimidate us with this cool reception. Duhem and I stayed a full fourteen days at the agency. We had our headquarters in the filthy, windowless room and dined at his inhospitable table, where a crossfire of pointed remarks between the "judge" and the "colonel," his clerk, on one side and Duhem and I on the other usually kept the conversation lively.

The "judge" was the typical Indian agent in the worst sense: callous, rude, brutal toward his subordinates, and, last but not least, stingy. He hated and despised the Indians with all the fire of his Yankee soul and found total agreement in the "colonel," a vehement opponent of Negro emancipation besides, who responded in monosyllables. At the same time the "judge" was a shareholder in the trader's store, where his son-in-law was the trader.[12] Everyone who has done any reading about Indian policy will realize what this says about an agency, where at the same time there are warehouses of goods that must be distributed weekly to the Indians on behalf of the government.[13] *Brisons là dessus* [Enough said already].

If these gentlemen of San Carlos were far from pleasant, their manor was even less so. From the unsightly agency building made of adobe, with whose "guest quarters" my readers are already familiar, to the slaughterhouse, the stores, and the prison; from the former school building without doors, windowpanes, or benches to the officers quarters—everything is in a state of disrepair and decay, a vivid reminder of the ruins of Ures, Ehrenberg, and the like. The entire complex is situated at the edge of an arid mesa covered with volcanic rocks, at the foot of which the shallow, muddy Gila disgorges its syrupy mass of water.

One can see mountains on all sides, but most of them arid and unattractive to the eye. One's gaze is first arrested by the mesas, as pale as heaps of ash. Then mountains rise in the distance, of which the Triplets to the north, three steep basalt peaks, are the most prominent ones. To the southeast the mighty slopes of Mount Turnbull, blanketed with firs, rise up high above the heat of the Gila Valley, dominating everything and caressing the blue sky, with its peak garlanded with vegetation. Luxuriant cottonwoods grow along the banks of the river, though farther away—as they likewise do along the dry bed of the little San Carlos River coming from the north.

San Carlos is 2,400 feet above sea level. The summer here is terribly hot, and I experienced the most extreme hot weather of my entire journey in San Carlos. It was during the afternoon that the scorching desert wind sent its searing, howling breath across the mesa and drove thick swirling dust clouds ahead of it so that the thermometer registered 120°F. The site is an unfortunate choice for an agency. The water there is bad. Malaria is quite prevalent, and the site is in too remote a corner of the reservation. The Indians are not happy there, but to a certain extent they are also compelled to stay in the area to obtain their weekly rations. The extensive San Carlos or White Mountain reservation has hundreds of spots more suited for an agency than San Carlos.

That same evening of the day I arrived, I visited Captain Crawford, who received me with the greatest courtesy. His bronzed features still clearly bore traces of the severe travails he had endured. In fact, he had just arrived from Mexico three or four days ago with his captives and escort. That evening there was supposed to be a dance of the Chiricahua Apaches to celebrate a girl reaching puberty.[14] The Chiricahuas had their encampment along the wooded banks of the San Carlos River. Before long, in the company of some officers, we make our way through the darkness, guided by the glimmering of the campfire and the faint sound of voices reaching our ears. Eventually we press through the dense throng of Indian spectators, and a colorful, vivid scene astonishes us.

To the monotonous drumbeat and savage shouts of an equally monotonous, dull chant, a number of Indians, men and women, are dancing around a huge flickering fire, whose glimmering illuminates the bronze-colored dancers in the most fantastic manner. The men and women dancers are packed tightly together in small rows, mostly in groups of four with the upper arm against each other, while the forearms are stuck forward with the fists against each other and the elbow resting on the chest. They stand facing away from each other, with the understanding that in every row two walk forward and two backward. The rows move up and down at a brisk, skipping pace. At intervals this movement momentarily comes to a halt. Then the men walk toward the circle of musicians, and the women also separate themselves for a moment only to ask their partners a moment later for another round with a tap on the shoulder. The young squaw, as the principal personage of the festival, dances through the rows alone decked out in a fine leather costume, shuffling slowly, but buoyantly moving her feet forward. Nearly all the men have red cloths tied around their heads like a band. Some, like Nané, who stands calmly watching the dance draped in a colorful serape, wear huge Mexican sombreros. Their attire is further a colorful and unsightly medley of red and white cotton, with the men wearing a white loincloth. Both sexes cover their legs with high chamois leather boots.

The Indian character is difficult to comprehend. The same Indians who suffered a defeat shortly before and were, in fact, flushed out of their hiding place as prisoners danced practically every evening while they were on the way to their place of banishment.

The greater part of these Indians, mostly Chiricahua Apaches, had already been on the San Carlos reservation before, following the abolition of the reservation at Fort Bowie, where the followers of Cochise had been brought together following their defeats.[15] But in 1881 the Chiricahuas broke loose en corps, making their way to the Sierra Madre in Mexico. From this time on they repeatedly eluded the fierce pursuits, both of Mexicans and of Americans, but sometimes suffered heavy losses until, as we have seen, they were brought back to the reservation by General Crook about two years later. Among them, though, were some who had never been on a reservation and had known nothing but untrammeled freedom.

The next morning I took a walk in the area around the agency to orient myself and here will try to give my general impressions. The huts *(khonge)* of the Apaches, hundreds of which were situated in the area around the agency, are nothing but wretched tree branch roofs with a blanket or a piece of canvas draped over them. They sag so much in the middle that one can barely stand upright. One must bend over quite a bit to go inside through the entryway. If a family moves, then the hut is trampled and partially incinerated. The few household implements, consisting primarily of a couple of grinding stones and basketry jars, are loaded on horses or carried by the women in a carrying basket with a flat bottom.

As for the Apaches' outward appearance, perhaps one can assume they include three original main types, in addition to a number of intermediate forms, the result of mixing. Assuming the northern origin of the Apaches, the first type, which I must regard as the most ancient and most primordial because of its Mongolian features, is distinguished by broad, flat faces with blunt noses and tiny eyes. That women, over the course of time, better preserve the original type than men proves to be the case among the Apaches as well because one finds the Mongolian type more widespread among them than among men. With angular features and aquiline nose, the second type bring to mind the traditional "redskin" type. Finally, the third has a straight and somewhat upturned nose and further corresponds to the second type. It vividly recalls the types I observed among the Pah-Utes. The Apaches with Mongolian facial features are, as a rule, smaller and more heavyset in stature than the other two, which are distinguished mostly by a rather tall stature and slender body build. In large part, however, most Apaches do not display these three types in their pure form, but hybrid forms instead. Only through a large number of observations and comparisons did I later come to posit three original primary types, all three of which are most likely brachycephalic, however.

As a rule, the Apaches are slender, and the muscles of the trunk and upper extremities are feebly developed. On the other hand, the hips and lower extremities, however slender, have powerful muscles. Many of them are more bandy-legged, and the women often sit with their feet pointed inward. Their gait is distinctive and marked by a pronounced oscillation of the hips and elastic body movement, recalling the gait of the tiger.

The Apaches' facial complexion most closely approximates no. 30, the hands and arms no. 43. But there are some, especially among the more elderly, who have a much darker facial complexion,

7. Loco, Chiricahua Apache chief
(after a photograph by Constant
Duhem, August 1883).

such as nos. 29, 37, and 43 on the chromatic scale. Others have an exceptionally light skin color on their upper body and arms, like nos. 26 and 33.

There is something shy, but at the same time something fierce, about many of their physiognomies. Their more or less squinting gaze is often piercing and unpleasant. It is not uncommon to find men with just one eye, and "pearl in the eye" (leukoma), especially, is a commonly occurring affliction. Numerous warriors are covered with heavy scars. Loco showed me the traces of at least five terrible wounds. The left half of his face and head bore signs of a terrible trauma, and the light had gone out for good in his glassy left eye. One of his thighs was once lacerated by bear claws. The Apaches' teeth are of medium size, often irregular, and heavily worn.

The men wear their hair fairly short, parted in the middle of the skull and hanging down half length from the neck. A fiery red or purple head cloth in the form of a broad band holds the loosely hanging hair together and covers the forehead at the same time. The women wear their hair the same way, but without the headband. The children's hair, which hangs down in tangled, disorderly fashion, is often severely faded, sometimes to such an extent that it has an ash gray or pale blond color. For their marriage young girls wear a special head ornament consisting of an oblong piece of wood covered with leather, which is adorned with numerous brass tacks. In the middle, where the little board becomes narrower, it is wrapped with red cloth and fastened from behind to the hair at the back of the head, covering part of the neck. Nevertheless, despite all my efforts to get one of these maidenly insignia for my collection, the mothers steadfastly refused to allow their daughters to give them up, the reason being that no one but the young spouse could remove the ornament from their hair on their wedding night. Because an Apache marriage did not fit in well with my prospective plans, I abandoned further efforts and contented myself with making a sketch of the item desired.

The Apaches are polygamous, but adultery is nevertheless severely punished with the outraged spouse cutting off his unfaithful partner's nose. In their daily life, however, additional mistreatment, whether of women or children, does not occur. The Apaches generally have few children, a characteristic they seem to share with all North American tribes.[16]

As I have already noted above in passing, distinctive articles of clothing among these Indians are rather rare nowadays. I noted the handsome chamois leather shirts with painted figures and long fringes just a few times, and I bought one from a young warrior for ten dollars. Leather war hats or caps *(sjach, tsjach)* decorated with eagle or wild turkey feathers, whose shape vaguely recalls Roman helmets, are still worn now and then.[17] However, the high white leather boots *(khé)* with turned-up toes are in widespread use among both sexes, and only occasionally does one find Apaches wearing a pair of crude American shoes from the store. They also buy in the stores all the red and colorful cotton (calico), now making up the prime component of their attire. The Chiricahuas, who arrived from Mexico practically naked, hastened to buy a few hundred yards of cotton with the money they plundered and thereby clad their nakedness.

The Apaches have few ornaments, and these consist primarily of necklaces and bracelets of beads, red beans, and the bark of a certain plant called *yerba del manso* (*Anemiopsis californica*?) by the Mexicans.[18] This bark, which has the color of cork, is characterized by a distinct, aromatic fragrance and astringent taste and is also chewed by the Indians because they maintain it is good for their gums. Not infrequently they suspend a couple of small feathers or a tweezers of Berlin silver on the necklace, which they use for carefully plucking out their facial hair. An object one encounters among most American tribes and among the Apaches, too, is an awl of bone, wood, or iron used for preparing of footwear, clothing, horse gear, etc., and kept in a leather sheath, which is often handsomely decorated with beads, little tin bells, etc., and is worn fastened to the belt. Under normal circumstances the Apaches evidently paint themselves little, if at all. Nor is there much tattooing, this being limited to small blue figures on the face, sometimes on the forehead.

The original weapons of the Apaches are bow and arrows; a long lance, with the iron tip taking up to a third of the entire length; a club *(zendízj)* covered with leather and movable lash; and a round leather shield, which is sometimes painted and adorned with feathers.[19] All these weapons, however, were very seldom used in war because in recent years the Apaches have learned the advantage of breechloaders. Springfield rifles are therefore in widespread use. They have fewer Winchesters and other weapons. Many—young adolescents, for example—also have revolvers of various calibers. To no small extent the Apaches certainly owe to their excellent arms the success that so often crowned their war raids in recent years.

According to the government report of 1882, the number of Indians on the San Carlos reservation is estimated at 4,133, but only 3,114 of them are actually Apaches because the 324 so-called Apache Yumas and 695 Apache Mohaves are physically as well as linguistically distinct from them. This reservation arose approximately fifteen years ago, and during this time various tribes of Apaches, from New Mexico as well, were concentrated there. These Indians are divided into a number of small tribes and bands, some of which are not clearly distinguished, however. Not uncommonly these names are used only for Apaches from the same tribe, though living in different areas. But the number of synonyms easily leads to confusion too. The White Mountain, Sierra Blanca, or Coyotero Apaches dwell in the north of the reservation; they are the most numerous tribe and amount to about 1,400. The Tonto Apaches or Deldzjé are about 600, the San Carlos Apaches about 800. In addition, there are also Pinaleño, Arivaypa, and Mogollones Apaches, of which the former two probably must be included among the "San Carlos" Apaches, the latter among the Coyoteros.[20]

What the government reports mean by "southern" and "mixed" Apaches is a mystery to me. The agent himself did not know; neither was he familiar with the dwelling places of the other tribes just mentioned. All these tribes are more or less "mixed." The Chiricahuas, a separate tribe in the days of the Apache Napoleon, Cochise, now consist in large part of Apaches from various tribes, including Hot Spring Apaches from New Mexico—Mescaleros and Coyoteros, in particular. Perhaps originally the most indomitable Apache tribe, the Chiricahuas, the more their members thinned out, were replenished by so-called renegades from other tribes, and after its annihilation in 1880, the feeble remnants of Victorio's band, under Nané, joined the Chiricahuas as well.[21] Other Apaches within the territory of the United States are the Jicarillas, who number about 700 and are established on the Fort Stanton reservation with the Mescaleros, numbering 900,[22] and the Apaches farthest east who reside in the Indian Territory, numbering about 300. The Lipans have apparently ceased to exist as a tribe: some of these Indians are scattered in the Indian Territory and Texas and probably in northeastern Mexico as well.[23] From these figures it appears that the number of Apaches in the United States definitely does not exceed 5,500.[24]

There is perhaps no Indian tribe in all America—and in civilized Europe as well—that is more well known than the Apaches. They really are one of the most remarkable peoples of the western hemisphere. As far as tradition goes back until the present day, their existence has been marked by an indomitable spirit, strife, and plundering. I cannot help but feel a certain admiration for the handful of savages who made their way from the frozen north to the scorching deserts of Mexico, always fighting and always in movement, falling and rising up again, always holding out to the very end.[25] Unquestionably the Apaches have played an important role in the history of Mexico and the United States, and their name will live on long after the last of their warriors has gone to the "happy hunting ground."

To no small extent the Apaches owe their popularity to novels in which they, more than any other of their racial compatriots, play the hero's role. This brings me to a subject that maybe I should have discussed earlier: I am referring to the romanticism of the American wilderness, the romanticism we have come to know from the works of Cooper, Aimard, Ferry, Mayne Reid, and others.[26]

The romantic era in the West is over. The undefiled wilderness of former days has shrunk to a region so small that it does not contain enough game to ensure the hunting nomadic tribes their sustenance, as it once did. The fierce spirit, the power of the once mighty tribes has been broken for good, and nearly everywhere "civilization" has taken root. Driven toward the brink, the "sons of the wilderness" had little choice but to surrender and eat the bread of charity or struggle and starve. Many tribes long held out in the unequal struggle, persevering with the spirit of desperation. Their ranks diminished from year to year, however; their territory shrank more and more, and thus gradually emerged the condition that we now encounter among the Indians in the West. The majority of Indians are kept alive by rations from the government.

I believe that many conditions, such as the above-mentioned writers have depicted them, may have been true, and individual characters among the Indians and border denizens could correspond to the heroes of these novels. But let no one now harbor any illusions about finding much of anything recalling the dream images of days past. The harsh prose of stark reality grips the observer irresistibly, and disillusionment and disappointment follow one after the other. Only occasionally during my journey did I see images evoking memories of what I had read about as a boy.

Another issue concerns the fidelity of the topographical description in Aimard, Ferry, and Mayne-Reid. Naturally I leave Cooper out of consideration because the wilderness described by him at the present time comprises a couple of the most civilized states of the Union, and in the case of the other writers I will strictly confine myself to what I became familiar with from my own observation. From my comparisons I conclude that as to topography, Aimard merits the least, Mayne-Reid the most confidence among the three. I could best characterize their description of places as *preposterous*. Though based on earlier observation and knowledge once held, it displays the greatest confusion.

The description of the Indians' morals and customs is often preposterous as well. In Aimard's case, in particular, a limitless confusion prevails. Moreover, the way he deals with distances is amusing. Distances that are hundreds of miles on the map are easily covered in a day by the heroes of his novels. As I am writing, a couple of examples come to mind:

Near El Paso and along the Rio Grande there are no dense primeval forests where panthers dwell, nor were there ever any. The only vegetation one encounters is occasional *cottonwoods* along the banks of the river. Aimard, just like Ferry, fantasizes when he has bison appearing south of the Gila River. Aimard has the Sioux Indians do battle near Casa Grande, with forests and stone oaks spreading out nearby. That is roughly comparable to saying that reindeer are encountered in Lombardy and having Estonians lay siege to the Colosseum, which is surrounded by forests of dwarf birch. Somewhere Aimard mentions Chichimec ruins. One could just as well say that the Vandals and Huns once built fortresses, the ruins of which can still be found.[27] At no single spot, not even at its mouth, is the Gila River "two miles wide," as Aimard assures; at Yuma its width barely reaches a quarter of a mile. Nor have the Apaches ever occupied a village along the river consisting of "huge tents of bison hide." Nor are these Indians familiar with the "calumet," or peace pipe, and the custom of scalping.[28]

If the Apaches do have a warlike and rather unruly nature, the Americans and Mexicans, for their part, do nothing to soothe their nature but are always doing whatever they can to make them more excitable and distrustful. For the most part the American government has deliberately pursued, sometimes in good faith, an abominable policy toward these Indians. Because of the continual capriciousness and treachery of which they have time and again been guilty toward the Apaches, these Indians must be exonerated from much of the blame. As for the Mexican government, it has never exercised a policy toward the Apaches but simply regarded them as wild beasts.[29]

What is said here regarding Indian policy is generally valid, and one could name the following as the most important reasons for the never ending complications between whites and Indians: 1. The government of the Union not honoring treaties; 2. Fraud by Indian agents; 3. The infringement of Indian rights by the whites generally. I could fill a book enumerating the various misdeeds perpetrated by whites, with or without the complicity of the American government, not just against the Apaches but against all their racial compatriots.[30] A single case among many, which I draw from the excellent book of Manypenny, can serve by way of illustration.[31] I shall, indeed, have the opportunity to return to these issues in the course of my narration.

In February 1871 a young Apache chief with twenty-five followers came to Camp Grant, saying that they wanted peace and wanted to have a home because they had none with the troops constantly harassing them. A young officer, Lieutenant Whitman, the post commandant, advised the chief to go to the White Mountains and settle there. But he refused, stating that he was an Arivaypa Apache and wanted to live in the land of his fathers. Lieutenant Whitman then agreed he could stay and also assemble the rest of his band near Camp Grant. A short time later approximately 500 Apaches—men, women, and children—had gathered. Meanwhile the lieutenant had sent a detailed report to the military commander of his department with a request for instruction on how to deal with these Indians, who were impoverished, unclad, and starving. After waiting more than six weeks, the lieutenant's document was returned to him without any response because it had not been submitted in the proper format.

Meanwhile the Indians had been receiving minor rations from the fort in return for which they cut grass every day for the horses of the garrison. Their conduct was exemplary, and they were confident Whitman would help them. He grew sympathetic to them and in an official report expressed himself as follows: "I came to feel respect for men who, ignorant and naked, were still ashamed to lie or steal and for women who would cheerfully work like slaves to clothe themselves and children, but, untaught, held their virtue above any price."

On April 30 the same Indians fell victim to a vile massacre, perpetrated by a band of citizens from Tucson—Americans and Mexicans. The misdeed occurred before Lieutenant Whitman could prevent it. When he came to the site of calamity, the camp was aflame and the ground was covered with the dead, mutilated women and children. To give at least the appearance of his sympathy, he allowed the dead to be buried, and around evening those who had escaped from the bloodbath gradually emerged.

Many of the men—says Lieutenant Whitman—whose families had been killed, when I spoke to them and expressed sympathy for them, were obliged to turn away, unable to speak and too proud to show their grief. The women whose children had been killed or stolen, were convulsed with grief, and looked to me appealingly, as though I were their last hope on earth. . . . The camp was surrounded and attacked at daybreak. So sudden and unexpected was it, that no one woke up to give the alarm, and I found quite a number of women, who were shot while asleep beside their bundles of hay, which they had collected to bring in on that morning. The women who were unable to get away, had their brains beaten out with clubs or stones. . . . The bodies were all stripped. . . . I have spent a good deal of time with them since the affair. . . . What they do not understand is, that while they are at peace, and conscious of no wrong intent, that they should be murdered. . . . One of the chiefs said: "I no longer want to live; my women and children have been killed before my face, and I have been unable to defend them. . . ." About their stolen children they say: "Get them back for us; our little boys will grow up slaves and our girls, as soon as they are big enough, will be diseased prostitutes to get money for whoever owns them. Our dead you can not bring to life, but those that are living we give to you, who can write and talk, and have soldiers to get them back.[32]

Shortly afterward Lieutenant Whitman was removed from his post; he had shown too much sympathy for the Indians.[33] A year later General Howard returned to the place of misfortune. The Indians showed him the graves of their dead and what was left of their camp. They spoke of Lieutenant Whitman, their friend, and about their devotion to him and asked for his recall so that he could provide his support. This officer was resented, however, because he had so clearly expressed his abhorrence of this murder, a murder "approved by men of prominence and influence in the territory." General Howard denied the Indians' request.

This affair at Camp Grant [says Mr. Manypenny] is not an isolated case. Expeditions of the same kind have been often fitted out and set on foot, with results as merciless and barbarous, and men who claim to give tone to the actions of the communities in which they reside, have openly participated in them. Even the governors of territories have organized bodies of men to go out and hunt down the natives, with authority to kill them wherever found; to destroy their villages, take possession of their property as booty, and to receive a premium for all Indian scalps taken.[34]

I had better luck photographing and measuring the Indians than I had first anticipated, but it required patience and tact to persuade them to do this. I got the most help from a Mexican, Antonio Díaz, who had formerly been a war captive for twelve years among the Pinaleño Apaches and was now a government interpreter at San Carlos. He had great influence over them, and he was obviously feared. Without him I would never have succeeded in getting a number of Chiricahuas to pose, including Loco, Nané, and other chiefs. Duhem had the best luck when he gave the Indians their small photographic portrait on tin (so-called tin type) as a present, and tobacco and small coins obviously proved helpful. As elsewhere, I had the most trouble with women; only very few of them could be persuaded to pose. Usually we were busy all morning, sometimes part of the afternoon as well, with the aforementioned activities, primarily at the officers' quarters, where a number of Indians were constantly coming and going.[35] In the afternoons and evenings I was in the Indian encampments, from the sullen Chiricahuas to the friendly Apache-Yumas. Visiting the camp of the former one afternoon, Duhem and I came to a hut, inside of which there was an individual among the Indians present who, to judge from his appearance, was a Mexican. Duhem made the not very complimentary remark that one ought to hang that fellow because certainly he was a bandit who had participated in the Chiricahuas' raids.

"Il me semble que ces messieurs parlent français" [It looks to me like these gentlemen speak French] all of a sudden issued, to our great astonishment, from the mouth of the putative Mexican, who before long told us he was a Canadian mestizo who had married an Apache squaw and was now a scout in government service and charged for the moment with keeping an eye on the Chiricahuas. With astonished looks the Apaches present peered at us when they noticed that we were speaking a language the sound of which they had never heard before. From that moment on the rumor spread among the Indians that there were two men who, though white, nevertheless spoke a different language from English or Spanish, and once a young buck turned to ask me whether I was not a "white man." Among the Indians a white is synonymous with an American; so they call a Negro "black white man" or "black American." Of other whites they have practically no conception. The sound of French seemed pleasing to many of them, and they often mimicked us in the most comical fashion. It also afforded them the greatest pleasure when I asked Antonio Díaz a number of Apache words and jotted them down.

The copper buttons from my hunting jacket decorated with small animal heads aroused the bucks' craving. They touched them and nearly yanked them off. When I left San Carlos, I had only one button left on my jacket. Otherwise I could not complain about their behavior. From the wide-open room, where our blankets, clothes, weapons, etc., lay, and which Indians repeatedly came to take a look at and ask for cigarettes, I never missed a thing.

Duhem had the splendid idea of bringing along a magic lantern to put the Indians in a favorable frame of mind toward us. During the evenings he put on performances at the agency or in the abandoned, windowless school building. Dense throngs of Indians—both sullen, taciturn warriors and happy, laughing squaws and children—then gathered around us and expressed their enjoyment and admiration with shrill cries and a prolonged laughter as one amusing scene followed the other in a vivid sequence. A strange thought! The same men who a month before had moved across the land mercilessly burning and killing were here enjoying themselves like innocent children with the images from a magic lantern.

Among each other the Apaches, and Indians generally, are mostly entertaining, animated chatterers, whose forte is in what one familiarly calls "cracking jokes." The looser the "jokes," the more appealing they are. Nevertheless, this is not to imply that the Apaches, and the Indians generally, are shameless. On the contrary, in many respects their sense of shame is a matter of no less sensitivity than among the whites.[36]

The Apaches, too, are great lovers of games and dancing, and not a day went by that I did not see men hour after hour playing *nazjózj* or *nazjoozj,* which at first sight recalls the *ohtoorbook* game of the Mohaves but is fundamentally different. Here, too, two men play at the same time, continually changing places. With big, slow steps, each one holding a long wooden pole in both hands, they go partway along a track across which rolls a ring tossed by one of them. This ring is evidently made of rope and is twisted together in such a way that the surface forms, so to speak, a number of joints. Suddenly the players extend their bodies forward and, with a forceful lunge, thrust the sticks next to each other across the sandy course after the ring, halting their running at the very moment the ring topples over. Now one of the players takes a blade of grass or a thin twig and counts the number of transverse joints of the ring with regard to the position of the poles, which have to fall over the ring. Depending on how the counting turns out, one of the players gets another turn or is replaced by another person. I usually saw them gambling with rifle cartridges, which lay in a small pile in the sand. There was always a large number of spectators present, both on foot as well as on horseback. Another favorite pastime is card playing, with Mexican cards always being used. Formerly the Indians made imitations of these cards in leather, but now hardly any more leather cards can be found.

The Apaches are no great virtuosi. But among them I found a musical instrument in vogue, which I have encountered nowhere else among Indians—namely the fiddle. It is a wooden instrument twenty to twenty-five centimeters long, furnished with a string made of a number of horse hairs bound together. When it is being played, it is placed on the left near the chest at stomach level, and with the small bow-shaped fiddle stick a number of scratchy sounds are coaxed from it. It is possible that originally the fiddle was not a musical instrument of the Apaches but came from the Mexicans.[37]

Captivity does not seem to be too oppressive for the Chiricahuas because they celebrated festivities many an evening, and twice I had the opportunity to observe their "peace dance." Around a huge fire several hundred Indians, crouching or standing, formed a gigantic circle, illuminated by the ruddy glimmer of the flickering flames. In rapid gait two men and a boy of eight or ten years trotted behind one another around the fire. These three were the principal personages of the evening.

The first Indian, a fellow of splendid stature, had drawn a chamois leather mask tightly over his entire face, and on his head he wore a large wooden contrivance, colored red and white, the principal contours of which recalled a trident. His muscular, toiling torso was painted completely white. From his shoulders hung long colored strips decorated with feathers. His hips and thighs were wrapped in a short animal skin skirt with long dangling fringes. Finally, his feet were covered with the usual high boots. In each hand he held a short crooked wooden sword. The second "dancer" was attired in nearly the same way, but the upper part of his trunk was colored black, the lower part white, while instead of a leather skirt he wore one of transparent white cotton. The boy was completely unclad, except for his breechcloth,[38] and painted from head to foot with white dye. He wore a mask, too, but wore no wooden contraptions on his head like the other two. In each hand he held a short slender stick.

The trotting about in buoyant double time was at once transformed into leaping, stomping, and crossing of swords. Now their movements resembled those of an enraged bull, who glances haughtily about the arena and suddenly lunges upon his enemy, and then again those of a prancing horse who recalcitrantly shakes its mane and, sniffing and snorting, tramples the ground with its stomping hooves. From time to time they utter an abrupt, shrill cry. The largest of the three was always in the forefront, the boy in the rear. After they had trotted around for a while, three other men joined in, two of whom were dressed more or less like the former, while one of them, entirely in white and likewise masked, played the role of clown. Running after the others, he mimicked their movements in the most ludicrous fashion. Sometimes he got in the way and danced out in front of them with provocative gestures. Sometimes all of them quickly ran away behind the row of spectators to catch their breath for a moment and then start anew in the same fashion. The music, which accompanied all this, was produced by a number of men hunkered down who were striking with long sticks on a hard cowhide lying on the ground and on small drums.

The longer the spectacle lasted, the more excited the dancers and spectators became. The latter eventually gathered in a tightly closed circle. Men, women, and children moved about monotonously chanting, slowly bounding around the fire with the painted figures—always in motion, more and more flushed—forming a spectacle as savage as it was bizarre. The climax of exuberant savagery was reached when the first "dancer" with a gigantic leap lifted himself above the flames and, uttering a fiendish cry, came down on the other side of the fire.[39]

It is a pleasure to view such a spectacle—but a savage, unfamiliar pleasure. Involuntarily one is carried along by the wild excitement. All that is savage and slumbers within oneself comes alive. One's muscles tense up. One's feet itch to move about in the whirling rows of fantastically illumined figures.

The Apaches understand the art of preparing an intoxicating drink, called *tiswin* or *toolch-paí*. They let corn kernels sprout in moist earth, then finely mash them and let the mash so obtained stand for several days in water until the fermentation has ceased. The American government does everything it can to prevent the preparation of tiswin because it is all too well known how this drink can incite and lead to violence.

Some of the Apaches till the soil; the primary crops are corn and watermelons. Also, the fruit of *Cereus giganteus* provides them with food, and my stay at the reservation was at exactly the same time they were collecting this marvelous succulent fruit.[40]

The Apaches are fond of meat. Indeed, meat was once their primary food, provided them by pillaged livestock from the settlers. Many have now started raising cattle on the reservation and have also come into possession of sheep supplied them by the government. As I have already noted in passing, a weekly issue takes place at the agency, consisting primarily of beef and flour. But only some of the Indians established on the reservation, mainly those living in the San Carlos area, derive any benefit from this. Many of my readers will perhaps say that the American government is acting in a humane way by maintaining so many "dead-eaters." To a certain extent, that is indeed the case. First of all, however, it is simply indemnification for taking away their lands and their freedom, largely depriving them of hunting, their original primary means of livelihood. Secondly, it is the sole means of winning the Indians to a different way of life, to attract them to a fixed location and gradually make them sedentary—something the government has in mind as the primary condition for civilization. It is unquestionably true that this measure has had influence, both on the Indians generally as well as on the Apaches in particular. With the exception of 300 to 400 Chiricahuas, by far the largest portion of the Apaches living in San Carlos is slowly but surely progressing along the path of civilization. The changes of the last twelve years have been extraordinary. Perhaps the 1883 Apache campaign is also the final one on a grand scale.[41]

That a significant part of the men at arms in government service exercises police surveillance, of a sort, on their own tribal compatriots, is proof by itself that unanimity has been shattered and that many of them, from their own self-interest, want to break with the past. However strange this may sound, during their last campaign the Chiricahuas had the public sentiment of the remaining Apaches against them. This is most clearly evident from the fact that hundreds offered to take on their rebellious tribal compatriots under General Crook, the "gray fox."

Likewise the guard at the prison (calaboose), where a number of Indians are locked up for the most varied offenses, consists of heavily armed Apache scouts who, if necessary, would have no qualms about shooting down their own fellow tribesmen. Thanks to the judge's foul, irascible temper, the calaboose was always well occupied, and several prisoners were even loaded down with heavy chains. Their clanking was the music that always woke us up in the morning at sunup, after we had spent the hot night outdoors on the inner courtyard and the prisoners were sent out to sweep. The punishment was well chosen because for an Indian there is practically nothing more demeaning than performing this kind of work.

That the "judge" was hated by the Indians, as was his clerk, the gruff "colonel," goes without saying. What restrained the former above all was that one could not hang or shoot the captive male Chiricahuas without the formality of a trial. That General Crook would thereby have broken his pledge to the Indians and would have scared off the still absent Chiricahuas from returning to the reservation the "judge," probably did not understand. Notwithstanding all his efforts to punish the "damned scoundrels" with death, the government this time was sensible and humane enough to turn down his request and follow the advice of General Crook, who was less shortsighted than the "judge" and also understood the Indian character infinitely better.[42]

For me the issue days were quite important because then I could move slowly along the long rows of waiting Indians at my leisure and, following the method of William Edwards, make observations about their facial features.[43] On a day like this the greatest commotion and activity at the agency prevails from 8 A.M. until late in the afternoon. Also, one can then form a better impression of their horses, on which they had arrived from distant camps to later return heavily laden with quivering meat, sacks of flour, and purchases from the store.

Whoever thinks that the Apaches have splendid horses and that they themselves are splendid riders, as the aforementioned novelists maintain, will find himself quite disappointed after a visit to San Carlos. As a rule, the horses are unimpressive, rather small rocinantes without beauty or spirit.[44] Usually they look as if they have been ridden too often and poorly foddered. Thus an Apache shows little solicitude for his horse and during raids, especially, he often rides them to death. Because spare horses are brought along, however, the horse that collapses is immediately replaced by another one, and a couple of strips of meat hurriedly sliced from the still warm body of the fallen horse provide food for the first twenty-four hours. The uninterrupted continuation of their long rides is the secret reason why they move so swiftly. To protect the hooves of the horses as much as possible from the rocky ground and the spines of the plants, the Apaches use coverings of thick, untanned leather with the hairy side facing outward, which are wrapped around when wet and, once dry, fit tightly around the hoof. The saddles now in vogue among them are the well-known Mexican saddles with high pommel and wooden stirrups. They are good riders only up to a point. Their main characteristic is that they sit firmly in the saddle, but I believe they are not capable of performing maneuvers with a horse, as an experienced white rider can. Nor are the Apaches elegant horsemen. Their wooden stirrups are short, and thus they sit with their knees drawn up. While riding, particularly in short trot (so-called dog trot) and galloping, their trunk, head, and arms are in motion, and the latter especially swing up and down alongside the body like the flapping wings of a bird.

One should not assume that the Apaches fight on horseback and make charges like the Cheyennes and Comanches of the plains do, for example. The Apache is above all a mountain Indian who feels at home in uneven terrain, where boulders and ravines protect him and he can kill his enemy in ambush. They never fight together in large bands but always spread out in small groups of five to twenty, which sometimes split up again into smaller parties. Precisely that dispersion of their warriors has always been their strength and advantage and always made pursuit by the whites so difficult and led them to the mistaken idea that the number of Apache warriors was far greater. In this way, not many more than 120 Apaches in 1883, for five months, kept the inhabitants busy in a region that is larger than England.

That thorough knowledge of terrain is a prime requisite for such raids goes without saying, and in this respect the Apaches are without peer. If one takes into account as well their cunning, indefatigability, and ability to endure hunger and thirst, then one can understand why they are a dangerous foe—however small in number. They have often been called cowardly because most of them creep upon on their foe and never venture an attack until they have a good chance of succeeding. One can call this tactic unchivalrous, but it is certainly not the result of cowardly fear. It seems to me that a people for whom war and conflict is second nature cannot be cowardly.[45]

The power of the Apache chiefs *(nahntáhn)* is not great and is entirely based on their success in leading raids. Every warrior, though acting mainly in accordance with a preconceived plan, can nevertheless frequently act on his personal initiative, without being accountable to anyone. Although the dignity of chief can be hereditary, this is no pat rule because every warrior who has provided examples of outstanding leadership can be chosen on a temporary basis to organize a raid. Nané and Loco, who once stood at the head of so many expeditions, have completely lost their influence—the latter in particular. Because they were no longer in a position to assume an active role as a result of "bodily defects arising from service," younger forces have taken their place and undercut their former authority. For years now the well-known chief Eskimentzin, a brother-in-arms of the great Cochise, has not trodden the warpath and has turned into a pacified reservation Indian.[46] When I saw him he reminded me of a respectable farmer with his close-cropped hair, a straw hat, and citizen's dress.

The Apaches' "field dress" is very plain: they are stark naked except for the breechcloth and the high boots. The bullet belt is fastened around their middle, and all the food and clothes they carry is suspended on the back side of this belt.

Some writers say that there is a strong Mexican element among the Apaches, originating from prisoners, and this has contributed markedly to altering the Indian type. On the basis of my own observation, I must dispute this. I have seen at least fifteen hundred adult Apaches. Among that number I encountered only four or five persons who appeared to be of Mexican origin. Except for the Chiricahuas coming from Sonora, only a few Apaches understand Spanish. That would not have been the case if the Mexican element were so strongly represented.

Some whites lived on the reservation, so-called squaw men, who had sought refuge among the Apaches, but the judge had them driven off and kept only those who had performed service as scouts. Besides the aforementioned French Canadian, McIntosh,[47] one of the most prominent was Micky Free, an Irish half-breed, who married among the Coyoteros, had turned totally Apache, and barely spoke English.[48]

William W. Turner, and Buschmann after him, demonstrated that the Apache language is closely related to that of Athabasca or Tinné people living in the far north, thereby indicating their northern origin, which was later established beyond all doubt.[49] The Kenai or, better yet, Tená (or Tinneh) tribes living in Alaska are again related to the Athabascans, from which it is evident that the Tinné language family is the most widespread in America.[50]

The Apache dialects have as yet been very little studied, and even their number is not accurately known. According to reports I received, primarily from the interpreter Antonio Díaz, the Apaches of Arizona and bordering regions of Mexico speak two dialects—one of which is spoken by the Chiricahuas, Hot Springs, and Coyoteros as well as by the Mescaleros in New Mexico, the second by the Arivaypas, Pinaleños, and others. Navajo, also a Tinné language, can be regarded as a third dialect.[51] Regarding the other dialects, I can say nothing with confidence.

Apache sounds odd and, once heard, is easy to recognize because of its distinctive guttural, sibilant, and mute sounds. The following words in the Pinaleño dialect may serve as an example: *Istséné,* "woman"; *sjisjásje,* "son"; *sjilasjósj,* "finger"; *sistích,* "body"; *'ndénasésj,* "a band of riders";

glhee, "horse"; *pesjnaghatéh*, "knife"; *inzjó*, "it is good"; *dasdzáh*, "dead"; *isghángho*, "morning"; *zjágho*, "much or many"; *tsjotlóh*, "laugh"; *bahdzeenee*, "give"; *estsjigá*, "kill"; *tlitsogee*, "yellow," "orange"; *tlootsjísjee*, "green," "blue," "purple"; *atechwonzay?* "what is your name?"

The Apaches call themselves *'Ndé*, that is, "people," "nation," but have special names for each of their smaller tribes and bands—thus *Ai-ahá* or *Ai-há* for the Chiricahuas, *Tisépán* for the Pinaleños, etc. The name *Apache* is most likely derived from a Yuma word.[52] Among the tribes familiar to the Apaches, I name just the Pápagos and Pimas, who they call *Saikinné*, i.e., "sandhouses," and the Navajos, who they call *Yootahá*.

There was nothing I could learn with any certainty regarding the Apaches' religious concepts. Years would have been needed for this, during which time I would have had to learn their language and gain their confidence. I do know, to be sure, that they have superstitions regarding bears, owls, and snakes, but I am not able to say why.[53] Just ask a people who do not know you and mistrust you, and with whom you have stayed just a short time, what they believe and why they do this or that! It is impossible to get anything out of them that one can rely on. What passing travelers like me, in no matter what part of the globe, may serve up regarding the religion of a people whose language they do not know deserves very little credence—this I can state without hesitation. And yet how often have the *"Stubenethnologen"* [armchair ethnologists] forgotten this! But more on this issue in a subsequent chapter discussing my stay at Zuni.

It is almost certain that the Apaches have a clan system because the Navajos, with whom they are closely akin, have it too. I did not succeed in learning the names of their clans. Not even Díaz knew them.[54]

At San Carlos one finds remnants of ancient Indian ruins, just as one does at the Pima reservation and near Tempe; these are barely recognizable, however. On the edge of the mesa, near the military quarters, huge stones are visible, which, according to the plan they are set in, indicate the site where a building once stood. Superficially observed, the other ruins, five or six miles north of the agency, are nothing more than mounds of earth. Nearby potsherds, most of them painted, lie scattered about; they are wholly identical to those found in Pima territory and at Casa Grande. I would have been delighted to visit these spots with Adolf [Adolph] Bandelier, who stayed at San Carlos shortly before me and subjected these ruins to a careful examination.[55] How odd that Mr. Bandelier and I were traveling close on each other's heels without being aware of this. Wingate, Fort Apache, Showlow, Zuni, Fort Thomas, etc., I visited shortly after Bandelier's departure. When I left Tucson for good, he arrived the next day.[56]

The Apache-Yumas and Apache-Mohaves on the reservation, who, for no good reason, are cited in government reports, etc., as Apaches, or as Tinné Apaches, belong to the Yuma linguistic family. They are two divisions of one and the same tribe, that of the Yabipaís. The former call themselves *Yavepé-Kutchán;* the latter only *Yabipaí* or *Yabipaíye*. Their former dwelling places were primarily in the valley of the Rio Verde and in the mountains west of there. Prolonged fighting with the American troops had so debilitated them that in 1873 they submitted and settled in a reservation assigned them in the Rio Verde valley. Barely two years later they were transferred to San Carlos, and although many resisted and some of them fled, they had to yield to superior power and accept the dispositions of the "Great Father" in Washington.

There is terrible confusion regarding the term *Tonto* as an Indian tribal name. There are namely Tontos (Spanish: "fools," "lunatics") who are Yumas in a wider sense and Tontos who belong to the Tinné. But according to my investigations, the name "Tontos" is applied preferably to the Deldzjé, a tribe of the Apaches, and the name, perhaps given earlier to the Yabipaís by mistake, is now almost unknown among them. The Tonto-Yumas are, in my opinion, identical with either the Yabipaís ("Apache-Yumas" and "Apache-Mohaves") or the Tolkepayá, a small band that has arisen from the mingling of Yabipaís with Tonto Tinné. Among other things, I reached this opinion for the following reasons:

When I asked the Tinné Apaches who the Góhun were, they replied "the Apache Mohaves." The name "Góhun" or "Kóhun" is now applied by other writers—by Loew, for example—to the Tontos, who speak a Yuma dialect, and the vocabulary I recorded among the "Apache Yumas" agrees in many respects with what Loew designates as "Tonto."[57] The language of the Yabipaís differs markedly from that of the Yumas—and, indeed, to such an extent that an "Apache Yuma" and an actual Yuma from the Colorado do not understand each other.[58]

In outward appearance and character, however, they have much in common with the Yumas and Mohaves, but they are, as a rule, not as tall in stature and recall the Hualpaís most of all. However, they sometimes wear their hair after the fashion of the Mohaves and Yumas; they also have the custom of cleaning it by using river mud. Their hats resemble those of the aforementioned tribes, with whom they are well acquainted. Sometimes I encountered individuals among them who came from the Colorado.

Two weeks had passed by quickly when, on July 12, I bid farewell to the hot San Carlos, abundant in tarantulas and scorpions, to continue my journey north. The previous day Duhem began the trip back to Tucson via the mining town Globe City. I would have gladly traveled longer with him to enhance the value of my investigation, but the financial resources I had at my disposal did not permit this, and *nolens volens* [whether willing or not] I went my own way again. Captain Crawford had directed two cavalrymen and a Mexican, who drove pack mules, to accompany me to Fort Apache and had himself provided me a splendid riding mule. With our things packed and bagged and us armed, at 3 P.M. we headed up beyond the former subagency toward the mountains, and I bade farewell to the parched regions for good.

By then I had spent nearly six months, with brief interruptions, in the hot desert regions and been able to test against my own experience much of what Oscar Loew reports about the effect of a sojourn like this on the body.[59] What he says about the dropping of body temperature in relation to the increase of air temperature—the reverse of what occurs under usual circumstances—is entirely correct. On the other hand, I have failed to note an increase in the number of pulse beats and respiration, nor the loss of 12 to 15 percent of one's body weight after a stay of a few weeks in a desert climate. Certainly the formation of fat ceases to some degree and the muscles grow flabby, but I have not been able to observe such a huge reduction on my own body. I can certainly attest that one suffers many nosebleeds. However, I must question whether this is, in fact, always the result of extensive thinning of the blood resulting from excessive drinking. The moisture absorbed is very quickly secreted through the skin. One is continually bathed in sweat, yet one does not feel fatigued or listless. Instead, I believe that the intense heat causes congestion in the head, and this causes nosebleeds. Loew assumes that the thinning of the blood caused by considerable drinking impedes digestion and that during defecation a not insignificant portion of food leaves the body little changed. Also, as far as I myself am concerned, I have not been able to observe this. What strongly affected me was the alkali-laden water I often had to drink—near Tucson, for instance. This usually caused a mild stomach catarrh, queasiness after eating, and diarrhea, which stopped with the intake of better water. I fully share Loew's opinion that in hot regions a vegetable diet is far preferable to a meat diet and that it checks the sensation of thirst much longer. Likewise one should abstain from alcoholic beverages and tobacco. Although a draught of whiskey or brandy can make the sensation of burning thirst vanish momentarily, it returns much more quickly and intensely. Smoking, too, encourages sensations of thirst. As a beverage and as a stimulant at the same time, I derived the greatest benefit from coffee and tea without milk. I always had crystallized citric acid with me, a small piece of which, held in the mouth for a while, wards off the sensation of thirst.

It is a rugged mountain path that leads us slowly out of the heat of the Gila Valley, along a hundred bends, into cooler layers of air. The rain, long menacing, which had soaked the scorched ground near San Carlos just a few times, here surprises us with shower after shower, mingling with the gray dust that covers us.[60] For a long time the eternal saguaros accompany my path, as does the greasewood, but both later make way for grama grass, yellowish gray in color, the mescal plant, and eventually juniper trees. Yellow sandstone, interrupted in many places by igneous rock, makes up the ground on which the hoofbeats of our animals monotonously reverberate. In many places we leave the big "road" and follow a rugged, winding bypath, so steep that I often prefer to dismount from my long ears, who, more often than not, glides with outstretched legs rather than trots. It is a long ride this first day because Ash Creek, the only place where there is water, is far away. We eventually reach it at 9 P.M., but we find no water at the place where we expect it and no grass either. We follow the stream banks for some distance, searching and groping under the glimmer of the half-moon, whose gleam now and then penetrates the dark clouds enveloping it. We search for half an hour and eventually, thirsty and exhausted after an eleven-hour ride, we set up camp. The fire is quickly kindled, and before long the bacon is sizzling in the pan and the coffeepot resting on the fire. A light downpour and a howling coyote, who is welcomed by a shot from the soldiers, momentarily disturb our sleep.

Before 8 A.M. we are on our way again, across high grassy meadows, surrounded by sycamores and oaks. Out in front of us extends a wall of mountains with eternally green woods, the scent of which is wafted in our direction. The sun again illuminates everything in a marvelous glow, bringing to life the vegetation on which the dew and raindrops are still glistening. Having reached the rim of the high meadow, we follow a rugged and tortuous path that brings us to the mountain plateau, winding through forests of oak and firs,[61] three and a half hours after leaving the campsite. Not far from there, where a little creek splashes from rock to rock and the dark foliage of age-old pine and cedar trees sways back and forth, we halt a couple of hours for our meal.

The spot is called Wild Water. A unique feeling of well-being and pleasure exhilarates one's body as one's lungs relax in the air filled with ozone and plant fragrances, a feeling sure to enchant one's soul and evoke slumbering images of felicity. This is what one has always dreamt of: a Valhalla all one's own to experience and relish and to be free.

On redevient sauvage à l'odeur des forêts
[One turns wild again at the scent of forests]

These are scents the city dweller has never known, scents replete with aroma and freshness, abiding in memory like the strains of a melody once heard. All around magnificent trunks arise, rugged and vigorous with their bark in a reddish hue, like gigantic pillars bearing capitals of broad-branched leafy crowns, rustling and whizzing through the gust of the mountain wind. The ground is blanketed with high, lush grass, which continues across the mountain plain and along the slope of the ravines, the soil of which forms a large, dense arbor.

All day we follow the road through forests and meadows, where there are open spaces in the forest and the eye can roam in the distance, fixing on mountain after mountain and forest after forest, losing itself along the distant horizon. We see not a trace of living things: not an Indian, not a deer, not a bird, not an insect—nothing. There is nothing but the endless silence. By 4:30 P.M. we have reached the northern rim of the mountain plateau and descend to the Rio Prieto, or Black River, which in heavily twisting bends winds its way through a canyon, the walls of which consist of igneous rock, with lovely oaks and firs rimming the banks. On a meadow close to the water, we set up camp. Before long I plunge into the cool stream, refreshing myself after the long ride, and then lie down to revel and dream. A lovelier stream than this never sang its refrain, a refrain sung in solitude full of simplicity, calm, and harmony and reverberating a hundredfold through the rocky green banks for all eternity.

The night is cool and, shivering, we arise in the morning, damp from dew. Early on we are back in the saddle again and continue the journey to the other side of Black River. At first our path leads across high meadows, then at Turkey Creek through forests again. We pass many graves, testimony to the struggle between the Fort Apache garrison and the Indians. At Seven Miles Hill we descend into a magnificent narrow valley with dense forest growth, where for the first time I see a grouse. The last miles of the ride lead through a landscape, lovely beyond all description, until we reach Camp Apache at 11:30 A.M. The commandant, Captain Dougherty, receives me in the most courteous fashion,[62] and before long I am installed in a cool room of the hospital. Camp Apache is situated on a wide, grassy plateau about 5,000 feet above sea level in the middle of an area that has the geological character of the Carboniferous formation but where pyrogenic rocks, especially basalt, have brought about noticeable change in the original position of the sedimentary rock. Water, too, has played a part in the formation of the landscape and hollowed out deep, sheer canyons in the soil of the valley. At the place where two such canyons merge and form the bed for the merging North and East Fork of the White Mountain River lies Camp Apache.[63]

In the middle of the post is a wide court, bounded on the south side by the soldiers' wooden barracks and the stables, on the north side by the officers' quarters. Many of these dwellings are simple log houses built from tree trunks of sturdy pine. As far as one's gaze extends, the eye descries mountains covered with splendid forests. To the east, in the East Fork Valley, the blunt but mighty peaks of Mount Thomas and Mount Ord, which are 11,496 and 10,266 feet high, arise behind a lake of dark forests, bounding the horizon.[64] Camp Apache's climate is exquisite, though the winters are quite severe. In the summer, during the rainy season, thunder and rain showers are frequent. Barely twelve years ago the area where Camp Apache is situated was an unfrequented wilderness, the undisturbed realm of the wild Coyoteros, until the founding of this post in 1872 put an end to their hostilities, which, however, flared up now and then, most recently in 1881.[65]

The Indians have their camps along the White Mountain River and its tributaries. Thanks to the good offices of Lieutenant Gatewood, the chief of the Apache scouts,[66] I obtained an interpreter and a mount for my use and visited some camps at various distances from the post. These camps look just like the ones near San Carlos already described, but the Coyoteros are more heavily engaged in agriculture, with the fertile banks of the streams providing a better opportunity than elsewhere.

I had to abandon an attempt to pilfer a skull from an Indian graveyard not far from the fort because, when I was on the verge of opening a grave, I suddenly espied an armed buck who had clearly been following me with suspicion and now stood stiffly watching me, leaning motionlessly on his rifle. When I left as quietly as possible in the direction of an Indian camp, he followed me awhile longer and then vanished just as silently and suddenly as he had appeared.

The Coyoteros have a very simple way of burying their dead. The body is brought to a place where a number of loose blocks of rocks are available—in a cleft, for example. A number of these blocks are removed until there is room enough to lie the body down. Then they are put back in place again, and at the same time some heavy branches are stuck between the chinks to prevent the coyotes from violating the grave. According to what I learned, the closest relatives mourn the deceased for thirty days, venting their grief in howls of anguish.

I could measure twenty of the Apache scouts, and I reached the same results as in San Carlos.[67]

On the northern wall of the canyon, in the immediate vicinity of the fort, high above the bed of the stream on a nearly inaccessible place are a number of deeply incised signs, many of which have a mysterious meaning. Some recalled the characters I had encountered among the Papagos on the fortified Cerro del Zorrillo, others some pictographs from Lower California. There were animal shapes, human hands and feet, curved lines, star-shaped figures. I can say nothing with certainty about their origin, but as far as I can determine, there is no reason to doubt that they come from the Apaches.

Fort Apache's environs are abundant in game. First there are the grizzlies *(Ursus ferox)*, who live high in the mountains.[68] Coyotes and gray foxes *(Urocyon cinero-argentatus)* appear frequently. Deer *(Cariacus macrotus)* and antelope are sighted not infrequently. Wild turkeys *(Meleagris gal-lopavo)* and grouse *(Canace)* are abundant. But the Apache, though he hunts, does not track game high in the mountains because he dreads the many storms that break above the densely overgrown peaks and avoids these areas when he can.

I spend four pleasant days at Fort Apache and on July 18 leave well before sunrise with a buckboard, which carries the mail a couple of times a week between the fort and Holbrook, a small station along the new Atlantic and Pacific railway, about ninety miles away. The route, which is quite good, winds its way mostly through splendid pine forests and grassy meadows. The farther down one goes, the more oaks dominate the scenery. In a log cabin on the boundary of the reservation, where a couple of Americans dwell, we have breakfast and at 1 P.M. arrive at Cooley's Ranch or Showlow.[69] I have to stay here the rest of the day and all of the night before I can head on. Here I encounter some soldiers who are on their way to Fort Apache. Among them is a young man who reveals himself to be a countryman, and for the first time in seven months I can speak Dutch again. He used to be a cadet in the academy at Breda and eventually, after varied fortunes, had entered American service, performing the duties of cavalry bugler. In the area around Showlow, I visited some remnants of Indian ruins and collected a number of beautifully painted potsherds, which again had the same character as the ones I had encountered earlier. I spend the night with my country-man outside, under the buckboard for protection against the rain, because the stuffy log cabin is full of soldiers.

At 6 A.M. we continue the journey. We first go through rolling park landscapes of pine and oak trees. Later, before we reach Taylor's Springs, juniper bushes make up the sole vegetation. The ground consists of a kind of white limestone and is covered with patches of grass. Now and then we see a prairie dog *(Cynomys)*, which rises up in curiosity at our approach and quickly ducks down in its burrow. At Snowflake City, a Mormon settlement, where we have lunch, we can see their bur-rows in the middle of the "city."[70] Fortunately for them, there is not much activity in Snowflake.

As we continue our ride northward, juniper becomes less frequent and sagebrush *(Artemisia)* appears, alternating with short grass, which sparsely covers the vast, rolling limestone flats. Here and there a drab funnel-shaped cloud of dust hovers along the ground, vanishing as suddenly as it appeared. An oppressive, sultry heat prevails, and no sooner have we passed the small town of Woodruff than a heavy downpour is unleashed. At 6 P.M. we reach Holbrook, situated in the middle of a dismal sandy region. Freakishly shaped red sandstone mesas, bearing clear traces of erosion, rim the desolate banks of the Colorado Chiquito [Little Colorado], which has almost no water. In the main, Holbrook resembles all other frontier towns but has good wooden dwellings, surrounded by sturdy cottonwoods.

·····

NOTES

1. George Crook (1829–1890) was probably the most capable Indian fighter in the American military during the late nineteenth century. After serving with distinction in the Civil War and in the Pacific Northwest, Crook in 1871 was transferred to Arizona. Here he subdued the Tonto Apaches by raiding with small units and heavy reliance on Apache scouts, then a very controversial procedure. In 1875 he was transferred to the Department of the Platte, where he was less successful in campaigns against the Sioux and Cheyennes. In 1882 Crook returned to Arizona, where he carried out the expedition Ten Kate describes leading to the surrender of Geronimo and his Chiricahua followers. The number of troops at his disposal, however, were considerably less than Ten Kate indicates: only forty-two soldiers, eleven officers, three chiefs of scouts, 193 Apache scouts, and a few muleteers and journalists. Roberts, *Once They Moved Liked the Wind: Cochise, Geronimo, and the Apache Wars* (New York: Simon & Schuster, 1994), 76–83, 122–31, 227–38; Dan L. Thrapp, *General Crook and the Sierra Madre Adventure* (Norman: University of Oklahoma Press, 1972); Pieter Hovens, *Herman ten Kate en de Antropologie der Noord Amerikaanse Indianen* (Meppel: Krips, 1989), 159–64.

2. Meant here is Peaches (Tsoe), a White Mountain Apache youth, who actually fled the Chiracahua band and voluntarily returned to the San Carlos reservation, where he was taken prisoner. Thrapp, *General Crook,* 119–23, 128–38.

3. Loco (ca. 1823–1905), a Mimbres Apache chief, got his Spanish name (= "crazy") from the fury he displayed in battle when he was young. Loco, together with Victorio, resisted American efforts during the 1870s to move the Mimbres from their domain in Ojo Caliente, New Mexico, to the San Carlos reservation in Arizona. Never a virulent enemy of the whites, he eventually reconciled himself to the transfer and did not take part in Victorio's final breakout in 1879. Victorio (ca. 1825–1880), a Mimbres Apache chief, is regarded by some as the most formidable of all Apache warriors. (See note 21 below.) In 1882 the Apache chief Juh (ca. 1825–1883, a chief of the Nednai Apaches), who had bolted the reservation the year before, returned and, probably by force, led Loco and his band off to Mexico as well. (See also note 4 below.) As Ten Kate notes, Loco was one of the first Apache leaders to return with General Crook, and he took no part in the final Chiricahua struggles in 1885. Nana (ca. 1800–1896), another Mimbres leader, was a companion of Victorio during his famous escapes and raids of the 1870s but escaped the annihilation of Victorio's forces in Mexico. In 1881 Nana, with a band never numbering more than forty, led several devastating raids in southern New Mexico, covering more than a thousand miles, repeatedly eluding American troops, and killing thirty to fifty Americans. Nana later joined the Chiricahuas who fled to the Sierra Madre. The less-well-known Bonito, a White Mountain Apache, was another leader of the Apaches who fled to the Sierra Madre. Dan L. Thrapp, *Encyclopedia of Frontier Biography* (Glendale, Calif.: Arthur H. Clark, 1988), 1:865–66, 2:1038–39. Dan L. Thrapp, *The Conquest of Apacheria* (Norman: University of Oklahoma Press, 1967), 211–16 and passim. On Apache wars and warfare, see also Donald E. Worcester, *The Apaches: Eagles of the Southwest* (Norman: University of Oklahoma Press, 1979), and Grenville Goodwin (Keith H. Basso, ed.), *Apache Raiding and Warfare* (Tucson: University of Arizona Press, 1971).

4. Juh was one of the greatest Apache war leaders, while Geronimo (ca. 1823–1909), a Bedonkohe leader, is certainly the most famous. The two Apache leaders both participated in raids and battles in Mexico during the 1850s, fought with Cochise, and resisted American efforts to resettle the Chiricahuas on the San Carlos Reservation. Juh and Geronimo both played a key role in the 1881

escape to the Sierra Madre. Juh, however, rather than the more famous Geronimo, was probably the dominant figure in the planning and execution of some of the more dramatic developments during this phase of the Apache wars, such as the daring 1882 raid that led to the bolting of Loco and the Mimbres Apaches. In November 1883 Juh died after falling from his horse into the Casa Grandes River. Thus he never returned to San Carlos, and his death more clearly left the leadership of the Chiricahuas to Geronimo. Thrapp, *Encyclopedia,* 2:547–49, 753; Dan L. Thrapp, *Juh: An Incredible Indian* (El Paso: Texas Western University Press, 1973).

5. HtK 1889, 238. Regarding the campaign of General Crook against the Apaches, see the book of Captain John G. Bourke, *An Apache Campaign in the Sierra Madre,* New York, 1886, the essence of which first appeared in the American magazine *Outing,* Boston 1885. Eds.: John Gregory Bourke (1846–1896), as an aide to General Crook, spent extensive tours of duty in the Southwest, participating in the Apache campaigns and undertaking important ethnological investigations. He later published memoirs on the Apache campaign and important ethnological works on southwestern tribes such as the Apaches and the Hopis. Joseph C. Porter, *Paper Medicine Man* (Norman: University of Oklahoma Press, 1986).

6. Crawford accompanied General Crook on the aforementioned Sierra Madre expedition in 1883 and brought back 400 Chiricahua prisoners. He also played an important part in the campaign that followed Geronimo's second escape and flight to Mexico in 1885–1886 but was killed by Mexican soldiers in January 1886. Bernard C. Nalty and Truman R. Strobridge, "Captain Emmet Crawford: Commander of Apache Scouts, 1882–1886," *Arizona and the West* 6 (1964):30–40. Also see introduction, note 15.

7. Constant Duhem was a photographer in New Mexico as early as 1868 and later had a studio in Denver. This French photographer was in Tucson in 1883 when Ten Kate hired him for two weeks in June and July to take pictures of Apaches on the San Carlos reservation. Ten Kate sent sixty negatives to the Museum of Ethnology in Leiden, but over the years many faded, partially due to inadequate storage. The World Museum in Rotterdam also received a number of prints, which equally suffered. Beyond these, few images attributed to him seem to have survived. William S. Johnson, *Nineteenth Century Photography* (Boston: G. K. Hall, 1990), 198; Pieter Hovens and Anneke Groeneveld, *Odagot: Photographs of American Indians, 1860–1920* (Amsterdam: Fragment Uitgeverij, 1992), 100; J. Heyink, *Dr. Herman F. C. ten Kate en de Apache Indianen* (Bennebroek: Kiva Reeks, 1983).

8. See Oscar Loew, "Lieutenant Wheeler's Expedition nach Neu-Mexiko und Arizona," *Petermann's Geographische Mittheilungen* 20 (1874):455.

9. We have been unable to locate any record of this place.

10. The settlement was named after Isadore E. Solomon who settled there in 1876. It was renamed Solomon in 1950. Will C. Barnes, *Arizona Place Names* (Tucson: University of Arizona Press, 1960), 132.

11. Fort Thomas was established in 1876. It never consisted of more than a few adobe buildings and was abandoned in 1892, when it was no longer needed, after the conclusion of the Apache Wars. Barnes, *Arizona Place Names,* 132.

12. The "judge" was P. P. Wilcox of Denver, who had been appointed Indian agent at the San Carlos reservation in September 1882, in the wake of scandals caused by the graft of his predecessor J. C. Tiffany. Wilcox tried to eliminate corruption but was hampered by the lack of adequate personnel to replace Tiffany's holdovers. Wilcox rationalized the appointment of his son-in-law as a step needed to ensure honest administration in Indian trading. Wilcox was often embroiled in

jurisdictional disputes with the army. He opposed the resettlement of the rebel Chiricahuas on the San Carlos reservation; that explains his hostile reception of Ten Kate, who was recommended by Gen. Crook. Wilcox resigned his position two years later. Ralph Hedrick Ogle, *Federal Control of the Western Apaches, 1848–1886* (Albuquerque: University of New Mexico Press, 1970), 199–229.

13. HtK 1885: I recommend reading a piece by the famous paleontologist Prof. Marsh regarding his observations in 1874 at one of the Sioux reservations, "A Statement of Affairs at Red Cloud Agency made to the President of the U.S." Eds.: Ten Kate is referring to Othniel Charles March (1831–1899), who, beginning in the 1870s, organized and led major paleontological expeditions to the West and was the first to describe fossil serpents and flying reptiles in this region. *Dictionary of American Biography,* 23 vols. (New York: Scribner, 1943–73), 6, pt. 2:302–3.

14. The girl's puberty ceremony, or *nai'es* ("preparing her," "getting her ready"), of the modern Cibecue Apache takes a young woman symbolically through the four stages of life and emphasizes the four major values to which she should aspire: physical strength, an even temperament, prosperity, and a sound, healthy old age. As Keith Basso notes, "The primary objective of the puberty ceremony is to transform the pubescent girl into the mythological figure . . . Changing Woman. At the request of the presiding medicine man, and 'traveling on his chants,' the power of Changing Woman enters the girl's body and resides there for four days. During this time the girl acquires all the desirable qualities of Changing Woman herself and is thereby prepared for a useful and rewarding life as an adult." Keith Basso, *The Cibecue Apache* (New York: Holt, Rinehart and Winston, 1970), 64. See also Keith Basso, "The Gift of Changing Woman," *Bureau of American Ethnology, Bulletin 196* (Washington, D.C.: U.S. Government Printing Office, 1966).

15. In June 1876, Indian agent John Clum removed 325 Apaches from the Chiricahua reservation, but at least 400 under the leadership of Juh and Geronimo escaped. The closure of this reservation was one of the key actions that aggravated Chiricahua hostility and resulted in the raiding and bloodshed that only ended with the final surrender of Geronimo in 1886. Thrapp, *Conquest,* 169–71.

16. HtK 1885: *Apud Apache-Indianos feminae parturientes genibus nixae solo insidere solent, alia muliere post eam sedente eique ventrem premente. Apud Apache-Yumas idem usuvenit, nisi quod parturientes identidem surgunt et ultro citroque cursitant.* [Among the Apache Indians, women about to give birth are accustomed to sitting propped on their knees alone, with another woman behind her pressing her abdomen. Among the Apache Yumas something like this occurs, except that those giving birth periodically sit up and run up and down.]

17. HtK 1885: The leather war cap, which I sent to the Ethnographic Museum in Leiden, is decorated with split leathers of *Otus americanus, Bubo virginianus,* a feather of *Aquila chrysaëtos,* juv., and a specimen of *Sylvicola citreola.* A head ornament of the Apaches-Yumas present at the same place consists of feathers of the wild turkey and *A. chrysaëtos.* Eds.: *Bubo virginianus* (Gmelin), great horned owl; *Aquila chrysaëtos* (Linnaeus), golden eagle; *Sylvicola citreola.* "*Otus americanus*" may be *Asio otus* (Linnaeus), long-eared owl, which is similar in appearance to the great horned owl.

18. *Amenopsis californica* (Hook), yerba manso.

19. HtK 1885: A shield I acquired is decorated with feathers from *Corvus americanus.*

20. There are today seven recognized Southern Athapascan or Apachean-speaking tribes: Chiricahua, Jicarilla, Kiowa-Apache, Lipan, Mescalero, Navajo, and Western Apache. Writing in 1885, Ten Kate attempts to sort out the very complex history and use of Apachean group names. Most of the people he refers to are "Western Apaches." However, the term "Sierra Blanca," for example, has been used for three different Apachean groups. In the nineteenth century the term "Gila Apaches" sometimes

included the Pinaleños, Mogollones, Arivaipas, and other groups as well. Like Ten Kate, some scholars regard the San Carlos group as including the earlier separate Pinaleno and Arivaipa Apaches but disagree with Ten Kate in saying the White Mountain group contains the Sierra Blanca and Coyotero. Morris E. Opler, "The Apachean Culture Pattern and Its Origins," in *Handbook of North American Indians: Southwest,* vol. 10 (Washington, D.C.: Smithsonian Institution, 1983), 387–92; Keith H. Basso, "Western Apache," 488.

21. During the 1870s Victorio and Loco, the other leading Mimbres chief, tenaciously resisted American efforts to relocate them from their homelands in New Mexico to the San Carlos reservation. In August 1879 Victorio and his band bolted for the last time. During the following year, Victorio and his band of less than a hundred repeatedly eluded American pursuit and carried out numerous bloody raids in New Mexico and northern Mexico. Victorio and his band were finally trapped and annihilated by Mexican forces under Colonel Joaquín Terrazas at Tres Castillos, Chihuahua, on October 15, 1880. Dan L. Thrapp, *Victorio and the Mimbres Apaches* (Norman: University of Oklahoma Press, 1974). See also note 3 above.

22. Fort Stanton was established on May 4, 1855, to control the Mescalero Apaches. Abandoned during the Civil War, it was reestablished in 1868. Robert W. Frazer, *Forts of the West* (Norman: University of Oklahoma Press, 1965), 103–4.

23. At various periods in the eighteenth and nineteenth centuries, the Lipans roved from the Rio Grande valley in New Mexico and Mexico eastward through Texas to the Gulf Coast, carrying out raids against other tribes and the white settlements in Texas and Mexico. They suffered greatly during the Texan wars between 1845 and 1856 and were eventually driven into Coahuila, Mexico. In 1903 there were only nineteen survivors. Frederick Webb Hodge, "Lipan," ed. F. W. Hodge, *Handbook of North American Indians,* 2 vols. (Washington, D.C.: Bureau of American Ethnology, 1907–10), 1:768–69.

24. There were over 5,000 Apaches at San Carlos in 1877. Basso, "Western Apache," 481. The 1890 census gives 4,870 (San Carlos) and 561 (Mescalero). Department of the Interior, *Report of Indians Taxed and Indians Not Taxed in the United States, Eleventh Census 1890* (Washington, D.C.: U.S. Government Printing Office, 1894), 82–83.

25. The Athabascan peoples appear to have arrived in North America ca. 3000 B.P. About 2000 B.P. these Nadene peoples seemed to separate into various groups, some moving to the Pacific coast, some to the Southwest. The migrations of the southern Athapascan people have become better understood as hunting sites have been documented and dated from the Northwestern Plains through the mountains and plains of Utah and Colorado into the Colorado Plateau and down the Rio Grande Valley at about the time of the Spanish entrada from the south ca. 500 B.P. J. Loring Haskell, *Southern Athapaskan Migration A.D. 200–1750* (Tsaile, Ariz.: Navajo Community College Press, 1987).

26. For Gustave Aimard (1818–1883), see introduction, note 8. "Gabriel Ferry" was the nom de plume of Louis-Gabriel Ferry de Bellemare (1809–1852), a French traveler well known for his books about Mexico who also wrote several novels, many of which appeared posthumously. *Dictionnaire de Biographie Francaise* (Paris: Letouzey et Ané, 1933–2001), 1:976–77, 5:1342. The works of Aimard and Ferry have been thus characterized: "Their plots usually feature a white hero, preferably of French origin, his equally heroic Indian friend, and the antagonism between friendly and hostile tribes (chiefly Comanche versus Apache)." Christian F. Feest, "The Indian in Non-English Literature," in *Handbook of North American Indians: History of Indian-White Relations,* ed. Wilcomb E. Washburn (Washington, D.C.: Smithsonian, 1988), 4, 582. Thomas Mayne Reid (1818–1883), an English writer, emigrated to the United States in 1840, worked as a journalist, and later fought in the Mexican War.

After his return to Europe in 1850, he authored over thirty adventure novels based on western themes and his experiences in the United States. Many were translated into other European languages. *Dictionary of National Biography* 16:875–76. Pieter Hovens, *Herman ten Kate*, 192–96, discusses Ten Kate's studies of literary imagery concerning North American Indians.

27. In pre-Columbian Mexico the Chichimecs were Indians from the north who occasionally overran the centers of civilization in the Valley of Mexico.

28. Ten Kate is not quite correct. The Apaches occasionally took scalps, though only as an extreme form of revenge. David Roberts, *Once They Moved*, 44.

29. HtK 1885: In his most recent campaign General Carbo, already mentioned in passing in chapter 3, had expressly given his troops the order they should take no Apaches prisoner, neither women nor children, but kill them inexorably and without exception.

30. HtK 1885: I already reported about this on an earlier occasion. See the magazine *Omnibus*, 1878, p. 366.

31. HtK 1885: George W. Manypenny, ex-Commissioner of Indian Affairs. *Our Indian Wards*, Cincinnati, 1880. In this work, which is based entirely on official data, the writer shows, among other things, the inhuman treatment that the Indians received at the hands of the troops. All in all, it makes a convincing case for the valid right of the Indian. HtK 1889, 238: Besides the book of Manypenny *(Our Indian Wards)* regarding the villainous policy of the American government toward the Indians, one should read *A Century of Dishonor* (new ed., Boston 1888), by Helen Jackson, and her *Ramona*, rightly called an "immortal work" by a competent judge. Compare my essay titled "A Foreigner's View on the Indian Question in the Council Fire," the organ of the National Indian Defense Association, vol. XII, no. 3, 1889, Washington, D.C. Eds.: Helen Hunt Jackson (1830–1885) was one of the most prominent nineteenth-century publicists against injustice done to American Indians. Her *Century of Dishonor* (1881) was an exposé, while her novel *Ramona* (1884), though mostly fictional, was based on the life of a Cahuilla girl of southern California. The latter work was popular for decades. Thrapp, *Encyclopedia,* 2:716, 3:1190.

32. George W. Manypenny, *Our Indian Wards* (Cincinnati: Robert Clarke and Company, 1880), 191–92 (repr., New York: Da Capo Press, 1972).

33. Royal Emerson Whitman (1833–1913) had participated in the Civil War, afterward enlisted in the Third Cavalry, and was then transferred west, where he became commandant of Camp Grant. The Camp Grant Massacre, which Ten Kate describes, was perpetrated by a group of ninety-two Papagos, forty-two Mexicans, and six Anglos, instigated by vengeful Tucson citizens. Whitman was later subjected to several courts-martial and, though not convicted, his reputation suffered so severely that he resigned his commission. Thrapp, *Encyclopedia,* 3:1560–61; James R. Hastings, "The Tragedy at Camp Grant in 1871," *Arizona and the West* 1 (1959):146–60.

34. HtK 1885: A repetition of the murder committed at Camp Grant had nearly occurred in April 1883, when a large number of citizens from Tucson had set out to kill every male Indian of the San Carlos reservation. But this time the Apaches were on their guard, along with the troops stationed at San Carlos, so that the armed gang of hunters of men had to turn back without carrying out their plans.

35. HtK 1885: All the negatives prepared by Duhem, as well as my own made in Isleta and Guaymas, are found in the Ethnographic Museum in Leiden. Eds.: Unfortunately most of this material has been lost due to natural decay and bad storage.

36. HtK 1885: *Nullius umquam Indiani pudenda adspicere mihi contigit nisi pueri. Nullo pretio vir sibi persuaderi sinat, ut ista monstret. Feminae itidem illo nomine pudicitiae sensu magis sunt praeditae quam vulgo creditur. Cacaturi (viri etiam micturi) Indiani recedere solent, quod genus vere-cundiae humi nixum, mingentem vidi. Multarum gentium feminae stantes mingunt.* [Never at any time did I get to see an Indian's private parts apart from the boys. For no price would a man let him-self be persuaded to show them. For that reason the women are likewise more imbued with a sense of shame than is commonly believed. Indians about to defecate (the men even when they are about to urinate) are accustomed to withdrawing, though I did see one person shyly urinating with his knee resting on the ground. The women of many tribes urinate while standing.]

37. Fiddles, made from century-plant stocks *(Agave),* have from one to three strings. They were played by men for their own entertainment or for a group of friends but not at dances or ceremonies. Alan Ferg and William B. Kessel, "Recreation," in *Western Apache Material Culture,* ed. Alan Ferg (Tucson: University of Arizona Press, 1987).

38. HtK 1885: Roughly the same thing as a G-string.

39. Ten Kate appears to described the masked dancers, impersonators of important protective mountain-dwelling deities, the Mountain Spirits, who appear in the early evening of a girl's puberty ceremony. Morris E. Opler, "Chiracahua Apache," *Handbook: Southwest,* 10:414–15.

40. The Chiricahua diet depended as much on wild plant harvests as on game, and much of the time and energy of the women went into gathering and processing this food. The most important plant was the agave, or century plant, which provided "mescal," a sweet and nutritious food that could be dried and stored. The Chiricahua moved seasonally and between different elevations to harvest available plants. These included mesquite beans, various berries, seeds, nuts, and, as Ten Kate observed, prickly pear and other cactus fruits. Opler, "Chiricahua Apache," *Handbook: Southwest,* 10:413.

41. HtK 1885: From a letter sent me, dated San Carlos, February 25, 1884, it appears that, except for Chief Geronimo and roughly eleven warriors, all the Chiricahuas who were absent at the time of Crook's attack on the Indian fortress have faithfully complied with the promise to come to the reservation. If I am accurately informed, then Geronimo and his followers, too, later came to the reservation. Also, all through the year 1884 the Indians behaved peacefully. HtK 1889: The Apache campaign in 1883 is not the final one on a large scale. In the course of 1885, the Chiricahuas once again left the reservation to go on the warpath. The celebrated chief Geronimo and General Miles played the principal roles in this campaign, which came to an end in the spring of 1886. The well-known Captain Emmett Crawford perished in it, from Mexican bullets, in the Sierra Madre. Several hundred hostile Chiricahuas—including Geronimo, men, women, and children—who were made prisoners of war by the Americans were exiled to Florida. Therewith the strength of the hostile element among the Apaches has been broken for good." Eds.: For an account of these events, see Thrapp, *Conquest,* 311–67.

42. HtK 1885: General Crook, for example, had not even disarmed his prisoners or taken away their plundered booty, knowing full well that with the slightest violent action the warriors still tarrying in Mexico would learn about this and be converted into a merciless and redoubtable foe for all time. Through fire and smoke signals—mostly giant cactuses set ablaze, which we saw at night, especially on the mountains—the captured Chiricahuas were in constant contact with their brethren in Mexico. Earlier in Tucson, I was already struck by the flickering columns of fire and the red glow I noticed far

to the south. I did not know then that this was the Chiricahuas advancing with Captain Crawford's escort, who were sending messages to their friends remaining behind about how they were doing and where they were. As for disarming an Indian tribe, this is completely pointless. Today all tribes have sufficient monetary resources to provide themselves in short order with a completely new and often better armament through the intermediation of squaw men and other inhabitants of the frontier bent on gain. This seemed most clear from a response of General Crook when he was interviewed by a newspaper writer upon his return from the Sierra Madre and was asked whether he thought the raids of the Apaches were now over for good. "That is difficult to say with certainty," the general responded, "because there are many whites who have an interest in the renewal of hostilities."

43. William Henry Edwards (1822–1909), an American entomologist known particularly for his works on butterflies, also traveled up the Amazon in 1846. His account, *A Voyage Up the River Amazon* (New York: Appleton, 1847), was a well-known travel book in its day. *Dictionary of American Biography* 3, pt. 2:46–47.

44. Rocinante was the name of Don Quixote's nag.

45. HtK 1889, 239. My opinion that the Apache, despite his distinctive tactics, is not cowardly is entirely shared by Captain Bourke, an officer who repeatedly was on the warpath against the Apaches. He says, among other things: "He is no coward; on the contrary, he is entitled to rank among the bravest."

46. Eskiminzin (ca. 1828–1895), an Aravaipa Apache chieftain, was blamed for many depredations, although it has not been proved he was really responsible for many of them. About a hundred of his people were killed in the Camp Grant Massacre, noted by Ten Kate. After a period of turmoil following this event, Eskiminzin was settled in the mid-1870s on the San Carlos Indian Reservation, where he became reconciled to white domination. Thrapp, *Encyclopedia,* 1:467; John P. Clum, "Eskiminzin," *New Mexico Historical Review* 3(1928):399–420; 4 (1929):1–27.

47. Here Ten Kate has confused the French Canadian with the Canadian-born Archie McIntosh (1834–1902), who had long served as a scout for Gen. Crook, played a key role in achieving the surrender of the Apache chieftains Juh and Geronimo in 1880, and served in the 1883 Sierra Madre expedition. Juana Fraser Lyon, "Archie McIntosh, the Scottish Indian Scout," *Journal of Arizona History* 3 (1966):103–22.

48. Mickey Free (1847–1915), who was born of mixed Mexican and Irish parentage, was kidnapped in 1861 by Apaches, an event for which Cochise and the Chiracahuas were unjustly blamed, with the result being the prolonged conflict between this famous chieftain and the Americans. He was later adopted by White Mountain Apaches and in 1872 entered the U.S. Army as a scout and interpreter, playing a role in the 1883 Sierra Madre expedition and other campaigns. Thrapp, *Encyclopedia,* 1:518.

49. William Wadden Turner (1810–1859) was an American philologist who also participated in the Pacific railroad surveys of the 1850s. His work conclusively demonstrated the link between the Apache language and the Athabascan languages of Canada. William H. Goetzmann, *Exploration and Empire* (New York: Knopf, 1966), 328. Johann Karl Eduard Buschmann (1805–1880) was a German scholar of Indian languages, a pupil of Wilhelm von Humboldt. Ten Kate is probably referring to his *Das Apache als eine athapaskische Sprache erwiesen,* 3 vols. (Berlin: Königliche Akademie der Wissenschaften, 1860–63). See Hovens, *Herman ten Kate, 96.*

50. The Apachean languages—consisting of Navajo, Western Apache, Chiricahua, Mescalero, Jicarilla, Lipan, and Kiowa-Apache—comprise the southernmost geographic division of the Athapaskan language family. The two related divisions are the Pacific Coastal, containing eight languages spoken or formerly spoken in California and Oregon, and the Northern, embracing twenty-three languages distributed over a wide area in western Canada and interior Alaska. The languages of the Apachean group constitute a dialect complex derived from a common ancestral prototype. Robert W. Young, "Apachean Languages," *Handbook: Southwest,* 10:393–94.

51. Navajo is close to Western Apache, followed by Chiricahua/Mescalero. Jicarilla, Lipan, and Kiowa-Apache differ to a greater extent from Navajo. Robert W. Young, "Apachean Languages," *Handbook: Southwest,* 10:393–400.

52. HtK 1885: *Apa* is likewise *pa, pá-a, pai, opa,* etc., "man," "person," or "nation." *Agwá, 'gwa (ahuá)* is "war"; *che,* a suffix that has substantive force. The word *Apache* should thus have arisen from *Apa-agwá-che.*

53. In Apachean religious thought, sickness and misfortune could be caused by the anger of a deity or the failure to treat respectfully some personified natural force, such as lightning. In addition, there were animals and birds—notably the owl, snake, bear, and coyote—that were intrinsically dangerous and caused sickness by sight, touch, or odor. The spirits of dead sorcerers and restless ghosts of relatives often appeared in the form of the coyote and the owl. Morris E. Opler, "The Apachean Culture Pattern and Its Origins," *Handbook: Southwest,* 10:373.

54. The Western Apache thought of the clan as that group of relatives descended, not necessarily from one ancestor, but from the group that established the first agricultural site with which the clan was associated. The clan name generally referred to this legendary place of origin. Clan members formed an exogamous group within which there was a bond of obligation almost as close as that of the family. The clan's main functions were to regulate marriage, extend obligatory relations of the family, control farming sites, and provide the basis for war party organization. Charles R. Kaut, *The Western Apache Clan System: Its Origins and Development* (Albuquerque: University of New Mexico Press, 1957), 39–40.

55. HtK 1885: See *Das Ausland,* 1883, no. 49. Captain Crawford told me that on the western slope of the Sierra Madre there are a number of ruins. Stone axes and potsherds coming from there, which I had a chance to see, completely resemble those found in the Gila Valley. Bartlett, op. cit., reports on the casas grandes near Janos and Corralitos along the eastern slope of the Sierra Madre.

56. Bandelier's diary does record his arrival in Tucson on June 26, 1883. Adolph F. Bandelier, *The Southwestern Journals* (Albuquerque: University of New Mexico Press, 1966–84), 2:141.

57. HtK 1885: See Gatschet, "Der Yuma-Sprachstamm," in *Zeitschrift für Ethnologie,* 1877 and 1883. HtK 1889: It would be more accurate if Gatschet ("Der Yuma Sprachstamm," *Zeitschrift für Ethnologie,* 1886, pp. 105, 109–13) had called this in his word list "Apache Yuma" instead of "Tulkepaya" because in my opinion the Apache Yumas and Tolkepayá, or Tulkepáya, are not completely identical.

58. HtK 1885: Gatschet incorrectly identifies the Yumas with the Apache Yumas.

59. HtK 1885: *Petermann's Geographische Mittheilungen,* 1876.

60. HtK 1885: According to Loew (*Petermann's Geographische Mittheilungen,* 1876, pp. 410, 411), the vast moist stream of air that brings rain to New Mexico and Arizona during the summer is a genuine monsoon and, indeed, nothing more than the equatorial stream extending from latitude 28°N to 28°S. It is diverted by the intensely heated region of SW America during the summer,

and it is the result of the earth's rotation, just like the equatorial ocean current. The prevailing winds in the SW of N. America are also, according to Loew, SE winds, while in the winter, at least along the California coast and in the Mohave Desert, NW winds are the prevailing ones, with an absolute humidity less than that of the SE winds.

Dutton (*American Journal of Science* XXII, no. 130, p. 247), on the other hand, maintains that the prevailing winds of the SW of the United States are W. winds, which he at the same time regards as the reason for the great aridity of these regions—basing this conclusion on the fact that winds that constantly blow from cold to warm regions, without having the opportunity to pick up moisture, become warmer and drier.

61. HtK 1885: Here perhaps it is not superfluous to recall that according to Loew, the Southwest is divided into four different vegetation zones depending on the altitude:

1. The zone of cactus, yucca, and agave at an altitude of 3,000–3,500 feet.

2. The zone of *Obione* and *Artemisia,* between 3,500 and 4,900 feet; diminution of cactus species.

3. The zone of *Juniperus occidentalis* ("cedar") and *Pinus edulis,* between 4,900 and 6,800 feet; few cacti. Two species of oak. *Q. acrifolia* and *Q. emoryi* occur in this zone.

4. The zone of pine trees, between 6,800 and 10,800 feet.

Although one can probably accept these distinctions in the main, important exceptions occur now and then, in my opinion. Prescott, for example, at an altitude of 5,000 feet and thus (according to Loew) not in the pine tree zone, is ringed by a sea of heavy pine tree forests. The surrounding region between Wild Water and Camp Apache—which, on average, is certainly not above 5,000 feet but is probably under this—is covered primarily with pine trees. Given such a distinction, a difference of 1,800 feet is hardly insignificant.

62. William Edgworth Dougherty (1841–1915), a veteran of the Civil War, came to Arizona in 1882, arriving at Camp Apache on October 24, 1882. He commanded the post until June 1885, when he moved to Camp Grant. Constance Wynn Altshuler, *Cavalry Yellow and Infantry Blue: Army Officers in Arizona Between 1851 and 1886* (Tucson: Arizona Historical Society, 1991), 106–7.

63. Camp Apache was established on May 16, 1870, near the present town of Fort Apache, Arizona. It became a permanent post in 1873 and was renamed Fort Apache in 1879. Frazer, *Forts,* 3.

64. Mount Thomas (11,590) is today called Mount Baldy. Captain George M. Wheeler (see chapter 1, note 36) had named it "Thomas Peak" for Gen. Lorenzo Thomas (d. 1875), who had served in the war against Mexico. Mount Ord (10,860 feet), the third-highest peak in Arizona, was named for Major General Edward Otho Cresap Ord (d. 1883), who was in charge of the Department of California during the Apache wars. Barnes, *Arizona Place Names,* 3–4.

65. What some have termed the "Cibecue mutiny" involved an Apache medicine man, Nock-ay-del-klinne, who had been leading dances with the purpose of raising from the dead those Indians who had been killed and inciting others. In August 1881, the Indian agent at the San Carlos reservation, Colonel Eugene Asa Carr, supported by two cavalry troops and an Indian scout company, arrested the medicine man. On August 31 a clash took place between American troops and Indian supporters, during which the medicine man and seven Americans were killed. False rumors then spread among the Apaches at San Carlos and elsewhere that Carr's entire command had been massacred, and the emboldened Indians then attacked Fort Apache, where they were repulsed. This was the last united effort to attempt hostilities by the Apaches. Thrapp, *Conquest,* 217–30.

66. Charles Baehr Gatewood (1853–1896), after graduation from Westpoint, was assigned to Arizona in 1877. He participated in most of the major Apache campaigns of this period. His most notable accomplishment was his pursuit of Geronimo into Mexico in 1885–1886 and persuading him to surrender. Thrapp, *Encyclopedia*, 2:543–44.

67. HtK 1885: The thirty-two Apaches of various tribes whom I measured were all brachycephalic: average 90.05. Ten Tonto Apaches had an average cranial index of 88.30. Also the Tontos were thus without exception short skulled.

68. *Ursus ferox = U. arctos.*

69. This place was named after Corydon E. Cooley, a scout with General Crook's army who settled there in 1875. Supposedly he and a partner, finding it difficult to work together, decided to let a game of seven-up decide who would leave. Cooley won by showing a low card, hence the alternate name. Barnes, *Arizona Place Names*, 249.

70. This settlement, established in the late 1870s, got its name from two leaders, Erastus Snow and William J. Flake. Barnes, *Arizona Place Names*, 250.

CHAPTER SIX

By Way of Albuquerque to Santa Fe and the Surrounding Region

AFTER MAKING INQUIRIES, I ALTERED MY ORIGINAL PLAN of going from Holbrook to the Navajo reservation and from there to the Zuni pueblo. In fact, I learned that the government agent for the Navajo Indians was away for a while and that Mr. Cushing of the Smithsonian Institution, who held the rank of chief among the Zunis,[1] was in Santa Fe with a number of his followers to celebrate that city's 333rd anniversary.[2] Because I could accomplish little among the Indians without assistance from the aforementioned gentlemen, I decided to pass through Albuquerque on my way to Santa Fe. In the first city I wanted to visit the Indian school. In the second town the large number of Indians from the surrounding pueblos, on hand in Santa Fe to attend the exposition, provided a fine opportunity for observations.

I took advantage of the first opportunity to leave Holbrook and the following afternoon took a seat on the train leaving for Albuquerque. The stretch of land we steam through is as dreary and isolated as can be. Endless sand flats, sparsely covered with *Artemisia,* unfold before the eye, while here and there a sandstone mesa, freakishly formed, rises up like a solitary island in this ocean without shores. A few miles after we crossed the New Mexico line, shortly before reaching the tiny station Manuelito, enormous sandstone mesas in all manner of colors arise along both sides of the route, varying from light reddish brown to a fine cream color. The walls and peaks of these leviathans are covered with piñon trees *(Pinus edulis)* and juniper. Not far from there one can follow a canyon of similar character, which runs from north to the south, onward toward the horizon.

We stop for a while in Manuelito, which gets its name from one of the most famous chiefs of the Navajos,[3] and take a hurried meal in a baggage car set up as a diner. After the departure from Manuelito, the countryside becomes more attractive. One encounters grassy meadows on which numerous herds of black–and–white goats and sheep are roaming about, with Navajo herders on horseback watching over them. In Gallup, a small frontier town, I count a dozen saloons. A band of drunken citizens are raging and cursing, perhaps over the coal beds that were recently discovered there. Once past Gallup, darkness, coupled with rain showers, overtakes us, putting a definite end to further reflections. At 4:30 A.M. the train halts in Albuquerque.

After a couple of hours' rest in the Hotel Armijo[4]—because this line still does not have sleeping cars—I head out to the street to view the city. Arriving at the station, I find a number of Indians, who differ markedly in appearance from others I have seen. They are wrapped in colorful blankets and wear leather trousers. With them is a Negro; an Indian of lavender countenance with blond locks, clearly an albino;[5] and a white man with long curly hair, who speaks the Indian language and directs them with animated gestures.

From the bystanders I learn that he is Frank Cushing, who is returning from Santa Fe with his Zuni Indians. Approaching him, I introduce myself, relying on a recommendation I have for him. With unaffected politeness he welcomes me, and after having addressed a few words to the Indians, he heads to the hotel with me, where I am introduced to his wife and sister-in-law. Because Mr. Cushing is staying in Albuquerque for the same reason as I am, to visit the Indian school, we spend a very enjoyable day together. Cushing is one of the most interesting people one could ever meet. His speech, which is lucid and eloquent as though it were flowing from his lips, is at once instructive and fascinating. Charming, with a handsome appearance and sharp, intelligent features, framed with reddish blond locks, he calls to mind now an artist, now a soldier. Even though he looks older, he is only twenty-seven. He is of medium height and rather slender, yet at the same time energy and nimbleness are his defining characteristics. As a representative of the Bureau of Ethnology in Washington, Cushing had been living for nearly four years now with the Zuni. Accepted as a member of the tribe under the name of Ténatsali, or Medicine Flower, he held the rank of lieutenant-governor of the pueblo and war chieftain. Being fully versed in the language and life of these Indians, he thus had ample opportunity to carry out his ethnological studies.[6] But more about him and his work in a later chapter.

Together we head to the Presbyterian school, where ninety Indian children receive lodging and instruction.[7] The head of this school is Mr. R. W. D. Bryan,[8] who—strange turn of fate!—had taken part in Hall's polar expedition as an astronomer and traveling companion of Emil Bessels.[9] The school is an ugly abode building with squat rooms, situated in a sandy tract well outside the Mexican quarter of the city. By far most of the children, from both sexes, are from the surrounding pueblos; Laguna, in particular, has supplied a large contingent. There are just a few young Ute Indians, who, with their ungainly figures and large faces, can be clearly distinguished from the more refined Pueblo children. We attend reading and arithmetic classes. We hear them reciting *locorum nuda nomina* [the bare names of places] to demonstrate their geographical knowledge, the Ten Commandments in time to the clapping of hands and the stomping of feet. We see the children marching in and out of the room to the jingling of a table bell, folding their hands at prayer, unfolding them and assailing the food standing on a long table. After all this I am still hesitant about judging whether the Indian is *culturfähig* [capable of civilization] or not. Professor Bryan and the ladies who provide instruction will tell you that this is, indeed, the case. Good—for the time being I accept that. We will discuss this later on.

I would have been delighted to learn what impression all these events in the school made on Palowahtiwa,[10] the governor of the Zuni, who had come at Cushing's request with some of his "younger brothers" to take a look. But not a muscle of their faces twitched as they sat deathly silent, nothing eluding their view. Their gaze brightened up, however, as we, whites and redskins, sat down to the well-provided table and the aroma from the foods caressed their Zuni olfactory organs. Cushing is leaving in the evening that same day with his wife, sister, and at least thirty "brothers," and we part hoping to meet again soon.

Although this school visit to some extent relegated the viewing of the city to the background, I could nevertheless gain an overall impression of Albuquerque. The city consists of two quarters that are widely separated from each other. The one that is the oldest and situated closest to the Rio Grande has a totally Mexican appearance, with its flat adobe houses and sandy streets. The other, close by the railroad, forms New Albuquerque, which has arisen only in the last few years and has all the characteristics of a small American town, with its stores, banks, drugstores, saloons, barbershops, and feed-and-livery stables. In this fashion one encounters two races and two cultures together in Albuquerque, each dating from a different century. The valley of the Rio Grande here is very wide and has no attractive features as bare, ash gray mesas and mountains appear everywhere, from the banks of the river to the horizon, where they stand out in sharp contrast to the fixed, immobile sky.

On July 22, at daybreak, I continue the journey to Santa Fe. Here the same unappealing landscape, which made its appearance yesterday, unrolls for mile after mile. Alamos are the only vegetation, which rim the flat riverbanks in places. The only significant settlements we pass are Bernalillo, whence a mail coach runs to the medicinal springs of Jemez, and Wallace, where we have breakfast. There is a group of Indians at the station. They come from Santo Domingo, a nearby pueblo, and offer turquoises and small painted pottery for sale. The turquoises, which are generally used as ornaments by the Pueblos, are mostly low quality, bluish green in color, and seldom pure. The pottery, most of which has the color of putty and is painted with black ornamentation, is not unattractive. One would have to be very unfeeling not to buy a small item from the dark Pueblo girls, with a blush on their cheeks as fresh as a peach while they ask me, bashfully and comically at the same time, for a *real*.[11]

At Lamy we change trains[12] and the railway heads northward, zigzag, steeply ascending an attractive mountainous region where *piñones* and juniper bushes cover the yellow, sandy soil, until a high dark mountain range emerges on our right. Shortly afterward, at the foot of the range, white houses, spires, and columns of smoke rise, and a few moments later we alight from the train at Santa Fe. In the huge, attractive Palace Hotel, actually out of place in a city such as Santa Fé, I find the comfort I had done without for seven months and could fancy myself in St. Louis or Chicago.[13] But as soon as one looks outside the window or views the street below, the illusion vanishes because everywhere there are nondescript adobe houses and sandy streets, serving as reminders that one is still in the Southwest.

As a sample of the tremendous fondness for titles in this country, I cannot fail to record that the porter of this hotel, a marvelous black man, had the title "general." How silly it sounded: "General, won't you bring my luggage here!" "General, where are my boots, did you shine'm?" By no means was he the only member of the hotel staff with a grandiose title. In the chief clerk he had a "comrade-in-arms" of the same rank. As for myself, during my journey I was once called "general," repeatedly "captain," and not infrequently "professor," even though, according to European notion, neither my outward appearance nor my age conformed to those titles.

In spite of its age—for Santa Fe (full name: Santa Fe de San Francisco) was founded approximately 300 years ago by Spanish priests—the city offers the foreigner very little of note. The ancient church of San Miguel,[14] a small, unsightly building that lies half in ruins, and a similar adobe house, which is thought to be the oldest in the city and is said to be of Pueblo Indian origin,[15] are the most important things one feels obliged to see. The city is predominantly Mexican in appearance, though with an American touch. Just as in Tucson and Albuquerque, the Americans run the most important businesses, and the German-Jewish element, too, is heavily represented in Santa Fe, as, indeed, it is in all cities of the Southwest. The Mexicans, by far the majority, make up the lower classes of the population, comprising approximately 7,000 souls.[16] The past few years have not been thriving ones for Santa Fe—and significantly less so than in the days of the "Santa Fe Trail," when there were vast caravans with long trains of ox wagons of immigrants and traders coming from the East. The completion of the Atchison, Topeka and Santa Fé railway[17] could not prevent its younger sister cities of Albuquerque and Las Vegas from outgrowing the more ancient Santa Fe.[18]

Santa Fe has a marvelous location. The climate is cool and bracing. Sprawled out, it lies along the broad flanks of the Rocky Mountains, on the banks of the Santa Fe River, a small rippling stream. The town is more than 7,000 feet above sea level. Behind the city the mighty elevation separating it from the prairies runs from north to south like a steep rocky wall. In the distance Mount Baldy, with its 12,000-foot peak, reaches up to the sky beyond its dark garb of conifers covering the slopes on all sides. In the immediate vicinity of the town, the foothills are covered with yellow sandstone with piñones and *Juniperus virginiana*. Farther up are stands of *Abies* and *Pinus* densely interspersed. During the period 1874–1880, the average yearly temperature in Santa Fe ranged from 46.6° to 50.6°F.

The "great attraction" during my stay in Santa Fe was the "Tertio-Millennial Celebration," a splendid example of American humbug.[19] Here one can find everything available at a mediocre provincial fair—from carved furniture to pickles, from agricultural implements to children's toys. The only item meriting special attention was the collection of ores from various mining districts in New Mexico. In the end, the numerous Indians, who perform one or more of their dances almost daily, nearly made up for the other shortcomings. Unfortunately for the promoters of the "Tertio-Millennial," the whole thing was a failure, and they ended up with heavy financial losses. In no small measure the heavy rain showers, which fell almost daily, definitely contributed to the limited success.

The Indians who were temporarily in Santa Fe were primarily Pueblos from various tribes. For monetary remuneration and free meals, they were present on the exhibition ground practically all day. A band of Mescalero Apaches, who had visited Santa Fe for the same purpose, left the city the very moment I arrived there.

The first dance I witnessed was the Deer Dance of the Picuris Indians.[20] Ten unclad, painted men, heads adorned with the splendid antler of the elk,[21] represented a herd of these animals pursued by hunters. With their arms they leaned on short sticks, so that their torsos assumed a nearly horizontal posture. All the movements were well studied. One moment the herd was peacefully grazing, then scurried away again frightened, ranks closed, with the antlers in the nape of the neck. The hunters, four or five in number, were armed with bow and arrows and tried to approach the stags slowly and undetected. Two women, wrapped in heavily woven black attire and with green branches in their hands, jumped up and down, without moving from their position. The music accompanying all this consisted of pounding on small, round drums, tapped by a number of Indians standing by.

Another dance, performed by the Indians of San Juan,[22] was no less distinctive. In this dance, too, the movements and expressions of animals are mimicked but of an eagle this time, and only three people, two men and a boy, take part. They are covered from head to foot with mottled eagle feathers. Every one of their movements—from the arrangement of their plumage with the beak, to flying away with a rustling sound from fluttering wings—is a study, a demonstration of the Indians' tremendous powers of observation. The Indians surrounding them shout softly, the slow rhythm keeping time with the rumble of a flat drum.

The matachina dance, which I had the chance to see performed twice by the Indians of San Juan, by far surpassed the others in liveliness and in the abundance of figures but did not have the typically Indian character that distinguished the Deer and Eagle Dance. *La matachina,* or *los matachines*[23] (actually the "clowns' dance" or the "clowns"), is clearly bastardized by Mexican influence, as the name and principal personages, Montezuma and Malinche, indicate.[24] One could call the matachina a historical pantomime dance representing the lovers' quarrel of Montezuma. As the height of confusion, here Malinche is Montezuma's lover instead of performing that role with Cortés, as was historically supposed to be the case.

All the dancers, roughly thirty in number, are masked, with the exception of Malinche, represented by the graceful Pueblo girl Requesita. She has heavy, dark, wavy hair hanging loosely over her shoulders. Her small graceful figure is enveloped in two fine white blankets that are sewn together, decorated with broad black borders, but in such a way that the left half of her fine bust and her bare left arm are visible. On her foot she wears leather moccasins. Montezuma, wearing a black mask, is wrapped in colorful garb. The two *ahuelos,* half beast, half devil, have large leather masks completely covering their heads—one black, the other brown, with long ears. They are also attired like the other dancers, who have loosely fitting white clothes ornamented with beads, shells, and colorful ribbons on their bodies. On their heads they wear a black or red cap shaped liked a miter, which is covered with numerous silver ornaments, crosses, and tiny bars. They have tied a white cloth in front of their faces. In their left hands they hold a rattle made from a gourd shell covered with a cloth, in the right a colorful wooden trident.

The dancers gather in three rows, standing a few paces apart from each other. Malinche has taken her place in the middle, between the rows. Montezuma stands on the same line, but outside the rows. The ahuelos and the *toro* (the bull), an Indian wrapped in bison hide whom they will eventually kill, flank the musicians and participate in the presentation only toward the end. Before long the violins can be heard, beginning with an allegro, fiery and catchy like a Spanish waltz, then reverting again to the sad, plaintive tones of an Indian chant. There is quivering and glimmering all through the colorful rows, which move forward twisting and twirling, to the stomping of feet in rhythm and the sound of little bells dangling from their knee joints, without their lineup undergoing any changes in the process. The shy Malinche dances gracefully along through the rows, slowly traipsing, her eyes downward, while the tridents wave like ornaments. Now the dancers kneel down, and Malinche and Montezuma take turns pursuing each other, in a winding, twisting line or wheeling about in sudden turns. Then, in a skipping gait, the dancers change places again. Eventually, the monsters, the toro, and the ahuelos intervene in the struggle, but Montezuma triumphs over all of them. Triumphantly he emerges from the arena, taking Malinche with him as his prize.

Every day I spend a few hours in the Pueblo Indians' quarters. They are friendly people, with something good-natured and intelligent in their expression, cheerful and quick to laugh, and fond of my cigarettes. Not one of them speaks English, but all of them speak good Spanish. Among them I encounter three main types: the first, which I could call the Pueblo type par excellence; the second being the ordinary "redskin" type; the third, which I encountered only a very few times, characterized by very large faces, light-colored skin and eyes, and robust, vigorous figures. Besides these men of large, vigorous stature, especially among the latter two types, one encounters at the same time short individuals especially, with heavyset body build. As a rule, the women are exceptionally light in complexion.

Just as I found these types present among various Pueblo Indians in Santa Fe, I likewise noticed considerable resemblance in their attire. The men wore their hair hanging loosely down to the neck and over the forehead, cropped above the eyebrows, or parted in the middle and in back into two thick braids hanging over the chest, thereby serving as a vivid reminder of the Plains Indians hairstyle. They wear corresponding attire as well, for example, chamois leather leg attire (leggings) with long fringes along the seam. The upper body is usually covered with a short cotton shirt.

The Pueblo women's attire is still wholly original and consists of a kind of short habit fastened around their middle and reaching down just over the knees. The sleeves are very ample and cover the arms down to about the elbows. The neck is rather low cut. The material of which this piece of clothing consists is fine black wool, very tightly woven, and decorated by interwoven red ornaments in along the edges. The feet and legs of the women fit into simple, plain leather moccasins, which are attached to pieces of clothing on the leg. These latter items consist of very long strips of soft white chamois leather, which are wrapped around the legs so that they thereby reach a size nearly twice as large as normal. The women let their hair hang loosely, always covering the forehead to just above the eyes (we would call this long "pony hair"), but sometimes parted in back into two thick braids hanging in front and at other times hanging loosely around the neck—indeed, in the same manner some artists and learned gentlemen in our country sport their hair. The women wear no ornaments in their hair. The men, on the other hand, often wear eagle feathers (from *Aquila chrysaetos*) stuck in their braids, which are sometimes wrapped in otter fur. This kind of ornamentation is also encountered among the Plains Indians.

Unquestionably a centuries-long interchange has been going on between the Pueblo Indians of the Rio Grande Valley and neighboring nomadic tribes. Indeed, it is likely that a certain number of Plains Indians have settled among the Pueblo Indians and mingled with them.[25] By way of example, here I will just note that the language of the Indians from the Pueblo de Queres (Kera) shows a clear resemblance to that of the Kiowas and that a number of Jicarilla Apaches have settled at Picuris. The vogue of the "dance of the Utes" among the Indians of San Juan and the frequently encountered bison hides in use among the Pueblo Indians demonstrates that an interchange has taken place between the hunting tribes and the sedentary Pueblos and that it is still going on, albeit to a much lesser extent. An Indian from the Tesuque pueblo, which is close to Santa Fe, told me that he was familiar with the Comanches, Cheyennes, and Pawnees from his own observation. He also spoke of a people, far off to the Southeast, who ate people and were detested by all the other tribes. Here he most likely meant the then nearly extinct Tonkaways in Texas.[26] It is also known that not infrequently the Comanches came to Santa Fe to carry on trade.[27]

It is a rather widespread belief that the present-day Pueblo Indians are descendents of the Aztecs. I do want to discuss the absurdity of this proposition in greater detail following my visit to Laguna, the Moqui villages, and Zuni. For now, though, let me simply state that among the Pueblo Indians—including the Moquis and Zunis—one can posit at least four linguistic groups, all four of which cannot possibly be related to the Aztec language.[28] More later on, as well, regarding the so-called Montezuma cult, which purportedly exists among the Pueblo Indians. The majority of Pueblo Indians are Catholic, and it is astonishing that people who have been subject to Spanish influences for so long cling so tenaciously in so many ways to ancient customs—here I will just mention their dwellings and attire.

As for the San Juaneros' adjectives for colors, I found that they label white, yellow, and orange with the same name, *tzéi*, and for brown, purple, and pink have recourse to a paraphrase, using the word *háypáygway* = "little," "a little." "Purple," for example, is called "a little red, a little black" (*háypáygway pay, háypáygway hàhndee*).

On July 26th I interrupted my stay in Santa Fe with an excursion to the pueblo Tesuque nine miles north. Though small, it has all the principal features of the Indian "towns." The entire area between the two places consists of a pronounced undulating terrain of sandstone and loose sand, which everywhere shows traces of heavy erosion and has identical vegetation as nearby Santa Fe.

Three rows of houses forming right angles to each other enclose a spacious plaza, which is open on the east side. These houses, built of adobe, form two terraces resting on top of each other, which are accessible by means of broad wooden ladders. The doors are small and the windows tiny. At various places on the roofs of the houses, one notices a number of ovens with the shape of large beehives. Next to them lies a pile of cakes of dry sheep dung, which serves as fuel. The houses' chimneys are of adobe but end in an olla from which the bottom has been tapped out. The rooms of these dwellings are, as a rule, small and low in height. In many there is a large chimney and four or five grinding stones (metates) in a row in wooden troughs. In addition, on the ceiling beams above the floor of the room are suspended a number of long sticks equal to a man's height, upon which articles of clothing, blankets, harnesses, and weapons are suspended. A number of sheepskins and blankets lie on the ground—this is the sleeping area. Further, a number of pots of painted clay and a couple of baskets are the sum total of native domestic utensils. Red peppers *(Capsicum annuum)* and watermelons can be found in practically every dwelling. In many dwellings I found pictures of Catholic saints and colorful, ugly prints with biblical scenes, which the owners displayed with a certain pride.

The Indians of Tesuque, barely a hundred in number, belong to the Tewa tribe. Agriculture is their primary livelihood, and fields of corn and watermelons extend outward in the area around the pueblo. In addition, they own herds of sheep and goats, the foul-smelling corrals of which are encountered outside the built-up area. Their agricultural implements are still quite primitive. A completely wooden plow assumes the most prominent place among them. It consists of a pointed beam terminating in a crude handle pointing upward, while a stick fastened to the front end of the plow serves for attaching the hauling straps of the oxen. A similar crude specimen of Pueblo industry is the wooden oxcart with massive, creaking wheels, which make an earsplitting squealing, squeaking racket, just like Basque oxcarts in Spain. The oxen are harnessed in front of these carts with long ropes of untanned leather. Indeed, untanned leather and wooden pegs and wedges are the only ways with which a right-minded Pueblo Indian connects things because the use of iron has hardly made its way here yet.

As far as I could determine, the pottery made in the various pueblos does not afford much variety, except for that of the Zuni and Moqui Indians, who are farther advanced in the art of pottery making than the other Pueblo Indians. The pottery I viewed in Tesuque, and a few small samples that I purchased, may serve as an example for purposes of description.

One encounters open vessels in the form of ollas[29] with some variety and vessels with animal shapes. From an aesthetic viewpoint the former is certainly the best because the second can only be characterized as monstrous. The basic colors are, as a rule, light gray and cream color, while sometimes reddish brown is used in part as a basic color. Not infrequently glossy black is the sole color for small vessels. Likewise, one now and then finds small pottery that, though reddish brown and yellowish in color, is covered with a thick glittering coat resembling mica. The ornamentation is usually black and consists of an endless variety of wavy lines, meandering figures, and arabesques, which show up quite well on the bright background. The animals imitated in pottery are usually birds and reveal the gracelessness and low-level artistic sensibility of these Indians. Frequently one finds people depicted as well, mostly representing dancers and clowns from their dances.

Having returned to Santa Fe on the 28th of July, I headed to Las Vegas before continuing my journey in the West. A train ride of nearly seven hours takes you there along a magnificent mountainous route, which slices through the Rockies. Red and gray sandstone and limestone with their bare walls now rise up alongside a babbling brook. Then, joined together, they extend endlessly outward again, clad in a dark, fragrant garb of pines, piñones, and juniper. Now and then a grassy mountain meadow unfolds, providing fodder for the cattle herds of a lonely ranchero.

Las Vegas, like Albuquerque, has two elements,[30] which are mirrored in the appearance of the inhabitants as well as in the building style of the dwellings. It is a town that can look forward to a bright future. Situated at the outer limit of the prairies, bounding the open horizon toward the east, on the western flank it abuts steep limestone hills, which are the outgrowth of the Rocky Mountains. The houses of Las Vegas are laid out widely separated from each other. Or rather, the newly built streets and squares, which cover a large area, still have many open spaces. That is why the town's appearance is somewhat drab and makeshift. Many houses, not infrequently with four or five stories, are built from red brick, while gray limestone from the soil is used as building material as well. Apart from that, Las Vegas has the typical appearance of modern American towns, of which I need not repeat the [already] familiar description.

I stayed at Las Vegas just half a day before heading on to Hot Springs, six miles northwest of there, on the 29th. Although the medicinal springs in Las Vegas were already known to the Indians, and although a small military hospital was built there as early as 1846, during the Mexican War, only in more recent years have they attracted more and more attention. At the present time Las Vegas–Hot Springs is one of the most frequented spas of the American West. Here there are nearly forty warm springs, which emerge seething and steaming out of the crevices of reddish granulite, which has penetrated the layers of limestone. The temperature ranges from 71 to 136°F. The water contains primarily chloride and sodium sulfates and sodium and calcium carbonates and among other things is used by sufferers from rheumatism, gout, various skin ailments, and dyspepsia. The entire spa mainly consists of a couple of hotels, including the gigantic "Montezuma," a bathhouse, and a couple of small stores. Although the aggregate is not unattractive, thanks especially to the lovely surroundings, it still lacks the variety needed to make a long stay pleasant.[31]

The climate is marvelously cool and the air, rich in ozone, as pure as can be. The elevation upon which the spa is situated is 6,767 feet at the entrance of a narrow valley, the walls of which, consisting of limestone, are covered with pine trees and small oaks. The Rio Gallinas, a muddy little mountain stream, wends its way toward the Pecos River, rippling along through the valley, in some places affording an exquisite spectacle. If one climbs to the top of the rocks surrounding the valley, one then perceives on all sides the endless craggy masses of the Rocky Mountains, crowned by dark clouds—except toward the southeast, where its immobile, barren stretches of land from the green prairie rise up.

The public in Hot Springs consisted primarily of patients and pleasure seekers from the fashionable middle classes of the central states of the Union. Hot Springs is still too new and too little known to draw a high-toned, elegant public, such as one finds in Saratoga and Newport during the summer.

Let me follow up here with some observations about Americans, both in the eastern states as well as the West. It occurs to me—and I am not the first to say so—that generally Americans of both sexes, perhaps from every class of society, individual differences aside, exhibit a distinct national type. Though akin to the concept "type" in the anthropological sense, it is still not to be confused with it. I do not find it difficult to distinguish at first sight an American from an Englishman, to mention nothing of the difference in speech and accent.

The American is thinner and gaunter than the Englishman. His facial color lacks the ruddiness one encounters so often among the English. His features are more angular and sharply etched. In facial expression there is something energetic, daring—at times something callous and something weary all at the same time. Underneath the mask of calm and insouciance, the American is, in reality, nervous and agitated, excited as they themselves put it—always in a kind of feverish state, in a hurry to work and earn money. What a tremendous contrast here with the Mexican, who does a minimal amount of labor and is content as long as he suffers no want. The passion for work and earning money at any cost—solely for the pleasure of earning money, but not in order to reap the fruits—is alien to the Mexican, as it is to his half brother, the Indian, whom he most resembles physically and psychologically.

The "professional type," if I may call it that, is much less common among the Americans than among the Europeans; for the very same person, with varying success, exercises now one, now another profession—all depending on whether it "pays better." In civilized Europe there is something about appearance and demeanor that allow the discerning observer immediately to recognize bureaucrats, schoolmasters, merchants, etc., etc.—the distinctive trait resulting from the long-term performance of their profession. In the Union that is far less common because the same person rarely exercises one and the same profession—or never does so long enough—so that its influence can be felt.

A couple of examples among many:

I have known people who without any preparation were by turns banker, cook, railway official, or in the cattle business; others who had been clerk, schoolmaster, physician, "colonel," Indian agent, or in the mining business. It scarcely needs to be said *how* all these professions were exercised. One could call this pathetic if it were not so ludicrous to the utmost degree. In particular, I shall not easily forget the "colonels," "judges," and "doctors"!

Having returned to Santa Fe on August 1st, I made the acquaintance of Prof. A. H. Thompson, who was heading a topographical survey in northeastern Arizona.³² Because my journey would take me there, Mr. Thompson invited me to visit his camp near Fort Defiance and at the same time declared himself ready to provide whatever help was needed. Because this traveler had to stay awhile longer in Albuquerque and I wanted to visit Laguna Pueblo, we agreed to meet at Fort Wingate. As quickly as possible, I made the needed preparations for my departure and sent off the collection I made. But when I wanted to depart on August 2, it appeared that the route was blocked because of a railway accident, and I could only undertake my journey on the evening of the 3rd.

⁙⁙⁙⁙⁙

NOTES

1. Frank Hamilton Cushing (1857–1900), a pioneer American ethnographer, worked in the Bureau of American Ethnology (part of the Smithsonian Institution) from 1879 until his death. He lived five years (1879–1884) among the Zuni Indians of New Mexico, among whom he carried out pioneering fieldwork. He was one of the first anthropologists to investigate a culture by living and participating in it rather than simply observing it as a bystander. Cushing and Ten Kate became close friends and later collaborators in the Hemenway Southwestern Archeological Expedition of 1887–1888, which Cushing headed. See Jesse Green, ed., *Zuni: Selected Writings of Frank Hamilton Cushing* (Lincoln: University of Nebraska, 1979), 3–34; Jesse Green, ed., *Cushing at Zuni: The Correspondence and Journals of Frank Hamilton Cushing, 1879–1884* (Albuquerque: University of New Mexico, 1990); also Pieter Hovens, "The Anthropologist as Enigma: Frank Hamilton Cushing," *European Review of Native American Studies,* 2:1–5; 1988.

2. In 1609 Don Pedro de Peralta, the governor of New Mexico, moved the colony's capital from San Gabriel near the pueblo of San Juan south to the site of an abandoned Indian pueblo, where he established the town he called La Villa Real de Santa Fé. Because the relocation of the Spaniards from San Gabriel to Santa Fe took some time, most historians have declared 1610 as Santa Fe's founding date. David Grant Noble, ed. *Santa Fe: History of an Ancient City* (Santa Fe, N.Mex.: School of American Research Press, 1989). At the time of Ten Kate's visit many thought the city had been founded in 1550 (see note 19). Reasonably accurate dating of its foundation came only later in the decade. See Adolph Bandelier, *The Gilded Man* (New York: Appleton, 1893), 282–88.

3. Manuelito (ca. 1818–1893) was one of the leaders of the Navajo during their fierce struggles with the U.S. Army during the early 1860s and one of the last to surrender. After 1866, however, he made peace with the Americans and for a time was head of the tribal police. *Biographical Dictionary of Indians of the Americas,* 2 vols. (Newport Beach, Calif.: American Indian Publishers, 1991), 1:392–95.

4. Armijo House, named for its owner, Mariano Armijo, was built during the 1880s after Albuquerque became linked to the railway. A three-story, mansarded building, in sharp contrast to the prevailing adobe structures, it was intended to be the most elegant hotel in the Southwest. It was destroyed by fire in 1897. Marc Simmons, *Albuquerque: A Narrative History* (Albuquerque: University of New Mexico Press, 1982), 226, 249, 297.

5. HtK 1885: This Indian is depicted in chapter 8, in lithograph 10, the seated figure on the right.

6. HtK 1885: See inter alia *Revue d'Ethnographie* of Hamy, vol. I, p. 168, and *The Century Magazine*, New York, 1882 and 1883, where Cushing, under the title of "My Adventures in Zuni," recounts in captivating fashion all about his stay in Zuni.

7. On January 1, 1881, Presbyterians founded the United States Indian Training School (better known as the Albuquerque Indian School) one mile north of Old Town Plaza. In 1882 it moved to a campus one-half mile east of Los Duranes. In 1886 the Presbyterians transferred management of the school to the U.S. government. Lillie G. McKinney, "History of the Albuquerque Indian School," *New Mexico Historical Review* 20 (1945):110–19.

8. R. W. D. Bryan became superintendent of the school in 1882, a post he held until 1886. Afterward Bryan practiced law in Albuquerque. He died in 1912. McKinney, "Albuquerque Indian School," 114–19.

9. American explorer Charles Francis Hall (1821–1871) led three expeditions to the Arctic in 1860–1862, 1864–1869, and 1871. He perished on the last of these. Chauncey Loomis, *Weird and Tragic Shores: The Story of Charles Francis Hall, Explorer* (New York: Knopf, 1971). German scientist Emil Bessels (1847–1888) had earlier explored the Spitsbergen region. In 1871 he immigrated to the United States and joined Hall's expedition, serving as its scientific adviser. *Allgemeine Deutsche Biographie*, 56 vols. (Berlin: Duncker & Humblot, 1875–1912), 46:479–81. Ten Kate visited Bessels shortly after his arrival in the United States and received a letter of recommendation from him for Frank H. Cushing.

10. Palowahtiwa (Patricio Pino) succeeded his father, Pedro Pino (see chapter 8, note 22) as governor of Zuni in the late 1870s. Father and son are remembered today as strong advocates of Zuni rights. Raymond S. Brandes, "Frank Hamilton Cushing: Pioneer Americanist" (unpublished Ph.D. diss., University of Arizona, 1965), 83, 126; E. Richard Hart, "Zuni Relations with the United States and the Zuni Land Claim," in *Zuni and the Courts: A Struggle for Sovereign Land Rights*, ed. E. Richard Hart (Lawrence: University Press of Kansas, 1995), 77–78.

11. HtK 1885: 1/8 dollar = a "bit."

12. In 1880, when the Atchison, Topeka and Santa Fe Railway built a spur line into Santa Fe, the rail junction was at a village in the center of the Lamy Land Grant, 16,547 acres that Archbishop Lamy (see chapter 1, note 62) had taken into trust, and the junction was named in his honor. Keith L. Bryant, *History of the Atchison, Topeka and Santa Fe Railway* (Lincoln: University of Nebraska Press, 1982), 60–63.

13. Built in 1880, the Palace Hotel was an elegant, three-storied French Second Empire structure with elaborate wooden ornamentation and a mansard roof. It burned down in 1926. John P. Conron and R. Patrick Christopher, "The Architecture of Santa Fe," *New Mexico Architecture* 20 (1978):5, 20–21, and Fig. 30.

14. The original chapel of San Miguel, built in 1626, was destroyed during the 1680 Pueblo Revolt but rebuilt in 1710. It had a triple-tiered tower that collapsed in the 1870s, hence Ten Kate's comments on its state of disrepair. The Historical Santa Fe Foundation, *Old Santa Fe Today*, 4th ed. (Albuquerque: University of New Mexico Press, 1991), 101–2.

15. In Ten Kate's day, this two-storied adobe house was known as the "oldest building" in Santa Fe. However, tree-ring specimens taken from beams in the ceiling show cutting dates of approximately 1740–1767, thus approximately 150 years after the initial construction of the Palace of the Governors, which is acknowledged as the oldest building in Santa Fe. Historic Santa Fe Foundation, *Old Santa Fe Today*, 74.

16. German Jews did, in fact, play an important role in the commercial expansion of New Mexico. See William J. Parish, "The German Jew and the Commercial Revolution in Territorial New Mexico, 1850–1900," *New Mexico Historical Review* 35 (1960):1–30, 129–50.

17. The Atchison. Topeka and Santa Fe railway line reached Albuquerque on April 15, 1880. Ira G. Clark, *Then Came the Railroads* (Norman: University of Oklahoma Press, 1958), 136.

18. Here the author is mistaken. According to the 1880 census, Santa Fe had 6,635 residents, while Albuquerque had only 2,135.

19. The "Tertio-Millenial" festival, the largest show staged in New Mexico up to this time, was celebrated in Santa Fe between July 2 and August 15, 1883. It derived its name from one-third of a millennium, i.e., 333 years. Its professed purpose then was to celebrate the supposed 333rd anniversary of the founding of Santa Fe in 1550. It was for this festival that Cushing also brought his Zuni Indians to Santa Fe, where they staged a mock ambuscade and battle and also performed ceremonial dances. Bruce T. Ellis, "Santa Fe's Tertio-Millennial," *El Palacio* 65 (1958):121–35.

20. HtK 1885: Picuris is a small pueblo situated in the mountains north of Santa Fe whose residents, about 100 in number, speak the same language as those in nearby Taos. Eds.: Picuris Pueblo is in the mountains of northern New Mexico. As a Northern Tiwa–speaking village, it is most closely related to Taos Pueblo, eighteen miles north. The population of Picuris was 127 in 1870, 108 in 1890. Donald N. Brown, "Picuris Pueblo," *Handbook of North American Indians: Southwest,* ed. A. Ortiz (Washington, D.C.: Smithsonian Institution, 1983), 9:268–77.

21. HtK 1885: *Cervus canadensis* (Briss).

22. HtK 1885: A pueblo situated northwest of Santa Fe, with approximately 400 inhabitants, who speak a dialect of the Tehua or Tewa language.

23. Derived from the Italian *mattaccino,* a charlatan, jester, or mimic. See María Moliner, *Diccionario de Uso del Español,* 2 vols. (Madrid: Gredos, 1989), 2:364. Most scholars agree that the Matachinas Dance, derived from medieval folk dramas representing conflict between Christians and Moors, was brought to the New World by Spain, where it merged with aboriginal practices in Central Mexico and was then transmitted to the northern pueblos, probably by Mexican Indians accompanying Spanish settlers. Richard J. Parmentier, "The Mythological Triangle: Poseyema, Montezuma and Jesus in the Pueblos," *Handbook: Southwest* 9:609–22; Sylvia Rodriguez, *The Matachinas Dance: Ritual Symbolism and Interethnic Relations in the Upper Rio Grande Valley* (Albuquerque: University of New Mexico Press, 1996); Hovens, *Herman ten Kate en de Antropologie der Noord Amerikaanse Indianen* (Meppel: Krips, 1989), 118.

24. Montezuma was the Aztec emperor when Cortés invaded Mexico. "Malinche" is the name Mexicans gave to Doña Marina, the Indian woman who served as guide and interpreter to the Spaniards and later became Cortés's mistress.

25. Ten Kate is correct. The Pueblo communities were aware of the Plains tribes to the east and northeast even before the Spanish conquest, and the Spanish colonizers encouraged trading between Pueblo and Plains tribes, with Taos, Pecos, and Picuris serving as important commercial centers. There were also Mexican traders from New Mexico, the so-called comancheros, who regularly traded with the Comanches. Charles H. Lange, "Relations of the Southwest with the Plains and Great Basin," *Handbook: Southwest,* 9:201–6; Charles Kenner, *The Comanchero Frontier: A History of New Mexican-Plains Indian Relations* (Norman: University of Oklahoma Press, 1994).

26. Originally the Tonkawas inhabited central Texas but in 1859 were transferred to the Indian Territory. In 1862 rival tribesmen massacred about half the tribe because of their reputation for cannibalism and their supposed sympathy with the Confederacy. Their remnants were resettled in what is now northern Oklahoma. W. W. Newcomb, Jr., *The Indians of Texas* (Austin: University of Texas, 1961), 133–53; John R. Swanton, *The Indian Tribes of North America* (Washington, D.C.: U.S. Government Printing Office, 1952), 326–27.

27. HtK 1885: Möllhausen, among others, relates (*Reis van den Mississippi naar de Kusten van den Grooten Oceaan,* I, p. 212, Dutch translation) that in the prairies of Texas he met Indians from the Santo Domingo pueblo who were traveling to carry out barter. Eds.: See English edition, Möllhausen, *Diary of a Journey from the Mississippi to the Coasts of the Pacific* (London: Longman, Brown, Green, Longman & Roberts, 1858), 1:226.

28. In spite of their apparent similarities, four linguistic stocks are represented in the Puebloan populations. Hopi is a Uto-Aztecan language, closely related to the Numic languages of the Great Basin. Zuni belongs to a different stock, perhaps distantly related to California Penutian. The Keresans (Acoma and Laguna to the west; Zia, Santa Ana, San Felipe, Santo Domingo, and Cochiti in the Rio Grande Valley) have no known linguistic affiliation. The Kiowa-Tanoan family has three Tanoan subgroups (Tiwa, Tewa, Towa) in the Rio Grande area. The Northern Tiwa (Taos and Picuris) and the Southern Tiwa (Isleta and Sandia) represent one group. Towa is represented at Jemez (along with survivors from Pecos, which was abandoned in 1838). The Tewa—the Rio Grande villages of San Juan, Santa Clara, San Ildefonso, Nambe, Pojoaque, and Tesuque as well as the Arizona Tewa of Hano on Hopi First Mesa, who fled the Rio Grande after de Vargas's reconquest ca. 1696—constitute the fourth group. Fred Eggan, "Pueblos: Introduction," *Handbook: Southwest,* 9:224–35.

29. *Olla* is a Spanish term usually applied to medium-size to large water storage jars. A single olla on a masonry base or a series of ollas cemented together with mud plaster also served as chimneys in Puebloan villages at that time. Stewart Peckham, *From this Earth: The Ancient Art of Pueblo Pottery* (Santa Fe: Museum of New Mexico Press, 1990), 159.

30. I.e., Mexican and American.

31. During the 1880s Las Vegas was a major western spa, and the Montezuma Hotel, opened in 1882, provided some of the most luxurious lodging and dining in the West. The depression of the 1890s and the building of other spas farther west led to Las Vegas's decline as a resort area. Lynn Perrigo, *Gateway to Glorieta: A History of Las Vegas, New Mexico* (Boulder, Colo.: Pruett Publishing Co., 1982), 22—25.

32. Almon H. Thompson, the brother-in-law of the famous western explorer John Wesley Powell, accompanied him on one of his western expeditions in the late 1860s and early 1870s and made important maps of the Grand Canyon and other nearby regions in the Southwest. William H. Goetzmann, *Exploration and Empire* (New York: Knopf, 1966) 535, 555–57, 559–63, 568.

CHAPTER SEVEN

By Way of Laguna to the Navajo Indians

A Visit to the Moqui Villages

BECAUSE OF THE RAILWAY ACCIDENT, THE TRAINS WERE RUNNING on a very irregular schedule. Having arrived in Albuquerque, I was obliged to wait there until the following night for the train that was to take me to Laguna Pueblo.[1] Because there is no station in Laguna, I was let out in the middle of the night along the track and had no choice but to grope my way to the foot of a telegraph pole, spread out my blanket, and wait for morning.

When the sun rose, it illuminated a dismal landscape of brown sandstone cliffs, and I descried at some distance the terrace-shaped houses of the pueblo.[2] Closer by stood a small dwelling where, according to information I received in Albuquerque, the missionary, a subagent of the Indians, supposedly lived. So as not to disturb the reverend during his sleep, I waited awhile before announcing myself and met him while he was just putting the finishing touches to his Sunday toilette. Whether this put Reverend John Menaul in a bad mood or whether things were not going smoothly with his sermon, which he was to deliver shortly, I cannot say. Whatever the case, I was received with more than just coolness. He let me know that I could not count on breakfast or other tokens of hospitality and that, furthermore, he had no time now and had to milk his cow. Thereupon the little red Irishman grabbed a pail and vanished while he left me standing with an empty stomach.[3] In a very ill humor, I now headed into the pueblo and ended up in a dwelling where an American, who was married to an Indian woman, provided me with breakfast. Rejuvenated, I now took a closer look at Laguna.

The pueblo, with its irregular construction, is situated on the slope of a sandstone hill, which has been eroded in many places by water. To the south of Laguna flows the San José, a small river, which propels its muddy water eastward between steep walls toward the Rio Puerco, while the railway line cuts across the outermost southern rim of the pueblo. The surrounding area consists of yellow- and pinkish-colored sandstone from the Cretaceous era, broken up in many places—on top of the hills, for instance—by basalt. From these hills one has a view to the northwest of 12,000-foot-high Mount Taylor or San Mateo, a spent volcano, which, judging from the shape of the terrain of these tracts, must have once played an important role. At this time it is an object of reverence for various Indian tribes.[4] The only vegetation, which covers the dry ground in patches, consists of grass and juniper bushes.

The pueblo itself is one of the largest in New Mexico and is inhabited by nearly a thousand people (512 men, 462 women), who speak a dialect of the Kera [Keres] language and call themselves *Kawáikäme.*[5] They call their city *Kawáik* or *Kawáika*. The pueblo takes the name "Laguna" from a large lake that suddenly vanished about sixty years ago, emptying into the nearby San José River.[6] Also, the name the Navajo Indians give to Laguna, *Tozjánne*—that is, "plenty of water"—points to this lake's former existence.

Because it was harvesttime, very few Indians were in the pueblo because those engaged in this labor now lived in the field outside the pueblo. Nevertheless, I visited various dwellings that, on the outside and the inside, greatly resembled those of Tesuque. I had the opportunity to form my own idea about the type of the inhabitants, who, in appearance and in attire, generally match the Indians of Tesuque. In physiognomy some Indians call to mind the Apaches and, most likely, were Navajos who had settled in Laguna and were incorporated into the Kawáikäme. There were also individual Indians with luxuriant, very curly hair, a peculiarity I had noticed several times among the Apaches.

To hear a sample of the language, I strolled inside the old church building, dating from Spanish times, where Reverend Menaul was reading to a dozen Indians in English and Laguna from a catechism book and had some children, whom he had taught to read, repeat it. The language was not unpleasant to the ear and particularly striking for its abundance of sibilants. The reverend, perhaps mollified by my appearance in the church, informed me, among other things, that the Indians never pronounce the name of the Supreme Being; in preparing his catechism, he had to use the Spanish *Dios*. Though busy for some years now, he had not made any converts among these Indians, even though a small number came regularly to hear him; another part was still "heathen." Just what those "heathen" ideas were the reverend could not tell me: all that mattered was that they were "heathens" and had to become Presbyterians.

Generally, comparative religion is no more a strong suit of these missionaries than sociology. Without any serious investigation, they display great contempt for the religious and social conditions of the people they want to convert—in their zeal forgetting that not every change is an improvement. And so, I was at the wrong office for information on that subject. Because I had had enough of Laguna and its shepherd, I bade farewell to the place around midnight and the next morning arrived at

Wingate station. From here the mail wagon brought me to the fort of the same name, three miles south, where I met Professor Thompson and a couple of members of the expedition.

This military post, founded in 1868,[7] is situated at an elevation of approximately 6,800 feet on the northern slope of the Zuni Mountains. As far as the eye can see to the north and west towers, pyramids, and pillars arise in the most freakish red shapes and colorful sandstone from the Triassic formation. One of the most remarkable of these colossi, the result of erosion, is the so-called Navajo Church. Between them juniper bushes *(J. occidentalis)* and oaks *(Quercus alba)* extend far and wide, while behind the fort the slopes of the mountain ranges are covered with the magnificent ponderosa pine. Although Wingate is outside the Navajo Indian reservation, a number of these Indians have their encampments in the area nearby. Actually there are many scattered across the tract of land extending between the pueblo Jemez and the Moqui villages.[8]

I had the fortunate opportunity of getting to know the first physician at the post, Dr. Washington Matthews, well known for his ethnographic and philological investigations among the Hidatsa Indians in Dakota and now undertaking the same kind of work among the Navajos.[9] With him I visited various *chogáns,*[10] or huts, where for the first time I saw the justly famous Navajo blankets being woven and silver being made. The Navajos' summer huts entirely resemble the Apaches' *khonge* made of branches. Their winter huts, on the other hand, consist of tree trunks lain against each other and covered with earth so that the chógan takes on the shape of a blunt, irregular cone. Sometimes, however, the style of construction recalls that of the Mohaves.

The loom with which the Navajos weave their blankets is made entirely of wood and is very primitive in shape. It is operated by men as well as women. The blankets they weave are usually thick and heavy and made from the wool of their numerous herds of sheep and goats.[11] They vary in price from two to 100 to 125 dollars, all depending on the quality. The most common ones are woolen and white in color with broad dark blue and black transverse stripes. Those of better quality are less woolen and blue with individual black or red stripes or white with black and red figures. The very best are smooth and multicolored with complicated patterns, like a Mexican serape. On the four corners of the blanket there are woolen tassels and straps to fasten them when they are being worn because seldom is a Navajo seen without his blanket.[12] In addition, they make saddle blankets with just as much variety in color and quality as in the case of [regular] blankets. Usually two or three of these covers are folded up and placed under the saddle.

The silver work of the Navajos consists of ear- and finger rings, bracelets, buttons for adornment of various articles of clothing, and big thin plates, with which they decorate their leather belts and the headstalls of their horses. The silver used for this purpose comes from American coins. Now and then one can also see red and yellow copper bracelets. These ornaments often attest to the good taste and high artistic value, wherein the Navajos have equaled and, in blanket weaving, even surpassed their masters, the Zuni Indians.[13]

We left the fort on the evening of the day of our arrival so we could take the train, which had to bring us to Manuelito the next morning at sunup, and spent an anything but pleasant night on the hard floor in the small station building of Wingate. Arriving in Manuelito on August 7th, we found mounts and wagons from the expedition led by Professor Thompson. At 9 o'clock, after breakfast, we saddled up to head for the camp on the Navajo reservation near Fort Defiance. Initially the route—nothing more than a miserable wagon track—leads through a long, wide canyon, sparsely overgrown with piñones and juniper bushes. Later, more on the ascent, we come upon the wide, elevated valley of Bonito Canyon, which is on our left. The ground consists of white, yellow, and red sandstone, which here and there, especially along the walls of the high valley, assumes the most freakish shapes, rising up above the dark green of the conifers like awesome towers and fortifications. Gigantic sunflowers and yellow *Heliopsis* [oxeye] spread out in dazzling profusion and with the Capparadiceae, perhaps no less numerous purple, lend a distinctive color to the landscape, already so colorful because of the multitinted soil. The only living things we see are a herd of half-wild Indian horses, whom we surprise rounding the so-called Haystacks, a couple of steep, isolated sandstone peaks. They stare at us with astonishment, ruffle their manes, and, stomping and snorting, take flight.

A mile before we reach the camp, an isolated cluster of dark steplike stones, which here have broken through the sandstone stratum, arise in the middle of the valley floor. Eventually we pass a pair of chogáns alongside splendid cornfields and gigantic sunflowers. We see a number of white tents and some adobe houses, and a moment later we dismount at Fort Defiance after riding nearly four and a half hours. Professor Thompson accommodates me in his own tent, and suddenly I am at home in the camp.

Fort Defiance is situated at an elevation of 7,000 feet at the opening of a quarter-mile-long canyon with steep sandstone walls, which are 300 feet high. The Rio Bonito has beaten a path through this chasm for ages and because of the tremendous drop speedily propels its muddy waters southward. Established in 1851 to curb Navajo Indian raids, Fort Defiance was abandoned by its troops fourteen or fifteen years ago, and now just the agency remains.[14] Here one finds a number of very low, decayed dwellings and adobe sheds—in addition a large stone schoolhouse, which is closed, however, and whose massive walls and heavy doors recall a fortress. At some distance behind the agency is the cemetery, where a number of American soldiers are buried. The more distant surroundings likewise consist of red sandstone from the Triassic formation, which is blanketed with various kinds of grass, including grama, as well as juniper bushes, piñones, and other conifers.

The government agent was still away, but with the doctor's help I got to know various Indians and spent every day in various chogáns, observing their activities there and bringing together items for my ethnographic collection. Because it was right in the middle of the rainy season, I was often impeded in my various outings. Once while sitting around the fire in a winter chogán in the company of some Indians, a very heavy downpour suddenly broke loose. It was so powerful that within a few moments a heavy torrent of water, like a roaring creek, surged through the entrance, forced us to our feet, doused the fire, and put everything in the hut underwater. Hurriedly the Indians tossed everything that could be found in the chogán through the hole that served as a chimney onto the roof and from there onto a nearby hill. Then we waded nearly up to our knees through the water, which had transformed the cornfield into a sprawling pond, and with my Indian guide I mounted the horse, which we rode together.

To avoid the flooded fields, we took the return route across the hills, but when we reached the spot where the crude wooden bridge across the Rio Bonito led to Defiance, we found it swept away and the water rushing through the canyon, making a roaring noise with sloshing and foaming. We had no choice but to wait awhile until the water had subsided enough so that we could wade through the river without peril. But having arrived in the middle of the riverbed, our nimble horse had a great deal of trouble holding its own with its double burden, and we narrowly escaped tumbling into the rough waters.

There are Navajos in our camp every day. The guides and the person tending the herd of horses from the expedition are from this tribe too. In the morning, as we emerge from the tents and, shivering, head toward the big wood fire, over which breakfast is cooking, a small group of Navajos is usually standing wrapped in their blankets, gazing eagerly at the warmed-up contents of the pots and pans. Luckily for them, the cook, like all the subalterns from the expedition, is a Mormon—in other words, a friend of the Indians—and they can be sure that the leftovers from our breakfast will be distributed to them.[15] The assistant cook is, I believe, the sole non-Mormon and a former Prussian cadet—the friend, it so happens, of one of my fellow students at the University of Göttingen.[16]

As a type, the Navajos strongly recall the Apaches, but the thin black mustaches, which nearly all adult men wear, and the hair on their heads, which is bound up in back, lend their physiognomy a somewhat different expression. In other respects, they have the squinting and penetrating gaze of the Apaches as well. They are also lean and supple, while their appearance exudes tenacity and hardiness.

In their attire, which has already been mentioned, they recall the Pueblo Indians in many respects, particularly the Moquis and Zunis. In this regard many women can hardly be distinguished from their sisters in the aforementioned tribes. As a rule, the men wear a purple or red head cloth after the fashion of the Apaches but differ in that a bundled-up lock of hair is suspended from the back of their heads. Except for the blankets, leg attire, and moccasins, their garb is a cheap, unsightly hodgepodge of cotton prints and cloth, and darker colors, black and dark blue, are particularly in vogue. The leg attire consists of large pieces of brown leather, which are tightly bound below the knee with a band (Sp. *faja*) woven from red wool and reaching down to the ankles. The moccasins envelop the feet like a stocking and consist of soft, smooth leather, with a sole, which is only a little harder and thicker than the leather covering the toes and the insteps. The sole ornamentation of their footwear consists of a pair of silver buttons, allowing it to close below the ankle. Sometimes the leggings, too, are ornamented on the outside with a row of silver buttons. Not uncommonly both leggings and moccasins are entirely black. Both sexes wear broad leather belts decorated with lovely silver plates. The men, in addition, often wear well-made bags of leather or puma *(Felis concolor)* over their shoulders. Painting or tattooing the face is apparently rare. Now and then one sees

Navajos with broad-brim gray felt sombreros, with an eagle feather (from *Aquila chrysaetos*) attached to them or, indeed, a leather cap decorated just like the Apache *tsjagg*.[17]

Besides blankets and saddle blankets in every chogán, one finds a number of sheepskins and goat hides, which serve as places for sleeping and sitting. In addition, there is basketry, primarily water baskets, which are coated on the inside with resin, and very crude black pottery in the form of oblong pots. Moreover, [they have] small painted pottery from the Moquis, which they acquired by bartering with them.

As domestic animals, here too one again encounters a badly treated, mongrelized breed of dogs and tame prairie dogs now and then.

The horse gear and weapons of the Navajos partly match those of the Apaches. Among them one encounters narrow wooden saddles covered with rawhide and wide stirrups of the same material, lassos or lariats of leather or horsehair, and fine headstalls for the horses, richly ornamented with silver and with heavy Mexican bits. Besides guns (especially Winchesters and Sharps), their weapons consist of bow and arrows with iron tips, which they usually sheath in fine quivers of puma hide. I do not recall seeing shields and lances, though they are probably familiar with them. The club seems to be unknown.

The Navajos are wealthy not just because of their silver work, but, even more, their tremendous livestock, which, according to the government report of 1882, consists of no less than 40,000 horses, 500 mules, 1,200 cows, and 1,100,000 sheep and goats. From this, it is clear that the Navajos are a true equestrian race and lead a nomadic existence. Nevertheless, they cultivate corn *(natáh),* wheat, watermelons, and peaches and possess extensive orchards of the latter fruit in the Cañon de Chelle [*sic*].

Of all the tribes I have seen, the Navajos unquestionably have the best and finest horses. They are better fed, more robust, larger, and nobler in shape than the wretched ponies so often seen in the Apaches' possession. Most Navajo horses are only half broken and skittish, so that the owner of a herd repeatedly changes riding horses; as a result, the same horse is frequently ridden only over a period of many months. Sorrels and brownish yellow ones with black manes, tail, and legs and an eel stripe are the most common. A couple of times I saw horses with black heads (rusty and red roans). In addition, one encounters colors and shades (of color) of every kind among these horses.

At the present time the Navajos are not only the most numerous tribe of the Southwest but the most prosperous one as well. Twenty years ago hostilities and raids were ended by transferring the greater part of the tribe—at that time much less numerous than now—to a reservation near Fort Sumner in New Mexico.[18] Because their herds were deliberately destroyed by the Union troops during the war, they nearly succumbed to starvation. Poor and dispirited, they headed to their place of banishment on the Pecos River, where a large number of them died. Then, after spending a few years there, they were brought back to their land in 1868 by General Sherman. Since that time their number as well as their prosperity have increased. And after this hard lesson there have been no large-scale hostilities. The Navajos want no more war because they have too much to lose. An incident that occurred during my stay on their reservation is proof of this. The Navajos, in fact, held several hundred slaves from various tribes, such as Apaches and Utes, with whom they had been at war. The government agent demanded these prisoners be surrendered to their tribes, and to put some force behind his demand, he summoned a detachment of cavalry from Fort Wingate. Although the Navajos showed their displeasure with this demand, and there were even voices calling for armed resistance, the general sentiment was for acceding to the demand, and no violence transpired.[19]

Just like the Apaches, polygamy is in vogue among the Navajos. Syphilis seems quite widespread as well. Indeed, when it comes to virtue, the Navajos squaws are not very scrupulous according to our concepts—the soldiers of Fort Wingate could tell more about that.

The arrival of the aforementioned detachment, under Lieutenant Huse,[20] and the return of a surveying party made things very lively and merry in our camp. At midday, races were frequently run between the troops' horses and those of the Navajos, with huge wagers being made on both sides—sometimes turning out favorably for one side, sometimes for the other one. At these races the Indians were always unclad, except for their breechclout, and the horses unsaddled. What an unparalleled spectacle as they, with diabolic cries, plied their leather whips to the panting flanks of the running horses. With their fluttering manes and quivering nostrils, they devoured the distance like a whirlwind.

In the evening we often had races pitting man against man. Here some Navajos, among them the expedition's scout, proved to be a formidable opponent. The evening's amusements usually ended with a tug-of-war when all of us, including the professor and the officers, after superhuman tugs on the thick rope, breathless and with burning, quivering hands, needed rest, which we promptly found in our tents. The nazjózj game, described in the section on the Apaches, is also in vogue among the Navajos.

Someone who does not understand Navajo cannot distinguish its sounds from Apache, but when one compares word lists, conspicuous differences catch the eye. Among a hundred and thirty words, I found not one in which an *r* appeared. I presume that the sound does not exist in Navajo, especially because they cannot pronounce this letter. For *American,* for example, the Navajos say "Melican," for *serape* "selape," etc.

The Navajos call themselves *Tinné,* that is, "men," "people," from which their northern origin is again apparent because, as I already noted above, countless tribes in British North America distinguish themselves by the same name. At the same time they share a linguistic affinity to the southern Tinné, *Dinné,* or *'Ndé*—the Apaches and Navajos. A tradition of the Navajos further bolsters the belief in their northern origin because they claim that their relations live in the far north: the *Tinné-Nehatlóni,* that is, "people from another place," from whom they once separated and whom they may never see again because they would otherwise go blind.[21]

The name *Navajo* is of Spanish origin, but its meaning is unclear. I do not think it is a corruption of *navája,* "knife"; the name "Knife Apaches" (*A. de navája*), in my opinion, should be rejected. The Navajos have no more knives than any other tribe. It is more likely that the name comes from *navájo,* "lake," "pool,"[22] though here the accent falls on a different syllable. In many regions of their land, though, such as the Chuska Mountains to the east of Defiance, there are numerous small lakes, and Coronado already mentions "lakes" in these regions.[23]

Already at Fort Wingate, I heard that on August 13th the Moqui Indians at Hual-pé would perform the sacred Snake Dance, a ceremony that is celebrated every two years and up to now had been attended just once by whites.[24] With two members of the expedition, Professor Powell[25] and the naval officer Marsh, I left on the 11th, at 9:30 A.M., on horseback headed toward the Moqui villages situated eighty-five miles to the west. Our Navajo scout brought us part of the way on a good road, and from there the three of us continued our ride. About 2 P.M. we passed through magnificent tall woods of gigantic pine trees and from there, after a brief halt, alternately through small sandstone canyons and then mesas covered with sagebrush *(Artemisia).* This plant, which grows to considerable size in these regions, lends a distinctive tinge to the landscape because of its greenish gray foliage and at the same time fills the air with a strong aromatic fragrance. The Navajos treat headaches by drinking a warm infusion from this plant. When it has cooled, they moisten the temples and forehead with it. In the forest along the grassy edges of the creeks white, yellow, and red composites, primroses, and cruciferous plants stand blooming in isolation because the landscape we are crossing through in Indian file, riding silently one after another, is secluded and desolate.

Not far from an abandoned group of chogáns along the green rim of a canyon, we suddenly discover, to our astonishment, a cliff house in this canyon, nestled against the sheer rocky wall like a swallow's nest. The low walls raised up from huge, rough stone blocks look like they are crammed between the wide fissure resulting from erosion, which runs horizontally along the wall of the canyon halfway up. A very long and narrow entrance and a couple of small, rectangular windows are the only openings of the small structure, but however much we would have liked to go inside to more closely investigate this rocky ruin, the spot is inaccessible because of the steepness of the rocky walls and the absence of ladders. Furthermore, we have no ropes with us, and though Mr. Marsh, like a true seaman, tries to reach the top following all the rules of the climber's art, after a few futile attempts he is compelled to abandon the plan for further investigation. A short distance from here, in the same canyon, we notice two other cliff houses, though larger. To our regret, these are also beyond our reach, and we continue our ride, musing about the mysterious people, the *Enahsázé,*[26] who built these suspended dwellings.

Marsh, who has already taken this route before, begins commenting that we have lost our way. We check the compass and eventually reach a more open terrain where we see a Navajo with a herd of sheep off in the distance. I ride there straightaway to ask where Pueblo Colorado is, but the poor shepherd, who is somewhat bewildered by my appearance, does not understand me. Fortunately, toward nightfall we encounter a little band of Navajos on horseback, one of whom agrees to take us to the rancho where we want to spend the night for a little money and some tobacco. Near an abandoned homestead we encounter a band of Indians who are making camp for the night. They have been on a puma hunt and show us a couple of marvelous hides from these animals, still bloodstained.

At 8 o'clock, tired and hungry, we reach Pueblo Colorado, a secluded rancho and the banks covered with cottonwoods of the small river with this name. We spend the night on a couple of beds so filthy that they fill us with revulsion the next morning. At 7 A.M. we continue our journey. The name *Colorado* is well chosen because the sandy ground is red everywhere, but slowly, the farther west we go, the more the red Triassic sandstone changes over to yellowish white sandstone from the Cretaceous era.

Until 5:30 P.M. we continue the ride through a dismal, deserted landscape, the embodiment of dreadful monotony. There are mostly grassy plateaus and mesas overgrown with juniper, across which our path follows a very sinuous course. A couple of times we cross a muddy little stream, which has cut deep furrows into the ground, the beginning of a canyon. We proceed with caution because most rivers of this region are hemmed with long expanses of quicksand. Fortunately, both horses and mules are wary of them and carefully put their hooves down onto the sand, anxiously snorting, impetuously tossing themselves backward as soon as they note that the moist sand is beginning to give way. It is oppressively hot, and we are suffering thirst because the water in our tin canteens is lukewarm, and the muddy liquid we find in the brook and a couple of water holes has a strong sandy taste or is brackish. The sole living creature we get to see during the entire day is a lone cottontail rabbit, who, frightened, takes flight at our approach.

More flushed than exhausted, we reach, after riding about eight hours, the trader's store in Keam's Canyon, which we leave the next morning, again at 9:30, to head to the Moqui villages thirteen miles away in the company of Mr. Keam, the trader.[27] Roughly half of the route leads through the long winding canyon, which, while steadily descending, eventually widens and opens out to the Moqui desert, an undulating sandy plateau, covered in spots with short grass and the cornfields belonging to the Moquis.

Before long, high rocky walls rise up ahead of us in the distance, and only when we have nearly reached the foot of the steep rocks do we discern the terrace-shaped houses and ladders of a pueblo, while dark figures are moving about on the roofs and along the edge of the mesa. One moment we ride under the shade of a peach tree orchard, then we cautiously climb the narrow winding path hewn out of sandstone rocks, which eventually lands us in Tehua.[28] Here we unsaddled our horses and took up quarters in the dwelling of an Indian friend of Mr. Keam. Before the Snake Dance began at 4 o'clock, we had some time to orient ourselves and take an excursion through the pueblo.

We found ourselves on a sandstone mesa about 600 feet high, running roughly from north to south, which with its yellowish white, bare walls rose perpendicularly above the plain. A lifeless, drab desert extended as far as the eye could see. In the Southwest along the distant horizon glistened the snow-covered peaks of the San Francisco Mountains. In between, though more to the south, at a distance of six or seven miles, arise the high mesas, on which the villages Moshóngnavé, Shepálavé, and Shongápavé are perched like eagles' nests. In the sand flats between our vantage point and the aforementioned pueblos skimpy cornfields and small clusters of sunflowers extend outward. The Moqui Buttes, a group of cathedral- and pyramid-shaped sandstone colossi, broke up the endless plain, which

8. Walpi, Hopi village on First Mesa.

rolled toward the south. Moreover, this was a series of mesas—once the shores of a sea—which bounded the horizon to the east and the north. A blue, fixed sky vaulted over the landscape, the image of which remains indelibly imprinted on my mind.

Three pueblos are situated on the mesa where we were staying: Tehua, Setshómové, and Huálpé.[29] The last-named is the southernmost and largest of the three and is situated somewhat apart from the other two. Setshómové is the middle one and the smallest and is in close proximity to Tehua.

The terrace-shaped architecture and the tiny rooms of the houses, the low doors and narrow windows, the wooden ladders and the pale, ash gray color pervading everything—all this recalls the other pueblos. The distinctive feature of the Moqui villages, though, is their lofty, secluded location. What may have motivated a people to settle on these barren rocky cliffs, where they must arduously fetch water and food from below, in a region that is one of the most arid in the Southwest? Probably it was the sense of security in the midst of hostile tribes, with whom their forefathers had to contend as well, just as they do today with the Navajos and Apaches. The residents of Tehua are proof of an exodus that occurred in historic times. Roughly sixty years ago they left their original homeland, San Cristóbal in northern New Mexico, driven off by the Mexicans, to seek a new home far off in the west and to alight in the rocky fortress of the Moquis, with whom they have since remained loyal allies.[30]

We make the round over the entire mesa and enter many dwellings, everywhere welcomed with hearty laughter. Repeatedly we bump our heads going in, and the tallest of us can barely stand upright in the rooms. Just like Tesuque and Laguna, here, too, we encounter the slanting row of grinding stones in wooden troughs, numerous baskets and basketry plaques, pottery, woolen blankets, sheepskins, and rabbit fur blankets. Not infrequently we encounter colorfully painted wooden dolls with grotesque faces and strange head coverings. Sometimes a row of these deformed images is suspended on a cord stretched above the chimney or elsewhere in the apartment. Sometimes some of them are also lying on the floor, and one of my comrades ventures the observation that the Moquis do not have a very reverent relationship with their household gods, treating them this way. Here he erred just like Oscar Loew[31] and others after him. The so-called household gods are nothing more than models of persons from the Corn Dance—a child's toy. The Moqui name for these dolls is *dicha* (*ch* aspirated).[32] The mere fact that a Moqui, with the greatest willingness, relinquishes one or more of these *dichas* to you in return for a quarter is enough to demonstrate the erroneousness of this opinion.

In every room hangs a so-called breath feather, a downy little feather, which is regarded as a *porte bonheur* [lucky charm]. At the same time, like the feathers of the prayer sticks, it is some sort of emblem—more about this soon. Frequently we find carefully closed small bundles of leather hanging on the wall. These are dance paraphernalia—sacred items. Just touch them and ask them whether they would like to sell, then you will see at once whether they treat them like their "household gods," the dichas. An unwilling, pained expression suddenly comes to the owner's face, a gesture of refusal with the hand, at best a *"no quiero"* (I don't want to), which he utters with a tone whose meaning is unequivocal—and you know exactly where you stand.

Only a few Moquis understand English. Spanish is somewhat better understood, but most of them can only speak their own language. Some also understand and speak Navajo.

At Huálpé, Mr. Marsh encounters an old acquaintance: Oyiwísha (He Who Plants Corn), alias Jeremiah Sullivan, M.D., an adopted son of the Moquis, among whom he has spent more than two years.[33] Oyiwísha is just the man I need, and when I inform him of my plan to spend a few days among the Moquis, he places himself completely at my disposal. He Who Plants Corn quickly takes me aside, leaves the house, and brings me to the edge of the mesa before the entrance to an *estufa*,[34] beckoning me to follow him down there on the ladder.

Having arrived below, I encountered a row of hideously painted Indians sitting along the wall in the small oblong, square room, busily putting the final touches to their dance toilette. Above their heads were suspended eagle feathers, fox hides, rattles, tortoise shells, and other necessities with which they, the priests of the Order of the Serpent, will initiate the dance later. In a corner lay a heap of live snakes, incessantly writhing about, which are kept under control by an Indian waving a bundle of feathers. In the middle of the estufa stood a clay basin, filled with a pale brown liquid that had an astringent taste and with a large white seashell, serving as a drinking bowl, floating on top of it. This liquid was an antidote for snakebite, which the priests had been drinking for four days while fasting.[35] The discontented expression appearing on the faces of some priests after my appearance in the estufa and the time already far advanced, which meant that the dance should soon start, prompted us to leave the room and take our place on the flat roof of a house on the east side of Huálpé, where we could have a good view of the dance.

If we are to believe a Moqui chief's account, provided to Mr. Keam regarding the origin of the Snake Dance, then it mainly comes down to the following:

A very long time ago there was a beloved chief of the Moquis who, returning from far distant journeys, had brought home his lovely bride from another tribe. The Moqui women, envious that an outsider had won the heart of the bravest and wisest of all Moqui warriors, were relentless in devising ways of hectoring and inflicting insults to make the poor woman's life miserable. Too proud to complain, she brought a brood of poisonous snakes into the world, immune to the arrows and clubs of the Moquis, who killed their children and women, forcing the survivors to flee to another land. Finally, a huge snake delivered them from their dreadful pursuers by slaying them and directed the Moquis to live in the land they now possess, at the same time admonishing them henceforth to live in peace with their natural companions, the snakes. In gratitude for their deliverance, the Moquis initiated the Snake Dance as a religious ceremony and since that time have never killed a snake.[36]

Whatever the origin of the Snake Dance, it is highly likely that its purport is to pray for rain, the life-giving force of their corn and melon fields, orchards and pastures—for water, the foremost and greatest necessity of their existence.[37]

As mentioned, the dance took place on the eastern side of Huálpé at the edge of the mesas, where a roughly twenty-foot-high sandstone column, which had defied the gnawing ravages of water and time, rises up. Near this column a dense shelter of green cottonwood branches was erected. In the shelter more than a hundred snakes were sprawled out for the priests to keep an eye on. A dense throng of spectators from both sexes and every age had gathered in an extended circle along the mesa and along the roofs of the houses. Among the many who had thronged there from afar were a number of Navajos as well and some shabby frontiersmen, prospectors, and cowboys.

Before long we hear a rattling noise, and a row of more than twenty Indians, walking one after another, emerge from the estufa. All are unclad except for their breechclout and a fox hide hanging down from behind over their hips. On their feet they wear beautifully ornamented leather moccasins. A wreath of cottonwood leaves adorns their heads. Their faces are painted white and black, the trunk pink, the arms and legs dark brown. In the right hand they hold a white rattle in the form of a T, in the left a bundle of eagle feathers. A tortoise shell is fastened under the right knee, together with a number of deer and antelope hooves, which make a peculiar hollow rattling noise whenever they move around. There are eight boys in the row. Up front moves an Indian, who with his right hand whirls around a leather sling, humming,[38] while in his left hand he holds a finely ornamented bow. Behind him moves a second medicine man firmly grasping a clay bowl with water, from which he sprinkles water on the ground now and then using a bunch of feathers. With nimble gait they all move around in a circle, while the medicine man with the water has positioned himself in the middle. Then they gather next to each other on both sides of the shelter.

Immediately afterward, a second row of serpent priests, roughly thirty in number, appears, attired almost like the previous ones but without garlands of leaves and without rattles, while on their heads they wear feathers dyed red. They, too, move around in a circle repeated times and then gather next to each other, facing the first row. In plaintive tone they strike up a gentle chant, at the same time waving their feather bundles up and down and stomping rhythmically with their right feet.

After this scene has gone on for a while, the latest row arriving divides up into small groups of three, which halt by the shelter, one after the other. A moment later one of them, who is partly stooped over, emerges from there again with a writhing serpent, which he holds crosswise in his mouth. One of the dancers now places his right arm around the neck of the one holding the snake, while, using his left hand, which is armed with a bundle of feathers, he continually fondles the snake's head and keeps it turned away from his companion's face. The last person from the group of three gathers behind these two dancers, who, in a crouching position, stick their upper bodies outward, moving along in the circle, leaping and stomping. Before long there are ten of these groups moving about, which over and over put fresh snakes in their mouths until the supply is exhausted and everyone is loaded up with several snakes in the mouth and hands. Every now and then a snake drops to the ground. Now they try to slither away and escape between the rows of spectators, thereby creating a commotion, but the Navajos have their thick blankets with them, which, cleverly, they suddenly drop at the spot the snake is escaping to, thus heading them off. Then they rear up again—eyes glittering, the forked tongue darting with lightning speed, the tail rattling—ready to strike their death-dealing fangs into the flesh of their attackers. But the fluttering eagle feathers of the priests work wonders. They seem to cast a spell as they whiz right past the monster's head so that a moment later they can be taken up without warning in a nimble grip to be led around once more, impotently twisting and writhing inside the row of dancers.

A number of women, grouped in two rows, are continually scattering sacred corn flour on the ground, which must charm the snakes, too. The medicine man has been standing in the middle all this time, sprinkling water and chanting slowly, assisted by the priests with leaf garlands, who alternately put their right foot forward and backward, their bodies gently bobbing up and down.

The longer the ceremony lasts, the more excited the dancers become. Their eyes radiate wild abandon. Their movements become more violent and savage. Their sweat mingles with the garish colors of their naked torsos and—shrieking, and yelling, and heaving—they jump around. One completely loses track of things. Breathless and tense, one gazes upon a scene that in dismal savagery knows no equal. One could shout from savage delight, but suddenly the enchantment gives way. With the white flour the women delineate a large circle on the ground and divide it into four segments. Immediately thereafter the dancers toss all the snakes together in a heap inside the circle, while at the same moment all the spectators spit on the ground, "so not to take the snake venom into their bodies and hence swell up"—as Oyiwísha informs me. Now a moment of indescribable confusion ensues. The snake dancers suddenly assault the heap of snakes slithering in hundreds of coils, take as many as they can carry in their hands, and run with their dangerous burden, as fast as their legs can carry them, down the mesa in all four directions to grant the snakes their liberty once more in the rocky plain.

Long before sundown everything is over, as the rite indeed prescribes.[39] Shortly afterward my traveling companions return to Keam's Canyon to continue the journey the following morning to Defiance. I alone remain with Oyiwísha at Huálpé.

Unforgettable is the view I enjoy that evening sitting on the roof of one of the highest houses and sharing the evening meal with a kindly Indian family, while the sun, like a fiery orb, sets, its rays casting a glowing farewell greeting on the mesa. Everywhere there is peace and calm: in the smoke columns around the pueblo, which rise up in stately fashion toward the sky; in the evening wind, which cools your temples; in the silent desert, which veils itself in the pale tints of the night; in the minds of the many people who, in the simplicity of their hearts, have performed a sacred duty; finally in the stars replete with splendor, which radiate in the firmament.

Through Oyiwísha's solicitude I obtained a little room all my own from the war chieftain of Huálpé. Long-haired goat skins and sheepskins are spread out on the floor for me, and the other residents, too, make preparations for the night by bringing their rabbit skin blankets up on the roofs and lying down. The priests from the Order of the Serpent—who have been fasting for four days and, now that the period of tension is over, are sitting down exhausted and emaciated—make a lunge for the piles of *píki,*[40] which the women bring to them. But they must spend the night together at the entrance of the sacred estufa. My sleep is disturbed by nothing other than the barking now and then of one of the numerous dogs, the everlasting bane of every Indian village. But here I am safe under the hospitable roof of these gallant people who would not touch a hair on my head.

The following day, with Oyiwísha as my guide, I have ample opportunity to get a closer look at the three pueblos of the First Mesa and form an idea about the inhabitants' type. One should not assume that despite their age-long isolation, there is uniformity of type among the Moquis. In physiognomy alone two main types can be easily distinguished—one of which is the usual "redskin" type, the other a type with an admixture of Mongolian-Celtic features. The former I found among the men especially, the second quite common among the women. The racial duality reveals itself less in figure, shape of cranium, and skin color than in physiognomy. As a rule, the Moquis can be called small. From twenty measurements (fifteen men, five women) the average was 1.57 m—1.61 for the former, 1.48 for the latter. The cranial index varied between 80.43 and 95.91, thus from subbrachycephalic to brachycephalic. Skin color was generally very light (no. 33). In the case of the women, the characteristic skin fold often appears in the interior corner of the eye. The Moquis' teeth are frequently small and irregular. Both sexes are quite slender in body build, though the women not infrequently are stocky. The gait of the Moquis, and the squaws especially, is unsightly and waddling. The entire upper body, which is strongly balanced, inclines forward. The knees are bent and the feet often pointed inward. Their facial expression is kindly and friendly, and they lack the fierce countenance one encounters among the Plains Indians, as well as the squint-eyed physiognomy characteristic of the Navajo and Apache.

Among the young women and girls there are quite often ones who could be called pretty. The raven black, thick hair contrasts favorably with the pale tinge of the fine skin, with a dark glimmering through in some instances. The finely penciled eyebrows arch above the dark, liquid eyes, which are overshadowed with long eyelashes. They are shy, and, laughing with embarrassment, they turn away with a hand in front of their mouths when I send a greeting their way. It is quite difficult to take some of their measurements, and their elation knows no bounds when I measure their noses and take a close look into their eyes to ascertain their color. It is my good fortune that I am a friend of Oyiwísha, who speaks on my behalf and jokingly persuades them to go stand or sit, all depending on what I need. Oyiwísha is besieged with questions: who am I and why do I want to measure them? He replies that I am doing this solely for my own diversion. That puts them at ease: as long as there is no "bad medicine" involved, that is fine.

If the men's daily attire, too, has largely been bastardized and the cotton prints from Keam's store have found their way to the Moqui mesas, then the hairstyle, the breechclout, the moccasins, leggings, and *fajas* [sashes] have remained. As a rule, the men wear their hair long, hanging loosely over the shoulders and combed forward over the forehead, cut above the eyebrows. Some wear it bound in back with the Navajo headband. Now and then I noticed individuals with thick, wavy hair, which to some extent recalled the hair of *quarterons* and their closest relations.[41] Among most of the tribes I have visited, I have sporadically encountered this variety. Also the footwear, the leg attire, and fine red knee bands resemble those of the Navajos. In addition, both sexes wear dark blue, woolen leggings reaching from the knee to the ankles and resembling stockings without a foot.

The women's attire is wholly original and consists of a thick black, woolen habit with wide sleeves, reaching just below the knee, like the one encountered among many Pueblo Indians. Another piece of clothing, worn only by the women, is a small woolen blanket, black or white, which is adorned with wide black and narrow red borders. As long as they do not leave the pueblo, the women remain barefoot, but if they go down from the mesa to draw water, then they wrap their feet and legs in leather moccasins and countless bandages, already noted above.

There is a great difference between the hairstyle of the married and unmarried women. The former part their hair in the back of the head into two thick, long braids, which from the side of the head hang down in front over their chest. The young women wear horns of sorts consisting of their own hair, which are held up by a large wooden hair pin. The Moquis, but the Zunis and Navajos too, keep their hair beautiful and glossy with a distinctive item. It consists of a bunch of straw dried hard in the sun, held together with a little string or band in the middle. The hard extremity of the bunch, where the blades are sliced crosswise, serves as a comb, the softer points of the blades at the other end as a brush. Not infrequently the Indians comb and brush each other with great thoroughness. There is, I think, no part of the body to which Indians devote more attention

9. Hopi girls with characteristic hairstyle.

than their hair. From the standpoint of cleanliness, too, they could serve as a model to many a European—including the "clean" Dutch.

Because I have no food with me, I depend wholly on the Moquis' hospitality. Though I am now and then invited to dine with the greatest possible generosity, the Moqui cuisine hardly captivates me, even though my palate has not been pampered by the food of the last few months. Corn in various forms is always the primary food: first of all [there is] the aforementioned *píki*, mostly baked from blue corn, which is soaked in water and eaten with the fingers, like the other foods I will mention; then *pígami*, a brown corn mush, whose flavor somewhat resembles pancake dough; then *nookweebee*, sheep bouillon, with huge pieces of meat and uncooked green peas and corn kernels floating in it; *nookpiki*, a fine porridge of cornmeal and red pepper, baked in corn husks; and finally *paywilpeekee*, large, wet clumps of undercooked, blue cornmeal, which always aroused my revulsion.

When breakfast is ready in the morning, my hostess comes up to my chamber upstairs and says, "Eat, eat"—the only English she knows. Coming down, I take my place on the floor, where four or five Indians are seated around a large bowl, bringing the contents to their mouths with their fingers. I follow their example, and when I have enough, I am encouraged by signs to eat some more. To mollify them, I take another bite, only to be encouraged again by the nodding of heads to help myself. Then I bring matters to a conclusion by standing up and, with the gourd shell that is floating in water in the olla, take a draught of the dirty gray, fetid liquid full of sand and dead mosquitoes—the water that the Moqui drinks and with which he prepares his food. In the morning I wash myself with the liquid I draw from the olla with a tin dish, an operation that my friendly hosts follow with rapt attention and smiles.

The Moquis drink remarkably little. Their constitution appears to have grown accustomed to living on a minimal amount of water because the few springs, which are at the foot of mesas, are far from the pueblos. Drawing water olla by olla, which requires surmounting the long, steep path, is difficult and time-consuming work. The Moquis irrigate the cornfields by means of acequias leading to a small river, which flows north to the Colorado Chiquito.

Their herds of sheep and goats—whose huge stone-walled corrals look as though they were suspended at the edge of the mesa and who infest the pueblos, particularly Huálpé, with a permeating sheep stench—are led every morning across the sandy plain to grassy canyons to graze there all day, returning toward evening. Although sometimes horses—more often burros (small donkeys)—come onto the mesa, these animals never stay there long because of the lack of water and fodder. The horse herds of the Moquis, tended by various herders, are continuously out to pasture as well.

The Moquis are masters in pottery making and basket weaving. Not only in form, but in ornamentation as well, the pottery of the Moquis surpasses that of the Pueblo Indians—except for that of the Zunis—and corresponds more closely to the pottery of the cliff dwellers. The basic color of the Moqui ollas is white, the color for decoration black, brown, or red. These decorations are frequently related to the Moquis' mythology and at the same time are symbols and signs for various things. Thus, not infrequently one finds the image of Balilekóa, the most important water god, depicted on the urns. He has the shape of a bird with teeth who carries a big horn, the lightning, and the clouds. The symbol of growing force is a composite figure of wavy lines (meanders), triangles, and stair-shaped figures. Black is the symbol of heaven, brown or red the symbol of earth. The whirlwind is a spiral. Standing water is expressed by a number of lines crossing each other at a right angle, flowing water by a number of slanting parallel lines. Clouds are indicated by semicircles with the chord facing downward, the curve upward. If one wishes to signify that it is raining, one has a number of parallel, perpendicular lines descend from the circle's chord.

Among the Moquis the ollas serve rather varied purposes. Besides holding food and drink, they serve as a certain item of furniture [i.e., a chamber pot], which usually has a less conspicuous place in our bedrooms than among the Moquis. In their case the object in question is, for the most part, a very large black olla of crude fabrication outside the house, not far from the door. Without diffidence both men and women make use of it (*stantes mingunt* [they urinate standing up]) and would give rise to the assumption among foreigners that the Moquis, too, know the *"qui se gêne est gêné"* and put the item in question to better use than we do.

In addition the ollas are used for that section of the chimney protruding from the roof. One knocks the bottom out of a number of large pots and places them one on top of the other, provided that the bottommost part of one olla fits into the topmost part of the next one. Four or five of these pots already form a rather long chimney, which is fastened at the bottom with adobe to the flat roof or wherever it may emerge.

The pottery and baskets are the most important item in the Moqui household, and a number of these items can be found on the floor in every room. The basketry in particular consists of flat, round dishes of varying dimensions, from a large fish dish to a tea saucer. They have the shape of a spiral winding tightly inward and are frequently colored in the most tasteful fashion with red, black, and white, but the most common colors are black and yellow. The Moquis of Oraybe, the largest and most westerly pueblo, prepare baskets differing notably from the aforementioned ones both in style of weaving and design and color.

Another type of basketry, no less lovely, samples of which one now and then finds in the Moqui houses, is derived from the Kochoníno or Havasúpai Indians,[42] a small tribe that lives far to the west in a deep canyon along Cataract Creek. Both tribes visit each other now and then and remain on the best footing. The Navajos and Apaches, on the other hand, have been enemies of the Moquis for ages.[43] They call the former *Tasáhmuhway* (bastards), the latter *Yostyaymuh.*

The Moquis call themselves *Hopíte* or *Hópitû* ("the good ones"?) and, according to Oyiwísha, not *Shínumo* or *Shínome,* as one finds in some writers (such as Powell, Gatschet).[44] This latter word signifies "people," "nation," and is with *hopí,* "good"—*Hopíshínome*—the name the Moquis give to the other Pueblo Indians. They call the Tehuas *Hánome* or *Hánom.* The name *Moqui* or *Móki* is derived from their own language and signifies "stinking" or even "dead," recalling a former smallpox epidemic.[45] The language of these Indians—with the exception, of course, of the Tehua—belongs to the Numa family and, according to Oyiwísha, who was busy compiling a dictionary during my stay, consists of a light dialectical variation from pueblo to pueblo. In Oraybe, for example, the words are pronounced in long drawn-out fashion. In the Moquis' company, the Tehuas (Teguas, Tewas, Tiwas) speak their language because Tehua is so much more difficult than Moqui. The Tehuas are largely accepted into the Moqui clans because there has been considerable intermarriage.

The name *Tusayan* or *Tuçayan,* which the old Spanish authors used to designate the land of the Moquis and which even appears on new maps, is unknown there. The name *Tusayan* seems to be of Zuni origin.[46] The Moquis call their land *Mahstootchkwùh,* "the land of Másawé" (the earth god).[47] Despite Oscar Loew's assumption,[48] I have not been able to find anything that corroborates the worship of Montezuma by the Moquis.

According to Oyiwísha, the Moquis have seven clans, of which the Water clan is the most numerous and the Warrior clan the most aristocratic.[49] The members of the Order of the Serpent—priests, if you will—could belong to any of the seven clans but at the same time form a body all by themselves.

Weapons are rare among the Moquis, whence is evident not just their pacific nature but their limited bent for hunting as well. Now and then one encounters bow and arrows—guns far less often and then of very ancient vintage. The Moqui's most typical weapon is certainly a flat wooden stick that is thrown *(peushkway),* closely resembling the Australian boomerang, and used by preference for hunting rabbits. Most of these tossing sticks are not ornamented, but sometimes one discovers a few that are finely decorated. One probably encounters this "boomerang" among all Pueblo Indians, though in some places it has fallen into disuse.

The third day of my stay among the Moquis, August 15th, I went on foot with Mr. Sullivan to the Second Mesa to visit Moshóngnavé and Shepálavé as well. Along a steep, breakneck little path we descended from the rocky colossus on which Huálpé is situated and, arriving at the base, passed some Indian graves. These are nothing more than crude piles of stones with a great number of branches and sticks protruding in between.[50] Although I was seized by the desire to remove a skull and even attempted to do this the following day, Oyiwísha urgently besought me to desist so as not to make his stay among the Indians untenable.[51] Now and then a white *Datura stramonium* blooms among the barren rocks, and before long we head through the loose sandy flats, through sparse cornfields where the Moquis have erected a little guardhouse, resting on long stakes, and past tall sunflowers whose stems bend under the weight of the huge flowers. Fortunately the air is heavily overcast because seven miles across a yellow sand flat with the sun shining down on it are anything but pleasant. At noon, when we arrived at the pueblos, a gentle rain was falling.

The mesa on which Moshóngnavé and Shepálavé are situated is less high and steep than those we have just left. Because of the greater space of the plateau, the pueblos are also built according to a somewhat different plan and have a small plaza, which is lacking in Huálpé and the other pueblos of the previous mesa. The architecture of the houses, however, matches that of the former. Everywhere Oyiwísha is warmly received, and at various places we are invited in to eat píki or pígami, watermelons, or nookpiki.

In three different families I encountered albinos, whom I examined to the extent that their mothers permitted their bashful, frightened children to be examined. Although the dark skin pigment was completely missing in the four children whom I could closely observe, as well as in a fully grown male individual whom I saw only in passing, their hair and eyes were colored. All of them had light blond hair, roughly like no. 23 from the chromatic scale. One had light brown (no. 3–4), the other three light blue (13–14) eyes, with a bright brown ring running around the pupil of two of the children. All of them had abnormally dilated pupils (mydriasis), and the eyeball was always trembling (nystagmus). When I asked whether the children had poor vision, I received an affirmative answer, as was indeed to be expected. In the case of two of the children, the skin on their face, hands, and feet was unusually red and burning and peeling in some places (erythema). They were otherwise normal in stature. I could see nothing special about their teeth either. Hair growth was abnormal in many respects. Although armpit hair was missing, the arms and legs of all four of them were covered with thin yellow hair. And even the entire body of a girl about three years old was nearly covered with yellow, silky hair, attaining a length of a few centimeters in the hip region, on the arms and legs. The parents of these children were completely normal.

Oyiwísha estimated the number of albinos among the entire Moqui population, which amounts to approximately 1,800 people, at twelve or fifteen—certainly an enormous proportion.[52] Albinism has been too little studied for me to venture a judgment about this condition's origin. Here it may be sufficient to note that it is encountered often among most, if not all, the Pueblo Indians, but that I encountered it later, though less frequently, among the Navajos, Kiowas, Cheyennes, and Arapahos. At Moshóngnavé, I once more witnessed the Snake Dance, which exactly paralleled that of Huálpé, described above. A full-grown albino was among the dancers and cut a strange figure in the row of dark figures with his yellow hair and light skin.

Heading across the surface of the mesa, which extends along the side of Moshóngavé, Oyiwísha directed my attention to a couple of small sticks dyed green, ornamented with downy feathers, which were planted in the ground. They were offerings of a priest from the Order of the Serpent and marked the spot where he had prayed for rain. Oyiwísha was later able to provide me a couple of these gems in the envelope of corn husks and sacred flour in which they were wrapped before making the offering. They closely resembled those I later obtained from the Zuni priests of the Order of the Bow.

After the sun had already set, we returned to Huálpé. That evening I felt very indisposed, which probably was to be ascribed to the various píki preparations in particular, which I had to eat over and over again this day for the sake of politeness.

The following day a few Mormons came into the pueblos, to the immense aggravation of Oyiwísha, who is all too aware of the influence of the "Latter-Day Saints" on the Indians.[53] But there is no denying that the influence of the Mormons is infinitely better than that of the frontiersmen, from whom they learn nothing but bad things. Thus far the Moquis are significantly free from this influence, but one day the stream of pseudo-civilization, with whiskey, debauchery, and homicide, will reach here, too. For it seems that the coal fields of these regions are rich enough to be exploited, while the settlements along the new railway, which runs sixty miles south of their villages, are expanding. From year to year the land is taking on a different appearance.

The Moquis seem to be declining in numbers, as one might, at least, infer from the empty houses, which are becoming ever more numerous. There is tremendous mortality among younger children, which must in part be ascribed to the foul water. Between the ages of three and five, especially, many are mowed down by death. The Moquis have few children. A family with more than three children (the Moquis are monogamous) is rare. Many childless marriages exist.[54] The number of male and female births seems roughly the same, though the distribution is unequal in the various pueblos. Thus, one finds more boys than girls in Oraybe, for example, and more girls than boys in the villages of the eastern mesa.[55] Similarly, the pueblos are very unequally populated. The inhabitants of Oraybe are estimated at 560, those at Shepálavé at around 100. Smallpox has done its part to decimate the Moquis and even given them the name "smallpox people," *Ah'mookwickwih,* as their Zuni neighbors brand them.

My horse, which was grazing with the Moqui herd, seemed as if it could not fit in with its new company because the young Indian whom I had sent there on the morning of the 16th to retrieve it returned only late that afternoon, saying that my horse had broken his hobbles and that he had found him thirteen miles away over toward Defiance, grazing by himself. Because I do not know just when the surveying expedition, to which my horse belonged, will break up, that afternoon, with an eye on the long ride ahead, I said goodbye to Oyiwísha and my Moqui friends and by evening had returned to Keam's Canyon.

I spent the 17th there resting, which I needed to do, and at the same time viewing the fine collection of Moqui and cliff dweller pottery of Mr. Steven,[56] Mr. Keam's companion. It is remarkable that the present-day Moquis understand much of the symbolic ornamentation adorning the cliff dwellers' pottery and that this partially matches their own ornamentation.[57] This may be interpreted as evidence of the relationship between these two peoples, further bolstered by the fact that the Moquis speak of the cliff dwellers as "our forefathers." Cranial features seem to support this opinion. What we know about the skulls from the cliff houses and other southwest ruins, particularly from the descriptions of Bessels and Hoffman,[58] allows one to see a close correspondence between the brachycephalic skull shape with parieto-occipital flattening, which is a widespread occurrence not just among the Moquis but also among the Zunis and Pueblo Indians generally. On the one hand, this matches the skull shape of the Olmecs, one of the oldest peoples of Anahuac, on the other hand, that of the mound builders. The opinion that the present-day Pueblo Indians are in the broadest sense descendants of the Aztecs—an opinion that is already open to doubt for linguistic, historical, and ethnographic reasons—is contradicted by craniological indices because the Aztecs are dolichocephalic.[59]

Without providing adequate reasons Oscar Loew places the homeland of the Aztecs, Aztlán, in the stretch of land now largely included in the Navajo reservation and deems it as highly likely that the numerous ruins along the Rio Mancos and Animas derive from the Aztecs as well.[60] This opinion was expressed eight years ago and must be taken with a great deal of caution at the very least. Later investigations suggest instead that we have to look for the mysterious Aztlán in Mexico, in the mountains of Jalisco, near Lake Chapála,[61] and that the ruins of the Southwest come from the ancestors of the Zunis and Moquis and other pueblos. It is known that the former even abandoned four of their cities in historical times,[62] that the Indians of Pueblo-Pecos sought shelter at Jemez,[63] that the Tehuas left San Cristobal to seek refuge among the Moquis,[64] and that Laguna is becoming more and more depopulated because the Indians, by living spread throughout the land, find conditions more commodious for their livelihood.[65] Probably contributing to the abandonment of the many cities and cliff houses is the diminution of the population by causes we are not aware of, and the climate is becoming steadily more arid, with the resulting disappearance of water.[66]

Roughly a half mile away from the store on the northern wall of the canyon some figures can be found that the Navajos ascribe to the Aynahsáhzay (cliff dwellers) but one of which—quite remarkably—forms a symbol from the former's "whirlwind legend." They consist of a number of straight lines carved into the sandy rock intersecting each other at various angles.[67] The other figures consist of a hand and a kind of full-moon face with three horns, not far from each other, on the ceiling of a shallow cave inside the rocky wall. The entire ceiling is black because of smoke and fumes, and the face seems to be drawn on it, but how the hand got there is not easily determined. In addition, on the walls of the canyon are a number of carvings, difficult to make out, which are situated on an inaccessible site and look as if they were being incised there before the canyon was hollowed out to its present depth by the water. One of the figures seems to represent a horse with some men on its back. That powerful erosion might have occurred in historic times may be deduced from the circumstance that directly opposite the trader's store, in a natural niche high in the canyon wall and on a now inaccessible site, an orderly pile of stones, which once must have been erected by human hands, can be found.

Keam's Canyon is a place that is heavily frequented by Indians, Navajos as well as Moquis, for carrying on trade. The Moqui agency was established there but abolished a year ago and then united with that of the Navajos in Fort Defiance—certainly a poor choice because this place is not as centrally located in the areas inhabited by the Indians as Keam's Canyon.

From a Navajo, with whom I spoke through the intermediation of the post trader, I learned that they have more than thirty clans in their tribe but that the number was originally far less.[68] A number of Moquis, Indians from Jemez, Coyoteros, etc., were slowly incorporated into the Navajos, however, and in this way the number of clans increased. Thus one of their clans, for instance, is called *Kizjáhnùh* (house people), a name they give to the Pueblo Indians as well.

Among the Navajos, too, one encounters the odd though widespread custom that a son-in-law may not look his mother-in-law in the eyes. This seems to be based on the legend that the sun had a secret love affair with Estsánatlayhi, who became the mother of the twin brothers Nagènazani and Thobadêstchín, later the saviors of the Navajos through routing of the terrible giant Yëïtso who dwelled in the mountain Tsòtsîl (San Mateo).[69]

On August 18th I returned to Defiance with an American companion. During the afternoon we were overtaken by heavy thunderstorms, which forced us to seek shelter in the Navajos' chogáns now and then. In one of the huts was Ganemucho, or Ganado-mucho, the most important chief since Manuelito, who has lost much of his influence because of drunkenness.[70] He bore a striking resemblance to Loco, the Apache chief (see chapter 5, lithograph 7). After we had spent the night at Pueblo Colorado, we continued our ride during the final hours under rain and hail, as heavy as any I have ever experienced. Thoroughly drenched, I reached camp at noon on the 19th.

I spent the time I still had before I could head to Pueblo de Zuni broadening my knowledge about the Navajos as much as possible by traversing the area on horseback and foot and spending a part of the day in their chogáns. They were cunning and cautious bartering with me. The knickknacks I brought for that purpose were, as a rule, turned down after attentive observation because they preferred the clang of pesos. They valued their fine necklaces of cut shells and small turquoises too highly for my European women's ornaments to compensate [for them], and the price they demanded in cash amounted to more than I had on hand.

Among the peculiar gestures I noticed, not just among the Navajos but among Indians generally, is the pronounced protruding of the lips combined with a simultaneous head movement for signaling one thing or another, with the gaze being directed toward the intended object. The cry of feminine amazement consists of a prolonged shrill sound combined with a deep inhalation. They often hold one of their hands in front of their mouth, a gesture the Indian women and girls usually make when they laugh.

The Indians, generally, do not always assume that mask of dignified calm and imperturbable indifference that most people think is inseparable from being Indian. Usually it is easy to make them laugh. I have seen Indians, even men, so little able to control themselves that they could barely speak because of laughter, this not infrequently resulting from embarrassment. Quite often they also spit on the ground when they are embarrassed. I had already observed Mexicans doing the same thing. Often I have clearly seen Indians of both sexes blushing, less commonly turning pale. During measuring and photographing sessions, not a few Indians betrayed signs of embarrassment. The attentive observer can read amazement, joy, desire, annoyance, and the like on their faces without difficulty. Individual differences aside, there is a considerable variation in this respect among the different tribes. For example, when I compare the Yumas, Mohaves, and Pueblo Indians with the prairie tribes—where I have the Cheyennes (chapter 10) especially in mind—then the latter correspond much more to the Indians from fictional books—stoically calm, proud, and noble—than the former, who have more of a childlike nature, as it were.

The Navajos have the reputation of being big thieves. Though all the bad things said about Indians are frequently exaggerated, the Navajos nevertheless seemed eager to show me before my departure that in this case this was not mere slander: one night they came into the tent where Prof. Thompson and I were sleeping and stole a splendid puma hide quiver, which I had bought from one of them shortly before. That same night they stole two fine blankets from another person in camp.

For my part, I made every effort to purloin a skull and, after a number of attempts, got hold of one, which was washed out of a grave by the heavy rains and had landed in a ravine. When somebody dies, they bury him in the same spot where he breathed his last breath. If this occurs in a chogán, they heave the entire hut on top of him, thereafter abandoning the area forever. For this reason I visited such abandoned, collapsed huts more than once. As though the Indians could guess my thoughts, before I was aware of this, they followed upon my heels and spied attentively on me.

The arrival of Mr. Stevenson and his wife, charged with a scientific mission from the Smithsonian Institution, and of General Armstrong, superintendent of the Native school in Hampton, Virginia, injected considerable liveliness into the camp. With an eye especially to the imminent departure of the surveyors we had a jolly good time.[71] First we went on a riding excursion with improvised racing and artistic riding. Then we again opened the abandoned school building and organized a ball, with the ex-cadet and cook forcing out of the seraphin organ the profane dance music of Strauss and Metra rather than sacred tones.[72] In the evenings we had readings. Then the gray-haired professor took Joaquin Miller or Coleridge in hand, and he guided our thoughts to the shadows of the Shasta Mountains, to the council fires of the Modocs, or to the secluded rocky wastes of Utah, the land of thirst and mirages. Or we roamed about on the vast sea, pursued by ghost ships and serpents. From the tone of his voice and from the fire in his gaze, one could hear and see that he himself had seen, struggled, and endured. Then one could feel the vigor of a raw poetry like that of Miller; then one could understand enchanted fantasies like those of Coleridge.

Finally, the day of departure had arrived, when each of us would go his separate way. With regret I said farewell to my fellow companions in a jolly camp, and particularly to the paternal friend who had so enlivened my lonely odyssey and had been my sterling counselor in so many ways. In the morning of August 26th I headed out to Manuelito to reach Fort Wingate that same evening.

That some Americans, too, had transplanted some superstitious beliefs, prevalent in earlier times among their European forefathers, was apparent to me on the way to Manuelito when we found a pile of stones, which had been heaped together by the Indians in remembrance of some sort of event and which was continually growing as each passerby tossed a stone onto it. In all seriousness, the three Americans accompanying me, including the government agent and a civil engineer, took a stone from the ground and tossed it onto the pile, claiming this would bring us luck. While I smiled, with a shrug of the shoulders, at their invitation to follow their example, I was told, by way of warning, that things would not turn out well for me. The same people who otherwise speak disparagingly of the Indians here shared their superstition and made offerings to a pile of stones erected by "savages." Stone piles in various shapes, which can be regarded as the original form of monuments and as such are spread across the entire globe, are repeatedly encountered in the Southwest.

I have already reported on the Piedra de los Viejos of the now vanished Indians of the California peninsula, about the stone piles erected by the Pimas on old ruins, and about the stone pile in Keam's Canyon. The Apaches toss a stone, a twig, or a handful of grass onto the piles of stones, which now and then are found in the areas inhabited by them; these are the stone piles that are called "Apache post offices" by the frontiersmen. The Zunis, too, are familiar with them, and the Mexicans along the Rio Grande show them a certain reverence, just like their [Indian] half brothers.

Another superstition, often encountered in the West in many instances and that clearly comes from Europe,[73] is the one concerning horseshoes as a means of warding off evil influences. On or above the door of many a rancho, I found one or several horseshoes firmly nailed in. Sometimes I found this kind of amulet on wagons as well.

•••••

NOTES

1. HtK 1885: On the great railway lines of the West only two passenger trains travel in the same direction every twenty-four hours.

2. Laguna Pueblo is situated on a knoll above the San José River about forty miles west of Albuquerque. It was founded in about 1697 by Keresan speakers who fled various villages in the Rio Grande after de Vargas's reconquest. Major changes in Laguna society and political structure occurred during the 1870s as a result of a highway, the railroad, Anglo settlements, and the influx of Anglo missionaries and teachers. Florence Hawley Ellis, "Laguna Pueblo," in *Handbook of North American Indians: Southwest,* ed. A. Ortiz (Washington, D.C.: Smithsonian Institution, 1983), 9:438–49.

3. A native of Ireland, John Menaul came to the Southwest in 1870, where he worked among the Navajos and Apaches before accepting a position as Protestant missionary and teacher at Laguna Pueblo, 1876–1889. In 1877 he obtained a printing press, which he used to print bilingual English-Laguna texts, including a catechism and McGuffey's readers. Mark T. Banker, "Presbyterian Missionary Activity in the Southwest: The Career of John and James Menaul," *Journal of the West* 23 (1984):55–61.

4. Mount Taylor (11,301 ft) is the Navajos' sacred mountain of the south, "turquoise mountain" in myth and ritual. Acoma Indians regard it as the home of the Rainmaker of the North. It also has religious significance for the Zunis and Tewas.

5. HtK 1885: The Indians of the nearby pueblos Acoma, Hasatch, Povuate, and Moquino speak the same language, which, according to Gatschet, does not have the slightest affinity with Aztec or any other Nahuatl idiom. Eds.: Even today ethnolinguists have not been able to relate the Keresan languages to any other group, although a link with Uto-Aztecan seems to hold some promise. Michael K. Foster, "Language and Culture History of North America," in *Handbook of North American Indians: Languages,* ed. Ives Goddard (Washington, D.C.: Smithsonian Institution, 1996), 17:96.

6. In 1697, Laguna Pueblo was situated near an old lake held by a beaver dam on the San José River. It drained, as Ten Kate notes, earlier in the nineteenth century. Ellis, "Laguna Pueblo," *Handbook: Southwest,* 9:438.

7. The fort was, in fact, first established in 1860 under the name Fort Fauntleroy but was later renamed after Captain Benjamin Wingate, who was killed in New Mexico during the Civil War at the Battle of Valverde. By the time of Ten Kate's visit, the fort had largely lost its military importance. Lance Chilton et al., *New Mexico: A New Guide to the Colorful State* (Albuquerque: University of New Mexico Press, 1984), 406.

8. The Navajo reservation in 1883 consisted of the treaty reservation of June 1, 1868 (3,414,528 acres), as well as additions to the west in 1878 (957,817 acres) and to the east and south in 1880 (996,403 acres). James M. Goodman, *The Navajo Atlas* (Norman: University of Oklahoma Press, 1982), 56–57; Robert A. Roessel, Jr., "Navajo History, 1850–1923," *Handbook: Southwest,* 10:519–20.

9. Irish-born Washington Matthews (1843–1905), a pioneer ethnographer, began studying Native American cultures while serving as an army physician in the West. He spent six years among the Hidatsa, in what is now North Dakota, and published a grammar and dictionary of their language. In 1880 he was transferred to Fort Wingate, where he began his investigations of the Navajo, later publishing works on tribal mythology and other aspects of Navajo culture. James Mooney, "In Memoriam: Washington Matthews," *American Anthropologist,* 7 (1905):514–23.

10. HtK 1885: The Americans say "hogán," because they cannot pronounce the acute [i.e., aspirated] *ch* sound. Likewise they say "Navahos" instead of "Navajos" *(j* like acute *ch),* "Hila" instead of "Gila," "Hosé" and "Huan" instead of "José" and "Juan," etc.

11. HtK 1885: The herds of the Navajos, Moquis, and Zunis probably originally came from the numerous sheep and goats that Coronado brought with him on his expedition in 1540 to the "seven cities of Cibola." Eds.: Actually the Navajo took livestock from the Spanish somewhat later, in the period between 1650 and 1700. Refugees from the Pueblo tribes, in turn, entered into closer association with the Navajos after the outbreak of 1680, the Pueblo Revolt. James F. Downs, *Animal Husbandry in Navajo Society and Culture* (Berkeley: University of California Press, 1964), 26.

12. HtK 1885: The two Zuni Indians (chapter 8, lithograph 10) both have wrapped themselves in similar Navajo blankets.

13. HtK 1889: For thorough reports regarding weaving and silver work among the Navajos, see the excellent descriptions of Dr. Washington Matthews in *Second and Third Annual Report, Bureau of Ethnology,* Washington, 1883 and 1886.

14. The first military post in what is now Arizona, Fort Defiance was established in 1851 as a base to control the Navajo Indians. In 1868 it was converted into the headquarters of the Navajo Indian agency. Robert W. Frazer, *Forts of the West* (Norman: University of Oklahoma Press, 1965), 8.

15. According to Mormon belief, the American Indians are descendants of the apostate son of the Jewish prophet Lehi who arrived in America in 589 B.C. The Mormons believed that they had a special obligation to convert the Indians and that their conversion would precede the millennium. John A. Price, "Mormon Missions to the Indians," in *Handbook of North American Indians: History of Indian-White Relations,* ed. W. Washburn (Washington, D.C.: Smithsonian Institution, 1988), 4:459.

16. Ten Kate studied at Georg-August University in the spring and summer of 1881. He took courses in anatomy, zoology, and geography. Pieter Hovens, *Herman ten Kate en de Antropologie der Noord Amerikaanse Indianen* (Meppel: Krips, 1989), 38–39.

17. Navajo warriors on raids and journeys wore helmet-shaped caps *(chahadilkhadi)* made of buckskin but sometimes also of mountain lion or wild cat skins. The cap was decorated with owl, turkey, crow, and eagle feathers with a strand of abalone shell in front. Clyde Kluckhohn, W. W. Hill, and Lucy Wales Kluckhohn, *Navajo Material Culture* (Cambridge, Mass.: Harvard University Press, 1971), 272–78.

18. In June 1863, after more than a decade of hostilities, Brigadier General James H. Carlton charged Colonel Christopher (Kit) Carson with the task of rounding up the Navajo, a campaign that employed a scorched-earth policy. During 1864 thousands of Navajos in convoys walked 300 miles to Fort Sumner. This episode, during which many died, is known as the Long Walk. Hundreds of others sought refuge to the north and west in Arizona. After four difficult years a treaty was signed on June 1, 1868, which permitted the return of the Navajo to a part of the land they had previously owned. Robert A. Roessel, Jr., "Navajo History, 1850–1923," *Handbook: Southwest,* 10:506–23.

19. It is estimated that thousands of Indians, including a great many Navajos, were held as slaves in the New Mexico Territory. In the summer of 1883, in the incident Ten Kate is referring to, Navajo agent Dennis M. Riordan, with an armed escort, obtained six Paiute captives who shortly thereafter returned to their former master. L. R. Bailey, *Indian Slave Trade in the Southwest* (Los Angeles: Westernlore Press, 1973), 134–35.

20. Guy Evans Huse (1855–1893) was a graduate of West Point who joined the 4th Cavalry in 1879 and later participated in the 1885–1886 Geronimo War. Dan L. Thrapp, ed., *Encyclopedia of Frontier Biography* (Glendale, Calif.: Arthur H. Clarke, 1988), 2:697.

21. Twenty-three versions of these stories of origin dating from 1883 are summarized in Katherine Spencer, *Reflections of Social Life in the Navaho Origin Myth* (Albuquerque: University of New Mexico Press, 1947).

22. Specifically, in Spanish the term means a pool formed by rain.

23. The Navajo people call themselves *Dine,* meaning "person," "people," or "human beings." The English word *Navajo* has its origins in the Spanish *Navajo,* first used in the seventeenth century to refer to the territory then occupied by the Navajo in northwestern New Mexico. This term, in turn, seems to be a borrowing of the Tewa *navahu,* a compound of *nava,* "field," and *hu,* "wide arroyo," "valley," used to designate a large arroyo in which there are cultivated fields. David M. Brugge et al., "[Navajo] Synonymy," *Handbook: Southwest,* 10:496–97.

24. The Hopi-speaking peoples of northeastern Arizona occupied six villages on three fingerlike projections from the southern escarpment of Black Mesa at the time of Ten Kate's visit. A seventh village of Tewa-speaking people was situated on the first or easternmost "mesa." Hopi architecture was built of sandstone, and most villages consisted of compact, plaza-focused house blocks. The larger villages of Shungopavi (Second Mesa) and Oraibi (Third Mesa) were situated on larger landforms, and the house blocks formed streets, one or two of which were used as dance plazas. The Hopi ritual calendar is divided in two halves marked by the summer and winter solstices. Masked *(katsina)* dances take place in the winter and spring; unmasked (priestly) ceremonies, including the Snake Dance, occur in the summer and fall. Richard Maitland Bradfield, *An Interpretation of Hopi Culture* (Derby, England: The Author, 1995), 3–25, 51–59; Louis A. Hieb, "Hopi," *Native America in the Twentieth Century: An Encyclopedia,* ed. Mary B. Davis (New York: Garland, 1994), 240–43.

25. The identity of "Prof. Powell" could not be established. We have found no record indicating that John Wesley Powell, the director of the Bureau of (American) Ethnology, was there at the time.

26. HtK 1885: Name the Navajos give the cliff dwellers, the former inhabitants of the cliff houses. Eds.: The term *Anasazi* (Navajo: *'anaasazi*) is generally translated as "ancient people," but more recent scholarship suggests a fuller understanding: *'anaa-* ("those who live beside us but not among us") and *-sazi* ("ancestors greater than five generations old, ones whose bodies have returned to the earth and are now scattered about"). Harry Walters and Hugh Rogers, "Anasazi and 'Anaasazi: Two Worlds, Two Cultures," *Kiva* 66 (2001):317–26. An early confirmation of this interpretation is to be found in H. C. Rizer's "Ga-Bi-Tcai," *The Eureka Herald,* November 29, 1883.

27. Born in Wales, Thomas Varker Keam (1841–1904) served in Kit Carson's Navajo campaign as an interpreter. From 1875 until 1902 he was licensed to trade with the Hopis and he operated a trading post in the canyon that bears his name, ten miles east of the Hopi First Mesa. Laura Graves, *Thomas Varker Keams: Indian Trader* (Norman: University of Oklahoma Press, 1998).

28. The Arizona Tewa-speaking people of Tewa or Hano have lived on the Hopi First Mesa since 1696, after continuous pressure from the Spanish following de Vargas's reconquest of New Mexico in 1693. At Ten Kate's time, the village was most frequently called "Tehua," referring to the language, which had its immediate historic origin in Galisteo Basin Tewa. Edward P. Dozier, *Hano: A Tewa Indian Community in Arizona* (New York: Holt, Rinehart and Winston, 1966), 3–12.

29. HtK 1885: *Huálpé* or *Wálpé*, from *uwalpé*, which in the Moqui language means "house of rocks." Perhaps the name also signifies "broken rocks" *(wálpi)*. *Setshómové* means "white house," the afore-mentioned *Shepálavé* "peach house." Eds.: The etymology for the First Mesa village of Walpi is "place of the gap," for Sichomovi, "flower hill place," for the Second Mesa village of Shipaulovi, "place of the mosquitoes." John C. Connelly, "Hopi Social Organization," *Handbook: Southwest,* 9:551–52.

30. The exodus actually occurred much earlier when Southern Tewas, probably from the pueblos San Cristóbal and San Lázaro, fled Spanish rule following the abortive Pueblo Revolt of 1696 and settled on the Hopi First Mesa in 1700. Michael B. Stanislawski, "Hopi-Tewa," *Handbook: Southwest,* 9:600.

31. HtK 1885: *Petermann's Geographische Mittheilungen,* 1873 [Eds.: Correction: 1874], p. 408. Also, after my return I saw, among a collection of ethnografica sent by the U.S. National Museum to the Trocadéro Museum in Paris, some of these dichas cited as "deities"!

32. The Hopi word is *tihu* (plural: *tithu*). *Tithu* or katsina dolls are small, carved wooden representations of the *katsinum,* benevolent spirits of the lower world. The katsina doll (tihu) is not a katsina, a spirit, and thus it is not an object of worship. Tithu have always been made of cottonwood. At the time of Ten Kate's visit the face, or mask, was painted in elaborate detail, but little attention was given to the form or decoration of the body. Modern dolls frequently represent the ritual impersonators of the katsinum in their more realistic portrayal of the entire figure. Helga Teiwes, *Kachina Dolls: The Art of Hopi Carvers* (Tucson: University of Arizona Press, 1991), 33.

33. Jeremiah Sullivan, M.D. (1851–1916), joined his father, John H. Sullivan, newly appointed Hopi agent, in December 1880. Sullivan lived in Sichomovi village from 1881 to 1888, where he earned his living primarily as a physician. The doctor wrote accounts of Hopi myth and ritual as well as of the Hopi language. Stephen C. McCluskey, "Evangelists, Educators, Ethnographers, and the Establishment of the Hopi Reservation," *Journal of Arizona History* 21 (1980):363–90; Louis A. Hieb, "The Beginnings of Ethnology at Hopi," in *Layers of Time,* eds. M. S. Duran and D. T. Kirkpatrick (Albuquerque; Papers of the Archaeological Society of New Mexico, 1997) 23:37–50; also Hovens, *Herman ten Kate,* 59–60, 82, 115–18.

34. HtK 1885: An *estufa* (Sp.) is the council chamber among the various Pueblo Indians and, at the same time, the place where a number of their religious and mystic ceremonies are performed. Under normal circumstances, the estufa is the working place where blankets are woven besides. Eds.: This structure is now referred to by the Hopi word *kiwa.* As ritual architecture, some kivas are round (e.g., eastern Pueblos), some rectangular (Hopi), some aboveground, some subterranean. All are entered through the roof and all serve as a vehicle for communication and exchange between the worlds of the various Puebloan peoples and the world of the spirits. Peter Nabokov, Robert Easton, *Native American Architecture* (New York: Oxford University Press, 1989), 376–79; Pieter Hovens, *Anasazi-Pueblo: Indian Architecture in the American Southwest* (Arnhem: NMB-Amstelland, 1997).

35. HtK 1885: According to Captain John G. Bourke, U.S. Army, who in August 1881 was the first white man to attend the Snake Dance in Huálpé, one of the four "medicines," which are are used in these dances, is probably the golondrina (see chapter 2, note 94). *The Snake Dance of the Moquis of Arizona,* London, 1884, p. 189. Eds.: The first published account of the Snake Dance is that of William R. Mateer, Hopi agent in 1878–1879. Mateer's account of the Walpi observances appeared in *The Long-Islander,* October 10, 1879. W. David Laird, *Hopi Bibliography* (Tucson: University of Arizona Press, 1977), 422–23. In 1881 Bourke was not the only white man to attend the ceremony:

Jeremiah Sullivan, Thomas V. Keam, Alexander M. Stephen (see note 56), the artist Peter Moran, and others were also present. John Gregory Bourke, *The Snake Dance of the Moquis of Arizona* (New York: Scribner, 1884). See also E. G. McIntire and S. R. Gordon, "Ten Kate's Account of the Walpi Snake Dance," *Plateau* (1968) 41:27–33; Hovens, *Herman ten Kate,* 115–18.

36. The fascination of the Snake Dance led to the recording of a number of versions of the underlying myth in the last two decades of the nineteenth century. In a text attributed to Alexander M. Stephen (but most certainly written by Jeremiah Sullivan), it is noted that there were "three legends concerning the feast": the popular version known generally throughout the village, another known to members of the Snake and Antelope societies, and a third known only to the chief priests. Given the stratified and privileged nature of Hopi sacred knowledge, what has generally been recorded is the popular version, as in Alexander M. Stephen, "Legend of the Snake Order of the Moquis, As Told to Outsiders," *Journal of American Folklore* 1 (1888):109–14. Earlier, in 1883, Keam published this version of the Snake clan migration narrative in his "An Indian Snake Dance," *Chamber's Journal* (January 6, 1883), 14–16.

37. Rain is the most common request in Hopi prayer and ritual; however, the gift, blessing, or benefit, may take other forms as well. Louis A. Hieb, "Hopi World View," *Handbook: Southwest,* 9:580.

38. For communication and exchange between the people of this world and the spirits of the other world, the Hopi use a variety of expressive media, not simply words spoken in prayer or sung in ritual but color, dance, masking, smoke, percussion, etc. The bull roarer (Stephen's "whizzer"), a rectangular wooden prayer stick attached to a cord, makes a roaring sound when whirled. Bull roarers were referred to as thunder prayer sticks, as they were used to call lightning (and rain), primarily in the Snake-Antelope ceremonies. They are often decorated with the symbol of lightning. Alexander M. Stephen, *Hopi Journal of Alexander M. Stephen,* ed. Elsie Clews Parsons (New York: Columbia University Contributions to Anthropology 23, 1935), 637.

39. HtK 1885: The description of Captain Bourke and Mr. T. V. Keam, who witnessed the Moqui Snake Dance before me, differ somewhat from mine. Bourke described it thoroughly in his work already cited; from Keam, I am familiar only with the short description of the dance that he provided in *Chamber's Journal,* part 229, Febr. 1883. [Eds.: "An Indian Snake Dance," *Chamber's Journal of Popular Literature, Science and Art,* 4th ser. 20, no. 993 (January 6, 1883):14–16.] Some details mentioned in their accounts I have not witnessed. Thus Bourke speaks of an idol image, which is supposedly in a niche of the sandstone column, in the vicinity of which the dance is performed. Bourke calls the sandstone column "sacred." Oyiwísha assured me, on the contrary, that the Moquis do not worship it at all. Both Bourke and Keam speak of a multicolored altar they saw in the estufa, etc. Because my description of the Snake Dance is limited exclusively to what I saw and many details could have escaped my attention, the description is, of course, somewhat deficient, but through mutual comparison of the various descriptions maybe one will be able to gain a better picture of this solemn ceremony. HtK 1889: A description by Cosmos Mindeleff of the Snake Dance of the Moquis in 1885 in Moshongnavé and Huálpé, which again differs somewhat from the descriptions of Bourke, Keam, and myself but supplements it, can be found in *Das Ausland,* 1886, pp. 1011, 1023. Eds.: The article in question appeared first in English: Kosmus Mendelieff [*sic*], "An Indian Snake Dance," *Science* 7 (174) (June 4, 1886):507–14.

40. HtK 1885: A cake prepared from cornmeal, as thin as a wafer but in larger, flatter rolls.

41. HtK 1885: Mr. Cushing later informed me that at Shepálavé he had seen two children, a boy and a girl, with hair that though "seemingly fine, was crispy to the feel, frizzled, and stood out—owing to its length as does that of the Fijians or their wigs—the latter of which it greatly resembled."

   At Moshóngnavé, Bourke, op. cit., p. 283, encountered a young man with "long woolly hair like a Hottentot." Obviously Bourke saw the same kind of hair as Cushing, though he could have easily omitted "like a Hottentot" without undercutting his assertion in the slightest. However, it is known that the Hottentots' hair is very short and leaves the impression of being implanted in small tufts.

   However tempting it may seem to speculate here about Melanesian influence, I am nevertheless less inclined than before, as I later investigated an individual in a remote village of Lapland whose hairstyle strongly recalled that of a Papuan. How could one conceive of a Melanesian influence there?

42. The Havasúpais are a Yuman-speaking group closely related to the Walapais and Yavapais, their neighbors in northwestern Arizona. During the late nineteenth century, white cattle ranchers began encroaching on Havasupai land, while prospectors became interested in copper deposits in Cataract Canyon, a traditional agricultural locale of the Havasupais. As a consequence, a reservation was established within the canyon in 1880. Changes in traditional culture took place immediately. Henry F. Dobyns, *The Havasupai People* (Phoenix: Indian Tribal Series, 1971), 14–28.

43. Navajos, Apaches, Utes, and Paiutes raided Hopi fields as early as the eighteenth century. The raids (for food, livestock, slaves) increased after the establishment of the Mexican Republic in 1823. After U.S. annexation of the region, the Hopis repeatedly complained to American authorities about Navajo depredations. Katherine Bartlett, "Hopi History, No. 2: The Navajo Wars, 1823–1870," *Museum Notes* (Flagstaff: Museum of Northern Arizona, 1937), 8:33–37.

44. Albert Samuel Gatschet (1832–1907), a Swiss-born ethnologist and linguist who emigrated to the United States in 1868, was a longtime member of the Bureau of Ethnology and the author of several works on Indian ethnology and linguistics in both German and English. *Dictionary of American Biography*, 23 vols. (New York: Scribner, 1943–73), 4, pt. 1:192–93.

45. The English name for the Hopi is their name for themselves: *hopi*. The meaning of this term is given variously as "good in every respect," "good, peaceable," "wise, knowing." It appears, however, that another form of self-designation has been *mokwi*, as this is how the Hopis are referred to in the languages of several groups in the area: the Paiutes, Zunis, and Keresans. In addition, Spanish accounts from the sixteenth century use a variety of forms of Moqui. As the word became Anglicized, it came to be pronounced "moki," which resembled the Hopi word *moki*, "dies, is dead," or *mokpu*, "(one that's) dead." "Moqui" was so offensive to the Hopi that Jesse Walter Fewkes recommended the change to Hopi, and in 1923 the agency name was changed. Albert Schroeder and Ives Goddard, "[Hopi] Synonymy," *Handbook: Southwest*, 9:550–51.

46. HtK 1885: See my "Synonymie ethnique."

47. This is the earliest record of the term by which the Hopis refer to their land: *Masawtutsqua*, Masaw's land. Today Hopis distinguish between *Tutsqua* (land as a geopolitical construct) and *Hopitutsqua* (Hopi land, a religious concept). Masaw is the god of the earth's surface and of death.

48. HtK 1885: *Petermann's Geographische Mittheilungen*, 1876, p. 217.

49. HtK 1885: Bourke, op. cit., pp. 116, 117, counts eighteen clans by the Moquis.

50. HtK 1885: According to Gilbert, the soul of the dead man leaves the grave along one of these sticks, which the body grips in its hand as it ascends. Yarrow, *A Further Contribution to the Study of Mortuary Customs,* etc., p. 114. Eds.: Grove Karl Gilbert (1843–1918) was a geologist on the Wheeler and Power surveys of the West during the 1870s. He was later chief geologist of the U.S. Geological Survey. *Dictionary of American Biography* 4, pt. 1:268–69. The correct title of the work cited by Ten Kate is H. C. Yarrow, *Introduction to the Study of Mortuary Customs Among the North American Indians* (Washington, D.C.: U.S. Government Printing Office, 1880). In the work cited, Gilbert was reporting an 1878 conversation with a Hopi chief.

51. HtK 1885: Almost nine months later, thanks to the effort and thoughtful solicitude of Dr. Sullivan, I was surprised to receive a magnificent male Moqui skull. At the present time this skull is found in the Rijks Ethnographisch Museum in Leiden and has been described and depicted by me in the *Archives Néerlandaises,* Haarlem, 1885. Eds.: The present North American collection of the National Museum of Ethnology in Leiden does not contain any human remains, except a number of hair samples collected by Ten Kate.

52. In 1891 the Hopi population was 1,996. The number of albinos identified in a 1900 survey was eleven. The population figures and estimates of albinism given by Sullivan, a physician, appear to be accurate. Albinism occurs at different frequencies in various human populations. The average for European populations is one in 20,000. It is estimated that one in 182 individuals was an albino at Hopi in 1900. Charles M. Woolf and Frank Charles Dukepoo, "Hopi Indians, Inbreeding, and Albinism," *Science* 164 (3875) (April 4, 1969):30–37. Ethnic pigmentation was a lifelong interest of Ten Kate and he studied it wherever his travels took him, publishing his findings in a series of articles; Hovens, *Herman ten Kate,* 85–86.

53. Jacob Hamblin visited the Hopi villages in 1858, and by 1873 the Mormons had sent fifteen expeditions to the Hopi. In 1875 the Mormons established a mission at Moenkopi, a farming colony of Oraibi forty miles west of Third Mesa. In 1878 Tuba City was established near Moenkopi as the Mormons' major outpost in northern Arizona. Charles S. Peterson, "The Hopis and the Mormons 1858–1873," *Utah Historical Quarterly* 39 (1971):179–94.

54. During the winter of 1853–1854 the Hopi population was "greatly diminished" by a smallpox epidemic followed by a severe drought. Another drought occurred between 1862 and 1868 with springs failing by 1866, followed apparently by another smallpox epidemic in 1866–1867. The loss of life among children and the elderly was significant and probably accounts for Ten Kate's statement, "Many childless marriages exist." Thomas Donaldson, *Moqui Pueblo Indians of Arizona and Pueblo Indians of New Mexico* (Extra Census Bulletin, Eleventh Census, Washington, D.C.: U.S. Census Printing Office, 1893), 28.

55. HtK 1885: *Feminae parturientes manibus humi nixae, mento ad genua appropinquante, quasi saltaturae sedere solent.* [Women giving birth, leaning with the hands on the ground, the chin approaching the knees, are accustomed to sitting as if they were about to dance.]

56. Alexander Middleton Stephen (1846–1894) was born in Scotland and came to the United States in 1862. He served in the New York Infantry, 1862–1866. In 1869 Stephen and another Civil War veteran, Thomas A. McElmell, began a decade of exploration and prospecting in California, Nevada, Utah, Colorado, and Arizona. Stephen visited Keam's Canyon in 1879 and lived there from 1880 until his death. He learned Navajo, the lingua franca of the trading post, and first recorded and published accounts of Navajo culture. In 1891 he was hired to assist Jesse Walter Fewkes, director of the second Hemenway Expedition, to document Hopi social and ceremonial life. Stephen, *Hopi Journal,* xx–xxiv.

57. While Stephen was away prospecting, Ten Kate examined an extensive collection of prehistoric and contemporary Hopi pottery assembled by Thomas V. Keam. Stephen had begun a descriptive catalog of the collection in preparation for its being offered to the U.S. National Museum in 1884. On behalf of Mary Hemenway and the Hemenway Expedition, Jesse Walter Fewkes purchased the collection in 1892 for $10,000. Alexander Paterson, *Hopi Pottery Symbols* (Boulder, Colo.: Johnson Books, 1994), 7; Edwin L. Wade and Lea S. McChesney, *America's Great Lost Expedition: The Thomas Keam Collection of Hopi Pottery from the Second Hemenway Expedition, 1890–1894* (Phoenix: The Heard Museum, 1980).

58. Emil Bessels, *The Human Remains Found Near the Ancient Ruins of Southwestern Colorado and New Mexico* (Washington, D.C., 1876); Walter J. Hoffman, *Report on the Chaco Cranium* (Department of the Interior, U.S. Geological Survey, Tenth Annual Report of the Survey for the Year 1876, Washington, D.C.: U.S. Government Printing Office, 1879), 451–78.

59. HtK 1885: See my "Sur quelques crânes du Nouveau-Mexique et de l'Arizona," *Revue d'Anthropologie* 1884, p. 486.

60. HtK 1885: *Petermann's Geographische Mittheilungen*, 1876, p. 212, table 12.

61. HtK 1885: Hamy in *Bulletins de la Société d'Anthropologie*, 1883, pp. 835, 836. Eds.: Aztec legends relate that they were not native to the Valley of Mexico but immigrants. They probably were an early agricultural people who had absorbed traits of the Toltecs, particularly in the spheres of religion and ritual. Michael Coe, Dean Snow, and Elizabeth Benson, *Atlas of Ancient America* (New York: Facts on File, 1988), 143.

62. During the early period of Spanish domination, the Zunis occupied five pueblos, but in 1692, after the suppression of the Pueblo Revolt, they returned to just one pueblo, Zuni. Richard D. Woodbury, "Zuni Prehistory and History to 1850," *Handbook: Southwest*, 9:470.

63. Inhabited by Towa-language speakers, the Pecos pueblo—with an estimated population of approximately 2,000—was one of the largest Pueblo Indian settlements during the sixteenth century, when the Spanish explored and later conquered New Mexico. During the eighteenth century, the Pecos pueblo population declined drastically as a result of epidemics and Comanche raids. By the beginning of the nineteenth century only about a hundred inhabitants remained. In 1838 the last inhabitants, slightly more than a dozen in number, abandoned Pecos and moved to Jemez Pueblo, also Towa speaking. John L. Kessell, *Kiva, Cross, and Crown: The Pecos Indians and New Mexico 1540–1840* (Washington, D.C.: U.S. Department of the Interior, National Park Service, 1979); Albert H. Schroeder, "Pecos Pueblo," *Handbook: Southwest,* 9:430–37.

64. See notes 28 and 30.

65. After 1880, when Navajo and Apache raids subsided, Laguna's farmers could settle permanently near their plots rather than retire nightly to the pueblo for safety. Florence Hawley Ellis, "Laguna Pueblo," *Handbook: Southwest,* 9:441.

66. HtK 1885: A. Bandelier says that he has known Pueblo Indians who in the last 300 years changed their dwelling place three times, leaving ruins behind in every case. He also states that when the area around a pueblo dries up, the inhabitants abandon it to seek out a tract better provided with water and to build a new pueblo. If a dwelling or a pueblo falls into decay, then, according to Bandelier, it is not restored but a new one built elsewhere. Thus, according to him, the numerous ruins of pueblos do not always indicate a numerous population *at the same time*. See *Das Ausland,* 1882, 641. Eds.: See Bandelier's article "Die historische Entwicklung Mexicos," *Das Ausland* 55 (1882):643.

67. Thomas V. Keam, apparently quoting from Alexander M. Stephen's manuscript on Hopi pottery symbols, provides the Hopi story of this rock art: "The single spiral is the symbol of Ho-bo-bo, the twister, who manifests his power by the whirlwind. . . . The myth explains that a stranger came among the people, when a great whirlwind blew all the vegetation from the surface of the earth and all the water from its courses. With a flint he caught these symbols upon a rock, the etching of which is now in Keam's Canyon, Arizona Territory. He told them he was the keeper of breath. The whirlwind and the air that men breathe come from his keeper's mouth." Garrick Mallery, "Picture-Writing of the American Indians," *Annual Report of the Bureau of Ethnology* (Washington, D.C.: U.S. Government Printing Office, 1893), 10:604–5; Patterson, *Hopi Pottery Symbols* (Boulder: Johnson Books, 1994), 27, 250.

68. HtK 1885: Bourke, op. cit., p. 279, says that the Navajos have more than forty clans.

69. HtK 1885: See Matthews, "A Part of the Navajos Mythology," in *American Antiquarian,* April 1883.

70. Ganado Mucho (1809–1893), a Navajo headman so named for his large herds of cattle and sheep, had generally counseled peace during struggles with the whites in the 1860s. After the defeat of the Navajos, it was he who led his people to the Bosque Redondo reservation along the Pecos River in 1865 and back to their homelands in 1868 after the failure of this disastrous experiment in Indian resettlement. Thereafter he attempted, not always successfully, to protect his fellow tribesmen against white encroachment. Thrapp, *Encyclopedia,* 2:531–32.

71. Samuel C. Armstrong (1839–1893), the son of missionaries in Hawaii, fought on the Union side during the Civil War, commanding black troops during its final phases. After the war Armstrong played a key role in financing and founding Hampton Institute in 1868, which became a leading institution of black education and which, after 1878, also took in Native Americans. *National Cyclopedia of American Biography,* 63 vols. (New York: J. T. White, 1892–1984), 38:427–29. Colonel James Stevenson (1840–1888) and Mathilda Coxe Stevenson (1849–1915) both came to the Southwest in 1879 as members of the first collecting and research expedition of the newly formed Bureau of Ethnology, a division of the Smithsonian Institution. As the first husband-wife team in anthropology, James Stevenson published accounts of collections made at Zuni, Hopi, and elsewhere in the Southwest while Mathilda Cox Stevenson wrote descriptions of Zuni social and ceremonial life. Nancy J. Parezo, "Mathilda Coxe Stevenson: Pioneer Ethnologist," *Hidden Scholars: Women Anthropologists and the Native American Southwest* (Albuquerque: University of New Mexico Press, 1993), 38–62.

72. Jules Louis-Olivier Metra (1830–1889), a French composer, wrote polkas, waltzes, and other dances and operettas popular in their own day but largely now forgotten.

73. HtK 1885: Among other places, in the Netherlands this practice is encountered in the Veluwe region.

CHAPTER EIGHT

Stay at Zuni

MY FIRST CONCERN THE NEXT DAY WAS TO PAY MY RESPECTS to the commandant at Fort Wingate and ask him to provide me some means of transportation to Zuni. Because I could not leave until the 28th, I spent most of the day in Dr. Matthews's company, undertaking a long riding and walking tour in the heavily wooded Zuni Mountains rising behind the fort. The doctor's goal was to compile Native names for plants and bushes and ascertain their properties, based on the Navajo pharmacopoeia. To this end, he was accompanied by a trustworthy Indian, who led us through thick and thin and filled the doctor's herbarium with herbs while reciting the name and various properties of each plant. I do not wish to anticipate Dr. Matthews's work[1] here and will only state that on this expedition I got a full impression of the Zuni Mountains in all their beauty.

In the silent ravines, where the ozone-filled air rustles through pine trees and fills up your lungs and the babbling brooks bask in the rays of sunshine, isolated flowers sway between blades of grass and chunks of rock strewn over the undulating ground. Lovely red calomias and rudbeckia vie with dainty penstemons and blue-violet delphinias to enchant your eye, while along the damp banks of the creeks Cariceae and Juncaceae [rushes] and, on the treeless patches, sprawling fields of *Helianthus* [sunflowers] and *Heliopsis* in fraternal fashion share the space left for them in the dense forest.[2]

The next morning at 8 o'clock I leave Fort Wingate in a military ambulance, which will take me to Zuni, forty miles to the southwest. For the first twenty miles the route leads across the Zuni Mountains, through magnificent woodland, across grassy meadows awash with flowers. Sometimes, when the forest is not so dense and a valley emerges, the bluish region of the Tsòstìl, the sacred mountain of the Navajos, glimmers far off in the east. Promptly thereafter you descend to the foot of the mountains, where a clear creeks winds its way through the valley and Nutrias, a small Zuni pueblo, lies ahead of you.

I stop for a moment to exchange greetings and a couple of words with nearby Indians and then continue the ride. The route now leads through a very broad valley, which is covered with dark firs and juniper trees, its sides consisting of reddish Triassic sandstone. Eventually two steep mesas facing each other, emerge on both sides of the plain. Between them looms a drab elevation, which from a distance resembles a gigantic anthill. Here and there columns of smoke arise and dissipate in the air still clear just a while ago, which is slowly filling up with storm clouds. The closer I come, the more clearly I can make out the terraces, doors, and windows on the anthill. Moments later I ride into Zuni, welcomed by the furious barking of dogs and pursued by the curious glances of the Indians, who are hunkered down by their doors and on top of the roofs.

A black man with a cook's hat on his head, who is standing by a door and whom I recall seeing not long ago in Albuquerque, points out Frank Cushing's dwelling to me. Although he has been in nearby St. Johns for a couple of days, I am received by his wife and sister-in-law with genuine, unaffected American hospitality. Before long I have brought my scanty luggage inside and installed myself in their dwelling for a few days.

Zuni is one of the high points of my journey. I hardly know where to begin now that I must recount the many impressions that overwhelmed me and I must talk about my stay in a place that holds unforgettable memories for me. I could fill an entire book about Cushing and the Zunis, but I must make a stab at it with the many items noted in my diary and with all that comes to mind again as I write.

Mr. Cushing lives on the lower story of the house of Pálawahtiwa, the governor of Zuni, situated at the southeastern[3] corner of the pueblo. The small, half-obscure rooms with their low doors and narrow windows offer a medley of Indian and Japanese artistic sensibility and Oscar Wilde's "esthetic."[4] The floor is covered with multicolored Navajo blankets and bear and puma skins, which also hang from the walls, while Cushing's armor as priest of the Order of the Bow is suspended above an Oriental divan. It is a magnificent trophy, that colorful round shield adorned with feathers and the delicate bow and quiver made of puma hide. Here your eye alights upon the breachloading rifles and revolvers; there on a book rack; here on a box with fine porcelain and Zuni pottery; yonder Japanese fans, peacock feathers, sunflowers, and colorful little Moqui baskets, which adorn the walls in places. A soft light penetrates the small square windows and envelopes the picturesque interior in shimmering half tints of profuse richness and intensity.

Before nightfall the two women and I take a walk through the pueblo, but rain showers and gusts of wind, which had already been threatening for a while now, force us promptly to return. Fortunately, the next few days I have a better opportunity to observe the town. In the main Zuni has the same character as all other pueblos, and the description, already provided, of the Moqui villages of Tesuque and Laguna is generally applicable to Zuni as well.

The ground plan of Zuni is longitudinal, and its axis runs roughly from north to south,[5] while the tallest houses—consisting of four stories—are situated in the southern center of the town. Only the color of the houses differs entirely from that of the aforementioned pueblos and is purplish reddish brown, just like the ground they rest upon. Here, too, hundreds of wooden ladders jut above the terraces and numerous sheep corrals are found along the outskirts of the pueblo, filling the air with their penetrating stench. On the east[6] side of the town flows the shallow, muddy Zuni River, a left-hand branch of the Rio Puerco. The only tree in the town is a small cottonwood. All around on the plain the eye perceives nothing but sand, sparse grass, and corn and melon fields.

Together with the two small pueblos Nutrias and Ojo Caliente, which are inhabited by the same people,[7] Zuni numbers roughly 1,600 inhabitants—the remnants of a once mighty tribe of the *A'shiwi*, which formerly inhabited no less than fourteen pueblos but have shrunk to a minuscule number due to numerous disasters, wars, and epidemics.[8] Except for a missionary, who lives a short distance outside the pueblo, and a trader, Mr. Graham, who has his store in one of the streets, the Cushings are the only whites in the town.[9]

The second day of my stay I had the opportunity to observe one of the dances that play such an important role in the religious and social life of the Zuni Indians. The *kâkókshi,*[10] or "good dance," is the type of the *"cachinas,"* or *kâ'kâ's*, of the Zuni. This is a type of worship and supposedly represents the dance the soul of the departed attends as an observer at its consecration in the presence of the god-priests and which, it is alleged, is later performed now and then in this life by the soul itself with the dancers. The tradition of the kâkókshi is too long and too involved with the mythology of the Zuni to be dealt with here without a thorough discussion.[11]

The dance began about 9 A.M. and only ended at 4 P.M. In the beginning I counted thirty-one dancers, all of them dressed in the same fashion, along with a dancer dressed as a woman—and a priest. The former were completely unclad, except for a blanket wrapped around the middle [of their bodies]. The upper body and legs were smeared with white flour. Heavy necklaces of shells, beads, and turquoise hung from their necks down to their chests, with a glittering haliotis shell shining in the middle. Light green masks with long black beards covered their faces. The long raven black hair hung down loosely over their backs. On top of their heads were stuck yellow parrot feathers from Mexico.[12] White feathers from a pelican were fluttering in back. The blankets, fastened around their hips and reaching almost down to their knees, consisted of finely woven white wool and were hemmed with dainty black-and-green borders, while the lovely hide of a gray fox was dangling from behind. Fastened below the right knee, but on the inside, was a tortoise shell with rattling deer and antelope hooves, while the left one was enveloped by a dark band at the same height. Their feet were clad in lovely leather moccasins, partially covered by spruce branches, which were fastened around their ankles. In the right hand they held a gourd shell rattle, and a broad silver bracelet adorned their wrists. Finally, they carried green spruce branches in their left hands.

The dancer disguised as a woman was wrapped in a magnificent white blanket fringed with black hems, reaching down to his knees, and wore his hair in more or less the same style as the Moqui girls, while a similar green mask covered his face. The priest was the only one without a mask. A single white feather was stuck in his hair, which was bound together in back in a knot. His torso was clad in a dark cotton jacket. His legs were attired with broad white trousers and leather leggings. On his feet he wore soft footwear from the same material. In his left hand he held a small vase with sacred flour and a staff with eagle feathers.

The ceremony begins at the south side of Zuni. Close behind one moment, then right next to each other, they stomp incessantly with their right feet, then with their left, which do not budge from position, with the upper body slightly stooped. After an initial silence, a robust chant with a powerful cadence chimes in soon afterward accompanied by the rattling of the tortoise shells and the shaking of the rattles.

The priest and the dancer dressed as a woman stand at the head of the long, stomping row. Only during intermissions does the former strew the sacred flour over the ground with his right hand, always chanting, and with his gaze fixed on the dancers. The second one stands at the right side of the first dancer and executes the same motion as the former.

After dancing for a while, the row suddenly stands still and heads to the three or four various open spaces (plazas) inside the center of the pueblo. There they repeat in succession the same movements and the same chant and after a short while eventually vanish together in an estufa.

In the intervening period some new personages appear, wearing the most ludicrous attire. Their heads are completely covered with a gigantic round mask of dried clay with round holes for eyes and mouth, strongly recalling a deep sea diver's mask. They are completely unclad except for a loincloth and are anointed from top to bottom with pinkish mud. These are the *keóyemoshi,* or "guardians of the sacred dance," whose task it is to amuse the spectators during the dance intermissions. For the most part they engage in coarse jests, comic dialogues, and practical jokes, performing almost exactly the same role as our clowns. The dignity of these keóyemoshi is sacred, and every year a number of them are selected from the priesthood.

Making all kinds of jokes, they go inside various houses to ask for *héwé*[13] for the dancers resting inside the estufa, who never tarry there for long and resume their dance with renewed ardor. Every time they come out of the estufa after a round dance, a new dancer disguised as a woman has been added to the others, so that by the end of the dance there are a half dozen. Moreover, in the middle of the day they were joined by a dancer who took his place in the middle of the row, clad for the most part like the other dancers but without being anointed white and with a gigantic mask on his head besides.

As time passed, the more numerous became the spectators, who had taken up position in colorful, picturesque groups on the flat roofs of their houses, from where they could view the plaza. Here, the longer time went on, the more the row of bronzed figures with their rattles were passionately moving up and down while droning out, *"Haha-hahajeha-haha!"*[14]

I can imagine the difficulty Cushing had to contend with in the beginning when he wanted to make sketches of the Zuni dances and notes of his observations in their presence; for I myself can still see from the onlookers' glaring how displeased they were that I "brought the shadows of the dance onto the pages of my book." Fortunately, though, there were no threats on my life as there were on Cushing's, and I could put what I wanted on paper, though only intermittently.[15]

Circumstances beyond my control were the reason why I could not attend the conclusion of the kâkókshi, but later I learned that the final scene consisted of a kind of pantomime, which in gross unseemliness would yield nothing to the immoral dances of the South Sea Islanders.[16]

That same noon when the kâkókshi was in full swing, Mr. Cushing returned. This time he was wearing a costume that was part Indian, part fantasy. He held together the long locks rolling down over his shoulders with a black headband. A short blouse of dark blue cloth, low cut at the neck, covered his torso. Tightly fitting trousers of the same material, ornamented at the seams with rows of silver buttons, reached down to his knees. In addition, he wore brown leather leggings with attractively woven red knee bands and closed moccasins. Around his neck, hanging down to the middle of his chest, he wore precious strings of fashioned shells and turquoises, around his right wrist an armband of small, attractive *Oliva* shells, the emblem of his dignity as Priest of the Bow.

The first tour I made with him through the pueblo very quickly convinced me that Mr. Cushing is completely at home here and was regarded as the Indians' full-fledged fellow tribesman. Everywhere a friendly greeting, a nodding of the head, or a breathing on each other's hand, a way of greeting as graceful as it is symbolic. While exchanging handshakes there is, for just a moment, a mutual lifting of hands to the mouth with breathing on them; this is exchanging the "breath of life."

By the time of my visit, Ténatsali (Medicine Flower)—to call Mr. Cushing henceforth by his Zuni name—had spent nearly four years among the Zunis. If I wanted to discuss in detail everything he had discovered in that period of time, then I would have to expand the scope of my work and could repeat only imperfectly what he himself described in such captivating detail[17] and what he was able to tell me so eloquently by word of mouth. Then I would have to speak of the illnesses and deprivations that he had to contend with. I would report the dreadful trials he had to endure before he won the full confidence of the Indians. I would have to tell how he took three scalps before he could be accepted among the warriors of the nation[18] and could be named after "a magic plant that only grows on a remote mountain in the west, whose flowers were the loveliest on earth and of varied colors and whose roots and sap cured all human ailments"—a plant whose name he should bear as "child of the sun" and as "son of the Coru people of the earth, as long as the sun shall rise and set." I would have to recount how Ténatsali acquired the knowledge of their language, traditions, and legends, how he gradually penetrated the psychic life and being of the Zunis, and how he was eventually initiated into their religious mysteries. Nor could I pass over in silence how the young warrior bought off his forced marriage into the tribe by leading the priests to the "ocean of the rising sun," the subject of their adoration, to draw water there, which they were nearly lacking. I would have to describe how he was baptized in Boston Harbor as a Zuni priest and finally how his young wife came to share his voluntary exile in the Far West.[19]

After his arrival in Boston and in the great cities of the East, Cushing's name spread like a wildfire across the land. But with fame came, on the one hand, disbelief and bitter mockery from the public, which, always wary of humbug, saw in the young ethnologist nothing more than a prankster who was making fun of the public's credulity, and, on the other hand, contempt for the white man who had debased himself by living with Indians. Later, hate and resentment were his lot because Ténatsali had successfully defended the sacred right of his brethren against the greedy, unjust demands of a politician.[20] But even fellow specialists in Washington would not leave him in peace. There was suspicion of the work of the young ethnologist but also envy about the rich treasure trove of knowledge he had brought to light.

From the people he lives among I have been able to observe Cushing and know him through his work. Two things I have particularly gained from this acquaintance: a profound admiration for a man who has suffered for the sake of science alone and the conviction that his method of studying the ethnology of a people is the only authentic one.[21]

Pálawahtiwa, the most important chief of the Zunis, whom one could call the governor, was the successor of the well-known Pedro Pino,[22] about whom every traveler who visited Zuni has reported. Pálawahtiwa, who is already advanced in years, has handsome, intelligent features. He is heavily stooped and his gait faltering, the result of a fight with his mortal enemies, the "wild coyotes" or Navajos. Now that he can no longer go on the warpath, he vents his lust for battle on the dogs of the pueblo, and I still vividly recall how he lay in wait, armed with bow and arrow, to give passing dogs a warm welcome. In Zuni, too, dogs were once again an unending nuisance, and several times I was so beset by them that I had to use my revolver, to the Indians' great annoyance. Pálawahtiwa lives on the floor above Cushing with his spouse, a small woman whose face, with its exceptionally short, blunt nose, recalls a bulldog's physiognomy. In the morning, when I get up, the first thing I see is Mrs. Pálawahtiwa's face peeping into the ceiling of my chamber through the small singular window.

The governor conforms to the Indian type in its most noble form. That is a type that is not very common among the Zunis and is found mainly among the chiefs and priests. Although the Zunis have lived for ages separately in the region they now inhabit, from an anthropologic standpoint they nevertheless do not form a homogeneous race. Apart from the type just mentioned, one finds broad faces with short, straight or slightly up-turned noses, recalling the Celts. This type is quite common, particularly among the women. A third type, which I encountered only a few times among the women, revealed unmistakably Mongolian features. In facial expression, figure, general body build, and skin color the Zunis match the Moquis. They, too, have friendly, open faces. Moreover, they are small, rather slender, and of light complexion. The gait of the Zuni squaws is as stumbling and ungainly as that of the Moquis, but not a few young women and girls from both tribes display the same charms. Likewise, the attire of the Zunis from both sexes resembles that of the Moquis, but men wearing headbands after the fashion of the Navajos is more common among the former than among the latter. Cotton materials from Mr. Graham's trader's store are already quite common apparel and, at least as far as daily attire is concerned, have replaced chamois leather. The distinctive hairstyle of the Moqui girls is not found among the Zunis. Married women, as well as girls, wear their hair hanging loosely, cut at the neck and parted on one side.

Wearing Navajo blankets is widespread among the Zunis, but in addition, they own other attractive blankets of their own make, including the picturesque white blankets, decorated with black-and-green borders, used only in dances. They also make blankets from rabbit skins sewn together, just like the Moquis. In addition, they weave multicolored sashes and knee bands and make dark blue stockings without feet, like the former do.

The Zunis have been familiar with the art of silversmithing for some time, and here the Navajos have undoubtedly learned a great deal from them.[23] Pálawahtiwa is one of the most expert silversmiths in the pueblo, and the rings, bracelets, buttons, and belt buckles he makes are models of fine, tasteful work. He is equally adept in polishing turquoise and shells, and the precious strings that adorn his neck and chest are magnificent specimens of Zuni artistic industry. The shells are cut into small round disks, perforated in the middle, and strung together by the hundreds, with disks of turquoise and red coral interspersed in places. Necklaces of this kind are quite precious, particularly because of the shells, which are items greatly valued and admired because they come from the sea. Another stone the Zunis wear as an ornament is a kind of ruby spinel, which is found primarily in the numerous anthills of these regions.

The Zunis are not well advanced in weaving baskets. These consist of young twigs whose bark has not been removed and are crudely woven. Nor is there anything distinctive about their shape.

On the other hand, the Zunis surpass all other North American tribes in the making of pottery. The form is more delicate and austere, the ornamentation purer, and the color lovelier than I have seen anywhere. It consists of pots, pitchers, bowls, dishes, and cups of the most varied dimensions. One cannot enter any dwelling without one's eye alighting upon a number of these objects. Large ollas for holding water are particularly prominent. From the rim to the base the outline forms a wavy line that, the closer it gets to the bottom, practically turns into a straight line. Generally, the basic color of all the pottery is a more or less glossy white, while the ornamentation is black in color—in many places combined with reddish brown. Except for those encountered among all peoples—decorations in the form of meanders, spirals, and wavy lines—decorations consist of figures that would be difficult to describe without detailed drawings because they are derived from Zuni mythology. The study of ornamentation alone should make a lengthy visit to Zuni quite worthwhile because in the images one encounters a vivid impression of the popular imagination, handed down and imitated from age to age, linking the hoary past with today.

Pottery with animal shapes, mostly of birds, displays neither the clumsiness nor the monstrosity in that of the other Pueblo Indians. For the saucers and little bowls as well as the oblong pottery eating bowls—spoons, if one will—light brown is frequently the basic color.[24]

One of the most picturesque images that comes to mind was when, in the bright light of the early morning sun, a group of women and girls, with lovely water pitchers on their heads, came down along the small pathways between the cornfields surrounded with low adobe walls to draw water from the sandy river. Merrily laughing and chatting, they passed each other along the pathway or lay kneeling down to fill the ollas scoop by scoop with the muddy liquid. There was something

Oriental in that tableau with its fixed sky, overarching above the yellowish reddish landscape, bounded in the distance by the bare perpendicular walls of the *Tâ-ai-yállone,* or Thunder Mountain, which rose silently in isolation like a gigantic fortress in the background.

The drinking water in Zuni is just as bad as that in the Moqui villages. As I already noted, it is very muddy, has a sandy taste, and has a strong aroma of fecal matter and sheep. It sickens those who are not used to it. By consuming it, Ténatsali contracted a stomach ailment. I, too, could sense its deleterious influence, even though I drank it just a few times because my host, wary from experience, had water drawn near a spring several miles removed from the pueblo—a precaution that proved very costly, though, because of the enormous effort [it required]. The mortality among the young children in Zuni was also very high then because of this water being used, but those who made it through the critical period of trial are hardy and once adapted no longer suffer from its influence.

The cornfields, which are along the edge of the pueblo and, in patches, stretch farther out into the plateau, supply the principal food of the Zunis, who know how to prepare it in a variety of ways, just like the Moquis. Such a role does corn play in the life of these Indians that the Zuni philosophy teaches that it is one of the five elements (the sun, the earth, water, fire, corn) vital for human existence. Mutton takes second place. The numerous flocks, which are taken out of the open corrals every morning for grazing and return there every evening, are the Zunis' most prized possession. Although they own horses and cows, they are seldom encountered in Zuni because the grass needed is lacking there, and they graze far away—in the valleys and mountain slopes and in the area around Nutrias as well.

As for the Zunis' agricultural implements, these consist primarily of the crude wooden plow, like the one I already described above in Tesuque, and a wooden digging stick *(táhssahqueen),* which is approximately one meter long. The broad flat point serves for making holes in the ground, which must hold the seed. The farmer rests his foot on a sidelong spur, while the tool is otherwise handled like a spade.

The small light gray donkeys (Sp. burros), which one sees daily in the sandy streets of the pueblo loaded with bundles of firewood, particularly should be noted as a Zuni mode of transportation, in addition to their horses. The oxcarts, too, with their cumbersome wheels have not yet been supplanted by the modern Caldwell and Springfield wagons in such widespread use out west, though some of these vehicles have already found their way to Zuni.

The Zunis are passionate cigarette smokers. To see an Indian, and particularly a Zuni, smoking, you'd swear that he enjoys it twice as much as a white man. He puffs rapidly. With hefty drags, one following almost immediately after the other, he blows the blue clouds about his head, as though he were again and again reveling in the smoke, and then lets the smoke escape through his nose again. In contrast to the women from many nomadic tribes, those of the Pueblo Indians generally do not smoke. Cigarette smoking among the Zunis, and in all likelihood among the Pueblos generally, is a very ancient custom, which was in vogue long before the coming of the Spaniards and taken over by them from the Indians.[25]

In caves to the south of Zuni, Mr. Cushing found cigarettes and other objects that pointed to a very distant past but otherwise fully matched those of the present-day Zunis. Before they bought tobacco and cigarette paper from the Americans, like they do now, they smoked a kind of wild tobacco, rolled in corn husks or reeds. In performing certain religious rites, though, this manner of cigarette smoking is followed. By distributing cigarettes I quickly won the Zunis' friendship and, thanks especially to Ténatsali's intercession, had relatively little trouble carrying out anthropometric observations. As recompense, I then gave them some pieces of seashell, which were accepted with immense satisfaction, as they let out a huge gasp as a sign of reverence for the "Ocean of the Rising Sun." What always surprised them was *why* I wanted to measure them. But when Ténatsali told them that I was a medicine man and was doing this to let my people, who had heard of the Zunis, see what they looked like, they were satisfied and willingly let themselves be examined. Once, on Ténatsali's request, I addressed them in Dutch. They were utterly astonished, and one of them exclaimed: "This is very odd: he is a white man and yet he speaks differently than a white man!" "Come here," another one cried. "See this stranger. Let him measure you because Ténatsali says that he is a friend!"

As a result of my measurements, here I will simply report that the Zunis (18 obs.) are moderately brachycephalic (84.03) and have an [average] height of 1.54 m.[26] The material cited in a previous chapter regarding the relationship of the Moquis with the cliff dwellers also holds for the Zunis.[27]

Zuni has its albinos as well. According to Cushing, there are a dozen in all, including six women. I myself could examine only three because the others were away for the time being. Two of them displayed the same features as those described among the Moquis; a third one, a woman approximately forty years old, showed merely traces of albinism. The eyes were light gray and the skin extraordinarily light in color, though lacking the distinctive flesh color characteristic of the other albinos. Although her parents were normal, she had two brothers who displayed all the traits of genuine albinism.

An albino who frequently visited Ténatsali and provided instruction in English was the young Arizona. He was very intelligent, also very gentle by nature and strongly attached to his white brethren, to whom he often complained about his distress over the difficult lot of an albino. For albinos are not esteemed in Zuni, and much is required before a ruddy, blond-haired Zuni finds his *yiluk'ianiha* ("his to be" = fiancée).

As a rule, it is the girl who takes the first steps toward engagement by telling her parents and other blood relations how she loves her chosen one. They, in turn, tell the young man's blood relatives about this, and he then becomes her yiluk'ianiha. From this time on they spend considerable time together. One of the most common features of the engagement period is that—during the summer on the terraces, during the winter by the hearth fire—she carefully combs the hair of her beloved while he busies himself making a "bundle" for the girl. In this bundle, which we could call a "trousseau," a pair of hard-leather moccasins are never missing. When the young man has gathered together enough items for the girl, he then proposes to her. If she gratefully accepts this tribute, her father

10. Zuni men, with Arizona (seated), an albino (after a photograph by William Henry Brown, ca. 1880).

then accepts the young man as *talah'i*[28] (ward) and takes him into their home. From then on the young couple are considered man and wife.

The Zunis are monogamous, and the woman's place is definitely not as abject as is assumed to be the case for Indians generally. All the children are the woman's children, and hereditary rights run in the female line. Her submissiveness and devotion are wholly voluntary, not imposed, and if her spouse misbehaves she has every right to send him back to his old home. Infidelity and adultery, however, rarely occur among the Zunis.[29] As a rule, the Zunis do not have many children, while the number of male seems to exceed that of female births. According to Ténatsali's estimate, which placed Zuni's population at 1,620, there are a hundred more men than women.[30]

What is remarkable is that the doctrine of the influence of the mother's imagination on the embryo is also known among the Zunis. Ténatsali told me of an instance that vividly recalls what Lessing in his *Laokoon* says in this regard about Greek women.[31] A pregnant woman once came to him and asked whether Ténatsali had anything lovely she could constantly gaze at so her child would be lovely as well. By chance he had a photograph representing the Venus de Medici and gave it to her. True to her line of conduct, she brought a well-built *Shi'wi* into the world.[32]

Just like their northern brethren, the Moquis, the Zunis too are slowly but steadily diminishing in number. They are not, however, dissolving into a race of mestizos, as is occurring with many other tribes, but vanishing completely without leaving behind traces other than numerous ruins in the vicinity of present-day Zuni. Let your eye wander across the plateau, just direct your gaze to the base and close to the plateau of Thunder Mountain, Tâ-ai-yállone. Everywhere you will notice doleful ruins, a silent testimonial to an epoch long gone. Of the "seven cities of Cibola," the fabulous land of gold the Spaniards searched so long for, just three are now inhabited.[33]

For the sake of completeness I will list the names of the Zuni cities as follows: *Kiä'kima* (Sp. Caquima), south of Thunder Mountain; *Ma'htsakùh* (Sp. Mastúki), the city discovered by the monk Marcus of Niza,[34] to the east of Zuni, northwest of Thunder Mountain; the original Zuni or *Ha'lonawan* (Sp. Alóna), a little to the south of the present-day Zuni; the most important and largest city of "Cibola," *Ha'wik'uh* (Sp. Aguíco), twelve miles southwest of Zuni, near Ojo Caliente; *Kia'anaän,* to the south of Ha'wik'uh, the city from where the Spanish monks took refuge at Zuni because of the Apache siege.

Before the arrival of the Spaniards, the Zunis still held the following cities: Haínpassawan,[35] six miles west of Zuni; Pi'nawan, two and a half miles west of Zuni; He'shotatsina (Sp. Pescado), fifteen miles east of Zuni; Tâiá (Sp. Las Nutrias), twenty-five miles northeast of Zuni; Heshotau'thla, nine miles east of Zuni; Heshotathlu'ptsina, seven miles east of Zuni; Wi'mian, eleven miles north of Zuni; Sho'pak'ia, five miles to the north; and finally Heshoktakwin or Heshohtakwin, four miles northwest of Zuni.

The name *Cibola* (or Shibola), at the same time the Spanish word for "bison," is derived from *Shi'wona* or *Shi'wina,* by which the Zunis meant their land, which still has the name *Shiwinakwin,* moreover. As I already said in passing, the Zuni call themselves *"A'shiwi"* (sing. *Shi'wi*) = "flesh" or "the flesh." The name *Zuni* (pron. "zunyi") was given them by the Indians from the Cochiti pueblo along the Rio Grande.[36] Of the various tribes the Zunis are familiar with, they generally call the Pueblo Indians *Thluëlla'kwe* (City People)—*kwe* = "people," "men"; the Navajos *A'patsjoe* or *Pátsjoe* (Image, the Images), the Tonto Apaches *Tsji'shekwe* (plundering people); the White Mountain Apaches *Wilatsu'kwe* (People with the Lightning Shell or Sudden Attackers).[37]

In the evening, as the sun, following a brief twilight, has splendidly set behind the Twin Mountain[38] and the heat of day has given way to the night wind with its cool exhalation, we gather in Ténatsali's small, cozy apartment. Pálawahtiwa, or Naíutshi, the high priest of the Order of the Bow, and even Ti'wahuishiwa come, sit down to sample the "medicine that gladdens the heart" (grog or toddy), and relate events from the hoary past "when the days were new" and "the world was young." Then there is stillness in the circle, and the only sound is the soft voice of the old Zuni priest, regularly alternating with Ténatsali's translation, until late at night. Then one heard strange legends and traditions, colored with all the savage ardor and all the poetic dreams of an Indian imagination.

Thus he spoke about the origin of the classes or orders and clans or gentes of the A'shiwi, institutions that play a significant role in Zuni society. The former, four in number, all have a semireligious character and are strict secret societies. They are the priesthood, *Shi'wanikwe;* the Order of Hunters, *Sániak'iakwe;* the Knives' or Warriors' Order, *A'tshiak'iakwe;* and the Medicine Order, *Ne'wekwe.* Of the four aforementioned classes, that of the warriors is the most important and powerful. They form simply one association, that of the *A'pithlanshíwani,* or Priests of the Bow, which in some respects recalls the order of Freemasons and has twelve grades, each with a distinctive emblem. Every year the Priests of the Bow have a series of rites to perform, one of the most important of which is that of placing new war gods next to those of previous years.

Cushing, who was accepted into the order after two years of trying, has since played the role of guardian for these gods and twice accompanied them to their secluded resting place in the mountains. These gods, Ahaïïuta and Matsailema, though dual in form are one in spirit. They are regarded as the child or children of the sun god and are thought to guard the valley of Zuni from year to year. These are wooden, misshapen images, colorfully painted and richly ornamented with shells and turquoises. Each year they are prepared anew to be deposited in a solemn procession by the many other gods from earlier days who slowly molder and disintegrate.[39]

Besides the annual ceremonies, every Priest of the Bow also has an obligation to perform each month—that is, offering a pair of prayer sticks to the war gods. A short distance to the east of Zuni rises the small hill on top of which a number of colorful sticks and staves decorated with feathers are stuck into the ground. These sticks, which are wrapped in corn husks, have a length of roughly fifteen centimeters and a cross section of nearly one-half centimeter and in the main resemble those of the Moquis. They are hewn from the wood of the mountain mahogany tree, the hardest wood the Zunis know, which at the same time is used to make their clubs. The hardness of this wood symbolizes the prayer for courage and strength against the enemy. The red color with which the sticks are painted is called *a'hokon* (depiction of war) and denotes blood. With one exception the feathers come from various birds of prey and are named *la'tsumaywuh,* or "powerful feathers." They have a dual signification: destruction and spiritual fortitude. One prays to be in a condition to pursue the enemy just as relentlessly as the birds of prey their victims.

The only feather that does not come from a bird of prey is the one from the wing of a wild duck, which is one of the Zuni water gods and thus the symbol of strength and swiftness on the warpath. The downy feathers are called *ha'showahn* (ear) and probably signify that the "misty spirits of the gods" may hear the prayer.[40]

Another artifact, a genuine fetish, demonstrating the animistic concepts of the Zunis, is a small stone image in the rough shape of a bird, which carries an arrowhead on its back. Whenever he travels in hostile country or is on the warpath, a Priest of the Bow directs prayers to it, and he carries it with him in a little bag. This fetish represents an eagle, the god of the "upper world." According to their beliefs, this god possesses "a spirit and a living heart."

The Zuni priest addresses his prayers to this spirit. He offers food to the heart (the arrowhead). He asks for protection against the enemy and against ambushes in particular. The arrowhead, the "magic war medicine" *(sáwanikia),* represents the shield, which must protect the warrior's vulnerable side (his rear), for "no one has eyes and hands on his back." "A warrior does not ask for protection on the side, where he has arms and legs."[41]

The Zunis are a preeminently religious people. Daily, at nearly every moment, they must pay heed to certain things because this is what religion prescribes. Thus no right-minded Zuni, for instance, would dare take food before he has tossed a few morsels from each dish into the fire while muttering a short prayer to his ancestors. He is continually harried by the absurdity we call superstition. While in our case this is usually the vestige of the religious notions from our savage ancestors, a legacy handed down to later generations, in the Zunis' case, and that of all peoples on a low level of development, it forms an essential component of their religion.

There is a notion among the general public that the people we view as uncivilized are scarcely aware of religion, have no laws, and know nothing about morality—and, in general, are totally carefree, free as birds in the sky. That is a great error. On the contrary, the natural man, the "savage," is in many respects much less free than we are. The belief in his numerous gods, good and evil, in apparitions, prophecies, omens, and the like never leave him a moment's rest. Where in our case laws and institutions and morals are based partly on a religious foundation, in the case of the "savages" they are based entirely on religion. Thus a "savage" who is faithful abides by what his religion prescribes for him, for fear of drawing down upon himself the wrath of the gods.

Remarkably enough, one does encounter freethinkers and skeptics, even among peoples standing at a low level of development. Ténatsali told me that among the Zunis there are some who do not believe in the teachings of their "forefathers" and who in their hearts despise the laws and institutions of their people. But—*tout comme chez nous* [just as is the case with us]—they are fearful of public opinion and do as others do out of self-interest.

Among the peoples of nature the fear of "people" is perhaps just as great, relatively speaking, as in a civilized society. A "savage" is just as much concerned whether he can do this or that without "people" "saying" something about it. In their case, too, one knows what is *bon ton* [good form] and fashion, though always suitable for their society, of course. Thus in Zuni, just as among the Moquis, it is not *comme il faut* [the proper thing to do] to live on the top stories of the pueblo. If Pálawahtiwa or Ténatsali had gone to live in the house at the top, the inhabitants would have said that this was not in keeping with their position, and there would have been long discussions about this.

Nor should one assume that a "savage," and particularly a North American Indian, is insensitive to mockery or ridicule. Notwithstanding his often seeming stoicism, the Indian is sensitive. If one also takes into account his self-esteem and pride, which is particularly distinctive among men from some tribes, then one can comprehend how much mockery offends him. Themselves disposed, by dint of their great power of observation, to recognize right away the ludicrous side of persons and things, it doubly offends them whenever they notice that they have done something worthy of ridicule or ludicrous in the eyes of others.

The same sensitivity and self-esteem are the reason an Indian never forgets a favor but never forgets an insult either. Perhaps his love of truth and fidelity to one's word, once given, are based upon the same qualities—to say nothing of a good part of the hatred and contempt he feels toward his white neighbors, people who, as a rule, do not excel in the aforementioned attributes.

Just as one finds among the Indians warlike and less warlike tribes, I also believe there are religious and less religious tribes, related in no small measure to their natural disposition. Between the serious, dreamy Zuni with his involved philosophy and the happy, carefree Mohave who, to judge by appearances, has no more interest in religious speculations than a child, the difference is striking.

As is the case with so many peoples, the Zunis, too, have a good, or sacred, number and a bad one. Four is the sacred number, just as it is for Navajos; five is the bad number. Four is probably related to the number of fingers, except for the thumb. The Zunis distinguish six regions of the world: north, west, south, east, above, and below, a distinction very closely connected with their mythology.

The Zunis are one of the few tribes southwest of the Rocky Mountains who take scalps,[42] and one of the preconditions for being accepted into the Order of the Bow consists in taking a certain number of scalps. Every priest of this order owns a bandoleer of braided leather, which is decorated with stone arrowheads, each of which indicates a scalp taken. Pálawahtiwa, for example, had a shoulder belt on which five arrowheads were attached because he had killed and scalped five Navajos.

The Navajos and Apaches are the Zunis' archenemies, but especially they were many times involved in conflict with the former, notably over the stealing of horses and sheep or the plundering of their fields. In more recent years the hostilities have steadily diminished. Bringing of the Navajos into a reservation near Fort Wingate has certainly greatly contributed to this outcome.

The most important weapons of the Zunis are bow and arrows and wooden clubs, but in their case, too, these means of defense have now been partly superseded by breech-loading weapons. Their round shields are of hard, thick leather and beautifully painted. A weapon that is actually used just for hunting and primarily for rabbit hunting is a flat piece of wood that is thrown—the same one that is also in vogue with the Moquis and strongly recalls an Australian boomerang. The Zunis call this tool *zjai-annùh*. It has the same dimensions as that of the Moquis.

The Zunis' judicial system is quite straightforward. There are only two cases where the death penalty is applied: sorcery and cowardice in battle. The Priests of the Bow are the judges, and the sentence is carried out by the war chieftain. To the Zunis' credit, let it be said that crimes rarely occur among them. Furthermore, it is obvious that those who are accused of sorcery are, as a rule, completely innocent of the misdeeds ascribed to them.

The Zunis are animal lovers, but the ones they keep are sometimes used for other purposes as well. The dark eagles, for example, that can be seen perched in big wooden cages near the sheep corrals serve to provide them decorative feathers for their dances. Similarly, in some dwellings one encounters small, tame sparrow hawks. Although the Zuni dogs now and then receive a good thrashing, they look infinitely better than their poor, starved natural compatriots in Mexico. Every neighborhood in Zuni has its permanent dogs. If an unknown intruder dares enter a ward where he does not belong, then a storm is unleashed, and he is driven off with an earsplitting barking by the neighborhood dogs, often seconded by their owners.

Game is scarce in the area right around Zuni. Only ground doves *(Chamapelia)* appear in number in the sandy plain and among the cornfields but are difficult to get a shot at. At the same time, one has to be very careful about rattlesnakes, which are frequently encountered. For this reason the Zunis very rarely go hunting in the plain.[43] Farther away, in the mountains overgrown with piñones and juniper trees, which the eye from Zuni can descry in every direction, live deer and antelope whose life is frequently menaced by the puma *(Felis concolor)*.

The Zuni language is melodious, due to the fact that it has an abundance of vowels and most words end in a vowel. But Zuni also has hard guttural sounds and sibilants, which are difficult to reproduce. To the best of our knowledge, the language of the A'shiwi is completely separate, and Zuni, with Nutrias and Ojo Caliente, forms a *Sprachinsel* [linguistic island].[44] According to Cushing, the language is very difficult to learn, both because of its enormous vocabulary and its countless forms. In their contacts with the Navajos, they consequently use their language because the Navajos have only a very imperfect mastery of Zuni.

I want to provide just a couple of samples of Zuni that I learned from Cushing in particular:

There are three words for "many": *emma, teutsja,* and *kohomashoko.* For the verb "know" there are no less than five different expressions, all depending on the meaning, and each can again be modified in three different ways. To say, "come inside" = *kwata,* one must keep in mind how many people and to whom one is speaking; *kwata* applies to a single person, *atsjkwata* to two people, *ukwata* to several people, while one says *ansamukwata* to various people who belong to one and the same class.[45]

In my personal contact with the Zunis the most frequently heard words included *elûia, élahkwá,* and *kókshi,* in particular. The first two they used when I gave them one thing or another because *elûia* means "splendid" and *élahkwá* "thank you." With these very few words the Zunis revealed their friendly and less reserved manner. Yet in the case of other tribes, as a rule one does not express gratitude and, in particular, one does not disclose what one thinks about the item given. *Kókshi* = "good" followed whenever they approved of something or other and was used entirely as the Mexican *bueno* or *esta bueno* [*sic*] ("good," "that is good"). There was no way I could appear at a door without the hospitable *"kwata"* reaching my ear. If I walked inside, "Sit down and eat,"[46] echoed in Zuni while a sheepskin or a blanket was laid down and a bowl with *héwé* or *mu'wé*[47] was pushed closer to me.

For a description of the interior of Zuni dwellings I refer to that of the Moquis to avoid being repetitive, but the rooms are usually much larger and more spacious, while in many windows gypsum slabs (so-called Mary glass) serve as panes. Regular glass has already replaced gypsum slabs in not a few dwellings, however.

In addition to their everyday spoken language, the Zunis have a more ancient language, known only to the highest priests, in which the prayers of their order are recited. Ténatsali, too, was in command of this language and had to learn a prayer that filled a roll of paper several meters long when he wrote it down. A couple of years ago Cushing established the remarkable fact that the language of the small tribe of Havasupai Indians displays some affinity with the Zunis' archaic language.[48] This is all the more remarkable because the Havasupais—called *Kúchnikwe* or *Kochninakwe* (people of the piñon nut?) by the Zunis—speak a Yuman language and, according to Cushing, still live in cliff houses of a later date. Furthermore, he found ruins of dwellings of these Indians, recalling those of the Pueblo Indians, though they had just one story. He was also struck by how many Havasupais match the Zunis' type.[49]

Zuni traditions regarding their origin seem to indicate the West or Northwest. That they were aware of the sea during their earlier wanderings seems to be the case not only because they worship it but because they are at the same time familiar with the octopus or one of the other cephalopods.[50] According to tradition, this animal is called "he with the rapidly moving hair *(tsit-sjahaja)*" because of its numerous moving arms. Through tradition they are also familiar with earthquakes. They are labeled with the name of "the sound from the shell of the gods." Whether this indicates their familiarity with America's western coast, so frequently affected by earthquakes, or with earthquakes occurring in the Southwest in historic times instead,[51] we cannot say with complete certainty. We should be inclined to the former view, though, particularly because the tradition in this respect refers to how "the ocean was whipped to a fury" by "the sound of the shell of the gods." Moreover, in former times they undertook pilgrimages to the coast of the Pacific Ocean for the purpose of collecting sacred shells, including the abalone *(Haliotis), Oliva,* and *Olivella,* just like the Moquis did.

The Gulf of California is also known to them, and tribes that are now astonishing distances from them they know by name—such as the Pawnees, who until recently lived along the Missouri, and the Comanches from the Texas prairies. The latter, however, appeared to have visited the Zunis in their high valley during their earlier wide-ranging ramblings, which extended to California.

Since 1877 the Zunis have a reservation, which has the shape of an oblong quadrangle running from the northeast to the southwest. As is already evident from the enumeration of their former cities, their territory has been far more extensive than that making up their present-day reservation. But Ténatsali got hold of a document that indicated exactly the boundary of the Zunis' territory and the location of their cities. That was a very old map, depicted on a half-decayed buffalo hide in the priests' possession, which became an important piece of evidence in Ténatsali's hands, with which he demonstrated the ancient right of the Zunis to Nutrias. That put him in a winning position in the vigorous, oft-mentioned struggle over this issue he had to carry on with Senator Logan, the well-known Indian hater.[52]

They do not receive rations or yearly gifts from the government. In general, a sum is merely allotted for the Pueblo Indians to be employed "for their education and civilization."

For several years there has been a school at Zuni, headed by a Presbyterian clergyman. He has no cause for rejoicing about the interest among the Indians because just a few children attend his school. The majority of the Zunis do not see why they should let their children be educated in a doctrine and concepts so vastly different from their own and those of their "forefathers." There can be no thought about being able to civilize the Zunis—and Indians generally—in our sense until they have completely forgotten their own religion. Many years will have to elapse before such a thing will happen. Consider the Iroquois and Cherokees, two tribes that have been in contact with civilization for more than two and a half centuries. Here there are still people who adhere to their old religion. Thus, to some extent, one can understand how long it will last with other tribes and especially with the Zunis, for whom religion, more than elsewhere, is bound up with social conditions.

During my stay at Zuni, I witnessed an example of just how minimal is the influence of civilization, even on young Indians—to say nothing of later experience here. In Albuquerque a girl approximately fourteen years old, who had been at the "Indian Training School" in Carlisle five years in succession,[53] had joined the Cushings. I saw her in Albuquerque when she was on the way back to Zuni. She did nothing but complain and bemoan having to go back to her people, from whose customs and practices she had turned away and whose language she had nearly forgotten. To console her, Cushing proposed that she should first live with him after her return to Zuni to get slowly reacclimated. Eagerly she accepted his suggestion and showed every intention of instructing her fellow tribespeople in what she had learned in Carlisle.

Everything went well during the first days of her stay. She preferred speaking just English and also retained her American attire and manners. But the more she came into contact with former acquaintances, the more she withdrew from contact with the Cushings until finally, a few weeks after her return, she had completely reverted: she put aside her American clothing, refused to speak English, and took her permanent place in the tribe again as an authentic Zuni. Such examples should give pause for reflection. The reason for her complete conversion we must seek in the ridicule she was subjected to for her attire and awkwardness in Zuni customs by her fellow tribespeople. As I already noted, Indians are very sensitive and strongly influenced by public opinion. So, this girl, too, stood isolated and dependent and realized that she could not have any influence on the old scheme of things. For this reason, and perhaps also because of old habits, she adopted Zuni customs again. Let us suppose that *all* Zuni children of this girl's age educated at Carlisle had returned together to their pueblo. Then, perhaps, things might have turned out differently and they might have had some influence on the young people and together might have better maintained attire and manners acquired while away.

Cushing, who knows the Indians better than anyone, believes in the possibility of their civilization, but only after the passage of a long period of time. When I speak here of civilization, I mean civilization of an entire race or of an entire tribe, not isolated individuals. An individual can be civilized in a short period of time, but just because he has been able to pass through the swift process successfully does not mean that an entire race or people can do the same.

Although for some time now I had been pondering acquiring a Zuni skull, I had to desist because the burial ground was situated in the middle of the pueblo, and it was virtually impossible to go digging there. But I know that hundreds of skulls and skeletons were buried on this small tract surrounded by an adobe wall in ruins, which was in front of the old Franciscan church, because for many years now the Zunis have been committing their dead to exactly that single small plot of earth. It is already so full that with every new interment, the bones of the blessed "children of the sun" must be disturbed in their rest. The burial ceremonial of the Zunis is quite simple and is attended by no one but the grave diggers. The body, which is sewed inside some blankets, is lowered into a shallow grave without any ceremony.[54]

The ancient church at Zuni, built around 1692 by Spanish Franciscans, lies partially in ruins and consists of nothing more than the remnants of an altar hewn from wood.[55] The Spanish influence among the Zunis has completely vanished and has left behind nothing but a doleful ruin.

✦✦✦✦✦

Eight days had quickly come to an end, and however much I would have liked to have stayed longer at Zuni, time, ever fleeting, compelled me to take up the pilgrim's staff again and leave a place where, for a time, I had felt at home. On the sunshiny morning of September 5th, I bade my two hostesses a hearty farewell and, accompanied by Ténatsali, turned the reins to Fort Wingate. Pálawahtiwa and another Indian had already left for there the previous evening with an oxcart, which included my baggage, to get provisions for Cushing from the fort.

At a gallop we scurried merrily through the sunny valley with piñon and juniper bushes until, after a short halt at the middle of the day, the sky became overcast and gusts of rain and wind accompanied us intermittently. Toward nightfall we reached Nutrias. On the way, in the "valley of the crooked pine trees" *(Äshik'ia-mót-ella),* we saw on the rocky wall some crude drawings, the largest and most distinct figure of which was a deer with giant antlers. These date from very ancient Zuni times.[56]

At Nutrias we met Pálawahtiwa and Arizona, the albino, in one of the dwellings. Meanwhile, when the sky cleared up, we tarried no longer than necessary here to smoke a cigarette with our friends. Instead, we sought shelter for the night over yonder in the mountain forest rather than staying till morning in one of the cramped, smoke-filled dwellings of the Indians, however hospitable. We hurriedly watered our horses, provided ourselves with drinking water, and shortly thereafter, by dark, had reached a densely wooded stretch on the mountain plateau. Before long the steeds were unsaddled and "hobbled" and large blocks of piñon wood crackled in the fire, filling the air with a distinctive fragrance, while the dancing apparition of the flames illuminated the tree trunks with fantastic light.

At the campfire after a meal is the time for social chatting, the hour of relaxation after an exhausting day. Ténatsali talked about his life, in weal and woe, and at the end, as the late hour clamored for repose, sang a couple of lovely Zuni songs, whose final strains eventually died away with the rustling of the night wind in the branches of the piñones above our heads.

The next morning we had barely saddled our horses when Pálawahtiwa went past our campground just a short distance away. He accompanied us on the journey to the "bear spring," as the Zunis call Fort Wingate.[57] On the way I had the opportunity to witness the Zunis' tremendous aversion for canned sardines. During a brief halt in the woods I had opened a tin of sardines and offered some to Pálawahtiwa and his traveling companion as well. With a gesture full of horror, the former said to Cushing: "If he doesn't want me to get sick, then he should move the things out of my sight." The Zunis also have a tremendous revulsion for pickled foods. These are not unique cases but are widespread. On the other hand, the Zunis, like all other Indians, are crazy about strong drink, and I promptly atoned for my error by allowing both Zunis to take a hearty draught from my whiskey bottle.

Around one o'clock in the afternoon we had reached Fort Wingate and made our entry under Dr. Matthews's hospitable roof. That same evening Pálawahtiwa and his companion made their way back to the mountains, driving with Cushing's provisions on the oxcart. Before Ténatsali himself returned to Zuni, he gave me a final token of friendship by handing over two Indian skulls, which, for reasons of security, he had concealed from the Indians in the military hospital. One skull came from the ruins of the Zuni city Heshotau'thla; the other one had belonged to a Navajo.[58]

On the afternoon of the following day I said farewell to Ténatsali. With the last exchange of handshakes I gave him as a memento the best thing I could give: my revolver, my trusty companion on so many journeys, which he had praised for its accuracy over yonder in the valley of Äshik'ia-mót-ella. When I had gazed after Ténatsali as long as I could, and the clacking of his mustang's hooves finally vanished, I felt that I had parted from a friend.

That same evening I took the train from Wingate station and the following morning had returned to Santa Fe.

✦✦✦✦✦

NOTES

1. Matthews later published "Navajo Names for Plants," *American Naturalist* 20 (1886):767–77.

2. HtK 1885: Consisting chiefly of *Pinus ponderosa, Abies douglasii,* and *A. concolor.* The *madroño (Arbutus menziesi)* also appears in the Zuni mountains. Eds.: *Pinus ponderosa* (Laws), western yellow pine; *Abies douglasii = Pseudotsuga menziesii* (Mirbel) Franco, Douglas fir; *Abies concolor* (Gord.) Hildebrand, white fir.

3. Later corrected by author to "southwestern" (HtK 1889). Eds.: Cushing lived in a large room on the ground floor of Palowahtiwa's house, "Casa del Gobernador" he called it, from September 1879 until the end of 1883. A room was added following Cushing's marriage and return from the east in the fall of 1882. Later they moved into a house constructed with Smithsonian Institution funds. Birgitta Brunder, "Frank Hamilton Cushing und das Königliche Museum für Völkerkunde in Berlin," *Baessler-Archiv,* 41 (1993), 386 (fig. 3), 400 (fig. 8); R. S. Brandes, *Frank Hamilton Cushing: Pioneer Americanist* (Tucson: University of Arizona, Ph.D. thesis, 1965), 31, 116–17; on Cushing and Ten Kate, see: Pieter Hovens, *Herman ten Kate en de Antropologie der Noords Amerikaanse Indianen* (Meppel: Krips, 1989), 81–82, 119–26, 138–47, 201–2; Hovens, "The Anthropologist as Enigma: Frank Hamilton Cushing," *European Review of Native American Studies* (1988), 2 (1):1–5.

4. The British playwright Oscar Wilde (1845–1900) was noted for his "flamboyant aestheticism," exotic tastes, and belief in art for art's sake. Margaret Drabble, ed., *The Oxford Companion to English Literature* (New York: Oxford University Press, 1995), 1077.

5. HtK 1889, 239. Correction: "from east to west."

6. HtK 1889: Correction: "south side."

7. HtK 1889: To the small Zuni pueblos Nutrias and Ojo Caliente, Pescado, not far from Nutrias, must be added. These three small pueblos are actually nothing more than summer dwellings. In the winter the population moves to the main pueblo, Zuni itself.

8. Although the cultural antecedents of the Zuni people are a part of broad regional traditions beginning before A.D. 400, only in the thirteenth century did a clear link exist to the historic villages encountered by the Spanish explorers in 1540. In the Zuni drainage alone, thirty-six large plaza-oriented pueblos were constructed between 1250 and 1540. Zuni Pueblo is one of these later sites and was probably founded about 1350. A pattern of aggregation, a movement into fewer, larger villages, continued, so that in 1540 there were probably only six Zuni villages. T. J. Ferguson and E. Richard Hart, *A Zuni Atlas* (Norman: University of Oklahoma Press, 1985), 24–27; T. J. Ferguson, *Historic Zuni Architecture and Society* (Tucson: University of Arizona Press, 1996), 25–26.

9. Taylor Filmore Ealy (1848–1915), a medical missionary with the Presbyterian Church, came to the Southwest in 1874. In 1878, with his wife, Mary, and two daughters, he moved to Zuni Pueblo, where they established a mission about a quarter of a mile north of the village. Douglas D. Graham of Fishkill-on-the-Hudson, New York, established a trading post in Zuni, perhaps a year before Cushing's arrival in 1879. Brandes, *Cushing,* 33; Norman J. Bender, ed., *Missionaries, Outlaws, and Indians: Taylor F. Ealy at Lincoln and Zuni, 1878–1881* (Albuquerque: University of New Mexico Press, 1984), 130–31.

10. HtK 1885: *Kâ* = sacred dance organization, *kókschi(ona)* = "the good name," and *(van)* = "the good dance."

11. More commonly termed *kachinas* (*kokko,* sing., *kokkokwe,* pl.). See chapter 7, note 32. Dennis Tedlock, "Zuni Religion and World View," *Handbook of North American Indians: Southwest,* ed. A. Ortiz (Washington, D.C.: Smithsonian Institution, 1983), 9:499–508.

12. HtK 1889: According to Bandelier (*La découverte du Nouveau Mexique,* etc., *Revue d'Ethnographie* of Hamy, vol. V, 1886, p. 46), the Zunis got the feathers from the Sierra Madre in Mexico, where Bandelier encountered *guacamayos* (a *Sittace* [*Arara*] variety; *mu'la* in Zuni) below latitude 30°. Eds.: See English translation: Adolph F. Bandelier, *The Discovery of New Mexico by the Franciscan Monk Friar Marcos de Niza in 1539,* trans. and ed. Madeleine Turrell Rodack (Tucson: University of Arizona Press, 1981), 53.

13. HtK 1885: Paper[-thin] or wafer bread of cornmeal, like the píki of the Moquis.

14. HtK 1885: That I merely heard *these* sounds does not imply that the Zunis had no actual chant with *words* for this dance. As Cushing later informed me, the words of this chant become a prayer for rain and an abundant harvest through the intercession of the spirits of their ancestors, especially whenever they are regarded as "makers of rain clouds."

15. HtK 1889: Although the Zunis now do not mind if Americans attend their public dances, they do not tolerate Mexicans viewing them because they believe that then there will be no rain and the harvest will thus be ruined.

16. HtK 1885: Another ceremony with prayers for rain is the Snake Dance after the fashion of the Moquis, but with the Zunis this never takes place outdoors but inside the estufas. As Mr. Cushing informed me, when it comes to dexterity in performing this perilous dance, the Zunis are far behind the Moquis.

17. HtK 1885: Among other things, in the already mentioned "My Adventures in Zuni," in *The Century,* 1882–1883.

18. Cushing obtained two scalps from Dr. Harry C. Yarrow, a surgeon and naturalist with the Wheeler Expedition, and another from his father, Thomas Cushing, M.D. It is difficult to imagine how he might have deceived his Zuni companions. It is also clear he had no desire to "take a scalp." Brandes, *Cushing,* 68, 73.

19. Between February 22, 1882, and early October of the same year, Cushing and a party of five Zuni and Hopi men traveled east to Chicago, Washington, and Boston. While there, in July, Cushing married Emily Tennison Magill of Washington, a banker's daughter. Brandes, *Cushing,* 89–90.

20. While Cushing was in the East in 1882, Senator John A. Logan came to Zuni with his son-in-law, Major William F. Tucker. It was soon reported that Tucker and Captain Henry W. Lawton, both officers at Fort Wingate, made claims on Zuni lands and were supported by Logan. The senator was criticized in the media for his actions. Cushing denied any role in the newspaper stories, even though Logan had attacked him as an imposter. After an investigation the Commissioner of Indian Affairs canceled all the land claims by Tucker and Lawton. Brandes, *Cushing,* 96–107.

21. HtK 1885: The investigative method of Cushing is fully responsive to the ideal that hovered in the thoughts of Pechuel-Loesche when in his "Ethnologische Forschung" (loc. cit.) he posed as a condition: *"jahrenlangen Aufenthalt bei dem betreffenden Volke, Einleben in dessen Existenzweise, Erlernung der Sprache, taktvolles Anschmiegen an die Eigenart der Individuen* [staying for many years among the people concerned, immersing oneself into their mode of existence, learning the language, tactful accommodation to the unique qualities of individuals]." Only in this way is it possible *"empirisch zu forschen* [to carry out empirical research]" and elevate ethnography to *"Erfahrungswissenschaft* [an empirical science]." See introduction, note 9.

22. Pedro Pino (Lai-iu-ah-tsai-lu) was the father of Patricio Pino (Ba-lawahdiwa, Ten Kate's Pálawahtiwa) and a governor of Zuni from 1848 to the 1870s. Myra Ellen Jenkins, "Zuni History During the Early U.S. Period," in *Zuni and the Courts: A Struggle for Sovereign Land Rights,* ed. Richard Hart (Lawrence: University Press of Kansas, 1995), 46–59.

23. Ten Kate errs, as the Zunis learned the craft of silversmithing from the Navajos in the 1870s. James Ostler, Marion Rodee, and Milford Nahohai, *Zuni: A Village of Silversmiths* (Zuni: A:Shiwi Publishing, 1996), 57–58.

24. HtK 1889: Regarding the pottery making and ornamentation of the pottery, among both the Pueblo Indians generally as well as among the Zunis, see the outstanding illustrated studies of W. H. Holmes and F. H. Cushing in *Fourth Annual Report, Bureau of Ethnology,* and in addition the illustrated catalog of J. Stevenson in *Second Annual Report of the Bureau of Ethnology.*

25. The two tobacco species of economic importance *(Nicotinia tabacum* and *Nicotinia rustica)* are native to the New World. Columbus noted Indians used tobacco for smoking, chewing, and snuffing. Considerable diversity of use exists among American Indians. Peter Nabokov, "Tobacco," in *Encyclopedia of American Indians,* ed. Frederick E. Hoxie (Boston: Houghton Mifflin, 1996), 633–35.

26. HtK 1889: Regarding the skull index and stature of the Zuni Indians, I can add that, based on my measurements in 1888 (also 18 obs.), the average index is sub-brachycephalic (81.83). The average stature (13 obs., men alone) = 1 m, 64 cm.

27. HtK 1885. Not only have the Zunis nothing in common with the Aztecs from an anthropological standpoint, but in religion and social attitudes, too, there is no relationship indicated between the two peoples. Moreover, Montezuma—who curiously haunts nearly all writings on the Pueblo Indians—is not revered by the Zunis. Nor does the sacred well in Zuni, nor the vessels associated with it, of which Whipple and Bell (cited in Lubbock, *Origin of Civilization,* p. 292) make mention, have any connection with Montezuma. The motive for the opinion that many Pueblo Indians revere Montezuma appears to be that the Zunis, Moquis of Oraybe, and Pueblos of Taos worship the god Pó-shai-an-k'ia, who was the father of their secret medicine order and their reformer on the path to civilization. They believe that he came to earth as a man and, after having fulfilled his reformer's task, returned to his abode in the land of the sun, *Shí-pä-pu-li-ma,* "city enveloped in mist (or clouds)." Cf. Cushing, "Zuni-Fetiches," in *Second Annual Report of the Bureau of Ethnology,* Washington, 1883.

28. Later corrected by the author to *"talak'i."* (HtK 1889, 240).

29. HtK 1885: *Nemo fere corporis quaestum facit nisi octo hermaphroditi, quorum statura robustissima, vestitus vero partim virilis est, partim muliebris.* [Seldom does anyone profit from his body except eight hermaphrodites whose stature is most robust but whose garb is partly masculine, partly feminine.]

30. Ten Kate's population figures are basically correct. The population of Zuni was 1,650 in 1880 and 1,621 in 1890. However, the 1890 census figures indicate only a slight difference in the numbers of men and women: 820 males, 801 females. Department of the Interior, *Report on the Indians Taxed and Indians Not Taxed in the United States, Eleventh Census: 1890* (Washington, D.C.: U.S. Government Printing Office, 1894), 420.

31. Gotthold Ephraim Lessing (1729–1781), a dramatist and critic, was one of the leading figures of the German Enlightenment. His *Laokoon* (1766) was a treatise on aesthetics. Ten Kate may be referring to the second chapter of this work, where Lessing recounts how many pregnant mothers of famous ancients dreamt of relations with a serpent, the symbol of deified power.

32. HtK 1885: *Feminae parturientes in tergo jacent, acervo arenae sub abdomine strato, ut illa pars corporis magis promineat. Complures exstant obstetrices, quae Lucinae artem profitentur, quamquam et senes interdum hoc munere funguntur.* [Women about to give birth lie on their backs with a heap of sand spread out below the abdomen so that part of the body protrudes most of all. Many midwives appear, who profess Lucina's art, though old women sometimes exercise this occupation.]

33. Documents from the Coronado expedition are not completely clear, but most historians now agree that there were probably just six Zuni villages occupied in 1540: Hawikku, Kwa'kin'a, Halona:wa, Mats'a:kya, Kyaki:ma, and Kechiba:wa, although a recent archaeological study shows the possibility that the Zuni village of Chalo:wa, near Kechiba:wa, was also inhabited then. European diseases reduced a population estimated at 8,000 by 66 percent between 1540 and 1604. After the suppression of the Pueblo Revolt by Diego de Vargas, the entire tribe was allowed in 1692 to settle in a single permanent village at Halona:wa on the north bank of the Zuni River. By the nineteenth century the three farming villages of Nutria, Pescado, and Ojo Caliente were established. Ferguson and Hart, *Zuni Atlas,* 29; Ferguson, *Historic Zuni Architecture and Society,* 25–37.

34. Marcos de Nizza (d. 1558), a Franciscan monk, led an expedition through present-day Arizona to New Mexico in 1539 to investigate the truth behind stories brought back by Cabeza de Vaca regarding the "seven cities of Cibola" and their putative wealth. Though Fray Marcos himself never reached this destination, the black slave Estevánico, who had originally accompanied Cabeza de Vaca, did reach the Zuni city of Hawikuh, where he was killed by its residents. Fray Marcos then turned back to Mexico, where his reports, greatly exaggerated, encouraged the more famous Coronado expedition of the following year. See the above-mentioned work by Bandelier (note 12).

35. HtK 1889: "Hámpassawan."

36. Ten Kate is correct. The English *Zuni* is derived from the Spanish *Suni* or *Zuni,* which in turn was derived from Keresan. See Fred Eggan and T. N. Pandey, "Zuni History, 1850–1970," *Handbook: Southwest,* 9:479–80.

37. HtK 1885: See also my "Synonymie ethnique."

38. HtK 1889: This must actually be "behind the Great Mountain," because the Twin Mountain is *behind* this and thus is not visible from Zuni.

39. These are the Twin War Gods of the Zunis. Many of these images were stolen from their depository. In the 1980s and 1990s the Zunis staged a successful repatriation policy and managed to obtain all known war god images from museums and even private collections in the U.S. and Canada.

40. HtK 1885: Before Cushing, a member of the Ethnological Bureau in Washington who visited Zuni in passing found a few of these prayer sticks in the Zunis' farmland. He was immediately ready with an explanation and named them "boundary markers between farmlands," and they are labeled as such in the museum!

41. HtK 1885: Thanks to Mr. Cushing, I came into possession of a pair of prayer sticks and a fetish, which now are kept in the Ethnographic Museum in Leiden. I have illustrated the fetish in *Revue d'Ethnographie* of Hamy, vol. III, p. 163.

    Worth consulting is Cushing's "Zuni Fetiches," loc. cit., where he describes the origin of the fetishism of the Zunis and various kinds of fetishes—of the Navajos too. Bourke, op. cit., p. 126, pl. XXX, describes and depicts "idols" that could hardly be anything but fetishes. Eds.: Ten Kate collected a whole series of fetishes, publishing "Zuni Fetishes," *Internationales Archiv für Ethnographie,* 3 (1890), 118–19.

42. Among southwestern groups, the Keresan warrior societies or "scalp takers" at Laguna, San Felipe, Santa Ana, and Zia are said to have taken scalps. Taking scalps is also reported at Isleta (Southern Tiwa) and among the Mohave and Cocopa on the Colorado River. The Apaches showed little interest in scalping, except in retaliation against Mexicans. *Handbook: Southwest,* 9 and 10:passim.

43. HtK 1889: Several miles west of Zuni, however, great drives are carried out every autumn on horseback against hares *(Lepus callotis);* for that matter, all game coming within range of the boomerangs *(thleánnuh)* is welcome. These communal hunts, in which hundreds of riders participate and which I had the rare privilege of attending twice (in August 1888), have a religious significance because they are connected with the kâ'kâ. They are opened by a priest with a prayer in the archaic language.

44. HtK 1889: Without jumping ahead of future conclusions in comparative linguistics, it is nevertheless evident that the Zuni language is related to other American languages. I want to provide just a minor example, which, though it has no scientific value, is still not without significance.

      According to Mr. Graham, trader at Zuni and a credible individual, they came into a contact with a Mexican from the state of Chihuahua, who could understand the Indians in Zuni—to the astonishment of both parties. The Mexican then explained that the Indians known to him from a place called Nayurachi or Niurachi in Chihuahua spoke the same or very close to the same language as the Zunis.

      With Zuni itself, Nutrias, and Ojo Caliente the other "summer pueblo," Pescado, also belongs, of course, to the Shiwi "Sprachinsel." Eds.: The Zuni speak a language with no close relatives in the Southwest, although perhaps distantly related to California Penutian. Fred Eggan, "Pueblos: Introduction," *Handbook: Southwest,* 9:226.

45. HtK 1889: The Zuni words for "many" are thus accentuated: *èmma, téutsja, kóhomashoko.* The forms of *kwáta* are as follows: *átsjkwá, ánsamukwâta.*

46. HtK 1889, 241: In Zuni "sit down and eat" is *"imoh, ito."*

47. HtK 1885: A kind of croquettes of fine cornmeal, ground red pepper, salt, and lard, cooked in corn husks. That is the nookpiki of the Moquis.

48. Havasupai is a Yuman language with no known connection (or "affinity") with Zuni. Martha B. Kendall, "Yuman Languages," *Handbook: Southwest,* 9:4–12.

49. HtK 1885: For more details about this tribe living in a deep canyon along Cataract Creek (Arizona), I must refer to Cushing's "The Nation of the Willows" in *Atlantic Monthly,* Boston, 1882, and Gatschet in *Zeitschrift für Ethnologie,* 1883, p. 126.

50. Ten Kate's brief account describes the Zuni conception of the world and their traditions of origin and migration. Dennis Tedlock summarizes a part of this worldview as follows: "Toward the north, west, south, and east are the oceans, which together bound the earth with a circular coastline. In the oceans are four mountains, each with the color of its direction. The oceans are connected by underground passages with all the seeps, springs, ponds, and caves of the earth to form a single water system; the Zunis compare this system with the hidden roots and runners that connect willow shoots into a single plant. At the water outlets and on mountain tops are the 'telassinawe,' or shrines, of the world." "Zuni Religion and World View," *Handbook: Southwest,* 9:499. For an account of the migrations and migration traditions, see Ferguson and Hart, *Zuni Atlas,* 20–23, 142.

51. HtK 1885: Bandelier, *Ausland,* 1882, p. 792, speaks of a legend of the inhabitants from Laguna Pueblo, regarding the year of light *(año de la lumbre),* which should indicate a recent volcanic eruption. HtK 1889: According to Cushing, Zuni traditions indicate that the land they now inhabit was frequently affected by earthquakes. The investigation of the Hemenway Expedition in s. Arizona revealed as well that "Los Muertos" and neighboring cities were abandoned because of earthquakes,

and some were even considerably damaged. So we found many roofs of houses fallen in and later burnt by the fire from the hearth. Now and then skeletons were found of persons who were buried under the fallen roofs. (See my *Eenige mededeelingen,* etc., loc. cit.) Recall at the same time the severe earthquake in Sonora and the Southwest in May 1887. Eds.: Cushing's narrative of the Hemenway Expedition has recently been discovered and edited by Curtis M. Hinsley and David Wilcox, *The Lost Itinerary of Frank Hamilton Cushing* (Tucson: University of Arizona Press, 2002), the second volume of their multivolume work on that pioneering archaeological enterprise in North America.

52. See note 20.

53. The first Indian boarding school was opened at the former military barracks at Carlisle, Pennsylvania, in October 1879. The school had a five-year program, offering training in both academic subjects and industrial arts, and instituted the outing system, whereby Indian pupils at the end of their second year boarded with white families during the summer. Those for whom this experiment proved successful then continued their third year attending local schools with white children. The hope of the school's founder, Richard Henry Pratt (see chapter 10), was that these methods would foster Indian assimilation to white life. As Ten Kate's story shows, however, many Indians eventually returned to their reservations and even readopted the culture of their fathers. Howard R. Lamar, ed., *The New Encyclopedia of the American West* (New Haven, Conn.: Yale University Press, 1998), 164.

54. HtK 1885: The description of a burial at Zuni provided by Cozzens (*The Marvelous Country,* Boston 1873) [p. 367] is, like many other things that he conveys about the Zunis, entirely fabricated. Naturally Montezuma is drawn in again.

55. The mission of Nuestra Señora de Guadelupe de Halona was originally built between 1630 and 1666 but destroyed during the Pueblo Revolt and then rebuilt. The Franciscans stayed in Zuni during the eighteenth century but abandoned the pueblo in the early nineteenth century because of Apache and Navajo incursions. The dilapidated mission Ten Kate describes was only rebuilt between 1966 and 1972. Lance Chilton et al., *New Mexico: A New Guide to the Colorful State* (Albuquerque: University of New Mexico Press, 1984), 610.

56. Given the location, Ten Kate is probably describing an image at what is now termed Site 7, east of Zuni. M. Jane Young, *Signs from the Ancestors: Zuni Cultural Symbolism and Perceptions of Rock Art* (Albuquerque: University of New Mexico Press, 1988), 205, fig. 79.

57. HtK 1889: In Zuni the "bear spring" (Fort Wingate) is *Aïn-shek'ianna.*

58. HtK 1885: Both skulls are described in detail in *Revue d'Anthropologie* 1884, p. 486.

CHAPTER NINE

In Southern Colorado

IN THE FIVE WEEKS I HAD BEEN AWAY THE TEMPERATURE HAD COOLED
perceptibly, and rainstorms were the order of the day.[1] Meanwhile the "Tertio-Millennial" had run
its course and despite the publicity had been an unfortunate fiasco. Visitors, bands, and Indians had
all left the city for good, and Santa Fe had thus reverted to its former moribund somnolence. I
spent nine long days there, partly to pack up what I had collected and send it on, partly to divest
myself of a number of onerous guests from the order of the *Hemiptera* [i.e., bedbugs], a souvenir
of San Carlos, who had embittered my life for some time now. On top of that, part of the mountain railway, along which my itinerary to Colorado was supposed to lead, had been devastated by
heavy rains. Only on September 17th could I leave Santa Fe for good.

My plan was to visit the Ute Indian reservation in southwestern Colorado and then head to
the Indian Territory via Trinidad and through Kansas. Originally my plans also included visiting
the Jicarilla Apaches, living not far from the Utes. In the meantime the government had decided it
had to make these Indians move to another reservation for the third or fourth time and, despite
their resistance, bring them under military escort to the Fort Stanton reservation, where the
Mescalero Apaches are established.[2] Shortly before my arrival in Santa Fé, they had moved through
this city, leaving behind nothing other than some ethnographic items, which I later purchased again
from the hands of an American merchant.

In the morning at 8 o'clock I headed with the mail coach to Española, twenty-one miles north
along the Rio Grande, from there to take the mountain railway to Ignacio, the Ute agency. We are
traveling through a dreary region in the four-wheel vehicle, which now rolls jolting and bumping
across the heavy sandy trail, then across bumpy rocky plains again. Loose yellow sand, sandstone
rocks, and trapezoid-shaped mesas of the same color, covered with small juniper and piñon trees
standing far apart, extend outward for a vast distance. On the right arises the dark mass of the Rocky
Mountains, half blanketed by dense clouds, on the left, off in the dusky distance, the mountainous

land between Abiquiu and Jemez. Now and then the sun penetrates the cloudy veil and gives rise to a marvelous play of changing colors on the slopes of the mountains: blue, gray, and yellow in every nuance, fluctuating again and again and metamorphosing, all depending on the way the dark cloudy shadows hover above mesas and valleys. At such moments there is something indescribably majestic in nature, especially when the landscape is desolate, dreary, and remote. Once more I can see Tesuque, but I can only greet it from afar, so likewise for Pojoaque and San Ildefonso, for we continue onward, now slowly plodding onward at a trot, then in a vigorous gallop, all depending on the condition of the terrain.

Five and a half hours after leaving the capital, we have reached Española. It has barely more houses and barracks than letters in its name but nevertheless has a station—the last one, in fact, because the Denver and Rio Grande Railway coming from the north does not run farther than Española. A fellow traveler and I have lunch with a railway official. Then I set myself down on the sandy bank of the Rio Grande until the two-hour waiting time has elapsed and I can take my place in the train to Antonito. There are just a few passengers in each of the few small coaches making up the train.

Climbing most of the way, the small mountain railway heads north with considerable winding. The ground always has the same color and the vegetation is the same as on the other side of Española. But here the landscape is more mountainous and barren than over there because for a long time we stay close to the western, high mountain wall of the Rio Grande, which with its many bends opens a passage deep into the interior. The old route leads along the other bank, and the large covered wagons hitched to numerous oxen, which the eye now and then descries along this route, recall a time already becoming part of history.

Before long we leave the river on our right and now follow the route across a broad mountainous plateau, which is covered with clusters of dark juniper and piñon bushes. The stations we stop at are all insignificant, consisting of only a few wooden houses. Before long darkness descends sooner than usual due to the gentle but dense rain that is falling steadily and calls a halt to further observations of nature.

It is 8:30 P.M. when I disembark from the train at Antonito in Colorado, just across the New Mexico boundary. There is a crowd of people in the little town. Impromptu judges pass sentence on a couple of rogues who are sitting down with bloodstained, bandaged heads in a large store, in the middle of a crowd of rough-looking men with spurs, whose restless tramping horses are tethered in front of the shed with a lasso. I do not succeed in making my way through the dense throng of spectators to see exactly what is going on. I am really hungry and search out accommodation, which I promptly locate among one of Antonito's citizens for a couple of dollars. The lawsuit seem to have run its course rather late because I am awakened at night by a chaotic sound of voices and the tramping of horses, moving off at a gallop. The night is very cool, and although I have no thermometer to register the number of degrees, I lie trembling in the tiny little room whose walls consist of thin planks. Because Antonito has nothing to set itself apart from other frontier towns, I am delighted that I can depart at 10 o'clock the next morning to continue the journey to Ignacio.

From Antonito, toward the west, a mountain railway heading north separates from the main line. That is the narrow-gauge route linking the southwestern mining towns of Colorado, which at the time of my visit extended to Silverton. The difficulties laying this route through the heart of the Rocky Mountains were many, but the knowledge and persistence of the American engineers succeeded in overcoming all obstacles—and the mountain route came into being. The Denver and Rio Grande Railway with its branch lines is one of the most high-priced lines in the United States. If, as a rule, one pays three cents (roughly $7^{1}/_{2}$ Dutch cents) per mile for the other lines, then the price for the Denver and Rio Grande is eight cents.

In sheer beauty this route far surpasses the Black Forest Railway; it is at least the equal of the Brenner Railway. We had gentle rain and sunshine in alternation and thus the opportunity to observe the splendid forest and mountain scenery that unrolled before our eyes in variegated lighting. The only alternation to dark green conifers of various shapes with their ageless memory are oak, aspen, and willows, whose foliage is already resplendent with the marvelous multicolored tints of Indian summer. Now a somber shadow rested on the silent forests and accentuated the solemn gravity of the landscape. Then the sun broke through the clouds again and cast its cheery light on the damp foliage, making it sparkle in all its majestic color. Not uncommonly, too, a mountain slope provided an image of devastation. A chaotic medley of charred tree trunks—some still standing upright, most, though, toppled over and partially consumed—showed the spot where a fire had obliterated a splendid forest. In the depths wild streams rustled over boulders and uprooted tree trunks—sometimes through a narrow, steep bed, sometimes along the grassy rims of a mountain meadow. The majestic, long undulating outlines of the mountains joined up in an endless chain, concealing the shape of their peaks in the clouds.

Like a gigantic snake the train moved slowly forward, winding its way in hundreds of bends along the flanks of the mountains, across ingenious, elevated viaducts spanning gaping chasms, through tunnels and crevices, across rolling high meadows and through blooming park landscapes, of endless variety, until the eye wearied of the sight. We are alternately in Colorado and in New Mexico and stop at a number of small stations, most of them consisting of just a few houses. One of the most important is Chama. Then comes Amargo, just shortly before the Jicarilla agency, so that shortly after 8 P.M. we reach Ignacio, my destination.

At the small wooden station building I find a buckboard from the agency, and after having covered two miles at a rapid trot, I am sitting before long by a crackling wood fire in the log cabin of the agent—again a "colonel"! Here there is an Indian inspector as well—a "lieutenant colonel"— who, as it later appeared to me, limited his investigation of the reservation just to the agent's office. In addition, there was a clerk, a doctor, and a trader, along with a couple of employees of lesser rank, including a person who performs the duties of woodcutter and swineherd but still holds the title of judge. The news of an outbreak of the Utes, which the newspapers are reporting about, appears to have been a false alarm because everything was calm on the reservation.

On September 19th there is a glorious dawn, and with the first rays of morning I cast a glance at my new abode. The agency buildings are just four in number. Three are crude log cabins, evocative of Cooper's novels; the fourth one is adobe and whitewashed. Ignacio—as the four build-ings are called, after the most prominent chief of the Utes³—has an enchanting location on a plateau along the Rio de los Pinos. In every direction the eye discerns mountains blanketed with piñones and junipers, which rise to considerable height, toward the north especially; their jagged peaks stand out against the spotless blue sky. The river sloshes over its rocky bed in graceful bends, while the shady cottonwoods are mirrored in the stream, bright as crystal. In the meadows scattered clus-ters of fragrant *Artemisia* bushes break up the monotonous plain.

Along the rim of the high meadow, which rises above the bottomland of the river, stand a couple of Indian tents. They have the familiar pointed shape that one sees in all illustrations regard-ing Indians: a number of poles standing in a circle with the top ends resting against each other and fastened together, serving as a frame for the material the tent consists of. These were the first Indian dwellings I encountered with this shape because one does not find these tents southwest of the Rocky Mountains.

The ground consists of sandstone, but in and along the river appear quartzites, metamor-phic and limestone rocks borne from afar. Originating between the wooded flanks of Simpson's Peak, the Rio de los Pinos flows in an almost purely southerly direction to the San Juan, which in its turn unites with the western Colorado after a long journey through the desert.

The atmosphere in these regions is exceptionally pure and bracing. You feel a new life cours-ing through your veins, which you imbibe with the cool mountain air. An odd feeling of well-being takes hold of you. Blood flows more swiftly through your veins, making you feel daring, and your capacity for thought and comprehension is enhanced to the utmost degree. The lucid, transparent air and the fixed, immobile sky make the sunlight seem more vigorous, and at night the stars twin-kle with unparalleled splendor.

On the first day I already had the opportunity to observe a goodly number of Ute Indians. It was "issue day," and dense throngs were pressing in and around the shed where the meat is weighed and the flour distributed. Before proceeding to describe the Utes, maybe it is useful first to make a couple of general observations about these Indians.

The Utes, Utahs, or Yutas, who call themselves Nutes, form a powerful nomadic tribe, num-bering about 3,200. Before 1868 they dominated not only the western section of present-day Colorado but large stretches of land in the adjoining territories of Wyoming, Utah, and New Mexico as well. Their southeasternmost tribe even held territory along the Cimarron River, bordering on that of the Kiowas in northern Texas. They are divided into a number of tribes, of which the Uncompahgres and Tabewaches, Wimmenuches, Capotes, and Muaches are the most important.⁴ In 1880 the two first-named tribes were forced by the American government to say farewell forever to their mountains and were placed on two reservations in northeast Utah.⁵

The Capotes and Muaches, who were at home in northwestern and northeastern New Mexico, were already transferred a couple of years earlier by the government to the Wimmenuches in the southwestern corner of Colorado. In the reports they were labeled with the name "Southern

Utes"; they barely number 1,000 in all. They belong to the tribes of the Union who have least changed their attire and way of life, who support themselves almost exclusively by hunting. That, at least, is the case with the Southern Utes, for many of the remainder have started practicing agriculture. The Utes are warlike and brave and also cavalier by nature. The Comanches, Cheyennes, and Arapahos are their mortal enemies, but because the tribes are established wide apart on reservations, their fierce wars belong to the past. Linguistically the Utes belong to the Numa family, to which, as I have already reported, Pah-Ute, Moqui, and Comanche among others also belong.[6]

In every respect the Southern Utes presented me with a wholly new type: the image of authentic Plains Indians, the knightly figure of the West, so often described, intoned, and depicted. Even here, though, civilization had made inroads. Among them I encountered shirts, vests, dyed cotton materials, and even hats in some cases.

The men wear their hair with a part on the top or on the side of the head and carefully divided in back into two long heavy braids hanging down over the chest. The braids are mostly wrapped with precious otter hides or decorated with red ribbons, while the part is frequently colored red or yellow. The women wear their hair hanging completely loose, though not as long as the men. In their case, too, the part is, as a rule, in the middle, while the long luxuriant tresses rest on the back and the shoulders as well as upon the chest.

The men still wear almost exclusively leather leggings of Indian make and moccasins, while the upper body, on the other hand, is usually covered by an ordinary shirt and a vest. The leggings of the Utes, and of the Indians generally, differ from our trousers in that they cover just the legs but not the abdomen nor the posterior. They are fastened by means of garters, which are tied onto a belt around the middle, as is the G-string running between the legs. These leggings are, as a rule, very handsomely ornamented with colored beads and are bordered with fluttering side flaps on the seam. The moccasins too are almost completely covered with porcelain beads. Blue and white beads are used almost exclusively. If the Utes wear American shirts, they wear them hanging out with the vest on top, so that the dandies thus attired cut a rather ludicrous figure in our eyes. The women wear a kind of long dress that hangs halfway down to the lower leg. Leather dresses are already rare because now they are made of cotton and cloth. The women also wear leather leggings and moccasins, but, as a rule, the latter are not ornamented.

The Utes' ornaments consist primarily of strings of beads, a type of plastrons from seashells, and, in addition, earrings, rings, and bracelets of silver and Berlin silver. They buy the beads and seashells, as they do the Berlin silver items, in the trader's store. The seashells, prepared in the manner of the former wampum, are white in color and prepared especially for the Indians in the eastern states and sent to various stores out west. They are quite precious. The Utes acquire silver work from the Navajos, their southwestern neighbors. Frequently they give them dollar coins to have them made into ornaments conforming to their own taste and instructions. And their harnesses and saddles are not uncommonly ornamented with Navajo silver work. In addition, Navajo blankets are very much in vogue among the Utes. Many Ute men smear their faces from top to bottom with a yellow and red dye, a custom that is in vogue among the younger Indians especially. In addition, they pluck out eyebrows and eyelashes, giving their painted faces a glaring, rather bizarre expression. This dye is kept in an oblong bag of coarse leather, which has the same shape as their purses and is ornamented with beads. As amulets, some men wear so-called medicine bags on their clothing fastened to their chests, not far from the armpits.

In a previous chapter I have already noted how many Indians from San Juan Pueblo recall Plains Indians—whom I then knew only from descriptions. Among the Utes I now found not only types but also attire strongly matching that of the San Juaneros. I cannot determine with certainty whether this—along with the already noted fact that the aforementioned Indians have a "Ute dance"—indicates a common origin or reciprocal mingling of Utes and Pueblos of San Juan.[7]

Among the Southern Utes, I noticed two main types, apart from the countless transitional forms. One of these types I had not encountered among Indians up to now. I later encountered it among the Kiowas. It was distinguished especially by the large proportions of the face in relation to the skull and the ungainly, straight, or slightly up-turned noses. The forehead was strongly receding and had pronounced heavy eyebrow arcs. Trunk and uppermost limbs were very vigorously developed, the neck short, the shoulders high and square. Even though the figure was above the median [height], there was something heavyset and massive about its appearance. Not infrequently I found stout individuals among this type, goiters as well. The complexion was light (33, 44, 45), as was the eye color (3).

The second principal type most closely corresponded to the well-known "redskin type," which, as I have earlier noted, is found in various proportions among most—perhaps all—tribes of North America. But now and then minor variations of this type possibly occur; the one I encountered among the Utes matched the Comanche Horse Back (chapter 10, lithograph 14).

According to my reckoning, approximately half the Utes I saw belonged to both these types, while the other half, in varying degrees, belonged to transitional types. Occasionally I encountered individuals who reminded me of the Apaches, particularly the Tontos. Because the Utes are on a very amicable footing with the Jicarilla Apaches and intermarry with them, I presume that the presence of this type among the Utes can be ascribed to this circumstance.[8] I also observed some individuals who had thick wavy hair. Generally speaking, the Ute women cannot boast of gracefulness and in this regard stand far behind other tribes. There is something ungainly about their countenances as well as their physiques.

Nowhere did I have more difficulty investigating Indians anthropometrically than among the Utes and at the outset encountered a certain opposition. There could be no thought at all about measuring women. Men, and just a few of them, very reluctantly allowed themselves to be examined. On the one hand, there was an undefined fear and suspicion, on the other, opposition I had to contend with. Only on the seventh day of my stay on the reservation could I measure an Indian. He only permitted me to touch his head—for generous payment.

Neither the influence of agency doctor J. J. White nor that of the Negro John Taylor, the interpreter and an adopted son of the Utes, could sway the obstinate Utes during the first few days.

Eventually, on the eighth day I was able to examine nine Ute warriors, after they had seen that I was visiting various camps with the doctor and Taylor and seemed well disposed to them—but especially after I accorded the interpreter as well as everyone who let himself be measured solid monetary remuneration and tobacco to ensure a speedy result. But Ignacio, the chief, an Indian of herculian build, and Severo, another chief, continued stubbornly to refuse. The former deemed it unnecessary to provide an explanation why; the latter attempted to dispute me on very philosophical grounds. In good Spanish he told me that it was wholly unnecessary to measure men because they, as well as all wild animals and all plants, had fixed proportions in their dimensions. "If a man is big, he has a big head; on the other hand, if he is small, then his head is small too," he repeated over and over again. Although I made every effort to provide this Ute anthropologist with more accurate insights about the doctrine of proportions, he remained unpersuaded.

Almost daily I rode out with the doctor and the Negro interpreter to visit Indian camps scattered in all directions but that are always near the mountain streams. In the past couple of years the tents *(kaní)* of bison hide have completely vanished because the Utes have had to terminate their bison hunts since settling on the reservation. Their tents now consist of white or yellowish canvas, which is supplied by the government. But some of their kaní are painted in the old manner with hunting and war scenes and other figures, which are difficult to explain to the uninitiated.

As a rule, several tents are situated close by each other, and such a small group of graceful wigwams,[9] from whose open tip a blue column of smoke rises upward, is ensconced among the dense vegetation along a babbling brook. It is an image so lovely and distinctive that one would not grow weary observing it, while it serves as a vivid reminder of the tableaux so vividly sketched in pencil by the Indian painter Catlin.

Three long sticks always stand a short distance from the tents, set crosswise against each other on top so that they form a kind of trestle. On it usually rest the best pieces of clothing and equipment because in the tent itself they would probably get soiled or damaged. In the tents there is a chaotic Babel of blankets, deer hides, clothes, weapons, household implements, and food that takes up practically all the surrounding space from the one side of the entrance to the other, while the center is occupied by the fireplace. Among the distinctive household items, which one could perhaps call field gear, long, flat, approximately one-meter-long valises of handsomely prepared tough white leather painted in bright colors take pride of place. Their primary function is keeping dried meat.[10] In addition, there is another kind of leather valise in the shape of a large quiver with a flap that holds various small items. The Utes make crude basketry and water jugs woven from twigs, resembling those of the Apaches.

Small children are fastened to a large carrying plank rounded off at the top by means of a sturdy leather cover, which covers the plank at the same time. A large part of the widely protruding plank sticks far above the papoose's head so that it is well protected when it is being transported. These carrying planks, though quite distinctive, lack the ornamental features of the other tribes, and there is obviously something heavy and cumbersome about them, just like the Utes themselves.

If I stepped or rather crawled inside a tent, then I found the inhabitants, both men as well as women, often playing cards, of which they are great devotees. Then again I saw young warriors who amused themselves *"en petit comité"* by dancing to the sound of a leather drum. One, then the other, took turns, and the figures that were performed consisted chiefly of turning and twisting the trunk of the body with hands on their hips while the shuffling feet barely moved from their spot. Not infrequently I also found women at work. Some of them were mending clothes, others were ornamenting moccasins with beads, still others were preparing meals.

Outside the tents were even more things to catch the eye. Here a band of young warriors, a short distance from the tent, were shooting with their Sharps rifles at a target, the trunk of a cottonwood, and every time that the sharp bang was repeated through the mountains, large chunks of bark and wood chips flew up into the air, followed by the mumbling approbation of the marksmen. Elsewhere some hunters were getting ready to ascend [the mountains] and go deer hunting to return several days, perhaps weeks later, amply laden with a supply of meat and fine hides. Everywhere I encountered a carefree attitude and good cheer, but I missed the childlike, kindly features that characterized the Yumas and Mohaves. The Ute, in contrast, must struggle more against man and nature. In the winter there is snow and icy cold, which reigns in the mountains, with which he must contend. The rest of the year it is game that he must pursue with difficulty, if he is to find food. Formerly his most dreaded enemies were the Comanches and Kiowas, who disputed with him the right to hunt bison on the plains; later he had to struggle with the whites.

The Southern Utes are unfamiliar with agriculture, nor do they want to engage in it despite the government's efforts to introduce them to it. But before long they will be forced to adopt it, as game becomes scarcer with the passage of time and they must abandon their primary activity, hunting, to engage in agriculture. Their northern brethren are already part of the way there. But the Utes will never be able to engage in large-scale agriculture on their present-day reservations because the terrain there is not suited for this. This is a high mountain area with splendid forests, of which the narrow river valleys alone could provide good agricultural land. In addition to venison and grouse *(Canace)*, the Utes feed themselves on marvelous trout, with which the streams abound, as well as prairie dogs *(Cynomys)*. Originally their vegetable nutriment consisted primarily of the cambium layer from pine trees, which contains glycoside, known by the name of coniferine. That is why one encounters numerous pine trees stripped of their bark in the Colorado mountains. Now, in addition to beef, the Utes receive a specific quantity of flour from the government every week. In addition, they acquire coffee and sugar in the trader's store, so that there is now more variety in their food than formerly.

It is a unique but repulsive spectacle when one visits the slaughtering ground of the agency on issue day. The cattle set aside for the Indians are found inside a high enclosure consisting of wooden tree trunks and are shot down one by one by a employee of the agency or an Indian. While the animals are in their death throes, a number of Indians, men and women, assault them with knives to disembowel them and in the meantime take a sample of the fresh meat. Here the women show the most zeal. With an astonishing deftness they skin the animal and cut it into pieces, interrupting their work now and then to stick a piece of still warm intestine with its contents into their mouths. Mingled with the shouting of the Indians are yelping dogs, shoved along by the throng, who greedily lick up the pools of blood; at the same time, though, they are repeatedly disturbed by kicks or blows from their masters. Although the Utes eat all the cattle's innards, they nevertheless make an exception for the liver. They are keen on pork, too.

Only in more recent years have the Utes acquired their own cattle and sheep, these supplied in accordance with a treaty with a government of the Union. There are approximately a hundred of the former, a thousand of the latter. Just as among the Navajos, they are pastured by women as well as men on horseback. Much more precious than their livestock, though, are their horses—about 2,200 in number, which in quality and vigor are perhaps on a par with those of the Navajos and generally of the same variety. The saddles—used by the women especially, who sit on their horses like men, just as all tribes do[11]—consist of a wooden frame that is covered with rawhide. A very high pommel, adorned with long fringes of white chamois leather, sticks out in front and back.

Besides card playing, the Utes are passionate lovers of races, two of which I attended. For a length of more than a mile the *Artemisia* bushes from the sandy plateau north of the agency had been yanked up, so that a magnificent straight racetrack had emerged. At the end, along both sides of this course, two sizable groups of Utes were sitting or standing, each with a pile of Navajo blankets, puma hides, and accoutrements, serving as prizes for the race, in front of them. The riders were all boys of ten to twelve years, practically unclad. What a pleasure to watch how splendidly they acquitted themselves of their duties as jockey and how they were fused with their steeds like modern centaurs. If the horses, flushed and snorting with their shouting riders enveloped in clouds of dust, had reached the end of the track and if one of them had carried off the palm of victory, then a warrior from the losing side stood up and carried some prizes to the winning side on the other side of the track. All this took place in a calm, quiet atmosphere, without shouting and quarreling, affording a marked contrast to the confused, noisy spectacles one often encounters among civilized peoples on similar occasions.

Some of the warriors sat silently on the ground, speaking softly now and then while smoking their peace pipes, which made the rounds from mouth to mouth. Others stood alone or in groups, smoking cigarettes, while behind them their fine horses stood huddled together in colorful little herds. A couple of Navajos, whose slender, lithe figures contrasted sharply with the athletic figures of the Utes, were present as spectators and observed the horses and riders with the eye of a connoisseur. With a background of mountains blanketed with vegetation vanishing into a blue horizon, with a fixed cloudless sky on high and a blazing sun shining on everything, the colorful throng provided a spectacle so picturesque and distinctive that one would have wished one had the talent of a Bodmer[12] or of a Catlin to put this on canvas and indelibly preserve it from oblivion.

Although the Utes have the peace pipe, or "calumet," they do not manufacture it themselves but obtain the pipe heads by barter with the Comanches. As is known, all the tribes who are in possession of the peace pipe use a single variety of rock, a variety of reddish brown soapstone (so-called catlinite) coming from a quarry on the Coteau des Prairies on the boundaries of present-day Minnesota and Dakota.[13] According to Catlin,[14] associated with the quarry (Red Pipestone Quarry) is the legend that the Great Spirit, weary of his red children's wars, summoned them all together to this spot and from the red stone of the cliff shaped a pipe that would be a symbol of peace for them.[15] Earlier, in the vicinity of the Cimarron River in New Mexico, the Utes found a stone that has much in common with the one from up north and was, in fact, used for the same purpose as well. These pipes are very precious. A Ute, whose pipe I wanted to buy, along with the leather sheath and lovely tobacco bag ornamented with colored beads, wanted nothing more or less than a horse in exchange for it. As much as I would also have liked to have enriched our Ethnographic Museum with a peace pipe, I had to let the warrior keep his treasure.

At the present time the Utes are supplied almost exclusively with firearms and, indeed, with the finest Sharps, Winchester, and Ballard rifles. Bow and arrows are no longer much used. They have never possessed lances and tomahawks or battle-axes, so it seems, differing in that respect from most Plains tribes. On the other hand, just like them, they practice the custom of scalping their enemies.

Notwithstanding all my efforts to learn whether the Utes possess a clan system, the responses to this question were so confused and evasive that it was not possible for me to obtain anything definite from them. Do not try to obtain ethnographic information from the agent or the employees because, even if they have been on a reservation for some time, they barely know more than a few words of the language and thus have only a very superficial notion of the character, attitudes, and customs of the Indians—and usually none at all.

Normally the Indian agents are familiar only with the immediate surroundings of the agency. Of the rest of the reservation they know nothing from their own observation. Thus it is no surprise how their *inhaltslose* [devoid of content] yearly reports arise, with those people preparing the latest report largely copying what their predecessor reported. According to the interpreter, there must be numerous Utes on the reservation and outside who know the Cross-Eye, as they reverently call the government agent and "colonel," only by name and are utterly unconcerned about the man whom the "Great Father" in Washington in his disinterested clemency has appointed to guide his red children. In particular, the western part of the reservation bordering on Utah is an area little visited, if at all, by whites, where the Utes live in total freedom. Indeed, that part of southeastern Utah, which is bounded to the west and south by the Colorado and San Juan rivers, is perhaps the most unknown region of the United States. It is probably an arid, rocky desert, where numerous old Indian ruins, primarily cliff houses, can be found, just as in southwestern Colorado.

The investigations (surveys) led by Hayden in 1874–1876 have for the first time made the ruins of this area more well known.[16] The cliff houses on Rio Mancos have since then gained classic status, so to speak. Time, alas, did not permit me to visit some of these interesting ruins. Besides, carrying out successful exploration would have required an expedition consisting of various individuals. It should be quite evident that I, with my limited resources, could not organize one.

11. Buckskin Charley,
Southern Ute chief
(after a photograph
by Matthew B. Brady,
ca. 1880).

According to the whites who come into contact with them, the Utes' language is very difficult to learn. Nevertheless, the Negro Taylor, who lived two or three years among these Indians, seems to speak their language with ease and understand it. For my part, I found Ute words much easier to write than Apache and Navajo though equally cacophonous, thanks to the accumulation of consonants. The association of *ts* and *tsj* is quite common.

Sign language, rather widespread on the plains, is little known among the Utes. The more they were driven to the mountains by their enemies, the more the Utes lost the habit of using this language. Spanish, too, which is now the only language they use in dealings with the whites and is quite well understood and spoken by many, will gradually fall into disuse now that they no longer enter New Mexico and Arizona and are surrounded more and more by Americans.

I do not recall having met so much as single Ute who spoke even broken English. Even the most prominent people in the tribe, such as Ignacio, Severo, Buckskin Charley, and Aguila, who understood Spanish rather well, knew just a few English words. I then conversed with them in Spanish and asked them about the tribes they knew, about their battles with the *Komáts* (Comanches) and *Pákanawa* (Cheyennes), and their hunts for bison and deer. With a savage gleam in his eye, Aguila admitted to me: *"Me gusta mucho pelear"* (I love fighting), and with delight pointed to his heavy trunk, which, according to him, he owed to eating the brains of a Cheyenne he had slain. In the most minute detail Ignacio described for me the Moqui villages he had visited as a young man. In rapt attention they listened as I told them about the Chiricahuas and their most recent campaign or about the Mohaves along the great stream of the West. With diplomatic tact I was asked what I thought of Cross-Eye and what the "other man from Washington" (the Indian inspector) was doing here.

An incident I witnessed one day threatened to disrupt the good understanding that existed between Utes and whites at the agency and even put our life in jeopardy. Ojo Blanco (White Eye), a powerfully built warrior, arrived at the agency on horseback in a frenzied state, heavily drunk, muttering all kinds of gibberish and playing suspiciously with his revolver. The agent immediately ordered some nearby Utes from the Indian police to seize Ojo Blanco's horse and weapons, to lead him to his *kani,* and to keep watch until he had slept it off. The police obeyed this order only reluctantly. The worthy agent, here aroused to fury, unleashed a torrent of vigorous abuse and curses, which every right-minded American from the West has at his disposal, and wanted to have a go at the drunken rider. Although Ojo Blanco understood little English, he seemed to comprehend the flattering epithets hurled his way because at once he seized the representative of the great republic by the throat and dealt him a hefty blow in the face with his iron fist. The agent and "colonel," in turn, oblivious of dignity, broke loose from the grip of his attacker and leaped up and dragged him from his rearing horse, whereupon both fell to the ground wrestling. Meanwhile the agency cook had hurried inside and returned with a loaded rifle, which he immediately pointed at Ojo Blanco, and certainly would have killed him had the doctor not yanked the weapon from his hand and probably spared all of us from a catastrophe.

The Utes, who themselves could see that the combativeness might prove infectious and preferred to avoid a bloody spectacle, rushed up to free the agent and to pinion Ojo Blanco. It was high time because he already had his finger on the trigger when his tribal compatriots seized him roughly by his long braids and pulled his head to the ground. Then they carried him off in the direction of the camp under powerful escort. If serious blood had been shed here, the Utes probably would have acted without regard for persons, shooting down us few whites and then setting the log cabins and storehouses ablaze. In the West whites and Indians usually both follow the maxim: give as good as you get.

This was also why the agency residents urgently besought me not to make any attempts to desecrate the Utes' grave sites. After I had nevertheless cast this exhortation to the wind and spent the whole afternoon vainly "hunting bones," reproach was heaped on me during the evening when a fire signal was seen on a nearby mountain, for they thought this was the signal for the Indians to surround our log cabins and kill us. Nevertheless, this did not happen that night. The Utes' graves are extremely difficult to locate because they conceal their dead under a pile of rocks and branches—to judge from their description, not unlike the previously noted graves of the Coyoteros.

In contrast to their southern and western neighbors, the Navajos and Pah-Utes, mestizos do not appear among the southern Utes; the very few who may be born are promptly killed. Even the children of the Negro Taylor were apparently not permitted to live. Laughing, Ignacio remarked that over yonder, near the Rio Florida, children were born with "buffalo hair," but that they had been killed like puppies. The Ute squaws, too, have no relations with white men. The instances when a white man successfully plays the role of Don Juan among the Ute "beauties" are extremely rare. On the other hand, the Ute women are by no means so reticent toward their fellow tribesmen and, according to our notions, often transgress against the dictates of morality.

The Utes are generally a healthy race, to which the mountain climate certainly contributes greatly, but perhaps at the same time they can thank the mountainous land for goiter, which many are afflicted with. It would be interesting to do a chemical analysis of the water from the mountain streams, though it is by no means certain that the lack of iodine in the water is the cause of this affliction.[17] Those who had goiters recalled in habit sufferers from torpid scrofula. It is possible that scrofula, which, as we know, can, among other things, be the result of the final stages of syphilis, is the cause of goiters among these Indians. Most of them suffer from an acute rheumatism, for which their style of life in the open air and the rapid temperature changes, paired with moisture, are the cause.

The days passed by pleasantly. The time I did not spend among the Indians, I passed fishing for trout in the Rio de los Pinos. But the stay at Ignacio had its dark side as well. The government blankets under which I slept in the log cabin were the preferred abode for a number of stinging insects, branded with the name of *eerits* by the Utes.

Before continuing my journey, on Dr. White's invitation I undertook a four-day foray into the high mountains in the neighborhood of the 14,000-foot-high Mount Simpson. Up there in the mountains the doctor and Mr. Merrill, the trader, had a prospect[18] that yielded copper and silver ore and was once given them by a Ute out of gratitude for a service rendered.

On the morning of September 27th, with a pack horse with blankets and provisions in the lead, I headed out on horseback along the north route with the aforementioned gentlemen, along with Mr. Francis Bentley, an English tourist, whom I had gotten to know in Santa Fe and who had come to look for me in Ignacio. It was a magnificent ride. Everywhere the eye alighted upon stately fir forests, alternating with clusters of oaks and aspen, covering the mountain slopes with their red and yellow foliage. After we had left the reservation, we off and on passed by prosperous wooden ranches because white colonists have streamed in to exploit the land since the Indians have left these regions. Only after we had covered twenty-six miles did we make a short stop in the shady, rustling firs to brew some coffee and have a go at a couple of our tins with food. Then, one behind the other in Indian file, we followed the banks of the Rio Vallecito, a right-side tributary of the Pine River. *Populus* species and dark conifers, primarily *Pinus ponderosa* and *Abies engelmanni*,[19] rim the banks of the calm, clear stream, and before we leave them to begin a long ascent of the mountains we encounter an abandoned summer camp of the Utes. Although these Indians may no longer settle in the region surrendered by them three years ago, the government has still allowed them to retain hunting rights as long as there is game enough to sustain them. The path, which can barely be followed, loses itself here and there in lush mountain bunchgrass *(Festucacea)* or among a series of tree trunks uprooted by a storm, which our horses know how to sidestep with just as much agility as caution. Spruces *(Abies* varieties) and lank aspen (quaking aspen: *Populus tremuloides),*[20] whose yellow leaves rustle incessantly because of a mountain breeze, become more numerous the longer we go and, with the constantly increasing darkness, make it extremely difficult to follow the trail, by now nearly invisible.

Eventually we are enshrouded in total darkness. Only the stars sparkle in the bright sky, still allowing us to see the tops of the tall firs, between which we slowly and hesitantly continue our journey. Mr. Bentley and Mr. Merrill already seem to have lost the trail for some time because there is no response to our call. The doctor, too, is at wit's end, but the packhorse we bring with us, which has already been in the mining camp, moves cautiously ahead with its nose close to the ground. Eventually it brings us to the glimmering of a fire, which reveals to us the place where both men, who work the prospect, are camping.

Upon our approach the huge watchdogs chime in with an ear-numbing barking, which caused both prospectors, already resting, to spring up weapons in hand because they think they might be under attack. Hungry and numb, before long we are sitting by the crackling wood fire and partaking of venison and cabbage. Because our stray companions have not turned up, we fire off rifle shots at short intervals; these are promptly answered in the distance, repeated a hundredfold in the still night through the mountains, with the arrival of both riders ensuing shortly afterward. Just like us, they had lost their way and had to search longer, due to lack of a guidebook, which we had found with the packhorse.

We slept like tops under the small linen tent, which sheltered four of us, and, upon awakening in the cool morning hour, noticed that we were encamped at the edge of a forest on the northern slope of a mountain saddle. On the east side of this saddle, in the immediate vicinity, arises the highest peak of Mount Rundlett, the mountain where we are situated. The rocks consist of a kind of gray limestone, while in many places the ground is covered with conglomerate, so-called pudding stones. From all sides we are surrounded by boundless dark fir forests, with Mount Simpson off toward the north shimmering in between.

On the rocks close by the tents small squirrels with pretty stripes (chipmunks: *Sciurus striatus)*[21] and gray rabbits resembling large tailless rats *(Lagomys princeps)* gaily frolic,[22] with the latter emitting a shrill cry from time to time. The camp and the two prospectors, brave, rough fellows with broad-brimmed felt hats, are evocative of Bret Harte's mining camp stories.[23] They are at home in the wild surroundings, by the dirty linen tent and the wood fire. Hospitable, brimming with jokes, fond of whiskey and gambling, frank and undaunted and excellent marksmen, they represent the embodiment of the carefree adventurers of the West—though in the best sense of the word.

After a hearty breakfast of magnificent roasted venison and a dark, bitter, turbid liquid, which is called "coffee" out west, we headed to the prospect, on which my good friends had staked all their hopes. At peril of breaking our necks, we descended into one of these natural grottos or caves that are a widespread phenomenon in this limestone mountain range. Alternately descending and climbing, creeping and panting, we moved along the original archways or the hewed-out pathways, following with smoldering lamps in hand the veins of the mineral in the rocky walls. Where one person fancied mountains with gold, the other shook his head incredulously. There is perhaps no means more uncertain of making one's fortune out west than prospecting for metals. I have known prospectors who since the discovery of gold in California, thus thirty-five years ago, have been engaged in the search with varying fortune but in the end had not gotten one step farther ahead. The same was true for the man guiding us around, who was once prosperous but was now laboring for a paltry daily livelihood in this pit.

Western Colorado is a land whose soil is extraordinarily abundant in various minerals and affords at least the chance that some individuals, among the many seeking their fortune here, will be favored by a lucky accident, discovering the kind of a treasure their fevered imagination dreams about. The first discovery of metal in Colorado—and, indeed, of gold—occurred in 1858 at the spot where Central City is now.[24] Since then discovery followed on discovery: silver, copper, iron, lead were excavated in huge quantities from the heart of these mountains, and the ever increasing stream of fortune hunters eventually forced the Indians to leave their mountains in 1880.

Having returned from our visit to the prospective mine, some people from our group went hunting, but even though bears and deer were numerous in this region, we did not get to see them, and we scared up only a couple of grouse *(Canace obscura)*[25] and some dark squirrels. The next day we were luckier, though. Five of us left camp and after about an hour of riding through an utter wilderness, involving a considerable climb, we "hobbled" the horses and separated into two parties. Here we had reached the limits of the timberline and thus an altitude of about 10,000 feet above sea level, where, according to Hayden, the timberline is between 11,000 and 12,000 feet.

The landscape left the impression of gigantic, rugged, and utterly abandoned parks, where the wavy fields of long yellow grass alternated with nothing but dense fir forests. In the distance one's gaze alighted on the dreary gray mountainous mass, which had no other garb than a sparse snow cover in places, while small clusters of white clouds slowly migrated along the peaks.

Although we proceeded slowly and as cautiously as possible, so as not to scare the game, the rarefied air at this altitude had its effect on me. My respiration grew very labored, and I was repeatedly compelled to stop and catch my breath, while heavy heart palpitations proved a huge impediment for me in moving about. We wandered around for five hours. Though we saw numerous, quite fresh tracks of deer and bears, at our rendezvous at the place we had gotten off, one party later brought back only a young deer *(C. macrotis)*,[26] the other party, to which I myself belonged, nothing but some grouse. Because of the increasing autumn coolness, the game had probably already descended to the lower reaches because during a milder season this mountain range, and western Colorado generally, is a genuine wildlife park. Besides the "mule deer," or black-tailed deer, the elk *(C. canadensis)* and the bighorn, the mountain sheep *(Ovis montana)*, appear in these mountains.

Bears include particularly the dreaded grizzlies, the "silver tips" of the hunters, so named for the light, silverish points on the hair of the pelt, and the cinnamon bear, a variety of *Ursus ferox*.[27]

After the return to the campfire at nightfall, "hunter's Latin" is primarily spoken, with one of the prospectors, who had the reputation of being a dead shot,[28] doing most of the talking. As a credible example [of his skills], I would simply recall that our hunter needed just seventeen bullets for the fifteen bears he killed in the Rocky Mountains.

We had planned on returning to Ignacio early the next morning, but our horses had wandered off. Only after they were found, following several hours of searching, could we head back, returning that evening. I would have very much liked to have accompanied Mr. Bentley on his journey through the magnificent mountainous regions of Colorado and visited Manitou Springs, the "garden of the gods," and other places—where, just as in Switzerland, one encounters a multitude of *"Touristen-Pöbel"* [tourist rabble] from the eastern states already during the summer. But my plans did not include merely searching for the delights of nature, and I proceeded on the paths originally delineated.

On the morning of October 1, I boarded the train to Cucharas [Cuchara] to head from there via Trinidad in southeastern Colorado and through Kansas to the Indian Territory. Because I had covered that part of the way that was new to me in utter darkness, I regrettably cannot provide a description of it. Let me just say that the route led across Conejos and Alamosa, and the train brought me around 4 A.M. to Cucharas on the other side of the Rocky Mountains. I had to wait several hours before I could head on. Because it was still dark and cold outside, I lay down to rest, wrapped in my serape, on the floor of the station building to wait for daybreak. To my astonishment, Cucharas did not have a single saloon, nor even a "hotel restaurant," even though it numbered six or seven dwellings situated along the edge of the rolling prairie. After having partaken of a frugal breakfast with a couple of workers on the railroad, I took my rifle and tried it out on the mountain plovers *(Aegialites montana),* which I found by the ponds on the prairie.[29]

Late in the morning I took the freight train that came from Pueblo and rode to El Moro, which is thirty-seven miles from Cucharas. The caboose of a freight train is not exactly the most pleasant and optimal way to move oneself, but I made a virtue of necessity and arrived at El Moro after three hours of thorough jostling. My patience was, indeed, put to the test this day because again I had to wait four hours before the mail coach left for Trinidad, five miles south. On October 3 continuous rain showers disrupted the splendid clear weather that had favored me for the last two weeks and transformed the unpaved streets of Trinidad into a quagmire.

Trinidad is a new city on the rise and a rather large town for the West. It owes its flourishing condition above all to the rich mines of bituminous coal nearby, and countless ovens where coke is prepared pollute the pure atmosphere with their black smoke clouds. Trinidad has a fine hotel and many stores and in other respects resembles Las Vegas. It, too, has a partially Mexican population. Indeed, the Mexicans appear to be slowly spreading north in the United States, seeking to regain the terrain, which in the southern region is being more and more overrun by Americans.[30]

The city itself has a quite charming location between the spurs of the Rocky Mountains, here consisting of limestone and covered with dark piñones and yellow grass. As soon as I had put my correspondence in order and made the necessary preparations for the journey ahead, I bade farewell late in the evening of October 5th to Trinidad and on the wings of steam sped eastward through the endless prairies.

·····

NOTES

1. This chapter was later slightly revised and republished in Ten Kate's *Over Land en Zee: Schetsen en Stemmingen van een Wereldreiziger* (Zutphen: Thieme, 1925), 18–35.

2. An Executive Order reservation was created for the Jicarilla Apaches on March 25, 1874. Pressures from white settlers led to its abrogation on July 10, 1876. Another Jicarilla Apache reservation was established in northern New Mexico on September 1, 1880. Pressure groups then advocated the movement of the Jicarillas to the Mescalero Apache reservation, near Fort Stanton in southern New Mexico. By August 20, 1883, all of the Jicarilla Apaches were moved there. However, growing tribal consciousness and the support of General Nelson A. Miles and others led to the permanent establishment of the 1880 area as the Jicarilla Apache reservation on February 10, 1887. Veronica E. Tiller, "Jicarilla Apache," in *Handbook of North American Indians* (Washington, D.C.: Smithsonian Institution, 1983), 10:451–52.

3. Ignacio (1828–1913), a Wimmenuche Ute chief, became leader of all the Southern Utes after the death of the celebrated Ouray. He favored peace with the whites. Dan L. Thrapp, *Encyclopedia of Frontier Biography* (Glendale: Arthur H. Clark, 1988), 2:699–700. Ouray (1820–1880), an Uncompaghre chief, was a famous warrior who, after becoming chief in 1860, maintained friendly relations with the whites, though there was some friction during the decade of the 1870s, when the U.S. government seized Ute treaty lands. He played an instrumental role in negotiating the end of hostilities after the 1879 Ute uprising. Dee Brown, *Bury My Heart at Wounded Knee: An Indian History of the American West* (New York: Holt, Rinehart and Winston, 1970), 367–90; on Ute-white relations, see also Virginia M. Simmons, *The Ute Indians of Utah, Colorado and New Mexico* (Boulder: University Press of Colorado, 2000).

4. There were eleven Ute bands at the time of Ten Kate's travels, six eastern bands, which had ranges primarily in Colorado, and five western bands, in Utah. Ten Kate lists four of the eastern bands: Uncompahgre (Taviwach), Wimmenuch, Capote, and Muache. Situated in the Great Basin, these Ute bands were primarily hunting-and-gathering peoples. Their subsistence was largely dependent on the seasonal availability of berries, roots, seeds, and nuts as well as crickets, grasshoppers, and locusts. In addition, the Ute territories included a plethora of land mammals, such as rabbits, deer, antelope, and buffalo as well as fish. As a result of the decimation of their population and the loss of their traditional lands—in the west by 1850 and in the east by 1870—Ute culture had changed radically by Ten Kate's time there. Donald Callaway, Joel Janetski, and Omar C. Stewart, "Ute," in *Handbook of North American Indians: Great Basin,* ed. W. L. D'Azevedo (Washington, D.C.: Smithsonian Institution, 1986), 11:336–67.

5. The 1863 Treaty of Conejas established a reservation for the Taviwach band along the Uncompahgre River in northeastern Utah, which was then included in a larger Confederated Ute Indian reservation set aside in 1868. The agency for the Taviwach was moved to Uncompahgre in 1876, and they were then referred to as the Uncompahgre Utes. In 1880 a government treaty council forced the Uncompahgre band to sell their lands in Colorado and move to an area just south of the Uintah reservation in Utah, where a new reservation was created for them in 1882 and named Ouray after the Uncompahgre chief. Callaway et al., "Ute," 339.

6. The Numic languages are a branch of the Uto-Aztecan family. Three closely related groups comprise the Numic languages. Comanche is one of the Central Numic languages; Ute and Paiute are Southern Numic. Hopi is only distantly related within the larger Uto-Aztecan family. Wick R. Miller, "Uto-Aztecan Languages," *Handbook: Southwest,* 10:118–19; Wick R. Miller, "Numic Languages," *Handbook: Great Basin* 98–106.

7. This seems less likely than a San Juan–Jicarilla Apache relation both in terms of geographical proximity and the presence of Apachean (rather than Ute) features in San Juan ceremonial life. Alfonso Ortiz, "San Juan Pueblo," *Handbook: Southwest,* 9:278–95.

8. HtK 1885: For example, Ouray, the great chief of the Utes who died in 1880, was a Jicarilla on his mother's side.

9. Europeans commonly designate the conical buffalo skin tents of the Plains Indians as "wigwams" instead of "tipis." The term "wigwam" in this case is a misnomer, as it designates the dome-shaped dwellings of the Algonquian tribes of the eastern woodlands.

10. These rawhide valises are more commonly known as "parfleches."

11. In the nineteenth century European and American female equestrians sat with both legs over to one side.

12. In 1833–1834 Swiss artist Karl Bodmer (1809–1893) accompanied German explorer Prince Maximilian of Wied (1782–1867) on a journey of exploration along the Upper Missouri. Bodmer painted almost 400 watercolors of American landscapes and Indian portraits from the Mandan, Hidatsa, and Blackfeet tribes. His original watercolors, only discovered and exhibited after World War II, were the basis for eighty colored aquatints that illustrated Maximilian's narrative of the journey and are still a definitive visual record of the Plains tribes of the era. See William J. Orr, "Karl Bodmer: The Artist's Life," in *Karl Bodmer's America* (Lincoln: University of Nebraska Press, 1984), 351–76.

13. This site is now preserved as Pipestone National Monument. See Theodore L. Nydahl, "The Pipestone Quarry and the Indians," *Minnesota History* 31 (1950):193–208.

14. HtK 1885: *Manners, Customs and Condition of the North American Indians,* vol. II, p. 160.

15. HtK 1885: This legend has received poetic treatment from Longfellow in his "Hiawatha."

16. Geologist Ferdinand Vandiveer Hayden (1829–1887) explored much of the American West during three decades from the 1850s through the 1870s. He is best remembered for his exploration of the Yellowstone Valley and successful advocacy for the creation there of a national park. In 1874 members of the Hayden Colorado Survey—William Henry Jackson (1843–1942) and his photographic crew—went to southwestern Colorado to explore the San Juan region. In the La Plata mining district a miner, John Moss, persuaded them to take a route along the Mancos River to the Mesa Verde. Here Jackson created one of the most outstanding images of this era of

exploration—a photograph of Two Story Cliff House. In the following seasons Jackson and others made extensive surveys of archaeological remains in the Mancos Valley. Hayden was not a participant in these explorations. William H. Goetzmann, *Exploration and Empire* (New York: Knopf, 1966), 487–529; Mike Foster, *Strange Genius: The Life of Ferdinand Vandeveer Hayden* (Niwot: Roberts Rinehart, 1994).

17. Today it is well known that iodine deficiency is the cause of goiter.

18. HtK 1885: By "prospect" is meant a mine that is being worked on a provisional basis, as though by way of experiment, to be continued or abandoned, all depending on whether output is good or bad. Every mine was once a prospect; not every prospect, on the other hand, always becomes a mine.

19. *Abies engelmanni* = *Picea engelmannii* (Parry) Engelman., blue Engelmann spruce.

20. *P. tremuloides* Michx., quaking aspen.

21. *Sciurus striatus* = *Tamias striatus,* eastern chipmunk. As the name implies, however, this species is native to the eastern half of the United States. Ten Kate probably observed either *Eutamias minimus,* least chipmunk, or *E. quadrivittatus,* Colorado chipmunk. See E. R. Hall and K. R. Kelson, *Mammals of North America* (New York: Ronald, 1959), 1:293–95.

22. *Lagomys princeps* = *Ochotona princeps,* pika.

23. American author Bret Harte (1836–1902), who lived in California from 1854 to 1870, wrote several stories such as "The Luck of Roaring Camp" and "Outcasts of Poker Flat" depicting life in gold rush camps. These are characterized by some sentimentality and sympathy for social outcasts. Howard R. Lamar, ed., *New Encyclopedia of the American West* (New Haven, Conn.: Yale University Press, 1998), 488–89.

24. In fact, the first significant discovery of gold, in July 1858, occurred closer to Denver. Carl Abbott, Stephen J. Leonard, and David McComb, *Colorado: A History of the Centennial State,* 3rd. ed. (Niwot: University Press of Colorado, 1994), 51.

25. *Canace obscura* = *Dendragapus obscurus* (Say), blue grouse.

26. *Cervus macrotis* = *Dama hemionus,* black-tailed or mule deer.

27. HtK 1885: The cinnamon bear of the writers is not the same as that of the frontiersmen because by "cinnamon bear," the former understand a variety of *Ursus americanus* [black bear].

28. HtK 1885: Someone who hits his target with every shot.

29. *Aegialites montana* = *Eupoda montana* (Townsend), mountain plover.

30. At time of the American conquest the state of New Mexico had a large Hispanic population of long date. During the late nineteenth century some Mexican emigrants were drawn to the Southwest by prospects of work in the mines or railways, but truly massive Mexican emigration to the region only began at the beginning of the twentieth century. Matt S. Meier, Feliciano Rivera, *The Chicanos: A History of Mexican Americans* (New York: Hill and Wang, 1972).

CHAPTER TEN

Through the Indian Territory
Part 1

WHEN I WAKE UP THE NEXT MORNING IN THE SPLENDID PULLMAN CAR, the train is speeding across a rolling prairie.[1] I step up on the platform of the wagon, and the fresh fragrance of dew-covered plains rejuvenates me after having spent a night in the stifling atmosphere of a sleeping car. Shortly afterward we stop at the small station Coolidge in Kansas, just across the Colorado border. We have a hurried breakfast and learn that a few days ago a train had been attacked there by some cowboys, who killed the engineer and fireman. But when they tried to plunder the wagon, which held the mail and the goods of Wells & Fargo Express Company, they received such a warm welcome from the company officials that they quickly took to their heels with bloodied heads. While there is no chance, as there once was, of being attacked by Indians on the great railway lines of the west, white robbers have now taken their place.

During the night since we left Trinidad, we have descended 3,616 feet because Coolidge is situated at just 2,418 feet above sea level. The farther east we go, the more we descend along the gigantic incline of the prairies. Its highest elevation is along the base of the Rocky Mountains, while Atchison, the eastern terminus of this line in Kansas and at the same time the boundary of the original prairie, is situated at an altitude of just 800 feet.

All day long the train proceeds on its way through endless rolling plains, which are blanketed with short and evidently rather parched grass. Not a trace of Indians or game can be seen, however. Fifteen years ago the tribes of the Cheyennes and Arapahos were still masters of these tracts, but the laying and completion of the railroad, and the immigration and settlement accompanying it, forced them to vanish for good from the country and dwell on a reservation set aside for them in the southern Indian territory.[2]

The bison disappeared later than these Indians, or rather they did not vanish but were literally exterminated by the thousands and tens of thousands by the whites who hunted them not simply for love of gain, for their hides and bones, but from sheer blood lust as well. Between 1872 and 1874 the slaughter was continued, delivering the coup de grâce to the vast southern bison herd. The district to the west of the Indian Territory and the adjoining regions of Texas took the sorry remnants. Dodge estimates at 3,158,730 the number of bison killed in the area during the time period mentioned.³ He arrived at this figure by keeping track of the number of bison hides transported each year by the Atchison, Topeka and Santa Fe Railway. The thousands of bleached bison bones and skulls that I saw lying around at various places along the line, as at Syracuse and Dodge City, still bear witness to the bestial slaughter.

Steadily we follow the northern bank of the Arkansas River, which propels its muddy, pale brown waters eastward. The only trees one sees are paltry cottonwoods, which rim the banks of the stream in places or stand in clusters by the ponds and now and then break up the monotony of the prairie. Isolated cattle ranches and homesteads are spread out far and wide, while at intervals little towns in miniature arise along the railway. They all look alike, differing only in size, and all have nondescript wooden, mostly whitewashed houses. The aforementioned Dodge City, which once had the reputation as one of the most notorious brawling and gaming dens of the West, a hard place par excellence, is one of the most important "cities" we stop at.

Later that afternoon we pass Pawnee Rock, a spot associated with many legends from days past. The bare rock, which rises up above the grassy plain a short distance from the station, was the gathering place of various Indians tribes from time immemorial. Later it was a landmark for the immigrant caravans, which defied the perils of the desert in search of a new homeland. But the railway has brought all that to an end, and with the Indian and the bison, romanticism and enchantment have vanished from these plains forever. Utilitarians may rejoice that the solitary wilderness is being transformed into a "farmers' paradise" and exult in the cultivated fields, homesteads, and herds of cattle. The person who views the matter more from the aesthetic standpoint, however, and compares the present day and the past of these places, cannot suppress a feeling of resentment—I should say melancholy. Now the enchantment of the solitary steppes is gone, the enchantment with all its perils and travails. Now, in the place of Indian wigwams and bison herds, one gazes upon hamlets with greedy Yankees, farms, and herds of motley cattle.

The rain, which had hovered threateningly over the landscape in dark, heavy clouds all day long, broke loose in a torrent that evening. It was still raining when I stepped from the train at Newton at 5 o'clock to spend the night there, to take the line the next morning to Caldwell, on the northern boundary of the Indian Territory. Suddenly I realize that no train is going there because October 7th is, alas, a Sunday. So I am forced to spend thirty-six hours in Newton—much to my annoyance. The Yankee who will swindle and rob his fellow man, when he can, puts so much importance on appearances and makes such an affectation of religious feeling that here he does not allow the trains to run on Sunday and closes some stores and saloons. Much to my chagrin, I pass the time in the town with its lounging, tobacco-chewing, spitting, cursing, oafish, loutish population. For Newton has nothing new to offer, looks like a thousand other western towns of 2,600 inhabitants, and the inhabitants all look alike.

Early on the morning of October 8th, I bid farewell to Newton. It is again as hot and oppressive as the previous day, and a tepid south wind wafts across the fields. The region we slowly steam through is settled with homesteads and ranches, which are situated in the middle of corn and grain fields. At the small stations liveliness and activity everywhere prevail. The packed railway wagons include a public that, it is true, has a more urban tinge and is less rude than that "west of the Rockies" but just as caddish and boring. It is a business public especially, and the conversations one hears concern cattle and slaughterhouses, the price of grain, and irrigation of landholdings.

For the first time one can again see cylinder hats and parasols and heavy golden watch chains and thick seal rings without coats of arms, so widespread among the businessmen of the American middle classes. It is as though it were the shop sign of their "worth." Someone who is not "worth" a certain number of dollars does not outfit himself with these bulky ornaments. We pass in succession Wichita and Mulvane, where we cross the Arkansas, and then follow the route along the other bank in a southwesterly direction: first Belle-Plaine, Wellington, and eventually Caldwell, the end of the line.

Only a few of the chewing, spitting, apple-eating public with dollars jingling in their bags head on to Caldwell, where a couple of Indians standing by the station remind me that I am still in the West. Because I have to wait until the next day to head on, I seek accommodations in the hotel of Caldwell, which is packed. Only with the greatest difficulty can I obtain a tiny room because a troupe of stage actors have arrived who want to try their luck in this "outpost of civilization."

Caldwell is a busy little town, situated on elevated terrain of the undulating prairie. Green bluffs arise to the south. A short distance behind them extends the Indian Territory. Caldwell has about 1,000 residents. There is something sociable in the street life with countless covered wagons, which are the sole means of transporting goods in the areas where there is no railway. Freighters, cowboys, and tramps with broad-brimmed felt hats, heavy spurs, and tattered clothing throng the wooden sidewalks, which bound the sandy "streets," to gain access to the numerous saloons and stores or to leave them. Here and there Indians mingle with this motley band. They are imposing figures with long raven black locks, which hang down over the colorful blankets in which they are picturesquely draped. Quietly and calmly they go their way; make their purchases of sugar, coffee, flour, or colorful calico; and promptly head back to their camp, which is pitched next to a row of freight wagons because they are Indians from the Cheyenne reservation who are performing services for the agency there.

That evening the roaming artists put on "The Octoroon" (a slave story from the south) in a manner vastly exceeding my expectation, in essence too good for Caldwell's public.

A regular mail line—which is quite irregular nonetheless—maintains traffic between Caldwell and Henrietta in Texas and vice versa and stops at the most important places in the Indian Territory, which it intersects from north to south over a length of more than 220 miles.

At 1 o'clock on October 9th I take a seat on a buckboard of this line to head to Darlington, the Cheyenne and Arapaho agency. The Indian Territory has cured me for good of any desire to ride on buckboards. I think of hard, narrow seats, shared with bad traveling companions, of long, sleepless nights, of cloudbursts and drenched clothing—to say nothing of other things. But let me try to recount the good as well as the bad. The sun, which in the morning hid behind a gray cloudy veil, broke through at noon and cast a benevolent gaze upon my entry into the "red man's" country. Besides me a black soldier whose leave has ended and who is heading to his new garrison, Fort Reno,[4] is the only passenger on the buckboard. In addition, there is the coachman. Although here I am free from that semiurban loutishness, which stripped me of all my illusions in Kansas, I am stuck with two traveling companions who perceptibly augment my knowledge of American curses and pithy expressions. The crinkly-haired cavalryman is, indeed, still half numb from sprees in Kansas City. Now and then, though, there is a *lucidum intervallum,* and he recounts for us episodes from his marvelous furlough, which he sorely misses.

With the three of us huddled together on the only bench of the light vehicle, we trot through the prairie, which stretches out in long green waves for an immense distance. We pass some small streams, including Bluff Creek, with red sandy banks and equally red and sandy water, bounded by luxuriant cottonwoods and elms. The grass *(Sesleria dactyloides)*[5] is short and once served as food for the bison, who themselves have departed this area a few years ago. Nothing more recalls their presence, except for the countless huge holes in the ground filled with water (buffalo wallows) where they wallowed around in the summer to cool off and rid themselves of the obnoxious mosquitoes.

Countless herds of cattle, which have been granted the right to graze here by the Indians, have now replaced the bison. They roam across the lush grass by the hundreds, and one would almost think one were in England if armed riders were not guarding the herds and one's attention were not diverted at the same time by the shrill shrieking of the frisky prairie dogs *(Cynomys ludovicianus)*—after the bison certainly the most typical animal of the West. They are larger than the ones I have seen in Arizona and New Mexico and more numerous as well. The exterior of their earth dwellings recalls miniature volcanoes, with a very wide crater and flattened sides. Twenty, fifty, sometimes more are together and form a large bare, gnawed-off spot in the middle of the sea of grass. At our approach they straighten up and sit like dogs. Then they partially duck away in their burrows and emit a rapid, piercing shriek—I would almost say chirping because it resembles that of a finch— while tiny tails bob up and down with lightning speed. Then, at once when they have stared at you with their huge bulging rodent eyes, full of goodness and innocence, and decide that they have braved the danger long enough, they cease their crying and suddenly vanish inside their burrows.

Because the prairies from the east to the west rise by degrees, though continually, the horizon is extraordinarily vast, and the impression of endlessness one receives is perhaps even more immense than that of the ocean. Especially now, at this time of year, the plain displayed the same monotony because the splendid floral garb, which adorns the grassy sea during the spring, had long since withered. Before long the season of icy winds will draw near and, unconstrained by any protective wall of high mountains in the north, will find a wide, open path into the boundless, open plains.

People have sought an explanation for the treelessness of these plains, where soil and climate ought to be suitable for the growth of forests, in the destructive winds—but incorrectly so. Neither the millions of bison, which like a stream moving up and down from north to south with the alternation of the seasons, nor the prairie fires with their destructive flames, swept forward by the wind with astonishing speed, scorching thousands of miles of the plant cover, are the reason for the steppelike character of this region, where forests have always been absent. Later investigations have, in fact, demonstrated that these plains were once covered by a sea, which dried up in a geologically short period of time. The moist surface of the soil, consisting chiefly of weathered lime, sandstone, and granite, was slowly blanketed with a garb of grass and flowers. Later on, seeds from trees, reaching the plains due to various circumstances, first germinated where the soil was softest and the most water was on hand, especially along the banks of rivers, brooks, and pools.

Before nightfall we stop at two different ranchos, inhabited by whites. In one of them, Corn Creek, we have a frugal meal and continue the journey with fresh horses. Twilight has given way to an evening rich in splendor. A clear sky strewn with twinkling stars, with the half-moon casting its silver-white rays upon the earth, arches above the silent, eternal plain. The horizon now is no longer sharply delineated as during the day but blends with the mysterious teeming half darkness, which envelops the gigantic circle of which we are the constantly changing midpoint. This enchantment does not last long, though. The more time passes, the more the firmament becomes overcast with clouds, and one star after the other vanishes behind the somber veil. Only the moon casts its pale, muted light a little while longer on the plain, which before long is concealed for good in a gray veil.

Now that there is no more diversion, sleep overpowers me. The Negro, with a hangover, has already been resting for some time under my wool Navajo blanket and leans on me so heavily that I can hold my seat only with difficulty. Eventually I position myself on sacks and luggage, which are placed at the rear of the vehicle. My serape provides no significant protection from the wet chill weather, which becomes more severe as time goes on. I doze a moment, then suddenly I am startled awake because I am on the point of sliding off the wagon and being left behind in the dark plain. Hour after hour passes with no other diversion than a band of camping Indians, who are escorting a number of covered wagons and welcome us with demonic yelling. Whether they have whiskey or something else is the cause of their merriment, I do not know. They seem elated, though, and for a moment a couple of dark figures run after us, yelling. Skeleton, a name possibly recalling a prairie drama played out here earlier, is another ranch, which we reach late at night. Then, around 4 A.M., another one emerges along Indian Creek, where we wait several hours for reasons unknown. A heavy mist, normally quite uncommon on the prairie, rises up and forces me to warm my numbed limbs by the wood fire, which is burning in the wretched wooden dwelling and where our breakfast is being prepared at the same time.

Under a heavy mist we eventually resume the journey later that morning. In some places the ground is drenched as a result of the heavy rains that have recently fallen. After a couple of hours, we reach the banks of the Cimarron River or Red Fork of the Arkansas. Here we must face the difficult question of how we can best reach the other bank. In the Indian Territory bridges are quite rare. One wades through the river, even the largest ones, or swims across them.

All the rivers on the prairies are very shallow and full of sandbanks, their shape continually transformed under the influence of wind and current. This time, though, the Cimarron has risen so much, and the red waves are surging vigorously between the high banks of red Triassic sandstone with such great swiftness, that we deem it advisable to first take this state of affairs into consideration. Indeed, we are not the only ones who dare not cross the stream. There are various drivers with heavily-laden wagons who had been waiting for days now along the bank until [the water level in] the river dropped.

An Indian of robust stature cautiously approaches from the other bank. Wherever he can keep his balance and is not wrestling with the current, he cleaves the waves with a robust blow; the water reaches to nearly below his armpits. Luckily he reaches the edge of the bank, while the water drips from his bronzed herculian limbs. It is obvious that we cannot cross here with our load. We spend a couple of hours waiting. Fortunately, the sunshine comes through again and fondly caresses the sand of the bank.

I am hungry because the breakfast, taken at the break of day, was bitterly bad. My saddle-bags, however, hold no more tins of sardines. So I head out to see whether I can outsmart a rabbit or prairie hen, but over yonder, behind this sand hill, I see smoke. Coming closer, I reach a camp of freighters who have meanwhile returned from the bank to their wagons to take their meal. I ask if I could share a little with them. Rudely, but without hesitation, they point me to a seat by the fire and I share their simple chuck,[6] which consists of fried bacon and sweet potatoes *(camotes)*.

After I return to the river, it looks like the water has subsided somewhat, and we make the attempt to reach the other bank. We unload the vehicle and put the cargo in a small boat, which lies unattended along the shore, to reach the sandbank in the middle of the stream. With the consoling thought of "*commune naufragium dulce* [sweet shipwreck together]" I board the feeble hulk and paddle with all my might to the sandbank. We bob ominously on the red stream, and at the same time the little boat takes on water and jets spurt through the gaps in the planks. But finally, after twisting and twirling, turning and changing direction, we land on the bank, where the wet sand swiftly slides over our shoes and we must walk without halting to avoid sinking. The driver, who has laid everything aside except his shirt and his hat, now returns in the little boat and brings the vessel with the mules to the sandbank. Of the snorting mules nothing can be seen but their heads protruding upward—of the buckboard nothing more than the driver, who sits with his feet in the water as he reaches the middle of the stream. However, lashes and cursing—but even more, the long ears' desire for self-preservation—bring the vehicle to the sandbank unharmed. As quickly as we can, we toss the cargo, which is already beginning to give way, onto the buckboard, hurriedly jump in, and, wading, hasten through the other shallow half of the river.

Drenched and abundantly covered with red mud, we promptly continue the ride to Kingfisher, nine miles south along the Cimarron. There is a small ranch in an enchanting prairie situated along the confluence of two small streams. The driver feels he has ridden enough and decides to go no farther. We passengers, the Negro cavalryman and I, must wait until another opportunity presents itself. It may be that another mail wagon will come that same night but maybe only the following afternoon. For my part, I do not regret finding a moment to catch my breath and to roam through the field for a change.

Over yonder by the edge of the creeks, near luxuriant cottonwoods and elms, white tents emerge. These are the Cheyenne wigwams,[7] as I see from the herder who is driving a herd of half-wild mustangs to the camp. Incessant rounds of firing soon draw my attention. It is a band of Texans, who are on their way to Kansas and, on their way, are testing the soundness of their six-shooters on the poor prairie dogs, who have confidently maintained their colony a short distance from the rancho. But there is other game, too, because at the same time a prairie hen succumbs to the murderous lead from their shotguns.

After the meal I seek the rest I had long been deprived of and lie down in my serape on the hay by the corral. The Negro joins me before long and asks for a blanket because the poor devil is shivering from the cold. We have slept barely a few hours when we are awakened because the buckboard from Darlington has arrived and is heading on right away. In a rather foul mood, due to the interruption of such sweet repose, we once again take our place between the wheels and in the morning at 4:30 have already covered the twenty-two miles separating Kingfisher from Darlington, though it is pitch black. I knock on the door of the "hotel," which is pointed out to me, but it is completely full. Then I go to the store, where I am granted accommodation, and I lie down on the floor and fall asleep until the gray day rouses me with a gust of wind from the open window.

Darlington, the post office name for the agency of the Cheyenne and Arapaho Indians, is the largest place I have seen on a reservation. It is situated on the prairie along the sandy left bank of the North Fork of the Canadian River and consists of large wooden stores, school buildings, and other government buildings. The largest of these is a huge redbrick shed, where the agent's offices are set up and the supply of merchandise for the Indians lies piled up. One would hardly think one was in the "Indian Territory," of which the name by itself ought to bring a howling wilderness to mind. As is evident from everything I have related about the West, however, the Indian is almost nowhere master. He must patiently watch as the government puts buildings and forts on the land that for the previous generation was undisputed territory all their own. So, too, have originality and romanticism vanished in the land of the Cheyennes and the Indian Territory generally—as will be evident from the following pages.

Apart from the government officials, the whites you see at Darlington are practically all cattlemen. These are not just ordinary cowboys, though, but wealthy owners of huge herds—genuine cattle kings, whose cattle may graze in the Territory thanks to a treaty with the Indians. The newspaper appearing in Darlington, the *Cheyenne Transporter,* is also primarily devoted to the interests of the cattlemen. It teems with numerous silhouettes of cows and horses that are covered with large white letters, numbers, and odd hieroglyphic signs indicating the various brands of every herd grazing in the Indian Territory. This way one can find the name and the address of the owner, a sign of the range where the herd grazes.

Later in the morning, after I have assured myself a small room in the "hotel," I visit the agent, one of the few gentlemen from this estate whom I have met.[8] A glance at the area around the agency quickly convinces one about the state of affairs among the Indians. Among the hundreds of tents, blanketing the plain from near and far, there is no longer a single one of bison hide. They all consist of white canvas furnished by the government. Just like all Indian tribes in the territory of the Union, the present-day Cheyennes and Arapahos, too, are completely dependent on the government and public charges. The bison have completely vanished, and other game as well—deer and antelopes—are too scarce to provide a living. Thus nothing remains for the Indian but to keep silent, eat the bread of charity, or struggle and starve.

The history of the Cheyennes, like that of many other Indian tribes, is a sorrowful history, but individual episodes have achieved greater notoriety than is the case for most of their racial compatriots. I am referring to the bloodbath of the Cheyenne camp along Sand Creek, in eastern Colorado, by Chivington in November 1864[9] and the battle in Fort Robinson in Nebraska in January 1879.[10] I only wish to recall them.

In peacetime a band of 500 Cheyennes and Arapahos—men, women, and children—were cravenly assaulted at the break of day and massacred by a powerful band of Colorado volunteers. Nobody was spared during this bloodbath; even women and children found no mercy in the eyes of their "Christian" attackers. Chivington made every effort to broadcast his "victory" and boasted he had made 500 Indian warriors bite the dust.[11] It is no cause for surprise that the massacre cried out for vengeance. An Indian war thus ensued, bringing death and destruction to the homesteads of the settlers and costing the American government no less than thirty million dollars.

The next great clash between the Cheyennes and the Union was in the winter of 1868. This time, in addition to the Arapahos, their steadfast allies—the Comanches, Kiowas, Apaches, and southern Sioux—were involved as well. The war broke out in connection with the treaty of Medicine Lodge (October 1867), according to which the above-named tribes—the latter excepted—agreed henceforth to settle in the western part of the Indian Territory, reserving the right to hunt in southwestern Kansas as long as there were still bison, with the stipulation that no white colonists could settle on this hunting ground for three years.[12]

Only in the summer of 1868 did the Senate in Washington begin deliberations on the treaty. Meanwhile settlers were streaming into the hunting grounds, which, according to the treaty, provisionally belonged to the Indians. Unaware of the delay, they waited to no avail for the payment in goods of all kinds, food, and money promised them. The Indians suffered from hunger and, dissatisfied by this kind of treatment, they sought to gain a hearing with General Sheridan, who then happened to be at Fort Dodge.[13] But he refused to become involved. Incited by people who had an interest in an Indian war, he managed to prevent the 50,000 dollars and the goods promised the Indians from being handed out, on the grounds that the Indians had broken the Treaty of Medicine Lodge and were hostile. Sheridan was speaking only a *half*-truth. A small band of disaffected Cheyennes, tired of the long wait, had headed north for a campaign against their enemies, the Pawnee Indians. On their way through Kansas, they came into conflict with white settlers and blood flowed.

That was the signal. In all haste preparations were made, not to punish the Cheyennes who had moved north *but those who had gone south of the Arkansas* and did not have the slightest involvement in this matter. In the middle of November 1868 Sheridan began his campaign against the "hostile Indians south of the Arkansas." Already on November 27th Sheridan, or rather Custer, initiated "the Battle of the Washita," which involved attacking and destroying a large united camp of Cheyennes, Arapahos, Kiowas, and Comanches. A hundred and forty Indian warriors bit the dust after a desperate resistance. Among the fallen were various chiefs, including Black Kettle of the Cheyennes.[14] Fifty-six women and children—in addition to those who perished in the melee—were captured and the entire camp supply, in addition to 875 horses, seized. The Indians were too weak to avenge themselves and promptly surrendered at Fort Cobb.[15]

Six years later, in 1874, the Cheyennes and their former allies, for reasons like those of the past, took up their tomahawks once more. This time, too, they suffered defeat and paid an even more harsh atonement for their audacity. A large number of their warriors were banished to Florida and shut up in a fort, where those who did not pine away languished in captivity for many years.[16]

In the year 1879 the Northern Cheyennes would gain renown as the most heroic warriors of the Plains. Separated from their southern tribal compatriots, these Indians shared the same hunting grounds with the Sioux, their allies and blood relations,[17] ever since anyone can remember. In 1877 they were brought to the Indian Territory, as a kind of so-called experiment, to return to their own land if they did not like it there. More than a year passed, though, without any prospect for change. Around 300 of the most disaffected Cheyennes left their campground one night in September and, under the leadership of the chief Dull Knife, set out to return to their northern homeland.[18] Heavily decimated by the troops pursuing them along their route of more than 600 miles, they finally surrendered at Fort Robinson in northwestern Nebraska on the condition that they would not be sent back to the Indian Territory. After two months of captivity, when they received word that they must return once again to their place of banishment, Dull Knife and his warriors steadfastly refused, stating that they preferred death to banishment. It was the middle of the winter and bitter cold, and as a means of forcing the Indians to submission, their blankets, food, and firewood were taken away from them. This situation lasted *five* days, but the Cheyennes endured this torture in a mood of desperation. Instead of surrendering, they ventured a desperate sortie.

During the night of January 9th, at a moment the guard was less numerous than usual, the men cleared a way through the windows of the shed, where they were kept prisoners, and attacked the sentries with a few revolvers they had been able to conceal. After putting them out of commission, they fled with women and children to the fields covered with frozen snow, where they were soon pursued and overtaken by the entire guard. In the bloody fight that ensued, forty Indians, including various women and children, were killed.

A hundred and sixty cavalrymen, bringing two cannons with them, set out after the remaining refugees. Only on the 22nd did the pursuit, which was continued with fresh troops, come to an end. On this day the Indians were encountered at the entrance of a ravine, fifty miles from Fort Robinson, where they had entrenched themselves. The troops surrounded the Indians and opened up on them with murderous fire. The Cheyennes, who had no more ammunition, hurled themselves at the rows of soldiers with hunting knives in hand, but before they reached them a hail of bullets had mowed them down. Of the 320 followers who left the Indian Territory with Dull Knife, seventy-five remained after this battle. The government had the generosity to allow the majority of the widows and orphans to seek their long-wished-for abode among the Ogallalla Sioux, their blood relations. The seven surviving men, however, were sent with their wives and children to Fort Leavenworth to stand trial for the hostilities their tribal compatriots had engaged in the previous fall!

On the return to their homeland, the remaining Northern Cheyennes, still in the Indian Territory, did not have to undergo the travails of their brothers who preceded them. The government allowed them to repatriate in two groups: one left the hated place of banishment in 1881 under the leadership of Little Chief,[19] the final one in the summer of 1883, except for the very few who elected to remain.

The last time the Cheyennes in Indian Territory resorted to arms was in the winter of 1881–1882, when they nearly starved because the government had reduced their rations. The energetic measures of the then commandant of Fort Reno, who distributed to the Indians what was due them, saved both whites and Indians from a precarious situation.[20]

I apologize for this long digression, but I found it difficult to remain silent about what should be fully publicized. The most recent history of this tribe again demonstrates the barbarity of our own race toward our natural compatriots, to whom we ascribe shortcomings we ourselves possess in no lesser degree. And then I could not fail to record feats whose heroes are worthy of an epic. In the ravine, too, and in the place where the last Cheyenne fell, let one "erect a monument and call the spot Thermopylae."[21]

There are about 4,200 Cheyennes and 2,300 Arapahos on the Darlington reservation. Among the Cheyennes there are around a hundred more women than men. Among the Arapahos the number of persons of both sexes is approximately the same. At the same time that the Northern Cheyennes were being transferred for the first time to the Indian Territory, the government sent roughly 900 Arapahos, who occupied the same territory with the aforementioned tribe, to a reservation in Wyoming, which they had to share with the Shoshone Indians.[22]

Let us first take a look at the outward appearance of the Northern Cheyennes and Arapahos. Both tribes embody the ideal Indian type. Bent noses and angular features are very widespread among them, as are tall, slender, and powerful figures. Nowhere did I find that the women bore so close a physical resemblance to the men than among these tribes. Another type, less slender and large, with

12. Little Chief, Northern
Cheyenne, ca. 1880
(after a contemporary
photograph).

a straight nose, occurs almost as frequently as the former. Sporadically I encountered types recalling the Apaches, others the broad, massive figures of the Utes. The complexion of both tribes is generally light brown, resembling no. 30 from the chromatic scale.

Partial albinism is not uncommon among these tribes. Although the skin color is normal, the
hair is pale brown or yellowish white; sometimes, too, with black and white intermingled.[23] The
eyes in these cases are not always light blue or otherwise light in color but are usually brown. Based
at least on superficial observation, their eyes were normal and did not display the phenomena I
observed among the Moquis and Zunis.

Just like the Utes, the Cheyenne and Arapaho men pluck out their eyebrows and eyelids,
giving their faces a bizarre, strident expression that immediately brings to mind the physiognomy
of a bird of prey. Far more common than I hitherto encountered among other tribes was the way
the feet pointed inward, both for women and men. Both had an elastic, stately, and quite rapid gait.

13. Bent Left Arm,
Cheyenne.

As for attire of both tribes, only the leggings and footwear are still original. Leggings and moccasins are of beautifully tanned soft leather, tastefully decorated with colorful beads, especially blue and white ones—the leggings with round disks of Berlin silver as well. The men generally wear trouser legs too—since the other features of trousers are missing—of thick dark blue cloth with broad fluttering hems and a wholly Indian couture. In addition, they wear a mantle, consisting of two blue woolen blankets sewed onto each other; this forms not only a cap for the head but is large enough to envelope their entire figure at the same time. Frequently they drape themselves in their blankets in picturesque fashion, as they once did in their mantles of bison hide. In this way they cover the lowest part of their faces and remain standing or sitting immobile in the position assumed, staring ahead of themselves for quite some time.

Indians wearing hats or those who have cropped their hair short are rare among the Cheyennes and Arapahos, but the Indian police, who wear light blue uniforms when they are on duty, and schoolboys constitute an exception in this respect. As a rule, the men wear their hair parted in the middle from the top and in behind in two long braids on both sides of their head or hanging loosely over the chest. The scalp lock, a thin, tightly intertwined braid, which is attached to a spot of the crown, rests either on the left, along the heavy side locks, or in the rear over their back.[24] The splendid garb with eagle feathers and otter hides such as of Bent Left Arm, an important Cheyenne, is worn only on special occasions such as big powwows and dances.

As is the case among Indians elsewhere, the attire and hairstyle of the women from these tribes is plainer than that of the men. Leggings and moccasins consist of one piece and are barely decorated, if at all. Jackets and short skirts of gray or colorful cotton have now replaced the leather garb from days past. The women's hair, parted in the middle, hangs in disorderly fashion shoulder length along the head.

How the government agent in his 1882 report can say that more than 6,400 Cheyennes and Arapahos wear partial citizens' attire is incomprehensible to me. Although the materials they use for their attire are partly of American fabrication, the style and cut are unmistakably Indian.

During my visits to various encampments in the vicinity of the agency, I was accompanied alternately by two young Cheyennes, Bullbear and Roman Nose, a former "Florida prisoner."[25] The seven days of my stay in Darlington were particularly inauspicious for my investigation. The season was exceptionally wet, and only two days was the weather favorable enough for undertaking an excursion. Heavy rain showers, accompanied by thunder, turned the plain into a vast morass, over which the somber, chill autumn wind bellowed, propelling dark, dank clouds ahead of itself through the turbulent sky. Not a ray of sun illumined the landscape, as dismal and dreary as a Dutch polder on a dark November day.

I visited the Cheyennes in particular. The Arapaho camp was situated along the other bank of the North Canadian River, and because there was no bridge, it was difficult to pay several visits. But the lack of an Arapaho interpreter, in particular, was the reason that I had a look at these Indians only once, and alone. However, because Cheyennes and Arapahos have lived together since time immemorial and speak languages from the same family besides, much of what I relate here regarding the manners and morals of the former is also applicable to the latter.

I have already spoken in passing of these Indians' tents (Chey, *wih*). They have the well-known—I should say, classic shape of Plains Indian dwellings—and wholly recall those of the Utes, which I described in the previous chapter. What was new for me, though, were the high enclosures of dry branches, which often surrounded the tents. They provide protection against wind and rain and in the winter against snow. The wide flap on the open top of the tent, from which the smoke can escape, is always turned away from the wind.

The household implements one finds inside the tents are largely of American make. In the wih of Bullbear Sr., an aged Cheyenne chief,[26] I even found three wooden beds! Only the white leather valises decorated with colorful drawings, described above for the Utes, recall days past, just as do the richly tanned carrying planks or cradles, with the beautiful covers belonging to them. The cradles of the Cheyennes have at their upper end two long flat wooden stakes diverging from each other, giving the whole contraption a light, graceful appearance.[27]

Except for firearms of the latest model, their weapons consist of bow and arrows, spears, and battle-axes. That the Cheyennes, as well as the Arapahos, take scalps is already evident from the aforementioned scalp lock.

Both also smoke the peace pipe, which is smoked not just at special ceremonies and gatherings, as one could imagine, but in the way other tribes smoke cigarettes. This latter habit is not in vogue with the Cheyennes, thus already betraying their northern origin. Many a warrior to whom I offered tobacco and paper did not know what to do with it, much less roll a cigarette.

In Bullbear's wih I smoked the calumet for the first time. The head *(heeoogk)* consisted of red catlinite, which the Cheyennes themselves now no longer retrieve from the sacred quarry in the north[28] but receive by mail from Sioux City, where these heads are manufactured by Americans and sold to the various Indian tribes. Now they buy their smoking tobacco from the Americans too, but with it they mix finely cut sumac leaves *(Rhus;* Chey. *mahénnohánye),* giving the smoke a mellow flavor. The pipe passed from mouth to mouth and eventually, after having made the round among six or eight persons present in the tent, came back to Bullbear, whose wife smoked with the men—something that certainly would not occur if women really were regarded as nothing more than beasts of burden. Before the old chief took the first draw, he pointed the stem *(heess)* of the pipe to the four winds, muttering a few words I did not understand.

Seldom have I seen an old man with a more venerable countenance. There was a trace of melancholy in the fine bronzed features; a cloud of earnestness hung over the wrinkled brow, enveloped by wavy locks. What must be going on in the soul of this chieftain who could perhaps recall more than seventy winters and could compare the past and present of his tribe—a comparison between a powerful, invincible nation, living from hunting and the booty of war, and a humiliated people, eating the bread of charity from its foe? Evidently he was flattered that I knew something about the heroic deeds of the Cheyennes and that I was more interested in their customs and mores than anyone he had encountered. He knew only very little English, but we spoke through his son as an intermediary, who rendered my questions into Cheyenne to the best of his ability.

The language has a harsh sound, is heavily staccato and full of sibilants. Although the languages of the Cheyennes and Arapahos were once included in the Dakota group, later investigations have indicated that they belong to that of the Algonquins.[29] But despite the mutual relationship of the two languages, a Cheyenne and Arapaho cannot understand each other if each person resorts to his own language. Not uncommonly, though, they have learned each other's language. Here intermarriage between persons from both tribes certainly helped a lot. Most of all, however, they resort to sign language.

The sign language is the lingua franca, I would almost say *volapük,*[30] of the Plains Indians from the British possessions to Texas. It has reached a high level of perfection and seems adequate in every respect for mutual contacts among these tribes. Thus I recall having attended a conversation between a Cheyenne and a Kiowa, which dealt with the theft of a horse and lasted twenty minutes without either person uttering a single word.

The sign language also includes signs for each tribe. For example, whenever Indians from different tribes meet one another, the first question both have is which people they belong to, whereupon a gesture ensues. So the Cheyennes' tribal sign is the crossing aslant of the index fingers, that of the Arapahos moving the right index finger up and down along the right edge of the nose. From Bullbear, I also learned what the tribal sign of the Utes was, something they themselves did not want to show me: both hands stretched out flat and rubbing each other are both stroked across the knee. The tribal sign of the Pawnees, as well as that of the Utes, the mortal enemies of the Cheyenne, consists in mimicking a wolf's ears because the Pawnees bear the name of "wolf people." That of the Sioux, friendly with the Cheyennes, consists of a cutting motion of the hand to the position of the throat because one of the appellations for this nation is "cutthroats."[31]

The Cheyennes call themselves *Tsetistás*, that is, "we." The name "Cheyennes" is most probably derived from *chiens*, given them by the first French trappers, because the Tsetistás eat a lot of dogs, just like their brethren the Arapahos, who have received from the Utes and Comanches the name of dog eaters.[32] The Arapahos are called *Hitannewóï-é*, that is, nipple people. The Utes are called *Mohgtawátan* or *Mohgtawaítan* (the black people), the Comanches *Shishiniwotsíhan* (the snake people). For the whites the Cheyennes have a name that possibly means "spider."

The Cheyenne nation numbers eight clans or gentes and four medicine societies. In days past, during the "making of medicine," which was associated with special, often secret ceremonies, these clans always camped in a fixed order. Presented in the form of a diagram schematically illustrated, three clans take the right side, four the left side, and one clan the upper end in a large circle, which is open at the bottom and whose midpoint is occupied by the medicine hut. The following clans were camped on the right, whose names I will try to relate as best I can: the eater people; a clan consisting of three divisions—the people from the bear's backside, the dog people, and the hill people; and the people of the red tents. The upper end of the circle is taken by a clan that consists of two divisions: the woolly and the mangy people. Finally, on the left camped the very destitute people, the eastern people,[33] the completely quiet people, and the bison people.[34]

Now that their style of life has changed, these customs are no longer observed. Even the medicine societies are slowly dying off because there are no longer any new members to replace the old ones. Possibly the Cheyennes have learned that the secret remedies of their magicians do not work and could not prevent the downfall of the tribe because there is more powerful "medicine" from the "spider people," the whites, who are as irresistible as the north wind and as numerous as blades of grass on the prairie. There are also seers and mediums among the tribe who predict the future from various signs and have contacts with the spirits of the dead. But in their imagination the ordinary members of the tribe constantly communicate, too, with their deceased relatives, of whom they are most fearful, sometimes to the point of dementia. Food is often placed in the ground so that nothing will be lacking the spirits and they will be favorably disposed toward the living. Both the Cheyennes and the Arapahos bury their dead in the ground. Their northern brethren, on the other hand, place the corpses in a recumbent position between the branches of a tree.

With the Sioux and other northern tribes the Cheyennes have—or rather had—in common the Sun Dance, a religious ceremony described many times.[35] In many cases the tortures the dancers thereby inflicted on themselves were a kind of expiation. A warrior, for example, whose wife was ill tried to free her from her sufferings and cure her by subjecting himself to frightful tortures. In addition, the Cheyennes had the Hunting Dance, whereby part of the Indians disguised themselves as bison, antelope, and other animals and another part played the role of hunters who, armed with ridiculously small bows and arrows, gave a parodied presentation of their usual hunts. Another dance, nowadays carried out only rarely, consists of a number of men jumping in and around a fire, constantly moving about, roasting pieces of meat that they pulled out of the fire with their fingers, placing them glowing hot on their bare shoulders, and eventually consuming them.

A game I saw being played not infrequently by the children in the camps of both tribes consists in casting forward a long stick, on the tip of which the point of a bison horn is attached. As soon as the stick *(sko, skaô)* stops moving, they toss another one, thereby trying to hit the first one.

That these Indians are addicted to card games and are also keen on strong drink hardly goes without saying. Presently, however, it is quite difficult for them to get the latter because of strict government measures. Ten years ago the large-scale whiskey trade between inhabitants of Kansas and Indians, particularly Arapahos, was broken up with the arrest and conviction of a number of people who were bent on swindling the Arapahos and thus exploiting them. Because of poverty, they were on the verge of taking up their tomahawks. The firm price one of these "pioneers of civilization" demanded for a gallon (roughly 4 1/2 liters) of bad whiskey diluted with water was a horse or five tanned buffalo hides.

Notwithstanding the many parallels one can draw between Cheyennes and Arapahos, in other respects they have a quite different character. The Arapaho is not as proud and cavalier and has more the Apache's character. The Arapaho women have very loose morals; the Cheyennes, on the other hand, are possibly the most chaste of all Indian tribes. The immorality of the former is not without influence on the tribe because congenital syphilis and scrofula are quite widespread, as is immediately evident from superficial observation. The modesty of Cheyenne women is limited not just to relations with whites but at the same time extends to their male tribal compatriots as well.[36] I noted above that the Cheyennes and Arapahos not infrequently intermarry but with the understanding that men from the latter tribe take Cheyenne girls. The opposite rarely occurs, probably because girls from the Arapahos lack the charms of their sisters from the Cheyenne tribe.

In contrast to other tribes, the Cheyennes do not kill twins but carefully rear them. Robert von Schlagintweit maintains that the Plains Indians generally take so little care of their children that all who are not naturally strong perish. This comment leads me to believe that when he was among the Indians, he never bothered to take a good look or did so in a biased frame of mind.[37] For my part, I have never witnessed anything but the most tender treatment of children, both by men and women, among all tribes I visited—even among the otherwise so pitiless Apaches.

I would also like to protest in the strongest terms against the same author's assertion—which probably parrots what many others have said—that the Indians regard their women as nothing more than beasts of burden and labor.[38] When circumstances are taken into account, her situation is no more abject and her lot no harsher than among the lower classes of the "civilized" nations from our own race, and indeed better.[39] Truly, almost everything the renowned writer reports about the character and customs of the Indians is a hodgepodge of often misleading generalizations. I would not have cited the aforementioned writing, any more than many others of similar content, were the author just some ordinary commodity, but he is the celebrated explorer of India and Tibet. Precisely because his observations could gain acceptance do I raise my voice, albeit a feeble one, in opposition. A few more times I will have the opportunity to return to Schlagintweit.

Among the Arapahos the worldwide custom that a man may not look at his mother-in-law is in vogue.

The Cheyennes' form of government, like that of the Arapahos, is democratic. Usually the bravest and wisest men are chosen as chiefs. This dignity appears to be hereditary only as an exception. Neither of these tribes possesses a supreme chief, but the chiefs, as a collective body, manage the whole [tribe] and call for a council in difficult cases. During my stay the Cheyennes had no less than thirty-six chiefs, including Whirlwind[40] and Bullbear; the Arapahos, on the other hand, had just two, but these were the well-known Powder Face and Left Hand, both of whom I got to know.[41]

I once had supper with them in the company of the government agent and Captain R. H. Pratt, superintendent of the Indian Training School in Carlisle in Pennsylvania.[42] They were splendid, impressive figures of dignified countenance, who inspired confidence. They used knives and forks and otherwise had impeccable table manners and carried on conversation with us, partly in their own language through intermediation of the agent,[43] partly in broken English. This concerned primarily the recruitment of children from the tribe for the aforementioned school. Generally the Indians nowadays are no longer as unwilling as in the past to have their children educated by whites. Most of them realize that the chance for continuing their old nomadic existence has gone forever and that they have only the choice between following "the white man's ways" or doom.

No fewer than eighty children of the Cheyennes, as well as of the Arapahos, are already receiving instruction in the eastern states, especially at Carlisle—and with beneficial results, so it seems. At the agency itself, where there are various schools, headed by missionaries, including Mennonites, more than 200 children of both sexes are receiving instruction. Most are just as intelligent as white children of the same age, and not a few display musical talent.

It is perhaps inconceivable how even adult Indians, since they have outgrown children's shoes, can change their way of life, but those whom I had in mind had gone through a hard school and languished long years in captivity in sweltering Florida, far from their homeland. Most who had survived the time of trial and had seen their land again had been transformed from savage warriors to peaceful, orderly men who were engaged in agriculture and livestock raising or performing work at the agency. But they had outstanding guidance—strict, it is true, but humane—from Captain Pratt, who had first fought against them as a cavalry officer, later became their educator, and spent several years with them in Florida. The most explicit example was one of the captives: He Who Makes Medicine, or, to call him by his Christian name, David Pendleton, who as an Episcopal deacon preaches Christianity to his tribal compatriots.[44]

More than 1,700 Indian households from the Darlington reservation are, as the government report puts it, "engaged in agriculture" or other "civilized pursuits." In comparison with other so-called savage tribes, this may have quite some significance. Their livestock consists primarily of 6,000 horses and about 3,000 head of cattle. The aforementioned facts contradict Schlagintweit's judgment that the bitterest poverty can, at most, turn the Indian into a thief and murderer and never into a useful worker who can earn his livelihood in honorable fashion.[45] He also seems to be unaware that many tribes in North America own large herds. It surprises him that not a single tribe became a pastoral people despite favorable conditions.[46] But how can there be any discussion about this before the arrival of the Europeans, who first introduced the animals needed to form herds?

For the Cheyennes and Arapahos' sake, I hope that the government will not again make them switch reservations, as it did a few years ago, when they were transferred from the northwest of the Indian Territory to their present domain. Nothing, however, more impedes their development and progress in civilization than the repeated compulsory change of residence.

Still another obstacle stands in the way of nearly all the tribes of the Indian Territory. These are attempts by a certain "Captain" Payne from Kansas to open the territory to white settlers and take from the Indians their final ground. This unprincipled adventurer repeatedly attempted to conquer the territory with armed troops, frontiersmen, but was just as frequently put back across the border, along with his entire army corps, by American troops and the Indian police. "Captain" Payne, better known as "Oklahoma Payne," based on the Choctaw name for the Indian Territory, is most likely supported by some big railway companies, whose lines run through Kansas and who would have a strong interest in opening the Indian Territory to white settlement. Payne is the greatest disturber of the peace for the Indians, who do not know how his efforts will play out. Paralyzed by uncertainty, they show no eagerness for tilling the soil, which they undoubtedly would display if they were assured of its undisturbed possession.[47]

During one of my walks through the Cheyenne camps, I had the opportunity to witness the much renowned stoicism of the Indians. A young man named Núchkium showed me a terrible wound he had inflicted on himself cutting wood with an ax. The wound was old, quite neglected, and looked very bad. In spite of the intense pain I subjected him to cleaning the wound, not a muscle of his face twitched, nor did he heave a sigh. With taut attention a band of Indians stood around him and observed even my slightest movements. When Núchkium withdrew his foot properly bandaged, I could read gratitude and contentment in everyone's gaze.

Repeatedly I was asked in various wihs about medicines that I could not always provide. I referred them to the agency physician, who preferred to sit and wait in his office for patients who did not come instead of going around in the camp, where he could have found hundreds who were laid up with malaria and rheumatism, at the mercy of their medicine men, in whom their faith was shaken. But it was more in keeping with the interests of the personnel at the stores that a large number of quack remedies such as painkiller and the like were provided to these poor, ignorant people at double the price. Who would have ever thought that I would again find quack remedies, so widespread in my homeland, in the Indian Territory, in the heart of the Far West! Along with various epidemic diseases and strong drink, one could with full justification also call the quack remedies one of the precursors of "civilization."

To return once more to Indian stoicism, I must note that a rather large number of children, even boys, do not display anything at all like the self-control of their fathers. They bawl and cry *tout comme chez nous* [just like our own do].

Although I was also quite fortunate in obtaining varied information about the Cheyennes and Arapahos, anthropometry made no headway with them. Great shyness was evident in this regard. I could measure only eight men.[48] As for investigating the Cheyennes' sense of color, I found, as I did elsewhere, that they have no separate expression for individual colors even though they can see differences between various ones. Thus for them "green" = "blue like grass." The name for "red" is derived from the word for "blood" = *mah-eet*.

One of the most exotic scenes one can witness near the agency is the ferry on the Canadian, where numerous Indian riders wade across the river every day. Frequently two, sometimes three people are sitting on a horse—whether men, women, or children. A couple of times I myself resorted to this method of crossing and in fraternal fashion shared with a colossal Indian the slender back of his horse. The horses of these Indians lack the handsome bridles and saddles of the Utes and Navajos but have tails fashioned in a distinctive way. The whole thing looks like some huge tassels, some shifting across each other, terminating in a sharp point.

Because the idea of continuing my journey on a buckboard again, after the experience just undergone, did not appeal to me, I sent a request to the commandant of Fort Reno, which is two miles southwest of the agency, to provide me a horse and an escort so that I could head to Anadarko. Although I requested Major D. first personally and later once more in writing, my request was turned down for no valid reason. This is the only time I could complain about American officers. Moreover, none of the cattlemen in the area wanted to risk his horses, without a definite need, on the long route with swollen rivers and streams, and the agency vehicles were temporarily gone. So, on October 17th, late in the afternoon, I was left with no other choice than to mount a buckboard once more—this time as the sole passenger—and undertake the ride to the agency of the Comanche and Kiowa Indians.

Taking the route across by way of Fort Reno, after having followed a rolling prairie and a sandy path, we have reached the northern bank of the Canadian within three and a half hours. A couple of campfires of freighters show that the water is very high and they dare not make the crossing. Meanwhile the full moon has risen and illuminates the swiftly rushing river, which provides a very enchanting spectacle at this hour, flowing along silent, heavily wooded banks. For a long time we deliberate whether we should cross or spend the night along the edge of the stream, when an Indian on horseback, who crossed the stream in huge zigzag lines, made us aware that crossing with a lightweight little wagon like ours was feasible. Ten minutes later we have reached the other bank safe and sound and there have our evening meal, which consists of a little corned beef and a draught of whiskey. Through rolling prairies, alternating with forests of post oak, we follow the route sixteen miles farther to Spring Creek to change mules.

Until 1 A.M. we continue our ride because we discover Sugar Creek so swollen that a crossing at nighttime is inadvisable. During the marvelous night, moon and stars are mirrored in the motionless watery surface and the dark trees along the bank join with the slender rushes, which are gently waving, while a fragrant breeze wafts across the fields. Here one can behold an image much like the kind Lenau has evoked.[49]

We have unhitched the mules and spread our blankets on the sand of the bank and sleep in expectation of the next morning. But over yonder, a short distance away, arise a couple of tall cone-shaped huts. There is a fire where we can get warm. We push aside the curtain of the low entryway and find ourselves in a spacious dwelling with sleeping, half-naked Indians, resting on beds, which are situated just above the ground along the wall. Without speaking a word, one of the Indians stands up and tosses more wood onto the fire, which occupies the middle of the hut and before long communicates its beneficial warmth. Then, comforted, we go to our beds outside.

After the sun had risen, we consulted with a couple of Indians, who came out of the huts and appeared to belong to the Wichita tribe, regarding the condition of Sugar Creek. It was a good thing we had not made the attempt during the night because after we had persuaded these Indians to bring both the vehicle and the mules to the other side, the former completely vanished beneath the surface of the water and the mules had to swim. Meanwhile the driver and I put the mailbag and the baggage on our backs and carried them a bit farther to a narrow stretch of the creek, then across on a tree trunk lying above the water to the other side, where we set our dripping wet carriage into motion again.

At 9 A.M. we reached Anadarko, where I stopped at one of the filthiest inns I have ever encountered—the rendezvous of cowboys. Anadarko consists of a number of wooden houses and stores, which are quite far apart and are distributed along both banks of the Washita or Wishita River. Although this place is much smaller than Darlington, it can, however, boast of a wooden bridge, definitely a tremendous luxury for this region.

In many places the landscape is quite enchanting. There is undulating, indeed almost hilly ground, and dense trees such as oaks, elms, and cottonwoods cover not just the banks of the river but the more remote region as well. But here, too, the water owes its dark brown-red color to the soil, which consists of Triassic sandstone. There are some scattered camps in the district, and with their bustling activity they form a picturesque backdrop to the landscape.

The reservation, of which Anadarko is the agency, consists of two sections: the region of the Wichitas and "affiliated bands" to the north of the Washita River and that of the Kiowas, Comanches, and Apaches south of it. There is perhaps no reservation in the realm of the Union with such a *"Völkergewirr"* [medley of races]. But the nine tribes of this reservation together number not quite 4,200, which becomes clear when one realizes that some number barely fifty, others scarcely a hundred people. My resources, alas, did not allow me to tarry longer than four days in Anadarko, and thus I was not in a position to study each tribe individually. Besides the Kiowas, whom I prefer to discuss during my stay in Fort Sill, I came into contact with members of the tribes of the Wichitas, Caddos, Delawares, and Penetéka Comanches. I enjoyed the cordial support of the agent, Mr. P. B. Hunt.[50]

With the Towaconies, Wacoes, Keechies, Caddos, Delawares, and Penetéka Comanches, the Wichitas form the so-called affiliated bands. The first four tribes are linguistically related and belong to the Pawnee language group. The Towaconies and Wacoes are in reality just subdivisions of the Wichitas. The name "Wichita," "Wishita," or "Washita" was given them by their enemies, the Osage. They call themselves *Kiddekuhdeessuh* and are called "dark huts" *(Toogcannuh)* by the Comanches, because of their dwellings. The first whites who came into contact with the Wichitas called them "Pawnee-Picts," because of their habit of painting themselves, a custom that has long since lapsed.[51] Their original domain was situated near the Missouri, it seems. From there they moved to the Arkansas and Neosho and once had one of their settlements on the spot where the city of Wichita in Kansas is now. Driven from there by other, more hostile tribes, they moved southward at long intervals to the mountainous region to which they gave their name. For a long time one of their bands established itself "at the bend of a river between red hills" and thus received the name "Towaconies." The three Wichita tribes together number about 400, the Keechies by themselves not quite eighty.

These tribes are peace loving by nature and have never been hostile to the whites. Certainly their limited number is a major reason for this situation. For a long time now they have abandoned their savage lifestyle and even partially embraced Christianity. No longer is there much distinctive about their finery and attire. Their long hair, the broad leather belts with large, round Berlin silver plates worn by the squaws, and leather moccasins are now the only things, apart from their distinctive huts, that recall the past. Their clan system, too, seems to have fallen into disuse.[52]

The huts I referred to above with a single word consist of pliant poles, approximately five to six meters long, which are bent over at the tip and attached to each other, while the stout bottom end of these poles, placed in the ground, occupies a circle of four to five meters. This frame is covered with willow branches and long grass so that the hut looks like a cross between a gigantic beehive and a pointed haystack. A hole in the top and the low entryway are the only openings of these huts, which are very dark inside. Now, though, many Wichitas live in American-style houses, which rise up in the middle of their cornfields. The members of this tribe whom I saw were of the "redskin type" without, however, the proud, martial expression of the Cheyennes.

Just like the Wichitas, the Caddos, too, have almost completely deviated from the lifestyle of their fathers. Merged with a number of small, kindred tribes, they number approximately 550. Sixty years ago they left their dwellings in western Louisiana and moved to the banks of the Brazos River in Texas, while part of them moved to the land of the Choctaws, later to join up again with the others and establish themselves in the Indian Territory. Among the remnants of the tribes now incorporated among the Caddos, I will name just the Nadákos or Naráko[53] and the Ionies or Haínai, originating from the Sabine River, the Naketoes Haïsh and the Beloxis, of whom the ten or twelve remaining members have lost their language and taken that of the Caddos.[54] The Caddos call themselves *Hasínai*. The name "Caddos" is probably derived from a word of the Nadáko's dialect.[55]

Apart from sign language, Comanche is the language understood and spoken by all tribes of this reservation in their dealings with one another. The tribal sign of the Caddos consists of imitating a movement like that of the nose being pierced, recalling their former custom of piercing the nose. That is why they are still called *Mósi*, which means "pierced noses," by the Kiowas.

Both hunting and war are part of the Caddos' history, as well as the custom of scalping and painting their faces red in their wars with the Osages.

An intelligent Caddo Indian, George Parton, whose Caddo name was Tátassi,[56] could not even name for me all the names of his former clans. He only knew those of the Wolf, Panther, Bear, Bison, Beaver, Raccoon, and Crow. As a distinguishing mark the members of the first clan cut off a piece of their ear. Members of the same clan could not intermarry. In contrast to many other tribes among the Caddos, succession is in the male line. The dignity of chief *(káhadi)* is not hereditary. The one with the best qualifications for this position is chosen.

Although only a few of the Caddos profess Christianity, polygamy is no longer in vogue.[57]

Their method of interment resembles that of the Wichitas: when the grave is filled, a number of stakes are driven into the ground in a slanting direction so that they intersect roughly in the middle above the grave and form a barrier against wild animals.

As for the names of colors, as they are provided me by the aforementioned George Parton, it seems that the Caddos indicate blue and purple with the same word—*hassahacoo*—but have a special word for green, namely *bághanosháhagh,* and for the concept of color have a special word, to wit, *pitjáwa*.

Near my "hotel," in a small branch hut, I encounter an elderly, sickly Indian woman, who squats and grieves. Through signs, she explains to me that she has been abandoned by her people, the Apaches, and has neither fire nor food. I give her what I have in my knapsack and visit her every day, watching with satisfaction as she warms her stiff limbs by a flickering wood fire and gratefully accepts my humble gifts. Leaving elderly, feeble people—and often, too, sick people of lesser age—to their fate is a prevailing custom among many Indian tribes and is connected to their nomadic lifestyle.

The Apaches of these regions, just a few of whom I was able to observe, seem to be related to the Mescalero Apaches. In attire they deviate somewhat from their tribal compatriots in Arizona and more closely correspond to the Plains Indians. They are best known under the names of *Táshi* and *Essekwitta*, given them by the Comanches. There are also some Lipan Indians among them, belonging to a small Apache tribe, whose members are scattered far and wide among other Indians. The Apaches of this reservation number approximately 340.

Among the Indians transferred from other regions to the banks of the Wishita are also about eighty Delawares, who are the remnant of the ancient, once powerful tribe immortalized by Fennimore Cooper. With approximately 700 others, they have sought an abode among the Cherokees. Driven from their forests in the New England states, they slowly moved west of the Mississippi to later establish themselves in the Indian Territory. Since their forced exodus, though, many of their warriors roam through the entire western region of the Union, from the eastern prairies to the Pacific Ocean, from the Missouri to the Rio Grande, spreading death and terror among other tribes, frequently returning years later and bringing a string of scalps as a trophy of these distant journeys. As trappers, trailblazers, and scouts, often in government employ, they gave rein to their wanderlust and warlike desire, demonstrating through their deeds that they were worthy of the ancient renown.

I have met just three Indians from this tribe: two adult men and a young man. The former were very ugly, with gross, repellent features and long, disheveled hair. Both wore leggings and a breechcloth, in addition to leather moccasins. And despite the fact that their people have been in contact with civilization for approximately two and a half centuries, they looked nearly as savage as the neighboring Kiowas and Apaches. The young man, on the other hand, was wearing citizen dress and spoke fluent English. When I learned that these Indians belonged to the Delaware tribe, I said, "Lenape?" to them by way of a question. With ill-disguised astonishment that someone who was utterly alien to them knew the name that they gave themselves, they uttered a deep guttural, *Auh, auh!* thereby nodding assent with their heads. However, when I told them through the young man's intermediation that I had seen their ancient enemies, the Iroquois, far out in the east by the great lakes and had crossed the ocean to learn about the red man's life, they then looked at me with distrust and refused to have anything more to do with me. From the agent I later learned, however, that the Lenape are very attached to tradition and not only speak their own language almost exclusively but have also preserved their religion and various ancestral customs.

Part of the Penetékas, or Honey Eaters, the southernmost tribe of the Comanches, numbering approximately 160, settled a few years ago among the "affiliated bands" and since then were reckoned among these tribes and reported as such in the government reports. One morning my attention was drawn by loud lamentation, which seemed to be coming from the woods along the riverbank. After I had made my way with difficulty through the terrain—which had been made impassable not only by high brush and long grass but also by the water from the river, which had suddenly overflowed its banks—I came to an open area where there was a small Comanche encampment. There I found a number of men and women in mourning, standing by a wagon hitched to mules. Looking more intently, I noticed that a body wrapped in blankets lay on this wagon and recalled having heard the day before of an old chief who lay mortally ill. Besides the unclad driver, an Indian sat at the head of the body, while on every rim of the wagon three men were standing at some distance from each other with their faces turned toward the body. Six or eight women, with their upper bodies and legs down to their knees unclad, stood behind the wagon and, as a sign of mourning, had thus slashed their faces and trunks with sharp knives so that blood was trickling down their faces, breasts, and shoulders. Both men and women were raising a loud, incessant commotion, consisting of a kind of prolonged wailing and sobbing. When my presence was noticed, I was given to understand by a discontented gesture and angry look that I must leave. Though I did not comply, the mourning took its course nonetheless. A number of unsaddled horses, whose tails had been almost completely cropped, stood scattered among the trees. Eventually the wagon rode away to the prepared grave over yonder behind the hills, and after the cries of lamentation had momentarily reached their climax, the mourners dispersed. When I returned to the spot a couple of hours later, the entire camp with all its inhabitants had vanished.

As I later learned, there was a particular reason for the use of wagons at this ceremony. When the chief lay dying, some Comanches came to the agent and asked him what he preferred, whether the body should be buried in the Comanche fashion, that is, on horseback and with the giving away of all the deceased's possessions, or in the white manner. When the agent had replied that he preferred the latter way, they had complied. Once again this proves how one distinctive custom after the other among these people is being lost and what was current yesterday has already vanished today. Mr. Hunt further informed me that shortly after the chief's death he had gone inside his tent and found the body in a sitting position, handsomely painted and attired, with a couple of bison hides adorning his head. Thus had he departed for *Apameen,* "the land of the fathers," which is what the Comanches call the place they all go to after their death.[58]

The schools affiliated with the agency at Anadarko certainly have contributed in no small measure to making these Indians gradually alter their lifestyle over the passage of time. One hundred and thirty children are already receiving instruction there, while approximately thirty are receiving their education at Carlisle. Because I lacked the time to visit these schools personally, I do not wish to expiate further on this topic. I only want to note that here, too, an ex-Florida prisoner, a Kiowa, made a useful contribution toward civilizing his tribal compatriots. But generally the Kiowas are less inclined to adapt to civilization than the Comanches.

However much I regretted having to leave Anadarko, because of the Indians, I was delighted to turn my back on it because of the wretched stay in the log cabin where I had to spend the night in the company of six or eight cowboys in an attic, in beds with straw sacks, the covers of which were of the most dubious white. The menu, too, left much to be desired, though one could hardly say my palate had been pampered during the last ten months. Half-cooked *camotes* or sweet potatoes, tough meat or rancid bacon, and the black, acrid coffee, without which I cannot imagine any meal in the West, were the steady fare that appeared on the rude table, only to vanish into the cattle herders' famished bellies in an incredibly short time. I got my money's worth because for board and lodging I paid the extraordinarily low price out west of a dollar a day.

So, on the evening of October 21 I said farewell to Anadarko once more—this time the last— to mount a buckboard, with Fort Sill as my destination. I would not forget the last ride. We had not been riding for very long when heavy, uninterrupted rainstorms broke loose, enveloping the prairie in a pitch-black night. When the last bit of candle burned out in the sole lantern, we went astray in the darkness and got lost. Thoroughly drenched and numbed, we wandered about for hours over unfamiliar hill and dale. At peril of drowning and losing baggage and everything else, we crossed the heavily swollen Cache Creek and after a dreadful, endlessly long night arrived early in the morning at the military post. The sun had reached its zenith before I had completely dried my togs in a small dwelling not far from the fort and I could decently pay my respects to the commandant and look the place over.

Fort Sill is the largest military post I have seen in the West. It is situated on a huge plateau 1,700 feet above sea level at the confluence of two small rivers, Cache and Medicine Bluff creeks.

14. Horse Back, Comanche, ca. 1880.

The surrounding area is quite enchanting. To the west arise the heavily wooded Wishita [Wichita] Mountains, like a secluded cluster of islands above the waves of the everlasting grassy ocean, which bounds the horizon in the other directions. Erected in 1868 under the name "Camp Washita," this post was selected during Sheridan's campaign that year as an important strategic point.[59]

The deputy commandant of Fort Sill promptly put me in contact with the military interpreter, Mr. Horace P. Jones, who had lived more than twenty years among the Comanches and enjoyed their complete confidence,[60] as well as with the former scout, Philip McCusker.[61] I owe it to them that I could visit various encampments without hindrance and meet a number of Indians, from whose accounts I have here culled the most important items.

After the Apaches, the Comanches are perhaps best known to the general public, who have read the latest novels about Indians and have in this way obtained a fairly accurate conception of this people. What may have been valid in the days of Mayne-Reid and Aimard is in large part now no longer the case. This proud and once mighty nation, too, has turned into a band of government beggars. Rendered powerless by lack of game, they have been tamed for good.

15. Solosa, son of Kiowa
chief Satanta, ca. 1880
(after a contemporary
photograph).

According to the Treaty of Medicine Lodge in 1867 they, along with the Kiowas and Apaches,
have come into possession of their present-day reservation. From 1874, when they last went on the
warpath, dates the tremendous transformation in their condition.[62] Some of the Comanches, however, just like a number of Kiowas, have become involved in cattle raising and some agriculture and
have thus shown that they have yielded to the inevitable. The Indian is philosophical by nature. As
soon as he realizes that nothing can be done in spite of his efforts, he submits with calm resignation, waiting for what may transpire.

The Comanches, reckoned at 30,000 forty to fifty years ago by Catlin,[63] estimated at 15,000
around 1850 by Schoolcraft,[64] now number barely 1,600 persons, including fewer than 350 men
at arms.[65] In historical times the Kiowas do not seem to have been as numerous. Schoolcraft estimates their numbers thirty years ago at 1,500. Now they number around 1,100, including approx-

Through the Indian Territory · Part 1

imately 270 men at arms. Among both tribes the women are far more numerous than the men, particularly among the Comanches.[66]

The Comanches or *Nimênim,* that is, "people of peoples," as they could once call themselves with pride, were the most powerful tribe of the southwestern prairies. Their plundering raids extended from Nebraska to over all of northeastern Mexico, though the greater part of Texas was their territory par excellence. Some dauntless warriors were not afraid to bid farewell to their tribe for years at a time and press ahead on their adventurous wanderings to California or the heart of Mexico. An old chief named Mowway[67] told me that about forty years ago he traveled so far south with some comrades that he encountered "little men covered with hair and with long tails, who lived in the trees." What Mowway saw, of course, were monkeys, and it is known that in America the northern limit of these animals is at a latitude of approximately 19°, that is, at the latitude of the peak of Orizaba. From this one can form an idea about the extent of their journey.[68]

Given the cosmopolitan nature of the Comanches, it can be no surprise that their language, after sign language, is understood and spoken by nearly all the nomadic tribes of the Southwest to some degree or another. There are even Sioux Indians who understand Comanche. As the dominant tribe, the Comanches were too proud to learn another language and forced the other tribes to use their own. Among their sworn enemies were the Utes and the Tonkaways; the latter they call *Nimêtéka* = "cannibals."[69] They also have waged many a bitter battle against the *Móhtawas* and *Wasahzj,* better known as Kaws and Osages.

In attire the Comanches, as well as the Kiowas, resemble the above-described Cheyennes and Arapahos. The most important difference I noticed consists in the Kiowas' footwear, which is especially lovely with fiery red square flaps that are ornamented along the edges with beads and hang down to the side of the foot below the ankles.

Among both tribes the "redskin type" is the dominant one such as in these two lithographs of a Comanche and a Kiowa, but with a number of Comanches, I noted a delicacy of features and a nobility of expression I have missed in most other tribes. Otterbelt, one of the most important chiefs, was an archetype of male beauty. A young warrior, *Monewístekwa* (He Who Strikes First), had facial features recalling a Greek image and was one of the handsomest people I have ever met.

As a rule, the Comanches are smaller[70] and less robust than the Kiowas, some of the men having gross features strongly recalling the Ute type. Both the Comanches and the Kiowas are generally quite light in complexion. Among the latter I found many with light brown eyes (roughly no. 2–4 on the scale). The Kiowas retain only the tips of their thin mustaches. Partial albinism is not uncommon among them.

Among both tribes live a number of Mexican captives, all told maybe fifty in number, who have almost completely adopted the manners and customs of the Indians and are treated by them as fellow tribesmen. When I once asked a couple of these people, including one with ash blond hair and light blue eyes, whether they were Mexicans, they replied: *"No, señor, somos indios!"* (No, sir, we are Indians).

In my investigation regarding the manners and customs of the Comanches, I attempted to determine the veracity of an article by Léon de Cessac that came to my attention before my journey.[71] The information from this traveler regarding the Comanches, which he claims to have obtained from a hunter who was their captive for thirteen years, seems upon investigation to be largely a hodgepodge of inaccuracies. Although I intend to discuss the aforementioned writing elsewhere and check it against my own experience, here I will only compare one item or another when the opportunity presents itself.[72]

The Comanches separated long ago from the Shoshones or Snake Indians, an event for which they have preserved in oral tradition. They are divided into seven small tribes of unequal strength, among which I would name just the Yampatéka, Tenéwa, and Penetéka.[73] The first and last tribes are named according to their favorite food, the *yampa* root *(Anethum)* and wild honey. *Téka* = "someone who eats" is derived from the verb *maréka* or *mareska* = "eat." The Comanches' tribal sign still recalls their origin: it is the mimicking of a writhing snake with the hand.

It appears that the Comanches already dominated the southwestern prairies before the Kiowas, who, according to their own tradition, came from the north on sleds with dogs harnessed in front. Although the oldest known dwelling places of the Kiowas were situated in the Rocky Mountains, in present-day Colorado, in historic times they have always lived among the Comanches.[74] Although both tribes since then have coexisted on an amicable footing, despite the great concord among them, they have, nevertheless, retained some distinct features. The greatest difference, though, consists in language. There are many languages related to Comanche. As far as we know, it belongs to the Numa group; Kiowa, on the other hand, appears to stand entirely on its own. With Apache-Navajo and Tuscarora,[75] Kiowa is one of those languages whose peculiar sound I will never forget. Kiowa, too, I could distinguish from a hundred other languages. Distinctive are the many nasal sounds and the absence of *r* and *v,* at the same time as the palatal consonants *dsj* and *tsj* and various gutturals appear—just as in many other American languages. A very distinctive sound—half nasal, half dental—that also appears in Wichita falls between the Arabic *dad* and *za.*

It is worth noting that the Kiowas constitute an exception to the custom of the Comanches and of various other Indian tribes of giving obscene personal names. Another Kiowa peculiarity is that they eat fish. While a Comanche will kill a bear without hesitation, a Kiowa will not do this except under great duress. The Kiowas' tribal sign consists of imitating the drinking of water by moving the hand up and down to mouth level with fingers spread out. The Indians toss water into their mouth with the hand, at least when they quench their thirst at a brook or pond while out in the field.

The tents of the Comanches and Kiowas resemble those of the other Plains tribes. In their case, too, canvas from "Uncle Sam" has replaced the painted bison hides. But it appears that tents (Com. *káni, kánik*) in the old style are still encountered on occasion. Among the Comanches, I found more huts and awnings made of branches than elsewhere. In days past, a village or encampment consisted of a large number of tents close together. But nowadays they do not go on their great bison hunts together, and for other reasons too this custom has lost its reason for being. So one only encounters camps consisting of a few tents.

Rides across the prairie to visit the encampments were enjoyable, all the more so because the weather was continually clear and lovely. A cool fall atmosphere had taken the place of the cold rainy days.

The soil of the prairies near Fort Sill consists primarily of clay and marl. In places where the grassy carpet does not cover the hard ground or where a stream such as Medicine Bluff Creek is surrounded by high rocky walls, a light gray, nearly white limestone comes into view. In the deep bottomland of the little rivers—frequently the source of malarial fevers, which ravage the inhabitants of Fort Sill—a fertile humus layer covers the ground. Here shady oaks pair up with stately cottonwoods and small willows, and already from afar they betray the capricious course of the numerous creeks, which intersect the land like a network of furrows. Here the pointed leaves of sumac, already colored red by autumn, flutter up and down through the wind. Over there a richly laden pecan nut tree has dropped its fruits. Yonder are numerous Chenopodiaceae with long grass blades all confusedly entwined together. Sometimes the eye espies once more old acquaintances from more temperate tracts: the prickly mesquite, where the ground is the driest, or the dark juniper trees framing the reddish bluffs along the water.

One moment a band of prairie fowl darts back and forth frightened, then a hare leaps up in front of your horse's hooves. Your greyhound companions, bent on a long race, gleefully go on the attack and pursue the game with dizzying speed. Your zest for the hunt and irresistible urge for space and movement make you thrust your spurs into your steed's flanks. Snorting, it shakes its mane and speeds onward with the swiftness of the wind. If only you could always ride so directly across the endless grass oceans, bathing in a sea of light. That is the steppe of the West, which you have dreamed of. At that moment you understand the poet's plaint, full of melancholy longing, when from afar he longs for the open spaces and movement and invokes the plains, his plains of America, without limit or boundary, and he chants:

> *Room! Room to turn round in, to breathe and be free,*
> *And to grow to be giant, to sail as at sea*
> *With the speed of the wind on a steed with his mane*
> *To the wind, without pathway or route or a rein.*
> *Room! Room to be free. . . .*[76]

But the bison, which he sees moving across the steppe in numberless herds, like a thundering storm cloud, have vanished. You can and must gaze toward the farthest horizon, off to the west, if you are still to see just one—but to no avail. At most, the light coat of an antelope appears as a tiny moving dot against the grass, to swiftly vanish for good.

After bison, antelope and deer were the most important food of the Comanches and Kiowas, and though the former animals are still hunted, the Indians now rely almost exclusively on their government rations and the small herd of cattle they have begun tending. Both tribes also eat the prairie dog, the Comanches a small tortoise as well. The liver of cattle or bison was never eaten—bone marrow quite often, however. Vegetable nutriment includes the fruits of the persimmon *(Diospyros),* from which a kind of cake is made and the flavor of which very much resembles that of our currant-rye bread. Only twenty-five years ago did the Comanches begin cultivating corn, and de Cessac's assertion that already well before this time they grew corn and watermelons seems without foundation.[77]

Once, while visiting the camp of the Comanche chief, Tabenánneke, at the foot of Mount Scott, in the Washita [Wichita] Mountains, I realized how much value Indians can sometimes attach to objects. When I asked whether I could buy a round leather war shield *(tope),* Tabenánneke responded that for no price in the world would he surrender this because it had shielded him since his youth and accompanied him on all his campaigns. Out of friendship for Koostjeravo (Bison Chief, as Mr. Jones is called) he would let me look, however. Then he beckoned to a squaw to remove the many pieces of cloth covering the shield. The precious object rested on three sticks, which were stuck in the ground outside the kánik and was covered as well with a leather case, which the chief did not remove, though. On the interpreter's advice, I did not touch the shield. Indeed, Tabenánneke himself did not do that either. When I had personally thanked him, it was again carefully covered.

There are clear distinctions regarding the Indians' property. Only the very ground they inhabit do they own in common. Many times it has happened to me that in buying or trading for ethnographic items I confronted the problem of the owners being absent, without the blood relatives being moved to enter into negotiation. Also, not infrequently it happened that a father or mother told me: "That belongs to my child; I cannot sell it; if my child wants to, that's fine."

As a rule, there is everywhere mutual respect for personal property by members of the same tribe. It is frequently the case that during their residents' absence, huts with household goods, weapons, etc., remain a whole day or longer without surveillance, without anyone else daring to go inside the hut, much less steal something from it. In this respect, too, the "civilized" nations could learn from the "savages." On the other hand, theft from other hostile tribes is deemed a kind of right of war.

The original weapons of the Comanches are the bow *(eth, hoomok)* and arrows *(páka),* which are kept in a quiver *(hóko)* of puma hide—as they are elsewhere—and a long lance *(tsjik).* The arrows now all have iron points. Some years ago, when the government gave the Comanches plows and other agricultural implements, they had no better idea of how to use them than breaking up all the iron and making it into arrowheads and lance tips. Some time ago they had the practice of coating their arrows with rattlesnake venom, but because they put themselves, as well as their children, in jeopardy, they gave up this practice. Apparently these Indians never used tomahawks. On the other hand, they had war whistles *(hoke),* prepared from the brachium of an eagle and used in attack. They were familiar as well with another kind of reed flute *(wónuh)* that serves as a musical instrument. The original saddles *(nárinno)* of the Comanches greatly resemble those of the Utes but here, too, have been almost completely supplanted by Mexican saddles.

The Comanches' disposition is ebullient and lively. They combine a great inclination to jesting with a keen spirit of observation that puts them in a position where they can immediately see the comic side of persons and things. Addicted to dice and horse races, like most Indians, they also spend a considerable part of their time singing and dancing and telling stories, with animal fables playing an important role. They engage in peculiar, organized debates, with the men putting each other to the test. These certainly contribute a great deal to their well-known acumen and insight at gatherings. At these debates each person poses in turn a question, which is discussed by the other participants. One will dispute, for example, over questions such as these: whom would you rescue from death, your wife or your child, if you could only rescue one of them? If someone gave you a choice of giving up your horse or your tobacco, which would you choose?

Thanks to their far-flung journeys and their frequent commerce with various tribes and with Mexicans, the Comanches have a more cosmopolitan, unbiased view of matters than other Indians and are in a better position to form accurate judgments of circumstances and things. That they are a step above many of their racial compatriots is evident from the women's participation in men's deliberations and conversations, something that, as far as I can see, is unknown to the aforementioned authority of de Cessac, who harps on the old, hundred-times repeated theme regarding the abuse of women.[78]

The Comanches are polygamous and, as a rule, marry very young, perhaps the reason why many marriages are childless and why they generally have few children. Although as a rule marriage is a contract, which is concluded after negotiations between both sides, abduction occurs now and then.

When twins are born, one of them is killed. Probably they find it degrading when a woman, like dogs, has more than one offspring. Or perhaps they proceed from the premise that it is better that one dies than that both suffer want. But maybe the belief originally had as its basis that each of the twins had a separate father. Although parturition occurs easily, as a rule, there are certain women in the tribe who practice Lucina's art.[79]

Women's lifestyle before marriage is quite liberated, but only with respect to fellow tribesmen. No more than in the case of Utes would they have liaisons with whites. Formerly, adulterous women were punished by shooting an arrow through the foot. Later the Apache practice of cutting off noses came into currency, but this custom, too, has for all practical purposes vanished. Whenever a Comanche squaw is suspected of adultery, she is forced to state under oath that she is innocent. In this case she makes an incision into her hand or arm with a knife and smears the blood on her lips, thereby avowing her innocence while invoking "the Father" (the Supreme Being, the sun) and everything that is sacred to a Comanche. Rarely if ever is such an oath false because they fear that otherwise the "Father" will bring down upon her sickness or a horrible death. But even without oaths one can rely on the assurances and promises of the Comanches and of Indians generally. Precisely their faith in one's word, once given, means that they do not understand the breaking of promises and treaties by the government, and their confidence, once shaken, gives way to distrust and disdain.[80]

Although I was only able to learn very little about the Comanches' religion, it is clear that it is a form of Sabianism. They worship—as do so many other primitive peoples—the sun, whom they call the "Great (Beneficent) Father" *(Tábe* or *Ta'ab Sétsja)* and to whom they ascribe the creation of all things. Montezuma or a sacred fire, which according to de Cessac is constantly maintained, they have never known, nor have they ever worshiped the Aztec ruler.[81]

Whenever a Comanche speaks of dying, he says, *"Apameen!"*—a combination of *ápa* = "father" and *mínam* = "go," "come," and signifying, "Father, (I) am coming (to you)." Apameen is the land he goes to after death. This is the "happy hunting ground" of the writers of Indian novels, a designation unknown to the Comanches. According to their beliefs, not just Comanches—men, women, and children—go to Apameen but all wild animals as well. When I asked the old chief Mow-wé whether he thought that the whites would go to Apameen too, he responded: "We do not know, but I suppose that they have their own place. We have enough trouble looking after ourselves. Let the whites search for their own Apameen." Whenever the sun is about to set and its final rays bathe the horizon in a red glow, the Comanches believe that the red dust clouds are driven up high by thousands of blessed Comanches dancing in rows in far-off Apameen.

The clear, calm nights in these stretches provided me the opportunity to learn something about the Comanches' knowledge of the stars. For the brightest stars and constellations they have special names, which is not surprising for a people living in endless steppes, who frequently had to use the stars as a guide on their long journeys. For them the North Star is the star par excellence; they call it *"the* star" = *Tatsinope.* The morning star is called *Tátatsinope;* Orion, *Tadémemo;* the Pleiades, *Soweté;* the Milky Way, *Essehabit;* Charles Wain, *Woeguhpoke,* etc. For the sun, as a heavenly body, and for day the Comanches have the same word = *tábe* or *ta'ab;* for the heavens they use the expression "blue cloud"; for thunder "the clouds cry out."

In one of his two works, Colonel Dodge states that the Indians have no special names for the seasons.[82] I can give no more credence to this assertion in regard to other tribes than I can as far as the Comanches are concerned. They make a distinction not only for our four seasons but also for a number of phases in each of them. Where observation of nature is concerned—whether of climate or conditions of soil or terrain, animals or plants—the Indians make even more distinctions than we do. Not infrequently their mythology provides an explanation for the wherefore of different phenomena.

A peculiarity of the Comanche language is the continual transformation some of its vocabulary undergoes. For example, if a person who is called "Eagle" or "Bison" and is the bearer of this name dies, then people will pick another term for these animals because it is impermissible to speak a dead person's name.[83] This custom is widespread not only among the American Indians but among a number of people in other parts of the world as well, as is the custom that a person may not cite his own name, probably based on the belief that a bad influence will result from this. Whenever I wanted to know an Indian's name, for either men or women, I always had to turn to another person because they themselves never respond.

The Comanches' form of government is democratic. Hereditary right, insofar as it concerns the dignity of the chief *(parávo)*, is unknown, even though de Cessac maintains the opposite.[84] Their law is the *talio* [i.e., *lex talionis*]: eye for an eye, tooth for a tooth. The exaction of blood vengeance can be bought off by the party who has committed the murder.

Among the dances of the Comanches, I will name just the "dance of the big house" *(pikáni niskêra* or *níthkâdo),* also in vogue among the Kiowas and called *káochtoo* by them. This dance is held every year when the cottonwood loses its leaves, and its intent is to entreat blessings for the nation. Those who take part in these dances must fast for four days and then may chew only willow bark. Besides a large hut, a bison head is necessary for this ceremony. This is stuck on a pole in the ground, and offerings are brought to it. Year by year the performance of this dance becomes more onerous, because of the difficulty finding a bison. Well ahead of time hunters head out to the chasms of the Llano Estacado (Com. *Piyánowit* = great range), where the last remnants of the great southern herd have sought a place of refuge.

The stay at Fort Sill remains one of my most pleasant memories from the West. The small, dilapidated dwelling at the edge of the woods bordering Cache Creek, where I had set up my headquarters, offered me a tranquil little nook where, after returning from a long ride, I surrendered myself to a dreamy repose in a hammock on the veranda. It was lovely there morning and evening, and after the roaring cannon shot, which rang across the plain at daybreak and the close of day, nature again returned to its calm repose, while the sun sent a splendorous greeting to the dew-covered grass and colorful foliage or bathed the sky in its evening gold, hastily making way for a bright night, wherein the heavenly lights shone with unaccustomed brilliance.

On the part of the officers and their ladies, too, I experienced the fullest hospitality, and it was with a sense of regret that eight days after my arrival I bade farewell to Fort Sill to head to Dallas, Texas, and from there to visit the eastern part of the Indian Territory.

·····

Notes

1. HtK 1885: By Indian Territory one understands the extensive tract of land that in 1825 was set aside by the American government for practically all Indian tribes east of the Mississippi. The Indian Territory then, which was acquired by treaty with the Osage and Kansas Indians, also included the present-day state of Kansas. The accommodation of various tribes from the east in their new residences took place, though, only after 1830, with long pauses, and gave rise to long wars. Eds.: An annotated summary of Ten Kate's explorations and researches in Oklahoma can be found in "Herman F. C. Ten Kate, Jr.: An Adventurous Dutch Ethnologist in Indian Territory, 1883," ed. Augustus Veenendaal, *Chronicles of Oklahoma* (1995), 73 (1):32–51.

2. The Cheyennes and Arapahos are Algonquian-speaking peoples who moved from the area of Minnesota into the Plains, where they became allied in the nineteenth century. Eventually both groups divided, forming the Southern and Northern Cheyennes and Arapahos. By the treaty of Medicine Lodge in 1867 (see note 12 below), the Southern Arapahos, together with the Southern Cheyennes, were placed on a reservation in Indian Territory (Oklahoma). However, it was not until 1875 that the Southern Cheyennes, upon threat of force, agreed to remain on the reservation. Donald J. Berthrong, *The Cheyenne and Arapaho Ordeal* (Norman: University of Oklahoma Press, 1976), 3–47; Loretta Fowler, "History of the United States Plains since 1850," in *Handbook of North American Indians: Plains,* ed. R. J. DeMallie (Washington, D.C.: Smithsonian Institution, 2001), 13 (1):282.

3. HtK 1885: *The Hunting Grounds of the Great West,* 2nd ed., London, 1878, p. 142. Eds.: Richard Irving Dodge (1827–1895), a colonel in the U.S. Army who participated in the Indian wars of the 1870s, was the author of *The Plains of the Great West* (New York: Putnam, 1877), one of the most widely read contemporary guides to the American West. *Appleton's Cyclopedia of American Biography,* 7 vols. (New York: Appleton, 1888–1901), 2:194.

4. Fort Reno, in central Indian Territory, was established in 1875, with the first buildings erected in 1876 (see note 20 below). H. Merle Woods, *Fort Reno: The Protector* (El Reno, Oklahoma: El Reno American, 1975).

5. *Sesleria dactyloides = Bulbilis dactyloides* (Nutt.) Raf., buffalo grass.

6. .HtK 1885: "Chuck" or "chuckaway" is the western expression for food and above all in vogue among the cowboys.

7. "Wigwams" is a common European misnomer for *tipis*. It is surprising that even Ten Kate fell victim to this.

8. John D. Miles, a Quaker, was the Indian agent at the Cheyenne-Arapaho reservation from 1872 to 1884. He sponsored a controversial program of leasing Indian lands to cattleman in hopes of raising adequate revenue for the Cheyennes. Their vigorous opposition eventually led to his resignation. Stan Hoig, *The Peace Chiefs of the Cheyennes* (Norman: University of Oklahoma Press, 1980), 148, 154, 156. See also Flora Warren Seymour, *Indian Agents of the Old Frontier* (New York: Appleton, 1941), 236–53.

9. The Sand Creek Massacre occurred on the morning of November 29, 1864, when the Third Colorado Volunteers under Colonel John M. Chivington (1821–1894) attacked the sleeping Southern Cheyenne at their reservation on Sand Creek. Over 200 Cheyenne (mostly women

and children) were killed. News of the massacre led to condemnation and investigations by the Committee on the Conduct of War, a joint congressional committee, and the military. Chivington resigned in 1865. In retaliation the Cheyenne twice sacked Julesberg, Colorado, halted travel to Denver, and participated in the fighting on the Plains in 1865. Stan Hoig, *Sand Creek*, 1961.

10. Fort Robinson, Nebraska, was established near the Red Cloud Agency in 1874. It played a significant role in the 1876 Sioux Campaign in which General George Crook disarmed the Sioux and Colonel Ronald McKenzie compelled the Northern Cheyenne under Dull Knife (see note 18) to surrender. In 1877 Crazy Horse was killed at the fort. In 1879, as noted later in Ten Kate's narrative, some sixty-four Northern Cheyenne who escaped from Fort Reno, Indian Territory, and had been recaptured and confined at Fort Robinson were killed during a second attempt to escape. Howard R. Lamar, *The New Encyclopedia of the American West* (New Haven, Conn.: Yale University Press, 1998), 391; George Bird Grinnell, *The Fighting Cheyennes* (Norman: University of Oklahoma Press, 1956), 414–27.

11. HtK 1885: It does not say much for the residents of Denver that they gave an ovation to the villain whom they called the "hero of Sand Creek" when he visited the city in the autumn of 1883. Moreover, the man who led the troops as a scout at this event is still alive. I met him in Darlington. His name is Robert Bent, and his mother was indeed a Cheyenne! Eds.: Robert Bent (1841–1889) was a reluctant participant in and devastating observer of the Sand Creek Massacre. He was married to a Cheyenne and later settled among them in the Indian Territory. Dan L. Thrapp, ed., *Encyclopedia of Frontier Biography* (Norman: University of Oklahoma Press, 1965), 1:99.

12. The Treaty of Medicine Lodge was negotiated on Medicine Lodge Creek, Kansas, during the autumn of 1867 as members of a federal "peace commission" met with leading representatives of the Southern Plains tribes: Comanches, Kiowas, Cheyennes, Arapahos, and other smaller groups. The Southern Plains tribes were allotted reservations in the western part of Indian Territory and were forbidden to occupy territory outside their bounds. Most Indian bands and groups of warriors ignored the treaty and refused to abandon their traditional hunting areas. Douglas C. Jones, *The Treaty of Medicine Lodge: The Story of the Great Treaty Council as Told by Eyewitnesses* (Norman: University of Oklahoma Press, 1966).

13. General Philip Sheridan (1831–1888), after achieving great distinction as a victorious cavalry commander in the latter phases of the Civil War, was appointed commander of the Department of the Missouri, with headquarters at Fort Leavenworth, in 1868. His major activities were the South Plains campaign of 1868 against the Cheyennes and the 1874–1875 campaign that finally forced the Cheyennes, Comanches, and Kiowas onto reservations. His policy was generally characterized by strong hostility, indeed brutality, toward the Indians. To him is attributed the expression that the only good Indian is a dead Indian. Roy Morris, *Sheridan: The Life and Wars of General Phil Sheridan* (New York: Crown, 1992).

14. Black Kettle (ca. 1803–1868), a Cheyenne chief, was a consistent partisan of peaceful relations with the whites, a position he continued to advocate even after the infamous Sand Creek massacre from which he barely escaped with his life. Stan Hoig, *Peace Chiefs*, 104–21.

15. The Battle of Washita took place on November 27, 1868. It followed widespread raids by Indians in Kansas during the summer of 1868. General Philip Sheridan decided on a winter campaign to force the Cheyennes and Arapahos onto a reservation near Fort Cobb, Indian Territory. The main

force was the Seventh Cavalry led by Lieutenant General George Armstrong Custer, which attacked and captured a large village on the reservation. The village turned out to be that of Black Kettle, a peaceful chief, who was killed in the brief fight. Although not a decisive battle, it helped persuade the Cheyennes to move onto the reservation. Stan Hoig, *The Battle of Washita: The Sheridan-Custer Indian Campaign of 1867–69* (Garden City, N.Y.: Doubleday, 1976).

16. In the Medicine Lodge Treaty of 1867 the Cheyennes, Comanches, and Kiowas had their hunting rights in northern Texas validated. However, white colonists and buffalo hunters interfered with their rights, and Texas politicians challenged the treaty. The eventual result was the Red River War in 1874–1875, in which the tribes were defeated by Colonel Nelson A. Miles and others. The Indian leaders were made prisoners and deported to Florida. Douglas C. Jones, *Treaty of Medicine Lodge*; J. L. Haley, *The Buffalo War: The History of the Red River Uprising, 1874–1875* (Garden City, N.Y.: Doubleday, 1976).

17. The Cheyennes and Sioux belong to two distinct linguistic groups, the Algonquian and Siouan. On the other hand, Ten Kate correctly notes that they were frequent allies during the Indian wars of the 1860s and 1870s.

18. Dull Knife (ca. 1810–1883), a Northern Cheyenne chief, had fought the whites in the 1864–1865 wars following the Sand Creek Massacre, and his warriors, although not he himself, may have been involved as Sioux allies in the 1876 struggles against Crook and Custer. An assault by Colonel Ronald Mackenzie on his village in 1876, which inflicted heavy losses, resulted in his surrender the following spring and the move to a reservation in the Indian Territory. After the events noted by Ten Kate, Dull Knife himself escaped and eventually found refuge among the Sioux under Chief Red Cloud, where he died broken and embittered. Thrapp, *Encyclopedia*, 1:429.

19. Little Chief, a Northern Cheyenne chief, had led his band to the Darlington agency in 1878. When it became apparent that the locale and conditions did not suit the Cheyennes, Little Chief actively urged the whites to allow his people to return to their homeland, even undertaking two journeys to Washington for this purpose. When permission was finally granted in 1881, he led his band to the Pine Ridge reservation, where they remained for ten years and were then permitted to return to their ancestral homelands in eastern Montana. Hoig, *Peace Chiefs*, 137–41.

20. In 1881 and 1882 Cheyenne-Arapaho crops failed because of poor soil and persistent drought, and the sun dances failed to bring back the buffalo herds. Rations were running low and starvation had become a reality. Commissioner Hiram Price ordered rations to be cut by one-third because of budgetary problems at his bureau. However, Indian Agent John D. Miles objected, as this would certainly result in Indian raids on cattle ranches and possibly a larger Indian uprising. Major Randall of nearby Fort Reno then offered the military herd of buffalo to feed the starving Indians. D. J. Berthrong, *Cheyenne and Arapaho Ordeal*, 68–77.

21. HtK 1885: See my composition "Amerikaansche toestanden" in the magazine *Omnibus*, 1878, p. 369. Eds.: Thermopylae was a pass in northern Greece where in 480 B.C. King Leonidas and 300 Spartans for a time held back the entire invading Persian army under King Xerxes. The Spartans were eventually betrayed and massacred, but their heroic delaying action has sometimes been credited with gaining time for the Greeks to rally, thus sparing Greece greater destruction or even eventual conquest.

22. In 1878 the U.S. government transferred a small band of Arapahos from the Red Cloud Sioux Agency to the Wind River (Eastern Shoshone) reservation in Wyoming. They settled in the southeastern corner, where St. Stephen's Mission was established among them by the Jesuits.

James I. Patton, "Report of Agent in Wyoming," *Annual Report of the Commissioner of Indian Affairs, 1878* (Washington, D.C.: U.S. Government Printing Office, 1878), 148–55; Pieter Hovens, "Moccasins and Wooden Shoes: St. Stephen's Arapaho Mission and Its Dutch Superiors," in *Annals of Wyoming* (forthcoming).

23. HtK 1885: A young white-haired Cheyenne named White Bison, a pupil at the Indian School in Carlisle, assured Captain Pratt, this school's director, that his father, a medicine man, at one of his "medicine days" had ordered that his hair should become white, and thus it happened one night. Before this time—until he was about ten years old—his hair had a yellowish, sandy color, just like that of his mother, three sisters, and brother. Eds.: Ten Kate studied albinism among Native peoples throughout his life and published a series of articles on the subject. Pieter Hovens, *Herman ten Kate en de Antropologie der Noord Amerikaanse Indianen* (Meppel: Krips, 1989), 85–86.

24. HtK 1885: It is incomprehensible to me how Dodge, op. cit., 399, can say that the Plains Indians wear no scalp lock, where any number of other tribes besides the Cheyennes and Arapahos do this. I would name just the Comanches and Kiowas.

25. Ten Kate here is referring to the son of the celebrated northern Cheyenne chief Bullbear (see note 26). By Roman Nose is meant not the more famous Northern Cheyenne chief and warrior but Henry Roman Nose, a Southern Cheyenne, who had been imprisoned in Fort Marion, Florida. In 1880 he returned to the reservation, where he became an advocate of acculturation. Hoig, *Peace Chiefs,* 79–80, 171 n.; Ellsworth Collings, "Roman Nose: Chief of the Southern Cheyennes," *Chronicles of Oklahoma* 42 (1964):429–57; Hovens, *Herman ten Kate,* 62–64.

26. Chief of the Dog Soldiers and an important Cheyenne leader by the 1860s, Bullbear was a participant in the Medicine Lodge Peace Council (1867) and supported the agency school. Grinnell, *Fighting Cheyennes,* 133; Hoig, *Peace Chiefs,* 85–96.

27. A general review and analysis of cradling practices with illustrations of cradles Ten Kate collected can be found in Pieter Hovens and Lilianne Krosenbrink-Gelissen, "Managing Papooses: The Anthropology of Cradling and Swaddling in Native North America," *Yumtzilob* 5 (4) (1994):283–314. See also Barbara Hail, ed., *Gifts of Pride and Love: Kiowa and Cheyenne Cradles* (Providence, R.I.: Haffenreffer Museum, 2001).

28. The quarry was in Dakota Indian territory in southwestern Minnesota. It is now Pipestone National Monument. See Theodore L. Nydahl, "The Pipestone Quarry and the Indians," *Minnesota History* 31 (1950):193–208.

29. Ten Kate is correct. See Ives Goddard, "The Algonquian Languages of the Plains," *Handbook: Plains,* 13 (1):73–74.

30. An invented language like Esperanto.

31. HtK 1885: In order to refrain from all compilation, I refer the interested reader to the interesting work of Garrick Mallery on this subject in *First Annual Report of the Bureau of Ethnology,* Washington, 1881.

32. The Cheyenne called themselves *Tsistsistas,* "people alike." The term "Cheyenne" is derived from the Sioux name *Sha-hiyena, Shai-ena,* or (Teton) *Shai-ela,* "people of alien speech." J. H. Moore et al., "Cheyenne," *Handbook: Plains,* 13 (2):881.

33. HtK 1885: According to tradition, "the eastern people" = *Sootai* is at the same time the name of a tribe in the north, from which the Cheyennes once separated, then heading south. The Cheyennes seem to come from the region by Lake Winnipeg, in present-day Canada, whence they were driven off by other tribes. Eds.: Historians now believe the ancestral home of the Cheyennes was in what

is now the southeastern part of the state of Minnesota and that they later moved, first to the region of the Sheyenne River in North Dakota and then into west-central South Dakota and in the early nineteenth century into southeastern Wyoming and southeastern Oklahoma. J. H. Moore et al., *Handbook: Plains,* 13 (2):863–65.

34. Ten Kate's findings differed substantially from those of James Owen Dorsey, an earlier observer; his data are almost mirrored in the results obtained by E. Adamson Hoebel in 1930. Hovens, *Ten Kate,* 112–13.

35. A calendrical ritual conducted primarily to ask the Great Spirit to bring the tribe a successful bison hunt, the Sun Dance also celebrates the creation of the world. At least thirty distinct tribal groups celebrate some form of the Sun Dance. George A. Dorsey's account of the Cheyennes (1905) provides rich ethnographic detail (*The Cheyenne Sun Dance* [Chicago: Field Columbian Museum Publications 101]). Glenn J. Schiffman, "Sun Dance," in *American Indians,* 3 vols., ed. Harvey Markowitz (Pasadena: Salem Press, 1995), 3:760–62; Joseph Epes Brown, "Sun Dance" in *The Encyclopedia of Religion,* 15 vols., ed. Mircea Eliade (New York: Macmillan, 1987), 14:143–47.

36. HtK 1885: *Puellae, tamquam custodem virgineum, involucra (telas) femoribus atque inferiori parti corporis trunci circumdant arcteque alligata gestant. Idem facere feminae menstruantes nec non illae, quarum mariti absunt. Puellis verecundia tanta est, ut primis matrimonii diebus involucra ista gestare pergant, maritumque a coitu prohibeant.* [The girls, as the safeguard of their virginity, surround the thighs and the lower parts of the trunk with woven coverings and wear them bound tightly. Menstruating women and those whose husbands are away do likewise. Such is the girls' sense of modesty that during the first days of marriage they continue to wear these coverings and refrain from coitus with their husbands.]

37. HtK 1885: *Die Prairien des amerikanischen Westens,* Cologne and Leipzig 1876, pp. 124, 125. Eds.: Robert von Schlagintweit (1833–1885) was the youngest of three brothers who gained great renown for their exploration of India, the Himalayan regions, and Central Asia in the 1850s. After this expedition, Robert, who became a geography professor at the University of Giessen, also delivered lectures on his journeys in over seventy German-speaking cities of Europe. An invitation to the United States in 1868 resulted in a transcontinental journey and several additional books, including the one cited by Ten Kate. *Allgemeine Deutsche Biographie,* 56 vols. (Berlin: Duncker und Humblot, 1875–1912), 31:336–47.

38. HtK 1885: Ibid., p. 112.

39. HtK 1885: J. W. Powell and J. Owen Dorsey, two of the most preeminent experts on Indian conditions, express themselves in the same spirit. *Transactions Anthropological Society of Washington,* vol. I, p. 29.

    In not a single one of North American tribes known to them are the children abused or the women treated as slaves. Because the woman always belongs to a different clan from the man, he dare not mistreat her for fear of vengeance on the part of her relatives.

    Likewise, among the Indians there is an appropriate division of labor. The man takes care of his family household and he is its head, but the woman carries out household duties.

    According to them, tender attachment between spouses, the elderly, and children is not at all uncommon.

    Also, Captain Bourke (*The Snake Dance,* etc., pp. 45, 46), a man who, through a long stay in the West learned to judge the Indian character according to its true worth, expresses himself as follows on the occasion of a scene he witnessed between two betrothed in the pueblo Santo Domingo:

"So much stuff and nonsense have been written about the entire absence of affection from the Indian character, especially in the relations between the sexes, that it affords me great pleasure to note this little incident."

40. More often called Old Whirlwind (He-vo-vi-tas-tami-utsts), Whirlwind was an important Cheyenne chief by the 1870s. Grinnell, *Fighting Cheyennes*, 104.

41. Powder Face and his band settled near Darlington in 1876. He traded in buffalo robes and used his profits to start a herd of horses and cattle, an example followed by other tribesmen. These activities brought him into conflict with the Indian agent, who preferred that the Indians till the soil, thereby adopting a sedentary and "civilized" way of life. There were two Southern Arapaho chiefs named Left Hand, the more famous one an advocate of peaceful coexistence with the whites who was mortally wounded in the Sand Creek Massacre. The less well-known chief Left Hand (1840–post 1889), whom Ten Kate met, was unrelated to his more well-known namesake and actually became chief of the Southern Arapaho with the death of Little Raven in 1889. D. J. Berthrong, *Cheyenne and Arapaho Ordeal*, 59, 68–69, 102–3, 143, 215; Margaret Coel, *Chief Left Hand: Southern Arapaho* (Norman: University of Oklahoma, 1981).

42. Richard Henry Pratt (1840–1924), a soldier and Indian educator, fought in the Civil War and in 1868–1869 and 1873–1874 campaigned against the Cheyennes, Comanches, and Kiowas. He accompanied Indian prisoners to Florida, where he began his educational work. In 1878 he transferred to Hampton Institute in Virginia, but, believing that it was better to separate blacks and Indians, he inaugurated in 1879 what became the Carlisle Indian School in Pennsylvania. During the period he headed the institutions, some 5,000 Indian pupils passed through. Pratt strongly favored separating his pupils from tribal influences and encouraging adaptation to the white man's ways. See his memoirs *Battlefield and Classroom: Four Decades with the American Indian, 1867–1904*, ed. Robert M. Utley (New Haven, Conn.: Yale University Press, 1964); Hovens, *Herman ten Kate*, 171–72.

43. HtK 1885: Agent J. D. Miles was the only government agent I met who understood something of the Indians' language and for that reason was also the only one who was respected and loved by them. When Schlagintweit (op. cit., p. 132) speaks of Indian agents as people of culture and education and in possession of "linguistic knowledge not at all easy to acquire," then I must assume that he only came in contact with persons who were the exception to the rule or rather that he never met an Indian agent at all.

44. David Pendleton was trained as an Episcopal minister in New York State. He returned to Darlington in 1881, preaching the Gospel to his people and opposing the Sun Dance. He also introduced Christian funeral rites. Berthrong, *Cheyenne and Arapaho Ordeal*, 85.

45. HtK 1885: Op. cit., p. 113.

46. HtK 1885: Loc. cit.

47. After the Civil War the land of the Five Civilized Tribes in the Indian Territory was reallotted to permit creation of a reservation for the Plains tribes. Some land in the center of the territory, however, remained unallotted. This land became the goal of white homesteaders or "boomers." David Payne (1836–1884), beginning in 1879, attempted eight unsuccessful raids into the Indian Territory to open unassigned Indian lands to white settlement. Carl Coke Rister, *Land Hunger: David L. Payne and the Oklahoma Boomers* (Norman: University of Oklahoma Press, 1942).

48. HtK 1885: I derived from the result of these measures the following:

Three Cheyennes had a cranial index of 78.46, 79.59, 83.60. The maximum body length was 1 m 76. Among three Arapahoes, I found 71.54, 80.58, 84.00. Maximum stature 1 m 87.

49. The verse of Nikolaus Lenau (1802–1850), an Austrian poet, was noted for its melancholy nature lyricism and themes of world weariness. *Neue Deutsche Biographie,* 20 vols. (Berlin: Duncker & Humblot, 1953–2001), 14:195–98.

50. P. B. Hunt was the Indian agent at Fort Sill from 1878 to 1885. Although personally honest, Hunt's tenure witnessed frequent food shortages at the reservation, repeated encroachments by Texas cattleman, unauthorized white residence, and poor school attendance. For these reasons and his strained relations with the Indians, Hunt was eventually forced to resign. William T. Hagan, *United States–Comanche Relations: The Reservation Years* (New Haven, Conn.: Yale University Press, 1976), 139–44, 146–57, 160–65.

51. In Roman times the Picts were a people living north of Hadrian's Wall, in present-day Scotland, whose most distinctive feature was their practice of painting their bodies.

52. HtK 1885: An old custom, still in vogue now is: *ut feminae, infantem lactanti nulla sit cum eius patre communio. Credunt alioqui infantem sive diarrhoea sive alio morbo moriturum esse. Apud eosdem feminae non ita diu post partum lignatum vel ligna fissum ire solent, quo facto balneo utuntur. Fortasse huius rei causa in eo quaerenda est, quod putent, sibi alioqui rigidiora futura esse membra* [that women nursing their children have no association with their father. They believe that otherwise the child will die of diarrhea or another illness. Among them, the women are thus not accustomed to fetching or chopping wood after delivery, but they resort to baths. Perhaps here is the reason to investigate why they believe that if they don't take baths, their members will be more rigid.]

53. HtK 1885: The name of the agency is derived from this tribe, also called "Anadakos" or "Anadarkos."

54. The Hainai (also Inie or Ioni) are a Caddoan group, whose name "Ayano" or "Hayano" means "people" in Caddo. The Biloxi are a small Siouan tribe that apparently lived with the Caddo. D. Parks, "Caddoan Languages," *Handbook: Plains,* 13 (1):84.

55. The name "Caddo" derives from the French abbreviation of *Kadohadacho,* a word meaning "real chief" or "real Caddo" in the Kadohadacho dialect. European chroniclers refer to three Caddo groups: Hasinai, Kadohadacho, and Nachitoches. Timothy K. Pertulla, "Caddo Indians," in *The New Handbook of Texas,* ed. Ron Tyler (Austin: Texas State Historical Association, 1996), 1:887.

56. Ten years later Parton acted as interpreter and informant for James Mooney of the Bureau of American Ethnology when he conducted his seminal research on the Ghost Dance. James Mooney, *The Ghost Dance and the Sioux Outbreak of 1890* (Annual Report of the Bureau of American Ethnology 14, Washington, D.C., 1896); Hovens, *Herman ten Kate,* 65, 111.

57. HtK 1885: What was or is still the custom among them *ut uxori, cuius infans nondum incedere possit, nulla sit corporis cum marito communio. Interea maritus voluptariis sensibus cum alia muliere indulget, donec, elapso intervallo, ad priorem concubinam redit, quam, si ei non amplius placet, repudiare solet* [is that the woman whose child is not yet able to walk has no physical association with her husband. Meanwhile, the husband indulges his voluptuous appetites with another woman until, after the passage of time, he returns to his former concubine, whom he rejects if she no longer pleases him.]

58. An English translation of this part of Ten Kate's itinerary was earlier provided by Thomas Hester and Fred Stross: "Herman ten Kate's Account of the Burial of a Penateka Comanche at Fort Sill," *Southwestern Lore*, 39 (1973):9–11. See also Thomas W. Kavanagh, "Comanche," *Handbook: Plains*, 13 (2):895.

59. Camp Wichita was created in January 1869. On August 1, 1869, General Sheridan renamed it Fort Sill in honor of his classmate Brigadier General Joshua W. Sill, who was killed at the Battle of Stone River, Tennessee, on December 13, 1862. Wilbur Sturtevant Nye, *Carbine and Lance: The Story of Old Fort Sill* (Norman: University of Oklahoma Press, 1969), 85, 100. In naming the camp, Ten Kate confused "Wichita" with "Washita" the river and also battle site, about a hundred miles northwest, where in November 1868 General Custer massacred the Cheyennes (see note 15 above).

60. Born in Missouri, Horace P. Jones (1829–1901) settled in Texas as a young man. Here he befriended the Comanches, learned their language, and was eventually adopted into their tribe. After the Civil War he served as a scout and interpreter for the army, eventually settling in Fort Sill and vicinity. Joseph P. Thoburn, "Horace P. Jones, Scout and Interpreter," *Chronicles of Oklahoma* 2 (1924):380–91.

61. Philip McCusker (d. 1884), a noted scout of the Fort Sill region, had married a Comanche woman, was fluent in the language, and was said to be also fluent in Kiowa and Kiowa Apache. McCusker was the principal interpreter at the Medicine Lodge Treaty Council in 1867. Thrapp, *Encyclopedia*, 2:896–97.

62. HtK 1885: Comanches were also among the Indians from other tribes who had joined Victorio's band of hostile Apaches.

63. Ten Kate is referring to Catlin's *Letters and Notes on the Manners, Customs, and Conditions of the North American Indians* (1841; repr., New York: Dover, 1973), 2:68. Catlin, however, qualified his estimate: "This estimate I offer not as conclusive, for so little is as yet known of these people, that no estimate can be implicitly relied upon other than that, which, in general terms, pronounces them to be a very numerous and warlike tribe."

64. Henry Rowe Schoolcraft (1793–1864)—author, ethnologist, and Indian agent—published *Historical and Statistical Information Respecting the History, Conditions, and Prospects of the Indian Tribes of the United States* (Philadelphia: Lippincott, Grambo, 1851–57), a six-volume compilation of miscellaneous articles and data on selected Indian tribes and archaeological investigations. Ten Kate here refers to vol. 1, p. 518 (1851). Helen Hornbeck Tanner, "Henry Rowe Schoolcraft," *American National Biography*, ed. John A. Garraty and Mark C. Carnes (New York: Oxford University Press, 1999), 424–25.

65. HtK 1885: In addition, there are some Comanches among the Mescalero Apaches, the Utes, and perhaps as well a couple of other tribes. It is highly probable that a small number are also in northeastern Mexico.

66. The significantly higher number of women among certain Plains tribes was due to the many casualties in intertribal and interethnic warfare.

67. Mowway ("Shaking Hand"), a chief of the Kochateka band, was one of the most formidable Comanche leaders of his day. Ensconced in the Staked Plains, Mowway waged war against white intruders until his capture in New Mexico in 1869. A railway trip as a captive convinced him that further resistance against the more numerous and better-equipped whites would be futile. Thereafter he advocated accommodation. Eventually he renounced his chieftain's dignity so he could live with his immediate family on a farm near Fort Sill. Nye, *Carbine and Lance*, 104–5, 159, 161–65, 253.

68. Compare with the account of Carrying Her Sunshade, who as a very young girl was made captive in a Comanche raid in Mexico during the 1850s. According to her reminiscences, she lived near "the highest mountain in Mexico," which is Orizaba. Ernest Wallace and E. Adamson Hoebel, *The Comanches: Lords of the South Plains* (Norman: University of Oklahoma Press, 1986), 260–63.

69. The Tonkawas of central Texas were best remembered for this practice, which apparently was primarily connected with ceremonial activities: victory celebrations, avenging the death of a Tonkawa, depriving the enemy of a second life, and acquiring courage of one's foe. Andrée F. Sjoberg, "The Culture of the Tonkawa: A Texas Indian Tribe," *Texas Journal of Science* no. 3 (September 1953):294–95.

70. HtK 1885: Seven male Comanches had an average height of 1.69 m; max. 1.77 m; min. 1.57 m.

71. HtK 1885: "Renseignements ethnographiques sur les Comanches," in *Revue d'Ethnographie* of Hamy, vol. I, pp. 95–118. Eds.: Léon de Cessac (1841–1891) participated in scientific expeditions to the Northwest in 1875 and California in 1879. He published little and died in poverty and obscurity. *Dictionnaire de Biographie Francaise*, 114 vols. (Paris: Letouzey et Ané, 1933–2000), 8:79.

72. Htk 1889, 241: I have since discussed the reports of Léon de Cessac more thoroughly in the *Revue d'Ethnographie* of Hamy, vol. IV, 1885. This composition of mine had additionally appeared in translation in *Das Ausland,* 1885.

73. HtK 1885: See, in addition, my "Synonymie ethnique."

74. In the 1780s the Sioux drove the Kiowas from the Black Hills, forcing them farther south into Nebraska, Kansas, and northern Oklahoma. The Kiowas at first met resistance from the Comanches living in this area, but during the early nineteenth century the two tribes formed an alliance against their common enemies, primarily the Apaches and Cheyennes. Jerrold E. Levy, "Kiowa," *Handbook: Plains,* 13 (2):907–8, 915–16.

75. HtK 1885: See my "Een bezoek bij de Irokezen," *Tijdschrift van het Aardrijkskundig Genootschap,* vol. VII. Eds.: See chapter 1.

76. HtK 1885: Joaquin Miller, *Songs of the Sierras.* Londen [*sic*], 1872.

77. Cessac, "Sur les Comanches," 105.

78. Ibid., 169–70.

79. HtK 1885: *Mulieres menstruantes a caeteris contubernalibus segregatae, in appendicula tugurii, ramis tecta, iisque destinata, degere solent. Apud Comanche-Indianos haud raro coitus fit, dum vir et mulier in latere jacent. Roganti, num coitum et more equino facerent (de Cessac), mihi responsum est: "numquam."* [Menstruating women, separated from other companions in a small annex to a hut, with a roof of branches, set aside for them, pass their time there. Among the Comanche Indians, coitus occurs only rarely, with the man and woman lying on their side. When I asked whether they engage in coitus in equine fashion (de Cessac), the response was: "Never."]

80. HtK 1885: Schlagintweit, op. cit., p. 111, errs when he asserts that one cannot place any confidence in the words of Indians. Countless people who lived a long time in the West, and are not friends of the Indian, assured me that an Indian seldom or never breaks his word.

81. Cessac, "Sur les Comanches," 116–17.

82. HtK 1885: Op. cit. and *Our Wild Indians,* Hartford, Conn., 1882.

83. Ten Kate is in error. It is not the names of the animals that were changed; rather names of deceased persons were not bestowed on children.

84. Cessac, "Sur les Comanches," 101.

CHAPTER ELEVEN

Through the Indian Territory
Sequel

THE MILITARY PHYSICIAN, DR. T., WHO WAS HEADING to his new garrison, Fort Elliott, proved to be a congenial traveling companion to Henrietta, sixty-five miles southeast of Fort Sill. This time, fortunately, I will not have to make the long journey with a buckboard but with a suitable covered wagon, which provides enough room for both of us and the driver. The sandy track we follow leads through a deserted region, consisting of grassy, undulating terrain, which is intersected with many streams and surrounded by lush oaks, elms, and red sumac bushes. The water level has fallen considerably, and we cross the West Cache Creek and later the Red River without problem.

The isolation of this area makes us focus our attention on the wildlife of the prairie. A pack of large wolves[1] and a rattlesnake, which meets its maker after a round of bullets from our revolvers, are the only dangerous animals we encounter, but along our route we also run across countless cottontail rabbits and prairie dogs. In some respects the correspondence between these two rodents is striking. At our approach, for example, the former duck away near the entryway of the prairie dog burrows, without going inside, though, as the rightful owners do a moment later. Instead they remain sitting motionlessly with their ears in the nape of their neck until we have passed. The prairie dogs display considerable confidence because countless burrows are situated not only alongside but on top of the broad riding path, where they frolic and go their merry way unperturbed.[2]

On the reservation is the small mail station, a lone ranch, where we change horses—the only inhabited place we can see. Shortly before we cross the Red River, we encounter a sizable herd of cattle, tended by several cowboys on horseback. They are trespassers, who are not in the slightest concerned about the prohibition against cattle grazing on the reservation. The commandant of Fort

Sill, who must repeatedly put such trespassers over the border, told me that in his opinion, some agents, generously paid off by cattlemen, deliberately close their eyes whenever they let their livestock graze on Indian territory. When the Indians get wind of this, they take the simple but effective expedient of setting the prairie ablaze over a certain area.

The Red River, *Piyahápe* in the Cheyenne language, fully deserves its name because here the muddy, reddish water flows along the high red sandstone banks. Nowhere does one better comprehend the validity behind Pliny's expression, *"Talis est aqua, qualis terra, per quam fluit,"*[3] than in the American Southwest and particularly in the prairies.

Shortly after we reach Texas territory, not far from Taylor's store, which also serves as a mail station, we encounter a band of Comanches on horseback who were engaged in trading. Probably they have also concealed whiskey, along with other items, under their blankets. The owners of the stores on the southern bank of the Red River are often the source of problems with the Indians, who, after using strong drink, even in small quantities, lose all their restraint and reach recklessly for their weapons. The "wild" Indians, Comanches as well as Kiowas, who want to cross the Texas boundary are required to have a pass from their agent because otherwise they run the risk of being shot as "hostile" by the Texans, without the formality of a trial. That is what it has come to with the tribes that once threatened to take by storm Austin and San Antonio, the most important cities of Texas, and barely ten years ago threatened the very existence of Henrietta.

The landscape on this side of the Red River has the same character as on the other side. But houses situated far apart from each other, and large fences for the cattle with a kind of thick galvanized iron wire outfitted with transverse points, are now widespread.[4] Off in the distance a number of antelope are grazing among the cattle. Willingly or not, they are shut in by any of various cattlemen. Yet they all have adequate space because it is impossible for us to make out the other side of the fence. Toward dusk, which follows a splendid, clear day, we notice the glimmering of a prairie fire along the western horizon, emblazoning a large part of the sky with a red glow.

Shortly before we ride into Henrietta, the driver shows us the spot near a thicket where the mail wagon he was driving was assaulted by robbers fourteen days ago. He came out of it with a blow to his head from a revolver while the passengers, some black soldiers on leave from Sill, had to surrender their last cent, as well as their pistols. Little wonder that the Indians harbor a profound contempt for these "buffalo soldiers."[5] Nothing happens to us, though, and, numbed by the chill evening, we ride unscathed into the sandy streets of Henrietta to the cheerful crack of a whip, and before long we are slumbering on the firm beds of "The National" [Hotel].

Henrietta is a small town on its way up, which will surely thrive when the railway line from Fort Worth to Denver, the capital of Colorado, along which it lies, is completed and the vast region of North Texas, so well suited for cattle raising, becomes more accessible.[6] During my stay this railway line was already laid to Wichita Falls, a town between Henrietta and Fort Elliott.

Because the stranger will find nothing worth seeing in Henrietta, and one thing looks like everything else in all western American cities this size, I left it as quickly as possible. My opportunity arrived with the train heading southeast on the morning of October 30th, while Dr. T. continued his journey to Fort Elliott. The railway runs through rolling prairies, with limestone appearing now and then, and through vast forests of low oaks, but everywhere one can see that the land is already—to use the American expression—"filled up" with ranches and small towns. Decatur and Aurora are even rather sizable towns, and in Fort Worth, where I arrived five hours after leaving Henrietta, hustle and bustle reigns in the station, the like of which I have not witnessed for quite some time. There, until 3 A.M., I have the time to deeply ponder the huge contrasts the West has to offer before I can continue the journey to Dallas, which I reach early in the morning.

Dallas, which numbers 10,000 to 11,000 inhabitants, though not a capital, reminds one of a large city more than Tucson or Santa Fe. The absence of the wretched adobe buildings greatly contributes to this impression. While the center of the city—consisting of three straight sandy main streets, more than a mile long and intersected by a large number of cross streets—resembles Little Rock, Trinidad, and other cities, around Dallas stretches a network of country avenues. Here rustic wooden dwellings and elegant stone villas lie hidden among the foliage of acacias and oaks, while farther up a belt of low green oak bushes surrounds the city. From the outward appearance of Dallas's residents, it is clear that for some time now this city has passed through its dangerous phase as a hard place because armed tramps and hoodlums have taken permanent refuge elsewhere. Greater order and cleanliness are everywhere evident, and here the distinctly provisional character, which marks all towns out west, has all but vanished.

On the other hand, one can encounter far more Negroes in all possible hues, from the darkest black to light blackish yellow, on the streets than elsewhere. That also indicates normal conditions because one seldom finds Negroes in the small frontier towns, and the ones who are there are not the best element. But apart from that, Negroes in the states west of the Mississippi are much less numerous than in the ones east of this river because they lack the qualities [required] of a settler. They seldom take the initiative in agriculture and livestock raising.[7] For the rough, conflict-ridden life of the white settler in desert regions, they have neither the energy nor capacity. In their case sloth prevails over eagerness for gain; they have much in common with Mexicans in this regard. Negroes can be found in the Union only where there is a relatively dense population and an ambience allowing them to earn a livelihood in a more or less menial relationship.[8]

I was forced to spend much more time in Dallas than I would have liked. But as much as I wanted, I could not continue the journey because the most vital necessity—money—was lacking. Due to various circumstances the money I had been waiting for in Dallas had not arrived, and for nine days I had to contend with the unpleasant situation of being wholly without resources in a totally strange place. It got to the point where I had to sell my watch to appease the hotel keeper, who would otherwise have put me "out on the street." But on the ninth day of dreadful boredom and inactivity, the ordeal was not yet over. They were unwilling to pay me for the money order I had at last received because I could not prove my identity. Letters, protestations were all to no avail, but eventually, after telegraphing back and forth with a banker in New York, I got hold of the money, and in the early morning of November 9th, with a sigh of relief, I turned my back on Dallas. Therewith I set out on the last leg of my journey: a visit to several of the civilized nations of the Indian Territory.

The train passes through rolling prairie land, alternating with corn and cotton fields and oak forests, past the little towns of McKinney, Sherman, and Denison and some other little hamlets along the route. Roughly a mile above the last-mentioned place, the train crosses the Red River, which here flows between high banks of whitish limestone and provides a stark but lovely contrast, with its red waters emerging from the west and with its forests, resplendent in their autumn garb, along the bank. So we have reached the Indian Territory once more. The variegated magnificent dense forest continues up to a short distance before Caddo, my destination. In its trees, evocative of the centuries, which are entwined by climbing plants, the moist foliage rustles over the tall grass of the abruptly undulating prairie. In Dallas everything was a harbinger of summer: over there a warm sun, which from a fixed, blue sky cast its glow on the green oak trees, here a fine whitish cloud, suspended above the multicolored forests like a diaphanous veil, beckoning toward autumn.

Colbert, Durant, and Armstrong—three stations—are likewise so many tiny, isolated hamlets of log cabins. Around 1:30 P.M. I step off the train in Caddo and have thus reached one of the most important places in the land of the Choctaw Indians.

The reason I had chosen Caddo specifically was based on the opinion that the population consisted exclusively of zambos, a mixed race of Indians and Negroes, and I thought I would have the opportunity to investigate them closely, something that thus far had never been done. Hepworth Dixon, for his part, asserts in his book titled *White Conquest* that in Caddo "these cabins in the fields and nearly all these shanties in the town" are inhabited by these colored people. On closer examination, though, I found that not a single zambo was present in Caddo and that zambos had never even dwelled there. I found only whites, blacks, and Indians numbering 350, who made up the entire population. I had even less luck finding the "billiard rooms" and "drinking bars" of which the aforementioned author speaks. The Indian Territory maintains not a single establishment of this kind.[9]

The whites I got to know in Caddo included my landlord, a member of the Odd Fellows, of which Caddo possesses a lodge consisting of seven people; the former riding master of the Grand Duke of Mecklenburg-Schwerin, now freight rider; a deserter from Kassel, who now repairs the Caddoans' shoes; a Swiss ex-cavalryman, now garçon [bellboy] in the Odd Fellows' "hotel"; and a pastor who taught the little black children their ABCs and often hunted wild turkeys as well. In the person of Mr. Folsom, a totally civilized Choctaw Indian, whose grandfather was white, I met someone who could tell me a thing or two about the former and present condition of his people.[10] For particular details on the past history and manners and morals of the Choctaws, I must refer the interested reader to the works of Adair,[11] Roman,[12] Jones[13] and others. Here I prefer briefly to investigate how far the Choctaws have deviated from the customs of their forefathers. The stay of nearly fifty years in their new homeland has led to the disappearance of practically every distinctive trait among these Indians. Their former dwelling places were primarily in the present-day state of Mississippi, where around 1,800 of them still remain and they are regarded as American citizens.[14]

The Chickasaws, who are most closely related, live north of them, primarily in the western part of the state of Tennessee. According to the government report of 1882, the Choctaws number 16,000, the Chickasaws 6,000. By far, though, this number does not comprise full-blooded Indians; instead a number of whites, mestizos, blacks, and zambos are among them.[15]

The precise meaning of the name *Choctaw,*[16] or better yet *Cháhta,* appears to be lost, but possibly it signifies "division," bearing in mind the separation of the Creeks and Seminoles, tribes together with which the Choctaws formerly comprised one people.[17] According to tradition, the Chickasaws, better *Chíkasha,* were once Choctaws, but as a result of an uprising—which is what the name means—they later formed a nation of their own.

The Choctaws' attire is entirely like that of whites, with the sole difference that the scarves they wear around their necks are redder and more colorful, and the men not infrequently stick red-colored ostrich feathers on their broad-brimmed felt hats. Their former dwellings, log cabins of sorts with pointed roofs or huts of mud and grass, have made way for the usual houses of the American rural population. With Christianity, all distinctive features—except for language—have vanished. On the basis of their own legal determination, their clan system was abolished in 1836. The *Kashápaokla* ("the separated people") and the *Okcoolaihooláhta,* their main clans, are known only by name.[18]

In addition, the national ball games were officially abolished because they gave rise to feuding and were "irreligious." Just as scalping and smoking of the clay peace pipe, handed around in assemblies by the *tisho,* have vanished, the Choctaws have likewise abandoned for good sun and fire worship, as well as their unique way of handling corpses.[19] Indeed, there are still probably old people here and there who secretly pay homage to the beliefs and customs of their fathers, but the Choctaw people has forever lost its original character, maybe even more than the Creeks and Cherokees.

The Chickasaws, however, seem to be more backward than their Choctaw brethren and give evidence of their old contentiousness by intestine bloody quarrels, which occur especially when they have indulged excessively in *oka homi* (strong drink). Moreover, among the Chickasaws the performance of the *peshófa,* a "medicine making" among sick people, has not entirely vanished.

It was on November 10th that I headed, with the ex–riding master as my guide, to Old Boggy Depot, twenty miles almost north of Caddo, to visit Allen Wright, the former governor of the Choctaw nation.[20] Almost uninterruptedly the sandy wagon track led through magnificent, dense forests of various kinds of oaks, walnuts *(Juglans nigra),* sycamores, and Osage oranges *(Maclura aurantiaca),* while the fresh forest fragrance that follows rainfall filled the air. Nameless quiet, babbling brooks often crossed our path, losing themselves in the mysterious depths of the forest, whose grandiose seclusion gives pause for reflection. At times a log cabin standing in isolation emerged, surrounded by a cornfield, in which countless dead tree trunks were still standing in the ground, in patches where the wood had been cut. The first hamlet we stopped at is New Boggy Depot, consisting of a couple of stores and small wooden dwellings; two miles farther on is Old Boggy Depot, likewise surrounded by a dense wooded zone.[21]

Mr. Allen Wright lives in a nice wooden villa, which is furnished with a veranda and a balcony. Although he did not know me at all and had only the former riding master with me for an introduction, Mr. Wright received me with the greatest courtesy. Due to a misunderstanding, he was under the impression that I wanted to lodge with him for a while, and he would have satisfied my wish without hesitation had I not promptly stated that I came only to make his acquaintance, because his name was known to me for some time because of his "Chahta Lexicon."[22]

Mr. Wright, though a full-blooded Choctaw fifty to sixty years old, is a completely civilized man, who no less than my Iroquois friends, the Parkers and Mount Pleasants, is at home in every salon. As it happened, they, as well as some scholars I know in Washington, belong to his circle of acquaintances, which also helps put us on the best footing right away. I sit at the hospitable table and make the acquaintance of Mrs. Wright, a white woman, who has eight children from her Indian spouse. Those I saw showed not a trace of their Choctaw origin. Their dishes include *tafula*, the national dish of the Choctaws, consisting of a kind of corn mush or hominy, as well as *banáha* and *paskahawvshko*, two types of Indian bread, the latter with soft, spongy dough.

My questions are answered with a torrent of words. With a satisfaction of sorts, my host relates how all the old customs have vanished, which is not surprising when one realizes that Mr. Wright is actually a preacher and has benefited from an education in the eastern states. The man whose grandfather, or perhaps father, bore the honorary title of *humma*[23] here was speaking in fluent English with satisfaction about the church and the school among his people, convinced that in Christian civilization alone lay the Indians' salvation.

The Choctaws were also the source for the idea about incorporating the Indian Territory into the Union as a separate state, under the name of "Oklahoma,"[24] an idea much discussed in 1870 when a number of deputies from various tribes convened at Ockmulgee, the capital of the Indian Territory. Its realization, though, still seems far in the distant future.[25] Oklahoma will maybe always remain a utopia, not because the Indians, once civilized, are incapable of forming a union among themselves, but because the racial hatred and greed of the Americans will not permit the "red man" to keep an inch of land for himself in the future. Other Oklahoma Paynes more fortunate than their predecessor, will come here and swoop down on their land like a swarm of vultures on carrion. The opening of Indian Territory to white colonization is only a matter of time, and the "permanent homes, for ever secured," to which the treaties refer, will ring like bitter parodies of a faithless nation.[26]

The Choctaws have a supreme chief *(chito mingo* or *miko)* and three district chiefs who are elected by the people and periodically hand over their office. Until a short time ago, the main place where the large council meetings were held every year was Doaksville, in the southeast of the Choctaw reservation, but now it is Tushkahoma, east of the Sans Bois Mountains. The Choctaws have a printed legal code. Just like their civilized neighbors the Creeks, Cherokees, etc., they hold the land in communal possession and are spread out in mostly scattered homesteads, as a result of which the land is largely a fallow wilderness. The forests, which make up 50 percent of the Choctaw territory,[27] and the sprawling coal fields in the east of the Indian Territory, approximately one-third of its total area, are unexploited.

The Choctaw language is very melodious because of its numerous vowels and to an untutored ear provides a marked contrast to the languages of the Tinné, Numa, and Algonquin groups. With Creek and Seminole and some other languages of less importance, Choctaw-Chickasaw makes up the group of the Appalachian languages.[28] *D, g,* and *r* are lacking in Choctaw; *ai,* and *au* are the only diphthongs. The *hl* sound is distinctive, as are the nasal sounds, which, except for *e,* occur with the other vowels. Some words are used only by women. Here I mention only *ehwá* or *ehwak* = "phooey!" Just as in Creek, other words are used only on solemn occasions—to such an extent that one could speak of them having a language of oratory.

According to tradition, the Choctaws came from the west, preceded by their prophets, who carried sticks in their hands to point the way. The legend reported in this regard by Möllhausen,[29] as well as the one about the dwarfs or crayfish people, was told to me by Mr. Folsom. I would have difficulty, though, in seeing, as Möllhausen does, a connection between the legend regarding their origin with that of the Flathead and Chinook Indians west of the Rocky Mountains. Just because the Choctaws also deformed their skulls does nothing to confirm this opinion. This custom is in vogue among any number of tribes from both Americas. Although this custom has been discontinued among the Choctaws for some time, and people could only *tell* me that the children's skulls could be shaped into a predetermined form by laying bags of gold on them, I did encounter occasional elderly individuals whose skulls still displayed notable traces of this deformation.[30]

The arrival in Caddo of a circus, whose director was a "colonel," provided me a suitable opportunity to make studies in physiognomy among the numerous Choctaws of both sexes and every age, who had streamed in from every direction to attend the performances. Here I got an idea of what the government reports sometimes mean by "Indians." Of the Choctaws present, who number several hundreds, by far the largest number were half-breeds without uniformity of type, including some who had a kind of dark drab, chestnut brown hair and a pale tint. In addition, there were numerous Negroes—former slaves of the Choctaws—and occasional zambos. The rest might be regarded as Indians, but not all as full-bloods. To judge from a superficial observation, there are two, perhaps three types among them, one of which has a straight, rather short nose, the other a crooked nose and falls somewhere between the "redskin type" and the Semitic physiognomy. The third type has some Mongolian features. Most of these Indians are of medium stature but of powerful build. In this respect the women differ little from the men. Some of the women were smoking brown clay pipes or chewing tobacco. This latter custom they have probably taken on with American civilization because I have never encountered tobacco chewing among the noncivilized tribes.

The enjoyment of the worthy Choctaws was dampened somewhat that evening because the circus's "doctor," who gave hypnotic performances, was suddenly indisposed. Gulping down the contents of a little bottle of "painkiller," the horrid quack remedy, which he was able promptly to procure from a store, did not alleviate the aching in his lower body. So, as the sole person who could provide assistance, I got the moaning "doc" on my account. To the satisfaction of his boss, the "colonel," however, I brought my "colleague" back, to the extent that late that night he could leave again. The "doc" was the last patient I had to treat in the West.

With the circus the Indians vanished too, and Caddo returned to its accustomed calm. Because I, for my part, had seen enough of the Choctaw nation, on the afternoon of November 13th, at 2 o'clock, I boarded the train to Muskogee, the capital of the Creek reservation. Unbroken woodland with oaks, hickory, and sycamore trees, most of them entwined with sturdy liana, is all one sees as long as the sun is up. Small stations such as Atoka, Limestone Gap, Mc Allister, and Eufaula, largely inhabited by whites, lie hidden in the sea of trees and linked by the railway, the only high road cutting through this wilderness. The darkness allows us to see vast prairie fires, which bathe the distant horizon in a marvelous fiery glow. During the evening they are whipped up to an immense scale by the fierce north wind and rage even more fiercely than on the 12th. In the course of the evening I reach Muskogee, which has a decent hotel, managed by the recently chosen chief, Mr. Perryman.[31] It is so packed, however, that I must take refuge in a wretched hostel nearby.

The purpose of my visit in Muskogee was to establish contact with the government agent for the "five civilized nations"[32] and to acquire some information about the best means of finding out a thing or two regarding the Indians. I visited him the following morning. It was readily apparent that I would find nothing of importance in Muskogee, and I had to retrace my steps to Eufaula to visit one of the most important members of the Creek nation, the Hon. G. W. Stidham.[33]

Muskogee, after Vinita the largest town in the Indian Territory, has 500 inhabitants and consists only of some sandy crisscross streets, whose houses mostly comprise stores of various kinds, including some shops with furriers, proof that game is abundant in these parts. Muskogee is situated on a rolling prairie but on the broad crest of one of the waves—so to speak. Only to the east do one's eyes alight on the heavily wooded Bayou Hills and on all other sides on the endless rolling prairie.

I then returned to Eufaula late on the afternoon of November 14th, where I arrived that evening under splendid moonshine and a penetrating chill. Before long I had found a tavern where a number of woodcutters and freight riders were sitting around a fire, warming themselves. The tavern keeper, married to an Indian, proved to be an ex-*Oberkellner* [head waiter] from the "Vier Jahreszeiten" [Four Seasons] in Wiesbaden, who after numerous twists of fate had eventually strayed to this forgotten corner of the world. It seemed difficult to discern in this bearded frontiersman a former obliging soul from a first-class hotel.

The next morning my first concern is to visit Mr. Stidham, who, in spite of his standing among his tribal compatriots, runs a store. This is just one of the many anomalies that are perhaps only possible in America. I already mentioned that the newly elected chief of the Creeks ran a hotel. The former governor of the Cherokee nation, whom I later met, was simply postmaster, while his daughter helped him with the job. The initial reception from the Creek headman was cool, in spite of—or rather perhaps because of—my letter of recommendation from the government agent. Later, when we got around to talking, the bad feeling evaporated, and he invited me over to his house, a short distance from Eufaula.

Here, too, as far as the history and former way of life and customs of the Creeks are concerned, I must refer to the writers mentioned for the Choctaws but add Bartram's travel narrative.[34] The Creeks, too, arrived about the same time as the other now civilized nations from the east, where they primarily occupied the states of Georgia and Alabama and inhabited a large number of so-called towns.

Among the Creeks are incorporated the remnants of a number of tribes, which also originally had their home in southern and southeastern states of the Union but are merged with them. These include the Hitchittees, linguistically related to the Creeks,[35] Coosadas, and Alabamas.[36] In addition, there are the Uchees[37] and the Natchez, whose language differs fundamentally from the previous tribes'. From the last tribe, especially, immortalized by Chateaubriand in his *Atala, René, and Les Natchez*,[38] only a very few individuals still survive, distributed not only among the Creeks but also among the Cherokees and perhaps among other neighboring tribes as well. Of the 15,000 "Creeks" from the government report, there are not more than 12,000 Indians from various tribes plus mestizos. In addition, there are approximately 2,000 people of black descent. The rest consist of whites, who in large part have intermarried with the Creeks.

The Creeks now live in homesteads, which are indistinguishable from those of the Americans. With the abandonment of their ancestral grounds, communal life in "towns" has vanished, though a number of places in the present-day reservation still have the old names—Ockmulgee, Tullahassee, Muskogee, Eufaula, etc., were towns in their former territory.[39] To Muskogee, actually Maskóki, the Creeks brought their name: *Maskokúlki* (*úlki* = "people"). As is known, the Creeks got their name from the English, because of the many creeks that are so abundant in their original homeland.[40]

The Creeks have retained somewhat more of their old customs than the Choctaws. Ball games and some dances, for example, though no longer widespread, still occur on occasion. That is also true, by the way, of the *pahnkehátsho*, or "crazy dance," previously danced during winter in the "sweat lodges," with a number of Indians from both sexes and every age describing a spiral figure while chanting. The clan system, too, is still partly in vogue among them. In addition to the usual names of Bear, Wolf, Beaver, Eagle, there are also gentes of Raccoon, Otter, and Alligator, as well as Corn and Potato. All told, there are seventy or eighty clans.[41]

In the evening, while I was sitting at Mr. Stidham's hospitable table, it seemed hard to believe that scarcely a lifetime ago his tribal compatriots made the woods of Alabama and Georgia reverberate with their war cries and deemed the taking of scalps as the highest honor. The same man whose children were reared in the eastern states in the spirit of Moody and Sankey[42] was proud of the Indian blood flowing through his veins. "It is their proudest feather," he said, referring to his seven children whom he had from a union with a white woman. In the Union, I have never encountered Indian mestizos who denied their origin, even though there was also practically nothing to remind one of this. On the contrary, they were proud of their Indian blood and provided a stark contrast to the Mexican *gente de razón*,[43] who, just like our *Liplappen,* look down with contempt on their half brothers.

Although the Creeks have broken with their past a long time ago, legends from days past and ancient customs still linger on in their memory. What my host told me about them almost uninterruptedly, as a *rudis indigestaque moles* [crude indigested mass],[44] I do not choose to repeat here and must refer to the older historians of these Indians.[45]

There has been no lack of intelligent chiefs among the Creeks. I will just mention McGillivray from the end of the previous century, a mestizo called the "king of kings" by his tribal compatriots[46]; Weatherford, whose participation in the grand venture of Tecumseh to unite all tribes of North America in a league against the whites came to nought with a severe defeat in 1813[47]; McIntosh, likewise a mestizo, who became famous as the ally of the Americans in the 1812–1814 war against the British but was later killed by his own fellow tribesmen because of treason.[48] Oceola, a Seminole, surpassed them all in courage and intelligence. He was the soul of the war in Florida, which lasted seven years (1835–1841) and in which no more than 1,200 Seminoles withstood a part of American land and sea forces and more than 20,000 volunteers. The Seminole War cost the United States more than 40 million dollars and at least 3,000 men. Oceola was captured and died in exile.[49] The Seminoles are a branch of the Creeks, whose language they speak, but must not be confused with the Lower Creeks. Their name, *Seminol-úlki,* means "the people who are (become) wild." Since their transfer to the Indian Territory the Seminoles have become steadily more civilized. Numbering 2,700, they live in a small reservation to the southwest of the Creeks. A few hundred have remained behind in the wilderness regions of southern Florida and have preserved the old customs and usages unchanged.[50]

Because of the numerous mestizos among the Creeks as well, and the minor tribes merged with them, forming a judgment about their type is extremely difficult. Not a few recalled Choctaws, others Cherokees. As a rule, moreover, the Creeks seem taller in stature than their southern neighbors. Among the mestizos or half-bloods, both men and women, very well-built people appear who could pass for Southern Europeans. The Creeks also have a printed law book, schools, and missions, for the use of which a number of books have been printed in their language.[51] Creek sounds just as melodious as Choctaw. *B, d,* and *g* are missing in this language. In contrast to Choctaw, it has the *r* and more diphthongs.

During my stay in Eufaula, I witnessed an Indian burial. This, indeed, provided a stark contrast with the procedure from days past because where now the coffin is lowered into the grave, wholly in accordance with our customs, formerly the body was buried in an occupied hut. As a result, the dwellers were quite often forced to abandon the area for a time because of the unbearable stench. Children's bodies were placed in hollow tree trunks, the opening of which was sealed.

Before continuing the journey on November 16th, I took a walk in the area around Eufaula. From a high hill, blanketed with tall grass, I had a limitless view across the landscape. Forests and savannas, with a lone farmstead on individual spots between them, spread out endlessly across the strongly undulating ground, while to the south the Canadian shimmered in the clear autumn sun. Where the terrain is not sandy, the ground consists of whitish limestone.

Northward from Muskogee, one encounters little forest along the railway. There is extensive prairie, which at this time of year has lost its fresh vegetation and flowery garb and, pale yellow in color, stands out sharply against the sky, now bright blue, then again gray from heavy clouds, heralding the approach of winter.

Roughly five hours after leaving Eufaula, I have reached Vinita, in Cherokee country. Vinita, which is situated at the junction of three railway lines, has 600 residents, mostly whites, and is the most important town in the Indian Territory. It has a pleasant, rural appearance, as it is situated in the undulating prairie, broken by forests. Probably it owes its name to Vinita or Vineta, a Mexican, one of the first settlers of these regions.[52] It consists entirely of wooden houses, which are separated by wide, sandy streets. There one finds a number of stores and warehouses, a couple of churches and schools, a photographic establishment, and a couple of "hotels," of which the "Frisco" is the most important one. The Frisco's host is a kind of failed man of letters, a writer of "Dreams of Obai," who now has sought his fortune among the Cherokees.[53]

My first concern is to visit Mr. W. P. Ross, a former chief of the Cherokees, for whom I have a letter of recommendation. Mr. Ross is a wholly civilized and very well-educated man, who listens to me with the greatest courtesy and in the evening invites me to his home. Neither he himself nor his wife and children bear nary a trace of their Indian descent. Yet the extremely small eyes and angular features, with Mr. Ross's fine bent nose, recall the Cherokee, an impression that once again is partially effaced by the snow white beard covering his face. The former chief divides his time between being postmaster in Vinita and editing the *Indian Chieftain,* a weekly newspaper dedicated to the interests of all the Indian tribes of the territory.[54]

The name Ross is renowned among the Cherokees. John Ross was, indeed, the iron-willed chief who resisted the surrender of ancestral land, which the Cherokees eventually gave up, to settle in the prairies along the Arkansas, mainly between 1833 and 1838, after a sorry exodus—during which a quarter of their number died.[55] The Cherokees were once the most powerful tribe in the Southeast. Spread over a number of towns, they occupied the greatest part of Tennessee and stretches of North and South Carolina, Georgia, and Alabama. The many mounds of these tracts, which now arouse the admiration of archaeologists, are probably to be ascribed to the Cherokees' ancestors. The Cherokees once played a role in the history of the surrounding nations that was nearly as important as that of the Iroquois in the Northeast.[56] What is the land the Cherokee now shares with whites, blacks, and other Indians compared with the vast mountainous land with its dark woods and grassy savannas where he was lord and master! Well might he exclaim in recalling the past:

Where is my home—my forest home?
The proud land of my sires?

If the Cherokees were once preeminent on the warpath, now they surpass all Indians in the "arts of civilization." Already at the time of their forced relocation to the west, the Cherokees had attained a certain level of civilization. They had schools and churches and were engaged in agriculture. The first newspaper ever published by Indians, the *Cherokee Phoenix,* saw the light of day in Georgia. The atrocity of forcing a peaceful people to abandon their homeland, leaving everything behind, and to banish them through wilderness regions inhabited by hostile tribes is a deed that will forever be a dark stain in the history of the Union. Gradually the Cherokees have recovered from the heavy buffeting of fate. The Osages and Kansas, who first disputed the new homeland with them, driven off in their turn by the whites, have now sought refuge in the land of their more civilized brethren. Agriculture and livestock raising flourish among the Cherokees, as among the best farmers of Kansas, and slowly but surely the tiny nation is progressing in civilization. But all this has not occurred without alien influence. The Cherokees have mingled their blood with the whites to such an extent that only roughly half of them speak the ancient language of their fathers. All of those who are listed in the Annual Reports as Cherokees are not Cherokees at all, even if all of them have acquired rights of citizenship in the nation. Of the "Cherokees" in the Indian Territory there are approximately 15,000 who have Cherokee blood in their veins, whether of pure race, whether half-breeds in various gradations. Furthermore, 900 whites and 974 Negroes live among them, while approximately 700 Delawares, 700 Shawnees, 200 Creeks, and some Natchez live on the Cherokee reservation—18,500 people in all.[57]

Among the Cherokees the number of full-blooded Indians is declining because, more than ever, they are mingling with whites. From these marriages more children are being born than from those where both parents are Indians of pure race. This is hardly a unique situation: among all tribes that heavily mingle with whites—among the Iroquois, Creeks, Choctaws, etc.—the same phenomenon occurs. The mestizo race, which diverges more from the Indian type as time passes, steadily increases because again it seldom mingles with the colored race. The full-blooded Indians, on the other hand, steadily diminish. Their total dissolution into the white element is only a matter of time. Not only the civilized tribes but all of them, those still uncivilized as well, will go the same path.[58]

I could quickly see that there was little for me to do in Vinita and that, if I wanted to see more of the Cherokees, I must go to Tahlequah, their capital, where the National Council was just gathering. Furnished with the necessary recommendations, on November 19th at 4 A.M. I retraced my steps to Muskogee to take the mail coach from there to Tahlequah, twenty-eight miles east-northeast.

It is eight miles to Fort Gibson, a small military post. The broad sandy trail leads first through rolling prairie land until one crosses the Arkansas and Grand River or Neosho, exactly at their confluence, with a ferry and the terrain becomes more wooded. The difference in color between the two rivers is clearly visible. The Arkansas is muddy and brown in color from the sand, which is carried along from the flat regions. The Neosho is clearer because its waters flow from the north over limestone terrain, which is less soluble than the softer ground of Triassic sandstone in the west. The same Neosho is the reason that Fort Gibson, situated along the eastern bank, was once called the "charnel house of the frontier." The fort, which is now situated on a hill, was formerly in the lowland. Because the Neosho rises every year during the summer and floods the bottomland, when its level drops, it leaves behind a morasslike ground, which is the source of dreadful malarial fevers. The inhabitants of the "town" Gibson, which is on the fort's former site, still suffer from malaria, while the garrison, now transferred to a hill, which is not higher than 600 feet above sea level, is much less subject to it.

If one has left Gibson, the trail then leads uninterrupted to Tahlequah (roughly twenty miles) through oak forests. On the right arise the densely overgrown Bayou Mountains, like a row of table mountains linked together. Dark rain clouds hover above them, heightening the desolate character of the region. Menard, a solitary post station consisting of one or two wooden houses, where I can fill my hungry stomach with nothing more than a couple of dry crackers, is the only place we pass by. Except for some Indians on horseback, whom we ran into by the ferry, we encounter no other living creature. We wade through three or four quiet little streams, which flow through the labyrinth of forests to the Arkansas, and at 4 o'clock arrive at Tahlequah.

Although it stands out on the map in large letters, Tahlequah is an insignificant place and smaller than Muskogee and Vinita.[59] Almost all the houses are made of wood and form not more than a half-dozen "streets," which are full of rough spots and strewn with large loose stones. The capitol, a large, redbrick building, which is situated on a rectangular grassy plain, surrounded by a wooden fence, forms the most important part of the city. Three rows of houses, including two "hotels"; the government printing office; and the most important stores, separated from the fencing by a street, surround the capitol plaza, beyond which the heavily wooded hills emerge toward the east side. Tahlequah is not situated, as the maps suggest, along the Illinois River, but roughly three miles west of there. Indeed, up to now a decent map of the Indian Territory has been a desideratum. On no map known to me, for instance, is there a satisfactory description of the character of the terrain. The Bayou Mountains and the hills near Caddo are nowhere to be found.

The population of Tahlequah consists almost entirely of Indians. It was good that someone told me this because in the beginning I regarded the majority of these "Indians" as whites, as I did the host and guests of the Tahlequah Hotel, where I stayed. The guests whom in the beginning I thought were cattlemen appeared to be members of the Cherokee Senate and the Lower House, who were in the capital temporarily because of annual meetings of the National Council. Tahlequah was thus extraordinarily lively, and I had a better opportunity than otherwise to gaze upon the comings and goings of the Cherokees.

Thanks to my letters of introduction, I made the acquaintance of the recently elected head chief, Bushyhead,[60] with all the members of the Senate and some other important members of the Cherokee nation, and I could attend the council deliberations. The Senate has its sessions in the left wing, the lower house in the right wing of the capitol, while the office of the principal chief and of other dignitaries is upstairs. In the Senate there are only a few members, whose outward appearance brings Indians to mind. In the more numerous lower house, on the other hand, are seated some full-blooded Indians and many who pass for such.

In both assembly halls the debates are held in Cherokee and in English because there are many who have only an imperfect understanding of the former language. Two interpreters are thus constantly busy translating. Except for the president, secretary, interpreter—in short, the management of both bodies—all the members sit on cane chairs next to each other along the whitewashed wall of the hall, whose floor consists of unpainted boards. A surprising *sans gêne* [informality] prevails over the whole affair, particularly in the lower house. The members smoke, chew and spit tobacco, and sit with their feet up in the air like real Americans. Now and then the debates break off for a moment, and every member of the assembly eats an apple, or, indeed, someone stands up to take a draught with a ladle from one of the buckets filled with drinking water, which are standing in the window frames. Otherwise everything proceeds calmly and peacefully. No one gets excited, and now and then the room reverberates with the peculiar idiom of the Cherokees, then again with American English, which most of them have completely mastered.

Although—as far as I could judge from a superficial observation—the majority of the Cherokee counselors were on a par with the communal counselors of our farming communities, there were still individuals who in manners and outward appearance bore the hallmarks of real gentlemen, including Mr. Bushyhead, the president of the Senate, Mr. Benge,[61] Mr. Eubanks, both Boudinots,[62] etc. I will not easily forget my astonishment when one of the latter asked me whether Motley was still well regarded in our country and whether one could rely on his works.[63] Mr. Daniel Ross, brother of the former chief in Vinita, is editor of the official organ of the nation, *The Cherokee Advocate*, a weekly, one quarter of which appears in Cherokee, the rest in English.[64]

As is known, since 1824 the Cherokees have a syllabic alphabet, invented by the mestizo George Guess or Gist, also named Sequoyah.[65] It has eighty-five characters, of which the smaller half consists of conventional signs, the other half of letters, which are derived from the Greek as well as the Latin alphabet but have a different meaning in Cherokee. The Cherokees are proud of their alphabet. In Bushyhead's "Message" directed to the National Council shortly before my arrival, one reads: "A lasting monument of the Nation's intelligence and public spirit and a memento of its origin and antiquity can be erected on the foundation laid by the genius of Sequoyah in the Cherokee Alphabet." Apart from the *Advocate,* the code of the Cherokees (of which an English edition is also available) and some primers are printed in native characters. In many instances Cherokee, too, is written by means of Sequoyah's alphabet.

Cherokee is not euphonic, but at the same time, owing to lack of labials and consonant clusters, it has something of the distinctive harshness characteristic of so many American languages. In addition, the protracted somewhat singsong tone, with which it is spoken, has something of an annoying quality to the foreigner's ear.

Cherokee has two dialects that differ little: the *Élete,* or dialect spoken by the Lower Cherokees, and the *Otale,* spoken by the Highlanders or Eastern Cherokees in North Carolina and surrounding states. The main difference consists in the letter *r,* which is missing in the Élete. For example, a Cherokee from the Indian Territory will say: *ootakwalóskuh* = "thunder"; his fellow tribesman from the

Alleghanies, on the other hand, *ootakwaróskuh*. That is why the Western Cherokees once branded the others with the epithet *Seghakawonîeske* = "people with a strange way of speaking."[66]

The language of the Cherokees is completely different from that of the Creeks and other Appalachian peoples and, as far as we can determine, appears to exist in total isolation.[67] The superficial resemblance of the name *Cherokees* with *Iroquois* has led certain "ethnologists" into conjectures regarding the relationship of both peoples. Nothing, however, is more erroneous. The name *Cherokee* is a bastardization of *Tsalakí* (sing. and plural), as these Indians call themselves. This name has nothing to do with *atsjíra (atsjíla)* = "fire," as Adair—who speaks of *cheera*—wrongly asserted, along with other writers following him. If the name were Ts*í*lakí or Tsjilakí, that would mean "he or she takes fire"; the meaning of Tsalakí is unknown, however. The name *Iroquois*, on the other hand, is derived from a Huron word: *ierokwa* = "those who smoke" or "those who use tobacco."[68]

It is certain, though, that the physiques of the few full-blooded Cherokees whom I got to see definitely brought the Iroquois to mind, particularly in view of the extremely small eyes, the caruncle of which is covered by a fold of skin, and the somewhat squinting look, as well as the shape of the nose. The Cherokees are also of tall and vigorous stature. The Cherokee women are large and stocky. Many of them smoke clay pipes, just like their sisters from the Choctaw tribe. A great many enchanting types can be found among the women and girls of mixed blood.

It scarcely need be said that as a rule, the Cherokees dress like Americans. A number of men, however, wear a kind of jacket of Indian make. These jackets consist of a kind of woolen material with colorful Scottish colors, which are intersected by broad, vertical stripes, while the edges of the article of clothing are trimmed with thick woolen bands, colored red or black.

In contrast to the Creeks and Choctaws, who distinguish the neighboring tribes with names that are only bastardizations of the ones these tribes give themselves, the Cherokees have given some variant ones for them. Thus they call the Creeks *Anicoosa*, based on the Coosa River in Georgia, and the Delawares *Akwanké*. The name they give the Senecas of the Indian Territory, *Nantewèki*, is clearly derived, though, from their own name, *Nandowahgaah*.[69]

My investigation of the sense of color and color names among the Cherokees furnished me the following results:[70] "Red" = *kay-gv-ka* is derived from the word "blood" = *kay-gv*. For "orange" there is no special word, but one says, just as one does for "pink," *kay-gv-ka-ay-stay*—the last two clusters of letters being an abbreviation of *ay-yu-stay* = "like"; *kay-gv-ka-ay-stay* thus signifies "reddish." "Yellow" = *tah-loh-nay-ka* from *tal-lo-nay* = "gall," and *ka*, which just like *aye-stay* means "like," "just as." For "green" and "blue" separate words exist. For the former color *ay-tsa* is used, which at the same time means "fresh," "tender," "young"; "greenish" = *ay-tsa-ay-stay*. "Blue" = *sah-koh-ne-ka*. "Purple" and "violet" are distinguished with the word *ah-deh-hah-lu-geh (ka)*. With the exception of the last syllable, this word's meaning is perhaps "beginning," "twilight," recalling the purple tints of morning and evening twilight. "Black" = *kv-nah-ka*. "White" = *oh-na-kv (kv = ka = geh)*. "Gray" = *oh-na-gah-ka-ay-stay* = "whitish." To express the intensity of a color one uses *oh-scoh-stv* = "deep," "bright," "powerful." "Dark blue," for example, is thus *sah-koh-ne-geh (= ka)-oh-scoh-stv*.

The only distinctive dishes I was able to try at Tahlequah were *kanohéna*[71] and *kawiseta,* which reminded me of Mexican pinole. Otherwise the Cherokee cuisine was wholly like the American. The Cherokees with whom I dined had, so it seemed, already adopted from their half brothers the custom of eating with extraordinary rapidity and without uttering a word.

A tame raccoon was the guest's pet and entertained us with its amusing behavior, which sometimes recalled that of the house cat. With all due respect for the level of civilization of the worthy Cherokees, they have not advanced far in modern comfort, not at least as far as hotels are concerned. Thus several guests slept in a small room, so divided up that each bed must include two or three people. With difficulty I obtained a wretched room on the top floor, where, it is true, I did not have to share my bed with others but where at night there was dreadful leaking because of the heavy rain. In the morning all the guests washed themselves, one after another, in the same tin basin, which stood outside on the porch, while they used a single hand towel.

It is obvious that among the Cherokees ancestral customs have largely vanished. Ball games and dances are still in vogue only among the Eastern Cherokees of Carolina and bordering regions. On the other hand, the clan system is still current among the full-blooded Indians of the western Cherokees as well. Here are the names of the seven clans, as they were given me by Mr. W. P. Ross and whose manner of writing I have adopted:

Ah-ne-Wo-te (Painted People)
Ah-ne-Chees-qua (Bird People)
Ah-ne-Oh-ne-sti-ti
Ah-ne-Sa-ho-ni
Ah-ne-Wah-he-yur (Wolf People)
Ah-ne-Ge-lo-hi (Long-haired People)
Ah-ne-Koti-ca-wah (Long Savanna People)

Like the clan system, the peculiar system of marriage relationships is also in vogue. Accordingly, they use completely different appellations than we do, a system that is, indeed, quite widespread among all Indian tribes.[72] As a rule, the full-blooded Cherokees have one name, their Indian name. Those who have English names have an Indian name in addition. French names occur now and then among the Cherokees, as they do among the Creeks and Choctaws, and come from the time that Louisiana—formerly meaning the entire South and Southeast of North America—was a French possession.

Even though the Christian religion is the national religion, as it were, among the Cherokee full-bloods, not a few are still attached to the beliefs of their fathers. They label their supreme being with the name of "Old White One" or "Old Clean One," "Pure One" *(Ah-gah-yv-lu-na-gv).* Other names are *Oh-neh-lah-nv-hay* = "Creator" and *Eh-quah-ah-dah-nv-doh-gay* = "The Great Spirit." Their cult consists of praying to this spirit and performing various secret rites. With a certain predilection my authority, Senator Eubanks, pointed to the fact that many Cherokee customs recall those of the Israelites, something that Adair had done his utmost to demonstrate in their case and that of the Creeks as well. Among other things, they consult certain sacred rocks as oracles that they may know the will of the Great Spirit and predict the future,[73] something that Mr. Eubanks compares with the *urim* and *thummim* from the Bible.[74] Furthermore, they had prophets and priests who predicted the future—from dreams too—and their favorite colors are blue and scarlet, just like those of the Jews. Moreover, what Adair reported concerning the "sacred syllables" *yeh-hoh-wah* was here imparted to me by a Cherokee in the following manner: Whenever a Cherokee sings any kind of song, he ends with the sounds *he-yah-yoh-wah-he-yeh, he-yah-yoh-wah-he-yeh, hoh-wah-yeh!* From the last three words one can now form the word "Jehovah"! More examples of this kind among the Cherokees and among the Osages as well were related to me.

Here we confront the strange fact, which I previously encountered among the Iroquois as well, that among the civilized Indians there are people who, with a kind of satisfaction, pay homage to the notion that they are descendants of the "lost tribes of Israel." It is not worth the effort disputing the "arguments" of Adair, who always calls the Indians "the red Hebrews," of Catlin, and others—arguments that are just as fatuous and unscientific as those of certain writers who want to draw a connection between the manners and morals of the Indians and those of the ancient peoples of Europe. Ethnographic parallels, though they *can* point to the relationship of various peoples in certain cases, usually prove nothing more than the psychological unity of mankind, independent of time and space.

Among the full-blooded Cherokees many ancient songs and legends, which pass by oral tradition from one generation to the next, are still current. The subjects of these songs and legends are mostly heroic deeds and love; some are of a religious character. Here I will pass on a couple of these legends, as they were told to me by Senator Eubanks, almost word for word:

"In very ancient times there lived among the Cherokees two strange beings—monsters in human form, who in every respect looked like Cherokees, apart from two or three exceptions. These two monsters, a man and a woman, lived in a cave. They were called by the Cherokees Nv-yu-noh-way[75] or, indeed, Oh-ilv-tv[76] because they had sharp, pointed steel hands.[77] These monsters killed the children, and sometimes adults, among the Cherokees. Because they were attired like Cherokees and spoke their language, it was difficult to distinguish them from that people. The man usually killed hunters or other people who were alone and far from home by assaulting them, but the woman used cunning to lure her victims into an ambush. She came into family households with friendly offers of one service or another, such as looking after the children and the like. Once she had a child in her arms, she ran away with it, far enough so as to be outside of hearing range, and stuck her steel hand into the child's brains, then took the liver out of the body and vanished. Indeed, the Nv-yu-noh-way evidently fed on their victims' livers.

"The older Cherokees, long despondent about this treatment by the monsters, deliberated over the best way to kill the Oh-ilv-tv. They eventually decided to try their luck with arrows, not knowing that the Oh-ilv-tv had a stony armor. When a favorable opportunity to kill the woman presented itself, they fired arrows toward her with all their might and were quite surprised that these did not have the slightest effect on her. Then a topnot bird, which was perched on a bough nearby, said: 'In the heart, in the heart.' Now the Cherokees fired their arrows toward the spot where they thought her heart was, but they still did not succeed in killing the monster. Finally a jay arrived and said: 'In the hand, in the hand.' Now they fired at her hand, and she dropped dead. At the very moment she fell, her stony arm shattered into pieces. The people now picked up the pieces and kept them as sacred amulets for good fortune in war, hunting, and love. The male monster vanished. Tradition says that it went north."

Similarly, the Cherokees have a tale about flying monsters shaped like falcons who kill their children especially. They, too, were successfully combated because a brave man, whose only son had been stolen by the monsters, visited the cave where they were holding his boy and killed them, whereupon the old ones vanished without a trace.

Here is another legend:

"Once there lived gigantic snakes, as brilliant as the sun and with two horns on their heads. To look at one of these snakes was certain death. So great was the enchantment·they emanated that whoever tried to run away dashed in confusion toward the snake, only to be devoured. But great hunters, who 'had made medicine' for that purpose, could kill these snakes. They always had to be shot in the seventh strip of the skin. The last one of these snakes was killed by a Shawnee Indian, who was a prisoner of war among the Cherokees. He had been promised his freedom if he killed the snake, and after looking for days, in caves and on barren mountains, he found the snake in the high mountains of Tennessee. The Shawnee now started a huge fire of pinecones in the form of a huge circle and went after the snake. When it saw the hunter, it slowly lifted its head high, but the man shouted: 'Freedom or death,' and shot his arrow through the seventh strip of skin, whereupon he hurriedly turned around and leaped inside the ring of fire, where he was safe because at the same moment a stream of poison issued from the snake's mouth, but the fire halted it. The Shawnee had regained his freedom. Four days later the people came to the place and collected pieces of bone and scales from the snake, which were carefully preserved, because they were regarded as bringing good fortune in love, hunting, and war. On the spot where the snake died emerged a lake, the water of which was black. In the water of that lake the women of the Cherokees used to dip twigs with which they wove their baskets."

To most mestizos many of these legends are barely known by name. But among the elderly pure-blooded Cherokees, whose hearts are still attached to the mountains and woods of their lost homeland, they live on. During the long winter evenings, as they are seated around the fire in their log cabins, the voice of the storyteller reverberates until deep into the night. However often heard, the legends from the hoary past are always told and listened to again and again with the same enjoyment. But with the full-bloods the songs and traditions of the previous generation will disappear if a rescuing hand does not preserve them from oblivion. The language, too, is spoken less and less and one day, in a not too far distant future, will cease to exist as a living tongue.[78]

The Cherokees have a large number of schools and other educational institutions, of which the two national "seminaries," situated not far from Tahlequah, are the most important. One is for male, the other for female pupils. I only had time to visit the "Male Seminary," which is one and a half miles west of the capital on a hill. It is a very large stone building with tall, sturdy columns, where 110 pupils receive instruction. This "Seminary," founded in 1850, is instituted in the fashion of the English and American colleges so that various degrees from baccalaureate to master's can be conferred.

I attended lessons in geometry, physics, Latin, and history and got the impression that the Cherokee Male Seminary can vie with the best institutions of this kind. Who would have ever thought that in the Indian Territory, I would hear an explanation of the Leiden jar and Ivy being translated! But neither the language nor the script of the Cherokees is taught at this institution. Nor can it be denied that most pupils display not a trace of Indian blood. The pupils have formed among themselves three literary clubs, one of which is named after Sequoia and where there are debates and speeches a couple of times a month.

With the Cherokees becoming civilized, a prison and a mental institution have become necessary as well. Just like their orphanages, they are paid for entirely from tribal funds. I cannot make any observations here about the state of finances, agriculture, and livestock and other economic questions because I would be limited to repeating things whose accuracy I cannot vouch for; in the government reports more or less complete data can be found regarding that subject.

The Cherokees, who, to the number of roughly 2,000, still inhabit the mountainous regions of North Carolina and the bordering districts of South Carolina, Georgia, and Tennessee, form the "Eastern Band of Cherokees," a segment of the Cherokee nation, and remain in constant contact with their western brethren. As already mentioned, a small number of these Eastern Cherokees have settled recently in the Indian Territory, partly compelled to this by the infringement of their rights by white settlers, partly at the insistence of the authorities of their western brethren. In all likelihood, all those remaining will gradually move to the Indian Territory as well.[79]

Will the Cherokee nation survive in the future, too, as a separate state? Does it have enough vigor to live? And will it be able to resist the continuous stream of whites who do not now respect many areas of its territory? I posed these questions to a civilized Cherokee who was proud of his people's civilization, which he loved like few others. His response, though, did not sound encouraging. He questioned the Cherokees' future existence as a nation. His concern was based partly on the firm law that a small minority cannot possibly offer prolonged resistance to an overwhelming majority. On the other hand, the modus operandi of the government of the Union as far as treaties are concerned is quite well known. Notwithstanding the "final guarantee" with which the code book of the Cherokees concludes, referring to their treaty of 1866 with the United States, the "guarantee to the people of the Cherokee nation the quiet and peaceful possession of their country," he did not believe in the inviolability of that treaty.[80]

After staying two and a half days at Tahlequah, on the morning of November 22 I bade farewell to that place and late in the evening of the same day had returned to Vinita. Days before, mist and rain had imbued the landscape with a dreary haze. The following morning it was as though they had been swept away, and a sunny blue sky arched lovelier than ever above the forests and prairies resplendent in their autumn colors. It was as though nature had conspired to make the last day I would spend in the West an unforgettable one.

Once more this morning I went out in the field to take a last look at the limitless plains, which perhaps I would never see again, and once more to breathe in deeply the fresh aroma from the meadows. In a kind of reflex, I looked back on the long journey of eleven months I had made in Mexico and the Far West. Although the keynote of these thoughts was joy at the hope of soon seeing blood relatives again in the distant homeland, a feeling of quiet melancholy nevertheless mingled with the joy now that I stood on the verge of leaving these regions where I had had so much to experience and ponder. And that afternoon when the train hurriedly brought me back to the bosom of civilization, my thoughts long remained with the invisible sojourn and at the same time reverted again to the past.

A month later I had safely returned to my homeland.

◆◆◆◆◆

NOTES

1. HtK 1885: Timber or buffalo wolf, *lobo* of the Mexicans *(Canis lupus occidentalis)*.

2. HtK 1885: Schlagintweit, op. cit., 167, states, with no justification whatsoever, that these animals act confidently in extremely rare instances. I would be able to cite not a few instances, which he claims are exceptions. Moreover, in the immediate vicinity of railway lines, in Texas as well as Colorado, I repeatedly saw colonies of prairie dogs. On the other hand, I must wholly agree with S. when he disputes the opinion that ground owls and rattlesnakes always share the prairie dog burrows.

3. "The water is like the land it flows through." Pliny the Elder (23–79), Roman writer primarily on natural history.

4. The first commercially marketable barbed wire was invented by J. F. Glidden of De Kalb, Illinois, in 1874. It immediately came into widespread use in the Great Plains and contributed in a major way to the agricultural settlement of the region. Walter Prescott Webb, *The Great Plains* (Lincoln: University of Nebraska Press, 1981), 295–317.

5. The Civil War effort enlisted 200,000 blacks in the Union army, and in the Indian wars of the Plains and Southwest several regiments of black soldiers played a major part. Relatively few blacks settled in the West after the Civil War, however, although more blacks were employed as cowboys. K. W. Porter, ed., *The Negro on the American Frontier* (New York: Arno, 1971). See also note 8 below.

6. HtK 1885: Usually called "the Panhandle" by the Americans because the shape, viewed on a map, somewhat resembles the handle of a pan, here represented by the remaining part of Texas extending to the east and west. This is an appellation on the order of the "boot of Italy."

7. See note 5 above.

8. Ten Kate is correct in his observation that most blacks in the West in the 1880s lived in the larger towns, where they took advantage of employment opportunities as domestic workers. While Ten Kate combated contemporary negative stereotypes about Indians, he clearly succumbed to the same kind of stereotypes about blacks. One wonders what his attitude would have been if he had had more than superficial contacts with blacks during his journey and investigations.

9. William Hepworth Dixon (1821–1879), an English historian and traveler, visited the United States in 1866, traveling as far as the Great Salt Lake. Ten Kate's comments would bolster the assessment that "Dixon was no scholar. He was always lively as a writer, and therefore popular, but inaccuracies and misconceptions abound in his work." *Dictionary of National Biography* (Oxford: Oxford University Press, 1885–1922), 5:1033–35. Ten Kate is quoting from Dixon's work, *White Conquest,* 2 vols. (London: Chatto and Windus, 1876), 1:272–73.

10. Possibly Alfred W. Folsom, a prominent rancher and landholder who at one time sat in the lower house of the legislature. Harry F. O'Beirne, *Leaders and Leading Men of the Indian Territory* (Chicago: American Publishers Assoc., 1891), 130–31. Another possibility is that this is Julius C. Folsom (1831–1914), who was a judge, senator, and representative of the Choctaw nation. J. B. Thoburn, *A Standard History of Oklahoma,* 5 vols. (Chicago and New York: American Historical Society, 1916), 3:1308.

11. HtK 1885: *History of the American Indians,* London 1775. Eds.: James Adair (ca. 1709–ca. 1783), probably born in Ireland, emigrated to the United States in 1735. He established trading ties with the Cherokees, Chickasaws, and Choctaws, which in turn helped him to undermine French influence among the latter tribe. Adair is remembered primarily for the dubious thesis that the Indians were descendants of the ancient Jews. Yet his work still has useful information on the manners, customs,

and languages of these peoples. *Dictionary of American Biography,* 23 vols. (New York: Scribner, 1943–73, 23 vols.), 1 (1):33–34. HtK 1889: Along with the works of Adair, etc., which are related to the history, morals, and customs of the Choctaws, the outstanding book of Albert S. Gatschet, *A Migration Legend of the Creek Indians,* etc., vol. I, first part, Philadelphia, 1884, can also be recommended. In this work there is, as well, an account of other works about the Choctaws, Creeks, Cherokees, and other southern tribes, and their ethnology is handled at the same time.

12. HtK 1885: *History of Florida,* 1775. Eds.: Bernard Roman (ca. 1720–ca. 1784) was a native of the Netherlands who studied engineering in England. In 1757 he was sent to the American colonies as a surveyor, carrying out surveys and botanical collections in west Florida (1769–1773), the basis for his work *A Concise Natural History of East and West Florida* (New York: Printed for the Author, 1775). *Dictionary of American Biography,* 8 (2):127–28.

13. HtK 1885: *Antiquities of the Southern Indians,* 1873. Eds.: Georgian Charles Colcock Jones (1831–1893), mayor of Savannah before the Civil War and a colonel in the Confederate army, was also a prolific author of works on southern history and ethnography. *Dictionary of American Biography,* 5 (2):165.

14. HtK 1889: In addition to the state of Mississippi a small number of Choctaws live in s. Louisiana, not far from New Orleans, a city where they have been coming for years to sell medicinal plants, spices, etc. In Sept. 1888 I encountered there some Choctaw women who, though apparently of pure race, still had something distinctive in their hairstyle and the cut of their jackets.

15. HtK 1889: As regards the meaning of the tribal name Chickasaw or Chíkasha, Gatschet (op. cit., p. 94) says: "No plausible analysis of the name Chicasa . . . has yet been suggested." Eds.: The name Chickasaw is derived from the Choctaw term "Chikasha," which means "those who have recently left," indicating that the Chickasaws were formerly part of the Choctaw. They probably separated in the early sixteenth century. Muriel Wright, *A Guide to the Indian Tribes of Oklahoma* (Norman: University of Oklahoma Press, 1986), 84.

16. HtK 1885: Some writers such as Balbi *(Elémens de Géographie Générale)* and A. H. Keane (*Ethnography and Philology of America,* appendix of Bates-Hellwald, Central America, etc.) claim that the Choctaws were immortalized by Chateaubriand in his "Atala." By confusing one of the principal *persons* of this work—Chactas, N.B. a Natchez Indian!—with the Choctaw *tribe,* they provide a clear enough glimpse of their limited reliability on this subject. Compare, as well, the deservedly harsh criticism by Gatschet of this appendix in *American Naturalist,* May 1881.

17. The name *Choctaw* is an Anglicized version of the tribal name *Chahta,* which is of Creek origin and means "red," referring to the red or war towns, in contrast to the white or peace towns. Ten Kate is correct in stating that the Choctaws and Seminoles were Creek groups split off from the parent body. Wright, *Indian Tribes of Oklahoma,* 84, 97–98, 128–29, 228.

18. HtK 1889: The Kashápaokla and Ocoolaihooláhta ("people of the chiefs"), which I incorrectly called clans or gentes, are in all probability phratries, each of which is again divided into a number of gentes. The difference between the "kinships" *(iksa, yéksa)* of the Choctaws, reported by Gatschet (op. cit., p. 104), and phratries of which, at the very least, one is called Kashápaokla *(Kúshap ókla)*—is unclear to me.

19. HtK 1885: The corpses were left for some time on scaffolds and then cleaned of all soft parts by old men, who made a profession of this, using their long nails. Afterward the bones were ceremoniously interred in the charnel house, which every village possessed.

20. Allen Wright (1825–1885), who was born in Mississippi but transferred to Indian Territory while still a boy, was educated in Union Theological Seminary in New York and ordained as a Presbyterian minister in 1865, after which he returned to his people. Wright was versed in Latin, Greek, and Hebrew—a very erudite man, as Ten Kate notes. He also published a Choctaw dictionary. From 1866 to 1870 he served as tribal chief. Harvey Markowitz, ed., *American Indians,* 3 vol. (Pasadena: Salem Press, 1995), 3:873. Pieter Hovens, *Herman ten Kate en de Antropologie der Noord Amerikaanse Indianen* (Meppel: Krips, 1989), 64–65.

21. The site of these towns is about fourteen miles southwest of Atoka. Old Boggy Depot's origins as an Indian log cabin reach back to 1837, but during the Civil War it developed into a flourishing trade center. Later it was bypassed by the railroad and from that point on declined. Few traces now remain. New Boggy Depot, the present-day town of Boggy Depot, took this name in 1872 but dropped it again in 1883. Kent Ruth, *Oklahoma Travel Handbook* (Norman: University of Oklahoma Press, 1977), 52.

22. HtK 1885: *Choctaw in English Definition for the Choctaw Academics and Schools,* 1st ed., St. Louis, 1880.

23. HtK 1885: *humma* = "red," hence "bloody," was the title granted a Choctaw warrior when he had taken a scalp.

24. HtK 1885: *Okla* = "people," *homa* = "red." In his "Hunting Grounds" Dodge provides an illustration of an Indian tree burial, under which stands the inscription, "Okolohama, the last home of the Indians." Apart from the fact that "Okolohama" has no meaning, "Oklahoma" should, in any case, have nothing to do with a final resting place. This is an example of the superficiality regarding ethnography at least displayed by his book, which enjoys some renown.

25. HtK 1885: Compare R. de Semallé, *Considerations on the Establishment in the Indian Territory of a New State of the American Union,* Versailles, 1876. Eds.: Oklahoma actually became a state in 1907.

26. HtK 1885: Cf. Manypenny, *Our Indian Wards,* chs. VI and VII.

27. HtK 1885: Approximately 8 percent of the entire Indian Territory consists of forest land.

28. This group of languages, including Apalachee, is now called Muskogean. Goddard, "Classification of Native Languages," *Handbook: Languages,* 17:321.

29. HtK 1885: *Reis van den Mississippi naar de Kusten van den Grooten Oceaan,* vol. I, pp. 34, 35, 37. Dutch translation. Eds.: Balduin Möllhausen, *Diary of a Journey from the Mississippi to the Coasts of the Pacific with a U.S. Exploring Expedition,* 2 vols. (London: Longman, Brown, Green, Longmans and Roberts), 1:35–39.

30. HtK 1885: To judge from skulls in the museums in Paris and London, this deformation consisted of a flattening between the *tubera parietalia,* the *obelion,* and the *apex squamae occipitalis.*

31. Probably Joseph M. Perryman, who was elected governor of the Creek Nation in 1883. Harry F. and Edward S. O'Beirne, *The Indian Territory: Its Chiefs, Legislators, and Leading Men* (St. Louis: C. B. Woodward, 1892), 120–22.

32. HtK 1885: Cherokees, Creeks, Seminoles, Choctaws, and Chickasaws, all falling under the Union Agency in Muskogee.

33. The Hon. George Washington Stidham (1817–1894) was born in Alabama, the son of a Scotch-Irish itinerant who settled among the Creeks and a Creek mother. He moved with the tribe to the Indian Territory in 1837 and became an important tribal leader among the Creeks and, after the Civil War, the chief justice of the Creek Nation, a post he held until his death. He was also a leading agriculturalist who is said to have introduced the cultivation of both wheat and cotton to the Muskogee area. O'Beirne and O'Beirne, *Indian Territory,* 185–87.

34. HtK 1885: *Travels through Carolina, Georgia, and Florida* in 1773 et. seq. Eds.: William Bartram (1739–1823), naturalist, artist, and explorer, traveled throughout the Southeast with his father, the naturalist John Bartram (1699–1777), in 1765 and 1766. He returned to the area on a four-year 2,400-mile journey from North Carolina to Louisiana, 1770–1773. His diary was published in 1791. *Dictionary of National Biography,* 22 vols.(Oxford: Oxford University Press, 1885–1922), 2:297–99.

35. HtK 1885: Part of the Hitchitees, called Mikasuakies or Mikkesooke, are incorporated among the Seminoles of the Indian Territory. Eds.: The Hitchitis, a Muskogean language tribe, were living in the lower Ocmulgee River region of what is now Georgia when the first Europeans arrived in the 1540s. In the eighteenth century they moved to Florida to escape the onslaught of white settlement. Here they became part of the evolving Seminole nation, and Hitchiti-speaking Seminoles were referred to as Miccosukees, after a town near Lake Miccosukee in northern Florida. When the Creeks and Seminoles were removed from their homelands, many Hitchitis were also transferred to the Indian Territory, but some remained in Florida. Markowitz, *American Indians,* 2:323–24.

36. HtK 1885: According to Stidham, in 1817 some of these Indians moved from Alabama to southeastern Texas, where they live in Polk County. According to other accounts, the Coosadas and Alabamas emigrated only after 1820. Eds.: The Alabamas, who are part of the Muskogean language group, originally lived along the Alabama River, just below the junction of the Coosa and Tallapoosa rivers. They were part of the Creek Confederacy. The Coushatta or Koasati, a tribe from the Muskogean linguistic group, originally lived near the Tennessee River. In the mid-eighteenth century some Alabamas fled to Louisiana near Opelousas. In the 1790s some Coushatta joined them. The Indians were transferred to the Indian Territory in 1836. Other Alabamas and Coushatta, though, moved to an area near the present-day town of Livingston, in east Texas. Stidham appears to be correct, as sizable numbers of both members of both tribes are recorded as living here in 1817. In 1840 the Republic of Texas granted this settlement the status of a reservation for both Alabama and Coushatta Indians. John R. Swanton, *Indian Tribes of North America* (Washington, D.C.: Bureau of American Ethnology, Bulletin 145, 1952), 154–56, 158–59; Markowitz, *American Indians,* 1:16–17, 196–97.

37. HtK 1885: Schlagtinweit, op. cit., p. 124, errs when he says that the last of the Uchees died in 1875. Perhaps the last of those who lived in Georgia, because he seems unaware that a number of Uchees live in the Indian Territory. Eds.: The Yuchi originally lived in what is now Tennessee but moved to Georgia in the eighteenth century. Though they were part of the Creek Confederacy, their language was entirely distinct from the Muskogean languages spoken by the other constituent groups. Perhaps for this reason, they developed a special identity that has persisted to the present day. Some Yuchi also affiliated with the Seminoles. In the 1830s and 1840s most Yuchis were transferred to the Indian Territory with the Creeks and Seminoles. Ten Kate is correct regarding their survival: even as late as the 1970s there were an estimated fifty Yuchi-language speakers in Oklahoma. Markowitz, *American Indians,* 3:882.

38. François René de Chateaubriand (1768–1848) was a leading exponent of French romanticism in the early nineteenth century. The aforementioned novels were written in 1801, 1802, and 1826. Also a leading conservative politician, Chateaubriand was briefly foreign minister of France (1823–1824). As one scholar has noted: "Chateaubriand's . . . Indian novels have little to do with their author's visit to America; rather, they center around traditional French concepts of Indians, to which the beneficial influence of Christianity is added." Chr. F. Feest, "The Indian in Non-English Literature," *Handbook: Indian-White Relations,* 4:582.

39. HtK 1885: The Cowetas and Abacoes, presented by some writers as separate tribes, were called Creeks according to "towns" of this name.

40. By the seventeenth century, the Creeks and Muskogees occupied large areas of Georgia and Alabama. According to William C. Lowe: "The name 'Creek' is of English origin and derived from Ochesee Creek, a tributary of the Ocmulgee River. English traders originally referred to the Muskogees as Ochesee Creeks but soon shortened the name to Creeks." Markowitz, *American Indians,* 1:201–3.

41. HtK 1889: On the other hand, Gatschet (op. cit., p. 155), just like my authority Hon. G. W. Stidham, mentions ninety clans that still exist and three or four that have died out.

42. Dwight Lyman Moody (1837–1899), a layman but also one of the most well-known and influential American evangelists of the day, was an effective organizer and administrator who also played an important role in the Young Men's Christian Association and in missionary recruitment. Ira David Sankey (1840–1908), a singing evangelist, accompanied Moody on many of his preaching crusades in America.

43. A Mexican expression for those who speak Spanish rather than indigenous languages, i.e., Indians.

44. From Ovid, *Metamorphoses,* 7, referring to the condition of the Universe before Creation.

45. HtK 1885: Here I will provide just the etymology of the name "Oceóla," the well-known chief of the Seminoles in Florida, as provided me by Mr. S. This demonstrates the inaccuracy of other writers' etymologies, including those of McKenney and Hall. The name is actually Assiahóla. *Assi* was a drink made from a kind of wild berry; *iahóla* was the cry uttered during the drinking of assi at a gathering. Two men, each holding a gourd shell filled with assi held out in front of themselves, run in stooped-over position directly toward each other. Once they meet, they rise up simultaneously from their stooped posture while lifting the bowl with the assi and uttering a drawn-out *iahóla!* Thus *Assiahóla* is supposed to indicate the form observed in drinking assi. Nowadays the Creeks understand by assi ordinary tea. Eds.: Between 1824 and 1830 Thomas Loraine McKenney (1785–1859) was the head of the Office of Indian Affairs and one of the authors of the removal policy. After he left this position he published between 1836 and 1844 his *History of the Indian Tribes of North America* (3 vols.). Dan L. Thrapp, ed., *Encyclopedia of Frontier Biography,* 3 vols. (Glendale, Calif.: Arthur H. Clarke, 1988), 2:912–13.

46. Alexander McGillivray (ca. 1759–1793), son of a Scottish trader-planter and a French-Creek woman, became chief and head warrior of the Creeks after assuming leadership in efforts to repudiate the Treaty of Augusta between the Creeks and the state of Georgia. After unsuccessful efforts to play the Americans and Spanish against each other, he signed the 1790 Treaty of New York with the United States, agreeing to cede some lands to Georgia. J. W. Caughey, *McGillivray of the Creeks* (Norman: University of Oklahoma Press, 1938); David Edmunds, ed., *American Indian Leaders* (Lincoln: University of Nebraska Press, 1980), 41–63.

47. William Weatherford (ca. 1780–1822), whose father was a Scottish trader and mother McGillivray's sister, led the Creeks in their 1813–1814 war against the United States. After his defeat by General Andrew Jackson at the Battle of Horseshoe Bend in March 1814, he retired to a farm in Arkansas. Markowitz, *American Indians,* 3:849.

48. William McIntosh (ca. 1775–1825), whose father was Scottish and mother Creek, belonged to the faction of the Creeks seeking good relations with the whites. During the Creek War he fought against the "Red Stick" traditionalists. McIntosh signed several treaties ceding Creek lands, climaxing in the 1825 Treaty of Indian Springs, ceding lands east of the Mississippi. For this the Creek National Council ordered his execution, which was carried out by the former Red Stick leader Menewa. Markowitz, *Americans Indians,* 2:449.

49. According to recent scholarship, Osceola (ca. 1804–1838) was the son of an Englishman, William Powell, and an Upper Creek woman, Polly Copinger. Dislocated from Alabama during the Creek Wars of 1813–1814, Osceola settled in central Florida and, like many other dislocated Creeks, became known as Seminole. During the Second Seminole War (1835–1842) Osceola became the leader of Seminole resistance to relocation. Eventually he was captured and imprisoned, dying a few months later. Markowitz, *American Indians,* 2:564–65.

50. The name Seminole derived from the Muskogee word "seminola," meaning "wild," in the sense of going to live in an untamed area. There were, in fact, three Seminole wars (1818, 1835–1842, and 1855–1858). About 3,000 Seminoles were removed to Indian Territory during the period of the Second Seminole War, with a few hundred taking refuge in the Everglades, who were subject of the final government effort at forced removal. Markowitz, *American Indians,* 3:703–6.

51. HtK 1885: To Mrs. A. E. W. Robertson of the Tullahassee Mission, I am indebted for some books in Muskokee.

52. The town of Vinita, which came into existence with the junction of the Atlantic and Pacific and MKT railways, was actually named after Vinie Ream (1850–1914), the sculptor of the Abraham Lincoln statue in the Capitol in Washington, D.C. Ruth, *Oklahoma Travel Handbook,* 234–35.

53. The editors have been unable to locate this work in either the Library of Congress or the National Union Catalog. However, it is cited in *Fiction 1876–1983: A Bibliography of U.S. Editions* (New York: Bowker, 1983).

54. William Potter Ross (1820–1891) was the son of John G. Ross, a Scot, and Eliza Ross, a Cherokee, the sister of Chief John Ross, the famous Cherokee leader (see note 55). Active in Cherokee public life after the tribe's transfer to the Indian Territory, Ross in 1866, after his uncle's death, succeeded him as tribal chief. He energetically opposed the conversion of the Indian Territory into a regular U.S. territory and was a committed supporter of the male and female seminaries. He retired from leadership in 1875 but continued, as Ten Kate notes, to edit the *Indian Chieftain* and other newspapers. See *The Life and Times of Hon. William P. Ross* (Fort Smith, Ark.: Weldon & Williams, 1893), preface.

55. See Gary E. Moulton, *John Ross, Cherokee Chief* (Athens: University of Georgia Press, 1978).

56. HtK 1885: Regarding the earlier history, morals, and customs of the Cherokees, see the writers cited for the Choctaws and Creeks, as well as Ramsey, *Annals of Tennessee,* Charleston, 1853. Eds.: James Gettys McGready Ramsey (1797–1884) was a Tennessee physician and author— and, during the Civil War, Confederate activist. His work, *Annals of Tennessee to the End of the Eighteenth Century,* was the first study of the pioneer period based on public and private papers. *Dictionary of American Biography* 8 (1):342–43.

57. HtK 1885: How the Annual Report of 1882 can now list the number of Cherokees as 20,336 (as opposed to 19,280 in 1881) is a mystery to me. Even leaving the nearly 3,500 whites, Negroes, Delawares, and other Indians regarded as Cherokees out of account, it is incredibly sloppy to give the number of Cherokees, or those placed on a footing with them, as approximately 1,800 more than is really the case. Even if one deducts the 160 Cherokees coming from the eastern states to the Indian Territory, the difference is still too great. The births among the Cherokees do not exceed the deaths to the extent that an increase of 1,640 would arise. I take these figures from Mr. Ross and Senator Eubanks, a prominent Cherokee, who deserve the fullest confidence.

58. HtK 1885: The Miami tribe here provides one of the most recent examples. Except for a segment who merged with the Peorias in the Indian Territory, the majority is distributed among the whites of the state of Indiana and intermarried with them. As a tribe, the Miamis, still powerful at the beginning of this century, have ceased to exist. Individual tribes, like the Kansas and Quapaws, are undeniably diminishing in number, even according to agents' reports. They will have died out before they can take part in the great process of absorption. Numerous tribes in the eastern states have vanished in one of the two ways.

59. HtK 1885: The meaning of this name has been lost. It is certain, however, that it derives from the original region of the Cherokees because one finds the Tellico River in southeast Tennessee, whose name is merely a corruption of Tahlequah.

60. Dennis Wolf Bushyhead (1826–1898), who was born in Tennessee and participated in the "Trail of Tears," grew to manhood in the Indian Territory. During the 1870s he founded the National Party, and in 1879 he was elected to the first of two four-year terms as principal chief of the Cherokees. During his tenure he attempted to put tribal finances in order, effectively dealing with cattlemen, railroads, and oil companies. H. Craig Miner, "Dennis Bushyhead," in *American Indian Leaders,* ed. R. David Edmunds (Lincoln: University of Nebraska Press, 1980), 192–205; H. Craig Miner, *The Corporation and the Indian* (Columbia: University of Missouri Press, 1976), 109–12, 122–23, 140–42, 145–47.

61. George W. Benge, a prosperous landowner from Tahlequah, between 1881 and 1885 was national auditor of the Cherokee nation. O'Beirne and O'Beirne, *Indian Territory,* 349–50.

62. Elias C. Boudinot (1835–1890), a political rival of John Ross, was one of the first Cherokees to realize the possibility for profit making in the Indian Territory. Benefiting from the exemption from the federal excise tax, he established a tobacco business that undersold out-of-state rivals. His factory, however, was seized in 1869, bringing the enterprise to an end. Boudinot nonetheless remained a prominent politician and landowner through the 1880s. His elder brother, William P. Boudinot, intermittently edited the *Cherokee Advocate,* engaged in politics, and wrote poetry. O'Beirne and O'Beirne, *Indian Territory,* 115–16, 266–68; Markowitz, *American Indians,* 1:119.

63. John Lothrop Motley (1814–1877), an American diplomat and historian, was the author of several tendentious works on Dutch history during the sixteenth and seventeenth centuries, which show partiality for the Orange family and the Protestants and hostility toward Spain and Catholicism. J. Gubberman, *The Life of John Lothrop Motley* (The Hague: Martinus Nijhoff, 1973).

64. The *Cherokee Advocate* was first published in 1844, and its first editor was William Potter Ross, a nephew of the principal chief John Ross and a Princeton graduate. Daniel F. Littlefield, Jr., and James W. Parins, *American Indian and Alaska Native Newspapers and Periodicals, 1826–1924* (Westport, Conn.: Greenwood, 1984), 1:63–75.

65. Sequoyah (George Guess or Gist, ca. 1770–1843) had a Cherokee mother and an Anglo-American father. Although without academic training, he developed an alphabet that facilitated the writing of the Cherokee language. The system was in widespread use by the late 1820s. In 1828 Sequoyah was party to the signing of the treaty establishing the Cherokee domain in what later became Oklahoma, where he actively tried to promote unity among the different Cherokee groups. Grant Foreman, *Sequoyah* (Norman: University of Oklahoma Press, 1938).

66. Ten Kate is correct. In addition, there are the Kituhwa (Middle Cherokee) and Overhill–Middle Cherokee dialects. The Elati (Lower) dialect is extinct. Diane H. King, "Cherokee Language," *Encyclopedia of North American Indians,* ed. Frederick E. Hoxie (Boston: Houghton Mifflin, 1996), 109–10.

67. Ten Kate is correct in his assertion that Cherokee is not an Appalachian (Muskogean) language. Later research by Horatio Hale and Albert S. Gatschet established Cherokee as an Iroquoian language. Wallace L. Chafe, "Siouan, Iroquoian, and Caddoan," in *Native Languages of the Americas,* ed. Th. A. Sebeok (New York: Plenum Press, 1976), 1:527–72.

68. HtK 1885: Bruyas in Horatio Hale, *The Iroquois Book of Rites,* Philadelphia, 1883. HtK 1889: When I labeled the conjectures regarding the Cherokees and Iroquois as erroneous, the important work of Horatio Hale, *Indian Migrations,* as evidenced by language (*American Antiquarian,* vol. V, 1883), was not yet known. There he provides good reasons for the linguistic affinity of the two peoples. Eds.: Cherokee is a Southern Iroquoian language, a group found primarily in the Northeast. Apparently a major war against the Delawares (Lenni Lenape) along the East Coast led to a separation of the Cherokees from other Iroquoian speakers and their movement into the southern Appalachian highlands before the sixteenth century. Markowitz, *American Indians,* 1:151–56; see also Ives Goddard, "The Classification of the Native Languages of North America," *Handbook: Languages,* 17:292, 320.

69. HtK 1885: See my "Synonymie ethnique" and "Een bezoek bij de Irokeezen," loc. cit. Eds.: See chapter 1.

70. HtK 1885: To avoid all confusion, here I will follow the method of writing of one of the Cherokees who aided me in this investigation.

71. HtK 1885: The *oohse-áfki* of the Creeks, the *tafula* of the Choctaws.

72. HtK—1885: To avoid repetition I must here refer to "Morgan's Systems of Consanguinity and Affinity in the Human Family," in *Smithsonian Contributions to Knowledge,* vol. XVII, 1871.

73. HtK 1885: Cf. Whipple, *Report on the Indian Tribes,* p. 35.

74. HtK—1885: See especially Exod. 28:30, Num. 27:21, and 1 Sam. 28:6.

75. HtK 1885: "Stone shields" or "rock jackets." A tradition of the Tuscaroras likewise speaks of monsters in human form who ate people and had armored skin. They were *Ot-nea-yar–heh,* or "stone giants." See E. Johnson, *Legends, etc., of the Iroquois and History of the Tuscarora Indians,* Lockport, N.Y., 1881, pp. 55, 56.

76. HtK 1885: "Sharp," "pointed."

77. HtK 1885: It is noteworthy that my informant spoke of "steel" because the opinion prevailing thus far is that the original inhabitants of America before the arrival of Columbus did not know how to work iron. But later investigations, of Dr. Hostmann, seem to prove the opposite of this opinion. Cf. *Das Ausland,* 1884, no. 52. Whether the origin of this Cherokee legend dates from the time that they learned to work iron, after the arrival of the whites, I cannot say. Eds.: Indians did shape naturally occurring metals (gold, copper, iron) in various areas but did not know the process for extracting metals from ore.

78. There are approximately 22,500 Cherokee speakers today, including about 13,000 in northeastern Oklahoma who speak the Overhill dialect. Davis, *Native America,* 95–98.

79. Ten Kate's prediction proved incorrect. The Eastern Band of Cherokee Indians (9,845 members, 6,500 on Cherokee lands in 1990) occupy 56,572.8 acres in five North Carolina counties. Their lands were placed in federal trust in 1924 to ensure continued Cherokee ownership. Davis, *Native America,* 95–98.

80. Ten Kate's Cherokee acquaintance was tragically prophetic. Through the Dawes Act of March 3, 1893, and the subsequent settlers' "run" of September 16, 1893, the Cherokee Nation lost the lands known as the Cherokee Outlet (8,144,722 acres west of the 96th meridian). To make matters worse, although 27,176 illegal "intruder" whites within the remaining lands of the Cherokee Nation were to be removed, this negotiated provision of December 19, 1891, was not only upheld but the Curtis Act of 1898 gave the squatters preferential purchase rights. By 1920 the Cherokees had lost 90 percent of lands seemingly set aside for them in the treaty of 1866. See Chadwick Smith and Faye Teague, "The Response of the Cherokee Nation to the Cherokee Outlet Centennial Celebration: A Legal and Historical Analysis, September 1993," ed. Rennard Strickland, Norman: American Indian Law and Policy Center, University of Oklahoma, 1993.

Concluding Remarks

SUMMING UP, AS BRIEFLY AS POSSIBLE, THE MOST IMPORTANT TOPICS discussed in the preceding pages regarding the Indians of the regions visited, I would come to the following tentative conclusions—reserving the option of dealing with individual points in more detail elsewhere.

As far as the results of my investigation in physical anthropology are concerned, Waitz's remark is quite appropriate.[1] He notes, however: *"Die Rasseneigenthümlichkeiten des eingeborenen Americaners anzugeben, hat beträchtliche Schwierigkeiten, da die Mannigfaltigkeit und Verschiedenheit der äusseren Charaktere, welche die americanischen Indianer besitzen, fast immer in demselben Grade gewachsen ist, in welchem man sie allmählich genauer kennen gelernt hat."*[2] Hence it follows that my differentiation of a part of the North American Indians into a certain number of types can be regarded only as the first endeavor along these lines.

Among the tribes inhabiting the southwestern United States and northwestern Mexico, there appear at least five main types or varieties, sharply distinguished from an anthropological standpoint,[3] all belonging to the yellow or Mongoloid race.[4]

These main types as well as their numerous hybrid forms, which arise from mixing, are distributed in very unequal proportion among the various tribes. The intermingling of these varieties is so complete that nowhere does one encounter a tribe consisting of a single variety or a single type.[5]

Of these, the classic "Indian" or "redskin type" with the prominent bent nose and the angular physiognomy is the most widespread. It seems to be of more general occurrence among the tribes to the east than to the west of the Rocky Mountains.

More unity of type is prevalent among the women of the various tribes than among the men. Among some tribes the difference in type and in sexual features is greater than among others; in other words, in one tribe the women more resemble the men than in the others. Generally, the women and children of the various tribes have more Mongoloid features than the men.

The anthropological features are unrelated to differences in language. In other words, a group of individuals, representing various features of the main types already mentioned, speaks one and the same language.

The variety that once lived in the south of the Californian peninsula, from which I have encountered no living unmixed representatives, in all probability stands completely on its own in the regions I traveled through. As I have tried to show in detail elsewhere,[6] though, this variety presents features that, on one hand, recall the race of Lagoa Santa and their kin and, on the other, the Melanesians.

•••••

The Pueblo Indians are not to be regarded as the descendants of the Aztecs. From an anthropological standpoint at least, they in part comprise one of those pre-Toltec races, the type of which we find among the most ancient Mound Builders, the Cliff Dwellers, the inhabitants of casas grandes, and the Tlaltelolcas.[7]

From an ethnographic standpoint, in particular, all Indian tribes I have visited are in a state of transition. Already some have almost entirely abandoned their way of life, views, customs, and religion—others to a lesser extent. In time the same will be true of language and appearance. Before long it will be impossible to make ethnographic studies or collect ethnographic specimens among these tribes. If there is any place where investigation must be speedily undertaken, it is in North America.

•••••

The Indians' sense of color is well developed, though, as a rule, the names for certain colors are lacking. Contrary to the opinion of others that the Indians have no term for the abstract concept of color, like the civilized European languages, it seems that individual American languages do, in fact, possess one. In naming colors, the Indians I investigated proceed in the main from the same fundamental principles that Gatschet investigated.[8] I have not encountered color blindness among the Indians.

•••••

Perhaps most of my readers will be surprised that I do not make any observations about the origin of the Indians. I deliberately wish to refrain from doing so because I have not devoted anywhere near the attention needed to the question to make any kind of assessment. There are solid grounds for theories according to which America is populated from Asia, Oceania, and Europe; various facts plead equally well for those that assume an autochthonous population for the western hemisphere. But the excess baggage of premature theories has also made it more difficult to resolve this

•••••

question. Anticipating that light will later be shed on this matter, I would prefer to take a neutral stance for the time being.

I am not one of those who see in the Indian a kind of idyllic child of nature, the "noble savage" par excellence, as he is often depicted, nor do I belong either to those who regard the Indian as an "inhuman wretch," a peculiarity, between man and beast. The Indian is a human being and has all the human qualities, good and bad. Psychologically he does not differ fundamentally from civilized man, only in degree. To judge him fairly, one should keep in mind his living conditions and his most recent history. For a long time and often the Indian has been treated with a lack of understanding and humanity by his white natural fellows. Accordingly, his bad qualities have developed more than his good ones; that he has still retained good qualities speaks in his favor. To deny the Indian all moral character, as Dodge does,[9] proves that he got to know him only from one angle, which is understandable for an officer who gained his knowledge less among the Indians themselves than on the warpath against them.

Whenever one compares the condition of the Indians in Canada with that in the United States, one would tend to assume that the policy the government of the Union pursues toward the Indians is wrong. In Canada the Indians, like all other citizens, are subject to the law. There the system of reservations and agents is unknown. The endless complications and wars between whites and Indians rarely occur there.[10] But I believe the Indian policy of the Union, as it is now practiced, could yield good results if the government carried out needed reforms and, in particular, appointed as Indian agents only people who had enjoyed an education more in keeping with the importance of the position they occupy.

•••••

Were it granted me to make a judgment, on the basis of my experience in America, as to whether the Indian is receptive to our civilization, then, with an eye to his intellectual and moral disposition, already so well developed in his present condition, I would lean to the opinion that he is in such a position; over the course of time, he can pass successfully through the difficult process of the state of nature to civilization. I consider this possible, assuming that the Indian would survive as a separate race, but we have to take into account the far more numerous white and black populations, which pursue their path of development in the same domain. Before Indians as a race can be civilized, they will be mingled as a race, especially with whites, so that one could no longer speak of a civilized Indian race but just of a race with various degrees of admixture. From the past we can also predict the future. The path the Iroquois, Cherokees, Creeks, and Choctaws followed, many other tribes will gradually follow as well. The Indians cannot be called *"Dämmerungsvölker"* [twilight people][11] because their fate will not be destruction, not disappearance without a trace—but dissolution, metamorphosis.

•••••

With some hesitancy I touch upon the question regarding the diminution or increase of Indians in the territory of the Union because that is a particularly confusing issue. Proceeding from the same statistical results, various writers who have concerned themselves with this question have reached totally different conclusions.[12] From the statistical data, I, at least, cannot make an assessment regarding the diminution or increase of the Indians. However, I have known people who are charged with preparing these statistics and through my acquaintance have become convinced that the data warrant very little confidence. I have no desire to enter into a more detailed exposition, but I do want to note that people, both Indians as well as whites, who stood aloof from politics were of the opinion that generally the full-blooded Indian had not increased but, on the contrary, decreased. Suffice it to say, all Indians listed in the Annual Reports are by no means Indians; rather whites, blacks, zambos, and mestizos in all gradations are reckoned in. The unions between whites or mestizos and Indians are more fruitful than those between full-blooded Indians. Gradually the number of mestizos is increasing, and these alone make the number of Indians appear to increase because they [i.e., the mestizos] bear the name of Indians.

De Semallé,[13] Gerland,[14] Wilson,[15] de Quatrefages,[16] and others who treat the "extinction question" with relative thoroughness and came to the conclusion that the Indians were increasing based their argumentation primarily on the official government reports but at the same time recognized that mingling with whites had substantial influence on the increase. In many tribes, I must admit, the dying off is only apparent because the full-blooded Indians mingled almost entirely with whites exclusively. In other tribes, the smaller ones above all, the dying out of the full-blooded Indians is a fact, however, though there, too, part of the tribe will live on in a number of mestizos.

◆◆◆◆◆

Much has been written regarding the causes of the Indians' dying out. Among other things, the limited fertility of the women, infanticide, immorality, and war have been cited as reasons. But these factors in all likelihood already existed long before the Indians came into contact with Europeans, although I assume that most tribes in the wars with the whites have suffered heavier losses than in those that the Indians had waged before this time with each other. What did not exist before the Europeans, though, was the compulsion to start a new style of life on the reservations, which are frequently situated far from their original homeland, where soil, climate, and food are different. The repeated removals of tribes always result in an increased mortality, which again declines when the tribe has surmounted the critical transition period through adaptation. Where the full-blooded Indians have decreased, I would then be inclined to view the reservation system with all its consequences as the most important cause for their diminution.

As an example of how some Indians themselves envision their future, allow me to cite the very words from a letter I received during my stay in America from the female sachem of the Senecas.[17]

Speaking of the disappearance of entire tribes, she says:

Among the names, the echo of which still resounds, is that of the once mighty Iroquois confederacy. . . . Oh, what are the poor Iroquois now! . . . Their land no longer lies "in the shadows." One by one oblivion snatches away their finest children. Swiftly their wise sachems follow each other to the grave; swiftly, very swiftly not one shall remain unless Providence intervenes. In vain does my spirit wander across mountains, lakes, and rushing streams to find anyone who is familiar with the old oral traditions of the Iroquois, but all have departed. Their council fires have died out and turned to cold ash and will never blaze again.

Oh, worthy brother, forgive me for dwelling on a subject that always saddens me. It makes me sad to know that my people are vanishing, like the summer passes into the stormy winter.

•••••

Notes

1. HtK 1885: *Die Indianer Nordamerica's: eine Studie*, Leipzig, 1865, p. 76. Eds.: Meant is Theodor Waitz (1821–1864), a German philosopher and pedagogic reformer who also wrote on ethnography. *Allgemeine Deutsche Biographie*, 56 vols. (Leipzig: Duncker und Humblot, 1875–1912), 40:629–33.

2. [One encounters considerable difficulties in specifying the racial characteristics of the Native Americans because the variety and difference of the external characteristics the American Indians possess have almost always increased to the same degree that one has steadily gotten more precisely acquainted with them.]

3. HtK 1885: By "type" I understand here *"un ensemble de caractères distinctifs."* Cf. Topinard, *Eléments d'Anthropologie Générale*, p. 189. With just as much justification, perhaps I might have used the word *race*. However, if we continue using the word *variety* here, then let it be understood as *"variété héréditaire"* in the sense of A. de Jussieu. Eds.: Antoine Laurent de Jussieu (1748–1836) was a botanist at the Jardin du Roi and later professor at the Musée d'Histoire Naturelle in Paris. In his "Genera Plantarum" (1789) he developed an alternative for the Linnean classificatory system of plants. *Dictionnaire de Biographie Francaise*, 114 vols. (Paris: Letouzey et Ané, 1933–2001), 18:1046–47.

4. HtK 1885: By "Mongoloids" I mean the original inhabitants of America, the population of E. and SE. Asia, the North Asians and their relations in N. and E. Europe, the Malayan population of the Indian archipelago, and the Polynesians. In the main synonymous with the "Mongolenähnliche Völker" of Peschel, the "races jaunes" of the French anthropologists, etc.

5. HtK 1885: Cf. Kollmann, "Die Autochtonen Amerikas," *Zeitschrift für Ethnologie*, 1883, p. 1.

6. HtK 1885: "Matériaux," loc. cit., in "Sur les crânes de Lagoa Santa," *Bulletins de la Société d'Anthropologie de Paris*, 1885.

7. HtK 1885: Cf. De Quatrefages in Hamy, *Crania ethnica*, p. 466; Hamy, *Anthropolodie du Mexique*, 1re partie, Paris, 1884, pp. 15 ff., and my "Sur quelques crânes," etc.

8. "Farbenbenennungen in nordamerikanischen Sprachen," in *Zeitschrift für Ethnologie*, 1879, p. 293.

9. HtK 1885: *Hunting Grounds and Our Wild Indians*.

10. Ten Kate's conclusions are a bit simplistic. While Canada experienced far fewer Indian uprisings than the United States, the reasons lie less in humane Canadian policy than in the vastness of the country and the slower pace of white settlement and economic exploitation, which reduced the potential for Indian-white clashes. See Robert M. Utley, *The Indian Frontier of the American West, 1846–1890* (Albuquerque: University of New Mexico Press, 1984), 270–71.

11. HtK 1885: Carus, *Über ungleiche Befähigung der verschiedenen Menschheits-Stämme*, Leipzig, 1849.

12. HtK 1885: Cf. Behm and Wagner, *Die Bevölkerungen der Erde*, vol. VII, pp. 67, 68, and De Semallé and Simonin in *Bulletins de la Société de Géographie de Paris*, 1883, pp. 279, 289. Eds.: René de Semallé published several treatises on the question of the future of the American Indians, including "Considerations on the Establishment in the Indian Territory of a New State of the American Union" (Versailles, 1876) and "De l'État Présent et Futur des Peaux Rouges" (Paris, 1883).

13. HtK 1885: "De l'état présent et futur de Peaux Rouges," in *Bulletins de la Société de Géographie de Paris,* 1883, p. 329.
14. HtK 1885: *Globus,* vols. 35 and 36.
15. HtK 1885: *Journal of the Anthropological Institute of Great Britain,* May 1879.
16. HtK 1885: *Revue Scientifique de la France et de l'Étranger,* 1880, no. 33. Cf. *Das Ausland,* 1885, no. 2, in reference to a study of Dr. Harvard, *The French Half-Breeds of the North West.*
17. HtK 1885: See my "Een bezoek bij de Irokeezen," loc. cit. Eds.: First part of chapter 1.

Index

Numbers in **bold** type indicate photos or illustrations.

The Editors

LOUIS A. HIEB (1939)
studied library science at Rutgers University and received a Ph.D. in anthropology from Princeton. He was head of Special Collections at the University of Arizona and director of the Center of Southwest Research at the University of New Mexico. His specializations include Hopi studies, vernacular architecture, and comparative historiography. He is currently completing a book on ethnologists at Hopi in the 1879–1894 period.

PIETER HOVENS (1951)
studied anthropology at the Catholic University of Nijmegen (Ph.D. 1989) and North American Indian Studies at the University of British Columbia. He was a policy assistant on gypsy and minority affairs with the Netherlands government. As curator of the North American Department at the Rijksmuseum voor Volkenkunde [National Museum of Ethnology] in Leiden, his research focuses on ethnographic collections in the Netherlands and the history of Indian-Dutch relations.

WILLIAM J. ORR (1944–2002)
received his Ph.D. in history from the University of Wisconsin at Madison and specialized in the American West. Before transferring to the U.S. State Department and working in Washington, D.C., Mexico, Russia, Belarus, and Italy, he taught at Beloit College and was Curator of Manuscripts at the Joslyn Art Museum in Omaha. He translated and edited several books by German and Italian authors on their experiences in the American West and Mexico.